As robust as it is creative, and rigorous as it is warm, George Guthrie's commentary on Philippians offers interpreters a prized resource for understanding as well as living one of Paul's most inspiring letters. Numerous charts and excursus sections make this an easily navigable research resource, all written in engaging prose. I look forward to learning from this commentary as a teacher and preacher and to sharing it with my students, who so often turn to Philippians to ground their understanding of God's majestic grace in Jesus Christ.

—AMY PEELER, professor of New Testament, Wheaton College

In a crowded field of Philippians commentaries, George Guthrie's volume stands out as one of the best. Guthrie's clear and accessible exposition of the letter is grounded in deep and thorough research. Particularly helpful is the attention he gives to the movement of the letter's argument—a matter of vital importance to effective teaching and preaching the letter.

—DOUGLAS MOO, Wessner Chair of Biblical Studies, Wheaton College

Guthrie brings Philippians to life with his exceptional discussion of the epistle's structure and extensive command of historical context. Guthrie's elegant prose conveys Paul's pastoral concerns. Every chapter contains gems of newly discovered information that will delight scholars and students alike.

—LYNN H. COHICK, distinguished professor of New Testament, Houston Christian University

George Guthrie's commentary on Philippians is thoroughly researched, in conversation with interpreters past and present, and yet highly accessible. Full of exegetical and rhetorical insights, helpful graphics and sidebars, and pastoral wisdom, it will be useful for anyone interested in seriously studying—and living—this wonderful Pauline letter. I will return to it again and again.

—MICHAEL J. GORMAN, Raymond E. Brown Chair of Biblical Studies and Theology, St. Mary's Seminary & University, Baltimore

George Guthrie excavates the depths of Paul's letter to the Philippians to bring forth precious insights old and new. This commentary has the right amount of detail without being convolutedly technical. It is a careful and methodical exploration of this letter and a fantastic resource for anyone serious about exegesis, preaching, or teaching this precious letter by the apostle Paul.

—MICHAEL F. BIRD, academic dean, Ridley College

George Guthrie's scholarship is a gift to both academia and the church. Taking in the breadth of scholarship even while offering fresh exegetical insights and relevant pastoral application, Guthrie's commentary on Philippians will be a valuable resource for pastors and teachers for years to come.

—L. MICHAEL MORALES, professor of biblical studies, Greenville Presbyterian Theological Seminary

Philippians deserves a special commentary to unveil fully its manifold treasures, and this commentary by George Guthrie admirably fits that bill. It is part of the highly praised ZECNT series that has unique features such as a graphical layout of the translation of the Greek text, exegetical outlines, and theology in application in addition to in-depth explanation of the text. Guthrie conveys his thoroughgoing analyses in a winsome style, and his theological discernment makes this work indispensable for preaching and teaching the text.

—DAVID E. GARLAND, professor of New Testament, Truett Seminary, Baylor Seminary

This commentary is exactly what every faithful expositor needs—careful and warm-hearted exegesis of the Greek text that is based on cutting-edge research, yet with a commitment to clarity, brevity, and practical application. Here is a commentary that is informative and inspiring, written by a scholar deeply devoted to Christ and the Scriptures. Highly recommended.

—CHARLES L. QUARLES, research professor of New Testament and biblical theology, Southeastern Baptist Theological Seminary

George H. Guthrie's ZECNT commentary on Philippians is an excellent addition to the field of Pauline and Philippians study. The introduction is thorough, well-written, engages with Pauline scholarship skillfully, and, in my view, accurate in its conclusions. The exegetical sections draw from the Greek text masterfully with sound conclusions and interpretations. Yet it is also easy to read, and the "theology in application" sections give contemporary readers wise insights for thought and life today.

—REV. DR. MARK J. KEOWN, senior lecturer, New Testament, Laidlaw College

In this exegetically insightful, theologically rich, and spiritually edifying commentary, George Guthrie's considerable abilities are on display. This careful and pastorally sensitive commentary should be in easy reach of any person preaching or teaching on this remarkable letter.

—ROY E. CIAMPA, S. Louis and Ann W. Armstrong Chair of Religion, Samford University

I wholeheartedly recommend George Guthrie's volume in the ZECNT series. Guthrie writes creatively and imaginatively, yet faithfully. He incorporates the latest scholarship in careful exegesis. Details are noticed and valued but not at the expense of the larger story and theological landscape. As well as anyone, Guthrie connects the ancient, yet timeless, text of Scripture with all the complexities of contemporary life. You are hearing both professor and pastor comment accurately and creatively on one of Paul's most precious letters. You will not be disappointed.

—J. SCOTT DUVALL, Fuller Professor of New Testament, Ouachita Baptist University

Philippians, Paul's most joy-filled letter, is full of encouragement for Christians experiencing pressure from the surrounding culture and struggling with damaging disunity. Guthrie's commentary, itself a pleasure to read, offers a lively and compelling account of Paul's teaching on how to live well for Christ under such pressures. He shows how Paul uses a soaring Christ hymn and inspiring Christocentric examples, including his own, to exhort followers of Christ to live faithful lives and to partner in mission. A timely message, this lucid commentary demonstrates how deep theology can transform troubled and messy lives.

—BRIAN S. ROSNER, principal of Ridley College, Melbourne, Australia

George Guthrie is well-known for commentaries and other scholarship with the most helpful historical-cultural background, thorough analysis of the meanings of words, and meticulous analysis of the structure of the text. This gem of a study of Philippians does all of these, but the "theology in application" section goes one step further with deeply encouraging and convicting syntheses. If you can own only one commentary on Philippians, buy this one. If you already have plenty, consult this one first nevertheless.

—CRAIG L. BLOMBERG, distinguished professor emeritus of New Testament, Denver Seminary

George Guthrie has prepared a feast. Virtually every page of this commentary is seasoned with astute interpretive skill, theological insight, and prayerful reflection for God's people.

—JUSTIN K. HARDIN, vice president for academic affairs and professor of biblical studies,
Ouachita Baptist University

Like Gordon D. Fee, to whom this commentary is dedicated, George H. Guthrie is an accomplished scholar and gifted commentator. Guthrie's stated aim in writing this valuable volume is to equip clergy and laity alike to teach, preach, and live out the letter more faithfully. His learned love for Philippians is both insightful and infectious. I warmly and enthusiastically commend this work to you and hope that you will join me in using it regularly to plumb the depths and to share the treasures of this dearly loved Pauline captivity letter.

—TODD D. STILL, DeLancey Dean and Hinson Professor of Christian Scriptures,
Baylor University, George W. Truett Theological Seminary

# PHILIPPIANS

# PHILIPPIANS

ZONDERVAN
# Exegetical Commentary
ON THE
# New Testament

GEORGE H. GUTHRIE

CLINTON E. ARNOLD
General Editor

ZONDERVAN ACADEMIC

ZONDERVAN ACADEMIC

*Philippians*


Published in Grand Rapids, Michigan, by Zondervan. Zondervan is a registered trademark of The Zondervan Corporation, L.L.C., a wholly owned subsidiary of HarperCollins Christian Publishing, Inc.

Requests for information should be addressed to customercare@harpercollins.com.

Zondervan titles may be purchased in bulk for educational, business, fundraising, or sales promotional use. For information, please email SpecialMarkets@Zondervan.com.

---

Library of Congress Cataloging-in-Publication Data

Names: Guthrie, George H., 1959- author.
Title: Philippians / George H. Guthrie.
Other titles: Zondervan exegetical commentary on the New Testament
Description: Grand Rapids : Zondervan, 2023. | Series: Zondervan exegetical commentary on the New Testament | Includes bibliographical references and index.
Identifiers: LCCN 2023001517 | ISBN 9780310243892 (hardcover)
Subjects: LCSH: Bible. Philippians--Commentaries. | BISAC: RELIGION / Biblical Commentary / New Testament / Paul's Letters | RELIGION / Biblical Commentary / General
Classification: LCC BS2705.53 .G88 2023 | DDC 227/.607--dc23/eng/20230412
LC record available at https://lccn.loc.gov/2023001517

---



*Cover design: Tammy Johnson*
*Interior design: Kait Lamphere*

*Printed in the United States of America*

---

25 26 27 28 29 30 31 32 33 34 35 36 37 /TRM/ 19 18 17 16 15 14 13 12 11 10 9 8 7 6 5

*In memory of Gordon Fee*

*same place*
*different time*
*same mission*

# Contents

# Series Introduction

This generation has been blessed with an abundance of excellent commentaries. Some are technical and do a good job of addressing issues that the critics have raised; other commentaries are long and provide extensive information about word usage and catalogue nearly every opinion expressed on the various interpretive issues; still other commentaries focus on providing cultural and historical background information; and then there are those commentaries that endeavor to draw out many applicational insights.

The key question to ask is: What are you looking for in a commentary? This commentary series might be for you if

- you have taken Greek and would like a commentary that helps you apply what you have learned without assuming you are a well-trained scholar.
- you would find it useful to see a concise, one- or two-sentence statement of what the commentator thinks the main point of each passage is.
- you would like help interpreting the words of Scripture without getting bogged down in scholarly issues that seem irrelevant to the life of the church.
- you would like to see a visual representation (a graphical display) of the flow of thought in each passage.
- you would like expert guidance from solid evangelical scholars who set out to explain the meaning of the original text in the clearest way possible and to help you navigate through the main interpretive issues.
- you want to benefit from the results of the latest and best scholarly studies and historical information that help to illuminate the meaning of the text.
- you would find it useful to see a brief summary of the key theological insights that can be gleaned from each passage and some discussion of the relevance of these for Christians today.

These are just some of the features that characterize the new Zondervan Exegetical Commentary on the New Testament series. The idea for this series was refined over time by an editorial board who listened to pastors and teachers express what they wanted to see in a commentary series based on the Greek text. That board consisted of myself, George H. Guthrie, William D. Mounce, Thomas R. Schreiner, and Mark L. Strauss along with Zondervan senior editor at large Verlyn Verbrugge, and former Zondervan senior acquisitions editor Jack Kuhatschek. We also enlisted a board of consulting editors who are active pastors, ministry leaders, and seminary professors to help in the process of designing a commentary series that will be useful to the church. Zondervan senior acquisitions editor Katya Covrett has now been shepherding the process to completion, and Constantine R. Campbell is now serving on the board.

We arrived at a design that includes seven components for the treatment of each biblical passage. What follows is a brief orientation to these primary components of the commentary.

## Literary Context

In this section, you will find a concise discussion of how the passage functions in the broader literary context of the book. The commentator highlights connections with the preceding and following material in the book and makes observations on the key literary features of this text.

## Main Idea

Many readers will find this to be an enormously helpful feature of this series. For each passage, the commentator carefully crafts a one- or two-sentence statement of the big idea or central thrust of the passage.

## Translation and Graphical Layout

Another unique feature of this series is the presentation of each commentator's translation of the Greek text in a graphical layout. The purpose of this diagram is to help the reader visualize, and thus better understand, the flow of thought within the text. The translation itself reflects the interpretive decisions made by each commentator in the "Explanation" section of the commentary. Here are a few insights that will help you to understand the way these are put together:

1. On the far left side next to the verse numbers is a series of interpretive labels that indicate the function of each clause or phrase of the biblical text. The corresponding portion of the text is on the same line to the right of the label. We have not used technical linguistic jargon for these, so they should be easily understood.

2. In general, we place every clause (a group of words containing a subject and a predicate) on a separate line and identify how it is supporting the principal assertion of the text (namely, is it saying when the action occurred, how it took place, or why it took place?). We sometimes place longer phrases or a series of items on separate lines as well.
3. Subordinate (or dependent) clauses and phrases are indented and placed directly under the words that they modify. This helps the reader to more easily see the nature of the relationship of clauses and phrases in the flow of the text.
4. Every main clause has been placed in bold print and pushed to the left margin for clear identification.
5. Sometimes when the level of subordination moves too far to the right—as often happens with some of Paul's long, involved sentences!—we reposition the flow to the left of the diagram, but use an arrow to indicate that this has happened.
6. The overall process we have followed has been deeply informed by principles of discourse analysis and narrative criticism (for the Gospels and Acts).

## Structure

Immediately following the translation, the commentator describes the flow of thought in the passage and explains how certain interpretive decisions regarding the relationship of the clauses were made in the passage.

## Exegetical Outline

The overall structure of the passage is described in a detailed exegetical outline. This will be particularly helpful for those who are looking for a way to concisely explain the flow of thought in the passage in a teaching or preaching setting.

## Explanation of the Text

As an exegetical commentary, this work makes use of the Greek language to interpret the meaning of the text. If your Greek is rather rusty (or even somewhat limited), don't be too concerned. All the Greek words are cited in parentheses following an English translation. We have made every effort to make this commentary as readable and useful as possible even for the nonspecialist.

Those who will benefit the most from this commentary will have had the equivalent of two years of Greek in college or seminary. This would include a semester or two of working through an intermediate grammar (such as Wallace, Porter, Brooks and Winbery, or Dana and Mantey). The authors use the grammatical language that is found in these kinds of grammars. The details of the grammar of the passage, however, are discussed only when it has a bearing on the interpretation of the text.

The emphasis in this section of the text is to convey the meaning. Commentators examine words and images, grammatical details, relevant Old Testament and Jewish background to a particular concept, historical and cultural context, important text-critical issues, and various interpretational issues that surface.

## Theology in Application

This, too, is a unique feature for an exegetical commentary series. We felt it was important for each author not only to describe what the text means in its various details, but also to take a moment and reflect on the theological contribution that it makes. In this section, the theological message of the passage is summarized. The authors discuss the theology of the text in terms of its place within the book and in a broader biblical-theological context. Finally, each commentator provides some suggestions on what the message of the passage is for the church today. At the conclusion of each volume in this series is a summary of the whole range of theological themes touched on by this book of the Bible.

Our sincere hope and prayer is that you find this series helpful not only for your own understanding of the text of the New Testament but also as you are actively engaged in teaching and preaching God's Word to people who are hungry to be fed on its truth.

*Clinton E. Arnold, general editor*

# Author's Preface

A few years ago, when I began focusing on the project you have in hand, I had just completed a commentary on 2 Corinthians.[1] As I noted in the preface to that work, Ralph Martin once called 2 Corinthians "both the paradise and the despair of the commentator."[2] I found it to be both, causing pain and ecstasy in equal measure. Moving from the exegetical and structural labyrinth of 2 Corinthians—so marked by a depth of emotional bruising in the apostle's ministry—to the relatively straightforward, joy-filled letter of Philippians was like a breath of fresh air.

Of course, Philippians has its challenges. We have in our hands an ancient letter, written in Greek, shaped by conventions of the Greco-Roman world, and replete with Jewish and Christian theology. How could it not push us out of our simplistic readings of this text? Time and again in the process of working through the book, I stumbled upon issues that I felt needed more study, at least for my own understanding. I discovered, for instance, a grammatical construction at 1:15 that has not been discussed by other commentators and may help unlock a particular conundrum at that point in the letter. I also have thoughts on the structure of the so-called Christ hymn of 2:6–11 (what commentator has not!), as well as a few suggestions on the structure of Philippians as a whole, which, admittedly, I am still trying to work through. But the greatest benefit for me personally has been to sit with this book over a period of years, trying to listen intently to the details and think through their implications for my life, as well as for the lives of my brothers and sisters in the church. Philippians is *rich*, and I come away from the writing of this commentary having been helped greatly by Paul's thought and exhortations.

Therefore, I am deeply grateful for the opportunity to have worked on this project. Having been on the editorial team for the Zondervan Exegetical Commentary on the New Testament from its inception, it has been a joy to work with my fellow editors and to see the series thrive. Clint Arnold, our general editor, and someone I consider a dear friend, has been inordinately patient as I have clicked off other writing projects in order to finally get to this one, and he had keen insights on how to make the manuscript better. The same can be said of Con Campbell, whose expertise on issues of New Testament scholarship and Greek grammar I greatly value. I have

1. George H. Guthrie, *2 Corinthians*, BECNT (Grand Rapids: Baker Academic, 2015).

2. Ralph P. Martin, *2 Corinthians*, WBC (Waco, TX: Word, 1986), x.

worked as an author with Zondervan for the past twenty-five years or so and have very much appreciated their partnership in this ministry of writing for the church. Katya Covrett, vice president and publisher for Zondervan Academic, has always been wonderfully encouraging, and editor Chris Beetham brought to this project a characteristic attention to detail in the final stages of production.

The writing of this commentary was initiated while I was at Union University in Jackson, Tennessee, and I owe a deep debt of gratitude to the administration, my colleagues in the School of Theology and Missions, and the librarians of that place I so love, where I served for almost three decades. While at Union, I also spent a number of months doing research on Philippians at Tyndale House in Cambridge, UK, and, as always, that great library and community of Christian friends provided a wonderful boost to my life and work.

The final phase of the commentary has been completed since moving to Regent College in Vancouver, BC. Regent has provided the perfect, joy-filled community I needed to see the final stages of the project through. Jeff Greenman, our president, and Paul Spilsbury, our academic dean, have been warm and encouraging, as have my faculty colleagues and students. Cindy Aalders and the library staff have always been eager to offer timely help, for which I am deeply grateful. I also had two excellent TAs who did research on the In Depth sections of the commentary, graduate students Alexi Chantziantoniou and Michael Seminutin. I dedicate this volume to the great Gordon Fee, also a part of our extended community at Regent, whose influence permeates this commentary. Although we have spent very little time together, we share a vision for the life-and-Bible integration of our college. Gordon's "mentoring" of me has been through his many books and articles, but his mentoring has shaped me nonetheless.

Finally, as Paul celebrated the Philippians' partnership in ministry, I wish to acknowledge the partnership in ministry provided by the members of my immediate family. Over the past few years, I have witnessed my children, Joshua and Anna, blossom into adulthood, and I could not be prouder of them. And Joshua now has brought to our family his lovely wife, Gillian. Our children's commitment to the church, the use of their skills for the kingdom, the theological conversations we have had, the books, music, and articles they share with me, and especially the love they offer have been a steady source of encouragement. And what can I say of my "Pats," my "sister," "coworker," "fellow soldier" in ministry (cf. Phil 2:25), my gifted friend and fellow runner of this race? More than any other, you are used by our Lord to help me continue toward the goal (3:12–14), patiently encouraging me and loving me every step of the way, for which I will always be grateful.

*George H. Guthrie*
*Regent College*
*Vancouver, BC, Canada*
*March 2023*

# Abbreviations

| | |
|---|---|
| AB | Anchor Bible |
| *ABD* | *Anchor Bible Dictionary*. Edited by David Noel Freedman. 6 vols. New York: Doubleday, 1992 |
| ACCS | Ancient Christian Commentary on Scripture |
| AcPB | Acta Patristica et Byzantina |
| AcT | Acta Theologica |
| *AJA* | *American Journal of Archaeology* |
| *ANRW* | *Aufstieg und Niedergang der römischen Welt: Geschichte und Kultur Roms im Spiegel der neueren Forschung*. Edited by Hildegard Temporini and Wolfgang Haase. Berlin: de Gruyter, 1972– |
| ANTC | Abingdon New Testament Commentaries |
| ASV | American Standard Version |
| AYB | Anchor Yale Bible |
| BapTheo | Baptistic Theologies |
| *BBR* | *Bulletin for Biblical Research* |
| BDAG | Danker, Frederick W., Walter Bauer, William F. Arndt, and F. Wilbur Gingrich. *Greek-English Lexicon of the New Testament and Other Early Christian Literature*. 3rd ed. Chicago: University of Chicago Press, 1999 |
| BDF | Blass, Friedrich, Albert Debrunner, and Robert W. Funk. *A Greek Grammar of the New Testament and Other Early Christian Literature*. Chicago: University of Chicago Press, 1961 |
| BECNT | Baker Exegetical Commentary on the New Testament |
| BHGNT | Baylor Handbook on the Greek New Testament |
| *BI* | *Biblical Illustrator* |
| *Bib* | *Biblica* |
| *BibInt* | *Biblical Interpretation* |
| BNTC | Black's New Testament Commentaries |
| *BSac* | *Bibliotheca Sacra* |
| BST | Bible Speaks Today |
| *BTB* | *Biblical Theology Bulletin* |

| | |
|---|---|
| BZNW | Beihefte zur Zeitschrift für die neutestamentliche Wissenschaft |
| *CBQ* | *Catholic Biblical Quarterly* |
| CECNT | Critical and Exegetical Commentary on the New Testament |
| *CIL* | *Corpus Inscriptionum Latinarum*. Berlin, 1862– |
| ConBNT | Coniectanea Biblica: New Testament Series |
| CSB | Christian Standard Bible |
| *CTR* | *Criswell Theological Review* |
| *DBI* | *Dictionary of Biblical Imagery*. Edited by L. Ryken, J. C. Wilhot, and T. Longman III. Downers Grove, IL: InterVarsity Press, 1998 |
| *DLNT* | *Dictionary of the Later New Testament and Its Developments*. Edited by R. P. Martin and P. H. Davids. Downers Grove, IL: InterVarsity Press, 1997 |
| *DNTB* | *Dictionary of New Testament Background*. Edited by Craig A. Evans and Stanley E. Porter. Downers Grove, IL: InterVarsity Press, 2000 |
| *DPL* | *Dictionary of Paul and His Letters*. Edited by Gerald F. Hawthorne and Ralph P. Martin. Downers Grove, IL: InterVarsity Press, 1993 |
| *DPL2* | *Dictionary of Paul and His Letters*. 2nd edition. Edited by Scot McKnight, Lynn H. Cohick, and Nijay K. Gupta. Downers Grove, IL: InterVarsity Press, 2023 |
| *EBib* | *Etudes bibliques* |
| *EDEJ* | *Eerdmans Dictionary of Early Judaism*. Edited by John J. Collins and Daniel C. Harlow. Grand Rapids: Eerdmans, 2010 |
| *EDNT* | *Exegetical Dictionary of the New Testament*. Edited by Horst Balz and Gerhard Schneider. ET. 3 vols. Grand Rapids: Eerdmans, 1990–1993 |
| EEC | Evangelical Exegetical Commentary |
| EGGNT | Exegetical Guide to the Greek New Testament |
| ESV | English Standard Version |
| *EvQ* | *Evangelical Quarterly* |
| *ExpTim* | *Expository Times* |
| *HALOT* | *The Hebrew and Aramaic Lexicon of the Old Testament*. Ludwig Koehler, Walter Baumgartner, and Johann J. Stamm. Translated and edited under the supervision of Mervyn E. J. Richardson. 4 vols. Leiden: Brill, 1994–1999 |
| *HTR* | *Harvard Theological Review* |
| HTS | Harvard Theological Studies |
| ICC | International Critical Commentary |
| *Int* | *Interpretation* |
| IVPNTC | InterVarsity Press New Testament Commentary |
| JB | Jerusalem Bible |
| *JBL* | *Journal of Biblical Literature* |

| | |
|---|---|
| *JETS* | *Journal of the Evangelical Theological Society* |
| *JSNT* | *Journal for the Study of the New Testament* |
| JSNTSup | Journal for the Study of the New Testament Supplement Series |
| *JTS* | *Journal of Theological Studies* |
| KEK | Kritisch-exegetischer Kommentar über das Neue Testament (Meyer-Kommentar) |
| KJV | King James Version |
| L&N | Louw, Johannes P., and Eugene A. Nida. *Greek-English Lexicon of the New Testament: Based on Semantic Domains.* 2nd ed. New York: United Bible Societies, 1989 |
| LCL | Loeb Classical Library |
| LEH | Lust, Johan, Erik Eynikel, and Katrin Hauspie, eds. *Greek English Lexicon of the Septuagint.* Rev. ed. Stuttgart: Deutsche Bibelgesellschaft, 2003 |
| LNTS | The Library of New Testament Studies |
| LSJ | Liddell, Henry George, Robert Scott, Henry Stuart Jones. *A Greek-English Lexicon.* 9th ed. with revised supplement. Oxford: Clarendon, 1996 |
| LXX | Septuagint |
| MGS | Montanari, Franco. *The Brill Dictionary of Ancient Greek.* Edited by Madeleine Goh and Chad Schroeder. Leiden: Brill, 2013 |
| $NA^{28}$ | *Novum Testamentum Graece*, Nestle-Aland, 28th ed. |
| NAB | New American Bible |
| NAC | New American Commentary |
| NASB | New American Standard Bible |
| NCB | New Century Bible |
| NEB | New English Bible |
| *Neot* | *Neotestamentica* |
| NET | New English Translation |
| *NIB* | *The New Interpreter's Bible.* Edited by Leander E. Keck. 12 vols. Nashville: Abingdon, 1994–2004 |
| NIBCNT | New International Biblical Commentary on the New Testament |
| NICNT | New International Commentary on the New Testament |
| NICOT | New International Commentary on the Old Testament |
| *NIDOTTE* | *New International Dictionary of Old Testament Theology and Exegesis.* Edited by Willem A. VanGemeren. 5 vols. Grand Rapids: Zondervan, 1997 |
| NIGTC | New International Greek Testament Commentary |
| NIV | New International Version (2011) |
| NIVAC | NIV Application Commentary |

| | |
|---|---|
| NJB | New Jerusalem Bible |
| NKJV | New King James Version |
| NLT | New Living Translation (2nd ed.) |
| *NovT* | *Novum Testamentum* |
| NovTSup | Novum Testamentum Supplements |
| NRSV | New Revised Standard Version |
| NSBT | New Studies in Biblical Theology |
| *NTS* | *New Testament Studies* |
| *OCD* | *Oxford Classical Dictionary*. Edited by Simon Hornblower and Antony Spawforth. 3rd ed. Oxford: Oxford University Press, 1996 |
| *OTP* | *Old Testament Pseudepigrapha*. Edited by James H. Charlesworth. 2 vols. New York: Doubleday, 1983, 1985 |
| P.Oxy. | *The Oxyrhynchus Papyri*. Edited by Bernard P. Grenfell, Arthur S. Hunt, et al. London: Egypt Exploration Fund, 1898– |
| PNTC | Pillar New Testament Commentary |
| *Presb* | *Presbyterion* |
| *PRSt* | *Perspectives in Religious Studies* |
| PW | *Paulys Real-Encyclopädie der classischen Altertumswissenschaft*. New edition by Georg Wissowa and Wilhelm Kroll. 50 vols. in 84 parts. Stuttgart: Metzler and Druckenmüller, 1894–1980 |
| REB | Revised English Bible |
| *RevExp* | *Review and Expositor* |
| RSV | Revised Standard Version |
| SBLDS | Society of Biblical Literature Dissertation Series |
| SBLMS | Society of Biblical Literature Monograph Series |
| *SCJ* | *Stone-Campbell Journal* |
| SGBC | Story of God Bible Commentary |
| SHBC | Smyth & Helwys Bible Commentary |
| *SJT* | *Scottish Journal of Theology* |
| SNT | Studien zum Neuen Testament |
| SNTSMS | Society for New Testament Studies Monograph Series |
| Str-B | Strack, Hermann Leberecht and Paul Billerbeck. *Kommentar zum Neuen Testament aus Talmud und Midrasch*. 6 vols. Munich: Beck, 1922–1961 |
| *TDNT* | *Theological Dictionary of the New Testament*. Edited by Gerhard Kittel and Gerhard Friedrich. Translated by Geoffrey W. Bromiley. 10 vols. Grand Rapids: Eerdmans, 1964–1976 |
| *TDOT* | *Theological Dictionary of the Old Testament*. Edited by G. Johannes Botterweck and Helmer Ringgren. Translated by John T. Willis et al. 8 vols. Grand Rapids: Eerdmans, 1974–2006 |
| *Thf* | *Theoforum* |

| | |
|---|---|
| THNTC | Two Horizons New Testament Commentary |
| *TJ* | *Trinity Journal* |
| *TLNT* | *Theological Lexicon of the New Testament*. C. Spicq. Translated and edited by J. D. Ernest. 3 vols. Peabody, MA: Hendrickson, 1994 |
| TNIV | Today's New International Version |
| TU | Texte und Untersuchungen |
| *TynBul* | *Tyndale Bulletin* |
| $UBS^5$ | *The Greek New Testament*, United Bible Societies, 5th ed. |
| WBC | Word Biblical Commentary |
| WGRWSup | Writings from the Greco-Roman World Supplement Series |
| *WTJ* | *Westminster Theological Journal* |
| WUNT | Wissenschaftliche Untersuchungen zum Neuen Testament |
| *ZNW* | *Zeitschrift für die neutestamentliche Wissenschaft und die Kunde der älteren Kirche* |
| *ZTK* | *Zeitschrift für Theologie und Kirche* |

# Introduction

Fair blows the wind across the plain. From my window I see farmers working the fields out toward the mountains. Clouds dot a bright blue sky. Birds play about my little garden, one dancing on a half-ripe melon. It is a peaceful scene, completely at odds with the raging turmoil I feel inside.

Since the meeting at Lydia's house last evening, my stomach has been upset, tied in knots. I have slept little and cried much. Nicolas took me for a walk after the new-day meal, sitting with me halfway up the acropolis on a path outside the city and talking to me about the situation. We looked down on our beautiful little Roman colony, the recently constructed buildings near the forum glorious in the sunlight. Butterflies and dragonflies flew about as we sat on a rock near an altar for Diana, but the fresh air and the beauty of our surroundings did not help much, for I was turned inward, consumed by my thoughts. How did we get to this place, with things in such a mess? Euodia and I used to be the best of friends, neighbors, partners in the cause of Christ; but she has wounded me greatly—shamed our family. I do not want to forgive her or even talk to her, though I know this is wrong. I am still very hurt, and very angry.

Of course, we all were glad to get Paul's letter. We had been worried sick when we heard that he still had not been released and needed further assistance; we were told that his case had become very public and politically charged, some rhetors making fun of the apostle and his message in the forum, calling him an enemy of Rome, thus calling for his execution. For weeks we had waited and prayed for some word, but news does not travel quickly, least of all when one fears the news may be the worst.

When the letter arrived two days ago, the overseers called a meeting, to be held the next day in the evening, so that Paul's words might be read to all. I went and asked Epaphroditus, who brought the letter from Paul, about the apostle's status, and he said that things were hopeful; but he looked at me with wrinkles of worry about his face. When time for the meeting arrived, we sat around Lydia's large gathering room as the letter was read. From the start, Paul commended "all" of us for standing with him (come to think of it, he used the word "all" a great deal in the letter). Throughout, the apostle kept emphasizing unity, having a common viewpoint on things, and I started to get uneasy, since, admittedly, there had been friction in the church lately, especially between Euodia and me. As Epaphroditus finished reading the main part of the letter, "the arrow fell," as they say. Paul singled out me and Euodia, publicly called each of us by name, and called on each of us, for the sake of the gospel, to set aside our differences. He even asked the elder to help us reconcile. The words were not accusatory, just stated straightforwardly, and Epaphroditus read them gently, but they were very clear and very specific, unmistakable.

I looked at the floor, my face flushed and hot. I felt so embarrassed, so shamed, even though Paul in the next breath celebrated my partnership in the mission. I barely heard that part. I could not look at Euodia, but Nicolas later told me that she was looking at me, an expression of sadness on her face. I got up and left at that point, not even waiting for the end of the letter. Some of my friends reached out to touch me in sympathy as I walked out of the room, flashing stern looks in the direction of Euodia.

Could Paul really have understood the situation? Six months ago, Nicolas and I had honored Euodia and Adonis with the proposal that their Sophia marry our Pericles—and, three days later, they had declined! They said their concerns had to do with the instability of Pericles's character and spiritual commitments. Admittedly, he has struggled to find his feet in the world, but as a girl of *pietas*, *pudicitia*, and *concordia*[1]—all good Roman virtues—Sophia could help him, and I am sure he would do well. A mother knows!

Adonis and Euodia are more financially well-off than we are (and proud of their success!), though their business, as with the businesses of other tradespeople in the church, has suffered a great deal of late. Lack of connections with one of Philippi's associations has hurt all of us economically, and, of course, this has affected everyone in the church, most of all the poor, who have a hard time getting day jobs. The financial strain is always there, looming in the background.

Euodia and Adonis also are relative newcomers to the city, arriving from the interior eight years ago, and, of course, they are not citizens. We could have helped them! Although my husband Nicolas has a minor role in the public

1. Piety, modesty, and relational harmony. These were the three most important values for women in Roman society.

life of Philippi—and that role has been lessened more by our commitment to Christ—we have tried to use our place as one of influence for the church and our fellow believers. I suspect that Euodia sees our civic pride as compromise, even though, as one of Jewish background, Nicolas has never offered publicly on the emperor's altar. It is true that we struggle at points to know what to do in terms of our responsibility as citizens of Rome—those of us who hold that status are a minority in the church. Although Paul emphasized our "heavenly citizenship" in his letter, from the beginning he showed us how to use our Roman status for good, and at the same time we have paid a price for our stand with God's people. Surely Euodia and Adonis can see that.

Our stand with the church . . . If I am honest, the friction in my relationship with Euodia, along with the swirl of social and economic pressures put on us all by powerful people in the city, has affected the church, causing relationships to fracture and our unity to fray in unhealthy ways. Last night Nicolas gently pointed out to me that I had sinned when, in a burst of anger, I called Euodia, "Foulodia," a "bad way."[2] I am ashamed to say it, but I also mentioned that her mother was Thracian. I was very wrong in that.

In my moments of clarity and honesty with myself, when the hurt recedes a bit, I see that the turmoil between me and Euodia is not only hurting us but is hurting our witness with those around us. We have not been of "one mind," so we have not been able to proclaim the message of Christ—a message of reconciliation—with integrity.

Euodia and I have walked together, worked together in the gospel, for many years; I hate being at odds with one with whom I have been so close! But why has she done this to me?! Perhaps I should go to her. What was it that Paul said in the letter—that we should consider the interests of others as more significant than our own interests? That we should humble ourselves, empty ourselves, like Christ? But how am I to pour out this hurt, this anger?

Of course, specifics concerning the strained relationship between Syntyche (the narrator of our monologue) and Euodia are lost to history. We do not know if their relational breakdown was due to a conflict about some ministry issue, or a personal matter (as reflected in our fiction), or something else. In the modern church, don't conflicts often stem from a combination of personal issues and questions related to ministry? My goal for this bit of historical fiction is not speculation but rather to draw us into the world these women inhabited, to begin firing our imaginations

2. Euodia's name means "good way" or "good journey."

concerning first-century Philippi, to alert us to what seem to be the challenges that the Philippian church was facing (e.g., disunity, persecution from the authorities), and to present their moment as "embodied," with real flesh and bones, emotions, and spiritual struggles. For while we are separated from the Philippians by millennia and miles, language and cultural context, they were real people with real struggles, seeking to serve Christ in a challenging time and place. They also struggled with interpersonal relationships. In other words, we have a great deal in common with them, and therein lies the hope and help offered to us by this letter.

As we take up Philippians, we encounter a wonderfully rich and greatly loved book of the New Testament. With only a moment's thought, many believers can call to mind familiar passages like, "He who began a good work in you will carry it on to completion until the day of Christ Jesus" (Phil 1:6 NIV); or "to live is Christ and to die is gain" (1:21 NIV); or "I press on toward the goal to win the prize for which God has called me heavenward in Christ Jesus" (3:14 NIV). And looming large at the front door of the book's center section, the so-called Christ hymn of 2:6–11, offers us one of the most celebrated, one of the most written about, and arguably one of the most theologically potent passages in all of Scripture. Indeed, the book as a whole has been celebrated as "one of the foundational texts of Western culture,"[3] and for many of us it has been a rock-solid foundation for our spiritual lives, an encouragement in challenging times, and a source of strength as we face the future. We have in our hands a book that is both profound and practical, one that deserves the detailed attention that we will give it in the following pages.

For Philippians is like a young, stunning, thoroughbred horse, full of power, carrying us toward the finish line. There is grace and strength here, and endurance for a long race. Philippians is like a feast, with nourishing, soul-filling delicacies in verse after verse. There is sustenance and delight here. Philippians is like a beautiful, unfamiliar stretch of a rocky coast. Difficult to navigate at points but compelling. An invitation to depth, to risk, to boldness. There is wonder and mystery and courage here. Philippians is like the richest, most comforting conversation you ever had with a friend over coffee or tea. There is familiarity, warmth, and encouragement here. Philippians is pure joy.

Our goal in the introduction that follows, therefore, is to lay a foundation for a robust engagement of this letter from Paul to the church, particularly to address various aspects of the letter's context—historical, political, cultural, religious, and literary—so that we might *hear* this beautiful, powerful, relevant book more clearly and thus *live* it more faithfully. Although I seek to draw on the fruit of the broader scholarly guild to which I belong, my primary audience consists of fellow Christ-followers, both those

3. Paul A. Holloway, *Philippians: A Commentary* (Minneapolis: Fortress, 2017), xi.

laboring full-time in ministerial roles and those ministering as laypeople in the church. If I have helped my brothers and sisters in the church teach and preach and live Philippians more effectively, my effort in these pages will not have been in vain.

## Philippi in the Mid-First Century CE

### *Political Background*

Euodia and Syntyche lived in a relatively small but politically well-connected city, which saw itself as thoroughly Roman. Yet, as with most ancient cities, the path to its political status, ethnic makeup, and cultural ethos in the middle of the first century CE was a winding one that took twists and turns along the way.[4] Philippi began in 360 BCE as a Thracian settlement of Greek colonists from the island of Thasos. At that time it was called Krenides, a name taken from the "many springs" bubbling up around the hill that loomed at the town's back (Appian, *Civil Wars* 4.105). To the south was a substantial swamp, and thirteen kilometers to the southeast was a port, Neapolis, at the northern tip of the Aegean Sea. Spread out before the city was a broad plain with fertile soil and mountains rising in the distance.[5]

In 356 BCE, just a few years after its founding, Krenides was conquered by Philip II of Macedon, who had become king of the Macedonians just three years prior. The strategic and defensible location of the city, the ready water supply, and the mines of Mount Pangaion, just to the southwest of the city, attracted Philip, and he put his stamp on the place by building new walls, increasing its population, and renaming the city after himself.[6] The mines, from which the Thracians had long extracted gold and silver, boosted Philip's wealth and enabled him to expand his army and thus tighten his hold on his Macedonian kingdom.[7] When Philip died, leaving the kingdom to his son Alexander, forces were set in motion that would profoundly shape the culture of the Mediterranean world. Alexander conquered Greece and spread Greek language and culture across the Mediterranean region and beyond, a legacy that would lead eventually to Philippians being written in Greek, since that language endured as the *lingua franca* of Paul's world.

4. Eduard Verhoef, *Philippi—How Christianity Began in Europe: The Epistle to the Philippians and the Excavations at Philippi* (London: Bloomsbury T&T Clark, 2013), 1–7.

5. Charalampos Bakirtzēs and Helmut Koester, eds., *Philippi at the Time of Paul and after His Death* (Harrisburg, PA: Trinity Press International, 1998), 5–7. On the archaeology and geography of Philippi and its surroundings, see the review of resources and overview by Peter Oakes, *Philippians: From People to Letter*, SNTSMS 110 (Cambridge: Cambridge University Press, 2001), 3–11.

6. Bakirtzēs and Koester, *Philippi at the Time of Paul*, 6–7; Craig Steven De Vos, *Church and Community Conflicts: The Relationships of the Thessalonian, Corinthian, and Philippian Churches with their Wider Civic Communities*, SBLDS 168 (Atlanta: Scholars Press, 1999), 234–36.

7. Lee Martin McDonald, "Philippi," in *DNTB* 787.

Yet, as the forces of power shifted over the next century and a half, the Greeks eventually were conquered by the Romans at the Battle of Pydna in 168 BCE, and Philippi passed into Roman hands.[8] Two decades later the significance of the city's location was enhanced with the building of the *Via Egnatia* (ca. 145–130 BCE), which cut right through Philippi from east to west, making travel easier to other cities in the region.[9]

After another century had passed, the city had its most visible moment on the ancient world stage, in 42 BCE with the Battle of Philippi. The broad plain that spread out before Philippi became a battlefield. There the armies of Brutus and Cassius, who had been instrumental in the assassination of Julius Caesar, were defeated by those of the triumvirs, Marc Antony and Octavian. Seeing their defeat as an inevitable outcome, both Brutus and Cassius committed suicide. In celebration of the victory, Philippi was renamed *Colonia Victrix Philippensium*, thus granting the city the status of a Roman colony, which conferred on its citizens significant civic benefits. A little more than a decade later, in 31 BCE, the political alignment between Octavian and Antony crumbled, and Octavian defeated Antony at the Battle of Actium. In the mass displacement of troops after this decisive victory, some, along with landed Italian farmers who had supported Antony, were settled in Philippi, which again went through a change of name, this time to *Colonia Iulia Augusta Philippensis* (Dio Cassius, *Roman History* 51.4.6).[10] Thus the city was set firmly on the road to thorough Romanization and her identity closely tied to the great city of Rome.

## Cultural Context

From a geographical perspective, as Paul moved westward it was natural that he would eventually make his way to Philippi. Appian called it a "gateway" between Europe and Asia.[11] When the apostle came to Philippi in the winter of 49/50 CE, he encountered a Roman colony with an immediate population of about ten thousand, which manifested deep cultural and political ties with the city of Rome.[12] Citizens of Philippi were, in fact, considered citizens of the city of Rome itself. It is likely that Romans, though only about 40 percent of the population,[13] owned most of the

8. Edgar M. Krentz, "Military Language and Metaphors in Philippians," in *Origins and Method: Towards a New Understanding of Judaism and Christianity: Essays in Honour of John C. Hurd*, ed. Bradley H. McLean, JSNTSup 86 (Sheffield: Sheffield Academic Press, 1993), 11–12; Markus N. A. Bockmuehl, *A Commentary on the Epistle to the Philippians* (Grand Rapids: Baker, 2013), 3.

9. Steve Booth, "Philippi: A Historical and Archaeological Study," *BI* 37 (2011): 40. The road stretched from the eastern end of the empire all the way to Rome.

10. Krentz, "Military Language and Metaphors in Philippians," 11–12; Peter Pilhofer, *Philippi: Band I. Die erste christliche Gemeinde Europas*, WUNT 87 (Tübingen: Mohr Siebeck, 1995), 78.

11. Appian, *Civil Wars* 4.106.

12. Other Roman colonies visited by Paul were Pisidian Antioch, Lystra, Iconium, Troas, and Corinth. See Cédric Brélaz, "First-Century Philippi: Contextualizing Paul's Visit," in *The First Urban Churches 4: Roman Philippi*, ed. James R. Harrison and L. L. Welborn, WGRWSup 13 (Atlanta: SBL Press, 2018), 153.

13. Roman citizens in Philippi would have either moved to Philippi as citizens from Rome, been *liberti* (former slaves of

land, monopolized political leadership (which was patterned on that of Rome and led by two chief magistrates), were those of the greatest wealth and highest social status, had legal advantages over the majority Greek population, and tended to use Latin in official inscriptions and documents. The library in Philippi would have had Latin as well as Greek scrolls, and many of the coins on the street would have been Roman in style. The city even employed the leader of a Latin-speaking group of actors.[14] The colonial status of Philippi and the civic pride of her citizens would have been showcased at every turn, since Roman citizenship granted property and legal rights as well as exemption from forms of taxation.[15] Thus, during his first trip to Philippi, when Paul threw his Roman citizenship in the face of the magistrates who had stripped him, beaten him publicly and brutally, and imprisoned him (Acts 16:19–40)—all illegal actions against a Roman citizen who had not been tried—the move was pure genius.

In Luke's account, he calls Philippi "a Roman colony and the leading city of that district of Macedonia" (πρώτη μερίδος τῆς Μακεδονίας πόλις, κολωνία; Acts 16:12). Technically Thessalonica was the capital of Macedonia, and Amphipolis was the capital of the provincial district in which Philippi was located. So Luke may be using the term rendered "leading" in some English translations (πρώτη) as an honorific, simply meaning that Philippi, as a Roman colony, was a city of highest status and respect.[16] In any case, when Paul arrived in Philippi, he found a city of modest size compared to its much larger cousins Thessalonica and Corinth, but a city exuding a sense of self-importance.

As Paul walked through the Neapolis Gate on the eastern end of the city, having traveled up from the port at Neapolis, he passed the large theater looming to the right. The structure, situated snugly at the foot of the acropolis, could seat about eight thousand people.[17] Further on along the foot of the hill, Paul would have noticed the *Capitolium* situated on a terraced area dedicated to the gods of the Roman state. As he made his way through the city, the apostle would have encountered Roman baths, an exercise track, a library, housing complexes, and a large forum, which was a public space with fountains, galleries, monuments, and stores. Behind the forum and to the south was a food/meat market, a gymnasium, and the latrines.[18]

colonists) or their descendants who had won or been granted citizenship, or Greeks who by some means became citizens (Oakes, *From People to Letter*, 71).

14. Peter Oakes, "The Imperial Authorities in Paul's Letter to Predominantly Greek Hearers in the Roman Colony of Philippi," in Harrison and Welborn, *First Urban Churches*, 226.

15. Oakes, *From People to Letter*, 74–75; Bockmuehl, *Philippians*, 4.

16. The text with by far the strongest textual support reads, πρώτη μερίδος τῆς Μακεδονίας πόλις, κολωνία. Yet others have suggested that the original text read, "a city of the first district [πρώτης μερίδος] of Macedonia," which would align with the political context of the time. On the debate concerning the textual variant here, see especially Bruce M. Metzger, *A Textual Commentary on the Greek New Testament* (Stuttgart: United Bible Societies, 1994), 393–95; Mikael Tellbe, *Paul between Synagogue and State: Christians, Jews, and Civic Authorities in 1 Thessalonians, Romans, and Philippians*, ConBNT 34 (Stockholm: Almqvist & Wiksell, 2001), 217; Brélaz, "First Century Philippi," 166.

17. Oakes, *From People to Letter*, 44–45.

18. Verhoef, *Philippi*, 60.

The city recently had undergone extensive remodeling as a result of a planning initiative. Beautiful, contemporary buildings and monuments dotted the city in every direction. To Paul and his traveling companions, Philippi would have looked very Roman and thus very impressive.[19] The streets teemed with a mix of Romans, Greeks, people indigenous to that part of Macedonia, and visitors who had arrived from across the Mediterranean by the *Via Egnatia* or sea. Paul would have passed a wide array of merchants from Philippi and elsewhere, slaves, craftsmen, farmers, priests, and others engaged in a myriad of different occupations.

As noted above, it is estimated that the city boasted a population of about ten thousand. Another five thousand people lived in the suburbs immediately outside the city, and a total of around forty-six thousand lived in the 1900 square kilometer territory as a whole. Peter Oakes suggests an approximate demographic breakdown as follows:[20]

- elite 3%
- colonist farmers 20% (half owning, half renting)
- service groups 37% (a mix of Greek and Roman)
- slaves 20%
- poor 20% (mostly Greeks)

Community or civic groups would have played a significant role in giving people a sense of group identity.[21] Although many commentators tend to make much of the city's military background and its early orientation to a veteran population, Paul came to Philippi almost a century after the founding of the city as a Roman colony, and the veteran population by his day would have been quite small, perhaps only 3 percent.[22] Its ethos was dominated primarily by two factors: 1) its relationship with the city of Rome, and 2) its agricultural context, as the city was located on a large, fertile plain. Whereas the wealth of cities such as Corinth, Athens, and Ephesus lay in their position as commercial hubs of the Mediterranean world, the "riches" of Philippi largely lay in her arable land.

## *Religious Diversity*

When Paul came to Philippi, he also found a city of religious devotion to a wide array of gods and goddesses of various cultural origins, as was typical of most Greco-Roman cities.[23] From what we can tell from the archaeological evidence, not only

19. Brélaz, "First Century Philippi," 156.
20. Oakes, *From People to Letter*, 40–54; Verhoef, *Philippi*, 16–17.
21. De Vos, *Church and Community Conflicts*, 287.
22. Oakes, *From People to Letter*, 53.
23. On the wide variety of religious cults in the city, see Pilhofer, *Philippi*, 92–113.

were Roman, Greek, and Thracian gods venerated, but also those of Egypt, Syria, and Anatolia. Among them was Jupiter, known as "the most high god" (cf. Acts 16:17). Tyche, Pan, Nike, Athena, Hercules, Enodia Hekate, Mercury, Mars, Apollo, Dionysus, Venus, Minerva, Cybele and Attis, Isis, and Serapis were all represented in Philippi.[24] Diana (the Roman name of the Greek goddess Artemis)—goddess of the countryside and the hunt—was adored in this rural community. Dozens of depictions of Diana or her devotees have been found, spread across the surface of the acropolis. Many of them face the city, and they make up 50 percent of all the pictures and inscriptions on the hill.[25] The worship of Dionysus (i.e., Bacchus)—god of fertility, vegetation, orchards, the grape-harvest, winemaking, and wine—was also an unsurprising preference in this agricultural context. Other popular gods included the Roman deity Silvanus and the Thracian Rider.[26]

Nevertheless, the Roman state religions—especially the imperial cult—seem to have dominated the heart of the city.[27] Philippi's grand place in Roman history and its association with Octavian, who birthed the empire, fostered devotion to Augustus, his wife Livia, and other members of Augustus's family. For example, their statues populated the forum in Philippi.[28] Government and religion were mixed, with the head of the administration also serving as a high priest of the emperor cult. Inscriptions that name the colony also celebrate the *domus divina* of a Roman emperor like Claudius, at times using divine titles.[29] The mix of government, religion, and business in Philippi fomented a potent cultural brew against which the small Christian community would have seemed strange and uniquely uncivil. As we make our way through Philippians in the commentary that follows, we find numerous places where Paul's words need to be read against the backdrop of Roman religion's dominance in Philippi, including where the apostle boldly proclaims that God has made Jesus "Lord" to whom every knee will bow (Phil 2:10–11)—a confession that had even reached into Caesar's own household (4:22).

## Paul's Ministry to the Philippians

Paul's authorship of the letter to the Philippians has rarely been doubted,[30] and there is little reason for doing so.[31] Although the *superscriptio*[32] includes Timothy,

24. Tellbe, *Synagogue and State*, 214–15.
25. Verhoef, *Philippi*, 62.
26. Bockmuehl, *Philippians*, 7.
27. Although his position is overstated, see Lukas Bormann, *Philippi: Stadt und Christengemeinde zur Zeit des Paulus*, NovTSup 78 (Leiden: Brill, 1995).
28. Tellbe, *Synagogue and State*, 214–15.
29. Tellbe, *Synagogue and State*, 216–17.
30. F. C. Bauer's radical position stands as an exception. See the discussion of Richard R. Melick, *Philippians, Colossians, Philemon*, NAC 32 (Nashville: Broadman & Holman, 1991), 30.
31. Morna Hooker, "Philippians," in *The Cambridge Companion to St. Paul*, ed. James D. G. Dunn (Cambridge: Cambridge University Press, 2003), 105.
32. Letters of the era often opened with a prescript that included a *superscriptio*, stating the sender's name, an *adscriptio*,

it seems clear that the letter was written from Paul's perspective. Throughout, the apostle uses singular forms of verbs and pronouns to refer to himself, and he refers to Timothy in the third person (2:19–23).

At least three aspects of Paul's own background fit well with what we find in Philippians and his ministry to that church. First, Paul was a Roman citizen (Acts 16:37–38; 22:27–28) who had grown up in Tarsus, a great educational center of the empire and a city with its own significance in Roman life and history. Thus Paul understood the orientation to Roman culture and politics found on the streets of Philippi. His mention of "the praetorian" (τὸ πραιτώριον; 1:13) and "Caesar's house" (ἡ Καίσαρος οἰκία; 4:22), as well as the use of a Latinized way of referring to the "Philippians" (φιλιππήσιοι; 4:15), employment of citizenship language (πολιτεύεσθε at 1:27 and πολίτευμα at 3:20), and the image of citizens standing together under the threat of opposition (1:27–30), all reveal familiarity with Roman life and culture.[33]

Second, Paul's Jewish background is reflected in his expressions and theology. Scholars increasingly recognize the apostle's Jewishness as a key to his identity. As we see clearly in Philippians 3:5–6, the apostle's Jewish heritage provides a profound reference point for his life and ministry.[34] That heritage shines clearly in a variety of elements found in this letter, such as Paul wishing the Philippians "peace" (1:2), patterns of his prayers for them (1:3–11), an orientation to the day of the Lord (1:10), hope of resurrection (3:11, 21), and a Scripture-saturated celebration of the exalted Messiah (2:6–11).[35] In fact, although Scripture quotations are not found in Philippians, Paul embeds a great deal of Old Testament language in the book,[36] as we will see in the commentary.

Third, and most importantly, Paul understood himself to be a uniquely called apostle and missionary, sent by the Lord Jesus Christ to advance the gospel cause throughout the Mediterranean world and especially among the gentiles (Rom 11:13; Gal 2:8). This calling thrust the apostle out into the Mediterranean world to plant churches, and the church at Philippi was among those with whom he was closest.

Acts[37] tells us that while Paul and his mission team were in Troas, the apostle had a vision of a Macedonian "standing and begging him, 'Come over to Macedonia and

the name of those addressed, and a *salutatio*, a formal greeting. See Hans-Josef Klauck and Daniel P. Bailey, *Ancient Letters and the New Testament: A Guide to Context and Exegesis* (Waco, TX: Baylor University Press, 2006), 17–18.

33. Oakes, *From People to Letter*, 65–66.

34. Jörg Frey, "Paul's Jewish Identity," in *Jewish Identity in the Greco-Roman World/Jüdische identität in der griechisch-römischen Welt*, ed. Jörg Frey, Daniel R. Schwartz, and Stephanie Gripentrog, Ancient Judaism and Early Christianity 73 (Leiden: Brill, 2008), 285–88; John Koenig, *Jews and Christians in Dialogue: New Testament Foundations* (Philadelphia: Westminster, 1979), 38.

35. On Isa 53 as the backdrop behind the Christ hymn at Phil 2:6–11, see "In Depth: Philippians 2:6–11 as Hymn," below in the comments on 2:5–11.

36. See Jeffrey T. Reed, *A Discourse Analysis of Philippians: Method and Rhetoric in the Debate over Literary Integrity*, JSNTSup 136 (Sheffield: Sheffield Academic Press, 1997), 291.

37. On the range of critical assessments of Acts as a historical source see Bockmuehl, *Philippians*, 11–12, and on the accuracy of Luke's depiction of Philippi in Acts 16 see Pilhofer, *Philippi*, 153–59. Recent scholarship has moved in the direction of an enhanced appreciation for Acts's historical value.

help us'" (Acts 16:9 NIV). In response they immediately prepared to make the journey across the northeastern corner of the Aegean Sea, concluding that God had called them to preach the gospel to the Macedonians (v. 10). Luke, the author of Acts, seems to have been among this group, for here we see the author shift from third-person referents to use of the first-person plural (16:10–17; 20:5–15; 21:1–18; 27:1–37; 28:1–16). Along the way, Paul and the mission team stopped at Samothrace and the port at Neapolis, but they quickly made their way to Philippi. Paul probably came walking through the Neapolis Gate on the east end of the city in the winter of 49–50 CE. Over the next several days he and his coworkers planted the church in Philippi.

The events recounted in Acts 16:12–40 are very familiar. On the Sabbath, Paul and his companions made their way to a "place of prayer" (προσευχή; v. 13) beside a river.[38] There they met a group of women, including the God-fearing Lydia, a businessperson from Thyatira, whose heart was opened to the gospel. Her household was baptized, and she invited the missionaries to stay at her home. Since Philippi did not have a Jewish synagogue in the mid-first century, Paul could not follow his normal pattern of first engaging people in a synagogue context (Acts 13:5, 14–15; 17:1–2, 10; 18:4; 19:8). Thus, from the beginning, the church at Philippi seems to have been founded without any significant Jewish presence, and one of its prominent members was a God-fearing businesswoman, who had a large enough home for a gathering.[39]

Later, again on their way to the place of prayer, the team was met by a demonized woman—a slave who made a substantial income for her masters through fortunetelling. Her shouting, "These men are servants of the Most High God, who are telling you the way to be saved" (16:17 NIV), continued over a period of days, and Paul finally had had enough, seeming more irritated than anything else (v. 18).[40] He cast the demon out of her. When her owners realized that the money-making spirit was gone, they dragged Paul and Silas before the magistrates, who had them beaten with rods, thrown into jail, and kept under tight surveillance in an inner cell (vv. 19–24). Yet as Paul and Silas sang hymns in the middle of the night, God delivered them by using an earthquake to open the cell doors. He also opened the heart of the jailer and his household to the gospel. The story ends with the missionaries released from jail and the magistrates alarmed at the news that they had beaten Roman citizens without a trial. The church that met briefly at Lydia's house was encouraged in their newfound faith, and the apostle and his coworkers then left for Thessalonica (vv. 25–40). In the years that followed, the Philippians supported Paul's mission to the Thessalonians on several occasions (Phil 4:16). From the information we have, it seems that the apostle did not return to Philippi until five years later, perhaps in the winter of 55 CE.

38. It is most likely that the river mentioned was just outside a southern gate of the city, only about fifty meters from the city wall. See Bockmuehl, *Philippians*, 15, who follows Pilhofer, *Philippi*, 171–73.

39. Charles B. Cousar, *Philippians and Philemon: A Commentary* (Louisville: Westminster John Knox, 2009), 6.

40. The verb διαπονέομαι could be used to communicate deep disturbance or annoyance. So BDAG 244.

So, after his initial visit to Philippi, Paul made his way to Thessalonica, then on to Berea, Athens, and eventually Corinth, where he spent eighteen months establishing a church that would become problematic (Acts 17:1–18:1). During his stay in Corinth, the Philippians once again sent support for the work (2 Cor 11:9). Much of the following three years was spent in Ephesus, as the apostle shifted the gravitational center of his mission to that great city of Asia from which "all the Jews and Greeks who lived" in the province "heard the word of the Lord" (Acts 19:10 NIV).

Then, in late summer of 54, a riot forced Paul to leave Ephesus. He traveled north to Troas and then on to Macedonia. Acts briefly recounts this trip to Macedonia—"He traveled through that area, speaking many words of encouragement to the people" (20:2 NIV)—and this certainly would have included the Philippians. In fact, although we cannot know for sure, it may be that 2 Corinthians, or part of it, was written from Philippi (see 2 Cor 9:1–2), during the autumn–winter of 54/55 CE. It seems likely that Paul ministered in Macedonia and perhaps even traveled around to Illyricum (Rom 15:19) during the following months, then made his way back to Corinth, where he wrote Romans in January–March of 56 CE. Later that spring, Paul, having planned to go to Syria by sea, was forced by opponents to abort his plans and reroute through Macedonia, where he again spent time with the church in Philippi, sailing from her port after the Festival of Unleavened Bread (Acts 20:3–6). When he returned to Jerusalem, he was taken into Roman custody.

| | |
|---|---|
| Winter 49–50 | Paul arrives in Philippi for the first time |
| Late summer 54 | The riot in Ephesus precipitates (Aug.?) Paul leaving the city after a sojourn of two years and three months (Acts 19:8–10) |
| Autumn-winter 54/55 | Ministry in Troas, then Macedonia; Paul writes 2 Corinthians while in Macedonia |
| Winter-autumn 55 | Ministry in Macedonia and Illyricum (Rom 15:19) |
| Autumn-winter 55 | Paul makes his way back through Macedonia to Greece |
| Spring 56 (end of March?) | A plot causes Paul to abort a trip back to Syria by sea and reroute travel through Macedonia |
| April 56 | Paul sails, leaving Philippi after the Feast of Unleavened Bread (Acts 20:6) on a trip that ultimately takes him back to Jerusalem, where he will be taken into Roman custody |
| Autumn 56–58 | Paul's arrest in Jerusalem and imprisonment in Caesarea |
| Winter 58–61 | Paul's transfer to Rome and imprisonment there for two years (the writing of Philippians?) |

Thus, according to Acts Paul had at least three face-to-face periods of ministry in Philippi, and it is clear from our letter (1:3–8; 2:12–13; 4:1, 15–17), as well as Paul's words about the "Macedonians" in 2 Corinthians (2 Cor 8:1–5), that he had great affection for this church. Yet even more importantly, the letter to the Philippians embodies a key aspect of the apostle's mission "to call all the Gentiles to the obedience that comes from faith for his [Christ's] name's sake" (Rom 1:5 NIV). Paul's instructions to the brothers and sisters in Philippi are meant to help them to grow in obedience to Christ and to challenge them to join in his mission to the broader gentile world (Phil 1:5; 4:15–18). So *when* and *where* did Paul write the letter to the Philippians? To these questions we now turn.

## Crafting of the Letter

### *Paul's Location When He Wrote Philippians*

If the authorship of Philippians has but rarely been doubted, the apostle's location when he wrote, and therefore the date, have been debated a great deal indeed. Since the discussions surrounding these issues have been both extensive and labyrinthine, our approach here merely seeks to provide a brief overview. However, let me begin with a few reflections on the place of such matters in our process of interpreting and teaching books of the New Testament.

History matters, for God has given us his word in particular times, places, and ways. Therefore, the study of the history behind our books of the New Testament is both important and, at times, directly related to issues of interpretation. In speaking about the provenance of Philippians, for instance, Moisés Silva suggests that "a different geographical (and therefore chronological) setting will . . . affect our identification of Paul's opponents, and hardly anything is more important to understand a polemical passage than to know what the writer is polemicizing against."[41] While this may be true, we need to keep in mind that in choosing between the mid-50s of the first century (if Philippians was written from Ephesus) and a half decade later (if written from Rome) constitutes a very brief period. The variety and aims of Paul's opponents—be they political, or religious, or both—would not have changed much in that period, nor would have Paul's posture toward the various opponent groups. No matter the

41. See Moisés Silva, *Philippians*, BECNT (Grand Rapids: Baker Academic, 2005), 5. In a recent article Michael Flexsenhar writes,

> The answer to where Paul wrote Philippians also influences entire reconstructions of early Christianity—from its geographic origins, to the status of the people who joined the movement, to the socio-political impact of Christ-followers and the force of the movement in the wider Roman world, to Paul's martyrdom traditions and notions of apostolic succession in Rome, even to Christianity's cultural power in the long term. In short, the provenance of Philippians is often tied up with larger narratives about early Christianity. So debating Phil 1.13 can feel like an ideological battle.

See Michael Flexsenhar III, "The Provenance of Philippians and Why It Matters: Old Questions, New Approaches," *JSNT* 42 (2019): 21. Although it may be true that the issue of provenance has in the history of interpretation led to such reconstructions and the framing of Christianity in particular ways, one cannot but help think this statement, in reaction to misappropriation, constitutes an equally unbalanced overstatement. We should not exaggerate the importance of the matter of provenance. The emphases of Philippians are discernible apart from a definite identification of provenance.

location, Paul would have been concerned about "Judaizers,"[42] or traveling sophists, or those who opposed him for political reasons in various parts of the Mediterranean world. Should we seek from the text to discern the nature of his opponents addressed by a particular letter? Of course. Should we do our best to discern the provenance of the letter? Of course. But we also must admit that the historical clues we have in hand are limited and may constrain our level of certainty on aspects of the historical setting of the work. We also need to be careful that we are not overinterpreting a historical context and then reading that context into other interpretive issues in the book.

Therefore, we should treat the specifics of date and place as secondary issues for Philippians, since they are not made clear in the text. What is crucial is that we discern the dynamics surrounding Paul's situation, as well as Paul's response to those dynamics. The apostle's theological posture and his hortatory challenge to the Philippians do not change with our understanding of exactly where and when the letter was written.

What do we know of Paul's situation from the text of Philippians? Well, a good bit. Paul is in custody, "in chains,"[43] on capital charges (1:7, 12–26, 30; 2:17),[44] so his life has been threatened (1:20–24; 2:17). He is imprisoned "for Christ" in the cause of the gospel (1:12–14, 16). As for fellow workers, Paul is with Timothy, whom he plans to send to the Philippians soon (1:1; 2:19–24), even as he has sent Epaphroditus with the letter (2:25–30). Also, in his immediate context are other believers (1:14, 16)—some of them in "Caesar's household" (4:21–22)—as well as opponents (1:15, 17). He also alludes to many others in the broader culture who are hearing the message of Christ (1:12–18). The latter include those in the whole praetorium (πραιτώριον; 1:13), variously understood as the emperor's personal "guard" or some type of building. It seems, moreover, that Paul has been in his current situation for some time, for the Philippians had been slow in sending help (4:10), and there had been time for correspondence back and forth (2:25–28). The apostle plans to visit Philippi when he is released and in fact is hopeful that he may be released soon (1:24–25; 2:24).

How, then, have scholars interpreted this data as they reflect on the provenance of our letter?[45] Three main options have been on offer: Rome, Ephesus, and Caesarea. A few scholars have suggested Corinth, and recently the possibility of an administrative or civic building elsewhere in Asia has been advanced.[46] Here we focus on the three main options in the history of investigation, addressing more recent proposals along the way.

42. Although "Judaizers" has commonly been used in the history of Pauline discussions, in this commentary I use the description "Jewish agitators" due to the problem with "Judaizers" as a label. See J. K. Hardin, "Judaizers," in *DPL2* 571–74.

43. As noted in the commentary, this may or may not be literally true. "In chains" may be a figure of speech meaning "in custody."

44. On imprisonment in the ancient world, see Holloway, *Philippians*, 19; Richard J. Cassidy, *Paul in Chains: Roman Imprisonment and the Letters of St. Paul* (New York: Crossroad, 2001); Craig S. Wansink, *Chained in Christ: The Experience and Rhetoric of Paul's Imprisonments*, JSNTSup 130 (Sheffield: Sheffield Academic, 1996).

45. For an accessible overview, see Melick, *Philippians, Colossians, Philemon*, 34–40.

46. So Flexsenhar, "Provenance," 32–36, who leans toward an Ephesian origin but holds out the possibility of a building in a town like Roman Dium, which was near Philippi.

### Caesarea

A number of scholars believe that Paul wrote Philippians from Caesarea,[47] and the position has merit when read in light of Paul's Caesarean imprisonment recounted in Acts 21:37–26:32. Using Gerald Hawthorne's argument as an example,[48] the case in favor of Caesarea can be summarized as follows. (1) Luke states clearly that in Caesarea Paul was kept in Herod's *praetorium* (ἐν τῷ πραιτωρίῳ τοῦ Ἡρῴδου; Acts 23:35; cf. Phil 1:13). The building had been constructed by Herod the Great, but during the time of Paul's imprisonment it served as the residence of the Roman procurator and the headquarters of the Roman garrison. Paul's statement in Philippians 1:13 would then mean that his incarceration, which he characterizes as being in the cause of Christ, had become known throughout the procurator's palace, even to the Roman official himself, a situation clearly reflected in Acts (24:14–16). The reference to "Caesar's household" at Philippians 4:22 would also refer to the administrative staff, who were employees of the emperor.

(2) This imprisonment in Caesarea was of long enough duration (at minimum two years; Acts 24:27) to accommodate multiple trips back and forth to Philippi by Paul's associates. (3) According to both a close reading of Philippians and the account in Acts, Paul had a good bit of liberty, and his friends could care for his needs (Acts 24:23; Phil 2:25–30; 4:10–20). (4) As implied in Philippians 1:7, 16, Paul had already given a defense of the gospel but was still in prison (Acts 24:20–21). (5) Paul's anticipation of being released soon, and being able, therefore, to visit Philippi (1:24–26; 2:24), fits the Acts narrative well (Acts 19:21; 23:11). A Roman imprisonment, on the other hand, has the difficulty of explaining why, when released, Paul would have changed his plans, deciding not to continue westward to Spain (Rom 15:23–29).

(6) According to Acts, Paul was attacked by fanatical Jewish religionists before and during that imprisonment (Acts 21:37–26:32), which some suggest corresponds to the intensity of Paul's polemic against those of "the circumcision" (Phil 3:3).[49] Acts reflects a very different situation during Paul's Roman imprisonment (Acts 28:19–28). And, finally, (7) in Philippians Paul never mentions "the collection," a topic much on his mind during the Ephesian ministry, which suggests a date after the collection had been completed. This point supports both the case for Caesarea and that for Rome, over against an Ephesian provenance for the letter. If Paul wrote Philippians from Caesarea, this would give us a date of composition during 57–58 CE, according to the chronology outlined above.

47. E.g., Gerald F. Hawthorne, *Philippians*, WBC 43 (Waco, TX: Word, 1983), xli, who notes that the proposal was first set forth by H. E. G. Paulus in 1779 and then was developed by F. Spitta in *Zur Geschichte und Literatur des Urchristentums* (Göttingen: Vandenhoeck & Ruprecht, 1930), 3–4, 15–16, 40–41, and more recently by J. J. Gunther in *Paul: Messenger and Exile* (Valley Forge: Judson, 1972), 98–120, and then John A. T. Robinson, *Redating the New Testament* (London: SCM, 1976; repr., Eugene, OR: Wipf & Stock, 2000), 60–61.

48. Hawthorne, *Philippians*, xli–xliv.

49. So Hawthorne, *Philippians*, xlii.

Other scholars have not been convinced, and their concerns are as follows. The distance from Caesarea to Philippi would make travel back and forth more difficult than a trip to and from Ephesus or Rome. Yet this argument must not be given too much weight. At certain times of the year, ships left Caesarea—one of the premier ports in the Mediterranean at the time—on a regular basis, and a journey to the Aegean could be made in a matter of weeks.

Another objection concerns how the Philippians would have perceived the context of Caesarea. Would they have been impressed with the fact that the gospel had spread through a provincial governor's palace out in the backwaters of the East?[50] Perhaps not, though it must be admitted that Caesarea itself was an impressive context and one of the leading ports in the Mediterranean world.

Finally, the main objection to a Caesarean origin for Philippians concerns the nature of Paul's imprisonment and especially the question of his life being under threat, seemingly from Roman authorities (Phil 1:20; 2:17; cf. Acts 24:26; 25:27). Those arguing against Caesarea as the place of origin for Philippians suggest that this does not match Paul's situation in Caesarea. The counterargument that Paul's life *was* threatened in Caesarea by Jewish extremists doesn't quite fit.[51] At Philippians 1:30 Paul draws an analogy between his situation and the persecution experienced by the Philippians, and opposition from a Roman political context seems to correspond better than opposition from Jewish leaders. So it could be that Paul wrote Philippians during his imprisonment in Caesarea, but this position has been a minority report in the history of investigation. Most scholars believe there are better options.

### Ephesus

Another proposal, first suggested by H. Lisco in 1900[52] and growing in popularity in recent decades, believes that Paul wrote Philippians from Ephesus, which would move the date of the letter to the mid-50s, two to three years prior to the apostle's Caesarean imprisonment.[53] Two primary arguments for Ephesus as Paul's location when writing the letter are (1) the considerable time that Paul spent there in ministry, parts of it fraught with intense opposition, and (2) the short distance from Ephesus to Philippi.

Acts tells us that Paul spent over two years in the province of Asia, his mission stationed during that time in the great city of Ephesus (Acts 19:10, 22). The Corinthian correspondence speaks of the difficulties Paul had in Asia, the apostle feeling that he had been under a death sentence during a particularly harrowing time (1 Cor 15:32;

50. So Bockmuehl, *Philippians*, 30; Gordon D. Fee, *Paul's Letter to the Philippians*, NICNT (Grand Rapids: Eerdmans, 1995), 36.

51. So Hawthorne, *Philippians*, xliii; Robinson, *Redating the New Testament*, 60.

52. Hawthorne, *Philippians*, xxxviii.

53. E.g., G. Walter Hansen, *The Letter to the Philippians*, PNTC (Grand Rapids: Eerdmans, 2009), 22–25, who leans toward this view; Frank S. Thielman, "Ephesus and the Literary Setting of Philippians," in *New Testament Greek and Exegesis: Essays in Honor of Gerald F. Hawthorne*, ed. Amy Donaldson and Timothy B. Sailors (Grand Rapids: Eerdmans, 2003), 205–23, who makes the case primarily on the basis of Philippians's literary affinities with Galatians and 1 Corinthians.

2 Cor 1:8–11). Proponents of the Ephesian position admit that we have no record of Paul being imprisoned during this period, but they suggest that such is plausible, for 2 Corinthians 11:23 indicates that the incarcerations recorded in Acts do not reflect all his imprisonments. Also, during the Ephesian ministry Priscilla and Aquila were with Paul (Acts 18:19, 26), and Romans 16:3–5 says that they had risked their necks for the apostle, underscoring the seriousness of the situation in Ephesus.[54]

On another note, the narrative of Acts and the data of Philippians correspond concerning interaction between Paul's mission and the Philippians; Paul sent Timothy to them and planned on visiting himself (e.g., Acts 19:22; Phil 1:1; 2:19, 23–24). And there is thematic correspondence between Philippians and other letters of the mid-50s, including Galatians and the Corinthian correspondence.[55]

For those who take Philippians to be a patchwork of multiple letters that were delivered during a number of trips back and forth, to and from Philippi,[56] both the length of Paul's ministry in Asia and the nearness of the two cities are important. The trip to Philippi from Ephesus was about 700 km (435 miles), which by land would take twenty-five to thirty days on foot and only four or five days by ship. Further, both Acts (16:12; 20:1–6) and 2 Corinthians (1:16; 2:13; 7:5; cf. 13:1) point out that Paul made at least three trips to Philippi, but the letter makes no mention of these multiple visits, simply referring to the beginning of gospel work in the city (Phil 1:5–6). It is reasoned that if the letter was written after the first trip and before the remaining trips to Philippi, an Ephesian provenance is most plausible.

Despite its popularity, the Ephesus proposal has had strong detractors. Of the argument from distance—tied as it is to theories regarding the letter's lack of unity—Fee, for example, states bluntly, "This is an example of one unlikely hypothesis building on another." In fact, of the case for Ephesus generally he writes that "there is not a single piece of *historical evidence* in favor of this view."[57] Similarly, Hawthorne proclaims that "the fatal flaw in the Ephesian imprisonment hypothesis is that it is totally built on conjecture."[58] It should be admitted that an Ephesian imprisonment must be hypothesized; there is no evidence of a praetorium in Ephesus, whether understood as a government building or a portion of the praetorian guard. If understood as a building, it would not be the headquarters of a proconsul, since Asia was a senatorial province,[59] and to understand it merely as a "palace"[60] would remove it

54. Bockmuehl, *Philippians*, 26.

55. Thielman, "Ephesus and the Literary Setting of Philippians," 215–21.

56. The Philippians had heard that Paul was in prison (1:12), had sent Epaphroditus to care for him (2:25), had heard that Epaphroditus was ill (v. 26), and had received Epaphroditus who brought the letter (v. 28). Those who hold to multiple fragments hold to more trips, which some suggest would be untenable with a significant distance.

57. Fee, *Philippians*, 35 (italics original).

58. Hawthorne, *Philippians*, xxxix.

59. Flexsenhar objects to this objection, suggesting that the term could be used for a proconsul's headquarters in a senatorial province. However, the examples he gives are from the third century CE rather than the early decades of the empire. See Flexsenhar, "Provenance," 31–32.

60. So Thielman, "Ephesus and the Literary Setting of Philippians," 222.

from the charged political context that seems to be reflected in Philippians (1:12–17). Further, while it is true that the members of "Caesar's household" (4:22) were spread throughout the Mediterranean—and thus a context like Asia is a possible location for such a referent—most inscriptional references to those belonging to Caesar come from Rome, Italy, or North Africa.[61]

Again, one of the main concerns about an Ephesian provenance has to do with the nature of Paul's imprisonment, which seems to have been of a long duration. According to Philippians, the apostle was held on capital charges, at times unsure of whether he would live or die (1:13–14, 20; 2:17). While it is true that Paul seems to have had a brush with death while in Ephesus (2 Cor 1:8–11), this does not necessarily entail imprisonment, and it is hard to imagine an Ephesian imprisonment that threatened the apostle with a death sentence—an imprisonment, moreover, that extended over a period of months, if not years. It is not impossible, but it seems unlikely.

Finally, although there are thematic correspondences between Philippians and Paul's letters to the Galatians and Corinthians, this does not necessarily mean that the letters were written at the same time. The difference, for instance, between the time during which the Corinthian correspondence was written and the time of Paul's Caesarean or Roman imprisonments would be no more than five to ten years, a fairly minimal period. Paul's reflections on the danger posed by his various opponents would not have changed drastically over that time. Also, the issue of thematic content cuts both ways. During the Ephesian ministry, Paul was keen to promote the collection for Jerusalem (e.g., 1 Cor 16:1–4; 2 Cor 8–9)—a matter on which Philippians is silent. It is admittedly an argument from silence, but the silence in our letter makes better sense if the collection had already been delivered to Jerusalem.[62]

Of course, Philippians *could* have been written from Ephesus, but it seems to me that the evidence for such is mostly circumstantial and strains to fit Paul's overt statements concerning his context.

### Rome

Finally, a number of scholars, such as Fee, Bockmuehl, Holloway, Silva, and others,[63] believe that Paul wrote Philippians during his first Roman imprisonment.[64] Of the three main options, a Roman provenance is generally considered the traditional position, especially since this is the only tradition that has survived from the earliest centuries of the church.[65] This is the position reflected in the commentary, and the following points are in its favor.

61. Bockmuehl, *Philippians*, 31, referencing Weaver.

62. Bockmuehl, *Philippians*, 27, 31.

63. Bockmuehl, *Philippians*, 32; Fee, *Philippians*, 34–37; Holloway, *Philippians*, 22–24; Silva, *Philippians*, 5–7.

64. For a defense of the position that Philippians was written in Paul's second Roman imprisonment, see Jim Reiher, "Could Philippians Have Been Written from the Second Roman Imprisonment?," *EvQ* 84.3 (2012): 213–33.

65. Silva, *Philippians*, 5. Hawthorne states that "from the second century Marcionite prologues attached to Paul's

(1) Acts records that Paul was imprisoned in Rome for a period of two years, guarded by a soldier while under house arrest but with a great deal of freedom for ministry (Acts 28:16, 20, 30). That length of time would allow for multiple trips by Paul's associates to and from Rome. (2) While the statements concerning the praetorium (Phil 1:13) and "Caesar's household" (4:22) could refer to locations or people outside of Rome, they certainly fit well, and perhaps best, referring to a location in the city of Rome itself. The Greek term translated "praetorium" (πραιτώριον) was a loanword from the Latin *praetorium*. It had various uses in the mid-first century, but one was as a reference to the Praetorian Guard[66] stationed in Rome, an elite group of six- to nine-thousand men who served as guards for the emperor but also as policemen, firemen, and government administrators, carrying out a broad range of duties for the empire.[67]

When Paul writes, "In the whole praetorium and to all the rest" (ἐν ὅλῳ τῷ πραιτωρίῳ καὶ τοῖς λοιποῖς πᾶσιν), we are offered several clues. First, the phrase most naturally is read collectively, referring to a group—in this case Caesar's elite guard—with "to all the rest" (τοῖς λοιποῖς πᾶσιν) referring to a broader group of people. Likewise, while those of "Caesar's household" could refer to people of a variety of statuses under the emperor elsewhere in the empire, the vast majority of Caesar's household would have been in the city of Rome. The Philippians, who hailed from a city that prided itself on its connections to the great city, would have been impressed with the advance of the gospel in that place, a point that makes sense of Paul's references both to the praetorium and to those in Caesar's household.

(3) As with the Caesarean position, the absence of any mention of the collection for God's people in Jerusalem makes better sense if the letter was written later than the Ephesian ministry, when the collection had already been delivered. (4) That Paul seems to be incarcerated in a charged political context, for a considerable period, with his life threatened—while also able to do ministry with considerable public impact—also seems to fit the Roman context well. (5) As argued by Bo Reicke, whereas the circumstances surrounding the production of Colossians, Philemon, and Ephesians fit the Caesarean imprisonment, the circumstances of Philippians fit the Roman imprisonment much better.[68]

---

epistles . . . until the eighteenth century, everyone accepted without question the 'fact' that the Philippian letter was written from Rome" (Hawthorne, *Philippians*, xxxvii). At the same time, the uniformity of the early tradition has been questioned; see Flexsenhar, "Provenance," 21–22.

66. See, for instance, Suetonius's *Nero* 9, which speaks of the "veterans of the praetorian guard" (*veteranis e praetorio*), whom Nero, after the death of Claudius, established in the colony of Antium. Also, Tacitus, *Hist.* 1.19; 4.2. See Sandra Bingham, *The Praetorian Guard: A History of Rome's Elite Special Forces* (Waco, TX: Baylor University Press, 2013), 16.

67. See esp. Bingham, *Praetorian Guard*, 81–114.

68. Bo Ivar Reicke, "Caesarea, Rome and the Captivity Epistles," in *Apostolic History and the Gospel: Biblical and Historical Essays Presented to F. F. Bruce on his 60th Birthday*, ed. W. Ward Gasque and Ralph P. Martin (Exeter: Paternoster, 1970), 277–86.

In some ways the Roman provenance of Philippians has been an increasingly embattled position in recent decades. The primary objections to the above arguments are as follows. First are arguments regarding geography. Scholars arguing for an Ephesian provenance often underscore the distance between Philippi and Rome. Yet the lines of travel between Macedonia and Rome were not so prohibitive. The distance could be covered in six to seven weeks (at a pace of 30 km/18.64 miles per day) by way of the *Via Egnatia*, a short trip on a ship across the Adriatic Sea to Brindisi on the heel of the Italian peninsula, and then up to Rome on the *Via Appia*.[69] With favorable weather, the trip from Philippi to Rome by ship could be managed in under three weeks, even with stops at various ports along the way.[70] Since Paul was under arrest in Rome for two years, multiple trips back and forth between Philippi and Rome would have been possible.[71] The argument from the standpoint of distance can be dismissed.[72]

The other geographical argument against a Roman provenance is that, since Paul planned to continue westward to Spain after visiting the city (Rom 15:23–24, 28), it makes little sense that, once released, he instead would return to Philippi—a desire expressed clearly in our letter (Phil 1:26; 2:24). Yet as Fee and others note, plans made as a free man can change, especially after several years in chains, and it would not be the first time Paul had changed his plans.[73]

Other arguments against a Roman provenance focus, for instance, on the reference to the "praetorium" (πραιτώριον; NIV: "palace guard") at 1:13. Cases have been made for Paul's use of the term as referring to a building in the Roman provinces. It is true that the term had a semantic range that could refer to a variety of building types during the imperial period, and this is a common use elsewhere in the New Testament.[74] Thus, it is *possible* that Paul could have used the term to refer to his incarceration in some other part of the empire.

The question is whether this position is more likely than the view that at Philippians 1:13 Paul was referring to the Praetorian Guard in Rome. Regarding this question, it has been suggested that the language Paul uses, "in the whole praetorium" (ἐν ὅλῳ τῷ πραιτωρίῳ), should be understood as speaking of a *place*, not a group of people. First, it can be pointed out that in several places the apostle uses "whole" (ὅλος) to speak of groups of people.[75] Second, the grammar of our phrase should not be read

69. See the discussion by Bockmuehl, *Philippians*, 31–32; Lynn H. Cohick, Philippians, SGBC (Grand Rapids: Zondervan, 2013), 6.

70. These figures were calculated using ORBIS, The Stanford Geospatial Network Model of the Roman World, found at http://orbis.stanford.edu.

71. See Reicke, "Caesarea, Rome and the Captivity Epistles," 284.

72. As asserted by Silva, *Philippians*, 5–7, and reiterated by Bockmuehl, *Philippians*, 32.

73. Fee, *Philippians*, 36. On Paul changing his plans, see, e.g., Guthrie, *2 Corinthians*, 103–9.

74. The term is used in the NT to speak of a governor's headquarters at Matt 27:27; Mark 15:16; John 18:28, 33; 19:9; Acts 23:35. On other uses of the term see especially Flexsenhar, "Provenance," 33–37. However, the examples used by Flexsenhar to demonstrate that even senatorial provinces might have a praetorium as the headquarters of a proconsul are very late (third century CE; see pp. 31–32).

75. It must be admitted that the *exact phrase*, translated

as pointing away from reading "in the . . . imperial guard" (ἐν . . . τῷ πραιτωρίῳ). Flexenhar, for instance, asserts that the form of our words here points toward Paul as referring to a building. He states, "As is well known, Paul uses the neuter singular form of the word πραιτώριον . . . . On its own, as Holloway rightly notes, πραιτώριον would most naturally refer to a building, since words ending in the neuter singular -(ε)ιον regularly refer to buildings."[76] Yet this perspective, particularly as it relates to the emperor's praetorian guard, is contradicted by hard linguistic evidence from the first century CE. For example, members of the guard were issued diplomas in Latin, by the emperor, which identified them as "those who served in my imperial guard" (*qui in meo praetorio militaverunt*).[77] A similar construction occurs in an inscription from the reign of Claudius, dated 46 CE, just a handful of years before Paul entered Philippi on his second mission trip. In the inscription, the emperor speaks of those who had served "in my imperial guard" (*in praetorio meo*; CIL 5.5050).[78] In both cases *praetorio* is neuter ablative and, with the preposition "in" (*in*) indicates *location*. Thus, this Latin phrase corresponds directly with Paul's Greek construction at Philippians 1:13, "in the . . . imperial guard": the preposition "in" (ἐν) + a reference to the praetorium in a neuter form (in Greek the case is dative; τῷ πραιτωρίῳ) to indicate location. Paul might be read as bringing over the construction from Latin to Greek almost woodenly. So words concerning the praetorium at Philippians 1:13 *can* be read as speaking of a *location as a group of people*. In this case that location consists of a very large body of people—an institution with thousands of members.[79] If this is correct, it most naturally aligns with Paul's location as being in Rome.

The argument that "Caesar's household" at Philippians 4:22 could refer to those of various positions or situations in locations other than Rome is well taken. But this does not constitute an argument against the reference being to followers of Christ in the employ of Caesar in the capital city. It merely speaks of other options, not contradictory information. Further, as I point out in the commentary on 4:22, there exist intriguing clues concerning the inroads of the gospel in Rome even before Paul's imprisonment there, found in the list of names in Romans 16. "The household of

here as "in the whole" (ἐν ὅλῳ), is universally used in the NT, the LXX, the broader Jewish literature, and in inscriptional evidence to describe a locale, not a group. See Angela Standhartinger, "Polis and Ekklēsia at Philippi: A Response to Kathy Ehrensperger, Paul Holloway and Julien Ogereau," in Harrison and Welborn, *First Urban Churches 4*, 145–46 and n24. However, if we focus on the adjective itself, the apostle employs the term rendered "whole" (ὅλος) several times to speak of people, e.g., "the whole church" (ὅλης τῆς ἐκκλησίας/ἡ ἐκκλησία ὅλη) at Rom 16:23 and 1 Cor 14:23, or "whole households" (ὅλους οἴκους) at Titus 1:11.

76. Flexsenhar, "Provenance," 29.

77. *CIL* 16.21.

78. See Bingham, *Praetorian Guard*, 16.

79. Further, as noted in the commentary on 1:13, there may be a stylistic reason that the wording there is awkward, for in that verse we have a balanced construction, with the infinitive flanked by two phrases built on the preposition (ἐν) translated as "in" and "among" respectively:

| | |
|---|---|
| "in the cause of Christ" | ἐν Χριστῷ |
| "to be" | γενέσθαι |
| "among the whole imperial guard" | ἐν ὅλῳ τῷ πραιτωρίῳ |

Notice how the balanced phrases, ἐν Χριστῷ (*en Christō*) and ἐν ὅλῳ (*en holō*) roll off the tongue. If Paul was speaking of a group of people, it would have been clearer to have written "to

Narcissus" (Rom 16:11) may refer to those in the house of Tiberius Claudius Narcissus, an influential client of Emperor Claudius (41–54 CE), and "Aristobulus" (v. 10) may be a reference to Herod the Great's grandson, who also had been a member of Claudius's court. Also mentioned is Paul's "relative" (συγγενῆ) Herodion, named between these two other influential households (v. 11). This may indicate that Paul had a family connection within the Roman civil service ranks.[80] These references in Romans may correspond to those in "Caesar's household" at Philippians 4:22, even if the believers to whom the apostle alludes were servants in those prominent households.

Thus, the objections to the Roman provenance of Philippians mostly extend our range of possibilities rather than constitute substantive arguments against a Roman location for Paul's writing of the letter. Is it possible that Paul was somewhere other than Rome when he wrote the book? Yes. Are there good reasons for thinking that he was in Rome? Undoubtedly. At the end of the day, does a particular position change our interpretation and appropriation of the theology and teachings of the book? Not really. The ways that Paul addresses the current needs in the Philippian church are clear from the text of Philippians itself, as detailed in our next section. So, who were the Philippians, and what needs among them prompted the writing of this letter?

### *The Church in Philippi and Paul's Reasons for Writing*

A number of individuals associated with the church in Philippi are mentioned in Acts or Philippians: Epaphroditus, Syntyche, Euodia, the brother who was encouraged to help Syntyche and Euodia, Clement, Lydia and her household, the jailer and his household, and possibly the slave girl from whom Paul cast the demon. Of those mentioned in the letter, Epaphroditus (Phil 2:25), Syntyche, and Euodia (4:2) have Greek names, while Clement's name is Latin. Lydia, mentioned in the Acts narrative, also bears a Latin moniker.[81] Thus it seems that the church consisted of a mix of those from Greek and Roman backgrounds, very much in line with the composition of the city in general.[82]

Peter Oakes has offered educated guesses concerning the makeup of the church,[83] suggesting the following:

- 1% of the Christian community came from the city's elite
- 43% of the church would have been those from service groups

*those* in the whole imperial guard" (τοῖς ἐν ὅλῳ τῷ πραιτωρίῳ), but that would have thwarted the balanced phrasing.

80. Bockmuehl, *Philippians*, 269–70. Of course, if Paul wrote Philippians after Claudius's rule, these families still may have been connected to the imperial house.

81. Some have taken Lydia's name as merely marking her place of origin, "the woman from Lydia," but archaeological and literary evidence suggests that "Lydia" was a known given name in the region.

82. Oakes estimates that a total of about 25–40 percent of the church were of Roman background and 60–75 percent Greek. See Oakes, *From People to Letter*, 62.

83. Oakes, *From People to Letter*, 60–61.

- 15% were colonist farmers
- 25% would have been poor
- 16% were slaves

Oakes admits that variables could greatly affect these percentages, so they are mere approximations. Yet these figures match what Paul tells us of the Macedonians generally—namely, that they were not of the elite and powerful but had given to Paul's mission out of their "extreme poverty" (2 Cor 8:2).

The Philippians' economic situation, along with their general status in Philippi, almost certainly played a role in the difficulties they were facing as a community, and signs of community stress are clearly reflected in the letter. For example, Philippians 1:27–30 serves as both a structural and thematic cornerstone for the whole document. With this passage, Paul launches the epistle's main body, writing:

> Make this your focus: Live out your heavenly citizenship in a manner worthy of the gospel of Christ, so that whether I come and see you or remain absent, I might hear about what is happening with you, particularly that you are standing firm in one Spirit, harmoniously striving together for the gospel faith, without being frightened in any way by those standing against you, which is a sign for them of destruction but of your salvation, and this [is] from God, because for Christ's sake you have been granted not only to trust him but also to suffer on his behalf, experiencing the same struggle that you saw I had and now hear that I have.

Here in this impressive single sentence, we have a foundational exhortation that contains several important clues about the Philippians' situation. The most salient points are as follows.

(1) *The Philippians' may have been perceived as strange and separatist in relation to the broader community, drawing the ire of the civic authorities.* Notice, first, that the matter of citizenship is front and center in Paul's statement.[84] The main verb, translated as "live out your heavenly citizenship" (πολιτεύομαι; 1:27), connotes discharging one's duties or obligations as a citizen. Bruce Winter has shown from inscriptions of the era that the word often was associated with "harmony" as a social virtue.[85] Almost certainly Paul appeals to the Philippians' understanding of "oneness" in a civic sense, yet applying the virtue to their commitment to Christ and his church. The apostle's use of this verb may also allude to the broader culture's demand for conformity (a forced "unity"). It is likely that those "standing against" (τῶν ἀντικειμένων; 1:28) the church in Philippi were doing so because of the civic disunity brought about by the believers'

84. On which, see the discussion of πολιτεύομαι in the comments at 1:27 below.

85. Bruce W. Winter, *Seek the Welfare of the City: Christians as Benefactors and Citizens* (Grand Rapids: Eerdmans; Carlisle: Paternoster, 1994), 102–3.

orientation to the countercultural gospel. In fact, it may be that the Christians' withdrawal from a variety of community associations—whether political, religious, or economic (or a combination of these), which often involved forms of pagan worship—and especially their refusal to participate in the Roman imperial cult had marked them out as dissident troublemakers and thus of concern to the civic authorities.[86]

(2) In a related vein, *the Philippians were being persecuted by those in authority in Philippi for their commitment to Christ as supreme Lord.* They live "for Christ's sake," not for the sake of the city or the empire. In Philippi the emperor, a deified man, would have been celebrated by the community with titles such as "Lord" and "Savior." To publicly refrain from such a confession was to mark oneself out as odd at best and treasonous at worst. Even more condemning, to confess as "Lord" and "Savior" one who, being God, took the form of a slave (Phil 2:7) and died on a Roman cross, was to invite ridicule and opposition.[87] In Philippians 1:30 Paul writes, "[You are] experiencing the same struggle that you saw I had and now hear that I have." As recounted above, the Philippians "saw" Paul's "struggle" when the authorities brutalized him and Silas during the apostle's first visit to the city (Acts 16:20–24). And as he writes Philippians, Paul is in chains again for the cause of Christ, seemingly at the hands of civic authorities (Phil 1:12–14).[88] The Philippians were experiencing a comparable form of persecution and had a reason to be "frightened" or intimidated by their opponents (1:28). Yet Paul affirms that they should face opposition together and understand their suffering on behalf of Christ as a gift ("you have been granted," ὑμῖν ἐχαρίσθη; 1:29).

(3) *The Philippians were struggling with disunity in the church.* The need for the Philippians to stand together, unified by the Holy Spirit, with one mind and gospel voice, forms another key element of our cornerstone passage (1:27–30). Paul wants to hear that the Philippians are "standing firm in one Spirit, harmoniously striving together for the gospel faith" (1:27). While the Philippians were challenged from without by public opposition to their movement, they also faced the fragmentation of their church from within. As Fee notes, this had yet to reach the level of outright division, but Paul clearly believed that the threat of disunity needed attention and decisive action.[89]

86. On community groups and associations in Philippi, see De Vos, *Church and Community Conflicts*, 287, who writes that "relations between the Christian and civic communities at Philippi involved quite serious conflict and oppressive measures because of withdrawal from the traditional cult practices." I believe this general statement likely to be true, but I am not as convinced of some of the author's conclusions concerning the nature of the fragmentation in Philippi. Where, for example, is the evidence that apostasy had taken place among the church members? On conflict with the civil authorities, see Mikael Tellbe, "The Sociological Factors behind Philippians 3.1–11 and the Conflict at Philippi," *JSNT* 17.55 (1995): 211; Bockmuehl, *Philippians*, 2–8; Bormann, *Stadt und Christengemeinde*, 217–24; Fee, *Philippians*, 30–31.

87. Fee, *Philippians*, 31–32.

88. So Fee, *Philippians*, 29–31. Fee notes that Paul's emphasis in the letter on his own sufferings and imprisonment (e.g., in the thanksgiving of 1:3–8 and the narrative of his affairs in 1:22–26) was to offer an example of how to handle such difficulties.

89. Fee, *Philippians*, 32–33.

In Philippians, this motif of being "one," of selflessly pouring oneself out on behalf of others, stands out clearly as we walk through the main body of the letter (1:27–4:4a). Following from the exhortation at 1:27–30, the apostle immediately extends his challenge to the Philippians to work toward unity; he speaks of oneness with Christ, participation in the Spirit, of "being like-minded, embracing a common love, having solidarity, sharing a common perspective" (2:2). The Philippians are called to turn from selfish ambition and conceit and to embody humility, putting the interests of others ahead of their own interests (2:1–4). Of course, Christ is the preeminent example of one who "humiliated himself" by not demanding the rights of his position, sacrificing all the way to the point of death (2:6–11). Having presented them with the example of Christ, Paul encourages them to work together "without grumbling and arguing" (2:14).

The center section of the letter continues with Timothy and Epaphroditus (2:18–30), and then Paul (3:4–14), offered as examples of humble, sacrificial ministry that leads to unity. This call for unity comes to a crescendo at 4:2–3, as the apostle pleads with Euodia and Syntyche to "align" their "perspectives in the Lord." In other words, they are called on to "get it together!" It seems significant that the calls for unity are consistently integrated with concern for the gospel (e.g., 1:27–28; 2:22, 30; 4:2–3). A fragmented church cannot present a unified voice to a world in need of the good news.

Thus, Paul writes his friends in Philippi in part to address both the pressure they are experiencing from the surrounding culture as well as the tearing of the church's relational fabric. Most of them were not well-off financially, and the tensions faced as they lived out a countercultural gospel would have exacerbated their economic challenges. What, then, does Paul do to minister to his friends who had ministered to him in his incarceration? He crafts the letter we know as Philippians, exhorting them to persevere in living well for Christ, offering compelling examples to imitate, celebrating their partnership in his mission, and giving them strong theological foundations for continued growth in the faith.

## *The Production and Genre of Philippians*

In our world of email and text messages, the writing of letters with pen and ink is an increasingly endangered medium. Yet for those of us who have dabbled in the arcane art (especially for intrepid souls who use a fountain pen!), we may feel that the experience offers us an affinity with the apostle. We imagine Paul under arrest, sitting quietly at a desk, jotting out his letter[90] to the Philippians. Yet letter writing in the ancient world was not normally such a simple affair.

90. As with the famous oil on canvas, "Saint Paul Writing His Epistles," a work of the early seventeenth century, attributed to Valentin de Boulogne.

To begin with, writing materials, like animal skins and sheets of papyrus (a paper-like substance), were expensive, and the writing of letters often was done by a professional, a trained scribe (the technical term is an *amanuensis*; that is, a secretary).[91] Writing with a clear and attractive script was not easy. The process of letter writing often went as follows. The scribe made ink out of gum, soot, and oil, and then took notes on the author's thoughts, scored the papyrus sheets, and wrote out the thoughts, conferring with the author on how the letter was to be expressed. The whole process, if done by a professional scribe, was expensive and took time, but it allowed the author to focus on the content rather than the mechanical process of writing, which was seen as a form of manual labor. At the very least, the writing of a letter like Philippians would have involved the *crafting* of thoughts and movements of the work, probably over a period of days.

Although we have no indication that Paul used an amanuensis for the writing of Philippians, it would not be surprising if he did so, since it was a very common practice and one often used by Paul himself.[92] In any case, we need to understand that the writing of Philippians, rather than a simple process of Paul jotting out thoughts in a matter of minutes, almost certainly involved an extended period of shaping the words that we have in this letter, the apostle working—alone or with a scribe—to produce a powerful message that would have a profound impact on the believers in Philippi.

As we look at the details of Philippians, it is clear that the book follows the general form of letters written during Paul's time. For example, letters often contained a "letter opening" that included a prescript and prayer report (1:1–11) and a "letter closing" with final words to the recipients, formal greetings, and a blessing (4:10–23). Yet, what kind of letter was Philippians? Just as we have templates for a "business letter" or a "reference letter" today, or use conventions like "Dear" at the beginning of a personal note or "Sincerely" at the close of a more formal letter, handbooks of the era spoke of elements to be employed in various kinds of communication. Examining Philippians closely, scholars have spilled much ink in recent years trying to determine its specific genre. Some have described Philippians as a general letter of exhortation;[93] others a letter of consolation, written because the Philippians were

91. E. Randolph Richards, *Paul and First-Century Letter Writing: Secretaries, Composition, and Collection* (Downers Grove, IL: InterVarsity Press, 2004), 59–80.

92. It seems clear from Rom 16:22, for example, that a fellow believer named Tertius wrote the letter to the Romans (cf. 1 Pet 5:12). In several other places, Paul closes a letter by noting that he writes his greeting with his own hand (1 Cor 16:21; Gal 6:11; Col 4:18; 2 Thess 3:17; Phlm 19), which almost certainly indicates that the rest of the letter was actually written by an amanuensis. In 2 Thess 3:17 the apostle even says that his personalized greeting is a "sign" (σημεῖον) in all of his letters, which probably means that he considered his own handwriting style a mark of authenticity.

93. See, e.g., Timothy C. Geoffrion, *The Rhetorical Purpose and the Political and Military Character of Philippians: a Call to Stand Firm* (Lewiston, NY: Mellen, 1993), 23, who suggests that the apostle, playing on military and political language, wrote Philippians as "an exhortative letter primarily in order to encourage the Christians in Philippi to remain steadfast in their commitment to God, Christ, and the gospel ministry and in order to show them how to do so."

demoralized by Paul's imprisonment and their own sufferings.[94] Most would admit that Philippians, as with all of Paul's letters, is a mixed bag, incorporating elements of various letter forms.[95]

Yet in recent years many have argued that Philippians best fits the shape and intent of what was known in the apostle's culture as a letter of friendship.[96] Normally such friendship letters include, for instance, mention of being "absent" from those addressed (Phil 1:27; 2:12), the current situation of the writer and the recipients (1:12, 27; 2:19, 23), and acknowledgment that the recipients in some way have participated in meeting the needs of the letter's sender (4:14).[97] The warmth and joy expressed in Philippians seem to mark it as a "friendly letter." Gordon Fee stresses, however, that Paul's letters should be seen as more than normal friendship letters of the day since they reflect a deeper level of friendship and partnership in mission. In fact, the apostle writes to his churches as to an extended family, and family letters of the era were also considered a subset of "friendly letters."[98] Moreover, as Fee points out, Paul's letters also contain healthy doses of exhortation. Thus Philippians, while expressing the warmth of deep friendship and even family relationship, also has been shaped by a good deal of moral exhortation, the apostle challenging these brothers and sisters to live well for Christ.[99] Considering this combination of dynamics found in the letter, Fee labels Philippians as a Christian "hortatory letter of friendship," which seems a good way to characterize this book.[100] The hortatory nature of the writing also suggests that we should give attention to the common rhetorical conventions the apostle used in the course of the letter's production.

94. Paul A. Holloway, *Consolation in Philippians: Philosophical Sources and Rhetorical Strategy*, SNTSMS 112 (Cambridge: Cambridge University Press, 2001), 161.

95. See John T. Fitzgerald, "Philippians in Light of Some Ancient Discussions of Friendship," in *Friendship, Flattery, and Frankness of Speech: Studies on Friendship in the New Testament World*, ed. John T. Fitzgerald, NovTSup 82 (Leiden: Brill, 1996), 143–44, who suggests that "Philippians is in part—indeed, in large part—a 'letter of friendship,' but it is also much, much more." Similarly, see David E. Aune, *The New Testament in Its Literary Environment* (Philadelphia: Westminster, 1987), 203, who suggests that Paul was "both a creative and eclectic letter writer."

96. E.g., M. White, "Morality between Two Worlds: A Paradigm of Friendship in Philippians," in *Greeks, Romans, and Christians: Essays in Honor of Abraham J. Malherbe*, ed. D. L. Balch, E. Ferguson, and W. A. Meeks (Minneapolis: Fortress, 1990), 201–15; S. K. Stowers, "Friends and Enemies in the Politics of Heaven: Reading Theology in Philippians," in *Pauline Theology, Volume I*, ed. J. M. Bassler (Minneapolis: Fortress, 1991), 105–21. Duane Watson pushes back on this label, pointing out that friendship was such a widespread social value in the Greco-Roman world that the designation proves unhelpful. See Duane F. Watson, "The Integration of Epistolary and Rhetorical Analysis of Philippians," in *The Rhetorical Analysis of Scripture: Essays from the 1995 London Conference*, ed. S. E. Porter and T. H. Olbricht, JSNTSup 146 (Sheffield: Sheffield Academic Press, 1997), 402.

97. Fee, *Philippians*, 3.

98. In part following Loveday Alexander, "Hellenistic Letter-Forms and the Structure of Philippians," *JSNT* 37 (1989): 87–101, who also includes letter elements such as a prayer for the recipients (Phil 1:3–11), reassurance about the sender (vv. 12–26), and information about the movement of intermediaries (2:19–30). On family dynamics in Philippians, see especially Joseph H. Hellerman, "Brothers and Friends in Philippi: Family Honor in the Roman World and in Paul's Letter to the Philippians," *BTB* 39.1 (2009): 15–25; see also Reed, *Discourse Analysis*, 169.

99. Fee, *Philippians*, 10–11.

100. Fee, *Philippians*, 12.

## Cultural Conventions, Rhetoric, and Paul's Timeless Message

As noted above, Paul's letters are shaped by language and forms that effected good communication in the Greco-Roman world of the first century. At the same time, the apostle claims to be working on behalf of God, whose message and intentions—his world-shaping gospel—are transcultural and not bound to a particular time in history. Paul's words are a fresh, ever-relevant message to us because they are ultimately God's words to us (as part of the people of God of all times and places), even though they were originally specific to the Philippians. Yet to hear these words for ourselves today, we first must *hear* them, understand them, and grasp what and how they communicated to the Philippians in their original context.

For example, a passage like Philippians 4:10–20 highlights the importance of understanding certain cultural dynamics, particularly how persons in Paul's world would have thought about friendship. That cultural perspective stands out as different from the way that we would think about such relationships today. Communication is always embodied in cultural expressions of various kinds, which convey particular messages.

At a number of points in this commentary, we read the text in light of Greco-Roman rhetoric, which was a major focus of education in that era.[101] From rudimentary levels to very advanced forms of public oratory, rhetoric taught the art of forceful, compelling communication, and thus a number of scholars have studied Philippians in light of various forms of rhetoric.[102] Such an approach tends to be attempted on at least two levels. Some, for example, have sought to read the letter *as a whole* in light of the normal forms of public oratory as reflected in the rhetorical handbooks of the time, as though the whole letter were shaped along the lines of a speech.[103] Others, however, are not convinced. Jeffrey Reed, for instance, suggests that while letters of the era could contain rhetorical *elements*, the theory of writing "rhetorical letters" is absent from the handbooks, and letter writing constituted a

101. See, e.g., Bruce W. Winter, "Rhetoric," in *DPL* 820–22.

102. In recent years attention has been given to Paul's use of rhetoric in Philippians. For example, see L. G. Bloomquist, "The Rhetoric of Suffering in Paul's Letter to the Philippians: Socio-Rhetorical Reflections and Further Thoughts on a Post-Colonial Contribution to the Discussion," *ThJ* 35.2 (2004): 195–223; Samuel Guy, "A Politeuma Worth Pursuing: A Rhetorical Analysis of Philippians 3:20 in Light of Philippi's Sociological Composition," *SCJ* 22.1 (2019): 89–100; A. H. Snyman, "Philippians 4:10–23 from a Rhetorical Perspective," *AcT* 27.2 (2007): 168–85; Andris H. Snyman, "A Rhetorical Analysis of Philippians 1:1–11," *AcT* 24.2 (2004): 81–104; idem, "A Rhetorical Analysis of Philippians 1:12–26," *AcT* 25.1 (2005): 89–111; idem, "A Rhetorical Analysis of Philippians 3:1–11," *Neot* 40.2 (2006): 259–83; idem, "A Rhetorical Analysis of Philippians 3:12–21," *AcPB* 17 (2006): 327–48; Duane F. Watson, "A Rhetorical Analysis of Philippians and Its Implications for the Unity Question," *NovT* 30.1 (1988): 57–88.

103. A leader in this approach is Duane Watson, who writes of Philippians that "of the three species of rhetoric, Philippians is to be classified as deliberative, for it exhibits the major characteristics of this species." See Watson, "Rhetorical Analysis of Philippians," 59. Watson broadly divides the letter into the *Exordium* (1:3–26), the *Narratio* (1:27–30), the *Probatio* (2:1–3:21), and the *Peroratio* (4:1–20). Watson, however, in a subsequent article seeks an integration of this form of rhetorical analysis with epistolary analysis. See idem, "Integration."

different discipline.[104] Nevertheless, in a letter like Philippians we find rhetorical elements on the microlevel of the book.

For instance, concerning 2:6–11, we see the rhetorical impact of the *hymnos* form. As noted in our introduction to that passage, such a piece of writing or speaking was used, in part, as a way of celebrating an individual while reinforcing Roman values. Yet part of the brilliance of the so-called Christ hymn is that it actually subverts Roman cultural values, turning them on their head by demonstrating that the path to ultimate status was shame and death—not a very Roman thought at all. Think of how such a message would have *communicated* on the streets of Philippi, even as it pushed hard against the assumptions of an honor-oriented society in which gaining status through honor was a supreme value.

At 1:18 we consider Paul's use of the rhetorical question, "What can be said in response?" (τί γάρ), and at 1:22b–23 we witness Paul's use of a rhetorical device known as *dubitatio*, by which an author or speaker would feign uncertainty on which of two options might be the best course of action. The effect was to draw the audience into the tension of the possible outcomes before revealing which the author thought would be better. We also see Paul use the examples of Timothy and Epaphroditus at 2:18–3:1, and alliteration at 3:2 (βλέπετε τοὺς κύνας, βλέπετε τοὺς κακοὺς ἐργάτας, βλέπετε τὴν κατατομήν), based on the *b* sound at the beginning of each exhortation, shaping a fine, punchy form of rhetorical writing. The apostle also uses alliteration at 3:13, the *e* sound (ἕν, ἐπιλανθανόμενος, ἔμπροσθεν, and ἐπεκτεινόμενος), shaping that powerful moment in the discourse with an exalted style.

All the above are aspects of the cultural clothing in which Philippians is dressed. Such cultural frameworks and rhetorical forms are not necessarily transferrable to our contemporary cultural contexts (although some have correspondences in some modern cultures), but they need to be understood to hear Paul's timeless message well as a powerful piece of discourse. The timeless message transcends cultural boundaries, but it was originally expressed in language, means of argument, and cultural conventions that we can and should work to understand.

## The Unity of Philippians

As a highly crafted work, Philippians presents a rich, unified writing that follows an identifiable trajectory from start to finish. Yet the letter also contains a number of elements—literary twists and turns—that have puzzled scholars seeking to discern its organization. In fact, in the mid-twentieth century, several scholars championed the position that Philippians consists of at least two or three letters, pieced together

104. Reed, *Discourse Analysis*, 453–54.

in a literary patchwork. For example, when at Philippians 3:1 Paul writes, "Finally, my brothers and sisters . . . ," it sounds like he is about to end the letter; yet 3:2–14 suddenly shifts to a rather harsh warning about false ministers and then to Paul's reflections on his own religious identity. Some have read such shifts as indicating a letter fragment. Nevertheless, the view that Philippians consists of shorter letters pieced together by an editor has been increasingly abandoned—and with good reason,[105] for the overall crafting, development, and cohesion of the book makes good sense as it stands. I seek to give an account of its structure below,[106] but let me first address the broader unity of the letter by offering two important examples of how it has been crafted to make the whole book "fit together."

First, Gerald Peterman has demonstrated that there are extensive verbal and conceptual parallels between 1:3–11 and 4:10–20, framing the book as a whole with reflections on the apostle's relationship with the Philippians, especially their partnership in his ministry.[107] The first of these passages functions as the "letter opening" and the latter as the bulk of the "letter closing," suggesting that the whole of Philippians is balanced by these beginning and ending thoughts on the brothers and sisters in Philippi. A number of these parallels may be seen as follows (especially as we pay attention to the words in Greek).[108]

105. Whereas in 1985 David Garland wrote, "Many still maintain that the epistle is a unity, but their numbers seem to be diminishing" (David E. Garland, "The Composition and Unity of Philippians: Some Neglected Literary Factors," *NovT* 27.2 [1985]: 142), in 2017 Paul Holloway could write, "A generation ago most critical scholars were agreed that Philippians as it appears in the manuscript tradition is a composite document pasted together from two or three originally separate Pauline letters. Today that view has largely been abandoned" (Holloway, *Philippians*, 10).

For the background of the discussion, see, e.g., Holloway, *Consolation*, 7–33. The external evidence for this patchwork approach is weak at best. The internal evidence focuses on the content of the letter—e.g., that "finally" (τὸ λοιπόν) at 3:1 normally marks the ending of a letter, but the letter continues, only to have "finally" (τὸ λοιπόν) repeated at 4:8. Yet as Margaret Thrall has pointed out, τὸ λοιπόν could be used in postclassical Greek as a transition device (though she concludes that in the case of Phil 3:1 it may be read as a closing formula). See Margaret E. Thrall, *Greek Particles in the New Testament: Linguistic and Exegetical Studies*, New Testament Tools, Studies and Documents 3 (Leiden: Brill, 1962), 25–30. Also, if we cannot make sense of an author's moves in crafting the letter as it stands, why hypothesize that an editor would craft a final product in this way? See Fee, *Philippians*, 22.

106. See especially the detailed discourse analysis of Philippians by Reed, *Discourse Analysis*, 412–13, who writes,

> The resulting evidence allows for a single-letter reading of the letter, that is, a reader is able to produce a coherent reading of the discourse as a single whole *via its linguistic structure and texture*. . . . The epistolary STRUCTURE (register) of Philippians . . . may be accounted for as a single whole when compared to other epistolary literature of its type.

In addition to the literary analysis described here, there have also been rhetorical analyses of the letter's unity, as with Watson, "Rhetorical Analysis of Philippians," 57–88. However, Reed concludes that, although letters of the era could contain rhetorical elements, the theory of writing "rhetorical letters" was absent from the rhetorical handbooks. Letter writing was considered a different discipline (Reed, *Discourse Analysis*, 453–54). Watson himself, a few years after the article noted above, sought to assess the rhetoric of the letter in light of epistolary dynamics; see Watson, "Integration."

107. Gerald W. Peterman, *Paul's Gift from Philippi: Conventions of Gift Exchange and Christian Giving*, SNTSMS 92 (Cambridge: Cambridge University Press, 1997), 91–92.

108. Peterman, *Paul's Gift from Philippi*, 91–93. I have included here those parallels that seem most clear with respect to terms used or strong conceptual correspondence.

| "joy" | "I rejoiced" |
|---|---|
| χαρᾶς (1:4) | Ἐχάρην (4:10) |
| "your participation" | "shared" |
| τῇ κοινωνίᾳ ὑμῶν (1:5) | ἐκοινώνησεν (4:15) |
| "the gospel" | "the gospel" |
| τὸ εὐαγγέλιον (1:5) | τοῦ εὐαγγελίου (4:15) |
| "from the first day" | "at the beginning" |
| ἀπὸ τῆς πρώτης ἡμέρας (1:5) | ἐν ἀρχῇ (4:15) |
| "the one who began a good work among you" | "the one enabling me" |
| ὁ ἐναρξάμενος ἐν ὑμῖν ἔργον (1:6) | τῷ ἐνδυναμοῦντί με (4:13) |
| "to think this way about all of you" | "giving careful thought to what might be done for me" |
| φρονεῖν ὑπὲρ πάντων ὑμῶν (1:7) | τὸ ὑπὲρ ἐμοῦ φρονεῖν (4:10) |
| "fellow participants" | "sharing" |
| συγκοινωνούς (1:7) | συγκοινωνήσαντές (4:14) |
| "imprisonment" | "in my difficulty" |
| δεσμοῖς (1:7) | τῇ θλίψει (4:14) |
| "might overflow" | "I have more than I need" |
| περισσεύῃ (1:9) | περισσεύω (4:18) |
| "having been filled" | "have been supplied/will supply" |
| πεπληρωμένοι (1:11) | πεπλήρωμαι/πληρώσει (4:18, 19) |
| "fruit" | "interest" (lit., "fruit") |
| καρπόν (1:11) | καρπόν (4:17) |
| "Jesus" | "Jesus" |
| Ἰησοῦ (1:11) | Ἰησοῦ (4:19) |
| "glory . . . of God" | "to . . . God . . . glory" |
| δόξαν . . . θεοῦ (1:11) | τῷ . . . θεῷ . . . δόξα (4:20) |

Why would an author use extensive verbal and conceptual parallels like the ones we have here? We need to remember that ancient writings consisted of mostly unbroken lines of letters—no headings, no punctuation, and no spaces between words. Consequently, authors had to mark movements of a document in different ways. One important convention they used was called *inclusio*, by which the beginning and ending of a discourse, or a subsection of a discourse, or even a brief passage, could be marked with distant parallelism, the same or similar words being used at the beginning and ending. In this way, ancient authors used *inclusio* to mark out a cohesive unit of text, much like we use subheadings in a book chapter today.

When we consider the parallels between Philippians 1:3–11 and 4:10–20, they are unmistakable and extensive, framing the entire book as a cohesive document.

Yet this is not the only use of distant parallelism in the book. In his 1985 article titled "The Composition and Unity of Philippians: Some Neglected Literary Factors," David Garland points out eight literary parallels between 1:27–2:4 and 3:16–4:3, marking 1:27–4:3 as an important and cohesive section of the document—the main body of the letter.[109] As we have already seen above in our section called "The Church in Philippi and Paul's Reasons for Writing," Paul launches the center section of the letter with 1:27–2:4. Garland notes that the language of this passage is echoed extensively in 3:16–4:3, the end of the letter's main body. I have expanded Garland's list to no fewer than seventeen lexical and conceptual parallels between 1:27–2:4 and 3:15–4:4a:

| | |
|---|---|
| "worthy of the gospel" | "in the gospel" |
| ἀξίως τοῦ εὐαγγελίου (1:27) | ἐν τῷ εὐαγγελίῳ (4:3) |
| "of Christ" | "of Christ" |
| Χριστοῦ (1:27, 29) | Χριστοῦ (3:18; cf. 3:20) |
| "live out your heavenly citizenship" | "citizenship . . . live/live a pattern of life" |
| πολιτεύεσθε (1:27) | πολίτευμα (3:20)/περιπατοῦντας/ περιπατοῦσιν (3:17–18) |
| "you are standing firm in one Spirit" | "stand firm in the Lord" |
| στήκετε ἐν ἑνὶ πνεύματι (1:27) | στήκετε ἐν κυρίω (4:1) |
| "striving together" | "worked hard alongside of me" |
| συναθλοῦντες (1:27) | συνήθλησάν μοι (4:3) |
| "for the gospel faith" | "in the gospel" |
| τῇ πίστει τοῦ εὐαγγελίου (1:27) | ἐν τῷ εὐαγγελίῳ (4:3) |
| "of destruction" | "destruction" |
| ἀπωλείας (1:28) | ἀπώλεια (3:19) |
| "of . . . salvation" | "Savior" |
| σωτηρίας (1:28) | σωτῆρα (3:20) |
| "those standing against" | "enemies" |
| τῶν ἀντικειμένων (1:28) | τοὺς ἐχθρούς (3:18) |

109. The parallels are as follows: πολιτεύεσθε (1:27)/πολίτευμα (3:20); στήκετε (1:27)/στήκετε (4:1); συναθλοῦντες (1:27)/συνήθλησάν μοι (4:3); ἀπωλείας (1:28)/ἀπώλεια (3:19); σωτηρίας (1:28)/σωτῆρα (3:20); παράκλησις (2:1)/παρακαλῶ (4:2); φρονῆτε/ἓν φρονοῦντες (2:2)/φρονῶμεν/φρονεῖν (3:15; 4:2); χαράν (2:2)/χαρά (4:1). See Garland, "Composition," 160–62. Garland also noted other elements that make the whole of Philippians cohesive. On the use of *inclusio* as a structuring device, see George H. Guthrie, *The Structure of Hebrews: A Text-Linguistic Analysis*, NovTSup 73 (Leiden: Brill, 1994), 15; H. Van Dyke Parunak, "Oral Typesetting: Some Uses of Biblical Structure," *Bib* 62.2 (1981): 153–68.

| "from God" | "God" |
|---|---|
| ἀπὸ θεοῦ (1:28) | ὁ θεός (3:15, 19) |
| "you saw I had and now hear that I have" | "Be imitators of me" |
| εἴδετε ἐν ἐμοὶ καὶ ἀκούετε ἐν ἐμοί (1:30) | Συμμιμηταί μου γίνεσθε (3:17) |
| "love" | "loved" |
| ἀγάπη (2:1, 2) | ἀγαπητοί (4:1) |
| "encouragement" | "I urge" |
| παράκλησις (2:1) | παρακαλῶ (4:2) |
| "being like-minded . . . sharing a common perspective" | "let us embrace this mindset . . . align their perspective" |
| τὸ αὐτὸ φρονῆτε/φρονοῦντες (2:2) | φρονῶμεν/τὸ αὐτὸ φρονεῖν (3:15; 4:2) |
| "my joy" | "my . . . joy"/"rejoice" |
| μου τὴν χαράν (2:2) | χαρὰ . . . μου (4:1)/χαίρετε (4:4a) |
| "with humility" | "of humiliation" |
| ταπεινοφροσύνῃ (2:3) | ταπεινώσεως (3:21) |
| "focused . . . on" | "pay careful attention" |
| σκοποῦντες (2:4) | σκοπεῖτε (3:17) |

These parallel elements play a significant role in highlighting the letter's main theme of unity while also framing the book's center section, which I have identified as extending from 1:27 to 4:4a. As we work through the commentary, we will deal with the details surrounding these elements as well as other uses of literary parallelism to craft subsections of the letter. But for now, I simply underscore that the letter *as a whole* has been strategically crafted, not only to reiterate key themes but also to mark major movements in the book. This use of extensive, distant parallelism offers us a compelling reason for receiving the entire letter as one, cohesive document.

Before leaving the question of how Philippians has been shaped, however, we need to consider one other interesting dynamic we find in the book, a dynamic that spans the book as a whole: Paul's use of the "rejoice/joy" theme. In the above treatment of the parallels at 1:27–2:4 and 3:15–4:4a, we note the repetition of "my joy" at 2:2 and 4:1. But we should also note that, at a number of key turning points throughout this letter, we find this theme of joy. In fact, at a few points the apostle *doubles* his statements or exhortations concerning joy, and this may offer one important clue to the book's organization.

For example, in the first pair of exhortations to "rejoice" found at 1:18, the first exhortation refers to what has gone before, while the second anticipates what the apostle will say next. In the first, Paul rejoices that Christ has been preached, even by those with false motives! In the second, the apostle continues to rejoice, anticipating his deliverance. In this way, the doubling of the rejoice theme at 1:18 may serve as a literary "hinge," transitioning from one movement of the letter to the next.[110] Paul doubles his statements about or exhortations to joy at three other key turning points in the letter: 2:17–18, 2:28–3:1, and 4:4. These seams also may be read as transitional,[111] the theme of joy playing a significant role in structurally shaping the book and contributing to the unity of the book as a whole. The seams highlighted by the motif may be depicted in the figure below.

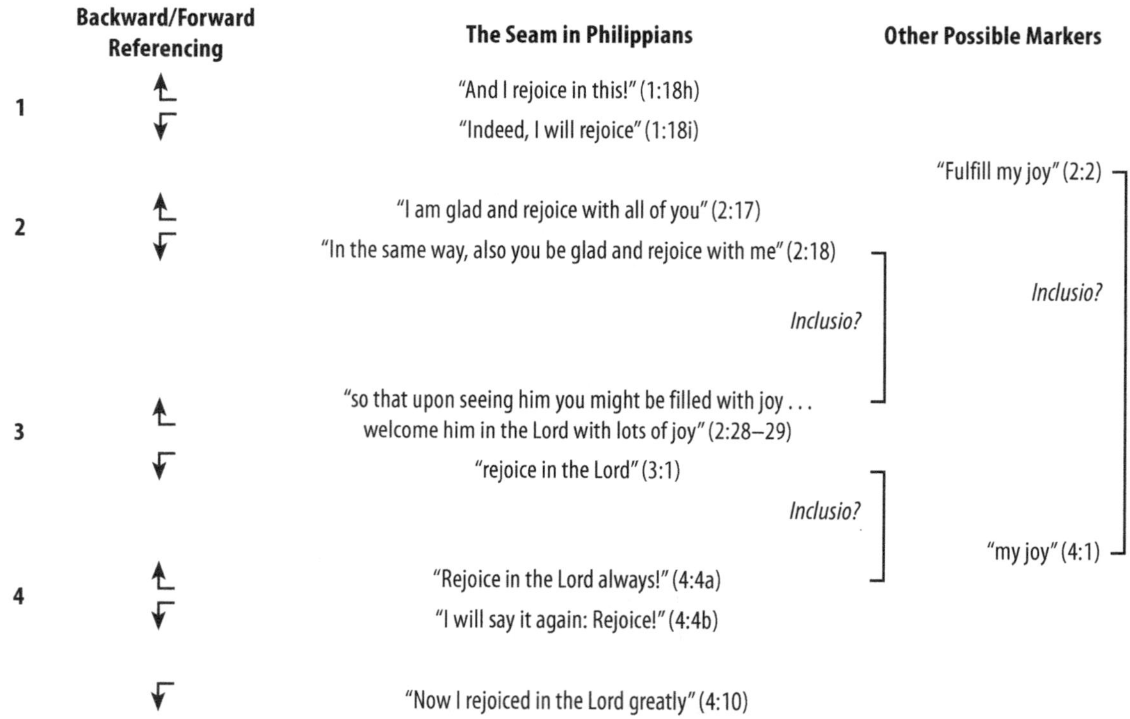


If this reading of the structural role played by the "joy" doubling motif at key points in the letter is correct, this important theme may also be seen as playing a part in crafting an *inclusio* around three important movements in the letter, also depicted in the figure. We have already noted the parallel between Paul's joy at 2:2 and 4:1. We

110. On a similar use of transition devices in another NT book, see Guthrie, *Structure of Hebrews*, 94–111, especially the material dealing with "hook words" and "overlapping transitions."

111. Admittedly, the backward and forward referencing in some of the seams are not as clear. As transition moments in the discourse, the *exact* placement of the end of one section and the beginning of the next is not as important as recognizing the marking of a transition. Thus, for instance, scholars have debated extensively whether the exhortation at 3:1 concludes the previous unit or introduces the one that follows, and we could quibble about placing a unit break between 4:4a and 4:4b. Yet transitions by their nature are meant to facilitate a smooth turning. Thus the "hard" breaks in our outlines of the book should not be the focus but rather should be considered as the marking out of major movements.

find similar parallels marking 2:18–30 and 3:1–4:4a. Notice that Paul first encourages the Philippians to have joy in 2:18, and this is echoed at 2:28–29, which specifically encourages them to embrace joy with the coming of Epaphroditus. Notice also the exact repetition of "rejoice in the Lord" (χαίρετε ἐν κυρίῳ) at 3:1 and 4:4a—the only two places in the book (indeed, in all of the NT) where this exact wording occurs. What then of the single use of the verb at 4:10, which does not involve a doubling of the motif, nor does it seem to be involved in the crafting of an *inclusio*? It is possible that with this iteration of the motif Paul breaks the pattern by returning to a reflection on his own act of rejoicing (1:18; 2:17) as he prepares to close out the letter. This expression of joy is forward referring, with the apostle now turning to the Philippians' concern for him and his joy in that concern.

The point of this section has been to demonstrate that the crafting of Philippians as a letter speaks to the question of the book's unity. Both the marking of broad sections of the book—indeed the book as a whole—with distant parallelism, and the consistent and strategic use of the "rejoice/joy" motif throughout, suggest that Philippians should be considered a unified whole. I started this section by stating that Philippians "follows an identifiable trajectory from start to finish." This is not to suggest that discerning the book's structure is easy—far from it! Consequently, we now turn to the question of the letter's organization.

## The Structure of Philippians

As we work our way through Philippians and in accordance with the conventions of this commentary series, we give detailed attention to both the literary context and the structure of each unit, and it is vital for the act of preaching and teaching that we orient the reader to the way various passages function and "speak." Yet, it may help to give an account of the big picture of the book, offering a sense of the letter's main movements and how they relate to one another. In broad terms Philippians has a letter opening, a letter body, and a letter closing. This overall development of Philippians, with subsections of the letter body, may be depicted as follows:

- The Letter Opening, involving a prescript and prayer report celebrating the Philippians' partnership in the gospel (1:1–11)
- The Letter Body (1:12–4:9), which includes:
    - The Body Opening, focusing on Paul's imprisonment (1:12–26)
    - The Main Body of the Letter, which gives a series of examples interspersed with exhortations (1:27–4:4a):
        - Exhortation to Live in Unity (1:27–2:4)
        - *The Example of Christ (2:5–11)*

Further Exhortations to Unity (2:12–17)
*The Example of Timothy and Epaphroditus (2:18–30)*
*The Example of Paul's Christocentric Life and Ministry*, with an initial series of exhortations (3:1–14)
Exhortations to Embrace *Paul's Christocentric Example* and Unity with One Another (3:15–4:4a)
The Body Closing, which offers a flurry of exhortations (4:4b–9)
The Letter Closing (4:10–23), involving reflection on partnership with the Philippians and a postscript

Notice the balanced way in which the letter develops. The letter opening, with its prescript and prayer report, is mirrored by the letter closing and its postscript, both focusing in part on the Philippians' partnership in Paul's ministry. The body opening in 1:12–26, which focuses on Paul's current situation and the advance of the gospel, is balanced by the body closing at 4:4b–9, where Paul challenges the Philippians to turn from anxiety and follow his example. At the heart of the letter stands the series of stellar examples of leadership—Christ, Timothy, Epaphroditus, and Paul—interspersed with exhortations to live well and in unity with one another. The mention of false teachers, or opponents, at 3:2–4 and 3:18–19, flank Paul's presentation of himself as an example, providing a contrast to the apostle's vision for true Christian ministers.

Thus, in Philippians we have a beautiful, powerful hortatory letter of friendship, shot through with expressions of joy and exhortations to joy. Paul generally follows the broad outline of the letter form but shapes it to address his relationship with this much-loved church, as well as key issues facing the Philippians. The heart of the book focuses on the need for unity in the church and encourages these friends to look to key examples of sound ministry, who will help them stand together against various forms of opposition and for the proclamation of the gospel in the world.

## An Outline of Philippians

I. The Letter Opening: A Prescript and a Prayer Report (1:1–11)
  A. The Letter Prescript (1:1–2)
    1. Senders and Recipients (v. 1)
    2. A Blessing (v. 2)
  B. A Joyful Prayer Report (1:3–11)
    1. Paul's Affectionate Appreciation for the Philippians (vv. 3–8)
    2. Paul Prays for the Philippians (vv. 9–11)

- II. The Letter Body (1:12–4:9)
  - A. The Body Opening: Paul's Current Situation (1:12–26)
    - 1. A Joyful Report on the Progress of the Gospel (vv. 12–18g)
      - a. Paul's Imprisonment Has Advanced the Gospel (vv. 12–14)
      - b. Proclamation of the Messiah Is Driven by Various Motives (vv. 15–18g)
    - 2. Paul's Hopeful Expectation concerning His Imprisonment (vv. 18h–26)
      - a. Confidence in the Outcome (vv. 18h–20)
      - b. Two Good Alternatives: Life or Death (vv. 21–24)
      - c. Paul Is Confident That He Will Live On to Fulfill His Ministry (vv. 25–26)
  - B. The Main Body of the Letter: A Call for Unity in the Church (1:27–4:4a)
    - 1. An Exhortation to Live Out the Unity of Community (1:27–2:4)
      - a. Stand Firm in Unity (v. 27)
      - b. Stand in Unity in the Face of Opposition (vv. 28–30)
      - c. Live in Unity by Self-Sacrificial Love for One Another (2:1–4)
    - 2. Be Like Christ Jesus, the Preeminent Example of Self-Sacrifice (2:5–11)
      - a. Adopt Christ's Mindset (v. 5)
      - b. Follow Christ's Example of Humility (vv. 6–8)
      - c. Attend to God's Great Reversal of Christ's Status (vv. 9–11)
    - 3. Further Exhortations to Unity and Exclamations of Joy (2:12–17)
      - a. Work Out What God is Working In (vv. 12–13)
      - b. Work Out Community Unity (vv. 14–16)
      - c. Paul's Joy in Ministry to the Philippians (v. 17)
    - 4. Timothy and Epaphroditus as Exemplars of Self-Sacrifice (2:18–30)
      - a. An Exhortation to Join Paul in His Joy (v. 18)
      - b. Timothy (vv. 19–24)
      - c. Epaphroditus (vv. 25–30)
    - 5. The Example of Paul's Christocentric Life and Ministry (3:1–14)
      - a. An Exhortation to Rejoice (v. 1)
      - b. False and True Standards of Relationship with God (vv. 2–6)
      - c. The True Nature of Relationship with God—Knowing Christ (vv. 7–14)
        - (1) Paul Considers All Things to Be "Loss" Compared to the "Gain" of Knowing Christ (vv. 7–8b)
        - (2) The "Gain" of Knowing Christ (vv. 8c–14)
    - 6. Exhortations to Embrace Paul's Christocentric Pattern of Life (3:15–4:4a)
      - a. A Call to Embrace Paul's Christocentric Pattern of Life (vv. 15–16)
      - b. Imitate the Right Leaders (vv. 17–21)
      - c. Final Exhortations to Stand Firm in Unity (4:1–4a)
  - C. The Body Closing: Exhortations (4:4b–9)

III. The Letter Closing (4:10–23)

- A. The Philippians' Gift and Partnership in Ministry (4:10–20)
    1. Paul's Joy in the Philippians' Gift (v. 10)
    2. Paul's Contentment in His Circumstances (vv. 11–13)
    3. The Philippians' Partnership with Paul (vv. 14–20)
- B. Postscript: Final Greetings and Blessing (4:21–23)
    1. Closing Greetings (vv. 21–22)
    2. A Blessing (v. 23)

# Select Bibliography


Alexander, Loveday. "Hellenistic Letter-Forms and the Structure of Philippians." *JSNT* 37 (1989): 87–101.

Allen, Pauline, ed. *John Chrysostom, Homilies on Philippians*. Writings from the Greco-Roman World 16. Atlanta: Society of Biblical Literature, 2013.

Anderson, Garwood P. *Paul's New Perspective: Charting a Soteriological Journey*. Downers Grove, IL: IVP Academic, 2016.

Arzt-Grabner, Peter. "Paul's Letter Thanksgiving." Pages 129–58 in *Paul and the Ancient Letter Form*. Edited by Stanley E. Porter and Sean A. Adams. Pauline Studies 6. Leiden: Brill, 2010.

Attridge, Harold W. *The Epistle to the Hebrews: A Commentary on the Epistle to the Hebrews*. Hermeneia. Philadelphia: Fortress, 1989.

Aune, David E. *The New Testament in Its Literary Environment*. Philadelphia: Westminster, 1987.

Bakirtzēs, Charalampos, and Helmut Koester, eds. *Philippi at the Time of Paul and after His Death*. Harrisburg, PA: Trinity Press International, 1998.

Balz, Horst Robert, and Gerhard Schneider. *Exegetical Dictionary of the New Testament*. Grand Rapids: Eerdmans, 1990.

Barclay, John M. G. *Paul and the Gift*. Grand Rapids: Eerdmans, 2015.

Barrett, C. K. *The Gospel according to St John: An Introduction with Commentary and Notes on the Greek Text*. London: SPCK, 1978.

Barth, Karl. *The Epistle to the Philippians*. Louisville: Westminster John Knox, 2002.

Basevi, C., and J. Chapa. "Philippians 2.6–11: The Rhetorical Function of a Pauline 'Hymn.'" Pages 338–56 in *Rhetoric and the New Testament: Essays from the 1992 Heidelberg Conference*. Edited by Thomas H. Olbricht and Stanley E. Porter. JSNTSup 90. Sheffield: JSOT Press, 1993.

Bauckham, Richard. *Jesus and the God of Israel: God Crucified and Other Studies on the New Testament's Christology of Divine Identity*. Grand Rapids: Eerdmans, 2008.

Becker, Ernest. *The Denial of Death*. New York: Free Press, 1997.

Begg, Alistair. *On Being a Pastor: For Pastors and Teachers*. Chicago: Moody, 2004.

Bengel, Johann Albrecht. *Gnomon of the New Testament, Tr., with Notes, Revised and Ed. by A. R. Fausset*. Edinburgh: T&T Clark, 1857.

———. *New Testament Word Studies*. 2 vols. Kregel Reprint Library. Grand Rapids: Kregel, 1971.

Bernat, David A. "Circumcision." Pages 471–74 in *Eerdmans Dictionary of Early Judaism*. Edited by John J. Collins and Daniel C. Harlow. Grand Rapids: Eerdmans, 2010.

Berry, Wendell. *A Timbered Choir: The Sabbath Poems, 1979–1997*. Washington, DC: Counterpoint, 1998.

Bingham, Sandra. *The Praetorian Guard: A History of Rome's Elite Special Forces*. Waco, TX: Baylor University Press, 2013.

Bird, Michael F., and Preston M. Sprinkle. *The Faith of Jesus Christ: Exegetical, Biblical, and Theological Studies*. Milton Keynes: Paternoster; Peabody, MA: Hendrickson, 2010.

Blass, Friedrich, and Albert Debrunner. *A Greek Grammar of the New Testament and Other Early Christian Literature*. Edited by Robert Walter Funk. Chicago: University of Chicago Press, 1961.

Bloomquist, L. G. "The Rhetoric of Suffering in Paul's Letter to the Philippians: Socio-Rhetorical Reflections and Further Thoughts on a Post-Colonial Contribution to the Discussion." *Thf* 35 (2004): 195–223.

Bockmuehl, Markus N. A. *A Commentary on the Epistle to the Philippians*. BNTC. Grand Rapids: Baker Academic, 2013.

———. "'The Form of God' (Phil 2:6): Variations on a Theme of Jewish Mysticism." *JTS* 48 (1997): 1–23.

Booth, Steve. "Philippi: A Historical and Archaeological Study." *BI* 37 (2011): 39–42.

Bormann, Lukas. *Philippi: Stadt und Christengemeinde zur Zeit des Paulus*. NovTSup 78. Leiden: Brill, 1995.

Bounds, E. M., and Edward D. Andrews. *Power through Prayer: A Healthy Prayer Life*. Updated and Expanded. Cambridge, OH: Christian Publishing House, 2018.

Brélaz, Cédric. "First-Century Philippi: Contextualizing Paul's Visit." Pages 153–88 in *The First Urban Churches 4: Roman Philippi*. Edited by James R. Harrison and L. L. Welborn. WGRW-Sup 13. Atlanta: SBL Press, 2018.

Brewer, Raymond Rush. "The Meaning of *Politeuesthe* in Philippians 1:27." *JBL* 73 (1954): 76–83.

Bridges, Jerry. *The Discipline of Grace*. Colorado Springs, CO: NavPress, 2006.

Briones, David. "Paul's Intentional 'Thankless Thanks' in Philippians 4.10–20." *JSNT* 34 (2011): 47–69.

Broneer, O. "The Isthmian Victory Crown." *AJA* 66 (1962): 259–63.

Bruce, Alexander Balmain. *The Humiliation of Christ in Its Physical, Ethical, and Official Aspects*. Edinburgh: T&T Clark, 1876.

Bruce, F. F. *Philippians*. NIBCNT. Peabody, MA: Hendrickson, 1989.

Buchanan, Colin Ogilvie. "Epaphroditus' Sickness and the Letter to the Philippians." *EvQ* 36 (1964): 157–66.

Buechner, Frederick. *Beyond Words: Daily Readings in the ABC's of Faith*. San Francisco: HarperOne, 2004.

Burk, Denny. "On the Articular Infinitive in Philippians 2:6: A Grammatical Note with Christological Implications." *TynBul* 55 (2004): 253–74.

Campbell, Constantine R. *Paul and Union with Christ: An Exegetical and Theological Study*. Grand Rapids: Zondervan, 2012.

Capes, David B. *Old Testament Yahweh Texts in Paul's Christology*. WUNT 2/47. Tübingen: Mohr Siebeck, 1992.

Capes, David B., Rodney Reeves, and E. Randolph Richards. *Rediscovering Paul: An Introduction to His World, Letters, and Theology*. Downers Grove, IL: IVP Academic; Nottingham: Apollos, 2007.

Cassidy, Richard J. *Paul in Chains: Roman Imprisonment and the Letters of St. Paul*. New York: Crossroad, 2001.

Cerfaux, Lucien. *Le Christ dans la Théologie de Saint Paul*. Paris: Éditions du Cerf, 1951.

Cicero. *The Verrine Orations, Volume II*. LCL 293. Translated by L. H. G. Greenwood. Cambridge: Harvard University Press, 1953.

Cohick, Lynn H. *Philippians*. SGBC. Grand Rapids: Zondervan, 2013.

Collins, Adela Yarbro. "Psalms, Philippians 2:6–11, and the Origins of Christology." *BibInt* 11 (2003): 361–72.

Colson, Charles W., and Ellen Santilli Vaughn. *The Body*. Nashville: Thomas Nelson, 1994.

Cornwell, Bernard. *Waterloo: The History of Four Days, Three Armies and Three Battles*. New York: HarperCollins, 2014.

Cousar, Charles B. *Philippians and Philemon: A Commentary*. Louisville: Westminster John Knox, 2009.

Crosby, H. Lamar, trans. *Dio Chrysostom: Discourses 37–60*. LCL 376. Cambridge: Harvard University Press, 1946.

Croy, N. Clayton. "'To Die is Gain' (Philippians 1:19–26): Does Paul Contemplate Suicide?" *JBL* 122 (2003): 517–31.

Cullmann, Oscar. *Peter, Disciple, Apostle, Martyr: A Historical and Theological Study*. Translated by Floyd Filson. London: SCM, 1953.

Culpepper, R. Alan. "Co-workers in Suffering: Philippians 2:19–30." *RevExp* 77 (1980): 349–58.

Dana, H. E., and Julius R. Mantey. *A Manual Grammar of the Greek New Testament*. New York: Macmillan, 1969.

Danker, Frederick W. "A Symphony of New Testament Hymns: Commentary on Philippians 2:5–11, Colossians 1:15–20, Ephesians 2:14–16, 1 Timothy 3:16, Titus 3:4–7, 1 Peter 3:18–22, and 2 Timothy 2:11–13." *CBQ* 60 (1998): 161–62.

Danker, Frederick W., Walter Bauer, and William Arndt, eds. *A Greek-English Lexicon of the New Testament and Other Early Christian Literature*. 3rd ed. Chicago: University of Chicago Press, 2000.

De Vos, Craig Steven. *Church and Community Conflicts: The Relationships of the Thessalonian, Corinthian, and Philippian Churches with Their Wider Civic Communities*. SBLDS 168. Atlanta: Scholars Press, 1999.

Denniston, J. D., and K. J. Dover. *The Greek Particles*. London: Duckworth [Bristol Classical Press]; Indianapolis: Hackett, 1996.

Droge, Arthur J. "Mori Lucrum: Paul and Ancient Theories of Suicide." *NovT* 30 (1988): 263–86.

Droge, Arthur J., and James D. Tabor. *A Noble Death: Suicide and Martyrdom among Christians and Jews in Antiquity*. San Francisco: HarperSanFrancisco, 1992.

Dunn, James D. G. *Beginning from Jerusalem*. Grand Rapids: Eerdmans, 2008.

———. "Christ, Adam, and Preexistence." Pages 74–83 in *Where Christology Began: Essays on Philippians 2*. Edited by Ralph P. Martin and Brian J. Dodd. Louisville: Westminster John Knox, 1998.

———. "Once More, Πιστις Χριστου." Pages 61–81 in *Pauline Theology, Volume IV: Looking Back, Pressing On*. Edited by E. Elizabeth Johnson and David M. Hay. Atlanta: Scholars Press, 1997.

Edart, Jean-Baptiste. *L'Épître aux Philippiens: Rhétorique et Composition Stylistique*. Études Bibliques 45. Paris: Gabalda, 2002.

Edsall, Benjamin A., and Jennifer R. Strawbridge. "The Song We Used to Sing?: Hymn 'Traditions' and Reception in Pauline Letters." *JSNT* 37 (2015): 290–311.

Edwards, Mark J., ed. *Galatians, Ephesians, Philippians*. ACCS 8. Downers Grove, IL: IVP Academic, 1999.

Ellicott, Charles John. *A Critical and Grammatical Commentary on St. Paul's Epistles to the Philippians, Colossians, and to Philemon, with a Revised Translation*. London: John W. Parker and Son, 1861.

Ellis, E. Earle. "Paul and His Coworkers." Pages 183–89 in *Dictionary of Paul and His Letters*. Edited by Gerald F. Hawthorne, Ralph P. Martin, and Daniel G. Reid. Downers Grove, IL: InterVarsity Press, 1993.

———. *Prophecy and Hermeneutic in Early Christianity: New Testament Essays*. Tübingen: Mohr Siebeck, 1978.

Erickson, Millard J. *Christian Theology*. Grand Rapids: Baker, 1983.

Fabricatore, Daniel J. *Form of God, Form of a Servant: An Examination of the Greek Noun μορφή in Philippians 2:6–7*. Lanham, MD: University Press of America, 2010.

Fee, Gordon D. *1 and 2 Timothy, Titus*. NIBCNT. Peabody, MA: Hendrickson, 1995.

———. *God's Empowering Presence: The Holy Spirit in the Letters of Paul*. Peabody, MA: Hendrickson, 1994.

———. *Paul's Letter to the Philippians*. NICNT. Grand Rapids: Eerdmans, 1995.

———. "Philippians 2:5–11: Hymn or Exalted Pauline Prose?" *BBR* 2 (1992): 29–46.

Fitzgerald, John T. "Philippians in Light of Some Ancient Discussions of Friendship." Pages 141–60 in *Friendship, Flattery, and Frankness of Speech: Studies on Friendship in the New Testament World*. Edited by John T. Fitzgerald. NovTSup 82. Leiden: Brill, 1996.

Fitzmyer, Joseph A. "The Consecutive Meaning of Eφ' Ω in Romans 5.12." *NTS* 39 (1993): 321–39.

Flexsenhar, Michael, III. "The Provenance of Philippians and Why It Matters: Old Questions, New Approaches." *JSNT* 42 (2019): 18–45.

Fowl, Stephen E. *Philippians*. THNTC. Grand Rapids: Eerdmans, 2005.

———. *The Story of Christ in the Ethics of Paul: An Analysis of the Function of the Hymnic Material in the Pauline Corpus*. JSNTSup 36. Sheffield: Sheffield Academic Press, 1990.

Frey, Jörg. "Paul's Jewish Identity." Pages 285–321 in *Jewish Identity in the Greco-Roman World/Jüdische Identität in der Griechisch-Römischen Welt*. Edited by Jörg Frey, Daniel R. Schwartz, and Stephanie Gripentrog. Ancient Judaism and Early Christianity 73. Leiden: Brill, 2008.

Furnish, Victor Paul. "The Place and Purpose of Philippians 3." *NTS* 10 (1963): 80–88.

Garland, David E. "The Composition and Unity of Philippians: Some Neglected Literary Factors." *NovT* 27 (1985): 141–73.

———. "Philippians 1:1–26: The Defense and Confirmation of the Gospel." *RevExp* 77 (1980): 327–36.

Garrett, James Leo. *Systematic Theology: Biblical, Historical, and Evangelical*. 2 vols. Grand Rapids: Eerdmans, 1995.

Geoffrion, Timothy C. *The Rhetorical Purpose and the Political and Military Character of Philippians: A Call to Stand Firm*. Lewiston, NY: Mellen, 1993.

Golden, Mark. *Sport in the Ancient World from A to Z*. London: Routledge, 2004.

Gorman, Michael J. *Apostle of the Crucified Lord: A Theological Introduction to Paul and His Letters*. 2nd ed. Grand Rapids: Eerdmans, 2017.

———. *Participating in Christ: Explorations in Paul's Theology and Spirituality*. Grand Rapids: Baker Academic, 2019.

Gundry, Robert H. "Style and Substance in 'the Myth of God Incarnate' according to Philippians 2:6–11." Pages 271–93 in *Crossing the Boundaries: Essays in Biblical Interpretation in Honour of Michael D. Goulder*. Edited by Stanley E. Porter, Paul M. Joyce, and David E. Orton. BibInt 8. Leiden: Brill, 1994.

Gundry Volf, Judith M. *Paul and Perseverance: Staying in and Falling Away*. WUNT 2/37. Tübingen: Mohr Siebeck, 1990.

Guthrie, George H. *2 Corinthians*. BECNT. Grand Rapids: Baker Academic, 2015.

———. "Paul's Triumphal Procession Imagery (2 Cor 2.14–16a): Neglected Points of Background." *NTS* 61 (2015): 79–91.

———. *The Structure of Hebrews: A Text-Linguistic Analysis*. NovTSup 73. Leiden: Brill, 1994.

Guy, Samuel. "A Politeuma Worth Pursuing: A Rhetorical Analysis of Philippians 3:20 in Light of Philippi's Sociological Composition." *SCJ* 22 (2019): 89–100.

Hamilton, James M. *God's Glory in Salvation through Judgment: A Biblical Theology*. Wheaton, IL: Crossway, 2010.

Hansen, G. Walter. *The Letter to the Philippians*. PNTC. Grand Rapids: Eerdmans, 2009.

———. "Transformation of Relationships: Partnership, Citizenship, and Friendship in Philippi." Pages 181–204 in *New Testament Greek and Exegesis: Essays in Honor of Gerald F. Hawthorne*. Edited by Amy Donaldson and Timothy B. Sailors. Grand Rapids: Eerdmans, 2003.

Hardin, J. K. "Judaizers." Pages 571–74 in *Dictionary of Paul and His Letters*. 2nd edition. Edited by Scot McKnight, Lynn H. Cohick, and Nijay K. Gupta. Downers Grove, IL: InterVarsity Press, 2023.

Harris, Murray J. *Prepositions and Theology in the Greek New Testament: An Essential Reference Resource for Exegesis*. Grand Rapids: Zondervan, 2012.

Harrison, James R., and L. L. Welborn, eds. *The First Urban Churches 4: Roman Philippi*. WGRWSup 13. Atlanta: SBL Press, 2018.

Hawthorn, T. "Philippians 1:12–19: with Special Reference to vv 15, 16, 17." *ExpTim* 62 (1951): 316–17.

Hawthorne, Gerald F. "In the Form of God and Equal with God (Philippians 2:6)." Pages 96–110 in *Where Christology Began: Essays on Philippians 2*. Edited by Ralph P. Martin and Brian J. Dodd. Louisville: Westminster John Knox, 1998.

———. *Philippians*. WBC 43. Waco, TX: Word, 1983.

Hawthorne, Gerald F., and Ralph P. Martin. *Philippians*. Rev. ed. WBC 43. Nashville: Thomas Nelson, 2004.

Hays, Richard B. *The Faith of Jesus Christ: An Investigation of the Narrative Substructure of Galatians 3:1–4:11*. Atlanta: Scholars Press, 1983.

Hellerman, Joseph H. "Brothers and Friends in Philippi: Family Honor in the Roman World and in Paul's Letter to the Philippians." *BTB* 39 (2009): 15–25.

———. *Philippians*. EGGNT. Nashville: B&H Academic, 2015.

———. *Reconstructing Honor in Roman Philippi: Carmen Christi as Cursus Pudorum*. SNTSMS 132. Cambridge: Cambridge University Press, 2005.

Hengel, Martin. *Crucifixion in the Ancient World and the Folly of the Message of the Cross*. Philadelphia: Fortress, 1977.

Hengel, Martin, and Roland Deines. *The Pre-Christian Paul*. London: SCM; Philadelphia: Trinity Press, 1991.

Hill, Wesley. *Paul and the Trinity: Persons, Relations, and the Pauline Letters*. Grand Rapids: Eerdmans, 2015.

Hofius, Otfried. *Der Christushymnus Philipper 2,6–11: Untersuchungen zu Gestalt und Aussage eines Urchristlichen Psalms*. WUNT 17. Tübingen: Mohr Siebeck, 1991.

Holloway, Paul A. *Consolation in Philippians: Philosophical Sources and Rhetorical Strategy*. SNTSMS 112. Cambridge: Cambridge University Press, 2001.

———. *Philippians: A Commentary*. Hermeneia. Minneapolis: Fortress, 2017.

Hooker, Morna D. "Another Look at πίστις Χριστοῦ." *SJT* 69 (2016): 46–62.

———. "On Becoming the Righteousness of God: Another Look at 2 Cor 5:2." *NovT* 50 (2008): 358–75.

———. "Philippians." Pages 105–15 in *The Cambridge Companion to St. Paul*. Edited by James D. G. Dunn. Cambridge: Cambridge University Press, 2003.

———. "Philippians." Pages 497–549 in vol. 11 of *The New Interpreter's Bible*. Edited by Leander E. Keck. Nashville: Abingdon, 2000.

———. "Philippians 2:6–11." Pages 151–64 in *Jesus und Paulus: Festschrift für Werner Georg Kümmel zum 70. Geburtstag*. Edited by E. Earle Ellis and Erich Grässer. Göttingen: Vandenhoeck & Ruprecht, 1975.

———. "Philippians: Phantom Opponents and the Real Source of Conflict." Pages 377–95 in *Fair Play: Diversity and Conflicts in Early Christianity: Essays in Honour of Heikki Räisänen*. Edited by Ismo Dunderberg, C. M. Tuckett, and Kari Syreeni. NovTSup 103. Leiden: Brill, 2002.

———. "ΠΙΣΤΙΣ ΧΡΙΣΤΟΥ." *NTS* 35 (1989): 321–42.

Hoover, R. W. "The HARPAGMOS Enigma: A Philological Solution." *HTR* 64 (1971): 95–119.

Hunter, W. B. "Prayer." Pages 725–34 in *Dictionary of Paul and His Letters*. Edited by Gerald F. Hawthorne, Ralph P. Martin, and Daniel G. Reid. Downers Grove, IL: InterVarsity Press, 1993.

Hunzinger, Claus H. "Zur Struktur der Christus-Hymnen in Phil 2 und 1 Petr 3." Pages 142–56 in *Der Ruf Jesu und die Antwort der Gemeinde: Exegetische Untersuchungen, Joachim Jeremias zum 70. Geburtstag gewidmet von Seinen Schülern*. Edited by Eduard Lohse, Christoph Burchard, and Berndt Schaller. Göttingen: Vandenhoeck & Ruprecht, 1970.

Hurst, Lincoln D. "Christ, Adam, and Preexistence Revisited." Pages 84–95 in *Where Christology Began: Essays on Philippians 2*. Edited by Ralph P. Martin and Brian J. Dodd. Louisville: Westminster John Knox, 1998.

Hurtado, Larry W. *Lord Jesus Christ: Devotion to Jesus in Earliest Christianity*. Grand Rapids: Eerdmans, 2003.

Jeremias, J. "Zu Phil. 2,7: ΕΑΥΤΟΝ ΕΚΕΝΩΣΕΝ." *NovT* 6 (1963): 182–88.

Jewett, Robert. "Conflicting Movements in the Early Church as Reflected in Philippians." *NovT* 12 (1970): 362–90.

Keener, Craig S. *Acts: An Exegetical Commentary, 15:1–23:35*. Vol. 3. Grand Rapids: Baker Academic, 2014.

Keller, Timothy. *Galatians for You*. Epsom, UK: The Good Book Company, 2013.

———. *Prayer: Experiencing Awe and Intimacy with God*. New York: Penguin Random House, 2014.

Keown, Mark. *Philippians 2:19–4:23*. EEC. Bellingham, WA: Lexham, 2017.

Klauck, Hans-Josef, and Daniel P. Bailey. *Ancient Letters and the New Testament: A Guide to Context and Exegesis*. Waco, TX: Baylor University Press, 2006.

Klijn, A. F. J. "Paul's Opponents in Philippians iii." *NovT* 7 (1964): 278–84.

Knight, George W. "Two Offices (Elders or Bishops and Deacons) and Two Orders of Elders (Preaching or Teaching Elders and Ruling Elders): A New Testament Study." *Presb* 11 (1985): 1–12.

Koenig, John. *Jews and Christians in Dialogue: New Testament Foundations*. Philadelphia: Westminster, 1979.

Koester, Helmut. "The Purpose of the Polemic of a Pauline Fragment." *NTS* 8 (1961): 317–32.

Köstenberger, Andreas J., and Scott R. Swain. *Father, Son and Spirit: The Trinity and John's Gospel*. NSBT 24. Downers Grove, IL: IVP Academic, 2008.

Krentz, Edgar M. "Military Language and Metaphors in Philippians." Pages 105–27 in *Origins and Method: Toward a New Understanding of Judaism and Christianity: Essays in Honour of John C. Hurd*. Edited by Bradley H. McLean. JSNTSup 86. Sheffield: Sheffield Academic Press, 1993.

Lau, Te-Li. *Defending Shame: Its Formative Power in Paul's Letters*. Grand Rapids: Baker Academic, 2020.

Lennox, John. *Gunning for God: Why the New Atheists Are Missing the Target*. Oxford, UK: Lion Hudson, 2011.

Liddell, Henry George, Robert Scott, and Henry Stuart Jones. *A Greek-English Lexicon*. 9th ed. with revised supplement. Oxford: Clarendon, 1996.

Lightfoot, J. B. *Saint Paul's Epistle to the Philippians: A Revised Text with Introduction, Notes, and Dissertations*. London: Macmillan, 1898.

Lohmeyer, Ernst. *Die Briefe an die Philipper, an die Kolosser und an Philemon*. KEK. Göttingen: Vandenhoeck & Ruprecht, 1928.

———. *Kyrios Jesus: Eine Untersuchung zu Phil. 2,5–11*. Heidelberg: C. Winter, 1928.

Longenecker, Richard N. *The Epistle to the Romans: A Commentary on the Greek Text*. NIGTC. Grand Rapids: Eerdmans, 2016.

Louw, J. P., and Eugene A. Nida. *Greek-English Lexicon of the New Testament: Based on Semantic Domains*. New York: United Bible Societies, 1988.

Macaskill, Grant. *Living in Union with Christ: Paul's Gospel and Christian Moral Identity*. Grand Rapids: Baker Academic, 2019.

Manson, T. W., and Matthew Black. *Studies in the Gospels and Epistles*. Manchester: Manchester University Press, 1962.

Marshall, I. Howard. *The Epistle to the Philippians*. London: Epworth, 1992.

Martin, Michael W. "Ἁρπαγμός Revisited: A Philological Reexamination of the New Testament's 'Most Difficult Word.'" *JBL* 135 (2016): 175–94.

Martin, Michael W., and Bryan A. Nash. "Philippians 2:6–11 as Subversive *Hymnos*: A Study in the Light of Ancient Rhetorical Theory." *JTS* 66 (2015): 90–138.

Martin, Ralph P. *2 Corinthians*. WBC 40. Waco, TX: Word, 1986.

———. *A Hymn of Christ: Philippians 2:5–11 in Recent Interpretation and in the Setting of Early Christian Worship*. Downers Grove, IL: IVP Academic, 1997.

———. *Philippians*. NCB. Grand Rapids: Eerdmans, 1980.

Martin, Troy W. "Investigating the Pauline Letter Body: Issues, Methods, and Approaches." Pages 185–212 in *How to Begin, and Why? Diverse Functions of the Pauline Prescript within a Greco-Roman Context*. Edited by Stanley E. Porter and Sean A. Adams. Leiden: Brill, 2010.

Matlock, R. Barry. "The Rhetoric of πίστις in Paul: Galatians 2:16, 3:22, Romans 3:22, and Philippians 3:9." *JSNT* 30 (2007): 173–203.

McCool, Matthew. *Writing around the World: A Guide to Writing across Cultures*. New York: Continuum International, 2009.

McDonald, Lee Martin. "Philippi." Pages 787–89 in *Dictionary of New Testament Background*. Edited by Crag A. Evans and Stanley Porter. Downers Grove, IL: InterVarsity Press, 2000.

McEntyre, Marilyn. *Caring for Words in a Culture of Lies*. Grand Rapids: Eerdmans, 2009.

Mearns, Chris. "The Identity of Paul's Opponents at Philippi." *NTS* 33 (1987): 194–204.

Melick, Richard R. *Philippians, Colossians, Philemon*. NAC 32. Nashville: Broadman & Holman, 1991.

Metzger, Bruce M. *A Textual Commentary on the Greek New Testament*. 2nd ed. Stuttgart: United Bible Societies, 1994.

Meyer, Heinrich August Wilhelm. *The Epistles to the Philippians and Colossians*. Translated by John C. Moore and William P. Dicksone. CECNT. Edinburgh: T&T Clark, 1875.

Michael, John Hugh. *The Epistle of Paul to the Philippians*. London: Hodder and Stoughton, 1928.

Miller, Ernest C. "Πολιτεύεσθε in Philippians 1:27: Some Philological and Thematic Observations." *JSNT* (1982): 86–96.

Mitchell, Margaret M. "New Testament Envoys in the Context of Greco-Roman Diplomatic and Epistolary Conventions: The Example of Timothy and Titus." *JBL* 111 (1992): 641–62.

Moo, Douglas J. *The Epistle to the Romans*. NICNT. Grand Rapids: Eerdmans, 1996.

Morgan, Christopher W., and Robert A. Peterson. *The Glory of God*. Wheaton, IL: Crossway, 2010.

Motyer, J. Alec. *The Message of Philippians*. Bible Speaks Today. London: Inter-Varsity Press, 1984.

Müller, Jac. J. *The Epistles of Paul to the Philippians and to Philemon*. Grand Rapids: Eerdmans, 1955.

Müller, Ulrich B. "Der Christushymnus Phil 2 6–11." *ZNW* 79 (1988): 17–44.

Nanos, Mark D. "Paul's Reversal of Jews Calling Gentiles 'Dogs' (Philippians 3:2): 1600 Years of an Ideological Tale Wagging an Exegetical Dog?" *BibInt* 17 (2009): 448–82.

Neusner, Jacob, and William Scott Green, eds. *Dictionary of Judaism in the Biblical Period: 450 B.C.E. to 600 C.E.* New York: Macmillan Library Reference, 1996.

Nongbri, Brent. "Two Neglected Textual Variants in Philippians 1." *JBL* 128 (2009): 803–8.

Oakes, Peter. "Jason and Penelope Hear Philippians 1.1–11." Pages 155–64 in *Understanding, Studying and Reading: New Testament Essays in Honour of John Ashton*. Edited by C. Rowland and C. H. T. Fletcher-Louis. JSNTSup 153. Sheffield: Sheffield Academic Press, 1998.

———. *Philippians: From People to Letter*. SNTSMS 110. Cambridge: Cambridge University Press, 2001.

———. *Rome in the Bible and the Early Church*. Carlisle: Paternoster, 2002.

Ogereau, Julien M. *Paul's Koinonia with the Philippians: A Socio-Historical Investigation of a Pauline Economic Partnership*. WUNT 377. Tübingen: Mohr Siebeck, 2014.

Ollrog, Wolf-Henning. *Paulus und Seine Mitarbeiterdand: Untersuchungen zu Theorie und Praxis der Paulinischen Mission*. Neukirchen-Vluyn: Neukirchener Verlag, 1979.

Osiek, Carolyn. *Philippians, Philemon*. ANTC. Nashville: Abingdon, 2000.

Packer, J. I. *Rediscovering Holiness*. Ann Arbor, MI: Vine Books, 1992.

Park, Mi Young Sydney. *Submission within the Godhead and the Church in the Epistle to the Philippians: An Exegetical and Theological Examination of the Concept of Submission in Philippians 2 and 3*. LNTS 361. London: T&T Clark, 2007.

Parunak, H. Van Dyke. "Oral Typesetting: Some Uses of Biblical Structure." *Bib* 62 (1981): 153–68.

Pascal, Blaise. *Pensées*. Penguin Classics. London: Penguin, 1995.

Peterlin, Davorin. *Paul's Letter to the Philippians in the Light of Disunity in the Church*. NovTSup 79. Leiden: Brill, 1995.

Peterman, Gerald W. *Paul's Gift from Philippi: Conventions of Gift Exchange and Christian Giving*. SNTSMS 92. Cambridge: Cambridge University Press, 1997.

Peterson, David. "Prayer in Paul's Writings." Pages 84–101 in *Teach Us to Pray*. Edited by D. A. Carson. Eugene, OR: Wipf & Stock, 2002.

Pilhofer, Peter. *Philippi: Band I. Die Erste Christliche Gemeinde Europas*. WUNT 87. Tübingen: Mohr Siebeck, 1995.

Plutarch. *Plutarch's Lives: Pericles and Fabius Maximus, Nicias and Crassus*. LCL 3. Edited by Bernadotte Perrin. Cambridge: Harvard University Press; London: W. Heinemann, 1916.

Porter, Stanley E., and Sean A. Adams, eds. *Paul and the Ancient Letter Form*. Pauline Studies 6. Leiden: Brill, 2010.

Porter, Stanley E., and Andrew W. Pitts. "Πίστις with a Preposition and Genitive Modifier: Lexical, Semantic, and Syntactic Considerations in the πίστις Χριστοῦ Discussion." Pages 33–53 in *The Faith of Jesus Christ: Exegetical, Biblical, and Theological Studies*. Edited by Michael F. Bird and Preston M. Sprinkle. Milton Keynes: Paternoster; Peabody, MA: Hendrickson, 2010.

Purves, Jim. "The Missional Doxology of the Philippian Hymn." *BapTheo* 3 (2011): 15–30.

Rapske, Brian. *The Book of Acts and Paul in Roman Custody*. Grand Rapids: Eerdmans; Carlisle: Paternoster, 1994.

Reed, Jeffrey T. *A Discourse Analysis of Philippians: Method and Rhetoric in the Debate over Literary*

*Integrity*. JSNTSup 136. Sheffield: Sheffield Academic Press, 1997.

———. "Philippians 3:1 and the Epistolary Hesitation Formulas: The Literary Integrity of Philippians, Again." *JBL* 115 (1996): 63–90.

Reicke, Bo Ivar. "Caesarea, Rome and the Captivity Epistles." Pages 277–86 in *Apostolic History and the Gospel: Biblical and Historical Essays Presented to F. F. Bruce on His 60th Birthday*. Edited by W. Ward Gasque and Ralph P. Martin. Exeter: Paternoster, 1970.

Reid, Daniel G. "Paul and His Coworkers." Pages 752–54 in *Dictionary of Paul and His Letters*. Edited by Gerald F. Hawthorne, Ralph P. Martin, and Daniel G. Reid. Downers Grove, IL: InterVarsity Press, 1993.

Reiher, Jim. "Could Philippians Have Been Written from the Second Roman Imprisonment?" *EvQ* 84 (2012): 213–33.

Reumann, John. "Church Office in Paul, Especially in Philippians." Pages 82–91 in *Origins and Method: Toward a New Understanding of Judaism and Christianity: Essays in Honour of John C. Hurd*. Edited by Bradley H. McLean. JSNTSup 86. Sheffield: JSOT Press, 1993.

———. *Philippians: A New Translation with Introduction and Commentary*. AYB. New Haven: Yale University Press, 2008.

Richards, E. Randolph. *Paul and First-Century Letter Writing: Secretaries, Composition, and Collection*. Downers Grove, IL: InterVarsity Press, 2004.

Robbins, Charles J. "Rhetorical Structure of Philippians 2:6–11." *CBQ* 42 (1980): 73–82.

Robertson, A. T. *A Grammar of the Greek New Testament in the Light of Historical Research*. Nashville: Broadman, 1934.

Robinson, John A. T. *Redating the New Testament*. London: SCM, 1976. Repr., Eugene, OR: Wipf & Stock, 2000.

Runge, Steven E. *Discourse Grammar of the Greek New Testament: A Practical Introduction for Teaching and Exegesis*. Peabody, MA: Hendrickson, 2010.

Ryken, Leland, Jim Wilhoit, and Tremper Longman, eds. *Dictionary of Biblical Imagery*. Downers Grove, IL: InterVarsity Press, 1998.

Sanders, Jack T. *The New Testament Christological Hymns: Their Historical Religious Background*. SNTSMS 15. Cambridge: Cambridge University Press, 1971.

Sapp, David A. "The LXX, 1QIsa, and MT Version of Isaiah 53 and the Christian Doctrine of Atonement." Pages 170–92 in *Jesus and the Suffering Servant: Isaiah 53 and Christian Origins*. Edited by W. H. Bellinger and William R. Farmer. Harrisburg, PA: Trinity Press International, 1998.

Schenk, Wolfgang. *Die Philipperbriefe des Paulus*. Stuttgart: Kohlhammer, 1984.

Schmittals, W. "Die Irrlehrer des Philipperbriefes." *ZTK* 54 (1957): 297–341.

Schnabel, Eckhard J. *Early Christian Mission*. Downers Grove, IL: InterVarsity Press; Leicester, 2004.

Shepherd, M. H. "Elder in the New Testament." Pages 273–75 in *Interpreter's Dictionary of the Bible: An Illustrated Encyclopedia*. Edited by George A. Buttrick. Downers Grove, IL: InterVarsity Press, 1962.

Silva, Moisés. *Philippians*. BECNT. Grand Rapids: Baker Academic, 2005.

Simmons, Charles. *Laconic Manual and Brief Remarker*. North Wrentham, MA: John D. Flagg, 1852.

Smith, David. *The Kindness of God: Christian Witness in Our Troubled World*. Downers Grove, IL: InterVarsity Press, 2013.

Snyman, Andris H. "Philippians 4:10–23 from a Rhetorical Perspective." *AcT* 27 (2007): 168–85.

———. "A Rhetorical Analysis of Philippians 1:1–11." *AcT* 24 (2004): 81–104.

———. "A Rhetorical Analysis of Philippians 1:12–26." *AcT* 25 (2005): 89–111.

———. "A Rhetorical Analysis of Philippians 3:1–11." *Neot* 40 (2006): 259–83.

———. "A Rhetorical Analysis of Philippians 3:12–21." *AcPB* 17 (2006): 327–48.

Spicq, Ceslas. *Theological Lexicon of the New Testament*. Translated and edited by James D. Ernest. 3 vols. Peabody, MA: Hendrickson, 1994.

Stendahl, Krister. "Paul at Prayer." *Int* 34 (1980): 240–49.

Still, Todd. *Philippians and Philemon*. SHBC. Macon, GA: Smyth & Helwys, 2011.

Stirewalt, M. Luther. *Paul, the Letter Writer*. Grand Rapids: Eerdmans, 2003.

Stowers, Stanley K. "Friends and Enemies in the Politics of Heaven: Reading Theology in Philippians." Pages 105–21 in *Pauline Theology*. Edited by J. M. Bassler. Minneapolis: Fortress, 1991.

Sumney, Jerry L. *Philippians: A Greek Student's Intermediate Reader*. Peabody, MA: Hendrickson, 2007.

Sussman, Max. "Sickness and Disease." Pages 6–15 in vol. 6 of *The Anchor Bible Dictionary*. Edited by David Noel Freedman. New York: Doubleday, 1992.

Talbert, Charles H. "A Hymn of Christ: Philippians 2:5–11 in Recent Interpretation and in the Setting of Early Christian Worship." *PRSt* 28 (2001): 141–42.

Tellbe, Mikael. *Paul between Synagogue and State: Christians, Jews, and Civic Authorities in 1 Thessalonians, Romans, and Philippians*. ConBNT 34. Stockholm: Almqvist & Wiksell, 2001.

———. "The Sociological Factors behind Philippians 3.1–11 and the Conflict at Philippi." *JSNT* 17 (1995): 97–121.

Thielman, Frank S. "Ephesus and the Literary Setting of Philippians." Pages 205–23 in *New Testament Greek and Exegesis: Essays in Honor of Gerald F. Hawthorne*. Edited by Amy Donaldson and Timothy B. Sailors. Grand Rapids: Eerdmans, 2003.

———. *Philippians*. NIVAC. Grand Rapids: Zondervan, 1995.

Thompson, Michael B. *Clothed with Christ: The Example and Teaching of Jesus in Romans 12.1–15.13*. JSNTSup 59. Sheffield: JSOT Press, 1991.

Thrall, Margaret E. *Greek Particles in the New Testament: Linguistic and Exegetical Studies*. New Testament Tools, Studies and Documents 3. Leiden: Brill, 1962.

Tite, Philip L. "How to Begin, and Why? Diverse Functions of the Pauline Prescript within a Greco-Roman Context." Pages 57–99 in *Paul and the Ancient Letter Form*. Edited by Stanley E. Porter and Sean A. Adams. Pauline Studies 6. Leiden: Brill, 2010.

Varner, William C. *Philippians: A Handbook on the Greek Text*. BHGNT. Waco, TX: Baylor University Press, 2016.

Verhoef, Eduard. *Philippi: How Christianity Began in Europe: The Epistle to the Philippians and the Excavations at Philippi*. London: Bloomsbury T&T Clark, 2013.

Vincent, Marvin R. *A Critical and Exegetical Commentary on the Epistles to the Philippians and to Philemon*. ICC. Edinburgh: T&T Clark, 1897.

Wallace, Daniel B. *Greek Grammar beyond the Basics: An Exegetical Syntax of the New Testament*. Grand Rapids: Zondervan, 1996.

Wallis, Ian G. *The Faith of Jesus Christ in Early Christian Traditions*. SNTSMS 84. Cambridge: Cambridge University Press, 2005.

Wansink, Craig S. *Chained in Christ: The Experience and Rhetoric of Paul's Imprisonments*. JSNTSup 130. Sheffield: Sheffield Academic Press, 1996.

Ware, James P. *The Mission of the Church in Paul's Letter to the Philippians in the Context of Ancient Judaism*. NovTSup 120. Leiden: Brill, 2005.

———. *Synopsis of the Pauline Letters in Greek and English*. Grand Rapids: Baker Academic, 2010.

Watson, Duane F. "The Integration of Epistolary and Rhetorical Analysis of Philippians." Pages 398–426 in *The Rhetorical Analysis of Scripture: Essays from the 1995 London Conference*. Edited by Stanley E. Porter and T. H. Olbricht. JSNTSup 146. Sheffield: Sheffield Academic Press, 1997.

———. "Paul and Boasting." Pages 77–100 in *Paul in the Greco-Roman World: A Handbook*. Edited by J. Paul Sampley. Harrisburg, PA: Trinity Press International, 2003.

———. "A Rhetorical Analysis of Philippians and Its Implications for the Unity Question." *NovT* 30 (1988): 57–88.

Watson, Francis. *Paul, Judaism, and the Gentiles: Beyond the New Perspective*. Grand Rapids: Eerdmans, 2007.

Watts, Rikki E. *Isaiah's New Exodus and Mark*. WUNT 2/88. Tübingen: Mohr Siebeck, 1997.

White, John L. "Introductory Formulae in the Body of the Pauline Letter." *JBL* 90 (1971): 91–97.

Wiles, Gordon P. *Paul's Intercessory Prayers: The Significance of the Intercessory Prayer Passages in the Letters of St. Paul*. SNTSMS 24. Cambridge: Cambridge University Press, 1974.

Windisch, Hans, and Georg Strecker. *Der Zweite Korintherbrief*. Göttingen: Vandenhoeck & Ruprecht, 1970.

Winter, Bruce W. *Philo and Paul among the Sophists: Alexandrian and Corinthian Responses to a Julio-Claudian Movement*. Grand Rapids: Eerdmans, 2002.

———. "Rhetoric." Pages 820–22 in *Dictionary of Paul and His Letters*. Edited by Gerald F. Hawthorne, Ralph P. Martin, and Daniel G. Reid. Downers Grove, IL: InterVarsity Press, 1993.

———. *Seek the Welfare of the City: Christians as Benefactors and Citizens*. Grand Rapids: Eerdmans; Carlisle: Paternoster, 1994.

Witherington, Ben. *Paul's Letter to the Philippians: A Socio-Rhetorical Commentary*. Grand Rapids: Eerdmans, 2011.

Wortham, Robert A. "Christology as Community Identity in the Philippians Hymn: The Philippians Hymn as Social Drama (Philippians 2:5–11)." *PRSt* 23 (1996): 269–87.

Wright, N. T. "ἁρπαγμός and the Meaning of Philippians 2:5–11." *JTS* 37 (1986): 321–52.

———. *The Climax of the Covenant: Christ and the Law in Pauline Theology*. Edinburgh: T&T Clark, 1991.

Yancey, Philip. *Vanishing Grace: What Ever Happened to the Good News*. Grand Rapids: Zondervan, 2014.

Zerwick, Max. *Biblical Greek*. Translated by Joseph Smith. Scripti Pontificii Instituti Biblici 114. Rome: Pontifical Biblical Institute, 1963.

Zoccali, Christopher. "Rejoice, O Gentiles, with His People: Paul's Intra-Jewish Rhetoric in Philippians 3:1–9." *CTR* 9 (2011): 17–31.

CHAPTER 1

# Philippians 1:1–2

## Literary Context

As an educated man of his time, the apostle Paul carried out long-distance communication through the medium of letter writing. Accordingly, his letter to the Philippians stands as a beautifully crafted composition, with elements common to letters of the broader Greco-Roman culture, as well as the apostle's specific religious contexts of Judaism and earliest Christianity.[1] Letters often began with a prescript,[2] followed by an introduction (called a "proem"), and Paul matches the pattern here. The prescript is found in 1:1–2, and the introduction—a thankful, joyful, prayer report—follows in 1:3–11.

**I. The Letter Opening: A Prescript and a Prayer Report (1:1–11)**
**A. The Letter Prescript (1:1–2)**
B. A Joyful Prayer Report (1:3–11)
II. The Letter Body (1:12–4:9)
III. The Letter Closing (4:10–23)

## Main Idea

Paul opens the letter to the Philippians in a way that is appropriate to his cultural context and nuanced for the pastoral need of the moment. He identifies himself and Timothy as the senders of the letter, addresses the Philippians and their leaders, and blesses them with grace and peace from God the Father and the Lord Jesus Christ.

1. On the form of first-century letters, see Stanley E. Porter and Sean A. Adams, eds., *Paul and the Ancient Letter Form*, Pauline Studies 6 (Leiden: Brill, 2010); Klauck and Bailey, *Ancient Letters*, 42; Richards, *Paul and First-Century Letter Writing*; M. Luther Stirewalt, *Paul, the Letter Writer* (Grand Rapids: Eerdmans, 2003).

2. On prescripts in ancient letters, see Philip L. Tite, "How to Begin, and Why? Diverse Functions of the Pauline Prescript within a Greco-Roman Context," in Porter and Adams, *Paul and the Ancient Letter Form*, 57–99.

## Translation

### Philippians 1:1–2

| | | | | |
|---|---|---|---|---|
| 1a | Senders | **Paul and Timothy,** slaves of | | Christ Jesus, |
| b | Recipients/General | **to** all of | | |
| c | Identification | **God's holy people** | | |
| d | | in | | Christ Jesus |
| e | Recipients/Specific | who live in Philippi, | | |
| f | | including the | overseers and | |
| g | | | deacons: | |
| 2a | Blessing | **Grace** to | you **and** | |
| b | | **peace** from | God our Father and | |
| c | | | the Lord Jesus | Christ. |

## Structure

Paul's prescript in Philippians has a *superscriptio* identifying the senders, an *adscriptio* addressing the Philippians and their leaders as the recipients, and a *salutatio* extending a blessing of grace and peace to the Philippians from God the Father and the Lord Jesus Christ. These three parts of the prescript may be seen as follows:

| | |
|---|---|
| *superscriptio* (the senders) | Paul and Timothy, slaves of Christ Jesus, |
| *adscriptio* (the recipients) | to all of God's holy people in Christ Jesus who live in Philippi, including the overseers and deacons: |
| *salutatio* (the greeting) | Grace to you and peace from God our Father and the Lord Jesus Christ. |

## Exegetical Outline

➦ **A. The Letter Prescript (1:1–2)**

1. Senders and Recipients (v. 1)
2. A Blessing (v. 2)

## Explanation of the Text

**1:1a Paul and Timothy, slaves of Christ Jesus** (Παῦλος καὶ Τιμόθεος δοῦλοι Χριστοῦ Ἰησοῦ). Paul begins his salutation by identifying himself and Timothy as the senders. Born with the Hebrew name "Saul" (שָׁאוּל, *šāʾûl*), the apostle at some point had been given, or had adopted, the Greek name we translate as "Paul" (Παῦλος; Acts 13:9), which sounds similar to his Hebrew birth name.

Six of Paul's letters name Timothy as a cosender (2 Corinthians, Philippians, Colossians, 1 and 2 Thessalonians, and Philemon). Notice that in the letter Paul refers to himself in the first person (e.g., Phil 1:3) and to Timothy in the third person (e.g., 2:19–23). So most commentators believe that the younger minister served as a corroborating witness rather than coauthor of Philippians.[3] It seems natural for the apostle to include his young protégé in this ministry missive, for Timothy had accompanied Paul when the church in Philippi was founded. In the intervening years, the younger man had continued to carry out vital ministry to the Philippians alongside his missionary mentor (Acts 16:1, 13; Phil 2:22).

In his letter prescripts Paul most often names himself an "apostle" (Rom 1:1; 1 Cor 1:1; Gal 1:1; Eph 1:1; Col 1:1; 1 Tim 1:1; 2 Tim 1:1), which he does not do here.[4] Commentators have wondered why Paul felt no need to assert his apostolic status in writing to the Philippians. It is notable that three of the four letters in which the apostle does not use the title are addressed to Macedonians (1 Thess 1:1; 2 Thess 1:1; Phil 1:1), with whom he seems to have enjoyed a high level of mutual respect and affection (1 Thess 2:7–8, 17–20; 3:1–10).[5] Further, only here in Philippians does Paul include cosender Timothy in the self-designation, naming both himself and Timothy as "slaves of Christ Jesus" (δοῦλοι Χριστοῦ Ἰησοῦ). Paul applies the label "slave" to himself or fellow ministers elsewhere at several places (Rom 1:1; 2 Cor 4:5; Gal 1:10; Col 4:12; 2 Tim 2:24; Titus 1:1).

For the original readers, the term rendered "slaves" would have brought to mind either their own life situation or the status of slaves serving all around them in the homes, shops, streets, and fields of Philippi. But the word also has a rich Old Testament background, referring to "servants of the Lord" in the Greek Old Testament[6]—a title indicating ministry on behalf of the Lord but also a title of honor for those who had served with distinction.[7]

In Philippians, the term "slave" is most ennobled by its use of Christ himself in 2:7, who, in the incarnation, took on the "outward appearance of a slave" (μορφὴν δούλου) before being exalted to

3. So, Bockmuehl, *Philippians*, 49; Silva, *Philippians*, 39. The general practice of naming a cosender might be related to the legal requirement of two witnesses confirming a testimony (Deut 19:15); so Hans Windisch and Georg Strecker, *Der Zweite Korintherbrief* (Göttingen: Vandenhoeck & Ruprecht, 1970), 26. In this sense, the cosender functioned to attest to the facts of the letter's origin and message. Fee follows Bruce in suggesting that Timothy may have been Paul's secretary; see Fee, *Philippians*, 61.

4. On the rationale for including the Pastorals as "Pauline," see Gordon D. Fee, *1 and 2 Timothy, Titus* (Peabody, MA: Hendrickson, 1995), 23–26.

5. Silva, *Philippians*, 39. The fourth was Philemon, and Silva notes the delicacy of that situation, seen especially in Phlm 17–20.

6. See, e.g., Josh 24:30; Judg 2:8; 2 Kgs 9:7; 10:23; 18:12; Ps 35:1; 133:1; 134:1; Jonah 1:9.

7. Chrysostom notes that Paul considers his and Timothy's service as slaves of Christ to be a great honor constituting true freedom: "One who is a slave of Christ is truly free from sin. If he is truly a slave of Christ, he is not a slave in any other realm, since then he would not be a slave of Christ but only half so" (Mark J. Edwards, *Galatians, Ephesians, Philippians*, ACCS 8 [Downers Grove, IL: IVP Academic, 1999], 217 [*Homily on Philippians* 2.1.1–2]).

kingship over the universe. Accordingly, Paul and Timothy minister to the Philippians on behalf of their humble master, Messiah Jesus.[8] Further, notice that Paul refers to Messiah Jesus three times in this brief prescript,[9] which alerts us to the Christocentric nature of the letter, flowing from the Christocentric nature of Paul's apostolic ministry.

**1:1b–e To all of God's holy people in Christ Jesus who live in Philippi, including the overseers and deacons** (πᾶσιν τοῖς ἁγίοις ἐν Χριστῷ Ἰησοῦ τοῖς οὖσιν ἐν Φιλίπποις σὺν ἐπισκόποις καὶ διακόνοις). The reference to the addressees might be considered in three parts. First, the apostle names the recipients generally with "to all of God's holy people in Christ Jesus" (πᾶσιν τοῖς ἁγίοις ἐν Χριστῷ Ἰησοῦ). As an address, "to . . . God's holy people" (τοῖς ἁγίοις; cf. NIV; NLT) seems roughly synonymous to "to the church" (τῇ ἐκκλησίᾳ; 1 Cor 1:2; 2 Cor 1:1; 1 Thess 1:1; 2 Thess 1:1; Phlm 2; plural at Gal 1:2), referring to the followers of Christ in a given location. A few modern English translations render the phrase as "to . . . the saints" (e.g., ESV, NASB, NRSV, NET). However, this translation struggles under a good deal of cultural baggage, both ecclesiastical and popular. Of course, Paul is not writing to a super-elite group who have attained exalted spiritual status, as the word has come to connote popularly for some people. In English speaking contexts generally, the English word "saint" has also struggled against both positive and pejorative uses, referring on the one hand to a person of good deeds (e.g., "she is such a saint!"), and on the other to the self-righteous (e.g., "he thinks he's a saint!").

Rather, we need an English rendering of the address that points to those who belong to God, set apart as holy people. Referring to all of Christ's followers, the phrase "to . . . God's holy people" is associated with God setting aside a people for himself by decisively cleansing them from sin and constituting them to be a people who live accordingly. By Christ's sacrifice, the Lord's followers are made "holy" people, who are set apart from humanity in general and live in a unique relationship to God (Heb 8:7–13; 10:14–17).

Of course, this relationship with God is made possible because these people are "in Christ Jesus" (ἐν Χριστῷ Ἰησοῦ), a favorite expression for Paul, used in this form eight times in Philippians (1:1, 26; 2:5; 3:3, 14; 4:7, 19, 21) and another thirty-eight times elsewhere in the apostle's writings.[10] The "in Christ" motif lies at the heart of Pauline theology, concerning believers' union with Christ as well as their transformation.[11] Michael Gorman writes, "Participation is not merely one aspect of Pauline theology and spirituality, or a supplement

8. Χριστοῦ Ἰησοῦ of Phil 1:1 can be read as a genitive of relationship, or perhaps a possessive genitive—Paul and Timothy belong to Christ.

9. Χριστός as a title refers to Jesus as Messiah and occurs thirty-five times in Philippians, twenty times in conjunction with Ἰησοῦς (if the inclusion of Ἰησοῦ at 3:12 is retained, as with $\mathfrak{P}^{46.61vid}$ ℵ A K L P Ψ 075. 81. 𝔐; note: throughout the commentary the symbols used in text-critical discussions stem from the NA$^{28}$, and the reader is referred to that edition for additional information. The evidence listed in the UBS$^{5}$ is also consulted). According to the NA$^{28}$ text, in thirteen of the pairings the order has Χριστός first, and seven have Ἰησοῦς in the primary position. The word order seems to make no difference semantically, but Paul follows a general tendency in Philippians to put Ἰησοῦς first when the pair is preceded by κύριος (Phil 1:2; 2:11; 3:20; 4:23), and the pair are inverted when preceded by the preposition ἐν (Phil 1:1, 26; 2:5; 3:3, 14; 4:7, 19, 21), in keeping with Paul's very regular use of the idiom ἐν Χριστῷ.

10. Rom 3:24; 6:11, 23; 8:1–2, 39; 15:17; 16:3; 1 Cor 1:2, 4, 30; 4:17; 15:31; 16:24; Gal 2:4; 3:14, 26, 28; Eph 1:1; 2:6–7, 10, 13; 3:6, 21; Col 1:4; 1 Thess 2:14; 5:18; 1 Tim 1:14; 3:13; 2 Tim 1:1, 9, 13; 2:1, 10; 3:12, 15; Phlm 23. Variations on the form include "in Christ," "in the Lord," "in the Lord Jesus," and "in him."

11. On the history of interpretation of the phrase, see Michael J. Gorman, *Participating in Christ: Explorations in Paul's Theology and Spirituality* (Grand Rapids: Baker Academic, 2019), xvii–xxiv. Gorman writes, "It is nearly impossible to engage Paul seriously today without recognizing the centrality of participation to his lived experience ('spirituality') and his theology" (xviii).

to something more fundamental; rather, it is at the very heart of Paul's thinking and living. Pauline soteriology (theology of salvation) is inherently participatory and transformative."[12] Constantine Campbell, in a thorough treatment of the theme, summarizes his findings on this rich and important thread in Pauline theology with the terms *union*, *participation*, *identification*, and *incorporation*:

> Union conveys faith union with Christ, mutual indwelling, trinitarian, and nuptial notions. Participation refers to the partaking in the events of Christ's narrative. Identification encapsulates believers' location in the realm of Christ and their allegiance to his lordship. Incorporation gathers up the corporate dimensions of membership in Christ's body.[13]

Particularly in Philippians, Paul hopes that believers' boasting with respect to his ministry might increase "in Christ Jesus" (1:26)—that is, in their mutual relationship to Christ. The Philippians should have the same attitude of serving one another that was modeled "in Christ Jesus" in his incarnation (2:5), or perhaps as may be experienced in their participation in Christ. "In Christ Jesus" constitutes the object of Paul's exultation in life and ministry (3:3), and the prize of the heavenly call of God is due to his relationship to Christ (v. 14). Further, one's relationship with Christ is the foundation of a life of peace (4:7), a life of provision (v. 19), and a life as part of the broader community of Christ (v. 21).

But why does Paul write "to *all* [πᾶσιν] of God's holy people in Christ Jesus"? The apostle often uses such language in his letter prescripts,[14] as well as in his letter closings.[15] He seems to address his readers with forms of this Greek term translated "all" (πᾶς) to stress inclusivity. Yet the word as used here in the prescript of Philippians may be especially significant, for it occurs thirty-three times in this relatively short letter,[16] seven times in the first eight verses. This drumming repetition can be understood as underscoring the apostle's "strong and repeated exhortations to unity" in the church.[17] He wants the Philippians to understand themselves as one, "all" working together under the lordship of Christ.

Further, the apostle identifies the specific location of these believers with "[to those] who live in Philippi" (τοῖς οὖσιν ἐν Φιλίπποις).[18] Later in the letter, the apostle will refer to them as "Philippians" (Φιλιππήσιοι; 4:15), and this city's special relationship with Rome will be an important point for

12. Gorman, *Participating*, xviii.

13. Constantine R. Campbell, *Paul and Union with Christ: An Exegetical and Theological Study* (Grand Rapids: Zondervan, 2012), 420. See also Grant Macaskill, *Living in Union with Christ: Paul's Gospel and Christian Moral Identity* (Grand Rapids: Baker Academic, 2019), who explores how Christian moral theology flows from Paul's thoughts on union with Christ.

14. For instance, he addresses his letter to the Romans with "to all those loved by God in Rome" (Rom 1:7–8). The prescript address in 1 Corinthians includes "all those in every place who call on the name of our Lord Jesus Christ" (1 Cor 1:2), and 2 Corinthians opens with "to God's church in Corinth, along with all of God's holy people throughout Achaia" (2 Cor 1:1). The word is also used at the beginning of Galatians (1:2) and in the thanksgiving of 1 Thessalonians (1:2)

15. Rom 16:15–16; 1 Cor 16:24; 2 Cor 13:12–13; Gal 6:16; Eph 6:24; Phil 4:21–22; 1 Thess 5:26–27; 2 Thess 3:18; Titus 3:15.

16. 1:1, 3–4, 7–9, 13, 18, 20, 25; 2:9–11, 14, 17, 21, 26, 29; 3:8, 21; 4:5–7, 12–13, 18–19, 21–22.

17. J. B. Lightfoot, *Saint Paul's Epistle to the Philippians: A Revised Text with Introduction, Notes, and Dissertations* (London: Macmillan, 1898), 83.

18. We have rendered the masculine present participle τοῖς οὖσιν, "to the ones being . . . ," straightforwardly as referring to those "who live" in Philippi. The verb εἰμί often is used with reference to a location (BDAG 284). The dative form is due to this participle referring to those being addressed.

consideration as we assess Paul's allusions to Roman citizenship in passages such as 1:27 and 3:20.[19]

Finally, in addressing his readers the apostle adds, "including the overseers and deacons" (σὺν ἐπισκόποις καὶ διακόνοις). This is noteworthy,[20] since only here and in the Pastoral Epistles does the apostle refer to church leadership with these terms (cf. Acts 20:28; 1 Tim 3:2; Titus 1:7). Yet, "overseer" (ἐπίσκοπος) has a fairly broad background in the literature of the Second Temple period. For instance, in Greco-Roman literature the term can be used of a guardian or of an office with responsibility for particular duties (e.g., Soph., *Ant.* 217; Plato, *Laws* 762d). In the LXX, the word can refer to those with responsibility to supervise some aspect of worship (Num 4:16; 2 Kgs 12:12; 2 Chr 34:12, 17) or officers over the army (Num 31:14; 2 Kgs 11:18). In short, an "overseer" could refer to a religious, military, or civil leader who provided supervision of some sort (e.g., Neh 11:9, 14, 22; Isa 60:17).[21] God, too, can be referred to as "overseer" as he judges the thoughts and actions of people (Job 20:29; Wis 1:6; cf. 1 Pet 2:25).[22]

At the very least, the reference in Philippians 1:1 seems to refer to a group of leaders in the church at Philippi—distinct within the general body of believers—as well as to another group called "servants" or "deacons." From our word study, it seems reasonable to assume that these "overseers" have some supervisory role in the congregation. If, as both Acts and Titus seem to indicate, they are synonymous to "elders" (which I think highly likely),[23] they follow a pattern of elders who offer spiritual oversight and leadership of the church, as in the earliest stages of the Jerusalem church (Acts 15:2, 4, 6, 22–23; 16:4; 20:17; 21:18; Jas 5:14)—a pattern that is evident in broader Judaism (e.g., Acts 4:5, 8, 23; 6:12; 22:5; 23:14; 24:1; 25:15). The mention of the "overseers" first probably indicates that they are the primary leaders in the church, functioning in a role normally associated with "elders" in earliest Christianity.[24]

On the other hand, διάκονος is used more broadly in the New Testament, with even less specificity. In the Gospels, the noun, whether used literally or figuratively, refers to someone performing the role of a "servant" (Matt 20:26; 22:13; 23:11; Mark 9:35; 10:43; John 2:5, 9; 12:26). In the epistles, the government (Rom 13:4), Christ (Rom 15:8), ministers of the gospel (1 Cor 3:5; 2 Cor 3:6; 6:4; Eph 3:7; 6:21; Col 1:7, 23, 25; 4:7; 1 Tim 4:6), and even false teachers (2 Cor 11:15, 23) can be referred to as "servants" (with reference to false teachers, the word is pejorative). When the term is employed of Phoebe, and of the "deacons" in 1 Timothy (3:8, 12), it seems to indicate a particular role within the church beyond its normal connotation—that these "servants" were focused on particular needs, which remain unspecified.

19. See Fee, *Philippians*, 66.

20. Paul's reference to the "overseers and deacons" has generated a great deal of discussion. See, e.g., Morna D. Hooker, "Philippians," in *NIB* 11:497–549; George W. Knight, "Two Offices (Elders or Bishops and Deacons) and Two Orders of Elders (Preaching or Teaching Elders and Ruling Elders): A New Testament Study," *Presb* 11.1 (1985), 1–12; John Reumann, "Church Office in Paul, Especially in Philippians," in McLean, *Origins and Method*, 82–91.

21. Josephus used the term of leaders appointed by Josiah during that king's reforms (*Ant.* 10.53) and of "overseers" who ensured Jewish conformity to the horrific demands of King Antiochus (*Ant.* 12.254).

22. Philo (*Alleg. Interp.* 3.43; *Migration* 135) and the Pseudepigrapha (e.g., *Sib. Or.* 21.3) also speak of God as the ἐπίσκοπος.

23. Citing Acts 20:28 and Titus 1:5, Theodoret notes that Paul applies the term "bishops to presbyters, for at that time they had both names." He refers here to our Greek terms ἐπίσκοπος and πρεσβύτερος (see Edwards, *Galatians, Ephesians, Philippians*, 218 [*Epistle to the Philippians* 1.1–2]).

24. The position that the Philippian "overseers" cannot be equated with the more developed role in the Pastoral Epistles is speculative. On "elders" in the early church, see M. H. Shepherd, "Elder in the New Testament," in *Interpreter's Dictionary of the Bible: An Illustrated Encyclopedia*, ed. George A. Buttrick (Downers Grove, IL: InterVarsity Press, 1962), 73–75.

We can't be sure why Paul mentions these leaders in the letter's prescript. It may be that they had led in the apostle's financial support and merited special mention.[25] Or it may be because of the key role they would play in facilitating unity in the church (e.g., 4:1–2).[26]

**1:2 Grace to you and peace from God our Father and the Lord Jesus Christ** (χάρις ὑμῖν καὶ εἰρήνη ἀπὸ θεοῦ πατρὸς ἡμῶν καὶ κυρίου Ἰησοῦ Χριστοῦ). Paul greets the brothers and sisters in Philippi with "Grace to you and peace from God our Father and the Lord Jesus Christ"—rich wording with which he consistently begins his letters (Rom 1:7; 1 Cor 1:3; 2 Cor 1:2; Gal 1:3; Eph 1:2; 2 Thess 1:2; Phlm 2).[27] The stylized greeting presents a balanced structure, with four Greek words per line:

| | |
|---|---|
| χάρις ὑμῖν καὶ εἰρήνη | "Grace to you and peace" |
| ἀπὸ θεοῦ πατρὸς ἡμῶν | "from God our Father" |
| καὶ κυρίου Ἰησοῦ Χριστοῦ | "and the Lord Jesus Christ" |

Gordon Fee points out that "grace to you," followed by "and peace," seems significant. Grace comes from God the Father and the Lord, and the result is peace.[28] The greeting thus hints at the foundational nature of the concept of "grace" in Christian life and thought. It is a rock on which believers stand in life and on which they stand with others in ministry. At Philippians 1:7, Paul celebrates the Philippians by calling them "my grace partners" (συγκοινωνούς μου τῆς χάριτος), since they had stood with him during his imprisonment and defense of the gospel.

As is often pointed out, the use of χάρις ("grace") is an adaptation—a meaningful, theological shift—from the pattern found in Hellenistic letters, which began with "greetings" (χαίρειν, e.g., Acts 15:23; 23:26; Jas 1:1). So the Christian tradition morphed "greetings" (χαίρειν) to "grace" (χάρις) and added the common Jewish greeting of "peace" (שָׁלוֹם, *šālôm*). This part of our salutation must have been common in the broader Christian movement, being used in the other Pauline letters,[29] as well as 1 Peter 1:2, 2 Peter 1:2, and Revelation 1:4.

Grace and peace come "from God our Father and the Lord Jesus Christ." Thus, Father and Son together constitute the source of grace and peace. Jesus taught the disciples to pray, "Our Father . . ." (Matt 6:9–13), which may be the origin of the confession here. Early Christian tradition follows in this vein, replete with references to the fatherhood of God (e.g., 1 Cor 8:6; 15:24; Gal 1:4; 4:6; Eph 1:3, 17; 4:6; Col 3:17; Jas 1:27; 1 John 2:14). Paul also refers to God as Father in Philippians at 2:11 and 4:20. It would have been shocking to Jews outside the apostle's messianic movement to include "the Lord Jesus Christ" alongside the Father as the dispenser of grace and peace. In this way, the salutation thus bears witness to the unique status of the Lord Christ[30]—the one exalted and given a name above every other (Phil 2:11)—and the blessings he and the Father bring to his people.

25. Lightfoot, *Philippians*, 82; Ralph P. Martin, *Philippians*, NCB (Grand Rapids: Eerdmans, 1980), 61.

26. So Davorin Peterlin, *Paul's Letter to the Philippians in the Light of Disunity in the Church*, NovTSup 79 (Leiden: Brill, 1995), 101–32. But see the reasoned objections to this view offered by Cousar, *Philippians and Philemon*, 26.

27. Colossians and 1 Thessalonians present shorter versions, if the textual decisions reflected in NA[28] are correct.

28. Fee, *Philippians*, 70.

29. In the Pastoral Epistles, 1 Tim 1:2 and 2 Tim 1:2 have the variation, "grace, mercy, peace" (χάρις ἔλεος εἰρήνη), and Titus 1:4 reads, "grace and peace" (χάρις καὶ εἰρήνη).

30. See especially Richard Bauckham, *Jesus and the God of Israel: God Crucified and Other Studies on the New Testament's Christology of Divine Identity* (Grand Rapids: Eerdmans, 2008), 107–51.

## Theology in Application

As noted in the introduction to our commentary on Philippians 1:1–2, Paul crafts the prescript to his letter in accordance with the forms found elsewhere in Hellenistic letters, including other letters of the New Testament. While we must take care not to overinterpret these formal elements,[31] Paul conforms to, and departs from, normal patterns, and this stimulates reflection. In application, we could focus on a number of elements—such as the divine identity of our Lord Christ, the "holy" people of God, local expressions of the church, and the need for grace and peace—but let us consider two points related to Christian leadership: the "humility" witnessed in Paul's prescript, and the shape of Christian leadership.

### *Humility in Formality*

The New Testament embodies the interaction of language and culture, both Greco-Roman and early Christian. Cultures have varying degrees of formality in communication. For instance, American culture, which emphasizes individual identity, values informality. But cultures with a greater sense of corporate identity, like those of the first-century Mediterranean world, tend to exhibit higher degrees of formality.[32]

Consequently, American culture often views formality as stuffy and inauthentic. But notice Paul's example in the letter prescript. Status was a vital concept in the Greco-Roman world, and a leader adopting the posture of a slave would have been unexpected and potentially offensive. By identifying himself and Timothy as "slaves of Christ Jesus," Paul joins his Lord (Phil 2:7) in a profoundly countercultural posture that sets the tone for the letter. Rather than stuffy and inauthentic, the apostle's approach exudes authentic ministry, with resonances from Old Testament literature—the "Lord's servant" does honorable work. Instead of presenting himself with apostolic authority (why he does so elsewhere is a question for another time), he bows as a servant of the Lord. We observe modesty and humility in the formality,[33] as Paul speaks with a different voice than would be expected from an authority figure in an official piece of correspondence.

31. When someone writes to me "Dear George" at the beginning of a modern business letter, should I ask, "What exactly was meant by the word 'dear'?" Of course not. But when my wife writes "Dearest," the greeting is infused with meaning, as it is a departure from her norm. The adjustment hints of something more.

32. Matthew McCool, *Writing around the World: A Guide to Writing across Cultures* (New York: Continuum International, 2009), 51.

33. McCool, *Writing around the World*, 53.

When we cooperate with certain cultural norms but do so in nuanced ways that shape communication, using or even bending the form to fit a particular need, the "formality" blooms into something vibrant, good, and beautiful. Perhaps we too could think about utilizing gracious formality, which in our day can be countercultural. A thoughtful "thank you" note, written after a delicious dinner and stimulating conversation, can prove a magical moment in relational bonding or a vehicle of ministry to a soul in dire need of encouragement. Simply extending a handshake can be a formality, but in the context of a strained relationship, the extended hand presents an openness of spirit. The form suddenly functions as something noble, even sacrificial. The formality thus expresses humility and an awareness of, and thankfulness for, one's place in the world. How we communicate with one another matters. Our words can be forms of "grace . . . and peace" if offered in humility.

## *The Shape of Christian Leadership*

As noted in our commentary on verse 1, Paul often uses the word translated "slave" (δοῦλος) to describe himself or other Christian ministers as "slaves" of Christ or others (Rom 1:1; 2 Cor 4:5; Gal 1:10; Col 4:12; 2 Tim 2:24; Titus 1:1). The backdrop for this idea, of course, is twofold. All believers live under the lordship of Christ as slaves of Christ, no longer belonging to themselves (e.g., 1 Cor 7:22; 2 Cor 5:15). In his earthly ministry, Christ gave his followers an example and a mandate to serve one another (e.g., Mark 10:45; John 13:12–17). This "slave" or "servant" orientation of leadership in the New Testament is a wonderfully countercultural concept in Paul's day and ours. And Paul's concept is not that "we are slaves of Christ who lord over you" but rather "we are slaves of Christ who, in service to him, serve you" (e.g., 1 Cor 9:19; 2 Cor 4:5; Phil 2:17). In writing about servant leadership, John Stott comments,

> The very first thing which needs to be said about Christian ministers of all kinds is that they are "under" people as their servants rather than "over" them (as their leaders, let alone their lords). Jesus made this absolutely plain. The chief characteristic of Christian leaders, he insisted, is humility not authority, and gentleness not power.[34]

Latin American theologian René Padilla tells of an early encounter with Stott, when the two of them had arrived in Bariloche, Argentina, in the middle of a heavy rainstorm. As they were shown to their room, mud from their shoes tracked the floor. Padilla records that as he awoke the next morning, he heard the sound of a brush. Rising, he found Stott brushing his shoes. Shocked, he exclaimed, "John!

34. As quoted in Richard Kauffman, "Quotations to Stir the Heart and Mind," *Christianity Today*, Oct. 1, 2001, 69.

What are you doing?!" The Christian statesman responded, "My dear René, Jesus taught us to wash each other's feet. You do not need me to wash your feet, but I can brush your shoes."[35]

As Christian leaders, it is too natural for us to allow status or position to cause a separation between ourselves and those to whom we minister, placing ourselves above the crowd. If we do not allow the New Testament theology of servant leadership to sink very deeply into our practices and attitudes, we will absorb the cultural values of "position," "pay," and "prominence" as the right of those who have moved up the leadership ladder. But as Michael Card writes in his song "The Basin and the Towel," a reflection on Jesus washing the disciples' feet (John 13:5), we need to bow as servants, tearing down our pride and sense of elevation, bridging the gap between us and others. I, for one, need more of an orientation to "basin and towel" leadership. Paul's example, even in the nuances of a letter prescript, serves as a good reminder.

35. Tim Stafford, "John Stott Has Died," *Christianity Today*, July 27, 2011, www.christianitytoday.com/ct/2011/julyweb-only/john-stott-obit.html.

CHAPTER 2

# Philippians 1:3–11

## Literary Context

Having opened Philippians with a theologically thick prescript, the apostle now moves to another typical feature of a letter opening, an introductory thanksgiving and prayer (1:3–11). In this part of the letter, authors could express thanksgiving and affection for the recipients, offer a prayer, and express joy[1]—all of which Paul does here. Philippians 1:3–11 flows in two primary movements, the first of which expresses the apostle's thanks and affection for this church (1:3–8); the second offers a powerful intercessory prayer on their behalf (1:9–11). Next Paul will turn to giving them a report about his own situation (1:12–26).

As we noted in the introduction to this commentary,[2] there are extensive verbal and conceptual parallels between 1:3–11 and 4:10–20;[3] in the latter passage, Paul specifically celebrates the Philippians' partnership expressed through financial support for his ministry. Among other things, this demonstrates that Paul had the Philippians' monetary gifts in mind from the beginning of the letter. Yet his appreciation for the Philippian church involved more than financial support, for he considered the Philippians his full partners and ready participants in the gospel mission.

**I. The Letter Opening: A Prescript and a Prayer Report (1:1–11)**
- A. The Letter Prescript (1:1–2)
- ➡ **B. A Joyful Prayer Report (1:3–11)**

II. The Letter Body (1:12–4:9)

III. The Letter Closing (4:10–23)

1. See especially Klauck and Bailey, *Ancient Letters*, 42; on thanksgiving and prayer reports, see Peter Arzt-Grabner, "Paul's Letter Thanksgiving," in Porter and Adams, *Paul and the Ancient Letter Form*, 129–58.

2. See pp. 31–32 above.

3. Peterman, *Paul's Gift from Philippi*, 91–93.

## Main Idea

Paul expresses deep, joyful affection for the Philippians, thanking God for their consistent participation in the gospel and voicing confidence in their future commitment to the Christian faith and mission. He also prays that they would continue in dynamic growth in the faith until the day of Christ, all to the glory of God.

## Translation

### Philippians 1:3–11

| | | |
|---|---|---|
| 3a | Thanksgiving | **I thank my God** |
| b | Temporal/ Frequency | every time I remember you. |
| 4a | Time | Always, |
| b | Context | in every prayer I pray for you all, |
| c | Manner | I pray with joy |
| 5a | Basis | because of your participation |
| b | Sphere | in the gospel |
| c | Inception | from the first day |
| d | Duration | until now, |
| 6a | Circumstance | being confident of **this very thing**, |
| b | Apposition | that the one who began a good work among you |
| c | Action | will perfect it |
| | Duration | until the day of Christ Jesus. |
| 7a | Assertion | **It is right for me to think this way** |
| b | Reference | about all of you |
| c | Basis of 7a | because I have you in my heart; |
| d | Context | in my imprisonment and |
| e | Context | in the defense and |
| f | | confirmation of the gospel |
| g | Assertion | . . . all of you are fellow participants |
| h | Associat. | with me |
| i | Reference | of grace. |
| 8a | Explanation of 7c | For |
| b | Oath | **God is my witness** |
| c | Content | that I long for all of you |
| d | Manner | with the affection of Christ Jesus. |

| | | |
|---|---|---|
| 9a | | And |
| b | Prayer | **I pray this** |
| c | | that your love might grow exponentially |
| d | | |
| e | Substance | in knowledge and |
| f | | penetrating |
| g | Substance | perception |
| 10a | Result | resulting in the discernment of what is spiritually valuable, |
| b | Purpose | in order that you might be sincere and |
| c | | faultless |
| d | Duration | until the day of Christ, |
| 11a | Circumst. | having been filled with the fruit produced by righteousness, |
| b | Agency | which comes through Jesus Christ |
| c | Result | to the glory and praise of God. |

## Structure

We see two main movements in this passage: verses 3–8 and verses 9–11. Philippians 1:3–8, in which Paul expresses thanks to God and deep affection for the Philippians,[4] presents a notoriously difficult, even convoluted, sentence structure.[5] Yet in terms of structure, we can begin by noting that a number of elements are found at the beginning and ending of the unit, forming an *inclusio*, a convention by which a writer "marked" the beginning and ending of a distinct passage or part of a discourse. These elements here include: the twin references to "God," "all/every," the first-person pronoun, and references to how Paul thinks about the Philippians with affection (1:3, 8).

Another clause, translated, "Accordingly, it is right for me to think this way about all of you" (καθώς ἐστιν δίκαιον ἐμοὶ τοῦτο φρονεῖν ὑπὲρ πάντων ὑμῶν; 1:7) functions as a "hinge," a structural turning point, dividing the first half of the unit from the second. But it also keeps the focus on the Philippians by using the pronoun "you" (plural forms of the Greek word σύ). Notice how these three clauses form the backbone of the passage:

4. For an introduction to Paul's letter thanksgivings, see Arzt-Grabner, "Paul's Letter Thanksgiving."

5. For instance, do the adverbial πάντοτε and the phrases that follow (ἐν πάσῃ δεήσει μου ὑπὲρ πάντων ὑμῶν) in v. 4 delimit the verb εὐχαριστῶ at the beginning of v. 3 or the participle ποιούμενος at the end of v. 4? The same question could be asked of the clause beginning with the perfect active participle πεποιθώς at the beginning of v. 6. Further, is the καθώς at the beginning of v. 7 the continuation of the sentence, as Fee suggests (Fee, *Philippians*, 88–89), or does it begin a new sentence, as with BDAG 494? These are but the beginning of woes.

I thank my God every time I remember you (1:3)
Accordingly, it is right for me to think this way about all of you (1:7)
God is my witness that I long for all of you (1:8)

Thus, our passage's first movement has at its heart the affection that Paul feels for the Philippian church. He thinks about them, thanks God for them, and longs for them with affection. Would that we all felt this way toward those to whom we minister!

These three main structural anchors of the passage are accented by four, evenly balanced subordinate clauses (1:4–5; 1:6; 1:7c; 1:7e–g), forming a chiastic structure as follows:

A **I thank my God every time I remember you. (1:3)**
  B praying for you with joy because of your participation in the gospel (1:4–5)
    C because I am confident of God's continued work in you (1:6)
      **D Accordingly, it is right for me to think this way about all of you (1:7a–b)**
    C′ because I have you in my heart (1:7c)
  B′ since you are grace partners with me in the gospel (1:7e–g)
A′ **God is my witness how I long for all of you . . . (1:8)**

In the second main movement of our passage, 1:9–11, the apostle offers a beautiful prayer consisting of a main clause followed by layers of subordinate clauses. The unit begins with "and I pray this" (καὶ τοῦτο προσεύχομαι), the "this" (τοῦτο) referring to what follows in the prayer. In verse 9, Paul uses "that" (ἵνα) to introduce the content of his prayer.[6]

Essentially Paul prays that the Philippians' "love might grow exponentially in knowledge and penetrating perception" (ἡ ἀγάπη ὑμῶν ἔτι μᾶλλον καὶ μᾶλλον περισσεύῃ ἐν ἐπιγνώσει καὶ πάσῃ αἰσθήσει). This "that" (ἵνα) clause is then followed by a result clause translated as "resulting in the discernment of what is spiritually valuable" (εἰς τὸ δοκιμάζειν ὑμᾶς τὰ διαφέροντα). In other words, as they grow in love they will discern what is best. Following on the heels of the result clause is a purpose clause that points to the fruit of discernment—"in order that you might be sincere and faultless" (ἵνα ἦτε εἰλικρινεῖς καὶ ἀπρόσκοποι). Discernment leads to sincerity and faultlessness. In a final subordinate clause (v. 11), Paul explains the circumstances behind the Philippians' sincerity and faultlessness "until the day of Christ"—they will be in a state of "having been filled with the fruit produced by righteousness." So, the logical relationships within this prayer may be depicted as follows:

6. As Fee notes, this is a common Koine idiom (Fee, *Philippians*, 98).

| | |
|---|---|
| I pray | this: |
| (content) | that your love might grow exponentially in knowledge and perception |
| (result) | discernment of what is best |
| (purpose) | that you might be sincere and faultless |
| (circumstances) | having been filled with the fruit of righteousness |

## Exegetical Outline

➡ **B. A Joyful Prayer Report (1:3–11)**

**1. Paul's Affectionate Appreciation for the Philippians (1:3–8)**

a. Paul Gives Thanks for the Philippians (vv. 3–6)

b. Paul Expresses Affection for the Philippians (vv. 7–8)

**2. Paul Prays for the Philippians (1:9–11)**

a. That Their Love Would Overflow in Perceptive Knowledge (v. 9)

b. That the Result Would Be Discernment of What Is Spiritually Valuable (v. 10a)

c. For the Purpose of: (vv. 10b–11)

(1) The Philippians Being Sincere and Faultless until Christ's Day

(2) Having Been Filled with the Fruit of Righteousness through Christ

(3) Their Lives Being for the Glory and Praise of God

## Explanation of the Text

**1:3 I thank my God every time I remember you** (Εὐχαριστῶ τῷ θεῷ μου ἐπὶ πάσῃ τῇ μνείᾳ ὑμῶν). In expressing thanks to God for the Philippians, Paul taps into a rich theme from Old Testament literature, especially the Psalms.[7] Expression of thanks to God for various blessings was standard in Jewish prayers of Paul's era, as reflected in the New Testament (e.g., Matt 15:36; Mark 14:23; John 11:41; Acts 28:15) and the letters of broader Hellenistic Judaism (e.g., 2 Macc 1:10–13). Paul incorporates this common expression of Jewish piety in the prologues of several of his letters.[8] Thanks for others constitutes a normal pattern of his life.[9] Of course, God, the creator and giver of all that is good, is the ultimate object[10] of the apostle's gratitude. The addition of the pronoun "my" (μου)[11] adds a personal

7. See 2 Sam 22:50; 1 Chr 16:8; 2 Chr 31:2; Ps 7:17; 9:1; 18:49; although the term commonly used in the LXX is ἐξομολογέω.

8. Rom 1:8; 1 Cor 1:4; Eph 1:16; Col 1:3; 1 Thess 1:2; 2 Thess 1:3; 2:13; Phlm 4.

9. The imperfective aspect of the present-tense verb translated "I thank" (εὐχαριστῶ), and the phrase rendered "every time" (ἐπὶ πάσῃ; ἐπί + the dative is temporal in this case) that follows, indicate that Paul's expression of gratitude is ongoing. On verbal aspect, see Constantine R. Campbell, *Basics of Verbal Aspect in Biblical Greek* (Grand Rapids: Zondervan, 2008), 65.

10. The phrase rendered "to God" (τῷ θεῷ) is a dative direct object.

11. This is perhaps a "genitive of relationship." The designation of genitive of possession is understandable, given Wallace's qualification that it be understood "in a broad sense" (Daniel B. Wallace, *Greek Grammar beyond the Basics: An Exegetical Syntax of the New Testament* [Grand Rapids: Zondervan,

touch to his expression of thanks, also drawing on common Old Testament language that Paul uses in similar expressions of thanks in other letters (Rom 1:8; 1 Cor 1:4; Phlm 4).[12]

In our passage, Paul always gives thanks to God when the Philippians come to mind: "I thank my God every time I remember you." The word translated here as "remember" (μνεία) occurs seven times in Paul's writings, and almost always in the thanksgiving at a letter's beginning.[13] This noun belongs to a family of words having to do with memory and can be rendered as "remembrance," "memory," or to make "mention" of someone.[14] Paul uses the word in context to speak of bringing the Philippians to mind in prayer. When the apostle thinks of this church, for whom he has so much appreciation and affection, he is filled with gratitude to God and is prompted to express his thanks for them.

Although some have suggested that Paul's intention here is to thank God for the Philippians' remembrance of *him*,[15] it is better to read the sentence as expressing Paul's thanks for the Philippians.[16] This accords with the fact that in the opening thanksgivings in his letters, the apostle normally thanks God for the recipients.[17] We might add that—as in our treatment of the "Structure" above—Paul's actions and attitudes *toward* the Philippians seem to form the backbone of the passage, shaping the consistent focus throughout the passage.[18] In reality, we observe a three-way relationship, in which Paul models a thankful posture toward God himself for the Philippians—a relationship that will be elaborated in 4:10–20.[19]

**1:4 Always, in every prayer I pray for you all, I pray with joy** (πάντοτε ἐν πάσῃ δεήσει μου ὑπὲρ πάντων ὑμῶν, μετὰ χαρᾶς τὴν δέησιν ποιούμενος). The apostle prays joy-filled prayers for the Philippians. Grammatically, the word "always" (πάντοτε) can be read as telling us something about the verb translated "I give thanks" in the previous verse (εὐχαριστῶ; "I always give thanks," as with 1 Cor 1:4; Eph 5:20; Col 1:3; 1 Thess 1:2; 2 Thess 1:3; 2:13; Phlm 4 [?]). Yet in a number of similar contexts, Paul uses "always" in relation to prayer generally

1996], 82). But "genitive of relationship" seems better, given the covenantal backdrop of a person's relationship to God in Scripture. This does not fit Wallace's "familial relationship" stricture (p. 83), but it seems more descriptive of what Paul has in mind, for whatever else the apostle means, covenant relationship is at its foundation.

12. E.g., Deut 26:3; Josh 9:23; 14:8; 24:27; 1 Sam 2:1; 2 Sam 22:30; 24:24; Ps 17:30; 103:33; 145:2; Hab 1:11.

13. Rom 1:9; Eph 1:16; Phil 1:3; 1 Thess 1:2; 3:6; 2 Tim 1:3; Phlm 4; with 1 Thess 3:6 the exception.

14. E.g., Jer 31:20 [38:20 LXX] reads, "Ephraim is my beloved son, a child to delight in; because, since my words are in him, I will remember him with remembrance [μνείᾳ]" (NETS).

15. Reading "you" (ὑμῶν) as a subjective genitive; part of the argument is that the preposition ἐπί + the dative should be read causally, not temporally, as is most often done with the objective-genitive interpretation. E.g., David E. Garland, "Philippians 1:1–26: The Defense and Confirmation of the Gospel," *RevExp* 77 (1980): 329–30; Peterman, *Paul's Gift from Philippi*, 94–96; Ben Witherington, *Paul's Letter to the Philippians: A Socio-Rhetorical Commentary* (Grand Rapids: Eerdmans, 2011), 56; John Reumann, *Philippians with Introduction and Commentary*, AYB (New Haven: Yale University Press, 2008), 148–49. Holloway, who holds to an objective-genitive interpretation, nevertheless suggests that the prepositional phrase should be interpreted causally, rendering the phrase "for every remembrance of you" (Holloway, *Philippians*, 69–72). Yet it may be suggested that a "cause" is inherent in the temporal reading of the phrase, as Paul thanks God *for* something *when* he remembers the Philippians.

16. As Fee points out, "Verbs and nouns denoting 'memory' take the genitive as their object," so the pronoun is better read as an objective genitive (*Philippians*, 78). So Marvin R. Vincent, *A Critical and Exegetical Commentary on the Epistles to the Philippians and to Philemon*, ICC (Edinburgh: T&T Clark, 1897), 6; Joseph H. Hellerman, *Philippians*, EGGNT (Nashville: B&H Academic, 2015), 20; Hansen, *Philippians*, 46; Hawthorne, *Philippians*, 19.

17. Fee, *Philippians*, 77–79.

18. Reed, *Discourse Analysis*, 200–201, 387.

19. See David Briones, "Paul's Intentional 'Thankless Thanks' in Philippians 4.10–20," *JSNT* 34 (2011): 47–69.

(Rom 1:10; Col 4:12; 2 Thess 1:11; Phlm 4 [?]). In the present context, it makes some sense to read the word "always"—a bit removed from the main verb—as modifying the prayer that follows (i.e., "I always pray"), since in relation to that prayer the apostle stacks up alliterative elements in a rapid-fire manner (notice the π at the beginning of words in the middle column):[20]

| | πάντοτε | "always" |
|---|---|---|
| ἐν | πάσῃ δεήσει μου | "in every prayer I pray" |
| ὑπὲρ | πάντων ὑμῶν, μετὰ χαρᾶς | "for you all, with joy" |
| τὴν δέησιν | ποιούμενος | "I pray" |

Paul prays constantly for the Philippian church, praying consistently and personally for these believers.

Praying "for"[21] others serves as a foundation of Christian life and ministry for the apostle.[22] And note the inclusiveness of his prayer: "I pray for you *all*" (ὑπὲρ πάντων ὑμῶν). As noted in our commentary on 1:1, Paul often uses the word "all" (πᾶς) to address people inclusively.[23] But the number of uses of this Greek word in the prologue (seven times in the first eight verses), and the thirty-three uses in this relatively short book, indicate that the apostle may have a bigger purpose in mind—namely, to underscore the need for unity in the church. Paul does not single out specific people or groups for special attention and concern (until 4:2!). Rather, he prays for all the brothers and sisters in Philippi.

Finally, Paul's prayer is infused "with joy" (μετὰ χαρᾶς). Ceslas Spicq calls joy "the distinguishing characteristic of the Judeo-Christian religion."[24] There is no religious parallel to the Jewish and Christian concept of joy in the ancient world, and as Markus Bockmuehl points out, in the Old Testament prophets "joy is especially characteristic of the age of redemption" (e.g., Isa 12:3, 6; 25:9; 35:1–10; 55:12).[25] The gospel of God forms the foundation of a joy-filled life. In Paul's case, not even prison could dampen his joy, as is evident in this joyful letter (Phil 1:18, 25; 2:2, 17–18, 28–29; 3:1; 4:4, 10), for he focuses on the progress of the gospel rather than his own discomfort.[26] So, not only does the apostle exhort these believers over and again to "rejoice in the Lord," he too knows the experience of joy firsthand and experiences that joy as he prays, reflecting on the Philippians' role in his mission. Thus, as expressed in Philippians 1:3–4, Paul's prayers are thankful, constant, inclusive, and joyful.[27]

---

20. The alliteration actually begins with πασῃ in v. 3 and continues in vv. 5–6.

21. The preposition ὑπέρ + the genitive here indicates an activity done in the interest of someone or something.

22. E.g., Rom 10:1; 2 Cor 1:11; 9:14; Eph 6:18; Phil 1:19; 4:6; 1 Tim 2:1; 2 Tim 1:3.

23. In letter openings: Rom 1:7–8; 1 Cor 1:2; 2 Cor 1:1; Gal 1:2; 1 Thess 1:2. In letter closings: Rom 16:15–16; 1 Cor 16:24; 2 Cor 13:12–13; Gal 6:16; Eph 6:24; Phil 4:21–22; 1 Thess 5:26–27; 2 Thess 3:18; Titus 3:15.

24. *TLNT* 3:498.

25. Bockmuehl, *Philippians*, 59. From the very beginning of telling the good news about Jesus, the word of salvation was proclaimed as a message of great joy (Luke 2:10–11), and Jesus's followers exuded joy as a normal aspect of their experience (e.g., Matt 13:20, 44; 28:8; Luke 15:7, 32; 19:6; John 15:11; 16:24; 17:23; Acts 2:46; 8:8, 39; 13:48–52). It is unsurprising, therefore, that joy characterizes the vocation of Christian ministry, marking a ministry as authentic (2 Cor 7:4, 13; Phil 2:2; 4:1; 1 Thess 2:19–20; 3:9; 2 Tim 1:4; Phlm 7).

26. Indeed, Paul often speaks of joy in his letters, either using the noun (Rom 14:17; 15:13, 32; 2 Cor 1:24; 2:3; 7:4, 13; 8:2; Gal 5:22; Phil 1:4, 25; 2:2, 29; 4:1; Col 1:11; 1 Thess 1:6; 2:19–20; 3:9; 2 Tim 1:4; Phlm 7) or the cognate verb (Rom 12:12, 15; 16:19; 1 Cor 7:30; 13:6; 16:17; 2 Cor 2:3; 6:10; 7:7, 9, 13, 16; 13:9, 11; Phil 1:18; 2:17–18, 28; 3:1; 4:4, 10; Col 1:24; 2:5; 1 Thess 3:9; 5:16).

27. Gordon D. Fee, *God's Empowering Presence: The Holy Spirit in the Letters of Paul* (Peabody, MA: Hendrickson, 1994), 62.

**1:5 Because of your participation in the gospel from the first day until now** (ἐπὶ τῇ κοινωνίᾳ ὑμῶν εἰς τὸ εὐαγγέλιον ἀπὸ τῆς πρώτης ἡμέρας ἄχρι τοῦ νῦν). Paul now explains the reason why his prayers are infused with joy when he prays for the Philippians. As here, the preposition translated "because" (ἐπί) can be used to mark the basis of an action.[28] Specifically, Paul points to the Philippians' "participation" (κοινωνία) in the gospel as that which has given him joy. He celebrates that they have participated with him in his gospel mission from the time they first met until the present. A rich word of relationship, the term rendered "participation" (κοινωνία) speaks of a close association, sharing, or fellowship with someone, which often issues in a strong sense of goodwill or altruism.[29] Thus the term came to be used of "sharing" with another or participating with them in a task, which is the sense here.

Consequently, the apostle celebrates that the Philippians have participated in his gospel mission, sharing with him for the advancement of the good news about Christ (see Rom 15:26; 2 Cor 8:4). Fee calls "the gospel" (τὸ εὐαγγέλιον), a word used nine times in the letter (Phil 1:5, 7, 12, 16, 27 [2x]; 2:22; 4:3, 15), "the singular passion of [Paul's] life" and "the glue" that holds Philippians together, for above all the gospel is centered in the person and work of Christ himself. To preach the gospel is to preach Christ (1:15–16), and to live worthy of the gospel (v. 27) is to live worthy of Christ.[30] We might say that the Messiah is the message, and the Philippians have participated unreservedly with Paul's mission out of a deeply rooted commitment to the gospel, as evidenced by the way they have shared materially in the apostle's work (4:15). From Paul's perspective, gospel mission needs to be a community mission, as it had been with the Philippians.

But we need to probe the issue of the Philippians' participation in Paul's ministry a bit further, as scholars have held two primary opinions. Some suggest that Paul primarily has in mind the Philippians' sharing in his mission by contributing financial support while he was in prison. Others suggest that the "partnership" primarily encompasses their suffering alongside him, as they too shared the gospel on the streets of Philippi.[31] Given the parallels with the end of chapter 1 and the broader parallels between 1:3–11 and 4:10–20, it seems prudent to suggest that *both* elements, suffering and giving, play a part in the "partnership" forged between Paul and the church, which the apostle here celebrates.[32]

Thus, the Philippians' participation in the gospel "from the first day until now" certainly includes their support of Paul as he has proclaimed the gospel around the Mediterranean world—even during his time in prison—but it also includes their active participation with him in the sharing of the

28. BDAG 364.

29. BDAG 552–53.

30. Fee, *Philippians*, 82.

31. See Peter Oakes's fictional account of the contrast between Jason and Penelope in Peter Oakes, "Jason and Penelope Hear Philippians 1.1–11," in *Understanding, Studying and Reading: New Testament Essays in Honour of John Ashton*, ed. C. Rowland and C. H. T. Fletcher-Louis, JSNTSup 153 (Sheffield: Sheffield Academic Press, 1998), 156–57. In Oakes's account, Jason hears Paul celebrating his sharing in the sufferings of Christ as he lives with difficulty in Philippi. Penelope, on the other hand, hears Paul thanking her and her husband for financially contributing so generously to his mission.

Examples of scholars who vie for suffering as the primary orientation are Ernst Lohmeyer, *Die Briefe an die Philipper, an die Kolosser und an Philemon*, KEK (Göttingen: Vandenhoeck & Ruprecht, 1928), 26; Lightfoot, *Philippians*, 85; and Oakes, all of whom point especially to the connections between 1:7 and 1:27–30. For a thorough treatment of the position that Paul has in mind financial help, as well as other possible nuances, see Keown, *Philippians 1:1–2:18*, 131–33. Keown rightly notes that we need not limit the scope of partnership.

32. So Fee, *Philippians*, 92–93.

good news (1:27–30; 4:2–3). These prepositional phrases, rendered "from the first day until now," are first of all temporal markers, celebrating the inception and duration of the Philippians' "participation." So these members of the church committed initially to the gospel mission by responding to the gospel themselves and embracing Paul, his missionary team, and the mission to which they were called. In Acts, Luke points out that Lydia opened her heart to the gospel as well as her home to the missionaries (Acts 16:14–15, 40). Similarly, after believing the gospel, the Philippian jailer took Paul and Silas home, cared for their wounds, and fed them (vv. 32–34). Once the missionaries left Philippi, members of the church made a public stand for the gospel, sharing it with others in the face of opposition.

**1:6 Being confident of this very thing, that the one who began a good work among you will perfect it until the day of Christ Jesus** (πεποιθὼς αὐτὸ τοῦτο, ὅτι ὁ ἐναρξάμενος ἐν ὑμῖν ἔργον ἀγαθὸν ἐπιτελέσει ἄχρι ἡμέρας Χριστοῦ Ἰησοῦ). The constancy of the Philippians' work with Paul and their support in the gospel mission gave him a great deal of confidence in their spiritual condition. The term translated as "being confident" (πεποιθώς) means "persuade" or "being persuaded." In this context, the word speaks of having confidence in something or someone, as seen in Greco-Roman literature (Herodotus, *Histories* 9.88; Sophocles, *Ajax* 769), and was increasingly common in the Second Temple period, especially in the LXX and Philo.[33] The sense of "confidence" is well attested in the New Testament, and Paul consistently uses the word with this meaning at a number of other places in the letter (Phil 1:14, 25; 2:24; 3:3–4). As portrayed in our diagram of the passage, the participle probably should be understood as telling us more about Paul's prayer of joy, mentioned at the end of verse 4. In other words, Paul's prayers are joyful because of the Philippians' past record of participation in his ministry (1:5), but his prayers are also hopeful as he anticipates God's continued work in their lives.[34] He prays with confidence.

Paul's confidence is expressed in "this very thing" (αὐτὸ τοῦτο), with αὐτό intensifying the pronoun τοῦτο ("this"). The apostle then employs a "this is that" construction, which can be diagrammed as follows:[35]

"Being confident of this
↓ *(Apposition)*
that the one who began a good work in you ..."

Of course, "the one who began a good work" refers to God, as Paul underscores the true and sure foundation for perseverance in the faith—a vibrant relationship with God himself. The juxtaposition of the apostle's commendation of the Philippians for their "work" with him in the gospel mission (1:5) and his celebration of the Lord's work in them (1:6) poses no problem for Paul's biblical theology, as these themes are fully integrated in his writings (see 2:12–13).[36] The golden-tongued church father, John Chrysostom, noted the deft pastoral balance in Paul's thought, stating,

> Having just given them a superb testimonial, in order that they should not feel down and out as human beings are so apt to feel, he immediately teaches them to refer both the past and the future—everything—to Christ, who will bring to

33. *TLNT* 3:66–77.

34. On this reading, the participle is understood as circumstantial.

35. The ὅτι clause relates to τοῦτο appositionally, as with A. T. Robertson, *A Grammar of the Greek New Testament in the Light of Historical Research* (Nashville: Broadman, 1934), 699.

36. Silva, *Philippians*, 45.

completion what he has begun in them. He does not take away anything from their achievement, for he has said, "I rejoice because of your fellowship," obviously pointing to their own very high level of accountability. But he does not imply that the achievement was theirs alone. Rather it was primarily God's work in them. (*Homily on Philippians* 2.1.6)[37]

That God "began[38] a good work among" the Philippians (ὁ ἐναρξάμενος ἐν ὑμῖν ἔργον ἀγαθόν) corresponds to "from the first day" (ἀπὸ τῆς πρώτης ἡμέρας) in the previous verse. God had begun his work among the Philippians when Paul first landed in Philippi, approximately a decade prior to writing the letter (late 49 or early 50 CE). According to Acts 16:12–34, that work began with the conversion of Lydia on a Sabbath day and continued with the conversion of the Philippian jailer and his family. Paul celebrates the work God accomplished "among" (ἐν ὑμῖν) them as a "good work" (ἔργον ἀγαθόν).[39]

Further, the apostle expresses his confidence that God "will perfect" (ἐπιτελέσει) the work for the duration of the age, "until the day of Christ Jesus" (ἄχρι ἡμέρας Χριστοῦ Ἰησοῦ). The verb rendered "will perfect" (ἐπιτελέω) means "to finish" something or "to bring it to completion."[40] For instance, elsewhere Paul can use the term to speak of finishing the collection for the saints (Rom 15:28; 2 Cor 8:6, 11) or of the "completion" of a process of Christian growth to maturity, as seen here (2 Cor 7:1; Gal 3:3).

The Old Testament prophets spoke of the "day" (or "days") of the Lord, which would bring deliverance for God's people and judgment for their enemies (e.g., Isa 2:2–21; Joel 1–3; Amos 8:9–11; 9:9–12). At times the Israelites called for the day of the Lord, thinking it would bring them a good outcome, but Amos foretold that it would not be what they expected, the day of "light" turning out to be a day of "darkness" (Amos 5:18). Apocalyptic literature spoke of it as a "day of judgment" (e.g., 1 En. 94.9; 4 Ezra 7.26–44), but in Paul's writings and in the New Testament generally, "the day" refers to the day of Christ's return (e.g., 1 Cor 5:5; 1 Thess 5:2; 2 Pet 3:10), which is clearly the case here. Paul anticipates that what God had begun among the Philippians in the mid-first century he would consummate at the end of the age. And he may have had in mind their resurrection from the dead—a grand "perfection" indeed!

**1:7a–c Accordingly, it is right for me to think this way about all of you, because I have you in my heart** (καθώς ἐστιν δίκαιον ἐμοὶ τοῦτο φρονεῖν ὑπὲρ πάντων ὑμῶν διὰ τὸ ἔχειν με ἐν τῇ καρδίᾳ ὑμᾶς). As we have seen, in verses 3–6 Paul expresses his thanks to God for the Philippians, experiencing *joy* in the Philippians' partnership in the gospel and confidence in their spiritual condition. As he turns to what we have in verses 7–8, he now expresses his *affection* for them as "fellow participants with" him "of grace." Yet how do these two parts of the passage relate, and specifically why does Paul connect the two with a word that we have translated as "accordingly" (καθώς), which introduces the apostle's statement, "It is right for me to think this way about all of you" at the beginning of verse 7?[41]

37. Edwards, *Galatians, Ephesians, Philippians*, 209–10.

38. The only other place this word for "begin" (ἐνάρχομαι) is used in the NT is at Gal 3:3, where Paul chastises the Galatian churches for their theological blundering: "Are you so foolish? Although you began [ἐναρξάμενοι] with the Spirit, are you now trying to finish by human effort?" (NET).

39. The "good work" should be understood as referring to the whole movement of the gospel among the Philippians rather than to the narrower sense of their financial support, as with Hawthorne, *Philippians*, 21.

40. BDAG 383.

41. As we turn to v. 7, the Greek text confronts us with a

When Paul says that the thought processes expressed in 1:3–6 are "right" (δίκαιον), the term means that they are "fair" or "appropriate." Although it is true that καθώς, which introduces this statement, can be read as causal (i.e., "because"),[42] this does not make sense here. Paul is not saying, "I have joy and confidence in you *because* it is right for me to think this way about you." Rather, he suggests that it is appropriate for him to "think this way about [ὑπέρ[43]] all of" them in terms of joy and confidence *because* of his affection for them ("because I have you in my heart"; διὰ τὸ ἔχειν με ἐν τῇ καρδίᾳ ὑμᾶς). The term καρδία is used 156 times in the New Testament and another 912 times in the LXX; it has a broad semantic range encompassing many aspects of a person's physical, spiritual, and mental life.[44] Yet, as here, it may describe the inner life or emotions (Rom 1:24; 9:2; 2 Cor 2:4), much as we may use the English word "heart" today. Here it expresses deep feeling of affection.

This affection matches and is in accordance with (καθώς) his joy and confidence expressed in the previous verses. Thus, the word rendered "this way" (τοῦτο) points back to the joy and confidence of the previous verses. This mix of affection, joy, and confidence that Paul feels when he thinks about the Philippians would be similar to a parent who experiences great joy and confidence in a child who does well in life, and that joy and confidence is bound up with deep affection the parent feels for the child. For Paul, his thanks to God for the Philippians and his joy and confidence in the Philippians are bound up with the deep affection he has for them. Paul expresses this affection with the clause translated, "I have you in my heart" (τὸ ἔχειν με ἐν τῇ καρδίᾳ ὑμᾶς).

**1:7d–g In my imprisonment and in the defense and confirmation of the gospel, all of you are fellow participants with me of grace** (ἔν τε τοῖς δεσμοῖς μου καὶ ἐν τῇ ἀπολογίᾳ καὶ βεβαιώσει τοῦ εὐαγγελίου συγκοινωνούς μου τῆς χάριτος πάντας ὑμᾶς ὄντας). As this verse continues, we learn the source of Paul's affection for the Philippians—it has grown out of the church's partnership in his mission. They have stood with him in gospel ministry and in the difficult contexts in which that ministry has played out.

Notice that Paul continues to address the Philippians with "all of you are" (ὑμᾶς ὄντας)[45] at the end of verse 7. This latter part of the verse explains[46] something further about the Philippians: "All of you" (πάντας ὑμᾶς) are "fellow participants with me of grace" (συγκοινωνούς μου τῆς χάριτος). Although some commentators understand the personal pronoun "me" (μου) to relate to "of the grace"

grammatical question. Does the clause fronted by the word we have translated as "accordingly" (καθώς) continue the sentence of v. 6, or does it start a new sentence? Greek grammars note that the word καθώς can be used at the beginning of a sentence; see BDF 236; Robertson, *Grammar*, 1382. This is the case even when the adverb is not used in a correlative relationship with οὕτως (e.g., Gal 3:6; 1 Tim 1:3). But Fee demurs, pointing to 1 Cor 1:6 and 1 Thess 1:5 (see also 2 Thess 1:3) as examples in which καθώς signals the continuation of a sentence in the thanksgiving at the beginning of a letter. Yet Fee's examples at 1 Cor 1:6 and 1 Thess 1:5 could be read as parenthetical statements and thus independent clauses, as with the NET's rendering of both verses.

42. So BDAG 493.

43. The preposition ὑπέρ marks "general content" (BDAG 1031), which is unusual in Paul. The clause φρονεῖν ὑπὲρ πάντων ὑμῶν forms an *inclusio* with τὸ ὑπὲρ ἐμοῦ φρονεῖν in 4:10 (so Bockmuehl, *Philippians*, 259), though the ὑπέρ construction in 4:10 seems to communicate advantage, which is the more common use for Paul.

44. BDAG 508–9.

45. Robertson notes that since ὑμᾶς is repeated, this is not an accusative absolute (Robertson, *Grammar*, 491).

46. The present participle translated as "are" (ὄντας) can be read as explanatory, delimiting the infinitive "have" (ἔχειν), and thus can be understood to answer the question, "Why does Paul have the Philippians in his heart?" (so NET, NASB, NRSV, ESV). It is because of their partnership in his ministry.

(τῆς χάριτος) that follows (i.e., "fellow participants of my grace")[47]—and the pronoun is ambiguous in context—it is better read as personalizing "fellow participants" (συγκοινωνούς), thus, "fellow participants with me."[48]

This term translated "fellow participants" (συγκοινωνός)—a term related to the word rendered "participation" (κοινωνία) in 1:5—could be used of a "business partner" in the ancient world.[49] If κοινωνία speaks of participation generally, the compound underscores "being participants together."[50] New Testament authors employ the compound three other times (Rom 11:17; 1 Cor 9:23; Rev 1:9), with stress on the idea of "participating" with others in some endeavor. For instance, at 1 Corinthians 9:23 Paul writes of doing all things because of the gospel, so that he can "share" in its benefits. In Revelation 1:9 John speaks of sharing with his readers in persecution, the kingdom, and endurance.

So, what does Paul have in mind at 1:7? He sees the Philippians as fellow participants with him "of grace." Of course, χάρις could refer to God's "grace" generally, but the article would seem to point to a particular expression of God's grace, and it may be suggested that he has in mind the Philippians' participation in his gospel ministry, as he has already mentioned in verse 5.[51] After all, his referent is clarified with "in my imprisonment and in the defense and confirmation of the gospel." Thus, as noted above on 1:5, the Philippians' participation with Paul was multifaceted. They gave of themselves in advancing the gospel, as well as their money. This interpretation would seem to correspond to 2 Corinthians 8:1–2:

> Now we make known to you, brothers and sisters, the grace of God given to the churches of Macedonia, that during a severe ordeal of suffering, their abundant joy and their extreme poverty have overflowed in the wealth of their generosity. (NET)

The common translation, "in my imprisonment" (e.g., ESV, NASB, NLT, NET), is a metonymy rendering "in my chains" (ἔν τε τοῖς δεσμοῖς μου; cf. Phil 1:13–14, 17; Col 4:18; 2 Tim 2:9; Phlm 10, 13). Paul almost certainly had literal chains in mind here, as only prisoners of high social status were incarcerated without them.[52] Since he speaks of his "defense" and "confirmation of the gospel," the apostle almost certainly had his current situation in mind.[53] Normally prisoners were held in custody while awaiting trial—to give them protection or to keep them until a sentence could be carried out—but incarceration could also be used as a form of punishment, and life under a guard could be brutal (e.g., Josephus, *Ant.* 18.203).[54] Paul experienced

47. E.g., see Brent Nongbri, "Two Neglected Textual Variants in Philippians 1," *JBL* 128.4 (2009): 805, who reads the later manuscripts that move the pronoun to follow χάριτος as seeking to clarify the ambiguity of the placement of μου in earlier manuscripts. Those who associate μου with χάριτος normally point to Phil 4:14.

48. This reading understands μου as a genitive of association (e.g., Rom 8:17; Eph 2:19; 5:7; Col 4:10; Rev 19:10). See the discussion of the matter in Bockmuehl, *Philippians*, 63, who notes that in the context of a letter being read publicly "in the case of ambiguity, the more common Greek usage would prevail in associating μου with the preceding noun (as also in v. 8 'God is my witness')."

49. So BDAG 952.

50. Fee, *Philippians*, 91.

51. Silva, *Philippians*, 47.

52. So Fee, *Philippians*, 92; Brian Rapske, *The Book of Acts and Paul in Roman Custody* (Grand Rapids: Eerdmans; Carlisle: Paternoster, 1994), 28; Cassidy, *Paul in Chains*, 45.

53. During Paul's first visit to Philippi, recorded in Acts 16:11–40, he and Silas were beaten and thrown into an inner cell with their feet fastened in stocks (v. 24).

54. Rapske, *Paul in Roman Custody*, 9, 16–20, 256–59; Craig S. Keener, *Acts: An Exegetical Commentary, 15:1–23:35* (Grand Rapids: Baker Academic, 2014), 2484, 2486.

imprisonment numerous times (2 Cor 6:5; 11:23), and he was deeply grateful when the Philippians stood with him in such dire circumstances, identifying with him in his suffering for, and defense of, the gospel.

Often used in legal contexts, a "defense" (ἀπολογία) was a speech offered as an argument on a person's behalf or was the act of making a defense (Acts 25:16; 2 Tim 4:16). Paul speaks here, however, of his defense of the gospel itself.[55] Another legal term, "confirmation" (βεβαίωσις), speaks of the proof demonstrating the validity of something (cf. Heb 6:16). In this case, Paul had given his life to bear witness to the established truth of the gospel. The use here is similar to the use of the cognate verb "confirm" (βεβαιόω) at Hebrews 2:3–4, where the word of salvation was "confirmed" by the original witnesses, who received it from Jesus himself, and God bore witness with them, "taking the witness stand" of history and validating the message by signs, wonders, miracles, and gifts of the Holy Spirit. So perhaps Paul proclaims the validity of the gospel by his testimony before the authorities. Paul's point, however, is that the Philippians have also been participants with him in these twin activities of defending and confirming the gospel.

**1:8 For God is my witness that I long for all of you with the affection of Christ Jesus** (μάρτυς γάρ μου ὁ θεὸς ὡς ἐπιποθῶ πάντας ὑμᾶς ἐν σπλάγχνοις Χριστοῦ Ἰησοῦ). Continuing with language from a courtroom context and specifically alluding to an Old Testament pattern (e.g., Josh 22:27; 1 Sam 12:5; Jer 42:5), Paul invokes God as his "witness" (μάρτυς . . . μου) to his affection for the Philippians. The Lord knows all actions, all thoughts. His Spirit discerns all motives and sorts out all intentions. There could be no better witness on the apostle's behalf, and Paul offers such sober oaths on numerous occasions in his letters (Rom 1:9; 2 Cor 1:23; 1 Thess 2:5, 10). In effect, the apostle assures the Philippians of his deep feelings for them in the strongest possible terms. The whole of verse 8, in fact, forms an explanation ("for," γάρ) of verse 7c, where Paul writes, "I have you in my heart."

The relative adverb translated "that" (ὡς) marks the content[56] of Paul's oath, and the clause it introduces coheres around the present-tense verb translated "I long for" (ἐπιποθῶ), which speaks of having a strong desire for something. In the broader literature of the time, the term could communicate a sense of eagerness but also anxiety or even fear.[57] Since its semantic range is somewhat broad, context is critical. Elsewhere in the New Testament the verb can be used to depict the image of longing for milk (1 Pet 2:2), of God's "jealous yearning" for people (Jas 4:5), and of the "desire" believers experience as they groan, longing for the resurrection body (2 Cor 5:2).

But this passage belongs to a thread in Paul's writings that speaks of relational longing, often with the sense of "missing" someone (when combined with "to see," ἰδεῖν; e.g., Rom 1:11; 1 Thess 3:6; 2 Tim 1:4) or "having deep affection for" someone (2 Cor 9:14).[58] Accordingly, in effect Paul says, "I really miss all of you." He again underscores the inclusivity of his affection—perhaps supporting his broader theme of the need for unity in the church—referring to the Philippians as "all of you" (πάντας ὑμᾶς). It is striking that he

55. Thus, "of the gospel" (τοῦ εὐαγγελίου) functions as an objective genitive. In the phrase ἐν τῇ ἀπολογίᾳ καὶ βεβαιώσει τοῦ εὐαγγελίου, the preposition and the article carry over to βεβαιώσει, and τοῦ εὐαγγελίου delimits both ἀπολογίᾳ and βεβαιώσει together.

56. BDAG 1105.

57. BDAG 377.

58. *TLNT* 2:58–60.

continues to define this deep longing for the Philippians as "with[59] the affection of Jesus Christ" (ἐν σπλάγχνοις Χριστοῦ Ἰησοῦ). The term rendered "affection" (σπλάγχνον) literally refers to the viscera—the internal parts of a body (Acts 1:18). It came to be used figuratively (often in the plural) of the seat of the emotions (as we use the word "heart" in English) or, as here, of the emotions themselves: "love" or "affection" (Luke 1:78; 2 Cor 6:12; 7:15; Col 3:12; Phlm 7, 12, 20; 1 John 3:17). Paul views his love for the Philippians as an extension of the love or compassion that Christ has for them.[60] As J. A. Bengel notes, "It is not Paul who lives within Paul, but Jesus Christ, which is why Paul is not moved by the bowels of Paul but by the bowels of Jesus Christ."[61]

## IN DEPTH: Prayer in the Letters of Paul

Not surprisingly, Paul often exhorts the recipients of his letters to pray,[62] or he requests prayer from them.[63] In his prayers we find an embodiment of Paul's theology of, and personal commitment to, prayer. The apostle's vocabulary of prayer is the richest in the New Testament, employing sixteen words for the activity, and he speaks of prayer more frequently than other New Testament authors.[64] Among his most frequently used words for prayer are προσεύχομαι ("to petition or pray"; nineteen times in seventeen verses),[65] προσευχή ("prayer," or "a place of prayer"; fourteen times in fourteen verses),[66] and δέησις ("request" or "prayer"; twelve times in ten verses).[67] All three terms are used in Philippians. Although he speaks of prayer at various places in his letters, his greetings, doxologies, and closings almost always include notes of prayer, often related to particular themes of the letter in hand.[68] Paul's writings, moreover, often include various forms of prayers, including what have been called "wish prayers" (e.g., Rom 15:5–6, 13; Gal 6:18; 1 Thess 5:23–24; 2 Thess 2:16–17; 2 Tim 1:16; 4:22; Titus 3:15), which give "living expression to the apostle's deeply responsible love—to his vital anxieties and burning hopes for each particular

59. The preposition ἐν is used as a marker introducing "instrumentality" (BDAG 328).

60. Todd Still, *Philippians and Philemon*, SHBC (Macon, GA: Smyth & Helwys, 2011), 33. Thus we read the genitive Χριστοῦ Ἰησοῦ as a genitive of source, or perhaps as a subjective genitive.

61. Johann Albrecht Bengel, *New Testament Word Studies*, 2 vols., Kregel Reprint Library (Grand Rapids: Kregel, 1971), 2:426.

62. E.g., Rom 12:12; Eph 6:18; Col 4:2; 1 Thess 5:17; 1 Tim 2:1, 8.

63. James P. Ware, *Synopsis of the Pauline Letters in Greek and English* (Grand Rapids: Baker Academic, 2010), 26–27; e.g., Rom 15:30–33; 2 Cor 1:11; Eph 6:18–20; Phil 1:19–20; Col 4:3–4; 1 Thess 5:25; 2 Thess 3:1–2; Phlm 22.

64. W. B. Hunter, "Prayer," in *DPL* 729.

65. Rom 8:26; 1 Cor 11:4–5, 13; 14:13–15; Eph 6:18; Phil 1:9; Col 1:3, 9; 4:3; 1 Thess 5:17, 25; 2 Thess 1:11; 3:1; 1 Tim 2:8.

66. Rom 1:10; 12:12; 15:30; 1 Cor 7:5; Eph 1:16; 6:18; Phil 4:6; Col 4:2, 12; 1 Thess 1:2; 1 Tim 2:1; 5:5; Phlm 4, 22.

67. Rom 10:1; 2 Cor 1:11; 9:14; Eph 6:18; Phil 1:4, 19; 4:6; 1 Tim 2:1; 5:5; 2 Tim 1:3.

68. Krister Stendahl, "Paul at Prayer," *Int* 34.3 (1980): 241; Gordon P. Wiles, *Paul's Intercessory Prayers: The Significance of the Intercessory Prayer Passages in the Letters of St. Paul*, SNTSMS 24 (Cambridge: Cambridge University Press, 1974), 229.

church."[69] Paul also gives "prayer reports," in which he recounts how and what he has been praying for his readers. We see such a prayer report at Philippians 1:3–4, 9–11, and in other passages, such as Ephesians 1:15–23 and Colossians 1:3–14. Other forms of Paul's prayers include doxologies, hymns, boasting, blessings, and praise.[70] His prayers are especially filled with thanksgiving to God (e.g., Rom 1:8; 1 Cor 1:4; 2 Cor 2:14; 9:15; Eph 1:15–16; Col 1:3; 1 Thess 1:2; 2:13; 3:9; 2 Thess 1:3; 1 Tim 1:12; Phlm 4).

As for other content, Paul prays for, or requests prayer for, himself and his ministry. For example, he prays/requests prayer for deliverance from enemies (Rom 15:30–32; 2 Cor 1:8–11); for the collection for Jerusalem (Rom 15:30–32);[71] for the ability to travel to see the Romans (Rom 1:8–10) and the Thessalonians (1 Thess 3:10–11); that God would take away his thorn (2 Cor 12:7–9); and that he would be able to proclaim the gospel fearlessly (Eph 6:19–20; Col 4:2–4).

His intercession for the churches includes prayer for their unity (Rom 15:5–6); for their joy, peace, and hope (Rom 15:13); that they would do the right thing and grow in maturity (2 Cor 13:7–9); that they would grow in wisdom and understanding so that they can know God better; that they would especially be established in love and be able to grasp the love of Christ, filled with the fullness of God (Eph 1:15–23; 3:14–21; Phil 1:9–11). Further, Paul prays that believers' love would overflow in a blameless life and that they would be made holy and be counted worthy of the gospel (1 Thess 3:12–13; 5:23–24; 2 Thess 1:11–12). He prays that God would fulfill every good purpose of the Christ-followers; that Christ would be glorified in them and they in him (2 Thess 1:12); that they would be encouraged and strengthened so that they might persevere in the faith (2 Thess 2:16–17; 3:5); and that they would live peaceful, godly lives (1 Tim 2:1–2). He expects that this will happen as God is with them (2 Thess 3:16).

Obviously, Paul's prayers have an epistolary function, playing a significant role in the shape of his letters. But at the core they are pastoral in nature, as Paul cares deeply about his readers. He prays to affect their spiritual lives and to teach them how to pray. In fact, Paul anticipates that his prayers will be a model for his fellow believers, as his life is permeated by prayer.[72]

69. Wiles, *Paul's Intercessory Prayers*, 154.

70. For the various forms of Paul's prayers and their place in his letters, see the catalogue in Wiles, *Paul's Intercessory Prayers*, 297–302.

71. Hunter, "Prayer," 726.

72. David Peterson notes, "This practice [of breaking into doxology during a theological argument] suggests that the life of prayer and thanksgiving should not be confined to set times and places, but that the acknowledgement of God's character and providence should be a natural part of everyday conversation for the Christians" (David Peterson, "Prayer in Paul's Writings," in *Teach Us to Pray*, ed. D. A. Carson [Eugene, OR: Wipf & Stock, 2002], 91).

This pastoral orientation of Paul's prayers is driven by two dynamics. First is the apostle's sense of mission.[73] His call by God undergirds his deep sense of responsibility for the churches. Just as the letters play a vital role in that mission, so the prayers that saturate them play an integral role in the mission. It is no exaggeration to say that prayer stands at the center of Paul's work of ministry, as his ultimate aim in prayer is to present his fellow believers to Christ at his return, to the glory and praise of God.[74] Second, Paul's constant, spontaneous Godward orientation in his prayers—thanksgiving, blessing, praise, and celebration of God's character and work—demonstrates a heartfelt love for God. For Paul, prayer is not just a religious activity but an expression of relational intimacy with the God who by grace saved him and called him.[75]

**1:9 And I pray this, that your love might grow exponentially in knowledge and penetrating perception** (καὶ τοῦτο προσεύχομαι, ἵνα ἡ ἀγάπη ὑμῶν ἔτι μᾶλλον καὶ μᾶλλον περισσεύῃ ἐν ἐπιγνώσει καὶ πάσῃ αἰσθήσει). Verses 9–11 offer a beautifully crafted prayer on behalf of the Philippians. As noted in the literary context of this passage, prayer was common in letter openings of the time. To some extent, this prayer parallels the one found at Colossians 1:9–11, where the apostle also prays for his readers to be filled with a perceptive knowledge that will shape their lives for God.

Literarily, we find important echoes here of elements observed earlier in the chapter, such as Paul's prayer for the continuation of that for which he had just given thanks,[76] continued references to the Philippians, and references to the Lord as "Jesus Christ" (as at 1:2). Paul speaks of Christ's "day" (as at 1:6), and of "God" (as with the three occurrences at 1:2–3, 8). Thus we see that the prayer in verses 9–11 flows from the rich, tightly woven, relational theology that marks the first eight verses of the letter. The prayer builds as follows. Paul prays for the Philippians to have:

a loving life, which must be integrated with
  a discerning life, resulting in
    a righteous life, which in turn results in
      a God-glorifying life.

First, he prays that they might have a loving life. As the subject of the "that" (ἵνα) clause, "love" (ἀγάπη) forms the bedrock request in the apostle's prayer, in line with his teaching elsewhere and New Testament teaching generally. Love forms a firm foundation.[77] Along with "faith" (πίστις) and "hope" (ἐλπίς), love forms a basic aspect of the great triad of the Christian life (e.g., 1 Cor 13:13;

73. Stendahl, "Paul at Prayer," 242–49.

74. Peterson, "Prayer in Paul's Writings," 100.

75. Peterson, "Prayer in Paul's Writings," 91–93.

76. Fee, *Philippians*, 97. The conjunction "and" (καί) at the beginning of v. 9 seems to be resumptive, as the statement on prayer reaches back to take up Paul's mention of prayer in v. 4. So Silva, *Philippians*, 49.

77. Paul uses the word seventy-five times in his writings, speaking variously of God's/Christ's love for believers (e.g., Rom 5:8; 8:39; Eph 1:4; 2:4; 4:2), of Paul's own love for those in his churches (e.g., 1 Cor 4:21; 16:24; 2 Cor 2:4), and of believers' love for one another (Rom 13:10; 14:15; 1 Cor 13; 14:1; Gal 5:13; Eph 1:15; Col 1:4; 2:2).

Col 1:4–5; 1 Thess 1:3; 5:8). Indeed, the call for brotherly love follows Jesus's own directive that love would mark out those who live truly as his disciples (John 13:35).

What Paul prays here, accordingly, is that the Philippians' love will "grow exponentially" (ἔτι μᾶλλον καὶ μᾶλλον περισσεύῃ). The verb sometimes translated "abound" or "overflow" (περισσεύω) is a favorite of the apostle, used twenty-six times in his writings. It refers to something "abounding," "excelling," or "existing in abundance."[78] Paul wants the Philippians to have loads of love in their community. He prays that this dynamic, superabundant love might be ever increasing, as the Philippians themselves grow in the faith and as the community grows in size through the advance of the gospel. Indeed, Paul amplifies the thought with the addition of "yet more and more" (ἔτι μᾶλλον καὶ μᾶλλον), which is translated here as "exponentially." Thus, they are to continue in a key expression of discipleship that has characterized them in the past.

The two terms translated as "knowledge" (ἐπίγνωσις) and "perception" (αἴσθησις) overlap semantically but have nuanced distinctions. In biblical literature the first of these words especially refers to a knowledge of God. For instance, in every case but one (1 Kgs 7:2), writers of the LXX employ the term to speak of knowledge that in some way relates to God (Prov 2:5; Hos 4:1, 6; 6:6; Jdt 9:14; 2 Macc 9:11). For instance, Hosea 6:6 reads, "For I want mercy and not sacrifice, and knowledge of God rather than whole burnt offerings" (NETS).

In general Paul employs the term to refer to a knowledge of the truth (1 Tim 2:4; 2 Tim 2:25; 3:7; Titus 1:1) or an understanding of sin (Rom 3:20). But he often takes it up particularly to speak of acknowledging God (Rom 1:28), or knowledge about God or the Son of God (Rom 10:2; Eph 1:17; 4:13), which is closely associated with knowledge of God's will (Col 1:9–10; 2:2; 3:10). Knowledge of God's will is probably in mind in our current context, given its ethical orientation. So Paul wants the Philippians' love to grow exponentially as it is integrated with, perhaps infused by, right Christian understanding of God and his will. Love needs to be informed by this kind of knowledge. Love unanchored from knowledge does not lead to "discernment of what is spiritually valuable" (Phil 1:10a).

Yet love also needs discernment, "penetrating perception" (πάσῃ αἰσθήσει), as translated here. The word αἴσθησις—a word used only here in the New Testament—refers to spiritual perception or discernment. In the broader literature of the Greco-Roman world, αἴσθησις could speak of sense perception, including picking up scents while hunting.[79] Josephus often uses the term of perceiving that some event has taken place (*J.W.* 3.326, 328, 332). In the LXX, however, the term most commonly refers to spiritual or intellectual discernment—the ability to grasp something mentally with a sort of spiritual consciousness or comprehension (e.g., Exod 28:3). It is often associated with understanding, insight, or wisdom.[80] It does not refer to mere knowledge but to a spiritual perception that leads to wise, righteous living. The addition of "penetrating" (more straightforwardly, "all," πάσῃ) may speak of discernment that is multifaceted or engaged in various situations—that is, "every kind of insight" (so NET; BDAG 784). But it may, rather, refer to a high degree of spiritual discernment (e.g., NIV: "depth of insight") or, translated here, "penetrating perception." So Paul

78. Rom 3:7; 5:15; 15:13; 1 Cor 8:8; 14:12; 15:58; 2 Cor 1:5; 3:9; 4:15; 8:2, 7; 9:8, 12; Eph 1:8; Phil 1:9, 26; 4:12, 18; Col 2:7; 1 Thess 3:12; 4:1, 10.

79. LSJ 42; see Philo, *Creation* 31, 53, 62, 112; Sir 22:19.

80. E.g., Prov 1:4, 7; 2:3, 10; 5:2; 8:10; 14:6–7; 15:7; cf. Col 1:9, which, in a similar prayer, speaks of spiritual wisdom and understanding.

prays that the Philippians' love might be "shaped and informed"[81] by knowledge and discernment. Knowledge without love is vapid (1 Cor 13:2), but love without knowledge can be misdirected, even destructive. This is not blind, sentimental, or indulgent love but a love infused with knowledge of the living God, sustained by discernment of how one should live for him in the world.

**1:10 resulting in the discernment of what is spiritually valuable, in order that you might be sincere and faultless until the day of Christ** (εἰς τὸ δοκιμάζειν ὑμᾶς τὰ διαφέροντα, ἵνα ἦτε εἰλικρινεῖς καὶ ἀπρόσκοποι εἰς ἡμέραν Χριστοῦ). In verse 10 we see the result[82] of that which is prayed for in verse 9. Paul understands spiritual discernment as the outcome of a knowledgeable and perceptive love. The infinitive rendered "discernment" (from the verb δοκιμάζω) could refer to the critical examination of something in order to determine its genuineness or worth.[83] Ancient Greco-Roman authors, for instance, describe legal cases in which evidence is presented to an authority, who then evaluates and discerns whether the evidence is valid.[84] Such discernment comes with examination and verification, as when a metal is tested (Prov 8:10; 17:3), or figuratively when God tests human hearts (Ps 66:10). This sense of "verification" is also found in the New Testament (e.g., 1 Cor 3:13; 1 Pet 1:7), but here in Philippians 1:10 it carries the nuance "to discern," and as in passages such as Romans 12:2 and Ephesians 5:10, the idea has to do with discerning what pleases the Lord or what is of real value.

Further, Paul prays specifically that the Philippians will discern "what is spiritually valuable" (τὰ διαφέροντα), a word referring to things "worth more than" or "superior to" something else.[85] Spiritual discernment demands that one must be able to distinguish one thing from another, deciding what is best or superior in quality or rank (1 Cor 15:41; Gal 2:6; 4:1). Here Paul has in mind the discernment of ideas and patterns of life that are spiritually valuable, sorting them out from those that are not. This may at times involve the discernment of the "good" over against the "bad," as well as the "best" over against what is "good."

The purpose has to do with Paul's desire for the Philippians to live out Christian character and integrity until the day Christ returns: "in order that you might be sincere and faultless until the day of Christ" (ἵνα ἦτε εἰλικρινεῖς καὶ ἀπρόσκοποι εἰς ἡμέραν Χριστοῦ). Both of these Greek descriptors, translated "sincere" and "faultless" respectively, are fairly rare in ancient literature. Used only here and at 2 Peter 3:1 in the New Testament, the first refers to sincerity, living a pure life, one without pretense or hidden motives. The term points to a right condition of the heart, which is vital as an appropriate foundation for one's actions. For instance, 2 Peter 3:1 speaks of "stirring up a sincere mind" or way of thinking. The second term (ἀπρόσκοποι) can speak of a "clear" conscience (Acts 24:16) or a life that is blameless and free of offense (1 Cor 10:32). Thus, Paul wants the Philippians to be people of integrity, sincerity, and innocence before God and a watching world.

His prayer is that they might live this way "until

81. Bockmuehl, *Philippians*, 67.

82. εἰς τό + the infinitive; scholars are divided as to whether εἰς τό + the infinitive + accusative subject of the infinitive communicates purpose (so the majority of commentators; so also ESV, CSB, Message, NIV, NET, RSV) or result (H. E. Dana and Julius R. Mantey, *A Manual Grammar of the Greek New Testament* [New York: Macmillan, 1969], 285–86; NLT?). The use of the construction is mixed in Paul, on which see Douglas J. Moo, *The Epistle to the Romans*, NICNT (Grand Rapids: Eerdmans, 1996), 105n66.

83. BDAG 255.

84. *TLNT* 1:354.

85. BDAG 239.

the day of Christ" (εἰς ἡμέραν Χριστοῦ). At 1:6, the apostle has already expressed his confidence that "the one who began a good work among" the Philippians would "perfect it until the day of Christ Jesus."[86] It is interesting to consider that only in Philippians is "the day" qualified as "the day of Christ." As noted in the commentary on verse 6, the Old Testament concept of "the day of the Lord" forms the backdrop for "the day" in early Christian thought. Here Paul writes "*until* the day of Christ" to speak of duration—"all the way to the day of Christ"—but also of anticipation. Paul longs for the Philippians to endure in the faith, but he also anticipates that last day as of preeminent importance, a moment of glory to God and utter transformation of God's people. Paul wants the Philippians to be ready for that moment.

**1:11 having been filled with the fruit produced by righteousness, which comes through Jesus Christ to the glory and praise of God** (πεπληρωμένοι καρπὸν δικαιοσύνης τὸν διὰ Ἰησοῦ Χριστοῦ εἰς δόξαν καὶ ἔπαινον θεοῦ). A righteous life that gives glory and praise to God is the ultimate aim of Paul's prayer for the Philippians. The perfect participle translated "having been filled" (πεπληρωμένοι) has "the day of Christ" as its temporal frame of reference, and it refers to the spiritual state of those who are sincere and blameless as they come to that climactic day. If Paul's desire for the Philippians comes to pass, their spiritual lives will have been filled by God[87] with "fruit produced by righteousness" (καρπὸν δικαιοσύνης; cf. Prov 3:9; 11:30; Amos 6:12; Eph 5:9; Heb 12:11). The term "fruit" (καρπός) offers a word picture communicating the "result, outcome, or profit" of some state or activity (BDAG 510; e.g., Rom 1:13; 6:21, 22; Gal 5:22; Eph 5:9; Phil 1:22; 4:17). The word "righteousness"[88] is in the genitive case (δικαιοσύνης) and thus could be translated in a few different ways: as fruit that "is righteousness" (appositional); "righteous fruit" (descriptive); or "fruit produced by righteousness" (a genitive of production[89]; cf. Matt 7:16, 20). Given the ethical[90] orientation of verse 10, the last of these interpretations seems most likely, and "the fruit" here, as at Galatians 5:22–23, has to do with Christian living and is "the spontaneous product of the new life implanted within" the Philippians.[91]

Of course, manifesting the "fruit produced by righteousness" is only possible "through Jesus Christ" (διὰ Ἰησοῦ Χριστοῦ).[92] Christ, through new-covenantal, faith-enabled transformation, has made it possible for people to live righteously by transforming them as they believe the gospel.[93]

86. There we see ἡμέρας Χριστοῦ Ἰησοῦ, while here at 1:10, and in 2:16, we see the abbreviated ἡμέραν Χριστοῦ.

87. The participle is a "divine passive," assuming the work of God, as reflected in the agency of Christ with the phrase διὰ Ἰησοῦ Χριστοῦ (Bockmuehl, *Philippians*, 69).

88. Paul uses δικαιοσύνη fifty-eight times in his writings. The term is complex and has fostered great debate, especially when the apostle speaks of "the righteousness of God." See especially the excursus in Moo, *Epistle to the Romans*, 79–90. Yet here Paul seems to speak of "the quality or characteristic of upright behavior" of a person (BDAG 248), as the Philippians live according to what pleases God (e.g., Ps 14:2 LXX; Matt 5:6, 10, 20; Rom 6:13, 16, 19–20; 10:5; 2 Cor 6:14; 9:10; Eph 4:24; Phil 3:6; 1 Tim 6:11; 2 Tim 2:22; 3:16; Jas 1:20). The backdrop of the idea lies in the Old Testament concept of covenant faithfulness. It refers to a life of godly behavior in accordance with God's ways, which bears fruit for God (so Moo, *Epistle to the Romans*, 80–81).

89. Wallace, *Greek Grammar*, 104–5.

90. Silva suggests the phrase is ethical rather than forensic for several reasons. See Silva, *Philippians*, 52–53.

91. F. F. Bruce, *Philippians*, NIBCNT (Peabody, MA: Hendrickson, 1989), 37.

92. The article that precedes the phrase (i.e., τόν) functions like a relative pronoun and relates back to the word "fruit" (καρπόν), thus the translation "fruit . . . which comes through Jesus Christ." Moreover, the construction διά + the genitive reflects agency; Christ is the one bringing about the fruit produced by righteousness.

93. So Fee, *Philippians*, 103–4; on "transformational interchange," see Guthrie, *2 Corinthians*, 315.

The thought is more overt at 3:9, where Paul sets the righteousness of law observance over against righteousness "through trust in Christ" (διὰ πίστεως Χριστοῦ)[94]—a righteousness that comes "from God on the basis of trust" (ἐκ θεοῦ δικαιοσύνην ἐπὶ τῇ πίστει). When believers are joined to Christ through the gospel, then God's righteousness manifests in their lives, for Christ is the source of righteousness (1 Cor 1:30), so that believers "embody righteousness and sanctification."[95]

To sum up verses 9–11a, then, Paul hopes that the Philippians will live lives of love infused by knowledge of God and acute perception, resulting in discernment that issues in righteous living, enabled by Christ. Ultimately, this fruit of righteousness in the lives of believers fills them "to the glory and praise of God" (εἰς δόξαν καὶ ἔπαινον θεοῦ).[96] Such praise expresses thoughts breathed regularly in the conclusion of Jewish prayers.[97] In a song of praise that uses these two terms, 1 Chronicles 16:27 LXX reads, "Glory [δόξα] and praise [ἔπαινος] are before him." God is the object of the glory and praise mentioned here, not human beings.[98] References to God thus bracket Philippians 1:3–11, as the apostle begins with thanks to God and ends with glory and praise ascribed to God. God's saving, sanctifying, and missional work among the Philippians—which the apostle has been celebrating since verse 3—thus comes to a crescendo with the focus on God.

## Theology in Application

In this first half of the letter's prologue, Paul's words embody a striking, theologically saturated mindfulness that should be considered carefully by all engaged in ministry. By "mindfulness," I mean a pattern of deep and reflective awareness of others' significance for our lives and the mission of Christ. A seventeenth-century Scottish pastor, Samuel Rutherford, once wrote, "My soul longeth exceedingly to hear whether there be any work of Christ in the parish. . . . I think of my people in my sleep. . . . My day thoughts and my night thoughts are of you."[99] Ministry mindfulness is "keeping others in mind" as we live, move, and have our being in various ministry contexts. Notice that a "prayer report" forms the context for such ministry mindfulness in Philippians 1. Paul thinks about the Philippians before God, thanking him for them, expressing his affection for them, and praying intentionally for their growth to the glory of God.

94. Or perhaps "through the faithfulness of Christ"; see the discussion in the commentary at 3:9.

95. Morna D. Hooker, "On Becoming the Righteousness of God: Another Look at 2 Cor 5:2," *NovT* 50.4 (2008): 373

96. The manuscript evidence here is a bit turbulent, as F, G, and Ambst read και επαινον μοι, and as 𝔓[46] reads θεου και επαινον εμοι. Silva notes the possibility that the latter reading is original but hesitates in light of having only one witness (Silva, *Philippians*, 58). Nevertheless, the depth and breadth of the manuscript evidence favor the reading as reflected in NA[28] and UBS[5] (א A B D[2] I K L P Ψ 075. 0278. 33. 81. 104. 365. 630. 1175. 1241. 1505. 1739. 1881. 2464 𝔐 lat sy co). So Metzger, *Textual Commentary*, 544.

97. So Hawthorne, *Philippians*, 29–30; e.g., 2 Sam 22:50; Ps 35:28; 41:13; Pr Man 15; 1QSb 4.25.

98. So, an "objective genitive." Contra, e.g., Witherington (*Philippians*, 67), Reumann (*Philippians*, 159), and Schenk, who reads it as a subjective genitive, the praise given by God to his people (Wolfgang Schenk, *Die Philipperbriefe des Paulus* [Stuttgart: Kohlhammer, 1984], 123–28).

99. Alistair Begg, *On Being a Pastor: For Pastors and Teachers* (Chicago: Moody, 2004), 150–51.

For many of us, ministry mindfulness—an expression of love for, and focus on, others rather than ourselves and our agendas—does not come naturally. Even as others are telling us about themselves, we may be thinking about what we need to do next or how to turn the conversation to our concerns. Especially for those who are more project oriented than people oriented, people under our sphere of influence may be assessed in terms of how they contribute to, or detract from, our project at that moment (e.g., a sermon, book, meeting, mission, institution, fund-raising campaign). People often "get in the way" of projects, and in the emotional clutter of a driven, project-oriented life or ministry, one struggles to carve out enough inner space for ministry mindfulness of others. Right now, are our lives characterized by being "other focused"? Or does our ministry to others give little thought to them as people? Notice the example of Paul in Philippians 1:3–11. The apostle thoughtfully communicates three overarching expressions concerning the Philippians: a genuine thankfulness for the past; an affirming affection for them in the present; and a prayerful hope for their future. Let's consider the significance of each.

## *Thank God for the Past*

Notice the expansiveness of the apostle's thanksgiving—and the fact that thanks-giving in a letter's prologue was normal in Paul's culture detracts nothing from the significance of what we see here. Paul consistently, joyfully, and confidently thanks God for the Philippians. When he says, "every time I remember you" (1:3), he notes that this is characterized by thanking God for the Philippians consistently. It is a normal feature of his practice of prayer. He prays joyfully because of the Philippians' consistent partnership with him in gospel ministry over the past decade. We know that the Philippians joined Paul in the work of gospel mission, supported his mission-ary work in the broader world, and gave to the collection for the saints in Jerusalem. Thinking about their "participation in the gospel" ministry gives the apostle joy. It feels good to have partners in a good work for a long time. Paul also prays confidently as he notes what God has done in their past. The fruit of their lives heralds good things ahead, for which Paul is grateful.

We might consider for a moment whether we give thanks for those with whom, and to whom, we minister. Is such thanks a consistent aspect of our prayer lives? Do we experience joy in the partnerships that God has put in our paths? Do we think about the implications of the faithfulness of those in our ministry sphere, recognizing such faithfulness as an encouraging indicator that anticipates the continued work of God "until the day"? Take a moment and thank God for two or three significant ministry partners in your life. If such thankful prayer is not yet a normal part of your prayer life, make it so.

For those of us in difficult ministry situations, an attitude of gratitude can be hard to cultivate. If you are being attacked, or questioned, or restricted in ways you had not anticipated, thanks doesn't come easily. But the grounding of this letter in joyful thanks is all the more striking because of Paul's current circumstances—he is in chains (1:13). And it is likely that the apostle, by this point, had been held in custody for at least three years. He was being attacked, and questioned, and restricted. Yet, he was thankful. Paul's posture brings to mind the words of Blaise Pascal, "Instead of complaining that God had hidden himself, you will give Him thanks for having revealed so much of Himself."[100] Such a pattern of difficult discipleship grows from the cultivation of character over time, and its glory shines all the brighter in dark places.

Such thankfulness shone brightly in the life of commander John Listerman, a marine and committed follower of Christ, who fought for the US during the Vietnam War. Listerman served alongside another commander, Charles Krulak, who was not a believer at the time but who later committed his life to Christ. In December of 1965, Listerman and Krulak found themselves in a battle zone. Krulak recounts what happened next.

> We were on patrol moving down a trail through the jungle. We came around a corner in that trail, and we ran into an ambush. John took the first round, a 50-caliber round right in his kneecap. As his kneecap burst, the crack was so loud it sounded like a mortar exploding. It threw him up in the air. As he was dropping, the second round hit him right below the heart and exited out his side. I was wounded also but nowhere near as badly. I saw John about 30 meters away on his back, his leg blown off.
>
> I crawled up to him, and I wanted to say, "Are you okay? Can I do anything?" but before I could do that, his head turned to me and he said, "How are you doing, Chucker? Are you okay?"
>
> I said, "Yes, John. I'm okay." He said, "Are my men safe?" I said, "John, your people are okay." At that point he turned his head and looked to the sky and repeated over and over, "Thank you, Lord. Thank you, Lord. Thank you for caring for my people. Thank you for caring for me."

Krulak remembers, "I was dumbfounded." Later, Listerman and Krulak were evacuated, and Krulak eventually became a Christian.[101] In that moment of crisis and pain, Listerman embodied thankfulness driven by his focus on others. Admittedly, ministry leadership is not easy. We get shot at and hurt at times. Yet a heart of thankfulness can focus our attention on the good that God has done and is doing

100. Blaise Pascal, *Pensées* (London: Penguin, 1995), 117.

101. As told by Linda M. Gehrs, Oak Park, Illinois; source: General Charles Krulak, from a message given at the Wheaton, Illinois, Leadership Prayer Breakfast (October 2000).

in the lives of those to whom, and alongside whom, we minister. Thankfulness for such good gifts should characterize us, as it did Paul, and give us confidence of good things ahead.

### *Express Affection in the Present*

Second, we should express affection for those who have been ministry partners with us. We might consider the ways in which the apostle expresses affection for the Philippians. He states, "I have you in my heart" (1:7), and says that God, who knows all things, knows that Paul longs for the Philippians "with the affection of Christ Jesus" (v. 8). The apostle's affection for this church had been forged in part by them standing with him as "fellow participants . . . of grace" as he ministered in his "imprisonment" and "in the defense and confirmation of the gospel" (v. 7). We grow in affection for those with whom we share significant ministry moments, especially difficult ones. Blessed are the ministers who have "fellow participants . . . of grace" walking with them in their challenges.

But Paul's words raise the question, "Do I have affection for those to whom and alongside whom I minister?" and "Do I express that affection?" Do I tell people that I care deeply about them, and when I am forced to be away, do I let them know that I long for them "with the affection of Christ Jesus"? You or I might respond, "Not my style." But perhaps it should be.

In his book on pastoral ministry, Alistair Begg notes that we must strive to love all people in our care with the same love, writing, "Love for the Lord Jesus and for His people is the preeminent motive for pastoral work (John 21:15–17)." He adds, "Those whom we serve should be in no doubt of our love, and we should take trouble, where necessary, to assure them of it (cf. 1 John 2:7; 3:2, 21; 4:1, 7, 11; 3 John 2, 5, 11)." Begg illustrates this key aspect of ministry with a story about Charles Warr, who at one time served as minister of St. Paul's Greenock in Scotland. One day, Warr was visited by one of his parishioners. Warr recounts,

> Mr. Arthur Caird . . . looked in to see me. He was always perfectly groomed, and as everyone said of him, was just as nice as he looked. After some desultory conversation, he ran his hand over his silver hair, turned on me his kindly eyes that always had a twinkle in them, and delivered himself of some flattering and heart-warming words about my first year's ministry at St. Paul's. Then he paused and after a short sentence went on: "Yes, everything in the garden's lovely—or nearly everything." I waited, now a little anxious. Arthur Caird rose and came over to me and laid a fatherly hand on my shoulder. "My boy," said he, "the garden's still waiting for the blossoming of one flower without which the garden of no minister can be perfect." Another pause. "I know we're not everything we ought to be, and no doubt we need a lot of scolding;

> but we'd all be a great deal better than we are if only you would try sometimes, instead of lecturing us, to show us that you love us!"

Charles Warr remembers, "These words were a turning-point in my ministry."[102]

If you are a pastor of a church, one possible application of this passage might be to preach on Philippians 1:3–11, explaining the original context and meaning, then moving to our modern context by expressing affection for your congregation. Take time to thank them for their participation in your ministry, expressing affection for them. Tell them that you love them in Christ.

### *Pray for a Fruitful Future*

Finally, we should pray for those to whom we minister, for their future growth in a knowledgeable and discerning love, which will bear spiritual fruit until the day of Christ and bring great glory to God. Many of us in the West are practical materialists and industrialists, working with the material stuff and the processes, programs, and principles of this world rather than working biblically with a strong, bedrock foundation of prayer. E. M. Bounds once wrote,

> It may be put down as a spiritual axiom that in every truly successful ministry prayer is an evident and controlling force—evident and controlling in the life of the preacher, evident and controlling in the deep spirituality of his work. A ministry may be a very thoughtful ministry without prayer; the preacher may secure fame and popularity without prayer; the whole machinery of the preacher's life and work may be run without the oil of prayer or with scarcely enough to grease one cog; but no ministry can be a spiritual one, securing holiness in the preacher and in his people, without prayer being made an evident and controlling force.[103]

Do we see prayer as essential in this way? Further, as we pray for people associated with our ministries, for what do we pray? It is understandable that we often focus on immediate needs, such as various difficulties, health issues, financial crises, or work-related situations. But as Tim Keller reminds us, "It is remarkable that in all of his writings Paul's prayers for his friends contain no appeals for changes in their circumstances."[104]

Notice that here, in Philippians 1, the apostle prays very specifically for a particular kind of love, shaped by knowledge and discernment, which ultimately would

102. Begg, *On Being a Pastor*, 150–51.

103. E. M. Bounds and Edward D. Andrews, *Power through Prayer: A Healthy Prayer Life*, updated and expanded (Cambridge, OH: Christian Publishing House, 2018), 29.

104. Timothy J. Keller, *Prayer: Experiencing Awe and Intimacy with God* (New York: Penguin Random House, 2014), 20.

result in "the fruit produced by righteousness." Paul prays for a very particular kind of love shaped by Christian thought, which issues in right Christian living, to the glory and praise of God in "the day of Christ" at the end of the age. The problem with the experiential "love" of modern Western culture, detached as it is from knowledge of God and discernment about godly living, is that it is shaped by other forces. Those who are not committed to Jesus Christ as Lord and to the knowledge of God revealed in him, who are anchored to nothing higher than personal experience and the cultural currents of the present age, can experience a "common grace" form of love—the joy of caring for another and being cared about. But they will never discern "what is spiritually valuable," or know what it means to be "sincere and faultless," or experience being "filled with the fruit produced by righteousness," which comes "through Jesus Christ" and ultimately results in "the glory and praise of God." Paul's prayer suggests that these things come from spiritual dynamics originating with God and work in specific ways for his praise and glory.

CHAPTER 3

# Philippians 1:12–18g

## Literary Context

As noted earlier in the commentary, an ancient-letter opening could express thanks and affection for a letter's recipients, offer a prayer, and express joy—all of which Paul does in the opening of Philippians (Phil 1:3–11). We now move to what may be called the "body opening"—the first movement of the letter body (1:12–26),[1] which contains two sub-movements: 1:12–18g and 1:18h–26. The whole of 1:12–26 is bracketed by an *inclusio* (the same or similar wording marking the beginning and ending of the unit) that speaks of the gospel's advance.[2] Notice the parallels of the following in 1:12–14 and 1:24–26: "to know" (γινώσκειν/οἶδα), forms of the pronouns translated "you" (σύ) and "I" (ἐγώ), "progress" (προκοπή), "in Christ" (ἐν Χριστῷ), "all/everyone" (πᾶσιν), "persuade" (πεποιθότας/πεποιθώς), and "much more/overflow" (περισσοτέρως/περισσεύῃ). Also, Fee points out that there are numerous elements in 1:12–26 that pick up on earlier themes or anticipate those to follow.[3] Thus, echoing the earlier theme from 1:5, 7, in verse 12 the apostle speaks of the advance of the gospel; he again mentions his imprisonment in the defense of the gospel (cf. 1:7) at 1:13, 14, 16–17; and the theme of love at 1:9 again surfaces at 1:16. In addition, themes such as "goodwill" (v. 15), "love" (v. 16), "selfish ambition" (v. 17), rejoicing (v. 18), and "the faith" (vv. 25, 27) foreshadow further expression of such themes in the balance of the letter. Thus, Paul's experience, detailed at 1:12–26, can be understood as an encapsulation of several key themes in Philippians.

Consider the first of two movements in the body opening (1:12–18g). Here Paul turns from celebrating and praying for the Philippians, to a report about his imprisonment. He speaks of his incarceration as an unexpected means by which the gospel has moved forward (vv. 12–18g). Paul may be locked up, but the gospel is

1. On the difficulty of identifying movements in the body of an ancient letter, see Troy W. Martin, "Investigating the Pauline Letter Body: Issues, Methods, and Approaches," in *How to Begin, and Why? Diverse Functions of the Pauline Prescript within a Greco-Roman Context*, ed. Stanley E. Porter and Sean A. Adams (Leiden: Brill, 2010), 185–212.

2. *Inclusio* was an ancient literary convention by which an author marked the beginning and end of a movement by the repetition of the same or related words. For more on the use of *inclusio* see Guthrie, *Structure of Hebrews*, 15.

3. Fee, *Philippians*, 107.

not. Paul's preaching of the gospel has made the reason for his imprisonment widely known among the imperial guard and others associated with the imperial household (vv. 12–13), as well as believing brothers and sisters, who have been emboldened to preach Christ fearlessly (v. 14). Even those who seek to hurt Paul by speaking negatively about his mission and message inadvertently spread the good news, and this too causes Paul to rejoice (vv. 15–18g).

In the second movement of the body opening (1:18h–26), the apostle expresses his hopeful expectation about his own future, offering us one of the Bible's most beautiful reflections on surrender to God amid difficult and uncertain circumstances. Paul is, after all, facing the possibility that he will be put to death. Yet in his surrender to God in the face of an imminent threat, the apostle confesses a willingness to go and be with the Lord or to stay and minister to the Philippians. The poignancy of Paul's perspective is beautifully captured in 1:21 with, "For as far as I am concerned to live is Christ and to die is gain." Nevertheless, in this unit he concludes with an expression of confidence that he will continue to minister among the Philippians for their progress and joy in the faith (vv. 25–26).

I. The Letter Opening: A Prescript and a Prayer Report (1:1–11)
**II. The Letter Body (1:12–4:9)**
A. The Body Opening: Paul's Current Situation (1:12–26)
➡ **1. A Joyful Report on the Progress of the Gospel (1:12–18g)**
2. Paul's Hopeful Expectation concerning His Imprisonment (1:18h–26)
B. The Main Body of the Letter: A Call for Unity in the Church (1:27–4:4a)
C. The Body Closing: Exhortations (4:4b–9)
III. The Letter Closing (4:10–23)

## Main Idea

Paul wants the Philippians to know that the Lord has used his incarceration for the advance of the gospel, and he notes two ways that the message about Jesus has gone forward. First, it has become public knowledge that the apostle's imprisonment is in the cause of Christ. Second, proclamation of Messiah Jesus has increased, both because the brothers and sisters have become much more daring in speaking God's word and because even those contentious people who talk about the Messiah out of bad motives inadvertently proclaim the Messiah! Thus, whether it is Paul's supporters or detractors who discuss his mission and message publicly, the apostle considers the public discussion a "win" for gospel mission.

## Translation

### Philippians 1:12–18g

| | | | |
|---|---|---|---|
| 12a | Wish | Now **I want you to know,** brothers and sisters, | |
| b | Content | that my circumstances actually have come about | |
| c | Advantage | for the progress of the gospel, | |
| 13a | Result (1) | so that 1) it has become public knowledge | |
| b | Place | among the whole imperial guard and | |
| c | | everyone else | |
| d | Fact | that my imprisonment is in the cause of Christ | |
| 14a | | and | |
| b | Result (2) | 2) the majority . . . | |
| c | | of the brothers and sisters, | |
| d | Circumstance | having become confident | |
| e | Object | in the Lord | |
| f | Reference | with reference to my imprisonment, | |
| g | Result (2) cont. | . . . are much more daring | |
| h | | to speak the word | |
| i | Manner | unflinchingly. | |
| 15a | Expansion | In addition to these, | |
| b | Description | **some people also,** motivated by hateful envy and | A |
| c | | factionalism, while | |
| d | Contrasting Descrip. | **others** motivated by goodwill | B |
| e | Action | **make public declarations** about the Messiah. | C |
| f | Assessment (of 15d) Explanation | **The latter** speak out of love, knowing that I am destined for the defense of the gospel; but | B′ |
| 16a | | | |
| b | Contrasting Assessm. (of 15b–c) | **the former** out of selfish ambition | A′ |
| 17a | Action | **speak publicly** about the Messiah | C′ |
| b | Manner | not from pure motives, | |
| c | Anticipation | expecting to stir up affliction in my imprisonment. | |

| | | | | |
|---|---|---|---|---|
| 18a | Rhetorical Question | **What can be said in response?** | | |
| b | Assertion | Only that | | |
| c | Manner/General | | in | each of these manners, whether |
| d | Manner/Specific | | from | false motives or |
| e | Alternative | | | true |
| f | Exclamation | **Messiah is spoken about publicly** | | |
| g | Response | and **I rejoice in this!** | | |

## Structure

Philippians 1:12–14 and 1:15–18g have distinct structures. The former begins with Paul expressing a wish—"I want you to know, brothers and sisters." The essence of what he wants them to know is stated in a content clause introduced with "that" (ὅτι): "that my circumstances actually have come about for the progress of the gospel." His incarceration has not hurt the mission; rather, it has advanced the mission. Paul then begins to unpack this assertion with the "so that" (ὥστε) at the beginning of verse 13, with which he introduces twin results: (1) the fact that Paul's imprisonment for the cause of Christ has become public knowledge, and (2) the brothers and sisters have grown more confident in the proclamation of God's word. Notice that the "my imprisonment" (τοὺς δεσμούς μου), which immediately follows "so that" (ὥστε) in verse 13, and the "my imprisonment" (τοῖς δεσμοῖς μου) in verse 14 mark out these parallel results. Both results are related to good outcomes of his imprisonment. So in verses 12–14 we have a wish statement, followed by a content clause, followed by parallel clauses expressing result.

In 1:15–18g we find a nicely crafted chiastic structure that draws attention to contrasting motivations of those who speak publicly about the Messiah.

| | |
|---|---|
| Some are motivated by hateful envy and factionalism | A |
| while others are motivated by goodwill; | B |
| the latter speak out of love | B′ |
| while the former speak out of self-centered contentiousness | A′ |

The outer two descriptions (A and A′) draw attention to those who are speaking publicly about Paul's ministry and teaching, and thus about Jesus. They are driven by a desire to fight against the apostle and his mission, "expecting to stir up affliction" for Paul while he is in prison (1:17c). These are those who inadvertently proclaim Christ, even though they do so from "false motives" (1:18f, h). The inner two descriptions in the chiastic structure (B and B′) speak of those who are aligned with

Paul, his mission, and his message. They are motivated by goodwill and love for the apostle, knowing that God has called Paul and destined him to defend the gospel at trial (1:15d–16). They are those who have "true" motives (1:18e). These contrasts are structurally built around parallel verbs that concern public proclamation, so that the structure of the whole is as follows:

| | | | |
|---|---|---|---|
| certain people | motivated by | hateful envy and factionalism, while | A |
| others | motivated by | goodwill; | B |
| **make public declarations about the Messiah** | | | **C** |
| the latter | out of | love | B′ |
| | knowing that | I am destined<br>for the defense<br>of the gospel but | |
| the former | out of | self-centered contentiousness | A′ |
| **speak publicly about the Messiah** | | | **C′** |
| | not sincerely | | |
| | expecting to stir up trouble in my imprisonment | | |

Neither Paul's context of imprisonment, nor contrarians who fight against his ministry, can contain the gospel. Thus, Paul rejoices in the proclamation of Christ, whatever the situation, whatever the vehicle.

## Exegetical Outline

**1. A Joyful Report on the Progress of the Gospel (1:12–18g)**

**a. Paul's Imprisonment Has Advanced the Gospel in Significant Ways (1:12–14)**

(1) His Imprisonment in the Cause of Christ Has Become Public Knowledge (vv. 12–13)

(2) The Majority of Brothers and Sisters Are Much More Bold in Speaking God's Word (v. 14)

**b. Proclamation of the Messiah Is Driven by Various Motives (1:15–18g)**

(1) Some Speak Publicly about the Messiah, Driven by False Motives (vv. 15a–c, 17, 18e)

(2) Some Speak Publicly about the Messiah, Driven by Pure Motives (vv. 15d, 16, 18f)

(3) Conclusion: Paul Rejoices That the Messiah Is Spoken of Publicly (v. 18g)

## Explanation of the Text

**1:12 Now I want you to know, brothers and sisters, that my circumstances actually have come about for the progress of the gospel** (Γινώσκειν δὲ ὑμᾶς βούλομαι, ἀδελφοί, ὅτι τὰ κατ᾽ ἐμὲ μᾶλλον εἰς προκοπὴν τοῦ εὐαγγελίου ἐλήλυθεν). Letter writing had many functions in the ancient world, including informing recipients of recent events experienced by the author. Thus authors might express what they "want" (βούλομαι) the readers to "know" (γινώσκειν), which is called a "disclosure formula."[4] The Philippians, whom he addresses as "brothers and sisters" (ἀδελφοί),[5] probably knew that their apostle was in prison. What they did not know—and Paul wanted them to understand—was that God had redeemed the apostle's incarceration wonderfully, turning his "chains" into a "chance" to spread the gospel. As he begins the letter body, therefore, he wants them to know that his imprisonment has had positive, if unexpected, results.

Unpacking the content (ὅτι) of his report, the apostle notes that his "circumstances"—literally, "the things according to me" (τὰ κατ᾽ ἐμέ)[6]—"have come about" (ἐλήλυθεν) for a reason.[7] The situation, Paul asserts, has worked out to be advantageous—"for the progress of the gospel" (εἰς προκοπὴν τοῦ εὐαγγελίου). Paul knows that this result is somewhat unexpected, and he acknowledges that another result was possible by use of the term rendered "actually" (μᾶλλον; so, e.g., ESV, CSB, NET, NLT, NIV).[8]

The word for "progress" (προκοπή) occurs in the New Testament only here, then at 1:25, and in 1 Timothy 4:15. At Philippians 1:25 Paul speaks of the Philippians' progress (προκοπήν) in the faith. At 1 Timothy 4:15 he writes of young Timothy's progress in ministry skills and character. That the gospel had made progress through Paul's imprisonment points to the gospel message moving out into the lives of the people in the culture.[9] After all, the "gospel" (εὐαγγέλιον) by its very nature is dynamic and on the move. Jesus went throughout Galilee proclaiming the good news (Matt 4:23; 9:35), expecting that the gospel would permeate the whole world (Matt 24:14; 26:13; Mark 13:10; 14:9).

4. E.g., P.Oxy. 1493 reads, "I want you to know, brother, that . . . ," and the author of P.Oxy. 50 writes, "I want you to know that we arrived in the city" (as related in David B. Capes, Rodney Reeves, and E. Randolph Richards, *Rediscovering Paul: An Introduction to His World, Letters, and Theology* [Downers Grove, IL: IVP Academic; Nottingham: Apollos, 2007], 61; John L. White, "Introductory Formulae in the Body of the Pauline Letter," *JBL* 90.1 [1971]: 93–94; cf. Rom 1:13; 2 Cor 1:8; Gal 1:11; 1 Thess 2:l).

5. The term ἀδελφοί referred to both men and women in religious contexts of the ancient world, so the translation needs both genders to be accurate. For example, Jesus refers to a disciple as "brother" (e.g., Matt 12:50; 28:10; Mark 3:35; John 20:17). That the women Euodia and Syntyche, leading women in the church at Philippi, are mentioned overtly at 4:2 demonstrates that there were men and women addressed by Paul's letter.

6. Paul uses this construction similarly at Eph 6:21 and Col 4:7. Cf. the different uses at Rom 1:15 and Col 2:14.

7. This perfect-tense verb (from ἔρχομαι) simply means that something has happened or taken place (BDAG 394), and the stative aspect of the perfect form indicates that Paul speaks of an event that has culminated in a current state of affairs.

8. The NASB's "have turned out for the greater progress of the gospel" seems misguided since μᾶλλον is an adverb, not an adjective, and thus should be read as delimiting the verb ἐλήλυθεν.

9. Both Philo (*Alleg. Interp.* 2.81) and Sir 51:17, for instance, use the term to speak of one making progress in wisdom, and Philo can claim that all true progress in life comes from God (*Alleg. Interp.* 2.93). The cognate verb προκόπτω can mean "to move forward" to a final stage (even one that is bad), or to make progress or advance in some way (Luke 2:52; Rom 13:12; Gal 1:14; 2 Tim 2:16; 3:9, 13).

Paul's gospel ministry spread from region to region on his mission outreaches (Rom 15:19; 2 Cor 2:12; 10:14; 1 Thess 3:2), and he rejects anything that would hold the gospel back (1 Cor 9:12). Indeed, the gospel minister's feet need to be fitted with "readiness" to move (Eph 6:15), since the gospel, by its very nature, must advance, accomplishing God's agenda for the world. Yet the means of its progress is sometimes surprising, as we see in the following verses.

## IN DEPTH: Paul and Imprisonment in the Roman World

From the book of Acts and Paul's own letters, we know that the apostle spent considerable time incarcerated. There are letters from the apostle that we categorize as "prison epistles" (Philippians, Ephesians, Colossians, Philemon), since Paul notes that he is a prisoner or "in chains" (Eph 3:1; 4:1; 6:20; Phil 1:7, 13, 14, 17; Col 4:3, 10, 18; Phlm 1, 9–10, 13, 23). Among the other letters traditionally ascribed to Paul, 2 Timothy, often styled a "pastoral epistle," could be added to the list (2 Tim 1:8, 16; 2:9). When speaking of imprisonment, Paul uses a variety of terms, including those for "prisoner" (δέσμιος; Eph 3:1; 4:1; 2 Tim 1:8; Phlm 1, 9), "confined" or "bound" (δέω; Col 4:3; 2 Tim 2:9), a "bond" or "chain" (δεσμός; Phil 1:7, 13–14, 17; Col 4:18; 2 Tim 2:9; Phlm 10, 13), "fellow prisoner" (συναιχμάλωτος;[10] Rom 16:7; Col 4:10; Phlm 23), and "chain" (ἅλυσις; Eph 6:20; 2 Tim 1:16). Although Acts records imprisonments in Philippi (16:19–40), Caesarea (23:23–24:27), and Rome (28:16–31), 2 Corinthians 11:23 indicates that the apostle's times in prison were "far more" than those experienced by the opponents in Corinth, evidently more than recorded by Luke, and Acts only speaks of one imprisonment prior to the time when Paul wrote 2 Corinthians. One early church tradition (1 Clem. 5:6) puts the number of the apostle's imprisonments at seven.[11]

Although there may have been exceptions,[12] in the Roman world imprisonment was not normally a punishment for a crime committed but rather a means of holding a prisoner awaiting trial or execution.[13] Rather than dedicated prisons, prisoners could be held in a variety of buildings, such as military barracks—as when Paul was taken into custody in Jerusalem (Acts 21:37; 23:16)—or a praetorium, such as the headquarters of the governor, where Paul was detained once he arrived in Caesarea (23:35).

10. It could be that the term συναιχμάλωτος was considered by Paul a designation of honor, reserved for those who had suffered imprisonment for gospel ministry with him. So Daniel G. Reid, "Paul and His Coworkers," in *DPL* 754.

11. Wansink, *Chained*, 200.

12. Rapske, *Paul in Roman Custody*, 16–20; Wansink, *Chained*, 32. Rapske notes several reasons for incarceration, including protection for the accused, to ensure that the accused would show up for trial, to hold a prisoner awaiting a sentence or execution, coercion, or punishment (10–20).

13. Reid, "Paul and His Coworkers," 753.

Also, imprisonment took a wide range of forms, as we see in our New Testament examples. In Philippi, for instance, Paul and Silas were stripped, severely beaten, thrown in an inner cell, and had their feet put in stocks (Acts 16:22–24). On the other hand, the apostle's imprisonment in Rome seems to have been a humane form of house arrest (28:16, 20). The worst form of imprisonment, referred to as *carcer*, involved being chained in vile conditions, such as in Paul's Philippian incarceration. Military custody, *custodia militaris*, on the other hand, was less severe; the chained prisoner could move about and be attended by friends or family (e.g., Josephus, *Ant.* 18.6.7 and 18.6.10). This seems to be the form of imprisonment reflected at the end of Acts, which Paul experienced in his first Roman imprisonment. A third form of imprisonment was "free custody," *custodia libera*, which involved the prisoner being supervised by agents other than military personnel, such as a magistrate (e.g., Suetonius, *Vit.* 7.3) or even a family member.[14]

The conditions faced in prison could be affected by a range of variables, including, for instance, whether a person was a Roman citizen, their social status, the nature of the crime, and the identity and status of the accuser.[15] A sense of justice, or the modern concept of fairness, often was not in play. A Roman citizen had the right to appeal to Caesar, but often an appeal was costly, as the appellant paid for the trip to Rome, the cost of living in Rome awaiting a hearing, and the cost of litigating the case.[16]

Although our data is slim, it seems that incarceration in a *carcer* could be horrendous, with prisoners herded together in dark, nasty, unsanitary conditions, which could be physically debilitating and psychologically devastating. Lucian (*Tox.* 29) writes, "Moreover, the stench of the room and its stifling air (since many were confined in the same place, cramped for room, and scarcely able to draw breath), the clash of iron, the scanty sleep—all these conditions were difficult and intolerable."[17] Prisoners were often chained, which could be a horrible aspect of incarceration. In fact, being chained was such a common experience that to speak of "bonds" or "chains" could simply be used as synonymous with being in prison.[18] In his work *Moralia*, and speaking of escape from the burden of chains, Plutarch writes, "Sleep makes light the chains of prisoners, and the inflammations surrounding wounds, the savage gnawing of ulcers in the flesh, and tormenting pains are removed from those who are fallen asleep."[19] At the same time, the practice and use of chains varied.

14. Cassidy, *Paul in Chains*, 39–43.
15. Rapske, *Paul in Roman Custody*, 37–59.
16. Rapske, *Paul in Roman Custody*, 55.
17. Wansink, *Chained*, 33–35.
18. Wansink, *Chained*, 46–47.
19. Plutarch, *Moralia*, translated by Frank Cole Babbitt, LCL (Cambridge: Harvard University Press; London: W. Heinemann, 1962), 459 (§165).

At times chains were used on arms and hands, while at other times on legs and feet. Some prisoners could be shackled with an iron collar. Nighttime might have brought greater restriction, and stocks were designed for almost complete immobilization. As noted above, chains could be used even in less severe forms of imprisonment.[20]

Prisoners in the Roman world often depended on friends or family for assistance, including the provision of basic needs like food and clothing. Friends could also "pay off" a jailer to procure better treatment or conditions for a prisoner. For example, Lucian writes of a person named Demetrius, who cares for his imprisoned friend, Antiphilus:[21]

> Then he bade him have no fear, and tearing his short cloak in two, put on one of the halves himself and gave the remainder to Antiphilus, after stripping from him the filthy, worn-out rags that he was wearing. From that time forth, too, he shared his life in every way, attending and cherishing him; for by hiring himself out to the shipmen in the harbour from early morning until noon, he earned a good deal of money as a stevedore. Then, on returning from his work, he would give part of his pay to the keeper, thus rendering him tractable and peaceful, and the rest sufficed well enough for the maintenance of his friend. Each afternoon he remained with Antiphilus, keeping him in heart; and when night overtook him, he slept just in front of the prison door, where he had made a place to lie and had put down some leaves." (*Tox.* 30–31)

This need for assistance makes sense of Paul's words concerning the Philippians' assistance sent through Epaphroditus: "I am amply supplied, now that I have received from Epaphroditus the gifts you sent" (Phil 4:18). Similarly, we can hear Paul's heartfelt desire for assistance and companionship at 2 Timothy 4:9–13:

> Do your best to come to me quickly, for Demas, because he loved this world, has deserted me and has gone to Thessalonica. Crescens has gone to Galatia, and Titus to Dalmatia. Only Luke is with me. Get Mark and bring him with you, because he is helpful to me in my ministry. I sent Tychicus to Ephesus. When you come, bring the cloak that I left with Carpus at Troas, and my scrolls, especially the parchments. (NIV)

20. Cassidy, *Paul in Chains*, 46.

21. Cassidy, *Paul in Chains*, 49–50.

Finally, in a world in which honor and shame were primary social-reference points, imprisonment represented a shameful existence for the prisoner and those who provided assistance. This reveals the irony of Paul boasting about his imprisonments in 2 Corinthians 11:23. Often the shame associated with imprisonment meant abandonment. In his *Life of Apollonius* (4.37), Philostratus tells of Apollonius's celebration of his imprisonment as an opportunity to test the mettle of the students who were learning philosophy from him. Of the thirty-four who started with him, only eight actually made the trip to Rome, the rest showing themselves to be cowards and not true philosophers![22]

Although Paul recognized the limitations of his imprisonment, its dangers, and the potential for shame, his perspective was profoundly shaped by a very different worldview. Imprisonment for Paul was an opportunity to share in the sufferings of the true king of the universe, for Christ to be exalted in his situation; shame would only occur if courage in proclaiming the gospel failed (Phil 1:20). Therefore, his imprisonment, rather than a setback, constituted an opportunity for the advancement of the gospel, a platform for mission (vv. 12–14), and thus a form of partnership with the Philippians (1:3–5; 4:14–19). Moreover, the apostle did not see himself as constrained by the Roman authorities. Rather, he consistently referred to himself as "a prisoner of Christ Jesus" (Eph 3:1; Phlm 1, 9) or a "prisoner for the Lord" (Eph 4:1; cf. 2 Tim 1:8). So, Paul celebrated his ultimate "imprisonment" under the lordship of Christ, the true Caesar of the universe. This is why, for Paul, imprisonment was a circumstance in which he and the Philippians could rejoice (Phil 1:18; 2:17–18).

**1:13 so that it has become public knowledge among the whole imperial guard and everyone else that my imprisonment is in the cause of Christ** (ὥστε τοὺς δεσμούς μου φανεροὺς ἐν Χριστῷ γενέσθαι ἐν ὅλῳ τῷ πραιτωρίῳ καὶ τοῖς λοιποῖς πᾶσιν). Verses 13 and 14 give the twin results ("so that," ὥστε) of Paul's imprisonment, both involving the gospel as publicly proclaimed. These twin results are (1) that Paul's imprisonment has become public knowledge, and (2) that "the majority" of the brothers and sisters have been emboldened to speak. The first result, found in verse 13, points to the progress of the gospel among those who do not yet know Christ; namely, "among the whole imperial guard and everyone else." As explained more extensively in our introduction, the apostle's reference to "the imperial guard" (τῷ πραιτωρίῳ) comes by virtue of a loanword, originating with the Latin term *praetorium*, and offers one of our key clues to the apostle's location when Philippians was written.[23]

Originally, the Latin *praetorium* referred to the tent of the praetor in a military camp, along with the area surrounding the tent. As the word

22. As recounted in Cassidy, *Paul in Chains*, 49.

23. See the introduction, pp. 19–21.

developed over time, it came to be used of a governor's official residence, normally in imperial provinces, which explains the way writers of the New Testament consistently employ the word (Matt 27:27; Mark 15:16; John 18:28, 33; 19:9; Acts 23:35).[24] Yet the word was also used of the imperial guard in Rome,[25] who carried out a wide variety of functions in the first century, including service as policemen, firemen, and government administrators. Their main role, however, was to live out service to the emperor as his elite, personal troops.[26] Our position here is that Paul probably refers to this group in Philippians 1:13.[27] Among other salient points in its favor, this interpretation fits well with the following phrase, translated "and everyone else" (καὶ τοῖς λοιποῖς πᾶσιν), which also seems to refer to a group of people.

Some might object that the praetorian guard was too large a body to be permeated by the "gospel awareness" that Paul mentions. After all, there were some six- to nine-thousand members of the emperor's guard. But "the whole imperial guard" need not mean that every single one of them knew of Paul's case. Rather "among the whole" (ἐν ὅλῳ), along with "everyone else," could constitute general references, meaning that the apostle's situation and its cause had become widely known among those at the heart of the Roman establishment.[28]

But in exactly what way had the gospel made progress among the members of the imperial guard and others (cf. 4:22)? Here Paul does not speak about acceptance of the gospel per se but rather an awareness of the message about Jesus because of the apostle's imprisonment. In learning about Paul, the elite guard and those in the vicinity of the imperial environs learned about Jesus. The wording of this part of our clause, "my imprisonment is in the cause of Christ" (τοὺς δεσμούς μου . . . ἐν Χριστῷ γενέσθαι), is awkward at best, but the sense is that "my imprisonment," literally "my chains," is a way of referring to Paul's incarceration.[29] As noted in the In Depth section above, prisons were often holding cells for those awaiting trial.[30] In Paul's situation, he probably was chained to a rotation of guards,[31] with a change in shift every four hours. Consequently, the apostle would have had generous opportunity to share with the guards about the message of Christ and how that message had brought him to his present circumstance. Somehow, his imprisonment became "public knowledge" (φανερούς), the term referring to that which was "visible" or "public" to those within proximity of Paul's imprisonment. The added phrase, "in the cause of Christ" (ἐν Χριστῷ), is an unusual use of this very common Pauline descriptor, as our translation suggests.[32] The phrase tells us something more about the word we have translated simply with "is" (γενέσθαι), giving us a balanced

24. Although scholars debate exactly which buildings the gospel authors have in mind (BDAG 859).

25. See, e.g., Suetonius, *Nero* 9; Tacitus, *Hist.* 1.19; 4.2. See Bingham, *Praetorian Guard*, 16.

26. See especially Bingham, *Praetorian Guard*, 81–114.

27. It should be noted that Paul does not say that he was being held by the guard but that his situation and message had become known throughout the guard.

28. This use of generalized language would be similar to someone in modern culture saying, "The whole town was in an uproar!" The point is not that every single person in the town was affected but that the impact of the situation was widespread.

29. Wansink notes, "Imprisonment so frequently involved being placed in chains that synecdoche was employed in texts, with the Greek and Latin words for 'chains' often interchangeably used with the words for 'prison'" (*Chained*, 46–47).

30. Wansink, *Chained*, 30–31.

31. We simply have no way of knowing whether the guards were praetorians or not.

32. Constantine Campbell lists this occurrence under "In Christ as a Periphrasis for Believers" but admits Phil 1:13 is difficult to categorize. See Campbell, *Union with Christ*, 124–25.

construction in Greek, with the infinitive flanked by two phrases built on the preposition "in/among" (notice the two uses of ἐν):

| | |
|---|---|
| "in the cause of Christ" | ἐν Χριστῷ[33] |
| "is" | γενέσθαι |
| "among the whole imperial guard" | ἐν ὅλῳ τῷ πραιτωρίῳ |

The sense is that Paul's imprisonment has become public knowledge, with people aware that it is in relation to Christ—that is, because of his Christian missionary activity. Thus the phrase seems to speak of Paul sharing a solidarity with Christ in his imprisonment, but it also communicates the purpose that has brought Paul to this place—"for the cause of Christ."[34] This certainly fits the emphasis in context on the proclamation of the Messiah. As Paul continues to identify with Christ and Christ's gospel, that identification shapes people's perception of Paul's imprisonment, even as they learn of the gospel itself. Paul sees this as a wonderful step forward for the mission, since his imprisonment has ushered him into the inner echelons of imperial power. Among those who stood at the very epicenter of the Roman Empire, Paul's cause, and thus Paul's Christ, was made known, and that constituted progress for the gospel.

**1:14 and the majority of the brothers and sisters, having become confident in the Lord with reference to my imprisonment, are much more daring to speak the word unflinchingly** (καὶ τοὺς πλείονας τῶν ἀδελφῶν ἐν κυρίῳ πεποιθότας τοῖς δεσμοῖς μου περισσοτέρως τολμᾶν ἀφόβως τὸν λόγον λαλεῖν). Still working off of the "so that" (ὥστε) at the beginning of verse 13, Paul notes a second way that the gospel has moved forward as a result of his imprisonment. This second result involves "the majority of the brothers and sisters" in Rome, who have experienced greater boldness in proclaiming God's word. "The majority" (τοὺς πλείονας, from the word πολύς), as our translation suggests, carries the sense of a majority, or "most" (e.g., 1 Cor 9:19; 2 Cor 2:6; 9:2), and in this case refers to the majority "of the brothers and sisters" (τῶν ἀδελφῶν), Paul's fellow believers, in Rome.[35] Thus, the apostle now focuses on the effect of his incarceration[36] on those in the church, especially those who are speaking about the gospel as it comes up in conversations about Paul's situation.[37]

In essence, the believers in Rome have "become

33. At least part of Paul's motivation for using this particular construction at this point may have to do with the construction of the *inclusio*, of which our phrase plays a part. I agree with Fee that the sentence seems somewhat elliptical, reflecting an understood verb of being, "[as being] in Christ"; so Fee, *Philippians*, 112–13 (see esp. n29).

34. Bockmuehl reads Paul's statement as "imprisoned in Christ," saying, "It is not clear how [Paul's participation in Christ's suffering] could be 'evident' to anyone but himself." Rather, he understands the apostle, in the vein of a prophetic dramatization, to be making an ironic reference to being Christ's prisoner, pointing to Phlm 1, 9, 13; Eph 3:1; 4:1; 6:20. In other words, Paul is "bound" to speak the gospel, under compulsion by Christ. See Bockmuehl, *Philippians*, 75. But it seems that the apostle's statement, rather than symbolic, is fairly straightforward, as his imprisonment and his service in the cause of Christ are directly related.

35. On the translation as "brothers and sisters," see above in the commentary on v. 12. *Contra* E. Earle Ellis, the reference here, rather than a technical designation for Paul's coworkers, refers to the general population of the church. See E. Earle Ellis, *Prophecy and Hermeneutic in Early Christianity: New Testament Essays* (Tübingen: Mohr Siebeck, 1978), 3–22. This is a partitive genitive, indicating the whole of which "the majority" were a part. See Wallace, *Greek Grammar*, 84–86.

36. The phrase τοῖς δεσμοῖς μου can be read as a dative of reference, thus the translation "with reference to my imprisonment."

37. On the makeup of the church in Rome, at least when Paul had written his letter to the Romans, see Moo, *Epistle to the Romans*, 9–13, who argues for gentile Christians as the majority, with a Jewish-Christian minority. We do not know the effect that Paul's imprisonment in Rome had on the makeup of the church, but it is clear from the passage before us that gospel

confident in the Lord" (ἐν κυρίῳ πεποιθότας) with reference to Paul's imprisonment. The verb[38] rendered here as "become confident" (πείθω) generally carries the sense of "convince" or "persuade" but in our passage speaks of being so convinced of something that one puts confidence or trust in someone (BDAG 792)—in this case, "the Lord."[39] It was not that the apostle's imprisonment caused the believers' confidence in the Lord to increase (so NASB, NLT, NIV, NET). Rather, they had grown in confidence despite the apparent setback for the gospel mission! It was *with reference to* Paul's imprisonment that they had grown in their confidence, not *because* of it. In other words, as they watched how the Lord had worked in and through Paul's imprisonment—seeing God sovereignly turn a "bad" situation for the good of the gospel—they were strengthened greatly in their own proclamation of the word. Undoubtably, the brothers and sisters grew in confidence as they witnessed Paul's own confidence in the Lord. Accordingly, Luke concludes the book of Acts by describing Paul's ministry during his Roman imprisonment with "[Paul] welcomed all who came to him, proclaiming the kingdom of God and teaching about the Lord Jesus Christ with complete boldness [μετὰ πάσης παρρησίας] and without restriction" (Acts 28:30–31 NET). Seeing the heroic courage of their apostle, and its effect in spreading the gospel, the Roman Christ-followers grew in courage, as Paul expresses in balanced clauses:

| | |
|---|---|
| "are much more daring" | περισσοτέρως τολμᾶν |
| "to speak the word unflinchingly" | ἀφόβως τὸν λόγον λαλεῖν |

Although the verb "to dare" (τολμάω) could be used in a negative sense (as in the English, "How dare you!"; e.g., Matt 22:46; Rom 15:18; 1 Cor 6:1; 2 Cor 10:12), it could also be employed positively to speak of boldness or courage; that is, "daring" to do something in the face of opposition or difficulty (Rom 5:7; 15:18; 2 Cor 10:2; 11:21). The adverb, translated here as "much more" (περισσοτέρως),[40] suggests that the believers were much more daring than they had been previously, seen in the way they talked openly about the gospel as they discussed Paul's situation.

Specifically, they dared "to speak the word"[41] (τὸν λόγον λαλεῖν) of God "unflinchingly" (ἀφόβως); that is, "fearlessly," in a hostile environment. The exact expression "to speak the word" (τὸν λόγον λαλεῖν) occurs only here in the New Testament, though variations of the expression are frequent.[42] Normally, the language is employed of

proclamation was aided. This, of course, reflects a situation prior to increased persecution in Rome in the mid-60s CE—a period addressed, perhaps, by the book of Hebrews.

38. The perfect active participle πεποιθότας is masculine plural accusative in form, relating grammatically to τοὺς πλείονας at the beginning of the verse. Its stative aspect suggests that the apostle speaks of a state of affairs that has been ushered in by his time in prison.

39. Thus the preposition ἐν at this point connotes close personal association, and Paul often uses the formula ἐν κυρίῳ with verbs that communicate conviction, hope, or confidence, as noted in BDAG 328 (e.g., Rom 14:14; 15:17; 1 Cor 15:31; Gal 5:10; Phil 2:19; 2 Thess 3:4; Phlm 8). This grammatical pattern offers a primary reason for reading ἐν κυρίῳ as related primarily to the participle rather than to τῶν ἀδελφῶν (i.e., "brothers and sisters in the Lord," as with, e.g., NLT, KJV).

40. The adverb is comparative and tells us more about the infinitive "to dare" (τολμᾶν).

41. The text "to speak the word" (τὸν λόγον λαλεῖν) is reflected in NA$^{28}$ and UBS$^{5}$, following 𝔓$^{46}$ D$^{2}$ K 630. 1505. 1739. 1881 𝔐 r vg$^{ms}$ Mcion$^{T}$. The variant that adds "of God" (τοῦ θεοῦ) has strong and varied support (א A B [D*] P Ψ 048$^{vid}$. 075. 0278. 33. 81. 104. 326. 365. 629. 1175. 1241. 2464 lat sy$^{p.h**}$ co; Cl), but it almost certainly presents a scribal addition, since the former, shorter reading almost certainly gave rise to the latter.

42. E.g., Mark 2:2; 4:33; 5:36; 8:32; Luke 24:44; John 12:48; 15:3; Acts 4:29, 31; 8:25; 11:19; 13:46; 14:25; 16:6, 32; Col 4:3; Heb 13:7.

the word of God, seen expressed as someone speaking "the word of God" (e.g., Acts 4:31; 13:46; 2 Cor 2:17; Heb 13:7) or "the word of the Lord" (e.g., Acts 8:25; 16:32; 1 Thess 1:8). Further, Paul elsewhere can refer to "the word of the cross" (1 Cor 1:18) or "the word of reconciliation" (2 Cor 5:19). From the references to "preaching" or "proclaiming Christ" in the immediate context (1:15, 17), it seems clear that speaking the word in 1:14 refers to some form of public utterance about the gospel.

**1:15–17 In addition to these, some people also, motivated by hateful envy and factionalism, make public declarations about the Messiah, while others are motivated by goodwill. The latter speak out of love, knowing that I am destined for the defense of the gospel; but the former speak publicly about the Messiah out of selfish ambition, not from pure motives, expecting to stir up affliction in my imprisonment**[43] (τινὲς μὲν καὶ διὰ φθόνον καὶ ἔριν, τινὲς δὲ καὶ δι᾽ εὐδοκίαν τὸν Χριστὸν κηρύσσουσιν· 16 οἱ μὲν ἐξ ἀγάπης, εἰδότες ὅτι εἰς ἀπολογίαν τοῦ εὐαγγελίου κεῖμαι, 17 οἱ δὲ ἐξ ἐριθείας τὸν Χριστὸν καταγγέλλουσιν, οὐχ ἁγνῶς, οἰόμενοι θλῖψιν ἐγείρειν τοῖς δεσμοῖς μου). Paul now describes two groups who have conflicting motives in speaking publicly about the Messiah. While a great deal of talk about Christ took place in the city as people discussed Paul's imprisonment,[44] some of that talk arose from impure motives. In fact, our passage alludes to those who not only disliked the apostle but were wishing him harm,[45] as we see in the language of verses 15–17.

Nevertheless, the way that Paul has crafted the transition from verse 14 to verse 15, as well as the ambiguity of the description of his opponents, raises an interpretive conundrum regarding Paul's "opponents." Were they a subgroup of the "brothers and sisters" mentioned in the previous verse? Or were they opponents mentioned elsewhere in the New Testament—perhaps akin to the Jewish agitators of Galatia or the interlopers of Corinth? Or perhaps Paul alludes to a problem group in Philippi?[46] And how are we to read the apostle's seemingly conciliatory tone in verse 18?

To untie this hermeneutical knot, we must move step-by-step through the text before considering which interpretation best fits the data, seeking to make the most sense of the apostle's point in context. The unraveling of our knot is a bit involved, and I beg the reader's indulgence as we work our way through a few key issues. We proceed by first looking at the structure of the passage, along with those elements that connect it to the previous verse. Then we consider the descriptions of each group, as well as their activity of speaking publicly about the Messiah.

43. In our diagram at the beginning of this unit, the main verbal clause, τὸν Χριστὸν κηρύσσουσιν, is positioned according to the flow of the sentence, since maintaining sentence flow highlights the parallelism and chiastic structure of the passage. However, here I offer a more readable rendering of the passage, which breaks with the structural flow of the text.

44. Notice that the reference to the imperial guard and others in v. 13, and the reference to the brothers and sisters in v. 14, relate directly to Paul's imprisonment. This sets the context for the speaking described in vv. 15–18, where, in v. 17, his imprisonment is again mentioned.

45. If we are driven by the understandable veneration of Paul that exists in some branches of modern Christianity, it may be difficult to imagine what a controversial figure the apostle was in earliest Christianity as well as in mainline Judaism of the day. E.g., Barth states, "The general esteem for Paul as the apostle of Jesus Christ set in relatively late in Christendom" (Karl Barth, *The Epistle to the Philippians* [Louisville: Westminster John Knox, 2002], 29).

46. On which, see the In Depth treatment of the opponents below on pp. 230–34.

## *The Structure of the Passage*

First, as noted in the "Structure" section above, in verses 15–17 we see a well-crafted unit built around contrasting parallelism and a chiastic structure:

| | | | |
|---|---|---|---|
| some people | motivated by | hateful envy and factionalism, while | A |
| others | motivated by | goodwill; | B |
| **make public declarations about the Messiah** | | | C |
| the latter | out of | love | B′ |
| | knowing that | I am destined for the defense of the gospel but | |
| the former | out of | selfish ambition | A′ |
| **speak publicly about the Messiah** | | | C′ |
| | not from pure motives | | |
| | expecting to stir up affliction in my imprisonment | | |

The contrast depicts two groups. Notice that those opposed to Paul are described in the first and last movements of the chiastic structure (A, A′), while he describes his supporters in the inner two movements of the structure (B, B′). Note also the parallel verbs at the heart of the unit, translated "make public declarations" (κηρύσσουσιν, C) and "speak publicly" (καταγγέλλουσιν, C′). So, in some sense, speaking about the Messiah publicly was an activity carried out by both Paul's supporters and by his opponents.

A key interpretive issue concerns how this highly crafted unit is connected to the previous verse, both in terms of grammar and meaning. Of first importance, Paul frames the contrasting parallelism in the passage with Greek constructions, both of which communicate "on the one hand . . . on the other hand" contrasts: μὲν καί . . . δὲ καί in verse 15, and μέν . . . δέ in verses 16–17. Yet it is the first of these, μὲν καί . . . δὲ καί, that effects the transition from the previous verse. This construction, which only occurs here in biblical literature, holds a possible key to unlock the interpretive knot.

Many commentators read the references to "some . . . others" (τινές . . . τινές) of verse 15 as referring to contrasting subgroups from within "the brothers and sisters" mentioned in verse 14. With this interpretation, those who have become confident in the Lord, who speak the word unflinchingly (1:14), are comprised of two factions: those who support the apostle and those who don't.[47] In this case, "in addition" (καί), the third word in verse 15, is read either as a mild connective facilitating a smooth transition from the previous verse or as an ascensive, "indeed," anticipating the content of verses 15–17, with its breakdown of the Roman evangelists into two groups.

Vincent, on the other hand, sees the opponents of verses 15 and 17 as distinct from the "brothers" mentioned in verse 14, stating that here Paul "introduces another and a different class, and not

47. So, e.g., Walter Hansen writes, "After announcing the good news about the brothers and sisters who dare to speak the word courageously, Paul tells the bad news that they are divided by their different attitudes toward him. Although Paul draws a sharp line of contrast between these two groups, he is clear that they have the same identity and the same message" (Hansen, *Philippians*, 71). Bruce, *Philippians*, 43, states, "Not all the Roman Christians who were preaching the gospel so energetically were animated by a spirit of fellowship with Paul." Also, e.g., Bockmuehl, *Philippians*, 76–77; Silva, *Philippians*, 63–64; Still, *Philippians & Philemon*, 36; Jac. J. Müller, *The Epistles of Paul to the Philippians and to Philemon* (Grand Rapids: Eerdmans, 1955), 52; Reumann, *Philippians*, 198; Gerald F. Hawthorne and Ralph P. Martin, *Philippians*, rev. ed., WBC 43 (Nashville: Nelson, 2004), 45; and many others.

the same class."[48] Similarly, Ellicott interprets the first "some" (τινές) of verse 15 as "exceptions to the foregoing" mentioned in verse 14.[49] Ellicott is likely correct that it makes little sense that some who have "become confident in the Lord with reference to" Paul's imprisonment (1:14) are, at the same time, aggressively opposing him, even wishing him harm—a point that will become clearer as we address the language used of the opponents in verses 15–17.

An additional point can be made, however, that strengthens the position that the opponents mentioned in 1:15–17 are distinct from the "brothers and sisters" celebrated in 1:14, and it has to do with the Greek construction mentioned above, which we have translated with "in addition . . . while" (μὲν καί . . . δὲ καί) in verse 15. The construction δὲ καί is a common one for Paul, used thirty-three times in his writings,[50] often showing an *alternative* to what has just been mentioned. The consistent sense is the meaning "but also" (BDAG 213). The other part of our construction, "in addition" (μὲν καί), does not occur elsewhere in the New Testament. Nevertheless, it is common in the broader Greek literature of Paul's day[51]—a point that has been overlooked in discussions on this passage.[52]

For instance, in Philo, μὲν καί occurs ninety-eight times, and in twenty-nine passages the construction is used in conjunction with δὲ καί, as here in our passage.[53] In Josephus, μὲν καί is employed eighty-three times, and in eighteen of these occurrences it is paired with δὲ καί. A search of Greco-Roman literature broadly demonstrates the same pattern, which apparently is common. In many cases, μὲν καί alone, or the construction in combination with δὲ καί (as it is at Phil 1:15), communicates that what follows is an element or person "added" to the discussion, sometimes in contrast to the group already mentioned (for examples, see the "In Depth" section below).[54] This adjunctive nuance is missing from the vast majority of translations (e.g., ESV, CSB, NIV, NLT, NET) and interpretations of the passage.

When used in combination with δὲ καί, as in Philippians 1:15, the construction also communicates the regular "on the one hand . . . on the other hand" sense of μέν . . . δέ. When we put the pieces together, we translate the "some" (τινές) + μὲν καὶ at the beginning of verse 15 as "in addition to these, some people also . . . ," as Paul distinguishes between the "brothers and sisters" of verse 14 and the opponents of verse 15. He adds this contrarian group to the discussion since they have come to mind as he reflects on public conversations

48. Vincent, *Philippians*, 18. Vincent's comment about the "familiar contrasting force" of καί must be taken with a grain of salt, since contrast normally is discerned on the basis of contextual matters.

49. Charles John Ellicott, *A Critical and Grammatical Commentary on St. Paul's Epistles to the Philippians, Colossians, and to Philemon, with a Revised Translation* (London: John W. Parker and Son, 1861), 17. Ellicott believes the opponents are Jewish agitators.

50. Rom 2:10; 8:26; 1 Cor 1:16; 3:8; 4:7; 7:3–4, 11, 28, 40; 14:15; 15:15; 2 Cor 4:3; 5:8, 11; 6:1; 8:11; 11:6; Eph 5:3, 11; Phil 1:15; 3:18; 4:15; 1 Tim 1:9; 3:7; 5:13, 24; 2 Tim 2:5; Titus 3:14; Phlm 9, 11, 22. The construction almost always conveys an adjunctive sense. Could it be that μὲν καί is also adjunctive, making the whole emphatically so?

51. The construction is discussed in J. D. Denniston and K. J. Dover, *The Greek Particles*, 2nd ed. (London: Duckworth; Indianapolis: Hackett, 1996), 371, where they note that it often has adjunctive force ("but also").

52. Most read μὲν . . . δὲ as repeated in identical fashion in v. 15, not noticing the significant addition of καί . . . καί. So, e.g., Cousar, *Philippians and Philemon*, 35. Silva only recognizes the first καί as facilitating the link with the previous verse, suggesting that "Paul's syntax is not always subject to precise logical analysis" (Silva, *Philippians*, 63).

53. At times δὲ καί precedes μὲν καί or is used more than once in the same context.

54. See Denniston and Dover, *Greek Particles*, 306, and the excursus below.

about Christ in the city.[55] Having thus made the transition to his detractors in verse 15a, Paul now contrasts his opponents and supporters in parallel fashion. The point of verse 14 is that evangelism is taking place among "the brothers and sisters." Verses 15–17 focus on Paul himself, specifically the very different postures of his detractors and supporters toward him. Based on our probing of the grammar, however, it seems more plausible that the detractors are not a subgroup *among* the speakers of "the word" celebrated in verse 14. Rather, they are another group altogether.

## IN DEPTH: A Grammatical Key for Interpreting 1:15

In our treatment of the unusual grammatical construction in 1:15, we already noted that often in Paul the construction "and also" (δὲ καί) should be read as adding to a discussion under way, carrying the nuance "also." In the broader literature of the Greco-Roman world, the same can be said of the first part of the "conjunction construction" we have translated as "in addition . . . also" (μὲν καί). This construction is only used once in the LXX, at Wisdom 7:1, and may be read adjunctively: "I myself *also* [μὲν κἀγώ] am mortal like everyone, and a descendant of the first-formed individual born on earth" (NETS). Two of the three occurrences of the construction in the Old Testament Pseudepigrapha (T. Ash. 2.5; Let. Aris. 13) clearly are adjunctive ("also"). For instance, in Testament of Asher 2.5 the author has been speaking about forms of evil that have "two aspects" (διπρόσωπον, that is, "two-faced"), having some form of good mixed with evil. He mentions this "two-faced" approach to good and evil twice in 2.1–4, giving examples. When he offers a third illustration of evil having two aspects, he states, "Another steals, does unjustly, plunders, defrauds, and pities the poor: this too has a twofold aspect [διπρόσωπον μὲν καὶ τοῦτο], but the whole is evil" (v. 5),[56] clearly using the construction to add to the discussion.

Further, the adjunctive use of the construction is evident in Philo, Josephus, and Epictetus. For example, it is made clear by its place in an "also many other things" construction in their works.[57] At *Creation* 170 Philo writes that in the account of creation given by Moses he teaches "many other things in addition" (πολλὰ μὲν καὶ ἄλλα; translation mine), and then mentions five beautiful lessons drawn from the Scriptures. He thus adds to the topic already under discussion.

Not surprisingly, these two constructions, μὲν καί and δὲ καί, each of which

55. It also can be pointed out that Paul often uses τινές to speak of opponents (Rom 3:3, 8; 11:17; 1 Cor 4:18; 6:11; 8:7; 10:7–10; 15:6, 12, 34; 2 Cor 3:1; Gal 1:7; Phil 1:15; 1 Tim 1:6, 19; 4:1; 5:15; 6:10, 21).

56. Craig A. Evans, trans., *The Pseudepigrapha (English)* (BibleWorks LLC, 2008).

57. E.g., Philo, *Creation* 53, 170; *Heir* 217; *Spec. Laws* 1.164; Josephus, *Ant.* 16.76; 19.65; Epictetus, *Diatr.* 2.10.17.

at times is used adjunctively when it stands alone, can also carry an adjunctive nuance—adding to a discussion or concept that has gone before—when used together in the μὲν καί . . . δὲ καί construction we have at Philippians 1:15.[58] As noted above, the construction occurs eighteen times in Josephus and twenty-nine times in Philo.[59] Some of these uses are clearly adjunctive,[60] adding people or topics "in addition" to what has just been under discussion. For example, at *Sacrifices* 6, Philo writes, "And Isaac, who was thought worthy of self-taught knowledge, of his own accord also [μὲν καί] leaves all the corporeal essence which was attached to his soul, and is added to and [δὲ καί; could be translated "and also"] made an inheritor with (not the people, as the others whom I have mentioned were), but with the 'race'" (Yonge). In this way, Isaac is added to the existing discussion.

From this review of these grammatical constructions, it is clear that an adjunctive reading of τινὲς μὲν καί as "in addition . . . some also" at Philippians 1:15 is not only plausible but very much in line with uses in the broader Greco-Roman literature of both μὲν καί and δὲ καί alone as well as μὲν καί . . . δὲ καί when used together. In our passage, this means that "some" (τινές) at the beginning of verse 15 may introduce an additional group rather than refer to a subdivision of the believers mentioned in verse 14. Paul does not write "some of whom" (τινὲς ὧν); he writes, τινὲς μὲν καί. The translation "some also," with the sense, "in addition to these, some also . . ." seems warranted, and the construction sets up the contrast embodied in verses 15–17. Concerning the exact identity of Paul's opponents and supporters, the text is ambiguous (though see the In Depth section below), and grammar can only take us so far. What is clear is that these two groups are driven by contrasting motives, which provide at least a hint of the identity of Paul's opponents.

## *The Contrasting Motives of Paul's Opponents and Supporters*

Now we consider the descriptions used of Paul's opponents over against Paul's supporters in 1:15–17, which focus on the posture of each toward the apostle, even as the message of Christ is spoken of publicly. The special focus of verses 15–17 rests especially on the motives manifested among these two distinct groups of people in relation to Paul's imprisonment, which has either been alluded to (1:12) or overtly mentioned (1:13, 14) three times

58. Let me stress that this is not *always* the case. My point here is that we have abundant evidence that an adjunctive reading at Phil 1:15 has ample support in the broader literature.

59. It does not occur elsewhere in biblical literature, nor in the OT Pseudepigrapha.

60. E.g., Josephus, *Ag. Ap.* 2.172; Philo, *Planting* 60; *Drunkenness* 141; *Heir* 243; *Dreams* 290, 297.

in the last three verses and is mentioned again in 1:17.

The motives of those who publicly oppose the apostle are described in verse 15. They are "motivated by hateful envy and factionalism" (διὰ φθόνον καὶ ἔριν).[61] These first two descriptors are introduced with the preposition "by" (διά), reflecting cause or motivation. The first, "hateful envy" (φθόνος), appears mostly in vice lists in the New Testament, referring to "envy" or "jealousy."[62] Yet as Bruce Winter points out, the term may reflect an active form of envy, not merely bad feelings about someone. That is, this term at times communicates an intense form of envy that involves hatred[63] and seeks the harm of its target.[64] This is clearly the case in a passage such as Matthew 27:18, where the religious leaders are said to have handed Jesus over to the Roman authorities "because of envy." They weren't merely jealous; they wanted to destroy the competition.

Pertinent to our passage, the term appears in Greco-Roman descriptions of conflict in the public square. In a writing ascribed to Dio Chrysostom but probably written by a Roman named Favorinus,[65] the author encourages rival cities to work in unity with one another. He points out that certain vices, which cause pain in civil relationships, should be eliminated. First among these, he mentions our term "hateful envy" (φθόνος) and groups it with "contentiousness" (φιλονικία). Both attitudes lead to "strife" or "discord" (στάσις), which in turn manifests in "your plotting against one another, your gloating over the misfortunes of your neighbours, your vexation at their good fortune."[66]

Similarly, in Philippians 1:15 Paul pairs "hateful envy" (φθόνος) with "factionalism" (ἔρις), which speaks of rivalry or discord. As with φθόνος, this term occurs frequently in New Testament vice lists,[67] the two terms occurring together at Romans 1:29 and 1 Timothy 6:4. Thus, "factionalism" (ἔρις) connotes the kind of attitude or posture toward others that ignites rivalry, divisiveness, or destruction of unity.

In verse 17 this same opponent group is described as speaking "out of selfish ambition, not from pure motives, expecting to stir up affliction in my imprisonment" (ἐξ ἐριθείας τὸν Χριστὸν καταγγέλλουσιν, οὐχ ἁγνῶς, οἰόμενοι θλῖψιν ἐγείρειν τοῖς δεσμοῖς μου). Thus, in 1:15–17 Paul notes a third inappropriate posture of his opponents, writing that they speak "out of selfish ambition" (ἐριθεία). This term he introduces with the preposition ἐκ, reflecting source.[68] This word speaks of a "party spirit" that disrupts community, but it also carries a note of "selfishness" or "selfish ambition" (Rom 2:8; 2 Cor 12:20; Gal 5:20; Phil 1:17; 2:3; Jas 3:14, 16). Spicq explains that the term originally had to do with work for hire but developed a more negative meaning:

61. As Morna Hooker points out, 1 Clement, a document associated with Rome, attributes the deaths of both Peter and Paul to "jealousy" (ζῆλος) and "envy" (φθόνος) (5:2), and that of Paul specifically to "jealousy" (ζῆλος) and "strife" (ἔρις) (5:5). See Morna Hooker, "Philippians: Phantom Opponents and the Real Source of Conflict," in *Fair Play: Diversity and Conflicts in Early Christianity: Essays in Honour of Heikki Räisänen*, ed. Ismo Dunderberg, C. M. Tuckett, and Kari Syreeni, NovTSup 103 (Leiden: Brill, 2002), 394.

62. E.g., Rom 1:29; Gal 5:21; 1 Tim 6:4; Titus 3:3; 1 Pet 2:1.

63. See, e.g., Dionysius of Halicarnassus, *Ant. rom.* 6.85.2.

64. Winter, *Welfare of the City*, 94.

65. H. Lamar Crosby, trans., *Dio Chrysostom, Discourses 37–60*, LCL 376 (Cambridge: Harvard University Press, 1946), 1.

66. Crosby, *Dio Chrysostom, Discourses 37–60*, 87–88. The author also notes the opposites of these as "sharing in things which are good, unity of heart and mind, rejoicing of both peoples in the same things" (κοινωνίαν ἀγαθῶν, ὁμοφροσύνην, ἐπὶ τοῖς αὐτοῖς ἀμφοτέρων χαράν; Dio Chrysostom, *To the Nicomedians* 38.43). It does not take much imagination to hear the virtues here as similar to Paul's exhortations to unity at Phil 1:27 and 2:2–3.

67. E.g., Rom 1:29; 13:13; 2 Cor 12:20; Gal 5:20; 1 Tim 6:4; Titus 3:9.

68. BDAG 392.

> As a result, the term *eritheia* ("paid work") originally had a positive sense; but it came to mean that which is done solely for interested motives ("What's in it for me?"). Hence the meaning: contrive to gain a position or a magistracy not in order to serve the state but to gain honor and wealth. From that developed two other meanings: dispute or intrigue to gain advantages, and the exclusive pursuit of one's own interests.[69]

Thus the word describes a person who is a "conniving ladder climber." In Greco-Roman literature, the word could be used in the context of a public figure attempting to get ahead through political maneuvering or intrigue.[70] Perhaps the apostle's opponents saw him as a rival leader of the messianic movement in Rome. They thus may have been comparable to the interlopers in Corinth with whom Paul had dealt a few years earlier. Or perhaps these were Jewish leaders, who saw him as a Jewish false teacher. What seems clear is that they were using sentiment against Paul in the public square to hurt him for their own advancement. Paul must have been standing in their way, thwarting their agendas. This fits the sense of "selfish ambition" (ἐριθεία) well.

This form of selfish ambition is contrasted with "purity" (ἁγνῶς);[71] thus, the opponents do not speak of the Messiah "from pure motives" but rather are driven by selfish ambition. Specifically, in 1:17 Paul states bluntly that the opponents hoped to negatively affect his political situation—"expecting to stir up affliction in my imprisonment." The opponents are "expecting" (οἰόμενοι) to hurt Paul in his imprisonment (τοῖς δεσμοῖς μου), thinking that they can "raise the level of" or "stir up affliction"[72] (θλῖψις ἐγείρειν) against the apostle. As Paul proclaimed the gospel throughout the Mediterranean, "affliction" was his constant companion.[73] In the biblical literature generally, the term we translate as "affliction" (θλίψις) could refer to adverse circumstances or events that cause intense distress—"oppression," "affliction," or "persecution." Although the word can have to do with a person's inner emotional state, in the context of 1:15–17 it suggests that the opponents were not merely wanting to unsettle Paul emotionally but wished to do him harm. Winter writes that "the stirring up of trouble was meant to prejudice the outcome of his case when it came to court. At least this much can be said—that Paul's opponents engaged in an activity calculated to aggravate his difficulties at trial."[74] It is clear that, at the time of writing, the apostle's life had been threatened (1:21–26). Thus, the opponents' ire must have been extreme enough to plot a worsening of his situation. Perhaps they wanted the apostle out of the way for good.

69. *TLNT* 2:70.

70. Winter, *Welfare of the City*, 95.

71. This seems to be the meaning consistently found in the Apostolic Fathers (Barn. 2.3; Herm. 13.1; 59.6; 102.2; 103.2; 104.2). Interestingly, the term is associated at Herm. 59.6 with the verb πολιτεύομαι, "to conduct one's life as a citizen," the same term Paul uses at Phil 1:27.

72. The word ἐγείρω could be used positively, e.g., to raise a person from a lower position to a higher one, or to raise from the dead, which is by far the most common use in Paul (e.g., Rom 4:24–25; 6:4, 9; 7:4; 8:11, 34; 10:9). But the object here (θλῖψις) points to uses of the verb that speak of the raising up of hostility. Further, the other use of θλῖψις in Philippians (4:14) shows that Paul had been experiencing affliction in his imprisonment for a while, and the Philippians had ministered to him in the past. The imperfective aspect of the present-tense verbs in our context indicates that at the time of writing, public talk about the Messiah was ongoing. Therefore, ἐγείρειν should not be translated "cause" (so CEV, NASB, NET), as if the affliction was not yet in existence. Rather, the idea here seems to be elevation, to increase or "stir up" the affliction that already was in existence (so NLT, NRSV).

73. LSJ 1208. See Rom 2:9; 5:3; 8:35; 12:12; 1 Cor 7:28; 2 Cor 1:4, 8; 2:4; 4:17; 6:4; 7:4; 8:2, 13; Eph 3:13; Phil 1:17; 4:14; Col 1:24; 1 Thess 1:6; 3:3, 7; 2 Thess 1:4, 6.

74. Winter, *Welfare of the City*, 95.

As for Paul's supporters, their motives stand in direct contrast to the opponents'. In the LXX, the word rendered "goodwill" (εὐδοκία; 1:15) often refers to God's benevolence, approval, or favor toward his people.[75] In the New Testament, Jesus celebrates the Father's "good pleasure" in revealing his truths to "little ones" (Matt 11:26; Luke 10:21). Paul at times uses the term in this vein (Eph 1:5, 9; Phil 2:13), but the word also can be used of one person's "goodwill" or favor toward another (e.g., Rom 1:10; 2 Thess 1:11; Pss. Sol. 3.4), as seems to be the case here.[76] Whereas the opponents are motivated by "hateful envy and factionalism," Paul's supporters are driven by a sense of goodwill toward the apostle.

Further, they speak "out of love, knowing that" (ἐξ ἀγάπης, εἰδότες ὅτι) Paul is "destined for the defense of the gospel" (εἰς ἀπολογίαν τοῦ εὐαγγελίου κεῖμαι, v. 16). Love stands as the foundational virtue of the Christian community, being a fruit of the Spirit and the hallmark of Christian conduct in the New Testament (John 13:34–35; Rom 12:9–21; Gal 5:22). Paul exhorts the Philippians to nurture loving relationships in the church (Phil 1:9; 2:1–2), since love builds unity as believers sacrifice for, and serve, one another. Here Paul acknowledges those speaking publicly about Christ who are motivated to speak "out of love." In other words, they want to help the apostle in his situation. Why? The answer is that they know that Paul is "destined for the defense of the gospel." Of course, Paul was "destined" (κεῖμαι)[77] to speak the gospel before rulers in his encounter with Jesus on the road to Damascus (Acts 9:15). In this context, however, he may mean that the believers are anticipating his public "defense" (ἀπολογία) of the gospel before the emperor and that they love him as a Christian brother who has been given such an opportunity to defend the Christian message on behalf of the church. Accordingly, they are speaking publicly and positively about Paul and about the Messiah as the apostle awaits trial in prison.

### *Preaching and Partisanship?*

This brings us to discern the activity that manifested the negative motives of Paul's opponents and the positive motives of his supporters. Paul states that both groups were "making public declarations about" (κηρύσσουσιν), or "speaking publicly about" (καταγγέλλουσιν), the Messiah. On the surface of it, this seems strange, for both the support of Paul and the attacks against him are set in the context of "preaching" or "proclaiming" Christ. Yet, as alluded to in our commentary, we need to think carefully about lexicology and the *context* in which this language was crafted. First, let's consider the terms themselves and their use elsewhere.

Writers of the LXX use the verb translated "announce, make known, proclaim aloud" (κηρύσσω)[78] thirty-one times, almost all of which refer to an official and public announcement of some sort (as with 1 Pet 3:19; Rev 5:2).[79] Among the prophets, we begin to find movement toward

75. E.g., 1 Chr 16:10; Ps 5:12; 19:14; 51:18; 79:17.

76. Contra Hooker, "Philippians: Phantom Opponents," 385, who sees the "goodwill" as having a divine component in that those supporting Paul were doing so because they were thinking of Paul's situation as grounded in the divine purpose. Yet all the contrasts here point to the posture of human beings, as does the parallel reference to the "love" driving the apostle's supporters, mentioned in v. 16.

77. This use of the verb is unusual in the NT, occurring elsewhere at 1 Thess 3:3, where Paul also speaks about persecution.

78. BDAG 543.

79. E.g., Gen 41:43; Exod 32:5; 36:6; 2 Kgs 10:20; 2 Chr 20:3; 24:9; 36:22; Esth 6:9, 11; Prov 1:21; 8:1; Dan 3:4; Hos 5:8; Joel 2:1, 15; 4:9; Jonah 3:5, 7; Mic 3:5; Zeph 3:14; Zech 9:9. See also 1 Macc 5:49; 10:63–64; Pss. Sol. 11.1.

the sense of "proclaiming," which involves bringing a word from the Lord (e.g., Isa 61:1; Dan 3:4; Jonah 3:7; Zeph 3:14; Zech 9:9). In the New Testament, among the sixty-one uses of the word—nineteen of which are in Paul—some refer to public declarations, such as the "preaching" of Jesus or John the Baptist (e.g., Matt 3:1; 4:17, 23), and some to testimonies responding to something Jesus had done for a person (e.g., Mark 1:45; 7:36; Luke 8:39), such as when the Gerasene demoniac "proclaimed" how much Jesus had done for him (Mark 5:20). Most of its uses involve "proclamation," or the public announcement of the gospel—that is, speaking about Christ and what he has accomplished.[80] Of course, Paul uses the term in this way consistently, but *he at times uses the word for false teaching, or the "preaching" of his opponents* (e.g., Rom 2:21; 2 Cor 11:4; Gal 5:11). So it can be used in a variety of ways, pointing to various forms of public announcement or proclamation. But most often in Paul it involves speaking about Christ in public, whether rightly or wrongly.

The second verb, καταγγέλλω, essentially means, "to make known in public, with implication of broad dissemination, proclaim, announce."[81] It, too, can be used of announcing something or someone. In Acts, the term speaks of the announcement of "these days" (Acts 3:24), the resurrection of the dead (4:2), the word of God or of the Lord (13:38; 15:36; 17:13), the way of salvation (16:17), customs (16:21), the unknown God (17:23), and light (26:23). So the list of announced objects is fairly broad, but the word is most often used of public proclamation of the Christian message. In Paul, the verb speaks of the proclamation of the Roman Christians' faith (Rom 1:8), the testimony of God (1 Cor 2:1), the gospel (9:14), the Lord's death (11:26), and of Christ (Phil 1:18; Col 1:28). So again, the list of the word's objects shows diversity, but the word often points to a proclamation or public discussion about things related in some way to the Christian message.

In context in Philippians 1:15–17, the parallel references to "the Messiah" (τὸν Χριστόν) clearly state the object of these verbs, but in what sense were the opponents and supporters of Paul "proclaiming" or "talking publicly about" the Messiah? As already noted, the message of the Messiah is discussed in association with Paul's imprisonment, a point the apostle has made in verses 12–14 and stresses again in verse 17, as seen in the following table.

| Verses | Paul's Imprisonment | Progress of the Gospel |
|---|---|---|
| 12 | "my circumstances" | "progress of the gospel" |
| 13 | "my imprisonment" | "in the cause of Christ" |
| 14 | "with reference to my imprisonment" | "to speak the word" |
| 17 | "stir up affliction in my imprisonment" | "speak publicly about the Messiah" |

It has become public knowledge that Paul's imprisonment is in the cause of Christ, so discussion of the Christian message and mission is "in the air." Accordingly, 1:15–18 has to do with public talk about the Messiah, but such discussion is carried out *with reference to Paul himself and his imprisonment*. This must not be missed. The context is the public square. His supporters speak about the Messiah in a way that expresses "goodwill" and "love" toward the apostle, while his opponents speak publicly about the Messiah in a way that harbors envy, factionalism, selfish ambition, and ill will. It would seem obvious that if the opponents were attacking Paul, seeking to stir up affliction for him in his imprisonment, their talk would concern *his message*

80. E.g., 1 Cor 1:23; 15:12; 2 Cor 1:19; 4:5; Gal 2:2; 1 Thess 2:9.

81. BDAG 515.

as well as the messenger and would *address* those in power, who could inflict further harm on the apostle. Thus, the talk was not only public but also political (since it addressed the political powers, who were holding the apostle). This, then, seems to be what Paul means when he says that both his supporters and detractors "speak publicly about the Messiah"—both detractors and supporters talk about Paul and his message—and Paul perceives this as a good thing, as we see in the next verse. Thus, the opponents are not "preaching Christ," as we would normally think of evangelism. Rather, in their public disputations about Paul and his mission, addressed to the political powers who had the apostle incarcerated, they talk about Messiah Jesus, even as they attack Paul's ministry.

**1:18a–g What can be said in response? Only that Messiah is spoken about publicly in each of these manners, whether from false motives or true, and I rejoice in this!** (τί γάρ; πλὴν ὅτι παντὶ τρόπῳ, εἴτε προφάσει εἴτε ἀληθείᾳ, Χριστὸς καταγγέλλεται, καὶ ἐν τούτῳ χαίρω). Verse 18 begins with a question that many commentators have found oddly mild as a response to aggressive opponents. The key here, however, is to focus on the object of this mild response. Paul's comment does not soften his usual concern about those fighting his ministry. Rather, he downplays the difficulties of his own circumstances. His joy lies not in the suffering itself but in "his ability to see every pirouette both for its own beauty and for its place in the whole dance" of God's redemptive process.[82] He rejoices that people are becoming more aware of the message about Christ, even if some vehicles of that awareness are driven by wrong motives and seek his harm.

The little question, "What can be said in response?" (τί γάρ;) has been rendered by English translations variously as "What then?" (ESV, NASB, KJV), "What does it matter?" (CSB, NRSV, NIV), and "What is the result?" (NET). The first of these seems rather wooden and obscure. The NET's "What is the result?" is possible,[83] fitting the context well, and the second, "What does it matter?" raises a question of the significance of these conflicting postures, downplaying the personal costs to Paul himself. How can we get at the apostle's nuance here?

Paul uses these words τί γάρ five other times in his writings (Rom 3:3; 4:3; 1 Cor 5:12; 7:16; 2 Cor 12:13), but only in one other instance do the two words constitute a question (Rom 3:3). There Paul seems to use the question with the sense, "How should we think about this?" or "What can be said about this?" which is followed by the apostle leading the reader in how to think about the situation.[84] In the LXX, this little rhetorical question is common to Job (e.g., 4:17; 6:5, 22; 16:3; 18:4; 21:4) with the similar sense of "What can be said in response?"[85] This rendering makes good sense in our context as well. The apostle has described a mixed situation, with both supporters and opponents speaking publicly about Christ. The latter are being used in some way to make Christ known, but they also seek to do Paul harm. So, with τί γάρ Paul asks the obvious question: "What can we say in light of this 'mixed' situation in which both good and bad are intertwined?"

82. Fee, *Philippians*, 124.

83. Cf. the use in Josephus (*J. W.* 3.401), where the construction seems to have the meaning, "To what end?"

84. Fee reads the γάρ as explanatory, which fits our reading. But he translates it, "What does it matter?" expressing significance (as e.g., CSB; NIV). I think rather that the nuance has to do with an appropriate or reasoned response: "How can we make sense of this?"

85. This parallel is strengthened by the recognition that Paul alludes to Job in the next verse (Job 13:13–18 LXX; see Silva, *Philippians*, 70).

Paul introduces his answer with "only that . . ." (πλὴν ὅτι), which brings in a note of contrast, riveting attention on a focused answer. The apostle's responses to the question could have varied, pointing, for instance, to the ungodliness of the opponents or the faithfulness of his supporters. He could have shared his sorrow and pain at being misunderstood and mistreated. Or Paul could have gloried in the goodwill and love of those who cared deeply about him, his Lord, and the gospel. But, like a linguistic funnel, "only that" narrows Paul's response to one, crystal-clear statement on the apostle's assessment of what is most significant in the situation: Christ is spoken about publicly in each of these manners, whether from false motives or true. The term translated "manners" (τρόπος) refers to the way in which something is done,[86] and the "each" (πᾶς), tells us that Paul still has the responses of both his supporters and detractors in mind. The construction rendered "whether . . . or" (εἴτε . . . εἴτε) distinguishes between these responses. The opponents are driven by "false motives" (πρόφασις), the word referring to a pretext. By contrast, Paul's supporters speak from "true" (ἀλήθεια), or what we might call "pure," motives. Nevertheless, both contrasting motives—whether false or true—result in the Messiah being spoken about publicly. For Paul, that is a win-win situation. This is how Paul's "circumstances actually have come about for the progress of the gospel" (1:12), and why the progress of the gospel is always to be celebrated!

## Theology in Application

In crisis ministry situations, right theology must provide a basis for right response. As Gordon Fee notes, "It would be easy to dismiss this passage (vv. 12–18a) either as anecdotal narrative or as Paul's simply putting the best possible face on a bad situation," but much more is going on here.[87] Of course, a rhetorical strategy is employed—Paul wants the Philippians to respond in certain ways—but based on what, and to what end? Several points are instructive as we think about application of this passage.

First, *when facing a crisis, seek to grow in theological perspective.* Rather than a bit of slick word-crafting or "detached theologizing," the apostle writes out of a significant crisis, under real threat, and manifests a set of deeply held theological convictions and priorities. In other words, his response to the crisis reaches deep down through the soil of his crisis to rest on the bedrock of his theology. He responds out of his *beliefs* rather than the emotions of the moment. His true values manifest in a message centered on the Messiah. In effect Paul says, "My situation and discomfort are not the center of the universe—the gospel is." To what end? That all things, beginning with the Philippians themselves, might work for the glory of God and the advancement of God's gospel in the world. Thus Paul sees his current situation, with its chains and challengers, from a spiritually high vantage point, looking down on

86. BDAG 1017.

87. Fee, *Philippians*, 125.

the messy struggles of his daily existence from a lofty, stable, theological mountain, seeing God's pattern of working out his will in the world.

I recently read Bernard Cornwell's historical account of the battle of Waterloo.[88] That decisive battle in 1815 Belgium, fought shortly after Napoleon's escape from Elba and brief return to military might, produced devastating losses on both sides. At a critical moment in the battle, when the French forces threw thousands of men at the ridge on which the Duke of Wellington's army was embedded, the air was so thick with smoke that many of the combatants could only see a few paces in front of them. In the brutal butchery of war, some on Wellington's side—their vision restricted by the casualties falling on every side—thought they were losing the battle, and they panicked. But the vast majority were clearheaded, keeping Wellington's command in view, always focused on the objective of winning the day. The future of Europe was at stake. Wellington himself was thoroughly engaged in the battle, directing from a high vantage point, apparently calm but never removed from danger. His decisions, and the decisions of other leaders under his command,[89] shaped the battle so that he and his allies became the conquerors of the "unconquered" Napoleon. The battle was shaped and won from a particular vantage point or perspective.

When we live according to a perspective that is deeply grounded in theology, we can then, secondly, *live as an example of boldness in the face of opposition*. Something in Paul's posture, presence, or pattern of response to his imprisonment was used by God to embolden the brothers and sisters so that they spoke the word of the Lord unflinchingly (1:14). God enabled the apostle to have that impact. Paul was much more experienced at handling threat than most of us (especially those of us in the West). Yet we might remember that our example—good or bad—in response to opposition is seen by others. We are training those under our ministerial care how to respond to difficult situations.

For a number of years, I have been privileged to work on the board of a ministry that trains house-church ministers in an Asian country. We have faced opposition to our ministry, but the brothers and sisters we have encountered there are wonderful exemplars of gracious boldness in difficult circumstances. When she was in her twenties, one sister, who has since gone to be with the Lord, was put in prison. She shared the gospel, prayed for fellow inmates—some of whom were healed—cast out demons, and generally worked for the improvement of the prison context. One day the warden came to her and said, "We don't understand what you are doing, but we are going to take you to another prison so you can do the same things there." She was used by God to change a dark and difficult place; oppression was changed to opportunity.

88. Bernard Cornwell, *Waterloo: The History of Four Days, Three Armies and Three Battles* (New York: HarperCollins, 2014).

89. Much credit goes to the leaders of the Prussian forces, alongside the critical mistakes of Napoleon's commanders.

The way in which this sister endured that period of her life, and the broad impact she has had on the church in that country, have been wonderful examples to others, including me. After leaving the venue where I had been teaching, I was profoundly encouraged and emboldened in my own faith, having been around this sister and others like her. Their boldness was infectious.

Such boldness comes, in part, as we see God redeeming our difficulties for the sake of the gospel. Thus we next *learn to see opposition as opportunity*. One of the striking dynamics in Philippians 1:12–18g has to do with Paul's upside-down perspective on the opposition he is experiencing. While most of us would focus on setback and on the threat of serious personal harm, Paul sees opportunity. Of course, one of the key interpretive questions about our passage has to do with the nature of this opposition. But it is clear that those opposing Paul were up to no good. His mild response to their threat has puzzled commentators, but his inverted values, seeing the good opportunity for the gospel as key, clarify his words at this point.

It may seem odd that public attacks on Paul and his ministry could be a vehicle for the spread of the gospel—the proclamation of Christ. Yet consider an analogous, modern example. The ministry One for Israel, located in Netanya, Israel, reaches out to millions of Jews and Arabs in the Middle East with the message of the gospel—a message of love, hope, and reconciliation. I have taught numerous times at the college associated with the ministry and know these brothers and sisters are deeply devoted followers of Christ. They are irenic in tone, sacrificial in service to the people of Israel, and theologically sound. Their media outreach is creative, excellent, and has been very effective.

Several years ago, one of the ultraorthodox, anti-missionary groups in the country became alarmed at the success of this ministry. They made public announcements attacking One for Israel, telling their followers, "Stay away from the Christian ministry's website!" They spoke publicly about Jesus and the Christian message of the gospel, attacking both and even threatening harm to those involved in the broadcast videos. What happened? Hits on the website soared! The public attacks had the opposite effect than that intended by the opponents, exposing thousands of people to One for Israel's ministry and the gospel. The public attacks on the Christian faith actually caused the spread of the message, and the opponents of the followers of Christ ironically served as an effective vehicle for the gospel's dissemination.

CHAPTER 4

# Philippians 1:18h–26

## Literary Context

Philippians 1:18h–26 constitutes the second and final movement of 1:12–26, the "body opening" of Philippians, which builds on the letter's prescript and joyful prayer report found in 1:1–11. In the body opening's first movement (1:12–18g), the apostle offers an enthusiastic perspective on his imprisonment, since he understands his circumstances to have worked for the advance of the gospel. Paul is under arrest, but the gospel is not arrested. Rather, the message about Christ has spread by virtue of the apostle's close proximity to the praetorian guard and perhaps others in Caesar's household (1:12–13; 4:22). Further, the brothers and sisters in the church have been greatly encouraged by witnessing Paul's response in his current circumstances and have been emboldened to preach the gospel without flinching (1:14). The apostle can even rejoice about opponents who speak publicly about Christ in order to do Paul harm, for at least Christ is being discussed in the public square (vv. 15–18g)! Thus, the whole of 1:12–18g offers a perspective-enhancing reflection on the ways in which God had redeemed an apparent setback for the Pauline mission.

In 1:18h–26, the apostle expands on his "posture of joy," expressing confidence that his imprisonment will result in his deliverance. He is also hopeful that he will not be shamed but will magnify Christ, whether through life or death (vv. 18h–20). In a sense, Paul's life hangs in the balance between continued ministry in the earthly body and a homegoing to Christ—with Paul clearly preferring the latter option (vv. 21–23). Yet, convinced that the more urgent need is to stay for the sake of the Philippians, the apostle expects that he will remain in his earthly ministry for the time being. Thus, as a result of his presence among them, he is convinced that the Philippians will make progress and know joy in the faith. This happy state, in turn, will result in an overflow of the godly pride they have in Jesus (vv. 24–26).

Once the body opening draws to a close with verse 26, Paul gets down to business with perhaps the letter's main theme—the unity of the church. Thus, in 1:27–2:4 the apostle repeatedly reiterates the need for the Philippian believers to be "one" (1:27; 2:2) or to be the "same" (2:2) in the way that they think, and especially in the unity of their community. This is one very important aspect of their "progress" in the faith, mentioned in verse 25. As Paul faces opposition, so the Philippians face opposition (vv. 29–30), but they can face it well as they stand together.

I. The Letter Opening: A Prescript and a Prayer Report (1:1–11)

**II. The Letter Body (1:12–4:9)**

- A. The Body Opening: Paul's Current Situation (1:12–26)
  - 1. A Joyful Report on the Progress of the Gospel (1:12–18g)
  - ➡ **2. Paul's Hopeful Expectation concerning His Imprisonment (1:18h–26)**
- B. The Main Body of the Letter: A Call for Unity in the Church (1:27–4:4a)
- C. The Body Closing: Exhortations (4:4b–9)

III. The Letter Closing (4:10–23)

## Main Idea

Paul is confident that, whether he is killed and goes to be with Christ or continues his ministry in his earthly body, the outcome will be good. Although he seems to hesitate in choosing which he prefers, the apostle thinks that staying and continuing his ministry to the Philippians—the form of "deliverance" he anticipates—constitutes the more urgent need and ultimately will result in the Philippians' spiritual growth.

## Translation

### Philippians 1:18h–26

| | | |
|---|---|---|
| 18h | Reiteration | Indeed |
| i | Declaration | **I will rejoice,** |
| 19a | Basis | for **I am confident** |
| b | Content | that for me |
| c | | this situation will result |
| d | Result | in deliverance |
| e | Means | through your urgent requests and |
| f | Means 2 | the provision of the Spirit of Jesus Christ, |

*Continued on next page.*

| | | |
|---|---|---|
| 20a | Accordance/Content 1 | in accordance with my eager expectation and |
| b | Content 2 | hope that I will not be shamed in any way but |
| c | Posture | with absolute boldness, |
| d | Time | even now as always, |
| e | Contrast (w. 20b) | will magnify Christ |
| f | Sphere | in my body, |
| g | Means | whether through life or |
| h | Contrast | through death. |
| 21a | Explanation | For |
| b | Reference | as far as I am concerned |
| c | Declaration | **to live is Christ** |
| d | | and |
| e | Alternative (sequence) | **to die is gain.** |
| 22a | Developmental conj. | Now |
| b | Condition | if I continue to live in a physical body, |
| c | Result | **this would mean for me fruit produced by the ongoing work.** |
| d | | And |
| e | Rhetorical Question | **which will I choose?** |
| | Confession 1 | **I don't know!** |
| 23a | Confession 2 | **I am torn** |
| b | | between the two, |
| c | Explanation/Desire | since I desire to depart and |
| d | Location | be with Christ |
| e | Comparison | —the better option by far! |
| 24a | Concession | Yet, |
| b | Action | to persevere in this physical body . . . |
| c | Advantage | for your sakes |
| d | | . . . seems the more urgent need, |
| 25a | | and |
| b | Basis | believing this to be the case, |
| c | Anticipation | **I am confident that I will remain and** |
| d | | **continue** |
| e | Association | with all of you |
| f | Result/Advantage 1 | for your progress and |
| g | Advantage 2 | joy |
| h | | in the faith |

| | | |
|---|---|---|
| 26a | Purpose | so that your pride in Christ Jesus might overflow |
| b | Cause | on account of your relationship with me |
| c | Means | through me being among you |
| d | Time | once again. |

## Structure

The passage contains two main movements, 1:18h–20 and 1:21–26. The first focuses on Paul's joyful confidence and makes a transition from the previous unit with "indeed" (ἀλλὰ καί). Now his joy is anticipatory, expressed as the apostle looks forward to his deliverance in the future. The remainder of this movement (vv. 19–20) is explanatory (γάρ). He tells his readers that this deliverance will come through their prayers and the help of Jesus Christ's Spirit, and that this deliverance will align with his eager expectation and hope that he will not be shamed but will "magnify Christ." As shown in the translation diagram, the phrases and clauses that make up 1:18h–20 are laid out with a cascade of subordinate clauses (called *hypotaxis*), a common feature of Paul's style.

By contrast, the second subunit primarily builds around coordinate, independent clauses (i.e., *parataxis*) that focus on the contrast between continuing to live for Christ in this world and experiencing the "gain" of dying and being with Christ. Verse 21 states this contrast; verses 22–23b express Paul's conundrum and uncertainty as he considers the two possibilities. This conundrum is expounded briefly in verses 23c–24, as the apostle sets his desire to be with Christ over against the Philippians' need for him to continue in ministry to them. The passage concludes in verses 25–26 with a string of subordinate phrases and clauses. Paul is convinced that he will "remain" and "continue" with the Philippians ("with all of you"), that the result will be their "progress and joy," and that his ministry will be for a particular purpose: "so that [their] pride in Christ Jesus might overflow."

Thus, the whole of 1:18h–26 begins with a statement of confidence, moves to the uncertainty of a rhetorically presented conundrum, and concludes with a statement of certainty, forming an A-B-A pattern.

## Exegetical Outline

➦ 2. **Paul's Hopeful Expectation concerning His Imprisonment (1:18h–26)**
- **a. Confidence in the Outcome (vv. 18h–20)**
  - (1) The Situation Will Result in Deliverance for Him
  - (2) Deliverance Will Come Through:
    - a) The Prayers of the Philippians and
    - b) The Help of Jesus Christ's Spirit
  - (3) The Deliverance Will Be in Line with Paul's Eager Expectation and Hope
    - a) That He Will Not Be Shamed in Any Way but Rather
    - b) That He Will Magnify Christ
      - i) with absolute boldness
      - ii) even now, as always
      - iii) in Paul's body
      - iv) whether through life or death
- **b. Two Good Alternatives: Life or Death (vv. 21–24)**
  - (1) Paul's Perspective
    - a) To Live Is Christ
    - b) To Die Is Gain
  - (2) The Conundrum: The Choice Is Difficult
    - a) Living Would Mean Fruitful Work
    - b) Leaving and Being with Christ Is Preferred!
    - c) Staying and Ministering to the Philippians Seems the More Urgent Need
- **c. Paul Is Confident That He Will Live On to Fulfill His Ministry (vv. 25–26)**
  - (1) He Believes the Philippians Need Him to Continue His Ministry to Them
  - (2) The Result Will Be Their Progress and Joy in the Faith
  - (3) The Intended Outcome Is So That Their Pride in Christ Jesus Might Overflow

## Explanation of the Text

**1:18h–19 Indeed I will rejoice, for I am confident that for me this situation will result in deliverance through your urgent requests and the provision of the Spirit of Jesus Christ** (ἀλλὰ καὶ χαρήσομαι, 16 οἶδα γὰρ ὅτι τοῦτό μοι ἀποβήσεται εἰς σωτηρίαν διὰ τῆς ὑμῶν δεήσεως καὶ ἐπιχορηγίας τοῦ πνεύματος Ἰησοῦ Χριστοῦ). In 1:18h–19 Paul expresses joyful confidence that he will be delivered from his imprisonment, believing that his release will be the work of the Spirit in tandem with the Philippians' prayers. The paired Greek conjunctions translated as "indeed" (αλλὰ καί) are progressive,[1]

1. And perhaps ascensive, as with our translation ("indeed"). Denniston and Dover, *Greek Particles*, 21. In Paul the construction is most commonly found in a "not only ... but also" (οὐ μόνον ... ἀλλὰ καί) construction, as at 2:27.

building on the apostle's first exclamation of joy in verse 18. With the future form of the verb for "rejoice" (χαρήσομαι), Paul repeats—almost in the same breath—the note on which he ended the previous unit, crafting a beautifully smooth "hook-word"[2] transition. Of course, "joy" stands as one of the book's most important themes. As noted in the commentary's introduction, the apostle also uses this "joy" motif at key transition points in the structure of Philippians (1:18; 2:17–18, 28; 3:1; 4:4, 10),[3] "coming up for air" in the onward romp of his letter and refocusing the hearers' attention Godward, exhorting them to a posture of joy. At 1:18h–19, the change in that posture is from a joy experienced in the apostle's present circumstances to an anticipation of joy in his future deliverance, as we see in the explanation (γάρ) that follows.

Paul most often uses the word translated as "I am confident" (οἶδα) to speak of understanding some aspect of theology,[4] but also of having knowledge about some event or situation (e.g., 1 Cor 1:16; 16:15; Col 2:1; 1 Thess 2:1, 5, 11; 3:4). Here we have a much less common use of the word, as the apostle speaks of "being confident" that something in the future will take place (see Rom 15:29; Phlm 21). Here the word has a sense similar to the Greek term πείθω ("I am persuaded, convinced, trust"), and Paul at times pairs these two terms (Rom 14:14; 2 Cor 5:11; Phil 1:25; 2 Tim 1:12; Phlm 21).

Particularly, he is confident that[5] his incarceration "will result in deliverance" (ἀποβήσεται εἰς σωτηρίαν). The verb rendered "will result in" (ἀποβαίνω) could mean "to depart" or "get out," but it here speaks figuratively of action leading to a particular "state or condition,"[6] and the condition in mind is freedom. The Greek word we commonly translate as "salvation" (σωτηρία, along with its cognate forms) has broad secular usage in literature of the Greco-Roman world. For instance, it can refer to deliverance from slavery (e.g., Acts 7:25), from death (e.g., 27:34), or from the hand of an enemy.[7] The term σωτηρία can also be used to speak of "deliverance" from imprisonment, as it does here.[8] Paul takes this part of the verse directly from Job 13:16 LXX, which speaks of vindication and deliverance from present, horrible circumstances. Paul in essence says he is confident that ultimately the outcome of his imprisonment will be his "deliverance" (εἰς σωτηρίαν),[9] most immediately a change from incarceration to liberation.[10]

For Paul, his release from prison will take place through (διά) both the prayers of the Philippians[11] and "the provision of the Spirit of Jesus Christ."[12] Thus both their "urgent requests" (τῆς ὑμῶν

2. With this type of transition, the same word or words are used at the end of one unit and the beginning of the next, thus stitching the two units together. For more on "hook words" as a transition device, see Guthrie, *Structure of Hebrews*, 12, 98, 102.

3. See the introduction, pp. 33–35.

4. E.g., Rom 2:2; 3:19; 5:3; 6:9, 16; 1 Cor 3:16; 5:6; 6:2–3, 9, 15–16, 19.

5. A "content" use of "that" (ὅτι), as the conjunction introduces that about which the apostle expresses confidence.

6. BDAG 107.

7. E.g., Plutarch, *Reg. imp. apophth.* 39.6; 72.2; *Sert.* 15.1; *Comp. Pel. Marc.* 3.1; Polybius, *Hist.* 11.9; Josephus, *Ant.* 2.331. For more on the topic, and some of the term's antonyms, see Guthrie, *2 Corinthians*, 171.

8. Certainly some scholars see broader, eschatological overtones in Paul's declaration, but the immediate context suggests he has release from incarceration in mind. Most notably, Paul would not see the prayers of the Philippians, mentioned in the next breath, as contributing toward his eschatological salvation, which does not seem to fit the immediate context. For the view that Paul speaks of eschatological salvation see, e.g., Bockmuehl, *Philippians*, 83. Cousar understands the referent as vindication rather than either deliverance or eschatological salvation. See Cousar, *Philippians and Philemon*, 38.

9. Also, μοι can be read as a dative of advantage, "for me."

10. The preposition εἰς + the accusative here marks a change from one state to another.

11. Here διά + the genitive functions as a marker of instrumentality—that by which something is brought about.

12. As Fee points out, here we have two nouns that serve as compound objects of the preposition δία, both introduced by a single article. Consequently, the prayers of the Philippians

δεήσεως) to God on Paul's behalf and the "provision of the Spirit of Jesus Christ" (ἐπιχορηγίας τοῦ πνεύματος Ἰησοῦ Χριστοῦ) play an important role in the apostle's deliverance. Paul has already mentioned his constant prayers *for* the Philippians (1:4), and he even caps off his letter opening with a moving, life-shaping prayer for these friends in Macedonia (vv. 9–11). But the partnership in prayer should move both ways. Later at 4:6 Paul exhorts the Philippians to be characterized by prayer and urgent requests to God (τῇ προσευχῇ καὶ τῇ δεήσει) rather than anxiety. They should be praying people, and he is confident that their prayers will result in his release from prison.

The word "provision" (ἐπιχορηγία) is found in the New Testament only here and at Ephesians 4:16;[13] it refers to something given, or supplied, or offered in support. The verb form of this word is more common (ἐπιχορηγέω; 2 Cor 9:10; Gal 3:5; Col 2:19; 2 Pet 1:5, 11) and speaks of giving something as a gift, supplying or furnishing what is needed, or providing support toward the well-being of another person.[14] If we think of the noun at 1:19 in terms of "provision," we probably are not far off the nuance.

But what provision does Paul have in mind? Some understand the provision as the Holy Spirit himself.[15] The interpretation accords well with Galatians 3:5, where Paul, using similar language, writes, "Does God then give you his Spirit [ὁ οὖν ἐπιχορηγῶν ὑμῖν τὸ πνεῦμα] and work miracles among you by the works of the law, or by your believing what you heard?" (NIV). Nevertheless, Paul's reference to the gift of the Spirit in Galatians 3 has to do with the Galatians' entrance into new-covenant relationship with God, so we do not have an exact fit with our passage.

Here, rather, Paul seems to allude to help by the Spirit, who has been sent from Jesus.[16] Consequently, it seems better to read "of the Spirit" (τοῦ πνεύματος) as speaking about "agency"—that is, the Spirit's help, indeed the Spirit's empowerment (i.e, provision "*by* the Spirit"), in the face of Paul's incarceration and interrogation. Given the context, Paul anticipates this provision by the Spirit in terms of support as he interacts with the Roman authorities (cf. Matt 10:20; Mark 13:11; Luke 12:12). The Spirit will embolden Paul to speak the word of Christ fearlessly, magnifying Christ in the process, which is the theme of verse 20.

**1:20 in accordance with my eager expectation and hope that I will not be shamed in any way but with absolute boldness, even now as always, will magnify Christ in my body, whether through life or through death** (κατὰ τὴν ἀποκαραδοκίαν καὶ ἐλπίδα μου, ὅτι ἐν οὐδενὶ αἰσχυνθήσομαι ἀλλ᾽ ἐν πάσῃ παρρησίᾳ ὡς πάντοτε καὶ νῦν μεγαλυνθήσεται Χριστὸς ἐν τῷ σώματί μου, εἴτε διὰ ζωῆς εἴτε διὰ θανάτου). Paul desires to handle his current crisis well, magnifying Christ, whether through life or death. As the apostle thinks about his release, he has a certain standard in mind concerning his own response to whatever public interrogations or proceedings may come. Unfortunately, the portion at the beginning of the verse, translated here as,

and the "help" of the Spirit are conceived by Paul as intimately related in bringing about the good effect he anticipates. See Fee, *Philippians*, 132n27; Max Zerwick, *Biblical Greek*, trans. Joseph Smith (Rome: Pontifical Biblical Institute, 1963), 59.

13. Where Paul refers to "every ligament of support" (πάσης ἁφῆς τῆς ἐπιχορηγίας) in describing the working of the body of Christ.

14. BDAG 387.

15. As Fee argues, with τοῦ πνεύματος read as an objective genitive. See Fee, *Philippians*, 133–34; Bockmuehl, *Philippians*, 84.

16. That the Spirit is described as "from Jesus Christ" (Ἰησοῦ Χριστοῦ)—a construction used only here in the NT—can be understood to connote "source," as the Spirit is sent from Jesus Christ (e.g., John 16:7).

"in accordance with,"[17] is simply passed over by a number of modern translations (e.g., NLT, NRSV, NIV, CSB, NET). Yet the wording is important. As explained in verse 19, Paul anticipates freedom. But the apostle is not interested in freedom at all costs. He will not buy his release with the currency of cowardice. Rather, he anticipates his freedom being attained "in accordance with" (κατά + the accusative) a particular posture on his part, a posture of "absolute boldness," through which Christ will be magnified.

Paul introduces this posture with "my eager expectation and hope" (τὴν ἀποκαραδοκίαν καὶ ἐλπίδα μου). The first of these nouns occurs only here and at Romans 8:19, where Paul writes of "the eager expectation" (ἡ . . . ἀποκαραδοκία) of the creation "for the children of God to be revealed" (NIV). The related verb (ἀποκαραδοκέω) could be used, for instance, of the intense emotion experienced by a soldier just before the start of a battle (Josephus, *J.W.* 3.264). In our verse, Paul speaks of his eager anticipation of boldly bearing witness to the gospel of the Lord Jesus. This interpretation seems more sure by Paul's addition of "and hope" (καὶ ἐλπίδα). In the present context, "hope" speaks of "looking forward to something with some reason for confidence."[18] When the time comes to be bold in the cause of Christ, Paul will continue his pattern of not flinching, as the remainder of the verse makes clear.

The apostle's bold response is expressed with a content (ὅτι) clause made up of two parts. The first part has to do with shame. The verb for "shame" (αἰσχύνω) could refer either to "being ashamed" of oneself or "being shamed/disgraced" by some person or situation.[19] The apostle expresses hope that he will "not be shamed in anyway [ἐν οὐδενί]"[20] when he has the opportunity to offer a public witness for Christ.

In Greco-Roman society, honor was to be achieved and shame avoided at all costs. Paul speaks of honor and shame against that backdrop, but his perspective has been shaped by knowing Christ, which turns the Greco-Roman value system on its head. What is honored by the world is shameful before God. What is honored by God is shameful before the world. Boldly standing in the shadow of the weak and foolish cross with the crucified and exalted Lord, the apostle eschews the "honor" of the world. He does not fear shame before the powers; he fears being shamed by a failure to speak openly about Christ.[21]

The apostle highlights the contrast with "but" (ἀλλ'). Rather than being shamed, Paul wants to magnify Christ publicly, as has been his pattern of life and ministry to this point (ἐν πάσῃ παρρησίᾳ ὡς πάντοτε καὶ νῦν μεγαλυνθήσεται Χριστός). Thus, the "shame" to be avoided finds its contrast in the phrase "in absolute boldness" (ἐν πάσῃ παρρησίᾳ). Acts has almost the same phrase at 28:31 where Luke records that Paul in Rome "proclaimed the kingdom of God and taught about the Lord Jesus Christ—with all boldness [μετὰ πάσης παρρησίας] and without hindrance" (NIV). In some New Testament uses, this word for boldness refers to "courage" or "confidence," and the nuance fits the current context, offering the antithesis of shame-worthy behavior.

Yet, in both Philippians 1:20 and Acts 28:31 we may see a related, if slightly different, sense,

17. The use of "according to" (κατά) + the accusative ἀποκαραδοκίαν, translated as "eager expectation."

18. BDAG 319–20.

19. E.g., Luke 16:3; 2 Cor 10:8; Phil 1:20; 1 Pet 4:16; 1 John 2:28.

20. More straightforwardly, "I will be shamed in nothing."

21. On honor and shame in Greco-Roman culture, see, e.g., Bruce W. Winter, *Philo and Paul among the Sophists: Alexandrian and Corinthian Responses to a Julio-Claudian Movement* (Grand Rapids: Eerdmans, 2002), 71–72.

παρρησία referring to plain speaking—that is, speaking with an open manner (e.g., Mark 8:32; John 7:4, 13, 26; 10:24; 11:14; 16:29; 2 Cor 3:12). If this is the nuance Paul has in mind, he means that, rather than responding in a public forum in a mealymouthed manner, he wishes to speak frankly, openly proclaiming the truth about Christ and the gospel. Of course, the ideas of "boldness" and "openness" are closely related, so we do not have to draw hard lines between the two. In any case, to speak openly of Christ as Lord, at the very heart of the Roman Empire, would demand a great deal of boldness, but this was nothing new to Paul.

In fact, with the phrase "even now as always" (ὡς πάντοτε καὶ νῦν), the apostle notes that he is characterized by responding courageously to public opportunities for the gospel.[22] Paul has the resolute hope that his posture of fearless proclamation in the current situation will conform to the pattern of life and ministry that has characterized him to this point. As he boldly magnified Christ in Damascus (Acts 9:19b–20), so now. As he publicly exalted Christ at Philippi, singing in the face of persecution (Acts 16), so now. As the apostle, having just been beaten by a mob, stood in the temple complex in Jerusalem, telling a hostile crowd of Christ's in-breaking on the Damascus Road (Acts 21–22), so now.

While the verb translated "will magnify" (μεγαλυνθήσεται)[23] could connote "to cause to make something large or great," here it speaks of causing Christ "to be held in greater esteem through praise or deeds."[24] The biblical use of the word has no true extrabiblical parallels. In the LXX it can be used of a person or a kingdom, which rises in position or power under God's favor.[25] God, his character, or his works may be "magnified" (1 Sam 12:24; Ps 57:10; 69:31); accordingly, Mary uses Old Testament language when she "magnifies the Lord" (Luke 1:46), as do those in Acts who magnify the Lord in other tongues (Acts 10:46).[26] Further, the "name of the Lord Jesus" could be magnified even by the witness of an evil spirit (Acts 19:15–17).

What, then, might it mean for Paul to magnify Christ in his body (ἐν τῷ σώματί μου, Phil 1:20)? At 2 Corinthians 4:7–15 we see the concept unpacked a bit. The apostle understands persecution—physical suffering for the sake of the gospel—to be a normal aspect of his mission. The gospel magnification of Christ before lost people moves forward in a hostile world via vulnerable, "embodied" servants, the "treasure" of the gospel presented in "terra cotta jars."[27] Thus Paul's chains—his suffering of persecution in the cause of Christ—are not a by-product of the ministry; they are systemic to his ministry. He might serve as a living carrier of the Christ-exalting message, or the witness may go forward powerfully and poignantly through his death. Although Paul speaks confidently about his impending deliverance, he does not speak presumptuously. He knows that his identification with Christ may lead to death eventually. So his goal is that "whether through life or through death" (εἴτε διὰ ζωῆς εἴτε διὰ θανάτου)[28] Christ might be exalted.

22. Wallace, *Greek Grammar*, 670–71. The comparative conjunction "as" (ὡς) functions in a correlative relationship with "even" (καί), and the latter should be read as ascensive ("even"), being the point of focus.

23. Technically "Christ" is the subject of this future passive verb ("Christ will be magnified"), but in our translation it is brought over as a first-person active ("I will magnify") for clarity in the English.

24. BDAG 459–60.

25. Gen 12:2; 1 Chr 29:25; 2 Chr 1:1; Sir 45:2; Wis 19:22.

26. *TLNT* 2:459–60.

27. For a more extended treatment, see Guthrie, *2 Corinthians*, 251–67.

28. The construction εἴτε ... εἴτε marks conditional alternatives, life and death, and διά + the genitives communicate means by which the magnification will take place. This contrast

**1:21 For as far as I am concerned, to live is Christ and to die is gain** (ἐμοὶ γὰρ τὸ ζῆν Χριστὸς καὶ τὸ ἀποθανεῖν κέρδος). Paul continues the contrast between life and death, sharing his own perspective—"as far as I am concerned."[29] The "for" (γάρ) itself may be read as leading into an explanation, and Paul seems especially to be playing off of the themes of "life" and "death" in the previous verse. The apostle makes clear why life and death are equally valid alternatives for him. He presents this contrast in beautifully balanced, minimalist language:

| | | | | |
|---|---|---|---|---|
| "to live is Christ" | τὸ | ζῆν | Χριστὸς | καὶ |
| "to die is gain" | τὸ | ἀποθανεῖν | | κέρδος |

Notice the similar sound in the first and last syllables of *Christos* (Χριστός) and *kerdos* (κέρδος). Moreover, the apostle seems to be engaging a play on words here. The Greco-Roman culture of the time had coined a popular motto, ζῆν χρηστός, "life is good." Paul, of course, uses Χριστός, subverting the value system of the broader culture and focusing on Christ rather than "the good life."[30] For him, all of life is centered on the Messiah.

The infinitival clause "to die" (τὸ ἀποθανεῖν), on the other hand, while presenting a sharp contrast, is still proclaimed in the most positive of terms.[31] In short, Christ is the sum of Paul's life and his whole reason for being. Death, as the door to life with Christ, is "gain" (κέρδος), an advantage rather than a loss (see 3:7).[32] Paul unpacks this theme further in chapter 3 (vv. 7–14).

The apostle's view of death stands as a stark contrast to the angst that many ancients experienced when confronted with the subject (and how many moderns feel as well!). Greco-Roman authors such as Cicero, Seneca, and Epictetus speak of the terror with which people consider the inevitable specter. Although holding a different worldview, Philo, a first-century Jewish writer, states, "Nothing is so calculated to enslave the mind as fearing death through desire to live" (*Good Person* 22). Similarly, cultural anthropologist Ernest Becker writes, "The idea of death, the fear of it, haunts the human animal like nothing else; it is a mainspring of human activity—activity designed largely to avoid the fatality of death, to overcome it by denying in some way that it is the final destiny for man."[33] Yet for Paul, both living and dying have positive outcomes. In the impending climax of his incarceration, the apostle faces a win-win situation.

**1:22a–c Now if I continue to live in a physical body, this would mean for me fruit produced by the ongoing work** (εἰ δὲ τὸ ζῆν ἐν σαρκί, τοῦτό μοι καρπὸς ἔργου). As Paul continues[34] to weigh these alternatives in the next two verses, he articulates the advantages of each. First, to continue to live would

of life and death initiates alternating reflections on the two: to live is Christ (1:21a), to die is gain (v. 21b), living in the flesh will mean fruitful labor (v. 22), to depart and be with Christ is better (v. 23), and to remain in the flesh is more necessary (v. 24). See Cousar, *Philippians and Philemon*, 38.

29. Thus, reading ἐμοί as a dative of reference ("with reference to me").

30. Arthur J. Droge and James D. Tabor, *A Noble Death: Suicide and Martyrdom among Christians and Jews in Antiquity* (San Francisco: HarperSanFrancisco, 1992), 121. With thanks to my student, Kylie Guenther, for this insight.

31. Paul sometimes uses a present-tense form of ἀποθνῄσκω, focusing on the ongoing vulnerability of being killed for the cause of Christ (e.g., Rom 14:8; 1 Cor 15:22, 31; 2 Cor 6:9). E.g., at 1 Cor 15:31 he writes, "I face death every day—yes, just as surely as I boast about you in Christ Jesus our Lord" (NIV). Each of these infinitives in v. 21 functions substantivally as the subject of its clause, with the verb "to be" understood in both cases.

32. The noun is taken from the world of commerce, speaking of "profits," but could be used of various advantages and acquisitions. But it took on spiritual connotations as well, as here. See *TLNT* 2:159.

33. Ernest Becker, *The Denial of Death* (New York: Free Press, 1997), xvii.

34. The conjunction δέ is continuative.

be fruitful for the kingdom of Christ. The conjunction translated here as "if" (εἰ)[35] sets up a "cause and effect"[36] possibility. That Paul would "live" (τὸ ζῆν) expresses the first possibility, echoing "to live" in the previous verse. Of course, if the apostle continues to live, it will be "in a physical body" (ἐν σαρκί). He often uses this little phrase—woodenly translated as "in flesh"—to refer to something related to the human body or to aspects of living as an "embodied" human being in the world (Rom 2:28; 2 Cor 10:3; Gal 2:20; 6:12; Eph 2:11; Phil 3:4; Col 2:1; 1 Tim 3:16).[37] The use here corresponds roughly to the phrase "in my body" (ἐν τῷ σώματί μου) in verse 20.

If Paul goes on living, fruitful labor will be the result (τοῦτό μοι καρπὸς ἔργου) as he continues ministering to the Philippians.[38] This offers a compelling reason for the Lord to keep his apostle in the land of the living. The expression combining "fruit" (καρπός) and "work" (ἔργου) could be translated straightforwardly as, "the fruit of work"; but almost all modern English versions translate these words as "fruitful labor" or "fruitful work" (e.g., ESV, CSB, NASB, NLT, NRSV, NIV, NET). Although this is a perfectly good rendering of the Greek text, we should pay attention to the emphasis here on the fruit rather than the work itself, the genitive "of work" (ἔργου) expressing production (i.e., "the fruit produced by work"). In other words, even though it would mean a delay in moving into Christ's presence, Paul embraces the possibility of continuing in his very difficult ministry, since the ongoing work would bear fruit for the kingdom of God.

**1:22d–23 And which will I choose? I don't know! I am torn between the two, since I desire to depart and be with Christ—the better option by far!** (καὶ τί αἱρήσομαι οὐ γνωρίζω. 23 συνέχομαι δὲ ἐκ τῶν δύο, τὴν ἐπιθυμίαν ἔχων εἰς τὸ ἀναλῦσαι καὶ σὺν Χριστῷ εἶναι, πολλῷ [γὰρ] μᾶλλον κρεῖσσον). The final clause of verse 22 continues the apostle's reflection on the "life or death" possibilities before him. Will he continue to live on in the flesh and thus carry out his fruitful work for the kingdom, or will he be killed as a witness to Christ, being released from his mission and stepping into the very presence of Christ?

Paul begins with a rhetorical question, "Which will I choose?" (τί αἱρήσομαι), employing a future form of the verb.[39] This verb (αἱρέω) is fairly rare in biblical literature, used only three times in the New Testament and ten times in the LXX. It universally has to do with the making of a choice, usually God choosing people or people choosing the ways of God.[40] "Which shall I choose?" the apostle asks. He confesses, "I don't know!" (οὐ γνωρίζω), with the verb in this case meaning "to have information

35. In place of εἰ δέ, $\mathfrak{P}^{46}$ and D* have "either/whether" (εἴτε), perhaps under the influence of that form as used in the contrast between life and death at the end of v. 20.

36. Wallace, *Greek Grammar*, 682–83.

37. This is similar to 1 Pet 4:2, which reads, "As a result, they do not live the rest of their earthly lives for evil human desires, but rather for the will of God" (NIV).

38. Again, the verb must be supplied, and "me" (μοι) probably should be understood as a dative of advantage ("for me").

39. Some translations have rendered the verb as communicating preference ("which is better"; "I prefer"; e.g., NLT; NRSV; NET). Various commentators prefer this as well, e.g., Cousar, *Philippians and Philemon*, 37. But this use seems unprecedented in the biblical literature, or at least it is rarely attested (1 Sam 19:1 LXX says that "Jonathan was very much choosing David," which could be understood to mean that Jonathan "preferred" David). There are rhetorical-background reasons to understand it to mean "choose" here, as will become clear below.

40. In the NT, see also 2 Thess 2:13; Heb 11:25. In the LXX see Deut 26:17–18; Josh 24:15; 1 Sam 19:1; 2 Sam 15:15; 2 Macc 11:25; Job 34:4; Isa 38:17; Jer 8:3. Cf. Pss. Sol. 17.21. The verse in Jeremiah specifically speaks of choosing death over life, but in a very different context from Paul's meaning here. Jeremiah deals with those who have abandoned the ways of the Lord and "chosen" destruction.

or be knowledgeable about something."[41] Broadly speaking, Paul most often uses this verb to speak of something being revealed or disclosed,[42] but here, in expressing perplexity, he employs a rhetorical convention discussed below.

The sense of uncertainty continues with the beginning of 1:23: "I am torn between the two" (συνέχομαι δὲ ἐκ τῶν δύο). The word translated here as "I am torn" (συνέχω) boasts a broad semantic range, meaning variously "to hold together," "to shut," "to crowd," "to guard," "to distress or torment" (i.e., emotionally torn), "to occupy someone's attention," "to urge," or "to direct/control."[43] Here the apostle uses the verb with the sense of being emotionally torn between his two options. The prepositional phrase "between the two" (ἐκ τῶν δύο) alludes to those two options, life or death.[44] It is striking that in all of this Paul seems to think he has a choice in the matter of whether he lives or dies, which has led some to conclude that the apostle was pondering suicide.[45] But there is a better way to interpret the passage. As Clayton Croy has pointed out, Paul here uses a common rhetorical device found elsewhere in Greco-Roman literature.[46] Using *dubitatio*, a public speaker—or in Paul's case, a letter-writer—would feign uncertainty concerning two options. This move emotionally pulled the audience into consideration of the options discussed. The options raised, for example, might involve which word would best be applied to a situation the speaker was describing or, as here, which of two outcomes would be preferable.[47]

What might this mean for our interpretation of the passage? It suggests that Paul had already made up his mind that, if the Lord willed him to continue in his ministry and defer his homegoing, he would gladly embrace continued ministry for the sake of the Philippians. This was the more noble, self-sacrificial choice. Accordingly, the apostle models what will be a key value exemplified in the heart of this letter (through the examples of Christ, Timothy, Epaphroditus, and Paul himself): laying aside one's own advantage for the sake of others. So Paul did not really have a choice as to whether he would live or die—that choice rested in the hands of God. But the apostle could choose to submit to God's will, embracing either life or death.

Clearly Paul desired "to depart and be with Christ" (εἰς τὸ ἀναλῦσαι καὶ σὺν[48] Χριστῷ εἶναι), which he describes as "the better option by far" (πολλῷ [γὰρ] μᾶλλον κρεῖσσον).[49] The word translated "to depart" (ἀναλύω) can be used literally

41. Although see the discussion in Bockmuehl, *Philippians*, 90, who renders the verb, "I cannot say," since γνωρίζω most often means "to make known" or "disclose."

42. Used twenty-five times in the NT, mostly in Paul's writings (e.g., Rom 9:22–23; 16:26; 1 Cor 12:3; 15:1; 2 Cor 8:1; Gal 1:11; Eph 1:9; 3:3, 5, 10; 6:19, 21; Phil 1:22; 4:6; Col 1:27; 4:7, 9). See BDAG 203. The verb γνωρίζω could also be used with the sense "to cause information to become known: make known, reveal," which is the first sense listed by BDAG.

43. BDAG 970–71.

44. The preposition ἐκ used with the genitive is like a partitive genitive, here meaning "between the two" or "one of the two."

45. Certainly there is a Greek philosophical tradition dealing with circumstances under which suicide was perceived to be appropriate, as well as some treatment in broader Jewish literature. For the background and interpretation of Phil 1:21–26 as a death wish, see Arthur J. Droge, "Mori Lucrum: Paul and Ancient Theories of Suicide," *NovT* 30 (1988): 264–75, and the survey of the position in Wansink, *Chained*, 97–100.

46. N. Clayton Croy, "'To Die is Gain' (Philippians 1:19–26): Does Paul Contemplate Suicide?," *JBL* 122.3 (2003): 517–531. See, e.g., Quintilian, *Inst.* 9.2.19. The device is known as ἀπορία or διαπόρησις (or in Latin *dubitatio* or *addubitatio*).

47. Croy offers an especially apt parallel to Paul's use here in Isocrates's speech *De pace* 38–39 ("'To Die is Gain,'" 528–29).

48. On not overreading σύν here, see Fee, *Philippians*, 146n33.

49. Fee calls this string of words "a remarkable compounding of superlatives" (*Philippians*, 146n34). There exists a good bit of textual turbulence in this part of the verse. In the $NA^{28}$ the word γάρ, which is explanatory, is supported by $\mathfrak{P}^{46}$ א A B among other strong witnesses and should be retained, however awkward the syntax.

of leaving a place (e.g., Jdt 13:1; 2 Macc 9:1; 12:7; 15:28; 1 Esd 3:3) and consequently was used figuratively of dying (e.g., Socrates, *Ep.* 27).[50] But Paul is "a man under orders" and cannot simply please himself. Consequently, another option—a noble one—must be put forward as the more urgent need.

**1:24–25 Yet, to persevere in this physical body for your sakes seems the more urgent need, and believing this to be the case, I am confident that I will remain and continue with all of you for your progress and joy in the faith** (τὸ δὲ ἐπιμένειν [ἐν] τῇ σαρκὶ ἀναγκαιότερον δι᾽ ὑμᾶς. 25 καὶ τοῦτο πεποιθὼς οἶδα ὅτι μενῶ καὶ παραμενῶ πᾶσιν ὑμῖν εἰς τὴν ὑμῶν προκοπὴν καὶ χαρὰν τῆς πίστεως). The conjunction translated as "yet" (δέ) marks this new development in the argument,[51] as the apostle transitions to focus on the Philippians' situation and how his anticipated freedom will affect their lives. Even though it is not his first choice, Paul believes he will "persevere in this physical body" (τὸ . . . ἐπιμένειν [ἐν][52] τῇ σαρκί) for the sake of this church he loves. In this verse and the next, the apostle uses three closely related verbs: "I persevere" (ἐπιμένω), "I remain" (μένω), and "continue" (παραμένω). The first, used here in verse 24, can mean simply "to remain" or "stay," but it can also connote "to persist," "persevere." Given Paul's context, and his preference to depart, persistence may be an important nuance, especially since he clarifies the verb by the prepositional phrase that follows. As we saw in verse 22, "in this physical body" ([ἐν] τῇ σαρκί) refers to continuing in a human body or living in the world.[53]

Why should Paul persevere, being willing for the Lord to delay his homegoing? He tells the Philippians that to stay "for your sakes seems the more urgent need" (ἀναγκαιότερον δι᾽ ὑμᾶς). "For your sakes" (δι᾽ ὑμᾶς) expresses the cause—the relational motivation driving the apostle. He would stay because his brothers and sisters in Philippi needed him. The term translated here as "more urgent" (ἀναγκαιότερον) is a comparative form of ἀναγκαῖος, an adjective meaning "necessary" or "pressing."[54] For instance, in Greco-Roman literature and the papyri, the term could be used of the demand to repay cash advances, or the pressure to fulfill an obligation of service as "necessary." The word also came to be used of "intimate" friends or relatives who were indispensable ("necessary") for one's personal well-being.[55] The comparative here intensifies the sense of necessity, as Paul describes remaining in the physical body as "more necessary"—that is, "more urgent" for the spiritual well-being of this church.

He continues ("and," καί) by elaborating on this thought with the participial phrase, "believing this to be the case" (τοῦτο πεποιθώς), expressing the apostle's conviction concerning the truth of what he has just written in verse 24. This perfect participle, translated as "believing" (from πείθω) connotes being "so convinced that one puts confidence in something."[56] This confidence is laid before the

50. BDAG 67.

51. Runge suggests that δέ is contrastive only in the sense that it works with a context that has contrast built into it. The function of the conjunction itself is to mark a new development in the argument. See Steven E. Runge, *Discourse Grammar of the Greek New Testament: A Practical Introduction for Teaching and Exegesis* (Peabody, MA: Hendrickson, 2010), 29–32.

52. A number of witnesses, including ℵ A C P Ψ omit ἐν, while 𝔓[46] B D F G K L retain it. So there are strong witnesses on both sides, thus the brackets around this word in the NA[28].

53. See Rom 2:28; 2 Cor 10:3; Gal 2:20; 6:12; Eph 2:11; Phil 3:4; Col 2:1; 1 Tim 3:16.

54. See Acts 13:46; 1 Cor 12:22; 2 Cor 9:5; Phil 2:25; Titus 3:14; Heb 8:3.

55. *TLNT* 1:97–98. Similarly, during a challenging moment in life we might say to someone, "I really *need* you right now."

56. BDAG 791.

Philippians in the words, "I am confident that I will remain and continue with all of you" (οἶδα ὅτι μενῶ καὶ παραμενῶ πᾶσιν ὑμῖν). In this case, as at 1:19, the sense of being "confident" (οἶδα) is roughly synonymous with "believing" (πείθω), meaning to "be convinced" of something, and these two terms are paired elsewhere.[57] So the apostle is convinced that he will "remain and continue with all" those in the Philippian church. The difference between the two cognates, translated as "remain" (μενῶ) and "continue with" (παραμενῶ), is that the first simply refers to Paul's conviction that he will continue living rather than going to be with Christ. The second, as the prefix hints, could be used to refer to remaining *with someone*, in this case the Philippians.

Further, the apostle is convinced that he will continue to be available to the Philippians for (εἰς)[58] the double benefit of their[59] "progress and joy" (προκοπὴν καὶ χαράν)[60] in relation to "the faith."[61] Pointing to the evangelistic impact of his imprisonment, the broader section started with Paul celebrating the "progress of the gospel" (εἰς προκοπὴν τοῦ εὐαγγελίου) in Rome (1:12). He now begins to wrap up 1:12–26 by focusing on the need for the Philippians to make "progress" in the faith, which will be realized through the embodiment of the gospel in their community as they do three things: (1) live their lives in a way that is "worthy of the gospel of Christ" (1:27), (2) become unified in standing boldly for the faith even to the point of suffering (1:27–30), and (3) grow in selfless sacrifice for one another (2:1–4).

Such progress will be accompanied by joy. Paul has crafted the sentence to communicate that "progress" (προκοπήν) and "joy" (χαράν) are profoundly interrelated. The Philippians will know joy as they make "faith-full" progress in following Christ. So whereas the progress of the gospel had come about by Paul's incarceration (1:12), his release will be used for the progress of the Philippians in their Christian lives. Both phases in his ministry advance the kingdom of God.

**1:26 so that through me once again being among you, the pride that you have in your relationship with Christ Jesus might overflow on account of your relationship with me** (ἵνα τὸ καύχημα ὑμῶν περισσεύῃ ἐν Χριστῷ Ἰησοῦ ἐν ἐμοὶ διὰ τῆς ἐμῆς παρουσίας πάλιν πρὸς ὑμᾶς). A result of Paul remaining alive and continuing in his role as apostle to the Philippians will be that their celebration of Christ will spill over when Paul returns to them. The "so that" (ἵνα) communicates the purpose, but also the natural result, of "remain and continue" in the previous verse.[62] The Philippians' celebration of Christ, Paul writes, will be brought about "through me once again being among you" (διὰ τῆς ἐμῆς παρουσίας πάλιν πρὸς ὑμᾶς). If, as we have suggested in the commentary's introduction, the apostle writes from Rome, what we have here constitutes a change of plans, since earlier Paul told

57. See Rom 14:14; 2 Cor 5:11; 2 Tim 1:12; Phlm 21. Thus οἶδα does not speak of "knowing" an aspect of theology, as, e.g., at Rom 2:2; 3:19; 5:3; 6:9, 16; 1 Cor 3:16; 5:6; 6:2–3, 9, 15–16, 19; nor of knowing about some past or current event or situation (e.g., 1 Cor 1:16; 16:15; Col 2:1; 1 Thess 2:1, 5, 11; 3:4). This is a less common use of the word, speaking of confidence concerning something in the future (see Rom 15:29; Phlm 21).

58. The preposition εἰς is probably used here as a "marker of a specific point of reference" (BDAG s.v. εἰς 5).

59. The inclusion of πᾶσιν ("all") with ὑμῖν ("you") may hint at the Philippians' need to address their problem of disunity. So Fee, *Philippians*, 152.

60. The preposition and accusative article relate to both προκοπήν and χαράν, as do the emphatically placed ὑμῶν and the delimiter τῆς πίστεως. Thus "progress" and "joy" are bound together and interrelated.

61. Perhaps τῆς πίστεως is a genitive of reference here.

62. BDAG 475; purpose and result often are nuanced differences in ἵνα clauses in this period.

the Roman believers of his intention to travel on to Spain after his time in Rome (Rom 15:23–28). Yet over time plans can change (see 2 Cor 1:15–17).[63] After an incarceration of two years, it is not difficult to imagine that the apostle felt a need to visit his network of churches again.[64]

One reason for the apostle to return to Philippi was that their "pride" (τὸ καύχημα ὑμῶν) in their "relationship with Christ Jesus might overflow" (περισσεύῃ ἐν Χριστῷ Ἰησοῦ). Paul uses this word for "pride" (καύχημα) several times in his writings,[65] and closely related words another forty-five times.[66] So the apostle considers what one "takes pride in," or "boasts" in, an important consideration for followers of Jesus. Used positively, this noun somewhat parallels a modern English speaker saying, "He is my *pride* and joy!"

In our modern, Western context, we have a more difficult time with the English word "boast," since boasting is considered unsavory behavior. Yet in both the broader Greco-Roman world and in the Judaism of the day, a person's "boast" could be viewed negatively or, as here, very positively. The background of the verse before us lies in the Old Testament, where celebrating the Lord and his work may be an act of witness and worship. Elsewhere the apostle makes a sharp distinction between "boasting" in human abilities and accomplishments and "boasting in the Lord" (e.g., 2 Cor 10:12–18). Furthermore, Paul writes a great deal about the "overflow" or "abundance" of things when the Lord is involved,[67] and Paul anticipates that, with his arrival (ἐν ἐμοί),[68] the appropriate pride the Philippians have in their relationship[69] with Christ will "overflow" (περισσεύῃ), spilling out onto the streets of Philippi.

## Theology in Application

### *To Live Is Christ*

Doug Hindmarsh, the father of my friend and colleague Bruce Hindmarsh, recently went to be with the Lord, now knowing the "gain" mentioned in Philippians 1:21. I did not know Doug, but I was moved by Bruce's eulogy for his dad, which paints a picture of a very *good* man. The recounting of his life's story challenged me, making me want to be better, to be more focused on the things that really matter in life. Doug was a business executive as well as a Christian leader and statesman. He loved his family, loved the church, and supported many Christian ministries.

63. On which, see Guthrie, *2 Corinthians*, 104–5.

64. So Bockmuehl, *Philippians*, 95.

65. Rom 4:2; 1 Cor 5:6; 9:15–16; 2 Cor 1:14; 5:12; 9:3; Gal 6:4; Phil 1:26; 2:16.

66. "Boasting" (καύχησις) ten times (Rom 3:27; 15:17; 1 Cor 15:31; 2 Cor 1:12; 7:4, 14; 8:24; 11:10, 17; 1 Thess 2:19); the verb "I boast, take pride in" (καυχάομαι) thirty-five times (e.g., Rom 2:17, 23; 1 Cor 1:29, 31; 3:21; 2 Cor 5:12; 7:14; Gal 6:13–14; Eph 2:9; Phil 3:3).

67. E.g., 2 Cor 1:5; 3:9; 4:15; 8:2, 7; 9:8, 12; Eph 1:8; Phil 1:9, 26; 4:12, 18; Col 2:7; 1 Thess 3:12; 4:1, 10.

68. This rendering understands "through" (ἐν) to connote cause, but this is only a nuanced difference from "agency" or "association" (i.e., "in connection with") or "relationship."

69. "In Christ Jesus" (ἐν Χριστῷ Ἰησοῦ) is interpreted here as communicating relationship. For this rich phrase in Philippians and interpretations of its use, see Campbell, *Paul and Union with Christ*, 99, 101, 104, 111, 370.

Yet, above all, Doug Hindmarsh loved Christ himself and was known as a person of consummate integrity whose life was given entirely to the service of Christ.

Bruce's cousin Stan recalls how he "came to a realization that Uncle Doug had somehow managed to live his life as one package—not divided," and Bruce writes that his dad "was the same loving Christian man of character and integrity wherever he was: at work, at home, on the road, at church, or wherever." Such integrity, such *integration* of the various strands of one's life, ultimately stems from life being about one thing: "To live is Christ." Doug taught Bruce, now professor of spiritual theology and history of Christianity at Regent College, the practice of what he called "'spiritual breathing'—that it should be as natural as breathing in and out, to experience the presence of God every moment." To live is Christ.

In the final years of his life, Doug faced a steady decline in health. One year before his death, Bruce took his dad for a radiation treatment. They went together into the treatment room at the hospital. The staff prepped Doug, placed him on the sliding table, and prepared his body to be radiated. When the treatment was finished and they were driving home, Bruce quietly asked his dad what he felt like God was teaching him in that season of his life. Bruce writes, "He said that as he lay there on the treatment table inside the rotating machines, he just kept praying under his breath, 'Every cell of my body belongs to you, Lord Jesus. Every cell of my body belongs to you.'" To live is Christ.

### *Boldness, Shame, and Magnifying Christ*

In the best sense of the word, public "pride," expressed in boldness, reflects very greatly on our values. A man who publicly celebrates his wife's gifts and virtues reflects how much he values her. On the other hand, shame marks that which we value the least, whether something about ourselves or something we find reprehensible in others. Paul was bold in his witness for Christ because he valued him more than anything and wanted Christ magnified before the world. It was not merely obligation but rather a manifestation of his deepest heart commitments. Those who shame Christ by shrinking before cultural forces, embracing the values of the culture for self-preservation or promotion, also reflect their deepest heart commitments to self rather than the Savior.

A while back in Nazareth, Israel, I taught a course on Hebrews to about thirty Christian pastors, half of them Jewish and half of them Arab. It was one of the richest experiences I have had in my ministry of teaching. One evening, one of the Arab brothers, who was from Nazareth, suggested that he give me a walking tour of the city. As we were leaving the hotel, three of the Jewish brothers asked if they could tag along. So, at about 9:00 in the evening, we went strolling through the alleys of Nazareth and made our way down to the Basilica of the Annunciation, the traditional site of the home in which Jesus grew up. As we came to the basilica, two older Arab men were coming up the street with a younger woman. One of the men, who informed us that he worked as a tour guide, introduced us to his grown daughter and proceeded to give us an impromptu history of the basilica, a wonderful presentation.

When the tour guide had finished, the other man, more from curiosity than animosity, asked my Arab brother, "You are an Arab, and these other guys are Jewish (I don't think he knew what to make of me); what is that all about?" Without any hesitation, all four of my friends enthusiastically proclaimed, "We are followers of Yeshua (Jesus)!" They explained that they are unified and brothers because of Jesus and his gospel! They were *bold*, and it was a boldness born of deep love and conviction, their simple impulse to magnify Christ. The apostolic witness to the living Christ, when embraced by true followers of Jesus, has the same fruit today.

## *Sacrificial Leadership and Discerning the Most Urgent Needs*

One of the touchstones of Philippians is sacrificial leadership, and Paul manifests this character strength in his willingness to delay his homegoing for the sake of his friends in Philippi. He assesses the need and sets his priorities accordingly. Recently I encountered this spirit in the person of Eric Liddell in an excellent biography written by Duncan Hamilton titled *For the Glory: Eric Liddell's Journey from Olympic Champion to Modern Martyr*.[70] Many people know about Liddell's Olympic triumph through the movie *Chariots of Fire*. Although I still love that movie even with its use of historical license, the fuller story of Liddell's life adds a depth and breadth and weight to his Christian commitment that the movie only begins to touch. Liddell turned his back on what almost certainly would have been increasing fame, high social status, and prosperity to serve those who needed him in a land he loved, halfway around the world.

At one agonizing point in his story, during Japan's WWII invasion of China, Eric is called upon by his mission organization to leave his family in the Chinese city where they lived and head to the dangerous, embattled, and resource-impoverished Shandong province. There Liddell would eventually be captured, interned in a camp for Westerners, and die of a brain tumor. Yet the depth of his commitment to Christ and his consistent, sacrificial service to everyone around him—even through long, harsh months of suffering—almost defy belief. What drove him? Need. He went to Shandong because the people needed him. After the war, many of his fellow prisoners bore witness to Liddell's posture of servanthood; he was widely known as resolutely

70. Duncan Hamilton, *For the Glory: Eric Liddell's Journey from Olympic Champion to Modern Martyr* (New York: Penguin, 2016).

focused on the needs of others, time and again stepping in to serve, often at great cost to himself. He discerned the urgent needs around him and acted accordingly.

Of course, need does not always constitute a call. Many a pastor's family has been wrecked on such an understanding. But at times, huge crossroads loom in front of us, and we are confronted with aching needs. Praise God for those who sacrifice comfort and status, fame and fortune, to meet the needs of Christ's church.

CHAPTER 5

# Philippians 1:27–2:4

## Literary Context

As noted above, the body opening comes to an end with verse 26, as the apostle now shifts from personal narrative to exhortation.[1] In that opening, Paul has given the Philippians a joy-filled report on his situation and the progress of the gospel (1:12–18g), and he has expressed his hopeful expectation that things would lead to his deliverance (vv. 18h–26). Now, with 1:27–2:4 the apostle turns to the letter's main theme—the unity of the church—and this unit functions as a hinge between the body opening and the main body of the letter. Paul picks up on the theme of "joy" amid persecution—already on such clear display in the letter—and points out that his joy will be made "complete" (2:2) as the Philippians live in unity.

Philippians 1:27–2:4 consists of two sub-movements (1:27–30; 2:1–4), Paul reiterating the need for the Philippian believers to be "one" as they struggle together for the gospel (1:27), to be "like-minded," loving each other in unity, embodying solidarity of community, and "sharing a common perspective" (2:2). They also are unified with their apostle as he and they stand firm in the face of opposition (1:29–30), but they can only face that opposition well as they live by the enablement of the Holy Spirit (v. 27) and in unity with one another.

What follows 1:27–2:4, spanning the rest of chapter 2 and 3:1–14, is primarily a series of examples: Christ (the preeminent example), Timothy and Epaphroditus, and Paul each offer a strong model of sacrificial, humble leadership that the Philippians should follow in their pursuit of unity. This heart of the letter body is then rounded off with 3:15–4:4a, which, as detailed in our introduction to the commentary, contains no fewer than seventeen lexical and conceptual echoes of 1:27–2:4, forming an *inclusio* around the book's center section.[2]

1. Fee, *Philippians*, 156.

2. For the specific parallels, see the introduction, pp. 32–33. On the use of *inclusio* as a structuring device see Guthrie, *Structure of Hebrews*, 15; Parunak, "Oral Typesetting," 153–68.

## Main Idea

Paul offers an introductory exhortation for the letter's main body, focused on building unity in the church, which is lived out in the face of opposition and built on the foundation of the Spirit's power and self-sacrificial love.

## Translation

### Philippians 1:27–2:4

| | | |
|---|---|---|
| 27a | Focus | Make this your focus: |
| b | Exhortation | **Live out your heavenly citizenship in a manner worthy of the gospel of Christ,** |
| c | Purpose | so that . . . |
| d | Possible Occur. | whether I come and see you or |
| e | Alternate Possib. | remain absent, |
| f | Hope/General | . . . I might hear about what is happening with you, particularly |
| g | Hope/Specific | that you are standing firm |
| h | Manner | in one Spirit, |
| i | Manner | harmoniously |
| j | Action/Means | striving together |
| k | Advantage | for the gospel faith, |

*Continued on next page.*

| | | | |
|---|---|---|---|
| 28a | Posture/Manner | | without being frightened |
| b | Degree | | in any way |
| c | Agency | | by those standing against you, |
| d | Evaluation/Infer. | | which is a sign |
| e | Recipient | | for them |
| f | Attribute | | of destruction but |
| g | Contrast | | of your salvation, and |
| f | Assertion | | this [is] from God. |
| 29a | | | Because |
| b | Advantage | | for Christ's sake |
| c | Basis (of 28f) | | you have been granted not only |
| d | Content | | to trust him but also |
| e | Expansion | | to suffer |
| f | Advantage | | on his behalf, |
| 30a | Circumst. | | experiencing |
| b | Description | | the same struggle |
| c | Indentification | | that you saw I had and now |
| d | | | hear that I have. |
| 1a | Inference | Consequently, | |
| b | Cause List | if there is | any encouragement in your relationship with Christ, |
| c | (1b–e) | if | any cheering up prompted by love, |
| d | | if | any participation stemming from the Spirit, |
| e | | if | any affection and compassion, |
| 2a | Exhortation | **complete my joy** | |
| b | Means List | in this way: | by being like-minded, |
| c | (2b–e) | | embracing a common love, |
| d | | | having solidarity, |
| e | | | sharing a common perspective, |
| 3a | Contrast | | not acting out of selfishness or |
| b | Alternate | | an elevated opinion of yourselves, but |
| c | Manner | | with humility, |
| d | Contrast (3a–b) | | thinking of others as more significant than you are, |
| 4a | Expansion | | each and every one of you focused |
| b | Object | | not on your own concerns but |
| c | Contrasting Object | | on the concerns of others. |

## Structure

Although it is possible to read 1:27–30 and 2:1–4 as separate units, the two function interrelatedly to a single purpose: to exhort the Philippians to unity, each approaching its hortatory task in its own way. Further, in considering the grammatical structure of 1:27–30 and 2:1–4, each unit is crafted around a single main clause.

At the heart of 1:27–30 we read, "Live out your heavenly citizenship in a manner worthy of the gospel of Christ" (v. 27). The main verb, having to do with "citizenship" (πολιτεύεσθε), anchors the clause in the manner of life that Paul wants the Philippians to follow, particularly that they would live a pattern of life that is worthy of their heavenly citizenship. The clause is flanked with "only," or "make this your focus" (μόνον), which introduces it, and a purpose clause offering the reason Paul wants them to live in this way. Namely, he wants to hear that they are standing firm in unity for the faith. The purpose clause ("so that," ἵνα) is also flanked on either side—Paul's circumstances, "whether I come and see you or remain absent," preceding it, and the balance of verses 27–30 unpacking it. In reality, the whole of verses 27–30 stands as one sentence in Greek, even though English translations break it up into two or more sentences for readability (e.g., ESV, CSB, NET, NIV). Further, there is some question about where the "this from God" (τοῦτο ἀπὸ θεοῦ) at the end of verse 28 fits in relation to the rest of the passage. To what exactly is Paul referring with "this" (τοῦτο)? Is it the "sign" earlier in verse 28? Or is it the content of the whole purpose clause to this point, especially the Philippians' act of "standing firm"? Is that the sign? What is clear is that the whole of verses 27–30 centers on the exhortation of verse 27 and flows from it.

Philippians 2:1–4 develops differently. The inferential conjunction translated "therefore" (οὖν) first connects 1:27–30 to a series of causal clauses in 2:1. At the heart of 2:1–4 stands the exhortation in 2:2, "complete my joy." The apostle then develops this exhortation to joy by explaining how the Philippians might do just that.

## Exegetical Outline

➦ 1. **An Exhortation to Live Out the Unity of Community (1:27–2:4)**
   a. **Stand Firm in Unity (1:27)**
      (1) Whether Paul Is Present or Absent
      (2) In One Spirit, with One Mind
      (3) Struggling Together in a Common Cause
   b. **Stand in Unity in the Face of Opposition (1:28–30)**
      (1) Don't Be Frightened by the Opposition
      (2) This Is a Sign
         (a) of Destruction for the Opponents
         (b) of Your Salvation
      (3) Suffering Is a Gift from God
   c. **Live in Unity by Self-Sacrificial Love for One Another (2:1–4)**
      (1) We Have Wonderful Resources in Christ
      (2) Be Unified in Every Way
      (3) Live Out Unity through Humility

## Explanation of the Text

**1:27a–b Make this your focus: Live out your heavenly citizenship in a manner worthy of the gospel of Christ** (Μόνον ἀξίως τοῦ εὐαγγελίου τοῦ Χριστοῦ πολιτεύεσθε). At the end of the body opening (1:12–26), Paul confesses his confidence that the Lord will allow him to stay alive so that he might continue his ministry to the Philippians. His presence among them would strengthen these brothers and sisters in the faith; they would make progress in, know the joy of, and experience pride in their relationship with Christ (vv. 24–26). He now draws into sharp focus what the Philippians should be about as a community, whether he is in Philippi or not. The apostle challenges the Philippians to live out their heavenly citizenship in a manner worthy of the gospel.

So, as he now turns from his circumstances to a very particular need the Philippians have, Paul draws that need into sharp focus with the word translated expansively with, "Make this your focus" ("only," μόνον). Here the term points to what one should seek out most particularly, marking a turn in the discourse,[3] as Paul in effect says, "Now give special attention to this!"[4]

With a forceful exhortation the apostle rivets the Philippians' attention: "Live out your heavenly

3. Reed, *Discourse Analysis*, 266.

4. In his homily 5 on Philippians, John Chrysostom explains μόνον as "the thing sought" (τὸ ζητούμενον μόνον). See Pauline Allen, ed., *John Chrysostom, Homilies on Philippians*, Writings from the Greco-Roman World (Atlanta: Society of Biblical Literature, 2013), 85. Pointing to Karl Barth's "lifted like a warning finger" (Barth, *Epistle to the Philippians*, 45), Bockmuehl writes of Paul, "One can imagine him pacing about and raising his index finger to make this point!" (Bockmuehl, *Philippians*, 97).

citizenship in a manner worthy of the gospel of Christ" (ἀξίως τοῦ εὐαγγελίου τοῦ Χριστοῦ πολιτεύεσθε). Positioned at the end of this clause, the present imperative verb, translated "live out your heavenly citizenship" (πολιτεύεσθε), has garnered a good deal of attention. Several versions render the verb along the lines of "conduct yourselves" or "live your lives" (e.g., ESV, CSB, Message, NIV, NET). Yet when exhorting his readers to a general pattern of living,[5] the apostle is most fond of the word picture of "walking."[6] So, why the focus on "living as a citizen" here?[7]

Philippi was a Roman colony, which gave it legal status in the empire, and citizens of the city would have celebrated that status. Thus, the verb can be read here with the sense of discharging one's duties or obligations as a citizen. Given Paul's emphasis on unity in Philippians, it is significant that in inscriptions of the era, the word often was associated with "harmony" as a social virtue.[8] Some have taken the admonition literally to mean "live as citizens of Rome in a way that honors Christ."[9] But in light of the apostle's use of the cognate noun (πολίτευμα) at 3:20,[10] where he writes, "our citizenship [πολίτευμα] is in heaven," Paul almost certainly intends to point to the believers' *heavenly* citizenship.[11] We find this thought reflected elsewhere in the New Testament at Hebrews 11:10, 16, where the great paragons of faith seek a city made by God (see also Philo, *Confusion* 78; *Giants* 61). On Paul's use of the term in our passage, Bockmuehl writes:

> Against the colonial preoccupation with the coveted citizenship of Rome, Paul interposes a counter-citizenship whose capital and seat of power are not earthly but heavenly, whose guarantor is not Nero but Christ. Philippi may be a colony enjoying the personal imperial patronage of Lord Caesar, but the church at Philippi is a personal colony of Christ the Lord above all (2:10–11).[12]

Stress is placed on the collective responsibility of the church as a whole rather than on individuals. The Philippians live out this heavenly citizenship as they stand together in unity against the onslaught of opponents who would divide them and overcome their faith.

The adverb rendered in our translation as "in a manner worthy" (ἀξίως) suggests how the Philippians, in community with one another, are to live out their heavenly citizenship. The adverb has to do with the qualitative measure of an action as suitable or appropriate in a given situation. Thus the

5. The aspect of the present imperative often conveys a general instruction.

6. So Fee, *Philippians*, 161. See, e.g., Rom 6:4; 8:4; 13:13; 14:15; 1 Cor 3:3; 7:17; 2 Cor 5:7; Gal 5:16; Eph 2:2.

7. Used elsewhere in the NT at Acts 23:1 and in the LXX at Esth 16:15; 2 Macc 6:1; 11:25; 3 Macc 3:4; 4 Macc 2:8, 23; 4:23; 5:16.

8. Winter, *Welfare of the City*, 102–3.

9. So Raymond Rush Brewer, "The Meaning of *Politeuesthe* in Philippians 1:27," *JBL* 73 (1954): 76–83; cf. Ernest C. Miller, "Πολιτεύεσθε in Philippians 1:27: Some Philological and Thematic Observations," *JSNT* 15 (1982): 86–96. Yet this position seems most unlikely, since many of those in the Philippian church would not have enjoyed the privilege of Roman citizenship. On Roman citizenship, see Carolyn Osiek, *Philippians, Philemon* (Nashville: Abingdon, 2000), 47–48.

10. See also its use in 2 Macc 12:7. Philo uses the cognate noun to speak of living appropriately as a virtuous person in a "city" or society (so *Creation* 143; *Agriculture* 81; *Confusion* 109; *Spec. Laws* 2.45). For Philo such a city may refer to the whole of nature or the human soul.

11. So Fee, *Philippians*, 162; Silva, *Philippians*, 80, 88. As noted by Silva, both Philo and Diognetus speak of heavenly citizenship (88). Only in these two places in Philippians does Paul use these related terms, making it appropriate that they be considered together. Thus Paul refers not to their citizenship in the Roman polis but their ultimate citizenship in heaven, which provides a point of orientation from which to live a life that is worthy of the gospel.

12. Bockmuehl, *Philippians*, 98.

Philippians are to conduct themselves in a way that is appropriate, specifically as they live out the "gospel of Christ" (τοῦ εὐαγγελίου τοῦ Χριστοῦ) before each other and the world. Rather than detract from the gospel, their lives should bear positive witness to the gospel. "Of the gospel" (τοῦ εὐαγγελίου) offers the point of reference. As good-news people they need to make sure especially that their manner of relating to one another matches their message, carried out with the gospel in mind. That this is the gospel "of Christ" (τοῦ Χριστοῦ) could be understood either as "originating with Christ" or perhaps "about Christ" and constitutes a common way of speaking about the gospel for Paul.[13] Jesus is the originator, mediator, finisher, main referent, and Lord of the gospel. The gospel, from start to finish, has to do with him as both its source and its primary referent.

**1:27c–k so that whether I come and see you or remain absent, I might hear about what is happening with you, particularly that you are standing firm in one Spirit, harmoniously striving together for the gospel faith** (ἵνα εἴτε ἐλθὼν καὶ ἰδὼν ὑμᾶς εἴτε ἀπὼν ἀκούω τὰ περὶ ὑμῶν, ὅτι στήκετε ἐν ἑνὶ πνεύματι, μιᾷ ψυχῇ συναθλοῦντες τῇ πίστει τοῦ εὐαγγελίου). Paul desires that the Philippians establish a powerful lifestyle of gospel unity rather than a momentary respite from bickering, and building a community of unity should not be dependent on circumstances. At 1:25–26 the apostle noted that his presence among them would be strategic for their growth, but the Philippians cannot be dependent on Paul for their growth in unity. Whether or not he comes to them,[14] they are called to be unified, fortified by their heavenly citizenship and working for the advance of the gospel.

As verse 27 continues, Paul writes of one reason why[15] the church members should live worthily of the gospel. He wants to "hear" (ἀκούω)[16] a good report of their spiritual resolve. First, the apostle speaks in general terms, saying that he wants to hear "what is happening with you" (τὰ περὶ ὑμῶν),[17] but then clarifies that he "particularly" (ὅτι)[18] is interested in whether they "are standing firm" (στήκετε, "you are standing firm").

The term meaning "stand firm" (στήκω) could be used literally of one's physical posture (e.g., Mark 3:31; John 1:26) but, as here, could also speak figuratively of living out a firm conviction or belief, whether "standing firm in the faith" (1 Cor 16:13) or "in the Lord" (Phil 4:1; 1 Thess 3:8). So the apostle wants to hear that this church, in the face of opposition, is taking their stand with and for Christ. At Philippians 4:1, the same verb echoes our current verse, as the apostle wraps up the letter body by exhorting the church to "stand firm" in their relationship with the Lord. The theme strikes to the heart of Paul's intention for the letter: standing together in unity flows from

13. E.g., Rom 15:19; 1 Cor 9:12; 2 Cor 2:12; 9:13; 10:14; Gal 1:7; Phil 1:27; 1 Thess 3:2.

14. Paul also uses "presence" and "absence" elsewhere in his letters. For instance, his presence and absence form a rhetorical framework for 2 Corinthians (see Guthrie, *2 Corinthians*, 47–48).

15. Here we have a purpose (ἵνα) clause. It could also be interpreted as a rare case in which ἵνα functions to introduce an intended result rather than purpose. See Wallace, *Greek Grammar*, 677. Read this way, that Paul would *hear* that they are living in unity is not the purpose for which they should live out a worthy citizenship. Rather it is the outcome, the result of such a pattern of life.

16. Several manuscripts attest an aorist subjunctive (ἀκούσω; ℵ[1] A C D[2] F G K L Ψ 0278. 33. 81. 104. 365. 630. 1175. 1505. 1739. 1881 𝔐), but it is the much weaker reading when compared to the text as it stands (𝔓[46] ℵ* B D* P 629. 1241. 2464). As Fee notes, the aorist form is more the default case, and scribes would have been less likely to depart from it and more likely to "correct" the present form. See Fee, *Philippians*, 158.

17. Literally "the things concerning you."

18. This is an epexegetical ὅτι clause.

a theologically grounded relationship with the Lord himself.

Next, through the end of verse 28, three primary phrases and clauses explain how the Philippians are to stand firm, with another seven phrases subordinate to one of these three. The Philippians are to stand:

in one Spirit
striving together
without being frightened

Fee has made a robust case for "in one Spirit" (ἐν ἑνὶ πνεύματι) as a reference to the Holy Spirit rather than a "community spirit of unity." His reasons are fourfold:[19] (1) there are no parallels in Greek literature, and particularly in Paul and the New Testament, where "in one spirit" is used with the sense of group solidarity. Paul simply does not use "spirit" as a word picture speaking anthropologically of a community's frame of mind. (2) When Paul employs "I stand" (στήκω), followed by a prepositional phrase headed by "in" (ἐν), he invariably has "sphere" in mind. So, according to Fee, rather than referring to the manner by which they are to stand, which has no parallel in Paul, the apostle writes of the "sphere" of the Spirit. (3) This idea of having a relationship grounded in the Spirit gets repeated in 2:1, and there, as in 1:27, there follows the admonition to have "solidarity" (2:2; σύμψυχοι). (4) Finally, the language of "in one Spirit," speaking of the common experience believers have through God's Spirit, occurs also at 1 Corinthians 12:13 and Ephesians 2:18. So reading the phrase as referring to the Holy Spirit is very much in line with Pauline usage.

Thus Paul grounds his exhortation to church unity in an appeal to the believers' common relationship with the Holy Spirit. In other words, there exists no unity in the church apart from the Spirit's work. As with 1 Corinthians 12:13, the one Spirit makes Christ-followers "one body." So "one Spirit" (ἑνὶ πνεύματι) underscores that the oneness of the community must, above all else, flow from this one Spirit.[20]

The apostle discusses a second way the Philippians are to stand firm, crafting his sentence around the present active participle translated "striving together" (συναθλοῦντες). The verb συναθλέω means "to contend" or "struggle along with"—that is, "to enter into a struggle along with others for the sake of something."[21] The only other place the verb occurs in the New Testament is at Philippians 4:3, where Paul says that Euodia and Syntyche "have participated in gospel work" (ἐν τῷ εὐαγγελίῳ συνήθλησαν) along with him, Clement, and other coworkers of the apostle.

Paul clarifies this commitment to "striving together" with two phrases, one preceding it and the other following. "Harmoniously" (μιᾷ ψυχῇ) speaks of the manner with which they are to strive, calling for a united community that is living together with a common purpose. The Greek word ψυχή could refer to the "soul" of a person or animal—the animating principle (e.g., Rev 8:9) or the inner life (e.g., Luke 12:19; John 10:24; Acts 14:2). It also could refer to a person as a whole (e.g., Acts 2:43; 3:23; Rom 2:9). At times the term speaks simply of "life," particularly the condition of being alive.[22] Here Paul probably calls for the Philippians to live out of a shared life orientation, striving as a unified community in a common mission.

19. Fee, *Philippians*, 164–66.

20. Fee speaks of this dynamic in terms of "source." See Fee, *Philippians*, 166.

21. BDAG 964; LSJ 1692.

22. BDAG 1099–100.

That mission can be summed up as "for the gospel faith" (τῇ πίστει τοῦ εὐαγγελίου). The term rendered "faith" (πίστει) can be read as a dative of advantage, the Philippians striving together for the promotion of the faith in the world—faith understood as roughly synonymous to the Christ-following movement, with its posture of trust in God. This faith has been "brought about by the gospel."[23] This interpretation reads "striving together for the gospel faith" in light of the similar thought that Euodia and Syntyche struggled together "in gospel work" (ἐν τῷ εὐαγγελίῳ) alongside Paul. What Paul probably has in mind in both places is standing with others as bearers of the gospel message before the world.

**1:28 without being frightened in any way by those standing against you, which is a sign for them of destruction but of your salvation, and this [is] from God** (καὶ μὴ πτυρόμενοι ἐν μηδενὶ ὑπὸ τῶν ἀντικειμένων, ἥτις ἐστὶν αὐτοῖς ἔνδειξις ἀπωλείας, ὑμῶν δὲ σωτηρίας, καὶ τοῦτο ἀπὸ θεοῦ). Our interpretation of "the gospel faith" at the end of 1:27 finds further support with yet another phrase clarifying the idea of "standing firm." The Philippians are to do so "without being frightened" (καὶ μὴ πτυρόμενοι; cf. NIV). The verb for "being frightened" (πτύρω), only found here in the New Testament, speaks of intimidation, being scared, or terrified by something,[24] and Paul wants to hear that no form of intimidation (ἐν μηδενί, "in any way") has worked to stop the Philippians from moving boldly forward with the gospel.

As noted in our In Depth section on the opponents of Paul,[25] while this passage offers an important glimpse into the Philippians' situation, the identity of the opponents ("by those standing against you," ὑπὸ τῶν ἀντικειμένων)[26] is less than certain. In light of what we know of the sociocultural context, it seems most likely that pagan civil authorities in Philippi were putting a tremendous amount of pressure on church members to conform to cultural and political values. One example might have been that believers were compelled to make public sacrifices to the emperor.[27] Or the letter's apparent allusions to Jewish agitators (e.g., 3:2–3) could suggest that false teachers were in the area and were causing trouble for the church. Yet these allusions in the latter case can be read as general cautions concerning a potential threat rather than particular, current problems in Philippi, and thus the former interpretation seems more likely. So Paul's hope is that rather than shrinking back in the face of intense public opposition, the Philippians will continue to stand their ground as they refuse to give in to intimidation.

This posture, holding to the gospel in the face of cultural pressure, will serve as a "sign" (ἔνδειξις)[28]

23. Hawthorne, *Philippians*, 57. With Hawthorne we read the genitive τοῦ εὐαγγελίου as a subjective genitive.

24. The word, e.g., could be used of startled or terrified horses; LSJ 1549; Hellerman, *Philippians*, 81. For example, during the Second Punic War as Hannibal threatened Rome, Gaius Flamininus, being overconfident and wishing to keep the battle away from the city, initiated an engagement with Hannibal's forces. As Flamininus jumped on his horse, however, "the animal was seized with quivering fright [ἐνροόμου τοῦ ἵππου γενομένου καὶ πτυρέντος], and he was thrown and fell head foremost to the ground." This was perceived by some as an omen, but Flamininus proceeded with his battle plan and was destroyed with his army (Plutarch, *Fab.* 3.1; Bernadotte Perrin, *Plutarch, Lives, Volume III: Pericles and Fabius Maximus, Nicias and Crassus*, LCL 65 [Cambridge: Harvard University Press; London: Heinemann, 1916], 125).

25. See this on pp. 230–34.

26. The verb ἀντίκειμαι connotes the act of an adversary or "to be in opposition" to someone or something; see BDAG 88. Cf. 1 Cor 16:9; 2 Thess 2:4.

27. E.g., Bockmuehl, *Philippians*, 100–101.

28. The term could carry the sense of "proof" or "demonstration" but here refers to "a pointer"—that is, an omen of something to come. See BDAG 332.

for their antagonists ("for them," αὐτοῖς),[29] and the sign carries a double message, pointing to both salvation and destruction. In Greco-Roman literature, "destruction" and "salvation" are often presented as binary opposites. For instance, they can be used in the context of warfare to speak of death and devastation, on the one hand, and rescue and liberation on the other.[30] Elsewhere, in 2 Corinthians 2:14–16 and 4:3, Paul uses related terms to speak, as here, of eschatological realities, pointing to judgment for the wicked and salvation for God's people.[31] In Philippians 2:12 the apostle exhorts the believers to work out their "salvation" with awe before God, and in 3:19 he notes that those who are enemies of the cross of Christ have an end that constitutes "destruction," which probably anticipates God's judgment of the wicked at the end of the age. Thus, as the Philippian believers stand for the gospel in the face of cultural opposition, they serve as a sign of things to come. Their gospel-embodied stance with Christ foreshadows the end of the age—when Christ will stand with his people, and their opponents will face the judgment of God.

Following these three key clarifications of how Paul envisions the Philippians "standing firm," 1:28 rounds things off with "this [is] from God." The "this" (τοῦτο) refers to the act of standing firm—specifically the Philippians' ability, by God's help, to endure in the face of opposition.[32] Just as they cannot live in unity apart from the Holy Spirit, so the Philippians cannot stand against opposition apart from the enabling of God himself.

**1:29–30 Because for Christ's sake you have been granted not only to trust him but also to suffer on his behalf, experiencing the same struggle that you saw I had and now hear that I have** (ὅτι ὑμῖν ἐχαρίσθη τὸ ὑπὲρ Χριστοῦ, οὐ μόνον τὸ εἰς αὐτὸν πιστεύειν ἀλλὰ καὶ τὸ ὑπὲρ αὐτοῦ πάσχειν, 30 τὸν αὐτὸν ἀγῶνα ἔχοντες, οἷον εἴδετε ἐν ἐμοὶ καὶ νῦν ἀκούετε ἐν ἐμοί). The Philippians have been blessed with a twofold gift: to trust and suffer for Christ, both of which parallel Paul's own experience. In verses 29–30 the apostle puts a theological "period" on 1:27–30, offering a "basis"[33] for the assertion in 1:28 that God is the one enabling them to stand firm. He positions the pronoun "you" (ὑμῖν) at the beginning of the clause for emphasis. He has in mind the special circumstance of the Philippians themselves—their particular gift of both trust and suffering.[34] They experience both "for Christ's sake,"[35] as twin privileges that they have "been granted" (ἐχαρίσθη). In Paul's writings, this verb (χαρίζομαι) can be used with the sense of

29. The text as we have it has strong external attestation (א A B C D* F G 0278. 33. 81. 365. 1175. 1241. 1739. 1881. 2464 lat). Some scribes seem to have felt the need for the addition of μέν, setting up a correlative construction with the δέ that follows later in the verse (e.g., K L 630 𝔐, the μέν prior to ἐστίν; D[1] P Ψ 075. 104. 1505, the μέν following αὐτοῖς).

30. See George H. Guthrie, "Paul's Triumphal Procession Imagery (2 Cor 2.14–16a): Neglected Points of Background," *NTS* 61.1 (2015): 89, citing Plutarch, *Apoph.* 2.22; 2.23.1; *Crass.* 25.11; Dionysius of Halicarnassus, *Ant. Rom.* 8.12.4; Herodotus, *Hist.* 3.14.11; Plato, *Leg.* 728b. See also Philo, *Cherubim* 130; *Alleg. Interp.* 3.225; *Flight* 27; and in the LXX see Amos 2:14–15; Jer 31:8; Wis 18:5–7.

31. E.g., the noun ἀπώλεια occurs at Rom 9:22; Phil 1:28; 3:19; 2 Thess 2:3; 1 Tim 6:9. The noun is used extensively in Paul: Rom 1:16; 10:1, 10; 11:11; 13:11; 2 Cor 1:6; 6:2; 7:10; Eph 1:13; Phil 1:19, 28; 2:12; 1 Thess 5:8–9; 2 Thess 2:13; 2 Tim 2:10; 3:15.

32. Similar to Silva, *Philippians*, 82–83, who states that the reference is not to "salvation . . . but rather to the whole complex of ideas: conflict, destruction, perseverance, and salvation. The true grounds for the Philippians' encouragement was the profound conviction that nothing in their experience took place outside God's superintendence."

33. So, e.g., Silva, *Philippians*, 83. Grammatically, this is an explanatory ὅτι clause.

34. So Cousar, *Philippians and Philemon*, 46.

35. The preposition ὑπέρ + the genitive indicates "interest," something done on behalf of or for the sake of someone or something (BDAG 1030). This is preferable to Hawthorne's interpretation of "in place of," "instead of" (Hawthorne, *Philippians*, 61).

"forgive" (2 Cor 2:7, 10; 12:13; Eph 4:32; Col 2:13; 3:13), but here and elsewhere the word connotes the act of giving, or being given, something (Rom 8:32; 1 Cor 2:12; Gal 3:18; Phil 2:9).

"To trust" Christ and "to suffer" on his behalf are expressed in a common "not only . . . but also" (οὐ μόνον . . . ἀλλὰ καί) construction. The "trust" side of this equation is foundational. The verb (πιστεύειν) basically has to do with believing something to the point of entrusting oneself in a particular way.[36] Although many English versions render the word as "believe" (e.g., ESV, CSB, NASB, NRSV, NIV, NET), in modern English "believe" can communicate a cognitive orientation and doesn't necessarily include the idea of commitment in any way. "Trust" (NLT, the Message), on the other hand, expresses the nuance of *active*, committed confidence in, or reliance on, Christ.

Suffering often follows on the heels of trusting Christ and weaves its way through the lives of believers, and God redeems this suffering. Paul does not treat suffering in the cause of Christ as abnormal or as a reason for panic. Rather than a sign that God has abandoned believers, those who suffer in his cause manifest their solidarity with the suffering Savior. Thus it is unsurprising that the Philippians are "experiencing the same struggle" (τὸν αὐτὸν ἀγῶνα ἔχοντες) that they had witnessed and are witnessing in the life of their apostle, who in turn saw his sufferings as conforming to a pattern established by Christ himself (2 Cor 4:10–14). The term translated as "struggle" (ἀγών) could be used of some aspect of athletic competition, with the imagery brought over to the spiritual realm as referring to a fight or struggle in the cause of the gospel.[37] The Philippians may have been experiencing "shunning, public embarrassment, nonrecognition of personal honor and status, discrimination in the patronage system because of their beliefs"[38]—along with other indignities. Nevertheless, they have Paul as a stellar example of how to handle such experiences. After all, he had suffered mob action and had been abused by the authorities when he first came to Philippi (Acts 16:19–24), and the Philippians now hear reports of his current imprisonment (Phil 1:12–14). Accordingly, Paul shows them how to suffer well for Christ.

**2:1 Consequently, if there is any encouragement in your relationship with Christ, if any cheering up prompted by love, if any participation stemming from the Spirit, if any affection and compassion** (Εἴ τις οὖν παράκλησις ἐν Χριστῷ, εἴ τι παραμύθιον ἀγάπης, εἴ τις κοινωνία πνεύματος, εἴ τις σπλάγχνα καὶ οἰκτιρμοί). The apostle here builds on his exhortation of 1:27–30 with further encouragement to be unified as a community, and he does so, beginning in 2:1, with a series of conditional clauses. The inferential conjunction,[39] translated here as "consequently" (οὖν), marks 2:1–4 as flowing from the thought of 1:27–30. These first four verses of chapter 2 present an emotional appeal for unity, instructing the Philippians on how to achieve it. As seen in our diagram of the passage, verses 1 and 2 are balanced on either side of the main clause, "complete my joy" (πληρώσατέ μου τὴν χαράν), with four thoughts preceding the main clause and four thoughts following.

The four conditional "if" (εἰ) clauses of 2:1 highlight foundational, relational dynamics that are necessary for unity: encouragement, cheering up, participation, affection, and compassion.

36. BDAG 816–17.

37. BDAG 17.

38. Osiek, *Philippians, Philemon*, 50; Hellerman notes, "Christians would have suffered for refusing to partake in public assemblies dedicated to civic and Roman gods, particularly those that honored Caesar as lord" (*Exegetical Guide*, 87).

39. Silva, following Schenk, tags the term as "resumptive" (Silva, *Philippians*, 85).

Each clause begins with "if" (εἰ) + "any" (τις) in parallel fashion, and none of these conditional clauses has a verb, making them crisp, punctuated descriptions that would have rolled off the tongue in a lyrical fashion. The first three can be read as expressing a Trinitarian framework, with references to "Christ" and the "Spirit" expressed overtly and the reference to God the Father implied.[40] Paul uses a similar trio of expressions referring to God at 2 Corinthians 13:13,[41] and in 2 Corinthians 1:3 God the Father is described with the terms "compassion" (οἰκτιρμός) and "encouragement" (παράκλησις), words also used here in Philippians 2:1. Thus Paul seems to employ this language to point to God as the source of these relational gifts. Also, as with the Spirit at 1:27, the work of God is prerequisite for spiritual unity in the church. In other words, when God promotes these dynamics of encouragement, comfort, community, affection, and compassion, they offer a solid foundation for solidarity among people, and such solidarity is the focus of 2:2–4.

The first clause in 2:1 reads, "if there is any encouragement in your relationship with Christ" (εἴ τις . . . παράκλησις ἐν Χριστῷ). The verbal idea is implied, and the clause begins with "if" (εἴ), which marks out a presupposition[42]—Paul assumes that this, and the following relational dynamics, exist. Ancient authors used the term παράκλησις to speak of "encouragement" or "exhortation," a "strong request" or "appeal," or "comfort" and "consolation."[43] Given the context of public opposition hinted at in 1:27–30, the word in this case could connote either "comfort" or "encouragement." The latter may be preferred since Paul almost certainly points to more than mere consolation and rather to an emboldening of these believers in their difficult public stance (1:27–30).[44] Such encouragement is found in their common relationship "with Christ" (ἐν Χριστῷ),[45] a favorite phrase of Paul, interpreted here as communicating "association."

The second clause reads, "if any cheering up prompted by love" (εἴ τι παραμύθιον ἀγάπης). The term rendered "cheering up" (παραμύθιον) has to do with consolation or encouragement of some sort, so its semantic range is similar to παράκλησις. Spicq states that the word group to which παραμύθιον belongs communicates "more than comfort or encouragement, but a real stimulation, strength for overcoming difficulties."[46] The genitive translated as "prompted by love" (ἀγάπης) may be read as a subjective genitive, referring to God's love as bringing about consolation.

If our interpretation of "in one Spirit" (ἐν ἑνὶ πνεύματι) at 1:27 is correct, Paul has already indicated that the role of the Holy Spirit is foundational to a community of unity. Now he writes of the "participation stemming from the Spirit" (εἴ τις κοινωνία πνεύματος), with the form of the word for "Spirit" (πνεύματος, the genitive) understood as communicating "source"—something originating with the Spirit. As pointed out above, although some have interpreted "spirit" anthropologically, the Trinitarian framework of the passage points to the Holy Spirit shaping "community" among the

40. Fee, *Philippians*, 179.

41. "The grace of the Lord Jesus Christ and the love of God and the fellowship of the Holy Spirit be with all of you." So Fee, *Philippians*, 179; Hellerman, *Philippians*, 92; Reumann, *Philippians*, 321.

42. Fee, *Philippians*, 177.

43. BDAG 766.

44. For a parallel context, see the treatment of 2 Cor 1:3–7 in Guthrie, *2 Corinthians*, 67–68.

45. For the extensive use of the phrase in Paul, with the interpretive options, see Campbell, *Paul and Union with Christ*.

46. *TLNT* 3:34. Spicq translates the term with "stimulation." Perhaps the idea of "bolstering" would be better. Thus Spicq interprets the term at Phil 2:1 as "stimulation to love," but we understand ἀγάπης to be a genitive of source, referring to God's love.

Philippians—a community that shares together in a common cause.

One possible reading of "participation" (κοινωνία) in 2:1 might be the sense of an attitude of good will, a feeling of generosity or altruism toward others in a group. Another possible interpretation recognizes that the term occurs in Paul's writings with the sense of "fellowship" or "close relationship" with others who share mutual interests (e.g., 1 Cor 1:9; 2 Cor 13:13; Gal 2:9). Although either of these two interpretations is possible, the broader context, including Paul's use of the term elsewhere in Philippians, commends an understanding of "participation," communicating a sharing in a common cause.[47] Paul uses the term with this nuance at Philippians 1:5, where he speaks of the Philippians' "participation" in the gospel, and it also seems to be the sense at 3:10, where the apostle expresses his passion to know Christ, to experience the power of his resurrection and "fellowship of his sufferings" (κοινωνίαν παθημάτων αὐτοῦ). Moreover, given the emphasis on standing "in one Spirit" for the gospel in 1:27–30, the broader context of the passage supports the sense of "participating" in a common cause, which Paul longs for this community to experience.

Verse 1 ends with the apostle pointing to "affection" (σπλάγχνον) and "compassion" (οἰκτιρμός), terms paired elsewhere at Colossians 3:12. The word for "affection" (σπλάγχνον) could be used literally to refer to internal organs, as with the spilling of Judas's intestines (Acts 1:18). But broadly in the ancient world the word was used figuratively to refer to the seat of the emotions, as we often use the English word "heart." Thus the Greek term speaks of feelings of love or affection in relationships, and this is a common use for Paul,[48] as seen at 1:8 where he speaks of cherishing the Philippians with the "affection of Christ Jesus."

"Compassion" (οἰκτιρμός), on the other hand, refers to concern or pity for another person. The term most often refers to an attribute of God, but as at Colossians 3:12 it can refer to the character of God's people.[49] Rounding out the series of causal clauses in Philippians 2:1, these two words could refer to God's affection and compassion for his church, but they could also refer to dynamics present among God's people as God builds them into a community.

**2:2 Complete my joy in this way: by being like-minded, embracing a common love, having solidarity, sharing a common perspective** (πληρώσατέ μου τὴν χαρὰν ἵνα τὸ αὐτὸ φρονῆτε, τὴν αὐτὴν ἀγάπην ἔχοντες, σύμψυχοι, τὸ ἓν φρονοῦντες). Paul's letter to the Philippians is infused with joy, as he expresses his own joy, mentions the joy of the Philippians themselves, or encourages them to "rejoice in the Lord."[50] Although his exhortation to "complete my joy" at the beginning of 2:2 isn't the *main* topic of 2:1–4, it does express an underlying, pastoral motivation driving the apostle's call to unity in the church—which is the main point. As Hellerman notes, Paul's "joy was not wholly unrelated to external circumstances, especially the spiritual state of his churches. So, although Paul is already taking joy in the Philippians (1:4; 4:1)," his joy will not be complete until this church thrives in a Christ-centered, Spirit-inspired unity.[51]

How are they to fulfill the apostle's exhortation

47. BDAG 552–53.

48. 2 Cor 6:12; 7:15; Phil 1:8; Col 3:12; Phlm 7, 12, 20.

49. BDAG 700; Rom 12:1; 2 Cor 1:3; Col 3:12; Heb 10:28. The term is used thirty-one times in the LXX. See, e.g., 2 Sam 24:14; 1 Kgs 8:50; 1 Chr 21:13.

50. For the use of the noun, see Phil 1:4, 25; 2:2, 29; 4:1; the verb: 1:18; 2:17–18, 28; 3:1; 4:4, 10.

51. Hellerman, *Philippians*, 97.

and thus his joy? "By being like-minded" (ἵνα τὸ αὐτὸ φρονῆτε). The verb φρονέω could be used, for example, to communicate the act of thinking, having an opinion, or being intent on something.[52] When Paul says, "Think the same" (τὸ αὐτὸ φρονῆτε), he does not call for uniformity (as with the CSB, "thinking the same way"). Rather, he calls for a *unity* within the diverse community (e.g., Rom 12:16; 15:5; 2 Cor 13:11). The term appears again at the end of 2:2 and again at 2:5, where it introduces the self-sacrificial example of Christ himself. With Christ, the Philippians should share a posture of single-minded, sacrificial commitment and a harmony of purpose in their approach to life under his lordship.[53]

Next, Paul explains how the Philippians are to embody such unity. First, the Philippians are called to live out unity by "embracing a common love" (τὴν αὐτὴν ἀγάπην ἔχοντες). Paul wants the Philippians to love each other, echoing the mention of "love" (ἀγάπης) in the previous verse. Again, if we are correct to read a Trinitarian framework in the clauses of verse 1, the love of God in that verse lays the foundation for the believers' mutual love in verse 2.

"Having solidarity" translates a rare single Greek word, σύμψυχοι, which underscores the notion of being "harmonious." This word may reiterate the call in 1:27 for members of the church to be harmonious (μιᾷ ψυχῇ). Philippians 2:2 concludes with "sharing a common perspective" (τὸ ἓν φρονοῦντες), the apostle again capitalizing on the verb we translated as "being . . . like-minded" (φρονέω) earlier in the verse and underscoring oneness, with the believers called to share a "common" (ἕν) way of thinking about their lives and mission.

**2:3–4 not acting out of selfishness or an elevated opinion of yourselves, but with humility thinking of the others as more significant than you are, each and every one of you focused not on your own concerns but on the concerns of others** (μηδὲν κατ᾽ ἐριθείαν μηδὲ κατὰ κενοδοξίαν ἀλλὰ τῇ ταπεινοφροσύνῃ ἀλλήλους ἡγούμενοι ὑπερέχοντας ἑαυτῶν, 4 μὴ τὰ ἑαυτῶν ἕκαστος σκοποῦντες ἀλλὰ [καὶ][54] τὰ ἑτέρων ἕκαστοι). Here Paul focuses on keys to attaining unity in the community: humility and selfless service on behalf of others. The content of these two verses relentlessly remains on the "being like-minded" statement of verse 2 and how that might be accomplished. The apostle employs a pair of contrasts that may be depicted in an A B A B pattern, with each pair separated by "but" (ἀλλά):

A **not** acting out of selfishness or an
elevated opinion of yourselves
*but*
B with humility thinking of the others as if
they are more significant than yourselves,
A each and every one of you focused **not**
on your own concerns
*but*
B on the concerns of others

The focus, of course, is on what must be driven out ("not . . . ") if the community is to thrive in unity.[55] The two "A" portions in this parallelism highlight the problem of self-centeredness, and the "B" portions emphasize an attitude centered on others.

What must be driven out, therefore, is "selfishness" (ἐριθεία) and its twisted sister, an "elevated opinion" of oneself (κενοδοξία). As we saw at 1:17, this term for selfishness (ἐριθεία) has to do with

52. BDAG 1065–66.
53. *EDNT* 3:439.
54. Following NA[28].
55. So Fee, following Meyer (Fee, *Philippians*, 186).

self-seeking, which by nature is divisive. This trait characterizes Paul's opponents, who work for his harm during the apostle's incarceration (1:17). Used just seven times in the New Testament,[56] the term is found nowhere else in Greek literature.[57] The word communicates a spirit of factionalism that is willing to tear others apart, climbing over the scattered pieces of community to advance one's own status. Of course, to take such an approach to life one must have an "elevated opinion" (κενοδοξία, "empty glory") of oneself, seeing others as dispensable in one's climb up the ladder of success. The word κενοδοξία connotes an "exaggerated self-evaluation" or "conceit" and includes the nuance of personal delusion.[58]

Humility and concern for others are the virtuous, Judeo-Christian alternatives to these twin community killers. The apostle defines "humility" (ταπεινοφροσύνη) as "thinking of others as if they are more significant than you are" (ἀλλήλους ἡγούμενοι ὑπερέχοντας ἑαυτῶν). The word is a compound of the concepts of being "humble" or "lowly" (ταπεινός) and "to think" (φρονέω). It thus relates to the φρον- word group in this section, which often expresses the notion of sharing a certain perspective and thus a certain posture in life. The antidote to an "elevated opinion" of oneself is to get one's mind right,[59] that is, to conduct oneself "with humility."[60] Self-promotion to one's own glory was a high cultural value on the streets of Roman Philippi; true biblical humility takes that value and turns it upside-down. The way "up" is "down," a posture of servanthood.

In broader Greco-Roman literature, "humility" often was used pejoratively to speak of a "groveling" posture, false humility (cf. Col 2:18, 23), or some form of weakness of character.[61] By contrast, biblical humility shows great strength of character, manifesting an awareness of who one is—and who one is not!—before God. With such a Godward attitude, a humble person can turn outward with an others-oriented perspective. Moreover, humbling oneself before God creates an important form of community among those who have been raised up together by the grace of God (Matt 11:29; Luke 1:48; 14:11).[62] As Paul emphasizes in Philippians 2:5–11, Christ himself is the supreme example of humility (Matt 11:29), since he gave himself on behalf of others. Thus, it is unsurprising that humility plays a significant role in the ethics of Christ-following (e.g., Acts 20:19; Eph 4:2; Col 3:12; 1 Pet 5:5).

Humility is fleshed out as each believer thinks "of others as more significant than" themselves (ἀλλήλους ἡγούμενοι ὑπερέχοντας ἑαυτῶν). The verb translated "thinking" in verse 2 (ἡγέομαι) was used by ancient writers with the sense of "to think, consider," or "regard."[63] Paul here promotes a certain posture toward "others" (ἀλλήλους) when compared to oneself.[64] The term rendered as

56. Rom 2:8; 2 Cor 12:20; Gal 5:20; Phil 1:17; 2:3; Jas 3:14, 16. The uses in 2 Cor 12:20 and Gal 5:20 are in vice lists.

57. *TLNT* 2:70. Spicq points out that the verbal cognate originally had to do with "work for hire"—a positive meaning—but later developed the negative sense of work done solely in one's own interest.

58. BDAG 538. Found elsewhere, e.g., in the LXX at 4 Macc 2:15; 8:19; Wis 14:14. Epictetus uses a cognate adjective to describe a person who is an imposter: "For what does this law say? Let him who pretends to things which do not belong to him be a boaster, a vainglorious [κενόδοξος] man" (*Diatr.* 3.24.43). In Galatians Paul uses the same adjective, warning his readers against such conceit: "Let us not become conceited [κενόδοξοι], provoking and envying each other" (Gal 5:26 NIV).

59. Silva, *Philippians*, 87.

60. The use here is a dative of manner.

61. Bockmuehl, *Philippians*, 110, who shows that humility could be a virtue in broader Judaism in the Second Temple period. See, e.g., Philo, *Alleg. Interp.* 3.82.

62. Bockmuehl, *Philippians*, 111.

63. BDAG 434.

64. Another participle, ὑπερέχοντας, reaches back to tell us

"[being] more significant" (ὑπερέχω) functioned as a status word in Greco-Roman society—for example, when referring to a person who excels or surpasses others.[65] That culture valued moving up the ladder of status almost above all other social dynamics. For Paul to suggest that the Philippians voluntarily consider others as above them in rank or importance would have been seen as radical and socially awkward, if not subversive! The call to move "down the ladder" of status was countercultural.

A related thought continues in verse 4 with "each and every one of you focused not on your own concerns but on the concerns of others" (μὴ τὰ ἑαυτῶν ἕκαστος σκοποῦντες ἀλλὰ [καὶ] τὰ ἑτέρων ἕκαστοι). Two parts of the verse parallel one another:[66]

| | |
|---|---|
| each and every one of you focused | ἕκαστος σκοποῦντες |
| not on your own concerns | μὴ τὰ ἑαυτῶν |
| but on | ἀλλὰ [καὶ] |
| the concerns of others | τὰ ἑτέρων ἕκαστοι |

Every member of the congregation—*each* (ἕκαστος) and every one!—should take personal responsibility for attending to the concerns of others in the congregation rather than being consumed with "their own concerns" (τὰ ἑαυτῶν; lit. "the things of themselves").[67] The verb translated as "focused on" (σκοπέω) refers to being especially attentive to something (e.g., Luke 11:35; Rom 16:17; Gal 6:1; Phil 3:17) or exerting "effort in continually acquiring information regarding some matter, with the implication of concern as to how to respond appropriately."[68] The apostle addresses our temptation to be consumed constantly with our own needs and agendas. If the καί in the passage is original,[69] Paul acknowledges that we should all give attention to our own needs and concerns. Yet to this personal responsibility (ἕκαστος) must be added a community dynamic (the plural ἕκαστοι at the end of verse 4)[70] of being attentive to the needs and concerns of others collectively, in the community (τὰ ἑτέρων). Such a pattern constitutes a form of living out humility, reckoning others as more significant than oneself.

something about ἀλλήλους, as the two words form an object-complement double accusative, while the genitive ἑαυτῶν communicates comparison. On this type of accusative, see Wallace, *Greek Grammar*, 182–83.

65. Elsewhere in Philippians, Paul will use the verb to speak of the "surpassing" worth of knowing Christ (3:8) and of the transcendent nature of God's peace (4:7).

66. We have a bit of textual turbulence here. First, in place of Paul's collective use of the singular ἕκαστος (𝔓[46] ℵ C D K L P 075. 104. 365. 630. 1241. 1505. 1739. 1881. 2464 𝔐 sy[(p)]), other witnesses, among them Alexandrinus and Vaticanus (A B F G Ψ 0278. 33. 81. 1175 lat), have the plural ἕκαστοι, as scribes undoubtedly brought the word in line with the other plurals in the context. The singular, though a common style variation in Paul, is the more difficult grammatically and thus the preferred reading. The evidence for the participial form σκοποῦντες (𝔓[46] ℵ A B C D F G P 075. 0278. 33. 81. 104. 365. 1175. 1241. 1739. 1881. 2464 latt) is strong, as is the evidence for the retention of καί (𝔓[46] ℵ A B C D1 L P Ψ 075. 0278. 33. 81. 104. 365. 630. 1175. 1241. 1505. 1739. 1881. 2464 𝔐 vg[st.ww] sy; Cass). Finally, in an apparent reversal of the situation with ἕκαστος above, some scribes seem to have felt the need to bring the plural ἕκαστοι in line with the singular ἕκαστος, as seen in a certain manuscript tradition (K L 0278. 630. 1505 𝔐 d sy; Hier).

67. The word can be read as a "distributive" or "collective" use of the singular. See Fee, *Philippians*, 175.

68. L&N 331.

69. It is retained by several strong witnesses, including 𝔓[46] ℵ A B C.

70. The repetition is both for emphasis and to add breadth in line with the other plurals in the passage.

## Theology in Application

### *Seek Unity for the Sake of Mission*

It is difficult to express adequately the importance of Philippians 1:27–2:4 in the development of the letter, since this text is a hinge, strategically placed at the beginning of the body proper to highlight the apostle's primary concern for the Philippians. Evidently the church in Philippi was struggling with disunity, with cracks in community manifested and extended under the weight of cultural opposition to the church. In answer, Paul calls the Philippians to think of themselves as a heavenly colony or outpost, which needs to shore up its Christian unity for the sake of the gospel. Alec Motyer sums up the significance of the verb translated "live out your heavenly citizenship" (πολιτεύεσθε) and writes:

> Philippi was a Roman "colony," a title seen as one of the coveted prizes of the Roman empire. "Colonial" status meant that the people of Philippi were reckoned as Roman citizens. Their names were on the rolls at Rome; their legal position and privileges were those of Rome itself. They were a homeland in miniature. But all this is also true of them spiritually as men and women in Christ. Grace has made them citizens of a heavenly city; in their far-off land they are the heavenly homeland in miniature; heaven's laws are their laws, and their privileges, its privileges. The life worthy of the gospel is an inescapable obligation: it is the essence of the homeland where the Lamb standing, as though it had been slain, forms the focal point of all life.[71]

When Christ truly stands at the heart of a community of believers and his law of self-sacrificial love governs the "little homeland," these prove to be powerful bases for standing in the face of opposition and a powerful platform from which to proclaim the transformative, unifying gospel.[72] People in deep community have lives that are pointed in the same direction, consumed by a common love and a common purpose. When living out their true citizenship, Christian believers stand side by side with arms locked, faces turned toward their Lord Christ and simultaneously toward the world. This is no contradiction. They must always face both Christ in his lordship and the world in its need if they are to live out their identity. Rather than a "unity at all cost," such constitutes a unity at great cost. The cost was great for Christ and can be great for us, for with such a stand comes suffering—one of the church's gifts (1:29).

71. J. Alec Motyer, *The Message of Philippians* (Leicester: Inter-Varsity Press 1984), 93.

72. Cohick, *Philippians*, 3; see especially her example in the first full paragraph on this page.

Earlier in the commentary I mentioned my ministry among Jewish and Arab believers in Israel. Two members of the group traveled to the US for a series of meetings a few years ago, and they agreed to speak to our students at the university where I taught at the time. In chapel, these brothers, one Jewish and the other Arab, stood side by side and explained to our campus community how the gospel breaks down unimaginable social barriers. The Jewish brother spoke on "Why God Loves the Arabs," and the Arab brother spoke on "Why God Loves the Jews." The impact on all of us was powerful.

Such living flows from a particular posture that is Christ focused, Spirit driven, and gospel saturated. It will always be a minority position in the world until Christ returns. In his book *Vanishing Grace*, Philip Yancey writes of a Muslim man who told the author, "I have read the entire Koran and can find in it no guidance on how Muslims should live as a minority in society. I have read the entire New Testament many times and can find in it no guidance on how Christians should live as a majority." Yancey reflects, "Christians best thrive as a minority, a counterculture. Historically, when [Christians] reach a majority they have yielded to the temptations of power in ways that are clearly anti-gospel."[73]

As we seek to apply Philippians 1:27–2:4, we might begin by asking ourselves: What is our focus in life? And what is the focus of the communities with which we are most associated? Are we truly focused on Christ and his mission in a way that unifies us against all odds? Does our common life manifest a counter-citizenship in the face of earthly powers? Are our lives appropriate to the nature of the gospel and the mission of the church, manifesting self-sacrifice, or is our ministry more about self-promotion? In other words, are our lives, and the life manifested by our communities, "worthy" of identification with the gospel?

## *Do Not Be Intimidated by Opposition*

If our patterns of life are "worthy" of the gospel in the sense described above, opposition certainly will come. The dominant culture in any given context *likes* dominance, likes flexing its cultural or political muscle, and may move against the heavenly colony in that place. The church makes counterclaims of a different kind of power, born of and for a different world, and thus born to different priorities and a different mission, taking orders from a different Lord. Eventually this will draw attention and perhaps overt opposition. We are gifted with belief and joy, but we are also gifted with suffering.

73. Philip Yancey, *Vanishing Grace: What Ever Happened to the Good News?* (Grand Rapids: Zondervan, 2014), 258.

Our temptation, of course, is to give in to debilitating fear, missing the moment of radical witness. We fear what could happen if the powers rise up against us. John Witherspoon notes, "It is only the fear of God that can deliver us from the fear of man."[74] Thus we should "serve the LORD with fear and celebrate his rule with trembling" (Ps 2:11 NIV). Being rightly related to God and holding a posture of deep reverence before him moves us to a place of joyful, unintimidated "fear" that quiets the intimidation of people. It is, then, an appropriately placed fear that makes the unintimidated church a "sign" to the powers, a sign of their destruction and of our salvation. Suffering becomes a sign, pointing beyond the moment.

I have known two friends who have died as martyrs—one in Afghanistan and one in Africa—both killed by extremists. I do not know what it was like for them to face their murderers, but I would guess that they struggled desperately against fear. I don't think that Paul's words here necessarily mean that we never feel fear but that we do not allow intimidation to stop us from making a bold public witness to the gospel. I am confident that my courageous friends stood for the gospel, under the hand and eye of the Lord Christ, until the very end. They were a sign, an eschatological notice, that evil will not win.

Years ago, I was teaching a course in a closed Asian country. We were on the seventh floor of a hotel with only conference rooms on that floor. I was there with another professor, the administrators of the course, and about sixty brothers and sisters from the house-church movement. Any of them could have been put in jail at any moment, but they sang songs to the Lord at the top of their lungs, completely unintimidated. Their joy-filled unity and boldness was infectious. Later as we left the hotel, a military unit was in the streets outside, but it did not phase the brothers and sisters at all, and miracle of miracles I felt absolute peace and joy as we walked past the soldiers and down the street.

For the church, opposition will always be a fact of life. But as we live in a selfless unity on mission for the Lord Christ in the world, we need not be intimidated. We are a sign; we will know the Lord's salvation.

74. As quoted in Charles Simmons, *Laconic Manual and Brief Remarker* (North Wrentham, MA: John D. Flagg, 1852), 192.

CHAPTER 6

# Philippians 2:5–11

## Literary Context

The main body of Philippians begins at 1:27 and extends to 4:4a. As noted above, 1:27–2:4 works as a hinge between the body opening (1:12–26) and the heart of the main body. In 1:27–2:4, we have two subunits, each calling the Philippians to unity. Philippians 2:1–4 focuses on the virtue of selflessness, looking out for the needs of others rather than one's own self-interests, and 2:5–11 flows from this exhortation. With 2:5–11, Paul uses the preeminent example of selfless service, Christ himself, as the first in his series of rich examples for the Philippians to follow. On the heels of this beautiful, powerful, christological reflection, the apostle follows with further exhortations to unity and exclamations of joy in 2:12–18. From there he will offer the positive examples of Timothy and Epaphroditus in 2:19–30, and finally he will offer himself as an example in 3:1–14.

As noted by David Garland, with use of striking vocabulary Philippians 3:20–21 demonstrates an intentional crafting of parallels with 2:5–11.[1] Given additional parallels with 3:19, we have expanded Garland's insights to include that verse as well.

| | | | |
|---|---|---|---|
| 2:5 | "be intent" (φρονεῖτε) | 3:19 | "intent" (φρονοῦντες) |
| 2:6, 7 | "form" (μορφῇ; μορφήν) | 3:21 | "like" (σύμμορφον) |
| 2:6 | "being" (υπάρχων) | 3:20 | "is" (υπάρχει) |
| 2:7 | "outward appearance" (σχήματι) | 3:21 | "will transform" (μετασχηματίσει) |
| 2:8 | "humiliated" (ἐταπείνωσεν) | 3:21 | "humiliation" (ταπεινώσεως) |
| 2:10 | "that . . . every knee will bow" (ἵνα . . . πάν γόνυ κάμψη) | 3:21 | "he is also able to subject" (του δύνασθαι αυτόν και ὑποτάξαι) |
| 2:10 | "heaven . . . earth" (ἐπουρανίων; ἐπιγείων) | 3:19 | "earthly things" (ἐπίγεια) |

*Continued on next page.*

1. Garland, "Composition," 158. Indeed, as Garland points out, there are parallels with 2:5–11 peppered throughout Phil 3 (p. 159). Nevertheless, they are especially concentrated in 3:19–21.

| | | | |
|---|---|---|---|
| 2:11 | "and every tongue will confess" (και πάσα γλώσσα ἐξομολογήσηται) | 3:21 | "all things to himself" (αὐτῷ τὰ πάντα) |
| 2:11 | "Jesus Christ is Lord" (κύριος Ἰησοῦς Χριστός) | 3:20 | "Lord Jesus Christ" (κύριον Ἰησοῦν Χριστόν) |
| 2:11 | "glory" (δόξαν) | 3:21 | "his glory" (τής δόξης αὐτοῦ) |

Whereas the Christ passage of 2:5–11 focuses on the incarnation and exaltation (i.e., the movement from heaven, to earth, and back again to heaven[2]), 3:20–21 celebrates the resurrection transformation of Christ-followers, a transformation effected by the Savior.[3] Believers' humble bodies will be brought into conformity with his glorious body. Thus, 2:5–11 provides the christological foundation for a vision of transformation as believers follow Christ, and their transformation ultimately culminates in their resurrection from the dead. This suggests that Christ is not only the paradigm for the Philippians to follow but also the "provider of the rights-renouncing, others-regarding, cruciform humility and love needed for existence in the Christian community."[4] In other words, we need not only an example to follow but also the spiritual power to follow the example; Christ models and provides the cruciform life for his followers.

I. The Letter Opening: A Prescript and a Prayer Report (1:1–11)
**II. The Letter Body (1:12–4:9)**
- A. The Body Opening: Paul's Current Situation (1:12–26)
- B. The Main Body of the Letter: A Call for Unity in the Church (1:27–4:4a)
  - 1. An Exhortation to Live Out the Unity of Community (1:27–2:4)
  - ➡ **2. Be Like Christ Jesus, the Preeminent Example of Self-Sacrifice (2:5–11)**
  - 3. Further Exhortations to Unity and Exclamations of Joy (2:12–17)
  - 4. Timothy and Epaphroditus as Exemplars of Self-Sacrifice (2:18–30)
  - 5. The Example of Paul's Christocentric Life and Ministry (3:1–14)
  - 6. Exhortations to Embrace Paul's Christocentric Pattern of Life (3:15–4:4a)
- C. The Body Closing: Exhortations (4:4b–9)

III. The Letter Closing (4:10–23)

2. On this pattern, see Harold W. Attridge, *The Epistle to the Hebrews: A Commentary on the Epistle to the Hebrews* (Philadelphia: Fortress, 1989), 78–81.

3. 3:19 sets the stage for this focus in 3:20–21.

4. Gorman, *Participating*, 35.

## Main Idea

Paul poetically presents Christ Jesus as the preeminent exemplar of and means to selfless sacrifice, who relinquished his exalted status and glory, becoming incarnate and humiliating himself to meet the needs of fallen humanity through death on the cross. As a result, God the Father exalted Christ as Lord to the preeminent place in the universe—an all-encompassing lordship that issues in glory to God the Father.

## Translation

### Philippians 2:5–11

| | | |
|---|---|---|
| 5a | Exhortation | **Be intent on this posture of humility** |
| b | Association | among yourselves |
| c | Identification | which we also see in Christ Jesus |
| 6a | Descrip./Concession | who being robed in divine glory |
| b | Posture | (1) **did not regard equality with God** |
| c | Correlation | as a status to be used for his own advantage |
| 7a | Contrast | but |
| b | Action 1 | (2) **stripped himself of the status,** |
| c | Simultaneous | taking the outward appearance of a slave |
| d | Means | by becoming like human beings; |
| e | | and |
| | Circumstance | looking like a normal person, |
| 8a | Action 2 | (3) **he humiliated himself** |
| b | Means | by becoming obedient |
| c | Extent | all the way to the point of death, even |
| d | Clarification | death on a cross! |
| 9a | Inference | For this reason |
| b | Action 3/Reaction | **God** also **highly exalted him** and |
| c | Simultaneous Act. | **gave to him the name above every name,** |
| 10a | Purpose | in order that at the name of Jesus |
| b | Response 1 | every knee will bow— |
| c | Sphere | whether of heaven, or |
| d | Alternative | earth, or |
| e | Alternative | under the earth— |

*Continued on next page.*

| | | |
|---|---|---|
| 11a | | and |
| b | Response 2 | every tongue will confess |
| c | Content/Title | that Jesus Christ is Lord |
| d | Goal | to the glory |
| e | Object | of God |
| f | Apposit. | the Father. |

## Structure

In 1975 Morna Hooker published a very influential essay on Philippians 2:6–11.[5] She introduces her reflections by delighting in a comment from A. B. Bruce, taken from his 1876 publication *The Humiliation of Christ*. Concerning this passage Bruce notes, "The diversity of opinion prevailing among interpreters in regard to the meaning . . . is enough to fill the student with despair and to afflict him with intellectual paralysis."[6] Hooker adds, "Nearly 100 years later, the cause of the despair has increased out of all proportion—but the paralysis has apparently still not overtaken us!"[7] Indeed. Four decades since Hooker's essay, thinking has shifted regarding various questions surrounding the passage, but its bibliography manifests "an uncontainable deluge of scholarly debate, quite possibly more so than any other New Testament text."[8] For instance, in the history of interpretation, numerous scholars have taken up the challenge of identifying the exact literary form of this so-called Christ hymn (on which, see the In Depth section below), and we only have space here to make a start on the topic. As a way forward, we reflect briefly on the grammatical structure of the text and then what might be called its poetic narrative development.

### *Grammatical Structure*

As for the grammatical structure of 2:5–11,[9] the diagram above shows that verse 5 introduces this christological reflection with an exhortation: "be intent on" (φρονεῖτε). The relative pronoun ("who," ὅς) in verse 6 launches a description of "Christ Jesus." The backbone of the description begins with three actions by Christ Jesus himself:

5. Morna D. Hooker, "Philippians 2:6–11," in *Jesus und Paulus: Festschrift für Werner Georg Kümmel zum 70. Geburtstag*, ed. E. Earle Ellis and Erich Grässer (Göttingen: Vandenhoeck & Ruprecht, 1975), 151–64. As an example of her influence on more recent reflections on the structure of the passage, see Bockmuehl, *Philippians*, 125.

6. Alexander Balmain Bruce, *The Humiliation of Christ in Its Physical, Ethical, and Official Aspects* (Edinburgh: T&T Clark, 1876), 8.

7. Hooker, "Philippians 2:6–11," 151.

8. So Bockmuehl, *Philippians*, 115. E.g., see Ralph P. Martin, *A Hymn of Christ: Philippians 2:5–11 in Recent Interpretation and in the Setting of Early Christian Worship* (Downers Grove, IL: IVP Academic, 1997), and the six hundred or so works noted by Martin have expanded further over the past two decades.

9. For an alternative approach, see Gordon D. Fee, "Philippians 2:5–11: Hymn or Exalted Pauline Prose?," *BBR* 2 (1992): 46.

A. he “did not regard equality” (v. 6)
B. he “stripped himself” (v. 7)
C. “he humiliated himself” (v. 8)

Philippians 2:9 is then introduced with “for this reason” (the inferential conjunction διό) and turns to twin actions by God the Father, who

A. “highly exalted him” and
B. “gave to him the name above every name”[10]

Notice that with the “in order that” (ἵνα) clause of 2:10–11, the exaltation of Christ elicits two responses from all creatures:

A. “every knee will bow” and
B. “every tongue will confess”

So grammatically the passage moves from Christ’s actions in his heavenly glory, to incarnation, to humiliation on the cross, and then to actions by God the Father, who exalted the Son and gave him a name above every name. This was so that the Son’s absolute dominion would be realized and God the Father would be glorified.

## *Poetic Narrative Structure*

Over the past few decades, proposals on the poetic structure of the passage have multiplied like rabbits.[11] As just two examples, my approach has a number of points in common with that of Robert Gundry,[12] on the one hand, and Markus Bockmuehl,[13] on the other. I differ with both by dividing the passage into two chiastic movements. The first comprises four narrative steps following the Son’s path from a preincarnate posture in glory, to his incarnation, to his passion, and finally to the Father’s response in exalting him (2:6–9b).[14] This narrative flow, or “way of the Son,” comprises a classic Christian understanding of Christ coming to earth from heaven and then, after the resurrection, being exalted back to heaven.[15]

10. All the verbs to this point are aorist indicative in form and thus perfective in aspect, which often functions to establish the backbone of a narrative. On that function see Campbell, *Verbal Aspect*, 38–39, though I am not convinced of Campbell’s view of “remoteness” being a factor in the form.

11. On this and other issues surrounding Phil 2:6–11 as a “hymn,” see the In Depth section below.

12. Robert H. Gundry, “Style and Substance in ‘the Myth of God Incarnate’ according to Philippians 2:6–11,” in *Crossing the Boundaries: Essays in Biblical Interpretation in Honour of Michael D. Goulder*, ed. Stanley E. Porter, Paul M. Joyce, and David E. Orton, BibInt 8 (Leiden: Brill, 1994), 271–93.

13. Bockmuehl, *Philippians*, 125.

14. Similar to Charles J. Robbins, “Rhetorical Structure of Philippians 2:6–11,” *CBQ* 42.1 (1980): 79–80, who divides the passage into two sentences.

15. On which, see Attridge, *Epistle to the Hebrews*, 78–81.

The second chiastic frame[16] begins with God's second action in verse 9, rendered "gave to him the name," which then conceptually opens the door for the "in order that" (ἵνα) clause in verses 10–11, which focuses on the name of Jesus. The thematic focus of these verses rests on the dominion of the Son and the ultimate glorification of God the Father.[17] The structure of the whole may be depicted as follows.

| | |
|---|---|
| A who being robed in divine glory, | PREINCARNATE |
| Did not regard equality with God | POSTURE IN GLORY |
| as a status to be used for his own | |
| advantage | |
| but | |
| B stripped himself of the status, | INCARNATION |
| taking the outward appearance of a slave, | |
| C by becoming like human beings | |
| and | |
| C′ looking like a normal person, | |
| B′ he humiliated himself | PASSION |
| By becoming obedient all the way to the point of death, | |
| even death on a cross! | |
| For this reason | |
| A′ God also highly exalted him | EXALTATION |
| and | |
| α gave to him the name above every name, in order that | |
| β at the name of Jesus | DOMINION |
| γ every knee will bow— | |
| δ whether of heaven, or | |
| earth, or | |
| under the earth—and | |
| γ′ every tongue will confess | |
| β′ that Jesus Christ is Lord | |
| α′ to the glory of God the Father | GLORIFICATION |

Several elements of the structure warrant attention, particularly the parallelism in the passage. The first chiastic movement begins and ends with references to God

16. The structure of vv. 9–11 proposed here is similar to that of Fee but with adjustments. See Fee, *Philippians*, 219n6.

17. Thus, my approach does not divide the passage on the basis of the actions of the Son over against the actions of the Father, as many do. Rather, my approach understands the first movement to highlight the narrative overview of the Son's journey from preincarnation to exaltation, with the second movement focusing on "the name" given to Christ at his exaltation. As we see below, this division of the passage also follows the use of two different OT contexts that lie behind Phil 2:6–11; Isa 52:12–53:12 lies behind the first chiastic movement, and Isa 45:23–25 behind the second.

(A–A′), as does the second chiastic movement (α–α′). Thus the whole moves from a reference to Christ's equality with God, to God's exaltation of Christ as Lord; from God bestowing a name at the exaltation, to glory being given to God.

The focus of each chiastic movement concerns a posture of submission. The Son's submission finds expression in his taking the form of a servant and humbling himself (B–C; C′–B′), and as a result of his exaltation everyone in all creation will be submitted to him (γ–δ–γ′). Also, the first movement goes from heaven, to earth, to heaven, while the second has a center that speaks of "heaven, or earth, or under the earth."

Further, other parallels are highlighted by this twin chiastic structure.

- the "in the image of God" (ἐν μορφῇ[18] θεοῦ) of verse 6 is balanced by "to the glory of God (εἰς δόξαν θεοῦ) in verse 11 (A and α′)
- that he "stripped himself" (ἑαυτὸν ἐκένωσεν) parallels he "humiliated himself" (ἐταπείνωσεν ἑαυτόν), and note the inversion of "himself" (ἑαυτόν) (B and B′)
- "becoming like human beings" (ὁμοιώματι ἀνθρώπων γενόμενος) forms an obvious parallel with "looking like a normal person" (σχήματι εὑρεθεὶς ὡς ἄνθρωπος), and again notice the inversion of "person" (ἄνθρωπος) in relation to the participle (C and C′)
- The double reference to "him" (αὐτόν/αὐτῷ) in verse 9 (A′ and α′)
- "the name of Jesus" (τῷ ὀνόματι Ἰησοῦ) is mirrored by "Jesus Christ is Lord" (κύριος Ἰησοῦς Χριστός) (β and β′)
- The confession that "every knee will bow" (πᾶν γόνυ κάμψῃ) finds an obvious parallel in "every tongue will confess" (πᾶσα γλῶσσα ἐξομολογήσηται) (γ and γ′)

Finally, each of these chiastic movements has a moment at which the reader is forced to slow down or pause. The expanding "of death" (θανάτου) with "death on a cross" (θανάτου δὲ σταυροῦ) in verse 8 creates an appropriate pause just before the climactic inference in verse 9.[19] And the triple "heaven, or earth, or under the earth" (ἐπουρανίων καὶ ἐπιγείων καὶ καταχθονίων) of verse 10 slows down the pace, putting space between knees bowing and tongues confessing, just before the final celebration of Jesus Christ as Lord.

18. On "image" (μορφῇ) as an allusion to the appearance of God the Son in his divine glory, see the commentary on 2:6 below.

19. As noted by Bockmuehl, *Philippians*, 125–26. Bockmuehl offers a modification of the proposal by Hooker, understanding the passage to be organized around six sets of three lines each. Moreover, he agrees with Fee that what we have in our passage is not formal poetry but "lyrical, exalted prose."

## IN DEPTH: Philippians 2:6–11 as Hymn[20]

One of the most voluminous discussions in New Testament studies concerns the nature of Philippians 2:6–11 as hymn. In considering the exact nature of the passage, several questions are raised. Is this a hymn? Where did this material originate? What is its purpose? Since the time of Ernst Lohmeyer,[21] scholars have offered a number of reasons for reading Philippians 2:6–11 as hymnic.[22] Among the reasons offered by interpreters through the years are (1) the passage is introduced by a relative pronoun (ὅς), as is the case with similar units in the New Testament (e.g., Col 1:15–20; 1 Tim 3:16b; Heb 1:2b–4); (2) the language normally is read as stylistically distinct from the wording of the rest of the book, making the passage seem a self-contained unit; (3) the words are arranged with a rhythm, or perhaps rhyme,[23] and have numerous points of parallelism; and for those who believe the hymn was a traditional piece adopted by Paul, (4) the passage includes words not normally used by the apostle. So, in the case of Philippians 2:6–11, the exalted Christology makes perfect sense as a standalone text, progressing from the pre-incarnate Christ to the confession of his universal lordship. Given its apparent function

20. Given the expansive literature on this topic, we can only outline the basic issues and make a few tentative suggestions. For more extensive treatments, see, e.g., Martin, *Hymn of Christ*; Matthew E. Gordley, *New Testament Christological Hymns: Exploring Texts, Contexts, and Significance* (Downers Grove, IL: IVP Academic, 2018); Reumann, *Philippians*, 333–83; Hawthorne and Martin, *Philippians*, 90–105. Fee laments the volume of material on this passage, writing that the profusion of debate "has sometimes tended to obscure rather than to enlighten, and, even worse, to bog down in debate a passage that should cause the reader to soar. It seems tragic that such a marvelous moment should get inundated by so much talk" (Fee, *Philippians*, 192n1).

On the identification of so-called hymns or hymn fragments in the New Testament, especially Phil 2, see, e.g., C. Basevi and J. Chapa, "Philippians 2.6–11: The Rhetorical Function of a Pauline 'Hymn,'" in *Rhetoric and the New Testament: Essays from the 1992 Heidelberg Conference*, ed. Thomas H. Olbricht and Stanley E. Porter, JSNTSup 90 (Sheffield: JSOT Press, 1993), 338–56; Frederick W. Danker, "A Symphony of New Testament Hymns: Commentary on Philippians 2:5–11, Colossians 1:15–20, Ephesians 2:14–16, 1 Timothy 3:16, Titus 3:4–7, 1 Peter 3:18–22, and 2 Timothy 2:11–13," *CBQ* 60 (1998): 161–62; Stephen E. Fowl, *The Story of Christ in the Ethics of Paul: An Analysis of the Function of the Hymnic Material in the Pauline Corpus* (Sheffield: Sheffield Academic Press, 1990); Otfried Hofius, *Der Christushymnus Philipper 2,6–11: Untersuchengen zu Gestalt und Aussage eines urchristlichen Psalms*, WUNT 17 (Tübingen: Mohr Siebeck, 1991); Claus H. Hunzinger, "Zur Struktur Der Christus-Hymnen in Phil 2 und 1 Petr 3," in *Ruf Jesu und die Antwort der Gemeinde: Exegetische Untersuchungen Joachim Jeremias zum 70. Geburtstag gewidmet von seinen Schülern*, ed. Eduard Lohse, Christoph Burchard and Berndt Schaller (Göttingen: Vandenhoeck & Ruprecht, 1970), 142–56; Martin, *Hymn of Christ*; Ulrich B. Müller, "Der Christushymnus Phil 2 6–11," *ZNW* 79.1–2 (1988): 17–44; Jim Purves, "The Missional Doxology of the Philippian Hymn," *BapTheo* 3.1 (2011): 15–30; Jack T. Sanders, *The New Testament Christological Hymns: Their Historical Religious Background*, SNTSMS 15 (Cambridge: Cambridge University Press, 1971); Charles H. Talbert, "A Hymn of Christ: Philippians 2:5–11 in Recent Interpretation and in the Setting of Early Christian Worship," *PRSt* 28.2 (2001): 141–42; Robert A. Wortham, "Christology as Community Identity in the Philippians Hymn: The Philippians Hymn as Social Drama (Philippians 2:5–11)," *PRSt* 23.3 (1996): 269–87.

21. Ernst Lohmeyer, *Kyrios Jesus: Eine Untersuchung zu Phil. 2,5–11* (Heidelberg: C. Winter, 1928), 4–13.

22. Fee, "Philippians 2:5–11," 30–31; Martin, *Hymn of Christ*, 25–28.

23. Adela Yarbro Collins, "Psalms, Philippians 2:6–11, and the Origins of Christology," *BibInt* 11 (2003): 368.

as reinforcing Paul's exhortation to selflessness, so the reasoning goes, the whole of its christological narrative could be read as theological overkill for Paul's contextual purposes.

Yet this confident program of identifying New Testament hymns, including Philippians 2:6–11, has been called into question of late on at least two primary fronts. First, some suggest that the so-called New Testament hymns do not match the style or conventions of broader Semitic, Jewish, or Greco-Roman hymnody.[24] Second, the linguistic and stylistic distinctions of these texts can be read simply as a type of exalted Pauline prose.[25] Those holding this position suggest that we simply do not have elements clearly marking the passage as a hymn.[26]

Nevertheless, more recent research has pushed back, proposing a mediating position. In their article, Michael Martin and Bryan Nash argue that *hymnos* was a prominent form addressed in the rhetorical handbooks of the ancient world, which followed specific, though flexible, conventions. Having examined the features of the genre, Martin and Nash conclude that Philippians 2:6–11 conforms completely to this type of composition, with one exception. The Christ hymn conforms in its inclusion of Christ's "origin" (amplified by *syncrisis*), birth, body, mind/virtues, deeds, manner of death, posthumous events, and names and titles (amplified with *syncrisis*). The exception is that whereas a *hymnos* normally included praise of values that reinforced the Roman vision of what might be worthy of adulation, Philippians 2:6–11 turns worldly values on their head. Martin and Nash explain:

> [The topoi] are handled in a manner that subverts conventional notions of what was—and was not—worthy of praise. Normally, such topoi were understood and employed in a way that served to reinforce the prevailing values of Roman culture. A subject was praised, for example, if he or she came from a noble family (origin), or possessed strength or beauty (body), or displayed courage (mind) in battle, or died in an honorable manner (death). And even when a subject lacked such conventional markers of status, innovative composition was encouraged that did not upset but reinforced the social order.... The Christ-hymn, by contrast, displays a kind of innovation that directly

24. Basevi and Chapa, "Philippians 2.6–11"; Fowl, *Story of Christ*, 31–32; Benjamin A. Edsall and Jennifer R. Strawbridge, "The Song We Used to Sing?: Hymn 'Traditions' and Reception in Pauline Letters," *JSNT* 37 (2015): 290–311.

25. Fee, "Philippians 2:5–11," 31.

26. Markus N. A. Bockmuehl, "'The Form of God' (Phil 2:6): Variations on a Theme of Jewish Mysticism," *JTS* 48 (1997): 3–4; Mi Young Sydney Park, *Submission within the Godhead and the Church in the Epistle to the Philippians: An Exegetical and Theological Examination of the Concept of Submission in Philippians 2 and 3*, LNTS 361 (London: T&T Clark, 2007), 11–13.

> challenges these markers. Christ is praised because he adopted what by every topos would normally be judged a more shameful station than was rightly his. And he did this, the hymn claims, because of his servant nature—because his mind was characterized by humility.[27]

Further, Martin and Nash demonstrate that such compositions were not limited to the poetic (though poetic elements may be identified in our passage). Rather, such topoi could be used to shape prose as well.[28] This fact, it seems to me, answers Fee's concern that the passage appears to embody "elevated prose" rather than known forms of poetry. Grounded in Martin and Nash's research, therefore, it seems that Philippians 2:6–11 can be read as *hymnos*, composed in a two-movement structure—verses 6–8 the first, and verses 9–11 the second. This does not necessarily mean that Philippians 2:6–11 was a "hymn" that was sung liturgically in churches of the first century,[29] but it does seem to follow or at least mirror the general pattern of *hymnos* as described by Martin and Nash. Nevertheless, despite Fee's objections noted above and in light of the extensive use of parallelism in the passage, the chiastic structures, and the narrative movement of the passage, I actually prefer Michael Gorman's language of "narrative poem"[30] to that of "hymn," and it may be suggested that the narrative-poetic nature of the passage has similarities to what we find in the poetic material of the prophets.

This brings us to a discussion of the traditional material behind Philippians 2:6–11. If the apostle used traditional material in his celebration of the Christ event—material shaped either by himself or someone else—it would explain uses of what seem to be non-Pauline vocabulary in the passage. Yet, what traditional material? Reumann has noted some fourteen different options in the history of interpretation![31] Nevertheless, the best evidence points us to the Jewish Scriptures. Specifically, recent work offers a compelling case for Isaiah 45:23–25 and 52:13–53:12 as extensively evoked in Philippians 2:6–11, perhaps drawing on the Hebrew form of these texts.[32] For instance, the following is adapted from Matthew Harmon and James P. Ware, noting the conceptual

27. Michael W. Martin and Bryan A. Nash, "Philippians 2:6–11 as Subversive *Hymnos*: A Study in the Light of Ancient Rhetorical Theory," *JTS* 66.1 (2015): 111–13.

28. Martin and Nash, "Philippians 2:6–11 as Subversive *Hymnos*," 136.

29. See Bockmuehl, *Philippians*, 116–17.

30. Gorman, *Participating*, 33.

31. Reumann, *Philippians*, 335–38, includes, for example, Iranian Zoroastrianism, gnostic redeemer myth, Greco-Roman hymnody or personages or social settings, enthronement rituals, or a variety of OT theologies. The best answer seems to lie in this final direction.

32. Especially, Bauckham, *Jesus and the God of Israel*, 43; Matthew Harmon, *Philippians: A Mentor Commentary* (Fearn, Ross-shire, Scotland: Mentor, 2015), 57–66, 201–3; J. Patrick Ware, *The Mission of the Church in Paul's Letter to the Philippians in the Context of Ancient Judaism*, NovTSup 120 (Leiden: Brill, 2005), 224–36.

links between Philippians 2:6–11 and the Isaiah texts while also pointing out language used in some Greek forms of these texts.[33]

| Verse | Word or Phrase in Philippians 2:6–11 | Passage from Isaiah |
|---|---|---|
| 2:6 | Form of God | 53:2a–b (Aquila uses μορφή) |
| 2:7 | Poured himself out | 53:12 |
| 2:7 | form of a servant/slave | 52:13–14; 53:11 (LXX δουλεύοντα) |
| 2:7 | likeness of men | 52:14; 53:2 (Aquila reads, μορφὴ αὐτοῦ ἀπὸ τῶν ἀνθρώπων) |
| 2:8 | found in appearance as a man | 52:14; 53:2–3 |
| 2:8 | humbled himself | 53:3–4, 7–8 |
| 2:8 | obedient to the point of death | 53:7–8, 12; see also 53:10 |
| 2:8 | death on a cross | 52:14; 53:3–8 |
| 2:9 | God highly exalted him | 52:13; 53:12 |
| 2:10 | every knee will bow | 45:23 |
| 2:11 | every tongue will confess | 45:23 |
| 2:11 | to the glory of God | 45:24–25 |

Such traditional material behind the poetic narrative in the passage would account for aspects of its vocabulary and style. The extensive conceptual correspondences between the passages supports the view that the Isaianic material lies behind Philippians 2:6–11. Further, it seems that the development of this narrative poem may have been based on the Hebrew text rather than the LXX. For example, in dealing with the "death" of the servant, the Hebrew text presents the servant as "pouring out his soul to death"—depicting the servant himself as carrying out this act—while the LXX reads more passively "his soul was handed over to death" (παρεδόθη εἰς θάνατον ἡ ψυχὴ αὐτοῦ). In Philippians 2:7–8, Christ actively took the path of obedience all the way to death. Further, the act of "pouring out" in the Hebrew text of Isaiah 53:12 (ערה) corresponds to Christ "emptying himself" in Philippians 2:7, the Hebrew and Greek terms having semantic overlap. At other points, the Greek wording in Philippians 2:6–11 differs from the LXX, while corresponding to concepts in the Hebrew text. Paul, on the other hand, uses the LXX elsewhere in quoting or alluding to Isaiah (e.g., Rom 4:25a), and he at times uses a form of the text

33. Harmon, *Philippians*, 202–3; Ware, *Mission of the Church*, 225–26; in correspondence with my former student, Taylor Brazil, who did the groundwork for this figure.

that does not conform completely—either to the LXX or to the Hebrew texts we have at hand. Thus, we cannot be certain, but we should not assume that Paul or someone else crafted this passage using the LXX as the source text.

## Exegetical Outline

→ **2. Be Like Christ Jesus, the Preeminent Example of Self-Sacrifice (2:5–11)**
- **a. Adopt Christ's Mindset (v. 5)**
- **b. Follow Christ's Example of Humility (vv. 6–8)**
  - (1) His Posture of Servanthood (vv. 6–7)
  - (2) The Extent of His Obedience (v. 8)
- **c. Attend to God's Great Reversal of Christ's Status (vv. 9–11)**
  - (1) The Exaltation (v. 9)
  - (2) God's Purpose, Our Response (vv. 10–11d)
  - (3) The Ultimate Goal, God's Glory (v. 11e–g)

## Explanation of the Text

This passage constitutes one of the most debated—as well as one of the most beautiful and powerful—texts in all the New Testament. Paul crafts (or incorporates) the full narrative arc of Christ's journey, from his preincarnate glory, to his exaltation, and finally to the consequent glorification of God the Father. Thus, the concise passage has been called "Paul's master story."[34] Yet its conciseness belies its complexity. In verses 6–7 alone, we find at least four massive flash points that have set the world of interpretation on fire and burned up loads of detailed commentary pages. These include the phrase "in the form of God" (ἐν μορφῇ θεοῦ), the term we translate as "status to be used for his own advantage" (ἁρπαγμόν), the verb "emptied" or "divested" (ἐκένωσεν), and the twin clauses "becoming like human beings" (ἐν ὁμοιώματι ἀνθρώπων γενόμενος) and "looking like a normal person" (σχήματι εὑρεθεὶς ὡς ἄνθρωπος). As we walk through our explanation of the text, we will need to give attention to these critical elements without getting bogged down in the history of interpretation.

**2:5–6 Among yourselves, be intent on this posture of humility, which we also see in Christ Jesus, who being robed in divine glory, did not regard equality with God as a status to be used for his own advantage** (τοῦτο[35] φρονεῖτε ἐν ὑμῖν ὃ

34. Gorman, *Participating*, xxiii, 34.

35. The omission of γάρ (א* A B C Ψ 33. 81. 1241. 2464. 2495 t vg^mss co; Or Aug) is probably original since there seems no good reason for a scribe to deliberately omit it, and its absence would explain the variety of conjunctions added by scribes. See Metzger, *Textual Commentary*, 545.

καὶ ἐν Χριστῷ Ἰησοῦ, 6 ὃς ἐν μορφῇ θεοῦ ὑπάρχων οὐχ ἁρπαγμὸν ἡγήσατο τὸ εἶναι ἴσα θεῷ). In seeking to call the Philippians to a posture of humility and service to others, Paul now turns to the example of Christ. He introduces this striking reflection with an exhortation: "Among yourselves, be intent on this posture of humility." The first word in the Greek sentence ("this," τοῦτο) serves as a pointer *back* to the pattern of humility that he has just been describing in 2:2–4.[36] Thus the apostle uses the pronoun, placed at the beginning of this new movement for emphasis and to link the exhortation of 2:2–4 to the example of Christ, which is laid out so beautifully in this passage.

As we saw in 2:1–4, Paul wants to get the Philippians' relationships right by getting their thinking right (cf. 2:2). Here he calls for the believers to "be intent" (φρονέω)[37] on the posture of humility he has just described. As we have already seen at 1:7 and 2:2, this term belongs to a lexical family having to do with thought or perspective. Ancient authors could use the word, for instance, to speak of having an "opinion" or thinking about a matter in a particular way (e.g., Acts 28:22; 1 Cor 13:11; Phil 1:7). Similarly, a writer might use the word to speak of "careful consideration" of something or the act of setting one's mind on something—as Paul does at Philippians 3:18–19, where he speaks of "the enemies of the cross of Christ . . . who are *intent* on earthly things." The exhortation at 2:5 seems to carry the nuance of giving careful thought to something, particularly the pattern of humility and service as embodied in the person and work of Christ himself.[38]

The apostle challenges the Philippians to cultivate such a posture in their community ("among yourselves"; ἐν ὑμῖν).[39] Given the parallel with "in Christ Jesus" (ἐν Χριστῷ Ἰησοῦ) that follows, we can also read the "among yourselves" as pointing to internal realities (i.e., "inside you")—after all, "thought" is internal to a person. Nevertheless, the emphasis probably lies in the community dynamic of sharing a certain perspective or posture as a group. Thus we understand the phrase as communicating "association" rather than internalization.

Specifically, the Philippians are to cultivate a posture of servanthood by following the example seen and power provided "in Christ Jesus" (ἐν Χριστῷ Ἰησοῦ). Paul uses this phrase to speak of believers' "union with Christ."[40] Yet in that relationship Christ also serves as a preeminent example for his people to follow.[41] Thus it is unsurprising that translations have varied between renderings that reflect imitation (e.g., CSB, CEB, CEV, NET,

36. At several places in Philippians, Paul follows the pattern of using the demonstrative pronoun to point *back* to what he has just mentioned (e.g., 1:7, 25; 3:7, 15; 4:8, 9). The adjunctive use of καί also suggests that here Paul picks up the themes of 2:1–4 and anticipates the example of Christ, which follows. Thus, τοῦτο should not be read as pointing forward to the content of the reflection on Christ. So Fee, *Philippians*, 199–200.

37. The present imperative form is the stronger reading based on external evidence ($\mathfrak{P}^{46}$ ℵ A B C* D F G 33. 81. 1175. 1739. 1881 latt sy). The present imperative often is used to communicate general instructions. See Campbell, *Verbal Aspect*, 70.

38. BDAG 1065–66.

39. That is, collectively, so ESV; similarly, "toward one another," NET; "in your relationships with one another," NIV.

40. Michael Gorman renders the phrase as "a community in the Messiah Jesus" (*Participating*, 91–92). The "union with Christ" interpretation may be seen in Martin's rendering: "As it becomes those who are 'in Christ Jesus' (i.e., as members of his community)." See the fuller discussion in Hawthorne and Martin, *Philippians*, 107–9. For arguments on both sides of this debate, see Hellerman, *Philippians*, 108–9, who in the end prefers the ethical ("example") interpretation "with some reservations." Against the ethical view as the only option here, see Silva, *Philippians*, 95–97, who suggests that the "union with Christ" view, which he sees as correct, can be built on with an ethical application.

41. On which, see Campbell, *Paul and Union with Christ*, 105–6. For ἐν Χριστῷ used of Christ as an individual person, see Eph 1:10; 2:15–16; Col 1:19; 2:9; so Murray J. Harris, *Prepositions and Theology in the Greek New Testament: An Essential Reference Resource for Exegesis* (Grand Rapids: Zondervan, 2012), 123.

NIV, NLT) and those that reflect participation or location (e.g., ESV, RSV). We have rendered this verbless phrase as "which we also see in Christ Jesus," which emphasizes imitation. Christ, the living, exalted Lord, offers believers an ever-present example of humility and service as they think of his path of humble sacrifice on their behalf, and this fits well with the center of the letter offering a series of examples to imitate (Christ, Timothy and Epaphroditus, and Paul). Yet the phrase "in Christ" should be understood as also drawing on Paul's broader theology of participation—that is, on believers' mutual relationship with Christ or participation in his life, which stands as the spiritual means for us living out the Lord's example.[42]

As we move to verse 6, the phrase we have translated as "being robed in divine glory" (ἐν μορφῇ θεοῦ) is as theologically rich as it is extensively debated.[43] The phrase tells us something about the state and circumstances of Christ Jesus prior to the incarnation.[44] The question is, What? Apart from the long ending of Mark (16:12), Philippians 2:6–7 boasts the only New Testament occurrences of the term often translated as "form" (μορφή), where it occurs twice, once referring to the "form of God" and then to "the form of a servant." This term appears in the LXX seven times,[45] almost always referring to outward appearance. For example, Isaiah 44:13 reads, "Having chosen a piece of wood, the artisan set it up with a measure and arranged it with glue; he made it like the form of a man [ὡς μορφὴν ἀνδρός], like human beauty, to set it up in a house" (NETS). In broader Jewish and Greek literature, the word communicates a variety of ideas, such as "stature, form, condition, feature," and "external appearance,"[46] but it overwhelmingly refers to an observable form or shape of something.[47]

Traditional interpretations have often read the phrase "form of God" as referring to the essential nature of Christ as God.[48] Other proposals vary widely, including extensive discussions that read in our passage an Adamic Christology (Christ as

42. For a fresh reading on the participation reading of this verse, see Gorman, *Participating*, 77–93. As my translation and comments reflect, I place more emphasis on imitation than does Gorman, and I am not yet convinced of his reading of the two words I have translated as "which . . . also" (ὃ καί). Yet I think his emphasis on participation in the risen Christ is helpful and meaningful in light of the transformation spoken of in the echoes of our passage in 3:10–21.

43. Gerald Hawthorne notes, "If the number and variety of interpretations given to this expression have any meaning it must be because it is of crucial importance for understanding the whole of the Christ-hymn, of fundamental significance for determining the Christology of the entire passage" (Gerald F. Hawthorne, "In the Form of God and Equal with God [Philippians 2:6]," in *Where Christology Began: Essays on Philippians 2*, ed. Ralph P. Martin and Brian J. Dodd [Louisville: Westminster John Knox, 1998], 97). More colorfully, as Markus Bockmuehl introduces an article on this phrase he notes, "Like proverbial vultures over a carcass, twentieth-century New Testament scholars have tenaciously continued to congregate around the supposed 'hymn' of Phil 2:5–11. As a result, this passage is one of the most overinterpreted texts of the New Testament" (Bockmuehl, "Form of God," 1).

44. The present participle of ὑπάρχω can speak of being present or, as here, "existing," thus being "in a state or circumstance" (BDAG 1029–30).

45. Judg [A] 8:18; Job 4:16; Isa 44:13; Dan 3:19; Tob 1:13; Wis 18:1; 4 Macc 15:4.

46. *TLNT* 2:520–21.

47. The most extensive lexical study to date was conducted by Daniel J. Fabricatore, *Form of God, Form of a Servant: An Examination of the Greek Noun* μορφή *in Philippians 2:6–7* (Lanham, MD: University Press of America, 2010), 27–98. In the second chapter, Fabricatore surveys six centuries of use of the term in Greek literature across a wide variety of genres. In his extensive lexical study he concludes (p. 87):

> μορφή is a term that had maintained a somewhat stable semantic range for 600 years. That semantic range includes the concepts of the physical form or shape of someone or something, which is the primary way μορφή is used. In some cases, it can refer to the essential nature of something, but even in these cases, that nature is perceived by the senses.

48. On which, see Reumann, *Philippians*, 334, 342. Lightfoot argued, on the basis of Aristotle and other Greek philosophers, that the term has a secondary, philosophical meaning that points to the "essential nature" of something (*Philippians*, 127–33). Several commentators and reference tools have followed this line of

the "new Adam," paralleling the narrative of Adam in Genesis, who was created in God's image) as the primary backdrop of this thought and the passage as a whole.[49]

Yet a better interpretation seems to be to understand Paul's words as referring to the "appearance" of Christ in his preincarnate, divine glory,[50] hence our translation, "robed in divine glory." This position assumes the preincarnate glory of Christ as God, but the emphasis lies on Christ's position or status as manifested in his appearance. Jewish tradition sometimes refers to God as having a "form." For example, several scholars have pointed to Philo's *On the Life of Moses* (1.66), where he writes of the burning bush theophany, "And in the middle of the flame there was seen a certain very beautiful form [μορφή], not resembling any visible thing, a most Godlike image, emitting a light more brilliant than fire, which anyone might have imagined to be the image of the living God." Thus, Philo, referring to the "form" of God, speaks of a divine glory, "emitting a light." He hedges a bit, not wanting to be dogmatic that we see an image of God himself, but he certainly points in that direction.[51]

Among other arguments for our phrase (ἐν μορφῇ θεοῦ) as speaking of Christ's glorious appearance, Bockmuehl points to Paul's own experiences of seeing the risen Lord, suggesting that the apostle stands squarely in the tradition of Jewish visionary experiences (e.g., Acts 9; 22; 26; 1 Cor 9:1; 2 Cor 12:1–9; Gal 1:12, 16).[52] This accords well with Old Testament material, where God often manifests himself in glory (e.g., Exod 16:10; 24:16–17; 33:17–23; 40:34–38; 1 Kgs 8:11; Isa 6:3). Given the extensive Isaianic backdrop behind Philippians 2:6–11,[53] Isaiah's majestic vision of God in Isaiah 6 certainly comes to mind. Further, although this word for "form" (μορφή) is not synonymous with the word for "glory" (δόξα), elsewhere Paul reflects on Christ as manifesting the divine glory of God (Rom 1:23; 1 Cor 11:7; 2 Cor 3:18; 4:6).[54]

With the emphasis on appearance, this understanding of "form" (μορφή) also syncs well with the parallel use of the word in the next verse, often translated as "form of a servant" (μορφὴν δούλου). In the incarnation, the Son takes on the "appearance" of a common slave.[55] The emphasis, then, seems to be on appearance reflecting a particular

thought; e.g., Louw and Nida arranged μορφή and its cognates under "A Nature, Character," as well as under "Appearance as an Outward Manifestation of Form" (L&N 586–87). See also, e.g., Silva, *Philippians*, 100–101; Fee, *Philippians*, 204–5. Yet, as shown by Fabricatore's study, when used in conjunction with φύσις ("nature"), Aristotle "almost always uses μορφή to denote something that is visible" (Fabricatore, *Form of God*, 50).

49. For these and other interpretations, see Reumann, *Philippians*, 342–43; Hawthorne and Martin, *Philippians*, 110–15; Bockmuehl, "Form of God," 6–11; Hansen, *Philippians*, 135–42. On Adam Christology see especially the summary in Hansen and the article by James D. G. Dunn, "Christ, Adam, and Preexistence," in Martin and Dodd, *Where Christology Began*, 74–83, as well as the response by Lincoln D. Hurst ("Christ, Adam, and Preexistence Revisited," also in Martin and Dodd, *Where Christology Began*, 84–95). It seems to me that the extensive parallels between our passage and Isa 45, 52–53 rule out Gen 3 as a primary backdrop.

50. So Bockmuehl, "Form of God"; idem, *Philippians*, 126–29; Fabricatore, *Form of God*, 209; Stephen E. Fowl, *Philippians*, THNTC (Grand Rapids: Eerdmans, 2005), 91–94; Joseph H. Hellerman, *Reconstructing Honor in Roman Philippi: Carmen Christi as Cursus Pudorum*, SNTSMS 132 (Cambridge: Cambridge University Press, 2005), 131–33.

51. Fowl, *Philippians*, 92.

52. In that tradition, as here in Phil 2:5–11, God's appearance is often associated with God's name. Bockmuehl concludes, "I would like to suggest that Paul stands in a similar Jewish mystical tradition in which it was possible to speak of the Lord's majesty and greatness by alluding to the inconceivable size and beauty of his bodily appearance" (Bockmuehl, "Form of God," 19). Think, for instance, of Jesus's appearance to Paul on the Damascus Road and the manifestation of Christ's name (Acts 9:5). See also Josephus, *J.W.* 2.142; Philo, *Confusion* 146. See the fuller argument in Bockmuehl, "Form of God," 17–23, and idem, *Philippians*, 127–29.

53. See above on pp. 158–59.

54. Fowl, *Philippians*, 92.

55. Hellerman makes the intriguing suggestion that, given the status-conscious culture of the Philippians, in which one's

rank or status. This view of 2:6 also fits well with our reading on similar language in 3:21, which refers to "our bodies of humiliation" (τὸ σῶμα τῆς ταπεινώσεως ἡμῶν), which Christ will "transform" (σύμμορφον) in accordance with his "glorious body" (τῷ σώματι τῆς δόξης αὐτοῦ).[56]

Having pointed to Christ's glorious appearance in his preincarnate state, Paul now turns to Christ's posture toward his own status of "equality with God" (ἴσα θεῷ).[57] The term translated as "equality" (ἴσος) could, for instance, refer to something equal in proportion or quality.[58] It also could speak of equality of position or status between individuals (e.g., 2 Macc 9:15), as it does here. John 5:18 seems to parallel Philippians 2:6 most directly: "For this reason they tried all the more to kill him; not only was he breaking the Sabbath, but he was even calling God his own Father, making himself equal [ἴσον] with God" (John 5:18 NIV). Both John and Paul speak of Jesus as divine,[59] but given the context of each, they approach that identity in slightly different ways. With his reference to God as Father, John underscores the intimacy of relationship between the Son and Father, and especially Jesus's profound dependence on the Father.[60] Philippians 2:6, on the other hand, stresses the Son's preincarnate position and the astounding thought that he, for a time, relinquished that position (rather than his divine nature) to meet a need that we could not meet for ourselves.[61]

So Paul writes to the Philippians that Christ did not "regard" this status of "equality with God as a status to be used for his own advantage" (οὐχ ἁρπαγμὸν ἡγήσατο τὸ εἶναι ἴσα θεῷ). To "regard" (ἡγέομαι) could carry the sense of "leading" but here communicates the common meaning of "consider" or "regard,"[62] that is, to think about something from a particular vantage point. What was it that Christ did *not* (οὐχ) consider in relation to his status of equality with the Father? This brings us to one of the most debated interpretive issues in the passage, specifically, how to understand the term we have translated as "a status to be used for his own advantage" (ἁρπαγμός).[63]

The term itself only occurs here in the New Testament, does not appear in the LXX, and only

---

rank was marked out by clothing, the contrast between the glorious appearance of the preincarnate Christ and his appearing in the "outward appearance of a slave" (which would indicate a certain manner of dress) would underscore to the Philippians a massive change in status. See Hellerman, *Reconstructing Honor*, 131–33.

56. The fact that 3:21 refers to the resurrection body of Christ rather than to his preincarnate glory does nothing to lessen these correspondences.

57. In terms of τὸ εἶναι ἴσα θεῷ, the article is not anaphoric in relation to what goes before in the verse; nevertheless, it embodies a "resonance" roughly parallel to ἐν μορφῇ θεοῦ ὑπάρχων. See Wesley Hill, *Paul and the Trinity: Persons, Relations, and the Pauline Letters* (Grand Rapids: Eerdmans, 2015), 91; Denny Burk, "On the Articular Infinitive in Philippians 2:6: A Grammatical Note with Christological Implications," *TynBul* 55 (2004): 253–74.

58. E.g., Exod 26:24; 30:34; Ezek 40:5; 4 Macc 13:20; Rev 21:16. It also could speak of something or someone like something or someone else (Deut 13:6) or corresponding to something else (Job 5:14; 10:10; 13:28) or that is level (Isa 51:23). Or it could speak of something identical to something else (Acts 11:17), equal in perception or treatment (Wis 14:9; Matt 20:12), or something consistent, as with a consistent testimony (Mark 14:56, 59).

59. See Bauckham, *Jesus and the God of Israel*, 41–45, 180; Andreas J. Köstenberger and Scott R. Swain, *Father, Son and Spirit: The Trinity and John's Gospel*, NSBT 24 (Downers Grove, IL: IVP Academic, 2008), 34–39.

60. See C. K. Barrett, *The Gospel according to St John: An Introduction with Commentary and Notes on the Greek Text*, 2nd ed. (London: SPCK, 1978), 256.

61. Cousar, *Philippians and Philemon*, 55; Osiek, *Philippians, Philemon*, 60–61. On "equal to God" as indicating rank or position of a king or emperor, bestowing honor and authority, see Hellerman, *Philippians*, 111–12.

62. BDAG 433–34.

63. The articular infinitive τὸ εἶναι plus the delimiter ἴσα θεῷ serves as the direct object of the verb and, in turn, ἁρπαγμόν serves as the complement. Thus we have here an "object-complement" form of the double accusative. So Wallace, *Greek Grammar*, 182–83.

rarely makes an appearance in extrabiblical Greek. It thus "has proved a sore trial to philologists and lexicographers, and to those who rely on their work."[64] Perhaps following the lead of the Latin Vulgate (*rapinam*, "robbery"), older English translations tended to translate the word as "robbery" (e.g., KJV, YLT, WEB). More recent English translations render the term variously as a thing "to be grasped" (NASB, ESV, NET, NIV [1984]), "something to cling to" (NLT), "something to be exploited" (NRSV; CSB), or something "used to his own advantage" (NIV [2011]).

The question has been rehearsed extensively, and those who wish to review a fuller discussion are encouraged to see the work of N. T. Wright, who builds on the work of R. W. Hoover.[65] In recent discussion, a consensus seems to be forming around the view that the word expresses the notion that Christ's preincarnate status was not "something to take advantage of, something to exploit," as reflected in the NRSV, CSB, and NIV (2011) translations.[66] The Roman cultural context of Philippians—indeed, the history of the world—is replete with examples of powerful people taking advantage of their positions at great cost to others. The apostle is leading the Philippians out of the soul-deadening suck of that cultural orientation, in which status means power and advantage over others (2:3–4). Paul calls them instead to the example of Christ, who held the highest possible status—that of God himself—but decided not to take advantage of his position by keeping himself from the vulnerabilities and suffering of human existence. Thus "Christ's decision does not imply that he gave up his equality with God but that he expressed his equality with God" in giving for others.[67] In other words, it was the Son's equality with God, his glory and status, that uniquely *qualified* him to carry out the work of sacrificial service, drawing humanity into God's redemptive purposes for the world. Only he could do it. Thus, God in Christ is revealed to be a condescending, sacrificial God, who has chosen to meet a need that we as human beings could not meet for ourselves. As Michael Gorman notes, here we have the "poetic narrative" of the gospel in miniature.[68]

**2:7–8 but stripped himself of the status, taking the outward appearance of a slave by becoming like human beings; and looking like a normal person, he humiliated himself by becoming obedient all the way to the point of death, even death on a cross!** (ἀλλ᾽ ἑαυτὸν ἐκένωσεν μορφὴν δούλου λαβών, ἐν ὁμοιώματι ἀνθρώπων γενόμενος· καὶ σχήματι εὑρεθεὶς ὡς ἄνθρωπος 8 ἐταπείνωσεν ἑαυτὸν γενόμενος ὑπήκοος μέχρι θανάτου, θανάτου δὲ σταυροῦ). With verses 7–8 we move from the Son's glorious, preincarnate humility (2:6) to his incarnation and passion. In verse 6 Paul focuses on what Christ did *not* do. Now he turns, by contrast

64. N. T. Wright, *The Climax of the Covenant: Christ and the Law in Pauline Theology* (Edinburgh: T&T Clark, 1991), 62.

65. R. W. Hoover, "The HARPAGMOS Enigma: A Philological Solution," *HTR* 64 (1971): 95–119; N. T. Wright, "ἁρπαγμός and the Meaning of Philippians 2:5–11," *JTS* 37 (1986): 321–52, now updated in idem, *Climax of the Covenant*, 62–98. By the end Wright overloads his interpretation, as he integrates into his reading of the term "Christ as Adam," "Christ as Servant," and "Christ as the pre-existent one" (pp. 90–91).

66. Wright, *Climax of the Covenant*, 97. So agree, e.g., Bauckham, *Jesus and the God of Israel*, 41, and Michael W. Martin, "Ἁρπαγμός Revisited: A Philological Reexamination of the New Testament's 'Most Difficult Word,'" *JBL* 135.1 (2016): 175–94, who confirms the position of Wright while suggesting that the word has no inherent sense of whether the thing exploited is already in the possession of the subject, which must be determined by context.

67. Hansen, *Philippians*, 145.

68. Michael J. Gorman, *Apostle of the Crucified Lord: A Theological Introduction to Paul and His Letters*, 2nd ed. (Grand Rapids: Eerdmans, 2017), 127–28.

("but," ἀλλ᾽), to what Christ *did* do. The main verbs here form the narrative backbone of the passage and are translated as "[he] stripped himself" (ἑαυτὸν ἐκένωσεν) and "he humiliated himself" (ἐταπείνωσεν ἑαυτόν). Each of these verbs is accented to clarify what Paul has in mind. Thus the narrative framework follows a logical, step-by-step progression:

The Son **stripped** himself of his preincarnate status, taking the (B)
outward appearance of a slave
by becoming like human beings (*incarnation*) (C)
looking like a normal person, (C′)
he **humiliated himself** by becoming obedient to the point of death (*the passion*) (B′)

Thus, the incarnation and the passion are the two means by which the Son accomplished his mission.

The verb translated as "stripped" (κενόω) could be used by ancient authors to express making something "empty," "to expend," "to throw away," "to strip," "to abandon," on the one hand, and "to destroy, render void" or to "make something of no effect" on the other.[69] Generally in the New Testament, the word carries the metaphorical meaning "to empty" something of its effect or meaning. For instance, 1 Corinthians 9:15 speaks of someone making Paul's boast (i.e., his preaching the gospel free of charge) "meaningless."[70]

Critical to understanding the apostle's intention in using this term (κενόω), we must keep in mind the emphasis on Christ's status in the passage.[71] One compelling reading understands the wording in light of Isaiah 52:13–53:12, which, as we have already noted, offers a primary backdrop for our passage.[72] According to this reading, the Son "emptying himself" to take the status of slave semantically parallels the thought in Isaiah 53:11–12 of the servant "pouring out" or "emptying out his soul" in order to justify many.[73] If this is correct, it may be that Paul (or whoever crafted the traditional piece adopted by Paul) uses "empty" (κενόω) instead of "hand over" (παραδίδωμι, the term used by the LXX translator), given its central notion of a change in status or rank. Thus a term was needed to communicate the idea of "divesting oneself of a position," and "to empty" (κενόω) expresses that nuance of ערה well.

This notion of Christ "divesting" himself of status is further clarified by the clause "taking the outward appearance of a slave" (μορφὴν δούλου λαβών), which indicates that the Son relinquished one status in order to take up (λαμβάνω) another.[74] Given the Isaianic backdrop of our passage, the word for "slave" or "servant" (δούλου) serves as a powerful allusion to the servant of Isaiah associated

69. BDAG 539; MGS 1113.

70. Similarly, both uses of the term in the LXX seem to be metaphorical as well (Jer 14:2; 15:9). Although Jer 14:2 could be read literally as the gates being emptied of people, the cry of the city of Jerusalem later in the verse seems to point to a metaphorical reading.

71. In response to the traditional reading of 2:6, κενόω at times has been interpreted as the Son giving up some aspect of his divine nature, emptying himself of some of his divine attributes. For an overview of interpretations of the "emptying" here, see Reumann, *Philippians*, 347–48.

72. E.g., Bauckham, *Jesus and the God of Israel*, 42–45; Lucien Cerfaux, *Le Christ dans la Théologie de Saint Paul* (Paris: Cerf, 1951), 283–98; J. Jeremias, "Zu Phil. 2,7: EAYTON EKENΩΣEN," *NovT* 6 (1963): 182–88.

73. Bauckham, *Jesus and the God of Israel*, 44, who follows Jeremias, "Zu Phil. 2,7," 182–88. The Hebrew term ערה ("pour out") is rendered with "hand over" (παραδίδωμι) by the LXX, a word that is used of Christ's "giving himself" (and in both cases ἑαυτόν is employed) for believers at Gal 2:20 and Eph 5:2, thus an act of self-sacrifice by Christ on behalf of others. It may be that in using κενόω at Phil 2:7 Paul wishes to express a similar idea but with a different nuance in the Hebrew, rendering the Hebrew, with its idea of "pouring out," quite literally into Greek.

74. Although not common, the aorist participle can be read as communicating purpose (telic), as with the translation, "in

with Isaiah 52:13–53:12. Mark 10:45, a passage that also has Isaiah's suffering servant as a backdrop,[75] comes to mind: "For even the Son of Man did not come to be served, but to serve, and to give his life as a ransom for many" (NIV).

Christ took on the slave status "by becoming like human beings" (ἐν ὁμοιώματι ἀνθρώπων[76] γενόμενος). In the New Testament, the word translated "becoming" (γίνομαι) often communicates the entrance "into a new condition," changing from one experience or state of existence to another,[77] and in the present context it gives us the means by which Christ changed his status to that of a slave. That he was "like human beings" (ἐν ὁμοιώματι ἀνθρώπων) does not mean that the Son only looked like a human but in fact was not.[78] It means that he shared in human nature, in our humanity, but was distinct as well (cf. Rom 8:3); no other human has been equal to God the Father prior to becoming human. The Son joined humanity in its human experience, adding humanity to his deity.[79]

The final clause of verse 7,[80] "and looking like a normal person" (καὶ σχήματι εὑρεθεὶς ὡς ἄνθρωπος), anticipates and tells us something about "he humiliated himself" (ἐταπείνωσεν) in the next verse, specifically pointing us to a circumstance of Christ's passion—he died as a human being.[81] The participle, which the NIV translates appropriately with "and *being found* [εὑρεθείς][82] in appearance as a man," we render a bit more periphrastically with "looking like[83] a normal person." This is the "set up" for Jesus's passion. He was a normal human being in appearance, but he, again, was no normal human being. He alone had added full humanity to his deity, and he had to become human to follow the path of obedience all the way to death on a cross. As with Hebrews 2:14,[84] the Son of God could not have died if he had not become human.

And thus, having lived a human life, "he humiliated himself" (ἐταπείνωσεν[85] ἑαυτόν) by taking the path to a dehumanizing death by crucifixion. The more common rendering of the verb, "he

order to take the outward appearance of a slave." On this use of the participle see Wallace, *Greek Grammar*, 634.

75. Rikki E. Watts, *Isaiah's New Exodus and Mark*, WUNT 2/88 (Tübingen: Mohr Siebeck, 1997), 271–72.

76. 𝔓[46] has the singular form, undoubtably bringing it in line with the singular in the next line.

77. BDAG 198.

78. For instance, docetism (from δοκέω, "to seem") was condemned as heresy for this idea in the early church. See Millard J. Erickson, *Christian Theology* (Grand Rapids: Baker, 1983), 712–14.

79. Similarly Hebrews uses the cognate verb to express the statement that "for this reason he had to be made like [ὁμοιωθῆναι] them, fully human in every way, in order that he might become a merciful and faithful high priest in service to God" (Heb 2:17 NIV).

80. I follow the versification in the Greek text. A number of English translations break the verse prior to this participial phrase (so, e.g., NASB, ESV, NIV; Fee, *Philippians*, 214; Hansen, *Philippians*, 153).

81. It is probably overinterpreting to read the word in terms of intellectual reflection, observation, examination, or investigation, as with Hansen, *Philippians*, 153–54.

82. The aorist passive participle of εὑρίσκω.

83. So he was found "in appearance" (σχήματι) as a human. The dative (σχήματι) comes from the word for "appearance" or "form" (σχῆμα), which only occurs in the NT here and at 1 Cor 7:31; it might be understood as a dative of reference—that is, "with reference to form." The word is similar to our reading of another word for "form" (μορφή) earlier in the verse, reiterating the notion of "outward appearance"—and that appearance was "as a man" or "person" (ὡς ἄνθρωπος). Thus Jesus entered his passion sharing the experience of being human (ἐν ὁμοιώματι ἀνθρώπων) and "looking like a normal person" (σχήματι . . . ὡς ἄνθρωπος).

84. "Since the children have flesh and blood, he too shared in their humanity so that by his death he might break the power of him who holds the power of death—that is, the devil" (Heb 2:14 NIV).

85. Josephus offers an example that combines the concepts of humility and "outward appearance." At *Ant.* 10.11 he tells about Hezekiah's response to the verbal abuse by the Assyrian commander. The king "put off his royal apparel, and clothed himself with sackcloth, and took the habit of a mourner" (Whiston). This last clause, καὶ σχῆμα ταπεινὸν ἀναλαβών, could be rendered more directly as "and taking a humble form."

humbled himself" (so, e.g., NASB, ESV, CSB, NET, NIV, NLT), might be regarded as a bit tame. Although the emphasis is on Jesus assuming a status as slave, humbly taking for himself a "downwardly mobile" posture in life, "humiliated" may be a better translation, especially given the cultural context of servants/slaves in the ancient world and the reference to crucifixion.[86] Again, the Servant Song of Isaiah offers a fitting backdrop. In Isaiah 53:4, 7 a key Hebrew term (ענה) has to do with "being humiliated" or "degraded,"[87] and the translators of the Greek Old Testament often render this word with our term used in Philippian 2:8 (ταπεινόω).[88] In the context of the Servant Song these verses speak of the servant's suffering and unjust treatment, which perfectly matches the passion embraced by Jesus.

So how did Jesus humiliate himself? He did so "by[89] becoming obedient," which of course is the role of a slave. This example of Christ's obedience calls to mind a culminating moment in the Son's obedient life—the great "not my will" moment in the garden of Gethsemane (Matt 26:39; Mark 14:36; Luke 22:42). In the immediate context, moreover, it also anticipates Paul's remembrance of the Philippians' obedience and his call for their further obedience at 2:12. Christ's obedience is a prime example to the church in their ongoing discipleship.

Further, his obedience had an excruciating duration, "all the way to the point of death" (μέχρι[90] θανάτου); death was the extent of Jesus's obedience, and this, too, was foretold in the Servant Song of Isaiah, as the servant's experience was riddled with death (Isa 53:3–12)—especially seen in the Hebrew form of the text.[91]

> For he was cut off from the land of the living . . .
> He was assigned a grave with the wicked,
> and with the rich in his death,
> though he had done no violence,
> nor was any deceit in his mouth . . .
> He poured out his life unto death.
> (Isa 53:8–9, 12 NIV).

Further, Jesus endured a very specific form of death, death on a cross, an engine of both humiliation and termination. The horror and social stigma of crucifixion in the ancient world is difficult to convey adequately in a short space. Cruel, purposefully drawn-out torture was combined with public humiliation in a way that communicated in no uncertain terms the fate of those who came into conflict with the purposes of the Roman Empire. The topic of crucifixion grated against the ears of the ancients, who regarded it a vulgarity that was best avoided in polite society.[92] In his work *Against Verres*, Cicero writes of the scandal of the crucifixion of a Roman citizen by Verres. He speaks of crucifixion as "the worst extreme of the tortures inflicted upon slaves. To bind a Roman citizen is a crime, to flog him is an abomination, to slay him is

86. E.g., Hellerman, *Philippians*, 116, who prefers "humiliated." See BDAG 990.

87. *HALOT* 853.

88. At 53:8 the Hebrew מֵעֹצֶר, "by oppression," is rendered in the LXX with ἐν τῇ ταπεινώσει. See J. Patrick Ware, *The Mission of the Church in Paul's Letter to the Philippians in the Context of Ancient Judaism*, NovTSup 120 (Leiden: Brill, 2005), 226.

89. This translation interprets the participle as communicating "means."

90. The improper preposition in this case is a marker of "degree or measure, to the point of" (BDAG 644).

91. As David A. Sapp points out, the emphasis on death is much more prominent in the Hebrew text than the LXX. See David A. Sapp, "The LXX, 1QIsa, and Mt Version of Isaiah 53 and the Christian Doctrine of Atonement," in *Jesus and the Suffering Servant: Isaiah 53 and Christian Origins*, ed. W. H. Bellinger and William R. Farmer (Harrisburg, PA: Trinity Press, 1998), 176–78.

92. See especially Martin Hengel, *Crucifixion in the Ancient World and the Folly of the Message of the Cross* (Philadelphia: Fortress, 1977), 9–10, 38.

almost an act of murder: to crucify him is—what? There is no fitting word that can possibly describe so horrible a deed" (*Verr.* 5.66.169–70).[93]

This is the great irony, the scandal of a crucified Lord of glory (Phil 2:6; see 1 Cor 2:8), "a stumbling block to Jews and foolishness to Gentiles" (1 Cor 1:23). Yet for Paul, this is the heart of God's wisdom and power (vv. 24–25). Gordon Fee writes:

> Here is the very heart of Pauline theology, both of his understanding of God as such and of his understanding of what God has done and is doing in our fallen world. Here is where the one who as "equal with God" has most fully revealed the truth about God: that God is love and that his love expresses itself in self-sacrifice—cruel, humiliating death on a cross—for the sake of those he loves. The divine weakness (death at the hands of his creatures, his enemies) is the divine scandal (the cross was reserved for slaves and insurrectionists). No one in Philippi, we must remind ourselves, used the cross as a symbol for their faith; there were no gold crosses embossed on Bibles or worn as pendants around the neck or lighted on the steeple of the local church. The cross was God's—and thus their—scandal, God's contradiction to human wisdom and power: that the one they worshiped as Lord of all, including Caesar, had been crucified as a state criminal at the hands of one of Caesar's proconsuls; that the Almighty should appear in human dress, and that he should do so in this way, as a "Messiah" who died by crucifixion.[94]

**2:9–11 For this reason God also highly exalted him and gave to him the name above every name, in order that at the name of Jesus every knee will bow—whether of heaven, or earth, or under the earth—and every tongue will confess that Jesus Christ is Lord to the glory of God the Father** (διὸ καὶ ὁ θεὸς αὐτὸν ὑπερύψωσεν καὶ ἐχαρίσατο αὐτῷ τὸ ὄνομα τὸ ὑπὲρ πᾶν ὄνομα, 10 ἵνα ἐν τῷ ὀνόματι Ἰησοῦ πᾶν γόνυ κάμψῃ ἐπουρανίων καὶ ἐπιγείων καὶ καταχθονίων 11 καὶ πᾶσα γλῶσσα ἐξομολογήσηται ὅτι κύριος Ἰησοῦς Χριστὸς εἰς δόξαν θεοῦ πατρός). Paul now celebrates the exaltation of Christ. Cosmically speaking, there is a great distance between the beginning of Philippians 2:6 and the end of 2:8, in which Christ Jesus took a path from "being robed in divine glory" and "equal to God" to the most ignoble, despicable death imaginable in the ancient world. The passage takes us from the highest of highs to the lowest place of human experience. And from broader New Testament theology we know that the experience was compounded by Christ bearing the unimaginable weight of human sin (2 Cor 5:21; Heb 9:28).

Yet, now comes the "great turning," which the text presents as a consequent focal event, introduced with "for this reason" (διὸ καί).[95] God did two things in response to Christ's obedient suffering:

| | | | |
|---|---|---|---|
| God also | highly exalted | | him and[96] |
| | gave | to him | the name above every name. |

Here, this lyrical, theologically rich narrative celebrates the Father's exaltation of the Son,[97] by

93. L. H. G. Greenwood, *Cicero: The Verrine Orations, Volume II*, LCL 293 (Cambridge: Harvard University Press; London: Heinemann, 1953), 655–57.

94. Fee, *Philippians*, 217–18.

95. BDF 229. The inferential (διό) is paired with "also" (καί) to highlight the result.

96. The καί can be read epexegetically (so, e.g., Fee, *Philippians*, 221; Hellerman, *Philippians*, 119). That is, God exalted Christ by giving him a name. Yet this would read "name" (ὄνομα) more in terms of a rank or position. It may be better to read the conjunction as coordinate, with the two clauses as describing simultaneous action.

97. On exaltation in NT and historical theology, see James Leo Garrett, *Systematic Theology: Biblical, Historical, and Evangelical* (Grand Rapids: Eerdmans, 1995), 115–30.

which Jesus was vindicated and given dominion over all things. As Richard Bauckham points out, the logic of this narrative parallels that of the Isaianic backdrop of the passage.[98] In Isaiah 53:12 we read, "Therefore I will give him a portion among the great . . . *because* he poured out his life unto death," and in 52:13, "He will be raised and lifted up and highly exalted" (NIV). Thus, the exaltation of Isaiah's servant comes as a result of his suffering, a thought also reflected in our passage.

Although occurring in the LXX,[99] the word translated as "exalted" (ὑπερύψωσεν) only appears here in the New Testament. Yet a related verb, "I exalt" (ὑψόω), is used of the exaltation of Jesus several times,[100] including in Acts 2:33 and 5:31 where the apostles proclaim the exaltation of Jesus as a result of his suffering of death.[101] John's Gospel, which also draws its inspiration from Isaiah, uses the image with the double sense of "lifted up" on a cross and "exalted," thus combining "suffering" and "exaltation."[102]

This passage, in line with broader New Testament teaching, presents Christ as exalted to lordship over all things, and the signifying act is when God "gave to him the name above every name" (ἐχαρίσατο αὐτῷ τὸ ὄνομα τὸ ὑπὲρ πᾶν ὄνομα). The word translated as "name" (ὄνομα), used three times in this passage, has a broad range of meanings, including "name," "status," "title," "office," "rank," "reputation," "fame," or even "person."[103] Further, "the name," used as a pious reference to God, came to be employed by early Jewish Christians as a designation for Jesus.[104]

Yet can we say more concerning "the name" given to Jesus? Although various suggestions have been made, there are three reasons the designation "Lord" (κύριος) seems to be the best interpretation.[105] First, as Larry Hurtado has pointed out, by the time that Philippians was written, the confession "Jesus Christ is Lord" was established as the earliest confessional formula of the early church (Acts 2:36; Rom 10:9; 1 Cor 11:23; 12:3; 16:22), and this against the backdrop in broader Judaism of the title "Lord" having become a common way of referring to Yahweh.[106]

Of course, in both the Septuagint and the broader New Testament, the term κύριος has various uses.[107] In the Septuagint particularly, κύριος renders the divine name (YHWH) in its various forms and in combination with various terms over

98. Bauckham, *Jesus and the God of Israel*, 43.

99. Given the clear Isaianic background of the passage, the verb may represent a periphrastic echo of the Hebrew at Isa 52:13b יָרוּם וְנִשָּׂא וְגָבַהּ מְאֹד ("will be elevated and lifted up and greatly exalted"). The verb is found in many "blessings" in the Odes of Solomon and Daniel, and twice in the Psalms. The use at Ps 97:9 [96:9 LXX] is consonant with Phil 2:9–11 and reads, "Because you are the Lord most high over all the earth, you were exalted far above [ὑπερυψώθης ὑπέρ] all the gods" (NETS).

100. John 3:14; 8:28; 12:32, 34; Acts 2:33; 5:31.

101. Acts 2:33 in context draws on Ps 110:1, a key OT text behind the NT's exaltation Christology. Quoted or alluded to twenty-two times in the New Testament, Psalm 110 plays a significant role in the substructure of New Testament Christology. See W. R. G. Loader, "Christ at the Right Hand: Psalm 110:1 in the New Testament," *NTS* 24 (1978): 199–217; David M. Hay, *Glory at the Right Hand: Psalm 110 in Early Christianity*, SBLMS (Cambridge: University Press, 1980). The pattern of glory-incarnation-exaltation, with Ps 110:1 at its heart, may be seen, for example, in the structure of the book of Hebrews. For a discussion of the treatment of this psalm in Hebrews, see Guthrie, *Structure of Hebrews*, 123–24.

102. Köstenberger and Swain, *Father, Son and Spirit*, 42. This combination of these motifs and logic is also found at Heb 2:9: "Now crowned with glory and honor *because* he suffered death" (NIV).

103. BDAG 711–14.

104. Richard Longenecker, *The Christology of Early Jewish Christianity* (Grand Rapids: Baker, 1981), 41–46. E.g., Acts 3:16; 4:7, 10; 16:18; 19:13–17; Eph 1:21.

105. On which, see Cohick, *Philippians*, 123.

106. The title "Lord" (κύριος) had for some time been used for Yahweh as a common religious expression in broader Judaism. See Larry W. Hurtado, *Lord Jesus Christ: Devotion to Jesus in Earliest Christianity* (Grand Rapids: Eerdmans, 2003), 21, 52, 112–13. In addition to Hurtado, see also Hawthorne and Martin, *Philippians*, 129.

107. See David B. Capes, *Old Testament Yahweh Texts in Paul's Christology* (Tübingen: Mohr Siebeck, 1992), 34–36.

six thousand times.[108] The pattern is established early on in Genesis, for example. God is referred to as "the Lord God" (κύριος ὁ θεός; e.g., Gen 2:15–16, 18, 22; 3:1), and later simply as "Lord" (κύριος; e.g., 4:3, 13; 10:9; 11:5–9). This common title for God, of course, also occurs throughout the New Testament (e.g., Matt 1:20, 22, 24; 2:13; 5:33; Mark 5:19; Luke 1:6, 9, 28, 46; 2:15, 22; Acts 4:26 [Ps 2:2]; 7:33; 8:24). Thus, calling Jesus "Lord" was no mere title but often rather a name of "divine significance."[109]

Second, as Hurtado also notes, Paul uses "Lord" as a name for God. For example, at times when he comments on an Old Testament passage, the apostle refers to God as "Lord"[110]—even when the Old Testament text does not use the title with reference to God (e.g., 1 Kgs 19:10 at Rom 11:3; Isa 28:11 at 1 Cor 14:21). It is highly significant, therefore, that at other points the apostle uses Old Testament "Yahweh" texts to speak of Jesus as the "Lord" referred to in the Old Testament passage of Scripture.[111] Note, for instance, that in the broader context of Isaiah 45:18–25—the passage alluded to overtly in Philippians 2:10–11—God refers to himself as "God," "Savior," and "LORD," with "LORD" used repeatedly.[112] It is the LORD who says, "Before me every knee will bow; by me every tongue will swear" (Isa 45:23 NIV), and in Philippians 2:9–11 these words are applied to Jesus. (The divine name is often rendered in English translations of the Hebrew text of the Old Testament as LORD in small caps.)

Third, the title "Lord" plays a climactic role in our Philippians passage. The parallel relationships in the chiastic structure of verses 9–11 may be seen as follows:

β at the **name** of Jesus
  γ every knee will bow
    whether of heaven, or
      earth, or
      under the earth—and
  γ′ every tongue will confess
β′ that Jesus Christ is **Lord**

Here, "the name" associated with Jesus in β parallels the full celebration of what every tongue will confess in β′ —"that Jesus Christ is Lord" (ὅτι κύριος Ἰησοῦς Χριστός). Note that for emphasis in the Greek text "Lord" (κύριος) comes first, prior to "Jesus Christ" (Ἰησοῦς Χριστός). Thus the "name" above every name is the name used of God himself throughout the Old Testament—the name "Lord."

Jesus was given the name above every name (i.e., "Lord") in order that, upon Christ's return,[113] "at[114] the name of Jesus every knee will bow." In the exaltation, God cast the covering of Christ's lordship over everything that is, and all knees bowing and all tongues confessing will be the ultimate result of his cosmic enthronement.[115] As noted above, this language presents an overt allusion to Isaiah 45:23. The broader passage from Isaiah reads,

108. Capes, *Old Testament Yahweh Texts*, 37.

109. Hurtado, *Lord Jesus Christ*, 52, 394.

110. E.g., Ps 32:1–2 at Rom 4:8; Isa 1:9; 10:22–23; 28:22 at Rom 9:28–29; Isa 53:1 at Rom 10:16; Isa 40:13 at Rom 11:34.

111. E.g., Joel 2:32 at Rom 10:13; Jer 9:23–24 at 1 Cor 1:31 and 2 Cor 10:17; Hurtado, *Lord Jesus Christ*, 112–13; see also David B. Capes, *Old Testament Yahweh Texts in Paul's Christology*, WUNT 2/47 (Tübingen: Mohr Siebeck, 1992).

112. Isa 45:1, 3, 5, 6, 7, 8, 11, 13, 14, 17, 18, 19, 21, 24, 25.

113. Fee, *Philippians*, 223.

114. The exact nuance of the preposition ἐν + the dative is difficult to determine. It can be used to communicate time (i.e., "when Jesus's name is called"), but as with our rendering, it might also communicate the means by which something is accomplished. What is clear is that "the name" has become an authoritative force.

115. Perhaps wishing to drive home the certainty of all things being put under Christ's lordship, or in an assimilation to the LXX ὀμεῖται (Isa 45:23), a scribe perhaps adjusted the subjunctive to the indicative form (A C D F* G K L P Ψ^vid 075. 0278. 6. 33. 81. 104. 365. 630*. 1175. 1241. 1505. 1739. 1881. 2464 *pm*; Ir^vl). The subjunctive seems to be the stronger reading both in terms of the parallelism in the passage and in terms of external witnesses (𝔓46 ℵ B etc.). See Metzger, *Textual Commentary*, 546.

> Turn to me and be saved,
>   all you ends of the earth;
>   for I am God, and there is no other.
> By myself I have sworn,
>   my mouth has uttered in all integrity
>   a word that will not be revoked:
> Before me every knee will bow;
>   by me every tongue will swear.
> They will say of me, "In the LORD alone
>   are deliverance and strength."
> All who have raged against him
>   will come to him and be put to shame.
> But all the descendants of Israel
>   will find deliverance in the LORD
>   and will make their boast in him.
>     (Isa 45:22–25 NIV)

Isaiah 45 proclaims the uniqueness of the Lord God: "I am the LORD, and there is no other" (v. 6; similarly, vv. 13, 21, 22). He alone created the earth and humankind (vv. 12, 18). He brings salvation (vv. 17, 21–22) and will gather the nations to himself to save them (vv. 20, 22, 24–25). In terms of the echo of Isaiah 45:23 at Philippians 2:10–11, Christ Jesus is the Lord of creation and salvation to whom Isaiah refers.

Of course, bowing to a lord and confessing a sovereign's lordship were acts of submission in the ancient world, and the point here is that every being in all of creation—including the enemies of God, those who have "raged against him" (Isa 45:24)—ultimately will acknowledge the lordship of Christ.[116] For the Philippians, this must have put their conflict with opponents in perspective (Phil 1:28), and it should give us perspective as well. Those who work and rage against God will one day bow the knee and confess that Jesus really is Lord. Accordingly, the triple locations, "of heaven" (ἐπουρανίων), "or earth" (καὶ ἐπιγείων), "or under the earth" (καὶ καταχθονίων), speak of the absolute nature of Christ's lordship. Although the language resists an overly specific interpretation, those "of heaven" (straightforwardly, "of the heavens") are probably the heavenly beings, including angels, Satan and the demonic, and perhaps those already with the Lord. Those of "earth" include humans throughout the earth (at the time of Christ's coming?); and "under the earth" probably points to the realm of the dead, which would have been especially impressive to those of a Greek background, for the Greeks held the underworld in awe.[117] The primary emphasis, however, rests on the comprehensive nature of Christ's lordship. Literarily, the triple, rhythmic reference to these places also pauses the flow of the passage, giving the reader space to absorb the implications of the proclamation.

Ultimately, the exaltation of Christ is "to the glory of God the Father" (εἰς δόξαν θεοῦ πατρός). Ceslas Spicq notes that the semantic development of the Greek word for "glory" (δόξα) is "probably the most extraordinary in the Bible."[118] A wonderfully complex and multifaceted concept in the Old Testament, "glory" is a common rendering of a Hebrew term (כָּבוֹד) that connotes "heaviness" or "weightiness" and can refer variously to respect, reputation, riches, glory, honor, splendor, majesty, or dignity. In his book *God's Glory in Salvation through Judgment*, Jim Hamilton summarizes God's glory as

> the weight of the majestic goodness of who God is, and the resulting name, or reputation that he gains from his revelation of himself as Creator, Sustainer, Judge, and Redeemer, perfect in justice and mercy, loving-kindness and truth.[119]

116. Witherington, *Philippians*, 153–54.
117. Fee, *Philippians*, 224–25.
118. *TLNT* 1:364.
119. James M. Hamilton, *God's Glory in Salvation through*

Thus, as with the great work of the suffering servant, Christ Jesus, God's glory can be directly related to his saving acts on behalf of his people (e.g., Exod 14:18; 16:7; Isa 12:2; 35:1–4; Ezek 39:21–29). This constitutes a primary way that God reveals his presence in the world (Isa 40:5) and his lordship over the world. Consequently, God's decisive actions in salvation and his presence have come to a climactic revelation in the incarnation, ministry, passion, resurrection, and exaltation of Christ, and all to God's supreme glory. In other words, God glorifies himself, brings deserved worship and focus to himself, and draws the nations to himself through the sacrifice and exaltation of Jesus Christ as Lord of the universe!

Of course, this confession has missional significance for the church. In fulfilling his absolute dominion over all that is (Isa 45) through the suffering of the servant (Isa 52:13–53:12), God has initiated his mission in the world, which will be consummated at the return of Christ. The eschatological drama portrayed in Philippians 2:6–11 is still playing out in the mission of the church, as she calls knees to bow and tongues to confess the "Lord Jesus Christ."[120] This reminds the Philippians (and us) that the exaltation of Christ is about the vindication of Christ over the powers of the world. But it is also an invitation to salvation.

> Christ above us.
> Christ come to us.
> Christ suffering for us.
> Christ over us.
> To the glory of God.

## Theology in Application

### *The Humility of the Servant God as an Example for Us*

We live in an age of laughable arrogance, as humanity looks down its nose at the frail, insipid, little gods of their imaginations, not knowing the one true God of unimaginable power and beauty. They breathe his air and look out on the complexity and grandeur of the world he has made with eyes he has shaped. They think about this world with a mind that God has wired beyond understanding, using the gift to think foolish thoughts, as if they could sit in judgment on the Lord and his ways. Even some who claim to be his conform to the world's values, rejecting God's Word, thinking they know better than he.

It is an old story, humankind knowing better than God, seeking to be like God (Gen 3:1–3), wishing to be the center of the universe, imagining that we can find freedom in ourselves and in the values of the world around us. We are powerful creatures with no true and lasting power.

*Judgment: A Biblical Theology* (Wheaton, IL: Crossway, 2010), 56. See also Christopher W. Morgan and Robert A. Peterson, *The Glory of God* (Wheaton, IL: Crossway, 2010), 153–87.

120. Ware, *Mission of the Church*, 235–36.

> The kings of the earth rise up
> and the rulers band together
> against the LORD and against his anointed, saying,
> "Let us break their chains
> and throw off their shackles." (Ps 2:2–3 NIV)

But the Lord has responded—and will respond—to the arrogant. The surprise is how he has responded. Not the part that reads, "I have installed my king on Zion, my holy mountain" (v. 6 NIV); that makes perfect sense. Ultimately, the arrogance of humanity must break before the Lord's laughter, his rebuke, and his unshakable power and rule (vv. 4–11). Proverbs 16:5 reads, "Everyone who is arrogant in heart is an abomination to the LORD; be assured, he will not go unpunished" (ESV). After all, he is God. To think that we as humans can hold any form of power in defiance of him is ridiculous. That part is not surprising at all.

What is surprising is how the Lord of glory came to be enthroned as the heir of the whole world (Ps 2:8). For it happened through utter humility, even *humiliation*. He did not move up but rather "down to his potential," and this provides a striking example for how we should live as we seek to build community with one another. The way to the throne of the universe was through the slaves' quarters. In a sermon, Martin Luther reflected on the surprising approach of humility taken by Christ.

> Even in that humanity he might have exalted himself above all men and served none. But he forbore and became as other men. And by "likeness of men" we must understand just ordinary humanity without special privilege whatever. Now, without special privilege there is no disparity among men. Understand, then, Paul says in effect: Christ was made as any other man who has neither riches, honor, power nor advantage above his fellows; for many inherit power, honor, and property by birth. So lowly did Christ become, and with such humility did he conduct himself, that no mortal is too lowly to be his equal, even servants and the poor.[121]

Not only did Christ step away from his status in heaven, refusing to use his position to his own advantage, but he chose not to take and wield power on earth. He who could have marshaled the armies of heaven did not take the throne of the universe that way. He who could command a storm did not assault the Roman Empire with raw power. Rather, he humbled himself, embracing the form of a servant, as a slave destined for a slave's death. John Chrysostom writes:

121. John Nicholas Lenker, ed., *Sermons of Martin Luther, Volume 7: Sermons on Epistle Texts for Epiphany, Easter, and Pentecost* (Grand Rapids: Baker, 1983), 177–78.

> He honored the Father all the more, not that you may honor him less but that you may marvel all the more. . . . The measure of his sublimity corresponds with the depth of his humility. (*Homily on Philippians* 8.2.5–11)[122]

He took the path of humility and sacrificial service. And he did this, not despite his equality with God but as an expression of his equality with God. In Christ's humility we begin to see the character of God himself, that we might respond to him and each other in humility.

Behold the condescension of God. That word, *condescension*, has taken on negative connotations in our modern world, but I am thinking of its earlier meaning, "to descend with" someone else. Christ lowered himself to be with us, to meet needs that only he could meet. He gave us an example of how we should love one another. How might we condescend, to "descend with" him, for the sake of our brothers and sisters, for the sake of unity in the church, imitating his humility?

This is Paul's purpose in sharing this big cosmic narrative writ small in a few short verses of Philippians. The grandest story of the universe is about choosing the route of a slave, a servant, refusing to take advantage of even those things that are our "rights," so that we might meet the needs of our brothers and sisters in the church. Each of us might stop and consider at this point:

> How am I promoting unity in the church through humility?
> How am I serving my fellow Christ-followers?
> Of what advantage am I letting go in order to serve?
> Is my way the way of power or of humble sacrifice?

## *The Divine Suffering*

Of course, we don't like the vulnerability of humility. We are befogged by the illusion that we control our lives, which gives some momentary comfort. All we need to do to disperse the thin fog of that illusion is to imagine our lives a hundred years into the future. We will have no ability whatsoever. We will not be able to do anything for ourselves. The curse of death makes no exceptions. Vulnerability is absolute. The suffering of our fallen world—bombs and cancer and viruses and the simple creep into old age, as overwhelming as it is unstoppable—climaxes in death. There is no decisive answer . . .

. . . but one. Again, it is staggering that God answered suffering by entering into it himself. The answer to those who say in their angry arrogance, "Why doesn't God

122. As cited in Edwards, *Galatians, Ephesians, Philippians,* 237–38.

do something about the suffering of the world?" is that he has. And he will. And this reality changes our perception of suffering, the world, and God himself.

Author and Oxford University professor John Lennox offers a perspective on suffering by sharing an encounter he had while touring a synagogue in Eastern Europe. There he met a woman from South Africa whose relatives had died in the Holocaust. The woman was there seeking information about her relatives and her own identity. As the rabbi explained the meaning of the Jewish festivals, Lennox and the woman noticed a jarring mock-up of the entrance to Auschwitz standing at the center of the exhibition. Over the doorway were the ironic, ugly words, "Arbeit macht frei" ("work makes one free"). Behind the display were photographs of children on whom Josef Mengele had carried out experiments in the death camp. At this point in the tour, this Jewish woman moved toward the doorway, reaching out to touch both sides of it. Looking at Lennox, whom she had learned believed in God, she said, "And what does your religion make of this?" In this woman's honest question rested the weight of the world's suffering and the existential weight of whether there is any meaning to life after all. Lennox reflects:

> What was I to say? She had lost her parents and many relatives in the Holocaust. I could scarcely bear to look at the Mengele photographs, because of the sheer horror of imagining my children suffering such a fate. I had nothing in my life that remotely paralleled the horror her family had endured.
>
> But still she stood in the doorway waiting for an answer. I eventually said, "I would not insult your memory of your parents by offering you simplistic answers to your question. What is more, I have young children, and I cannot even bear to think how I might react if anything were to happen to them, even if it were far short of the evil that Mengele did. I have no easy answers; but I do have what, for me at least, is a doorway into an answer."
>
> "What is it?" she said.
>
> I said, "You know that I am a Christian. That means that I believe that Yeshua is the messiah. I also believe that he was God incarnate, come into our world as savior, which is what his name 'Yeshua' means. Now I know that this is even more difficult for you to accept. Nevertheless, just think about this question—if Yeshua was really God, as I believe he was, what was God doing on a cross?
>
> "Could it be that God begins just here to meet our heartbreaks, by demonstrating that he did not remain distant from our human suffering, but became part of it himself? For me, this is the beginning of hope; and it is a living hope that cannot be smashed by the enemy of death. The story does not end in the darkness of the cross. Yeshua conquered death. He rose from the dead; and one day, as the final judge, he will assess everything in absolute fairness, righteousness, and mercy."
>
> There was silence. She was still standing, arms outstretched, forming a motionless

cross in the doorway. After a moment, with tears in her eyes, very quietly but audibly, she said: 'Why has no one ever told me that about my messiah before?'"

Lennox ends his story by noting, "There are no simplistic answers to the hard questions thrown up by human suffering. The answer that Christianity gives is not a set of propositions . . . it is, rather, a Person who suffered."[123] This is why, instead of making an argument, Paul lyrically overviews a story—one with a magnificent climax.

## *Every Knee Will Bow, Every Tongue Confess*

When we step back and look at what we have read about Christ Jesus in Philippians 2:5–11, the view is breathtaking and hard to take in in all its details. Equal with God, wrapped in glory, the ground and center of all that is, he did not treat his status as something to be used for his own advantage but poured himself out to the point of death. God died. Then he was exalted to a place beyond which there is no higher place. He has absolute authority and complete dominion, expressed in a name—the "Lord," the name by which God is addressed in much of the Bible.

The picture of absolute rule—every knee and tongue acknowledging his lordship in every possible corner of reality—leaves no space for dissent. But the verbs of the Greek text are formed as if waiting with bated breath, telling us that the kingship has been inaugurated but not yet consummated. The stark, and at times oppressive, reality weighs on some of us more than others: the enemies of our Lord still walk around and wag their tongues throughout the earth. In many dark corners of the world, the power seems to be all on their side. It is an illusion, but it does not feel that way. That is why Paul and the other writers of the New Testament remind us of these things. They had seen the Lord. They knew him raised. They believed he was exalted to the right hand of God. They died for him at the hands of defeated powers, knowing that their deaths pointed beyond the illusion to a greater reality—a greater day when all the powers will bend the knee, when all of sin and death and evil and rebellion will fall before the Name. And, of course, the turning of the tide comes in the passage just after verse 8, just after death had closed over Christ. The turning comes with resurrection, for in this broken world he broke the back of death, heralding that life would one day rule over all.

In his book *The Body*, Chuck Colson writes of a moment when the USSR was still a seemingly unbreakable power in the world:

123. John Lennox, *Gunning for God: Why the New Atheists Are Missing the Target* (Oxford, UK: Lion Hudson, 2011), 141–42.

> It was May Day, 1990. The place, Moscow's Red Square. "Is it straight, Father?" one Orthodox priest asked another, shifting the heavy, eight-foot crucifix on his shoulder. "Yes," said the other. "It is straight." Together the two priests, along with a group of parishioners holding ropes that steadied the beams of the huge cross, walked the parade route. Before them was passed the official might of the Union of Soviet Socialist Republics: the usual May Day procession of tanks, missiles, troops, and salutes to the Communist party elite. Behind the tanks surged a giant crowd of protesters, shouting up at Mikhail Gorbachev, "Bread! . . . Freedom! . . . Truth!"
>
> As the throng passed directly in front of the Soviet leader standing in his place of honor, the priests hoisted their heavy burden toward the sky. The cross emerged from the crowd. As it did, the figure of Jesus Christ obscured the giant poster faces of Karl Marx, Friedrich Engels, and Vladimir Lenin that provided the backdrop for Gorbachev's reviewing stand. "Mikhail Sergeyevich!" one of the priests shouted, his deep voice cleaving the clamor of the protesters and piercing straight toward the angry Soviet leader. "Mikhail Sergeyevich! Christ is risen!"[124]

Christ is risen! High and exalted is the Messiah! Fallen are the kingdoms of this world, whether they know it yet or not. Every knee will bow, every tongue will confess that Jesus Christ is Lord to the glory of God the Father. Christ is risen indeed!

124. Charles W. Colson and Ellen Santilli Vaughn, *The Body* (Nashville: Nelson, 1994), 231.

CHAPTER 7

# Philippians 2:12–17

## Literary Context

The main body of Philippians, begun at 1:27, continues with 2:12–17. At 1:27–2:4 we observe two sub-movements calling for the church to embrace unity by (1) standing together in the face of a hostile world (1:27–30) and (2) taking a countercultural, selfless posture toward one another (2:1–4). Paul then offers Christ Jesus himself as the first and foundational example of how to live this out, with the lyrical and deeply moving narrative poem of 2:6–11. This beautifully crafted passage traces the history of Christ's outpouring of himself—from being equal with God in status prior to the incarnation, to his incarnation and death, and through to his exaltation and confession as "Lord." Then, with Christ as their supreme example, in 2:12–17 Paul now calls for the Philippians to work out their salvation in community, even as they shine like lights in a distorted world. Notice that unity within the church and the unified church's stand together in facing the world continue as interrelated themes. Following 2:12–17, the apostle then turns to Timothy and Epaphroditus as exemplars (2:19–30), and finally he will use himself as an example to follow (3:1–21). Yet interspersed in the seams surrounding these examples—Christ, the ministers Timothy and Epaphroditus, and Paul himself—we find practical exhortations and instructions, as we have here in 2:12–17.

I. The Letter Opening: A Prescript and a Prayer Report (1:1–11)
**II. The Letter Body (1:12–4:9)**
  A. The Body Opening: Paul's Current Situation (1:12–26)
  B. The Main Body of the Letter: A Call for Unity in the Church (1:27–4:4a)
    1. An Exhortation to Live Out the Unity of Community (1:27–2:4)
    2. Be Like Christ Jesus, the Preeminent Example of Self-Sacrifice (2:5–11)
➡ **3. Further Exhortations to Unity and Exclamations of Joy (2:12–17)**
    4. Timothy and Epaphroditus as Exemplars of Self-Sacrifice (2:18–30)
    5. The Example of Paul's Christocentric Life and Ministry (3:1–14)
    6. Exhortations to Embrace Paul's Christocentric Pattern of Life (3:15–4:4a)
  C. The Body Closing: Exhortations (4:4b–9)
III. The Letter Closing (4:10–23)

## Main Idea

Paul now draws out the practical implications of Christ's example and exaltation (2:5–11), exhorting the Philippians to work out the salvation that God has worked in the world and continues to work in them. They will do so by holding to God's word, even as they live together in unity, shining like lights in a twisted world. Paul takes great delight in seeing the Philippians persevere in the faith, confident that his ministry to them will be well spent.

## Translation

### Philippians 2:12–17

| | | |
|---|---|---|
| 12a | Implication | So, my dear friends, |
| b | Accordance | just as you have always followed my instructions— |
| c | Circumstance | not only in my presence but |
| d | Altern. Circumst. | now all the more in my absence— |
| e | Exhortation | **continue working out your salvation** |
| f | Manner/Posture | with fear and |
| g | | trembling; |

| | | |
|---|---|---|
| 13a | Basis | for |
| b | Assertion | **God is the one working** |
| c | Sphere | among you |
| d | Object | both to will and |
| e | | to work |
| f | Advantage | for his pleasure. |
| 14a | Exhortation | **Do everything** |
| b | Manner/Posture | without grumbling or arguing, |
| 15a | Purpose | in order that you might be faultless and innocent, |
| b | Description | children of God who are virtuous |
| c | Context | in the middle of a morally twisted and |
| d | Description | perverted |
| e | | generation, |
| f | Action | among whom you shine |
| g | Simile | like stars |
| h | Place | in the world |
| 16a | Means | by holding out the word of life, |
| b | Result | resulting in my boast on the day of Christ, |
| c | Content/Action | that I neither ran |
| d | Manner | for nothing nor |
| e | Action 2 | worked hard |
| f | Manner | for nothing. |
| 17a | Ascensive | Indeed, |
| b | Hypoth. cond. | even if I am poured out like a drink offering |
| c | | on the sacrificial service |
| d | | for your faith, |
| e | Exclamation | **I am glad and** |
| f | | **rejoice** |
| g | Association | with all of you. |

## Structure

As reflected in the translation diagram, 2:12–17 develops grammatically in three main stages. The first, 2:12–13, builds around the challenge, "continue working out your salvation" (τὴν ἑαυτῶν σωτηρίαν κατεργάζεσθε), and the basis for that exhortation, "for God is the one working among you . . ." (θεὸς γάρ ἐστιν ὁ ἐνεργῶν ἐν ὑμῖν). A second movement, 2:14–16, flows from the exhortation to "do everything without grumbling or arguing" (πάντα ποιεῖτε χωρὶς γογγυσμῶν καὶ διαλογισμῶν), which is followed by a multileveled purpose clause, "in order that you might be faultless and innocent. . . ." (ἵνα γένησθε ἄμεμπτοι καὶ ἀκέραιοι). Finally, Paul's expression of joy at 2:17 constitutes the third and final movement. This is fairly typical Pauline style, with exhortations supported by strings of subordinate clauses before or especially following the main clause. The invitation to joy also bridges to the next movement, with a parallel, though inverted, invitation to joy at 1:18. These "joy-full" exhortations form a transitional seam between the two sub-movements.

## Exegetical Outline

➡ **3. Further Exhortations to Unity and Joy (2:12–17)**

- **a. Work Out What God is Working In (vv. 12–13)**
  - (1) Work Out Your Salvation! (v. 12)
  - (2) Basis of the Exhortation: God Is Working among You (v. 13)
- **b. Work Out Community Unity (vv. 14–16)**
  - (1) Don't Grumble and Argue (v. 14)
  - (2) Purpose: So That You Might Be Blameless and Innocent (v. 15a–c)
  - (3) Context: Amid a Morally Twisted Generation (v. 15d–e)
  - (4) Action: Among Whom You Shine as You Grasp the Word of Life (vv. 15f–16b)
  - (5) Result: Paul's Boast on the Day of Christ (v. 16c–f)
- **c. Paul's Joy in Ministry to the Philippians (v. 17)**

## Explanation of the Text

**2:12–13 So, my dear friends, just as you have always followed my instructions—not only in my presence but now all the more in my absence—continue working out your salvation with fear and trembling; for God is the one working among you both to will and to work for his pleasure** (Ὥστε, ἀγαπητοί μου, καθὼς πάντοτε ὑπηκούσατε, μὴ ὡς ἐν τῇ παρουσίᾳ μου μόνον ἀλλὰ νῦν πολλῷ μᾶλλον ἐν τῇ ἀπουσίᾳ μου, μετὰ φόβου καὶ τρόμου τὴν ἑαυτῶν σωτηρίαν κατεργάζεσθε· 13 θεὸς γάρ ἐστιν ὁ ἐνεργῶν ἐν ὑμῖν καὶ τὸ θέλειν καὶ τὸ ἐνεργεῖν ὑπὲρ τῆς εὐδοκίας). Paul now encourages the Philippians to work out the salvation God has brought to them in Christ. The passage begins with the term translated as "so" (ὥστε), which functions inferentially,[1] introducing what follows even as it builds on what has gone before. Consequently, we should read the exhortation "continue working out your own salvation" (τὴν ἑαυτῶν σωτηρίαν κατεργάζεσθε), as well as what follows, as building logically on the firm foundation of the truths about Christ in 2:6–11. We live in particular ways—make

1. Similar to "so then" (NASB); "therefore" (NRSV, ESV, NIV).

particular choices in life—because of who Christ is, what he has accomplished for our salvation, and his status as Lord of the universe.

Paul often addresses his congregations with the affectionate "dear friends" (ἀγαπητοί),[2] especially when making urgent appeals (e.g., 1 Cor 10:4; 15:58; 2 Cor 7:1; 12:19).[3] In Philippians he only uses the word here and at 4:1, where, using it adjectivally, he writes to his "brothers and sisters" in Philippi as "loved" (ἀδελφοί μου ἀγαπητοί),[4] just before his gentle but firm call for Euodia and Syntyche to reconcile. Here in 2:12, Paul's address of the Philippians as dear friends "renews the warm tone of 1:3–11,"[5] where he had written to them very personally.

The apostle calls the Philippians to "continue working out" (κατεργάζεσθε)[6] their salvation in meaningful ways in the world. In Paul's writings, the word is used either of a pattern of life being "practiced" or "lived out,"[7] or of something being prepared or produced by someone.[8] The former appears to be the nuance here in 2:12. We have translated the term as "working out," not with the sense of "working to earn" salvation but rather to place the emphasis on active engagement in living out the implications of salvation in daily life. Paul exhorts the Philippians to work out "your own salvation" (τὴν ἑαυτῶν[9] σωτηρίαν), that is, they are to embrace a pattern of life in accord with the salvation God has brought them in Christ. The thought here echoes the call for the Philippians to live out their "heavenly citizenship in a manner worthy of the gospel of Christ" at 1:27.

Again, this does not mean that the Philippians in some sense are working *for* their salvation, to procure salvation for themselves. Earlier at 1:19 Paul used this term "salvation" (σωτηρία) with the sense of his "deliverance" from incarceration. Here in 2:12 we have more eschatological overtones, having to do with "being saved" from judgment at the end of the age and saved to new life in Christ. As Hansen points out, Paul has already underscored that their salvation is "from God" (ἀπὸ θεοῦ, 1:28),[10] and the apostle consistently notes that salvation cannot be brought about by human effort; rather, it is the product of God's grace on the basis of faith (Rom 4:5; 10:10; Eph 2:8–9). Salvation comes through the life of Christ (Rom 5:10; 2 Cor 6:2) and will be worked in us, by God, until Christ returns (Rom 13:11; 1 Thess 5:8). Further, the obedience of the faithful works exists in tandem with, and results from, the work of God, a dynamic

2. Rom 1:7; 11:28; 12:19; 16:5, 8–9, 12; 1 Cor 4:14, 17; 10:14; 15:58; 2 Cor 7:1; 12:19; Eph 5:1; 6:21; Phil 2:12; 4:1; Col 1:7; 4:7, 9, 14; 1 Thess 2:8; 1 Tim 6:2; 2 Tim 1:2; Phlm 1, 16.

3. Hellerman, *Philippians*, 128.

4. In Philippians he more commonly refers to them with the familial "brothers and sisters" (ἀδελφοί; Phil 1:12, 14; 2:25; 3:1, 13, 17; 4:1, 8, 21).

5. Jerry L. Sumney, *Philippians: A Greek Student's Intermediate Reader* (Peabody, MA: Hendrickson, 2007), 52.

6. So, e.g., ESV, CSB, NIV, NET, all of which render the verb with the sense of "work out." Paul uses the verb nineteen other times in his writings, often having the sense of "to commit or do something" or "to produce or bring something about"; all but two of these occur in Romans or the Corinthian correspondence (e.g., Rom 1:27; 2:9; 4:15; 1 Cor 5:3; 2 Cor 4:17; Eph 6:13). The verb also appears at Jas 1:3, 20; 1 Pet 4:3. The verb occurs thirteen times in the LXX (e.g., Exod 15:17; Num 6:3; Deut 28:39).

7. E.g., Rom 1:27; 2:9; 7:8(?), 15, 17, 20; 15:18; 1 Cor 5:3; 2 Cor 12:12(?); Eph 6:13(?). In his commentary on Romans, Doug Moo points out the considerable overlap between this verb and the verbs for "practice" (πράσσω) and "do" (ποιέω). See, for instance, the overlap of these terms with κατεργάζομαι at Rom 1:27–28; 1 Cor 5:2–3; and here in Phil 2:12, 14. See Moo, *Epistle to the Romans*, 455.

8. Rom 4:14; 5:3; 7:13; 2 Cor 4:17; 5:5; 7:10; 9:11; 12:12; Eph 6:13(?).

9. Paul has been using the reflexive pronoun since the beginning of ch. 2 (2:3–4, 7–8, 12, 21), and here it probably is possessive in the sense of "the salvation given to you as a community."

10. Hansen, *Philippians*, 172; on which, see Cohick, Philippians, 136-38.

we see here in 2:12–13. Thus, "working out their salvation" in 2:12 equates to "living out obedience to the Savior[11] as a community."[12] The supporting material surrounding the exhortation points in this direction from various angles.

First, *working out their salvation has to do with following Paul's instructions, whether the apostle is with them or absent*: "Just as you have always followed my instructions—not only in my presence but now much more in my absence" (2:12). Paul taught a pattern of life for his congregations to follow (e.g., 3:17), and the Philippians have lived consistently according to Paul's teaching. This part of the Greek sentence is awkward, speaking of the "accordance" (καθώς/ὡς)[13] between the pattern of faithfulness they have held to in the past (e.g., 1:5–6) and how they are to continue "working out their salvation" as they move into the future. They are to be consistently living for Christ whether Paul is present or absent,[14] and the apostle encourages them in their vigilance in holding to his teaching "now all the more" (νῦν πολλῷ μᾶλλον) in his absence. Since Paul is not with them to give face-to-face encouragement and instruction, they will need to be especially attentive to live according to his pattern of Christian life and ministry.[15]

Second, *working out their salvation is to be carried out in a particular manner—with "fear and trembling."* The language here reflects an idiom from the Greek Old Testament that, for instance, could refer to the "fear of God" in light of his work on behalf of his people (Exod 15:16), or fear of military conquest (Jdt 2:28), or just terrors associated with the threats of an enemy (Ps 55:5 [54:6 LXX]). Paul normally uses the language, as here, of an appropriate posture before an authority, as at 2 Corinthians 7:15 and Ephesians 6:5, where he speaks respectively of the way the Corinthians had received Titus and how slaves should show respect to their masters.

However, in our current passage the conjunction toward the beginning of verse 13 ("for," γάρ) suggests that here we should read "fear and trembling" with reference to God, particularly as speaking of awe or reverence before him. As we saw in the narrative poem about Christ, the glorious Lord humbled himself to bring us the salvation of which Paul speaks. And he sits enthroned above all that is, equal with God the Father. Believers attend to their salvation with fear and trembling because the stakes for them in life are so high. "Fear and trembling"—a deep, deep reverence and sobriety stemming from a desire to know and obey the one true God—should keep believers from falling in the ditch of dread on the one side of the road (he has intended to save us, after all!) and the ditch of

11. Similar to Fee, who notes that the discussion on whether the emphasis is corporate or individual is a false dichotomy. Yet it is also a false dichotomy to sort out soteriology, "how people get saved," from ethical obligations of saved people. The better recent treatments integrate the "theological" and "ethical" or "sociological" interpretations for this passage. As Fee points out in response to Silva (Silva, *Philippians*, 120–21), it is always a "both/and." See Fee, *Philippians*, 234–35; Hellerman, *Philippians*, 130–31.

12. John Hugh Michael, *The Epistle of Paul to the Philippians* (London: Hodder and Stoughton, 1928), 98.

13. The omission of ὡς (B 33. 1241 vg[mss]; Ambst) may have been accidental but could have been judged by some scribes as superfluous. The inclusion has strong external support (𝔓[46] ℵ A C D G K P Ψ 81 614 1739 Byz Lect); so Metzger, *Textual Commentary*, 546.

14. In his letters Paul at times uses "presence" over against "absence" as points of reference for his interface with a church, challenging them to live well (e.g., 1 Cor 5:3; 2 Cor 10:1, 11; 13:2, 10; Phil 1:27). For example, in 2 Corinthians, the whole of the confrontation of the false teachers in the final four chapters of the book is framed with an *inclusio* using the "presence-absence" theme. The apostle offers a form of accountability, noting that eventually he will be present among them. Consequently, they—especially those who have yet to repent—need to adjust their lives to be ready for his coming. See Guthrie, *2 Corinthians*, 47–48, 464.

15. So Bockmuehl, *Philippians*, 152.

casual familiarity on the other. The appropriate place to be is joyfully living in deep reverence and appreciation for God who is working out his holiness in his people.

Third, *the Philippians' salvation is manifested as God works to will and to do his good pleasure among them*. As seen in the explanatory "for" (γάρ) toward the beginning of verse 13, here we have the basis for the imperative in verse 12.[16] The work of God *on behalf of* his people is foundational for the work *of* his people in the world. Paul crafts his letters with this understanding, often laying a foundation with theology and then building on it with ethical exhortations (e.g., Rom 12:1; Col 3:1). Rather than a division of labor between divine sovereignty and human responsibility, God's work enables and facilitates the work of believers.[17]

God is identified as "the one working among you" (ὁ ἐνεργῶν).[18] Paul uses the term translated "working" (ἐνεργέω) eighteen times in his writings, always referring to spiritual dynamics. In all but three cases[19] the word refers to some aspect of God's work or empowering,[20] pointing to spiritual dynamics taking place for some divine purpose. In this passage, moreover, God is working "among you"—that is, in the Philippians collectively—and the work therefore constitutes, among other things, the fostering of community among the believers. In context, this work of God among the Philippians will be manifest as they walk in unity, rejecting "grumbling or arguing" (v. 14).

God is working to accomplish two things: "both to will and to work for his pleasure" (τὸ θέλειν καὶ τὸ ἐνεργεῖν ὑπὲρ τῆς εὐδοκίας). Both[21] willing and working are needed to live out salvation. We need to *want* to please God (volition) and to *be active* in pleasing God (engagement). The word translated as "to will" (θέλειν) could speak of "having a desire for" or "wanting" something, of resolve or readiness to be engaged in an activity, or even of taking pleasure in something.[22] Here it speaks of volition and expresses the wonderful reality that God works in believers, giving them the will to do his will. Without the work of the Spirit of God, we lack the ability to live for God (Rom 7:15–22).[23] Yet Paul proclaims that God not only gives us the will to live out his will but works in us "to work" (τὸ ἐνεργεῖν) for his good pleasure, bringing desire and action together in a way that has a pleasing result. So the extent of God's work in the Philippians has to do with both their volition to engage in what pleases God and the God-pleasing engagement itself.

In context, "pleasure" (εὐδοκία) refers to what gives God pleasure—a common meaning in the Greek Old Testament and the Gospels. Both the Gospels and Paul also use the related verb (εὐδοκέω) to refer to what pleases God (e.g., Luke 12:32; 1 Cor 1:21; Col 1:19). Here Paul speaks of the volition and work done by believers as an outflow of the work of God and "for"[24] the sake of God's pleasure.

**2:14–16 Do everything without grumbling or arguing, in order that you might be faultless and innocent, children of God who are blameless in the middle of a morally twisted and perverted**

16. Bockmuehl, *Philippians*, 153–54; Reumann, *Philippians*, 406.

17. Hellerman, *Philippians*, 132.

18. Wallace, *Greek Grammar*, 602–3.

19. Rom 7:5; Eph 2:2; 2 Thess 2:7.

20. 1 Cor 12:6, 11; 2 Cor 1:6; 4:12; Gal 2:8; 3:5; 5:6; Eph 1:11, 20; 3:20; Phil 2:13; Col 1:29; 1 Thess 2:13.

21. The καὶ τό . . . καὶ τό coordinate construction can be rendered in English as "both . . . and."

22. BDAG 447–48.

23. Bockmuehl, *Philippians*, 154.

24. The preposition ὑπέρ + the genitive communicates advantage.

**generation, among whom you shine like stars in the world by holding out the word of life, resulting in my boast on the day of Christ, that I neither ran for nothing nor worked hard for nothing** (πάντα ποιεῖτε χωρὶς γογγυσμῶν καὶ διαλογισμῶν, 15 ἵνα γένησθε ἄμεμπτοι καὶ ἀκέραιοι, τέκνα θεοῦ ἄμωμα μέσον γενεᾶς σκολιᾶς καὶ διεστραμμένης, ἐν οἷς φαίνεσθε ὡς φωστῆρες ἐν κόσμῳ, 16 λόγον ζωῆς ἐπέχοντες, εἰς καύχημα ἐμοὶ εἰς ἡμέραν Χριστοῦ, ὅτι οὐκ εἰς κενὸν ἔδραμον οὐδὲ εἰς κενὸν ἐκοπίασα). With verse 14 comes another exhortation: "Do everything without grumbling or arguing," which is one very tangible way that the Philippians can "work out" their salvation and please God. Grammatically, the lack of a connecting particle (asyndeton) presents the imperative as closely related to the exhortation of verse 12 and the explanation of verse 13.[25]

We have already seen that the theme of unity in the church lies at the heart of the letter, and verse 14 picks up the theme as a specific expression of how they are to live in a way that is pleasing to God. With its focus on relational health, this little verse plays a big role in this movement of Philippians. After all, the Philippians cannot be "like-minded, embracing a common love, having solidarity, sharing a common perspective" (2:2) if they are grumbling and arguing. Thus the Philippians are "to live out" the Christian life by doing (ποιέω) and willing (θέλω) particular patterns of life. Accordingly, when the apostle says, "Do everything" (πάντα ποιεῖτε), he simply means "let your life be characterized by . . . ," and in particular they are to be characterized by a "lack" (χωρίς) of poor behavior, keeping their relationships in the church clear of "grumbling or arguing" (χωρὶς γογγυσμῶν καὶ διαλογισμῶν). Simply put, the apostle is saying, "Don't grumble and argue!"

The word for grumbling (γογγυσμός) could refer either to positive or negative murmurings "made in a low tone of voice"; that is, "behind-the-scenes talk."[26] Negatively, the word speaks of complaining and discontent (e.g., Acts 6:1; 1 Pet 4:9), and that is the sense here. Paul uses the cognate verb at 1 Corinthians 10:10 in speaking of the negative and dangerous example set by the wilderness wanderers, and the exhortation in Philippians 2:14 probably echoes those Old Testament narratives as well.[27] This is made more sure by the reference to a "morally twisted and perverted generation" (γενεᾶς σκολιᾶς καὶ διεστραμμένης) at 2:15, which alludes to Deuteronomy 32:5—a passage about the wilderness debacle.[28]

The second noun speaks of "arguing" (διαλογισμός). The term could be used to speak of the "process of reasoning," or an "opinion," or the "content of an argument," or even "doubt," but given the context of relational conflict in the church (e.g., Phil 4:2–3), the word here almost certainly has to do with "arguing" or "disputing,"[29] a manifestation of conflict in the community (cf. 1 Tim 2:8).

Verse 15 tells us why the Philippians should establish healthy patterns of relating to one another, turning away from "grumbling or arguing": "in order that" (ἵνα) they "might be faultless and innocent" (γένησθε ἄμεμπτοι καὶ ἀκέραιοι). These are the virtues they need as they interact with a morally twisted world. The first of these adjectives (ἄμεμπτος) speaks of being "blameless" or "faultless"; it is a word that Paul also uses at 3:6 where he proclaims that he had been "blameless" in terms of the righteousness based on the law. As seen by its

25. Fee, *Philippians*, 243.

26. BDAG 204. Both positive and negative whispering can be seen at John 7:12, where people are reported to have been whispering good and bad things about Jesus.

27. E.g., LXX Exod 17:3; Num 11:1; 14:27, 29; 16:41; 17:5; see Ps 105:25.

28. Silva, *Philippians*, 123–24, 131.

29. BDAG 232.

use in the LXX, the word basically points to a pattern of living righteously before God and others.[30]

The second adjective (ἀκέραιος) refers to being "innocent" or "pure."[31] At Matthew 10:16 Jesus tells his disciples, "Be as shrewd as snakes and as innocent [ἀκέραιοι] as doves" (NIV). Paul also uses this word at Romans 16:9, where he encourages the Romans to be "innocent [ἀκεραίους] concerning what is evil." In our current passage, being "faultless and innocent" contrasts sharply with "grumbling" and "arguing." In other words, rather than normal relational struggles that might be expected in any Christian community, grumbling and arguing should be seen as "unrighteous" or even "evil." Relational breakdown, after all, is antithetical to Jesus's "new" command that his disciples love one another, a primary orientation for true Christ-following in the New Testament.[32] As the world looks at believers caught up in grumbly, conflict-ridden churches, they understandably say, "They are no different from us!"

So that they might live well as God's children (τέκνα θεοῦ),[33] Paul also encourages the Philippians to be "unblemished" or "blameless" (ἄμωμα), a word very much related to the term translated as "faultless" (ἄμεμπτος) at the beginning of verse 15. This term is very common in the LXX, used often of the need for "spotless" sacrificial animals.[34] Yet the word also is used to speak of the character of God himself or of God's ways, or of the righteous person who walks with God in a way that is "blameless."[35]

Thus, in rapid-fire succession, we have three descriptors of Paul's desire for the Philippians, that they would be "faultless," "innocent," and "blameless." Rather than offering carefully nuanced distinctions between these three adjectives in verse 15, the alliteration of the Greek terms (ἄμεμπτοι, ἀκέραιοι, and ἄμωμα) should be read as "stylistic reinforcement"[36]—the drumming home of multiple, similar, potent, rhetorically crafted descriptions to make a point. In short, the Philippians are called to live lives that are above reproach, characterized by God's "right" way to live, demonstrating patterns of relating to one another that are free from accusation before a watching world.[37]

Further, the reference to "children of God" who are "blameless" (ἄμωμα) almost certainly points intentionally to Deuteronomy 32:5, a verse alluded to by Paul in verse 15. In the LXX, the Deuteronomy passage refers to the "blemished children" (τέκνα μωμητά) who make up "a generation, crooked and perverse" (γενεὰ σκολιὰ καὶ διεστραμμένη; Deut 32:5 NETS), which is clearly behind Paul's reference here to "a morally twisted and perverted generation" (γενεᾶς σκολιᾶς καὶ διεστραμμένης).[38] The term for "generation" (γενεά) could refer either to a "race" of people, or to "an age" (i.e., a temporal frame of reference), or to all the people "living

30. In Gen 17:1 LXX the Lord says to Abram, "Be well pleasing before me, and become blameless [ἄμεμπτος]" (Gen 17:1 NETS), on which see Fee, *Philippians*, 244–45. It is used especially in Job, where it is stacked up with other descriptors of living well before God (Job 1:1, 8; 2:3; 4:17; 9:20; 11:4; 12:4; 15:14; 22:3, 19; 33:9; cf. Wis 10:5, 15; 18:21).

31. Philo could use the word with the sense of "unmixed" (*Embassy* 334), and Epictetus could use it with the sense of a person who was "harmless" or even "unsophisticated" (*Diatr.* 3.23.15).

32. John 13:34–35; Rom 12:10; 13:8; 2 Cor 13:11; Gal 5:13; Eph 4:2; 1 Thess 4:9; 2 Thess 1:3; Heb 10:24; 13:1; 1 Pet 1:22; 3:8; 5:14; 1 John 3:11, 23; 4:7, 11–12; 2 John 5.

33. Used elsewhere as a designation for believers at John 1:12; Rom 8:16; and 1 John 3:1–2. At Rom 8:16 Paul writes, "The Spirit himself testifies with our spirit that we are God's children" (NIV).

34. E.g., Exod 29:1, 38; Lev 1:3, 10; 3:1, 6, 9; Num 15:24; 19:2; 28:3. The antonym is μῶμος = "blame" or "blemish, defect."

35. E.g., 2 Sam 22:24, 31, 33; Ps 14:2; 17:24, 31, 33; cf. 1 Macc 4:42.

36. Silva, *Philippians*, 132.

37. Hansen, *Philippians*, 181–82.

38. In Paul's form, the nominatives of the LXX have given way to genitives, and γενεᾶς may be read as an attributed genitive, with μέσον read as an adjectival accusative (see Robertson, *Grammar*, 488).

at a given time" (= "your contemporaries").[39] In Deuteronomy 32:5, those who rebelled and fell in the wilderness—that "generation" of Israel—are in mind, and they serve as a stark example of the folly of rebelling against God (cf. 1 Cor 10:1–13). The allusion could indicate that a particular form of rebellion was plaguing the church in Philippi—rebellion against godly leaders in the church.[40] Nevertheless, the primary reference here seems to be to the "world at large," the broader culture of Philippi and the Roman Empire generally (cf. Phil 1:28). Accordingly, Paul takes the scriptural allusion to rebels who oppose God and expands it to encompass people in a lost and fallen world.[41] Accordingly, the believers of Philippi are said to be amid this "generation," referring to lost humanity all around them on the streets of Philippi.

That generation, moreover, the apostle describes as "morally twisted and perverted" (σκολιᾶς καὶ διεστραμμένης), graphic terms pointing to issues of character and lifestyle. The first of these descriptions is an adjective, used in the ancient world to refer to something that was physically bent, curved, or crooked, such as a bent sword or a crooked post. The word came to be used figuratively of a person's character as "morally twisted"—that is, "dishonest" or "unscrupulous."[42] Similarly, the second description speaks of something "deformed" or "distorted" (from the verb διαστρέφω), but it, too, could be used figuratively, picturing a person as departing from an "accepted standard of moral or spiritual values," thus meaning "to pervert."[43] Here we have a two-pronged characterization of a culture out of sync with the ways of a holy God. It is "twisted and perverted," bent and distorted in relation to God's design for human beings.

Amid such a culture the church must live out a brilliant counterculture: "among whom you shine like stars in the world" (ἐν οἷς φαίνεσθε ὡς φωστῆρες ἐν κόσμῳ). Since God is doing a good work in this church (e.g., 1:6; 2:13), they "shine" brightly "like stars" against the dark backdrop of the world's moral distortions. At this point the apostle draws on Daniel 12:3 LXX, which reads, "And those who are intelligent will light up like the luminaries of heaven [φανοῦσιν ὡς φωστῆρες τοῦ οὐρανοῦ]" (Dan 12:3a NETS). Yet whereas Daniel's words have a more apocalyptic ring to them—the persecuted followers of God are vindicated in glory[44]—Philippians 2:15 brings to mind the very "down-to-earth" words of Jesus at Matthew 5:14–16, where the Lord says,

> You are the light of the world. A town built on a hill cannot be hidden. Neither do people light a lamp and put it under a bowl. Instead they put it on its stand, and it gives light to everyone in the house. In the same way, let your light shine before others, that they may see your good deeds and glorify your Father in heaven. (NIV)

39. BDAG 191–92.

40. Osiek, *Philippians, Philemon*, 71.

41. As Hansen points out, this is not a move by Paul to "replace" Israel with the church. Rather, Paul extrapolates out the posture of rebellion seen in Deut 32 to rebellion as characteristic of all those in the world who have yet to bend the knee to King Jesus (Phil 2:10–11). See Hansen, *Philippians*, 182. Interestingly, the suffering servant is also said to have suffered as a part of a "generation" (Isa 53:8).

42. BDAG 930.

43. BDAG 237.

44. As Osiek points out, the allusion to Daniel could point to an eschatological orientation, for in apocalyptic thought the righteous will be rewarded by being enthroned in glory in the heavenly realm. See Osiek, *Philippians, Philemon*, 71. Yet the imperfective aspect here, and the juxtaposition to the "world" (which admittedly could be rendered as "cosmos"), probably indicate that a "this world" orientation is in mind. The "shining" is further delimited in v. 16 by "holding out the word of life," which seems to place the context as this life.

Very much in line with Jesus's words, Paul tells the Philippians exactly where they are to shine. First, they are to shine among (ἐν οἷς, "among whom") the morally twisted generation just described; second, they are to shine "in the world" (ἐν κόσμῳ). The term translated as "world" has a broad range of meaning and could here refer to "humanity," "the universe," or planet earth. With the word picture of shining stars, the apostle seems to be crafting a play on words, using the word picture of stars shining in "the universe" to point to the Philippians' role vis-à-vis the people around them in the broader culture. The apostle calls for the church to present a clear, countercultural, moral witness before a dark and watching world.

How then are they to shine? With the beginning of verse 16, Paul tells them the means of doing so—"by holding out the word of life" (λόγον ζωῆς ἐπέχοντες).[45] In recent discussions among commentators, interpretation of the participle, translated here as "holding out," has focused on two primary meanings—"hold on" and "hold forth."[46] Between the two, the latter, which is often interpreted with an evangelistic emphasis, has the stronger case.[47] Read in this way, the Philippians are said to "shine like stars in the world by holding out the word of life." Of course, they have the ability to "hold out" the word because they *hold onto* the word. This orientation to God's word of life fits perfectly with the context, which emphasizes their "blameless" behavior in contrast to a world "morally twisted" and "perverted." The "word" is key to our closeness to God, our moral compass, and our impact on the world. In fact, there is no truly "Christian life" apart from the word of God. The term translated "word" (λόγον) in the phrase "word of life" (λόγον ζωῆς) comes first for emphasis, and "of life" can be read as an objective genitive, "the word that produces life." Although the "word of life" phrase is found nowhere else in Paul, his proclamation and teaching of God's word[48] certainly was central to his ministry and understood as giving life.[49]

The remainder of verse 16 expresses the desired outcome that will take place as the Philippians live out their lives as people attentive to God's word: "resulting in my boast on the day of Christ, that I neither ran for nothing nor worked hard for nothing" (εἰς καύχημα ἐμοὶ εἰς ἡμέραν Χριστοῦ, ὅτι οὐκ εἰς κενὸν ἔδραμον οὐδὲ εἰς κενὸν ἐκοπίασα). In our comments on 1:26 we have already discussed the concept of "boasting" as used by Paul. When a

45. I agree with Fee (Fee, *Philippians*, 247) that, rather than ἐπέχοντες reaching back to γένησθε at the beginning of the verse, it tells us more directly about the act of "shining," communicating "means."

46. When we consider the use of the word in biblical literature, neither of these two meanings has a significant place. In half of the twenty-two occurrences in the LXX the word means "to hold back" or "refrain" (Gen 8:10, 12; 1 Kgs 22:6, 15; 2 Kgs 4:24; 2 Chr 18:5, 14; Job 18:2; Jer 6:11; 2 Macc 5:25; 9:25), the same sense as in Acts 19:22; this meaning would make no sense in our Philippians context. The other primary meaning in the LXX, however, does make a great deal of sense in our context, having to do with "paying careful attention to" or "being attentive to" something (e.g., Job 30:26; Sir 5:1, 8; 15:4; 16:3; 34:2; 35:11; 37:11), and this is the same meaning found in three of the remaining four occurrences of the verb in the NT (Luke 14:7; Acts 3:5; 1 Tim 4:16; the fourth is Phil 2:16). However, this sense almost always occurs with the object in the dative, not the accusative as we have in Phil 2:16.

James P. Ware has done an extensive study demonstrating that the word has the two primary meanings of "hold back" and "hold forth." For instance, Aristotle uses the term of an octopus "extending" a tentacle. Theocritus employs the word of someone holding out a water pitcher to a spring (Aristotle, *History of Animals* 550b; Theocritus, *Idylls* 13.46; see Ware, *Mission of the Church*, 262).

47. See the extensive discussion in Reumann, *Philippians*, 393–94, and the options presented in LSJ 619–20. For the word in the lexicons and the broader Greco-Roman world, see Ware, *Mission of the Church*, 256–70.

48. E.g., Rom 3:2; 1 Cor 14:36; 2 Cor 2:17; Eph 6:17; Col 1:25; 1 Thess 2:13; 1 Tim 4:5; 2 Tim 2:9; Titus 2:5.

49. E.g., Rom 2:7; 5:10, 17, 21; 6:4, 22; 8:2, 10; 2 Cor 2:16; 4:11; Gal 6:8; Phil 4:3; Col 3:4; 1 Tim 1:16; 6:12; Titus 3:7.

person "boasted" in the ancient world, including the Jewish world, it could be perceived as an inappropriate expression of human arrogance.[50] Yet Paul at times uses "boast" (καύχημα) to speak of "celebration" of the Lord's person and work in the lives of his people (e.g., 1 Cor 9:15; 2 Cor 1:14; 5:12; 9:3; Phil 1:26), and that is the sense here. Whereas at 1:26 the focus was on the Philippians' boast in Paul when he joined them again, here in 2:16 the focus is eschatological, as Paul anticipates being able to celebrate the Philippians' faithfulness "on the day of Christ." The quadruple use of the preposition translated in the first instance as "in order that/on" (εἰς) is a bit difficult to sort out, but the first can be read as communicating purpose.[51] The second use of this preposition (εἰς) communicates a timeframe: "on"[52] the day of Christ.

Ancient Judaism spoke of a "day" of the Lord that would bring in divine judgment on the ungodly and salvation for God's people (e.g., Isa 2:2–21; Joel 1–3; Amos 8:9–11; 9:9–12). Paul, and the New Testament generally (e.g., 1 Cor 1:8; 5:5; 1 Thess 5:2; 2 Thess 2:2; 2 Pet 3:10), equates the day of the Lord with "the day of Christ," particularly referring to the Lord's return. That was a day of hope for Paul, who anticipated being able to celebrate a fulfilled ministry to the Philippians. This is stated negatively in our passage: "That I neither ran for nothing nor worked hard for nothing" (ὅτι οὐκ εἰς κενὸν ἔδραμον οὐδὲ εἰς κενὸν ἐκοπίασα). So the apostle longs to come to the day of Christ and see that all his work—a life spent, poured out for the salvation of others—was not empty of meaning, that he did not carry out his ministry "for nothing" (οὐκ εἰς κενόν . . . οὐδὲ εἰς κενόν). The doubling of the phrase translated "for nothing" rhetorically drives home the intensity of Paul's desire.[53] The term translated as "nothing" (κενόν) connotes the idea of being "empty," either literally ("empty-handed," e.g., Gen 31:42 LXX) or figuratively (e.g., Job 27:12 LXX). Here the figurative sense is extended to speak of an effort that has been done "in vain," that is, "without a meaningful result," or as we might say in English, "I did all that work for nothing!" As the Philippians persevere in the faith, coming to the day of the Lord with a life of faithfulness behind them, Paul's extensive, exhausting labors, his pattern of hard work, will not have been "for nothing."

The apostle speaks of his ministry labors as "running" and "working hard." The first, "running" (ἔδραμον, from the verb τρέχω), offers a metaphor for the "effort" the apostle has exerted in the process of ministry. Paul uses this word picture several times to connote human effort or engagement in living or ministering for God (e.g., Rom 9:16; 1 Cor 9:24, 26; Gal 2:2; 5:7). The second term speaks of ministry as "working" (ἐκοπίασα, from the verb κοπιάω). In both the LXX and the New Testament, the term often refers to being exhausted,[54] but more

50. For negative uses of the term καύχημα and its cognates in Greco-Roman literature, see *TLNT* 2:295–302. See also Duane F. Watson, "Paul and Boasting," in *Paul in the Greco-Roman World: A Handbook*, ed. J. Paul Sampley (Harrisburg, PA: Trinity Press International, 2003), 77–100. Watson writes:

> Paul's understanding of boasting is a unique mix of boasting as understood within Judaism and within the dominant Greco-Roman culture. Paul uses boasting in the situations prescribed as appropriate by the Greco-Roman culture, and he uses boasting according to its conventions for those situations. However, his understanding of the content of boasting itself is borrowed from his Jewish heritage and his newfound faith in Christ. (94)

51. See the discussion in Hellerman, *Philippians*, 138; Fee, *Philippians*, 248. The dative personal pronoun ἐμοί can be interpreted as a dative of agency (lit. "by me"; or perhaps a dative of possession, "my boast"). See Hawthorne and Martin, *Philippians*, 147.

52. BDAG 289.

53. The third and fourth uses of the preposition εἰς in the passage mark the result that the apostle wants to avoid.

54. E.g., Deut 25:18; 1 Sam 14:31; Ps 6:6; John 4:6.

often simply refers to the act of "working hard."[55] Paul consistently employs the term with this latter meaning, as he does here. These twin activities, "running and working," tell of the difficult, labor-intensive nature of Paul's ministry. He quite literally worked hard at tentmaking, which was a grueling form of manual labor that provided a platform for his ministry (Acts 18:3). Yet beyond his manual labor, the apostle faced a complex of work-intensive and emotionally draining activities—difficult travel, constant persecution, evangelistic encounters, teaching and ministering, and the emotional burden of the churches. These would have taken a physical and emotional toll (see, e.g., 2 Cor 11:22–12:10), but the labor was *purposeful*, and Paul was confident that his fruitful work among the Philippians would have a joy-inducing outcome.

**2:17 Indeed, even if I am poured out like a drink offering on the sacrificial service for your faith, I am glad and rejoice with all of you** (ἀλλ' εἰ καὶ σπένδομαι ἐπὶ τῇ θυσίᾳ καὶ λειτουργίᾳ τῆς πίστεως ὑμῶν, χαίρω καὶ συγχαίρω πᾶσιν ὑμῖν). Paul's intensive work on behalf of the Philippians is worth it from his perspective. Looking back on his life from our vantage point, his sacrifice went far beyond a "normal" pattern of laborious ministry (e.g., 2 Cor 11:23). Indeed, when the Lord called Paul on the Damascus Road, he proclaimed that Paul's ministry would be shaped by suffering: "I will show him how much he must suffer for my name" (Acts 9:16 NIV). Nevertheless, now, in a period of incarceration, embodying the severe extremes to which ministry could lead, Paul rejoices.

Thus Paul begins verse 17 with "indeed,[56] even if I am poured out like a drink offering . . ." The sense communicated by the apostle could be rendered as "indeed, even if this be the time that will bring me to my end . . ."[57] Thus read, the construction is used to build on the previous thought and add a potential situation that could arise.

In the conditional clause, the verb translated "I am poured out" (σπένδομαι) could be used by ancient authors of pouring out a drink offering on a sacrifice, which was a common practice both in Judaism and in the broader Greco-Roman world. Paul almost certainly draws on the LXX, in which the word finds expression nineteen times, all of which refer to pouring out drink offerings, either to the one true God or to false gods;[58] so language related to priestly ministry seems to be in play here, as the phrase "on the sacrificial service"

55. E.g., 1 Sam 17:39; Judg 5:26; Eccl 2:18; Matt 6:28; Luke 5:5; John 4:38; Rom 6:6; 1 Cor 4:12; 15:10; 16:16; Eph 4:28; 1 Thess 5:12; 1 Tim 4:10; see *TLNT* 2:327–28.

56. We can read ἀλλ' εἰ καί as at least progressive and indeed ascensive, even though the two conjunctions are separated by εἰ, which introduces a conditional clause. Perhaps Paul has in mind a combination of ἀλλά used emphatically (i.e., "certainly") and an adjunctive use of καί ("even"). See Thrall, *Greek Particles*, 13–16. Many understand ἀλλά to be contrastive, but we have to ask, with what is the "rejoicing" of the main clause being contrasted? Certainly not with "for nothing" of v. 16 (so, Reumann, *Philippians*, 397), and I would suggest neither is it being contrasted with Paul's "boast" on the last day. Fee reads the conjunction as building a contrast with "what has preceded," rendering the conjunction "but." He finds the interpretation of ascensive force ("not only labors, but even death") attractive but urges caution on the basis of the grammatical construction. See Fee, *Philippians*, 240, 250. This exact construction (ἀλλ' εἰ καί) finds expression numerous times in both Josephus and Philo, and some of these occurrences seem to be ascensive, as they introduce a conditional clause in the protasis of the sentence. See the construction in Philo, *Drunkenness* 198; *Heir* 23; *Names* 222; *Joseph* 24; *Moses* 1.245; *Embassy* 158; *Providence* 2.62; Josephus, *Ant.* 8.278; 12.425; 16.93; 18.243; *J.W.* 3.359; 4.281; 7.351; *Ag. Ap.* 1.284. The construction can be read as ascensive and progressive (e.g., Philo, *Names* 222; *Joseph* 24; *Embassy* 158), building on a previous thought to make an additional point. The same can be said for passages in Josephus (e.g., *J.W.* 7.351).

57. Reading εἰ καί with Fee as intensive rather than concessive; see Fee, *Philippians*, 240n2.

58. Gen 35:14; Exod 25:29; 30:9; 38:12; Num 4:7; 28:7; 2 Sam 23:16; 1 Chr 11:18; Hos 9:4; Jer 7:18; 19:13; 39:29; 51:17, 19, 25; Ezek 20:28; 4 Macc 3:16; Sir 50:15.

(τῇ θυσίᾳ καὶ λειτουργίᾳ) suggests. The terms for sacrifice (θυσίᾳ) and "service" (λειτουργίᾳ) draw on passages involving worship in the Old Testament (e.g., together at 2 Chr 31:2 LXX; 2 Macc 3:3; 4:14). These two words used in tandem can be read as a hendiadys—"sacrificial service"—Paul crafting a powerful word picture, drawing an analogy between the practice of Old Testament sacrifice and his extensive and "sacrificial" work of ministry to the Philippians. In this regard, the phrase "for your faith" (τῆς πίστεως ὑμῶν) can be read as communicating "advantage," Paul's sacrificial ministry carried out for the building up of the Philippians' relationship with God.[59]

There is debate concerning whether the apostle's language of being "poured out . . . on the sacrificial service" speaks of his ongoing ministry of suffering or of his martyrdom.[60] But I think, given our interpretation of the transitional words at the beginning of verse 17 (ἀλλ᾽ εἰ καί), that martyrdom is the likely meaning, since that construction seems to indicate a heightening or intensification of his themes of "running" and "working hard." Paul's life is poured out in ministry in such a way that death is always a threat (e.g., Phil 1:20–21; cf. 2 Cor 1:8–9; 4:10), and death through martyrdom was simply a natural culmination of a persecuted life. Further, at 2 Timothy 4:6, the only other use of the term translated "poured out" (σπένδω) in the New Testament, the apostle employs the word to speak of being "poured out" in martyrdom at the end of his ministry. The apostle's point here, accordingly, is that even if his life ends in martyrdom, he rejoices that the ministry will have accomplished its intended effect of the Philippians' endurance in the faith to the day of Christ.

Consequently, Paul's response to the prospect of martyrdom is "I am glad and rejoice with all of you." The first of these cognate terms, χαίρω, occurs seventy-four times in the New Testament. It could mean "to be glad," as the closely related term at Matthew 5:12 (ἀγαλλιάω, "exult, be glad") shows, or it could be used as a greeting (as in "I am glad to see you!").[61] The former is the case here. The related term, "I rejoice with" (συγχαίρω), is much less frequent, appearing only six other times in the New Testament (Luke 1:58; 15:6, 9; 1 Cor 12:26; 13:6; Phil 2:18) and, as our translation suggests, refers to rejoicing with someone else. The "someone" in this case is the inclusive "all of you" (πᾶσιν ὑμῖν). So we translate the whole as "I am glad and rejoice with all of you." Paul rejoices, not in the prospect of death at this point (cf. 1:21–22) but in faithfulness and the fruit of faithfulness in relation to the gospel. "Fidelity in the face of death or any other enemy is a cause for joy."[62] Further, in "rejoicing with" the Philippians, Paul draws them into—and includes them in—his sense of joy in his ministry of the gospel. The logical development in Philippians 2:16–17, therefore, is this:

> The Philippians' faithfulness will result in Paul's celebration on the day of Christ that his ministry was effective,
>
> **and**
>
> even if he is martyred in the course of his continued ministry, this does nothing to dampen the celebration.

59. Some commentators, on the basis of the same "service" language at 2:25, 30, suggest that what Paul has in mind here is the service of the Philippians themselves, not Paul's service to them (e.g., Hellerman, *Philippians*, 140; Silva, *Philippians*, 129). Yet the genitive in v. 25, "my need" (τῆς χρείας μου), and the associated pronoun "me" in v. 30 (με in τῆς πρός με λειτουργίας) both refer to Paul. The "service" of 2:17, on the other hand, is "the service stemming from your faith" (λειτουργίᾳ τῆς πίστεως ὑμῶν). This suggests that between 2:17 and 2:25, 30 there is a reciprocal relationship of ministry—Paul's ministry to the Philippians in v. 17, which is foundational, and the Philippians' ministry to Paul in vv. 25, 30.

60. For an overview of the debate, see, e.g., Hansen, *Philippians*, 187–88.

61. BDAG 1074–75.

62. Fowl, *Philippians*, 129.

## Theology in Application

### *Live Out Salvation as a "Process"*

I grew up in a tradition that emphasized the moment of salvation, often marked by when a person prayed "the sinner's prayer" or walked the aisle of the church in response to an invitation—or both. Punctuating my teen years were "revival" meetings, sometimes in big tents, and once even a "brush arbor," which was a rough, open-sided structure made of a wooden frame and covered with brush (such structures had been used in America beginning in the 1700s). The success of the revival was judged by how many people "got saved." I am thankful for that tradition, which taught me that God wants to save people through the work of Jesus in the gospel, that the gospel is something to which people should respond (and special moments when people are challenged to consider their response to the gospel can be important), and that God hears and answers when we cry out to him, professing him as Lord (Rom 10:9–10).

Yet as I have continued to read and study the Bible, I have found that salvation is so much more beautiful, powerful, life transforming, and comprehensive than I had ever imagined. It forms a profoundly rich tapestry of varied theological threads, beginning with Israel and coursing through the pages of the New Testament in a kaleidoscope of actions, word pictures, and time frames. God has, is, and will save his people in a variety of ways. In fact, as theologians such as Millard Erickson and J. I. Packer have pointed out, that beautiful tapestry points to the salvation we experience in Christ as having a past, a present, and a future.[63] In short, those who are a part of the new covenant *have been saved* from the penalty of sin, *are being saved* from the power of sin, and *will be saved* from the presence of sin. Of course, there is much more to it than that, but it's a beginning.

For example, speaking in the context of salvation as an already accomplished fact in the life of a believer, Titus 3:5–6 states that "he saved us, not because of righteous things we had done, but because of his mercy. He saved us through the washing of rebirth and renewal by the Holy Spirit, whom he poured out on us generously through Jesus Christ our Savior" (NIV; cf. 2 Tim 1:9). Ephesians 2:8, on the other hand, points to our having been saved but focuses on our salvation as a present reality: "For it is by grace you have been saved [ἐστε σεσῳσμένοι], through faith—and this is not from yourselves, it is the gift of God" (NIV). Notice the periphrastic perfect construction, which points to the current state of the believer—you have been and are being saved. Second Corinthians 2:15 also seems to refer to salvation (as well as the

63. Erickson, *Christian Theology*, 929; J. I. Packer, *Rediscovering Holiness* (Ann Arbor, MI: Vine Books, 1992), 46–47.

destruction of those who reject the gospel) as an ongoing reality when Paul writes, "For we are to God the pleasing aroma of Christ among those who are being saved and those who are perishing" (NIV). Finally, several New Testament passages place the emphasis squarely on salvation as a future event, concurrent with the coming of Christ. Hebrews 9:28 is one of these and reads, "So [Christ] will appear a second time, not to bear sin, but to bring salvation to those who are waiting for him" (NIV).

As we reflect on Philippians 2:12–17, this means that we should not speak of our salvation merely as a rescue from sin in the past. Nor should we only think of our salvation as a future rescue from the presence of sin and evil when Jesus returns. In addition to these, we need to think well about how God is working the gospel of our salvation in and through the dark corners of our lives and in our communities in the present. You and I are being saved right now!

So, ask yourself, "How am I being saved by God today as he works in my will and my actions?" "How am I living out my salvation, with appropriate 'fear and trembling,' in a way that is robust?" and "How is that salvation being manifested particularly in my community of faith?" Do our relationships in our church manifest our salvation, or are we characterized as being grumbly and conflicted? Do our relationships in our families and in our communities manifest our salvation? In what ways?

In some circles an exhortation from Jerry Bridges (which he picked up from a friend named Jack Miller) has caught on: "Preach the gospel to yourself every day!"[64] I kid my wife about her talking to herself while she is doing various things around the house. I shout from the next room, "Who are you talking to?!" And she replies, "Myself." I follow with, "Let me know if yourself starts answering back!" Yet the practice of talking to oneself—we could say, of "preaching to oneself"—is a very old one and should be encouraged.

> Why, my soul, are you downcast?
> Why so disturbed within me?
> Put your hope in God,
> for I will yet praise him,
> my Savior and my God. (Ps 42:5 NIV)

We need to preach the gospel to ourselves with the psalmist—and with the writers of the rest of Scripture—every day, for we need saving every day. Once we have been "saved" by entering Christ's new covenant, we need a present manifestation of salvation from sin and selfishness and discouragement and depression and bad habits of mind, heart, and body, and physical disintegration and relational dysfunction and

64. Jerry Bridges, *The Discipline of Grace* (Colorado Springs, CO: NavPress, 2006), 8, 45.

societal fragmentation. We need to "work out" our salvation with "fear and trembling" even as God continues to work in us "both to will and to work for his pleasure."

## *Shining in a Dark and Twisted World*

As we see in 2:15–16, Paul wants the Philippians to be "faultless and innocent, children of God who are blameless in the middle of a morally twisted and perverted generation." The world, of course, can be a terribly dark and violent place—soul crushing, in fact. In recent years it seems the moral fabric of many cultures around the world is fraying at the edges, pulling at the seams, intent on ripping apart. Yet, we must remember that the world is charged with the glory of God! This is not only true of creation but should be true of *us*, God's people, as its pinnacle and stewards. We should "shine," as Philippians 2:15 says.

Of course, every generation of Christ-followers has its challenges in attempting to shine "like stars" in such a world as ours. The key, however, has to do with our relationship with the living God, by his Spirit, through his good word. For in the word of God we find our moral moorings—how God would have us live as "faultless and innocent" in a morally twisted world. There is our source of light in the darkness, as the Spirit kindles the word in us.

Michelangelo completed the Sistine Chapel in 1512, and it was used as a house of worship from that point. At that time, the chapel was lit by candles, and over the years soot from those candles obscured Michelangelo's masterpiece. The black, sooty layer of grime on the ceiling created a dark veil that obscured the elaborate details of the artist's work. So, from 1984 to 1999 a team of restorationist artists worked on the ceiling. Kevin Miller explains the backdrop of the restoration:

> Prior to the restoration process, many in the art community thought that Michelangelo was a genius at composition. After all, how did he think to have Adam's hand stretching out, yearning to find the finger of God, which was already reaching out for him? But it was also widely believed that Michelangelo's coloration was mediocre. It was too dark, monochromatic, and blah. And yet when they restored those frescoes to their original state, everyone could see the beautiful, fresh, and even spring-like colors—pale pink, apple green, vivid yellow, and sky blue against a background of warm pearly grey. When the maker's true brilliance and goodness were revealed, people had to change their assumptions about Michelangelo.[65]

65. Kevin Miller, "Restored Sistine Chapel Reveals Maker's True Splendor," Preachingtoday.com, October 2013, www.preachingtoday.com/illustrations/2013/october/5100713.html.

Analogously, the world is a burning place offering its version of light, but it is a corrosive light, obscuring more than illuminating God's good creation. But in the kingdom come, with the advance of the gospel, God carries out a grand restoration project, restoring all the colors and dimensions of the image to which we as human beings were born. And God brings transformative light that fills and exudes from the believer, as he or she lives in a word-saturated way that reveals and shapes the moral fabric of life. And from that place, the word is held forth to the twisted world, drawing it toward a great untwisting to come.

CHAPTER 8

# Philippians 2:18–30

## Literary Context

We continue our trek through the main body of Philippians, which started at 1:27 and continues to 4:4a. The two sub-movements of 1:27–2:4 call for unity in the church, encouraging the believers in Philippi to live with a common purpose in life, worthy of the gospel in the face of a world in opposition to their message (1:27–30). Unity builds through selflessness and humility toward one another (2:1–4). As we saw in 2:5–11, the Lord Christ provides the ultimate example of selfless sacrifice, as the lyrical and deeply moving narrative poem of 2:6–11 follows Christ's pattern of pouring himself out for others in his incarnation and death. He consequently is exalted by God the Father, and at the name of Jesus all creation will bow the knee and confess Jesus as "Lord." Then in 2:12–17, the Philippians are exhorted to live in healthy relationships, shining like stars in a twisted and morally bent world, so that on the day of Christ, Paul might celebrate that his ministry was not empty of meaning and good results.

Now in 2:18–30, picking up on the themes of joy, the threat of death, and sacrificial service in 2:17, Paul builds on the example of Christ by pointing to Timothy and Epaphroditus as exemplars of true Christian ministry.[1] These fellow ministers of Paul, each of whom has a significant role as an apostolic representative to the Philippians, embody the virtues that Paul wants the Philippians to embrace. They prepare the Philippians for the coming of their apostle and literarily open the way for Paul to use himself as an example in 3:1–21.

1. On the significant role of this section in the execution of Philippians, see R. Alan Culpepper, "Co-Workers in Suffering: Philippians 2:19–30," *RevExp* 77.3 (1980): 349–58.

I. The Letter Opening: A Prescript and a Prayer Report (1:1–11)
**II. The Letter Body (1:12–4:9)**
A. The Body Opening: Paul's Current Situation (1:12–26)
B. The Main Body of the Letter: A Call for Unity in the Church (1:27–4:4a)
1. An Exhortation to Live Out the Unity of Community (1:27–2:4)
2. Be Like Christ Jesus, the Preeminent Example of Self-Sacrifice (2:5–11)
3. Further Exhortations to Unity and Exclamations of Joy (2:12–17)
➦ **4. Timothy and Epaphroditus as Exemplars of Self-Sacrifice (2:18–30)**
5. The Example of Paul's Christocentric Life and Ministry (3:1–14)
6. Exhortations to Embrace Paul's Christocentric Pattern of Life (3:15–4:4a)
C. The Body Closing: Exhortations (4:4b–9)
III. The Letter Closing (4:10–23)

## Main Idea

Timothy and Epaphroditus serve as exemplars of the type of selfless service seen in Christ himself, even as they serve as Paul's representatives of the mission, preparing for his imminent return to Philippi.

## Translation

### Philippians 2:18–30

| | | |
|---|---|---|
| 18a | | In the same way, |
| b | | also |
| c | Exhortation | **you be glad and** |
| d | | **rejoice** |
| e | Association | with me. |
| 19a | Desire | Now **I hope . . .** |
| b | Relationship | in the Lord Jesus |
| c | Content | **. . . to send** |
| d | Object | Timothy |
| e | Ind. Obj. | to you |
| f | Timeframe | soon, |
| g | Purpose | in order that I also may be encouraged |
| h | Time | when I learn what is happening with you. |

| | | |
|---|---|---|
| 20a | Explanation | For |
| b | Assertion | **I have no other kindred spirit available**, |
| c | Description | who genuinely will be concerned |
| d | Object | about what is happening with you. |
| | | |
| 21a | Explanation cont. | Indeed, |
| b | Assertion | **they all look out for their own interests** |
| c | Dissimilarity | rather than the things that interest Jesus Christ! |
| | | |
| 22a | General/Appeal | **You know** his proven worth, |
| | | |
| b | Analogy | that, like a son with a father, |
| c | Specific Example | he has served |
| d | Relationship | with me in advancing the gospel work. |
| | | |
| 23a | Inference | So **this is the person I hope to send** |
| b | Time | as soon as I determine |
| c | Object | what will happen with me; |
| | | |
| 24a | Confidence | and **I am confident in the Lord** |
| b | Content | that I myself will come soon. |
| | | |
| 25a | Explanation | Now **I considered it necessary . . . to send** |
| b | Indirect Obj. | to you |
| c | Identification | Epaphroditus, |
| d | Apposition/ | my brother and |
| e | List (d–h) | coworker and |
| f | | fellow soldier, who also is |
| g | | your messenger and |
| h | | minister attending to my need, |
| | | |
| 26a | Basis/Emotion 1 | since he was longing for all of you and |
| b | Emotion 2 | was very distressed |
| c | Cause | because you heard that he was sick. |
| | | |
| 27a | Expansion | Indeed, **he was sick** |
| b | Extent | to the point of death, |
| c | Alternate Outcome | but |
| d | Interpretation | **God had mercy** on him, and not only |
| e | | on him, but also |
| f | | on me, |
| | | |
| g | Purpose | so that I would not have sorrow piled on top of sorrow. |
| | | |
| 28a | Result (of 27d–g) | Therefore, **I sent him** |
| b | Manner | as soon as possible |

*Continued on next page.*

| | | |
|---|---|---|
| c | Purpose | so that upon seeing him |
| d | Outcome | you might be filled with joy again, and |
| e | | I might have less grief. |
| | | |
| 29a | Inference | So, |
| b | Exhortation | **welcome him** |
| c | Relationship | in the Lord |
| d | Manner | with lots of joy, |
| e | | and |
| f | Exhortation | **honor leaders like him,** |
| | | |
| 30a | Basis | since he came very close |
| b | Extent | to death |
| c | Cause | because of the work of Christ, |
| d | Circumstance | risking his life |
| e | Purpose | in order that he might fulfill |
| f | | what was lacking in your ministry to me. |

## Structure

As we consider the structural dynamics surrounding 2:18–30, we note first the repetition of lexical items having to do with joy that shape the transitions to and from this broader unit of text. At a number of places, Paul marks a "seam" or transition in the letter with this theme.[2] Although it is difficult to make a definitive case, it can be suggested that the double exhortation at 2:17–18 functions transitionally, marking the ending of one unit and the beginning of the next, much as the double references to joy at 1:18. At the end of 1:12–18g, Paul rejoices that Christ is preached, clearly pointing back to his comments just made with reference to his opponents. At the beginning of 1:18h–26, Paul proclaims, "Indeed, I will rejoice," and goes on to say why.

Similarly, at the end of 2:12–17 the apostle writes, "I am glad and rejoice with all of you." If we understand "in the same way, also you be glad and rejoice with me" of 2:18 as transitional, beginning the next unit, we have a very smooth transition. Why then would we suggest that the twin exhortations of 2:18 facilitate a transition to the next unit?[3] The answer is that the exhortations to "be glad and rejoice" in 2:18 accomplish two things in relation to the following unit. First, if as Fee suggests 2:19 picks back up on Paul's travel narrative, paused after 1:25–26,[4] then 2:18 can be read

2. The terms χαίρω, συγχαίρω, and χαρά occur a combined sixteen times in the book, often at the beginning or ending of units: 1:4, 18, 25; 2:2, 17–18, 28–29; 3:1; 4:1, 4, 10.

3. Understanding 2:18 to facilitate the transition at 2:17–18 also follows Paul's pattern of introducing a fresh unit, or a sub-movement, either with an exhortation to rejoice (2:18; 3:1; 4:4) or his own rejoicing or joy (1:4; 2:1–2; 4:1, 10). He ends a unit or sub-movement with corresponding expressions of joy at 1:18, 25–26, and 2:17.

4. Fee, *Philippians*, 263.

as containing a literary link or "distant hook word,"[5] aiding the resumption of thought that Paul will again be present with the Philippians. At 1:25–26, the apostle says he will remain (in his ministry) for the Philippians' "joy in the faith" (v. 25). As we have seen, at 2:18 Paul exhorts the Philippians to "be glad and rejoice" with him as he moves back to a discussion that involves his imminent return to Philippi.

Second, this double exhortation to rejoice at 2:17–18 also anticipates the "rejoicing" and "joy" of 2:28–29, which show one way that the Philippians will be glad and rejoice with Paul—by joyfully welcoming Epaphroditus back into their midst. Importantly, in his discourse analysis of Philippians, Jeffrey Reed has demonstrated that the "rejoice" theme in the book has, in part, a social function in relation to the Pauline mission. The theme occurs where the apostle speaks of his future visit (1:18–19), being poured out in ministry for the Philippians (2:17–18), Epaphroditus's arrival (2:28), his attempt to help them sort out relationships as part of his mission (4:3–4), and the receipt of their gift (4:10).[6] They will rejoice and be glad with Paul in the ongoing, meaningful interaction they have with him, his envoys, and their mutual, ongoing work for the gospel.

In the immediate context, the Philippians enter the joy of the apostle as they interact in a healthy manner with Epaphroditus (2:28–29). For Paul, mutuality is key when it comes to joy in the body of Christ,[7] for joy is stimulated and multiplies in Christian community. Thus, having encouraged the Philippians by his own example of rejoicing (1:18; 2:17), Paul reiterates this exhortation as he introduces the sending of envoys to Philippi and then brackets off the end of the section with further exhortations to embrace joy (2:18, 28–29). Thus, in challenging the Philippians to rejoice in 2:28–29, the apostle crafts the back end of an *inclusio*[8] opened at 2:18 and sets up a transition to the next unit. Both 2:18 and 2:28–29 concern the Philippians' joy:

| | |
|---|---|
| 2:18 | "In the same way, also you be glad and rejoice with me" |
| | (τὸ δὲ αὐτὸ καὶ ὑμεῖς χαίρετε καὶ συγχαίρετέ μοι) |
| 2:28–29 | "you might be filled with joy . . . welcome him in the Lord with lots of joy" |
| | (ἵνα ἰδόντες αὐτὸν πάλιν χαρῆτε . . . προσδέχεσθε οὖν αὐτὸν ἐν κυρίῳ μετὰ πάσης χαρᾶς) |

When Paul then transitions to the next unit, 3:1–14, he again exhorts the brothers and sisters to rejoice. So once again we find that double calls for rejoicing occur at a seam of the letter. These references to joy in 2:17–3:1 are depicted in the diagram

5. See Guthrie, *Structure of Hebrews*, 96–100; idem, *2 Corinthians*, 25.

6. Reed, *Discourse Analysis*, 257. Reed focuses on 1:18–19, 2:28, and 4:10 as examples in Philippians.

7. Cousar, *Philippians and Philemon*, 63.

8. For the use of *inclusio* as a common convention in ancient literature, see Guthrie, *Structure of Hebrews*, 76–89.

below. The *X*s represent references to rejoicing that "hook" 2:12–17 to 2:18–30 and 2:18–30 to 3:1–14.

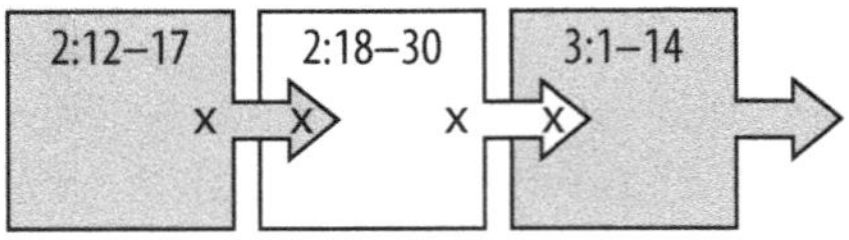


Further, at 2:17–19 and 2:30–3:1 the repeated phrase "in the Lord" (ἐν κυρίῳ), the repetition of "the same" (τὸ . . . αὐτό/τὰ αὐτά), the cognates "to be encouraged" (εὐψυχῶ) and "life" (τῇ ψυχῇ), and uses of "you" (ὑμῶν/ὑμεῖς/ὑμῖν) also can be considered to play a role in marking out transitions and the successive seams in the letter. The distant parallelism forms a significant marking of the discourse, almost certainly highlighting key transition points in the letter.

Yet there are other structural dynamics internal to 2:18–30 to which we also should give attention. The units about Timothy and Epaphroditus have a few features in common, presented in roughly parallel fashion. Both have:

- Introductory statements about "sending":
  "I hope . . . to send Timothy to you" (2:19)
  "I considered it necessary to send to you Epaphroditus" (2:25)
- An explanation concerning why Paul would send Timothy and had sent Epaphroditus (2:20–21; 2:26–27)
- A statement concerning the worth of each coworker (2:22; 2:29–30)
- A restatement near the end of each unit about the "sending":
  "So this is the person I hope to send" (2:23, Timothy)
  "Therefore, I sent him as soon as possible" (2:28, Epaphroditus)

Finally, regarding the structure of the unit, the "travelogue" in 2:18–30, with the anticipated sending of Timothy and the accomplished sending of Epaphroditus, highlights the coming of Paul himself to Philippi. At several places in his letters, Paul builds a sense of anticipation (and accountability) for the church to whom he writes by mentioning his own coming.[9] Accordingly, here in Philippians 2 at the end of the unit about Timothy, Paul expresses his confidence in his own coming: "And I am confident in the Lord that I myself will come soon" (v. 24). Given Paul's other correspondence with similar statements, this announcement can be regarded

9. Rom 15:22–29; 1 Cor 4:17–21; 2 Cor 12:14–13:10; 1 Thess 2:17–3:11; Phlm 22; Hansen, *Philippians*, 191–92. On Paul's travelogues and how he uses envoys, letters, and his own presence in relating to churches, see Richards, *Paul and First-Century Letter Writing*, 203, who follows Margaret M. Mitchell, "New Testament Envoys in the Context of Greco-Roman Diplomatic and Epistolary Conventions: The Example of Timothy and Titus," *JBL* 111.4 (1992): 641–62; Klauck and Bailey, *Ancient Letters*, 367.

as more important than might be seen at first blush. In sending these coworkers, Paul reinforces his own authority as the Philippians' apostle and prepares for his return to the city.

## Exegetical Outline

→ **4. Timothy and Epaphroditus as Exemplars of Self-Sacrifice (2:18–30)**
  **a. An Exhortation to Join Paul in His Joy (v. 18)**
  **b. Timothy (vv. 19–24)**
    (1) Paul Hopes to Send Timothy Soon to the Philippians, to See How They Are Doing (v. 19)
    (2) Timothy Shares Paul's Concern for the Philippians, while Others Look Out for Their Own Interests (vv. 20–21)
    (3) Timothy's Proven Worth (v. 22)
    (4) Timothy and Then Paul Should Come to Philippi Soon (vv. 23–24)
  **c. Epaphroditus (vv. 25–30)**
    (1) Why Paul Sent Epaphroditus (vv. 25–26)
    (2) Epaphroditus's Illness and Its Outcomes (vv. 27–28)
    (3) An Exhortation to Welcome and Respect (vv. 29–30)
      a) Welcome Epaphroditus with Joy (v. 29a–d)
      b) Respect Leaders Like Him (vv. 29e–30)

## Explanation of the Text

**2:18–19 In the same way, you also be glad and rejoice with me. Now I hope in the Lord Jesus to send Timothy to you soon, in order that I also may be encouraged when I learn what is happening with you** (τὸ δὲ αὐτὸ καὶ ὑμεῖς χαίρετε καὶ συγχαίρετέ μοι. 19 Ἐλπίζω δὲ ἐν κυρίῳ Ἰησοῦ Τιμόθεον ταχέως πέμψαι ὑμῖν, ἵνα κἀγὼ εὐψυχῶ γνοὺς τὰ περὶ ὑμῶν). Paul tells the Philippians of his plan to send Timothy to them and explains his motivation for doing so. Philippians 2:18 obviously continues the thought of the previous verse, and so most commentators consider it the conclusion to the previous unit.[10] Yet the exhortation to joy in verse 18 can be seen as a transition to 2:18–30. In verse 17 the apostle writes, "I am glad and rejoice with all of you" (χαίρω καὶ συγχαίρω πᾶσιν ὑμῖν), and then turns this around in 2:18 with "you be glad and rejoice with me" (ὑμεῖς χαίρετε καὶ συγχαίρετέ μοι[11]). The "in the same way . . . also" (τὸ δὲ αὐτὸ καί) at the beginning of 2:18 is constructed both to reach back to the previous verse (τὸ δὲ αὐτό) and to lead into what follows (καί, read as adjunctive, "also").

10. So, e.g., Hawthorne and Martin, *Philippians*, 135; Reumann, *Philippians*, 384; Bockmuehl, *Philippians*, 149; Cousar, *Philippians and Philemon*, 60.

11. The dative may be considered a dative of association.

To "hope" (ἐλπίζω) anticipates the future with a measure of confidence and resides in the hearts of God's people because of the Lord whom they serve. Thus the apostle expresses "hope" at a number of points in his letters, sometimes with reference to eschatological hope,[12] and at other times with reference to more mundane events of life,[13] as we see at the beginning of 2:19. Yet Paul expresses his hope as "in the Lord Jesus" (ἐν κυρίῳ Ἰησοῦ), which Harris tags as communicating "location"—that is, as being "grounded in the Lord Jesus."[14] Yet it seems better in our current verse to read "in the Lord" (ἐν κυρίῳ) as pointing to Christ as the object of hope.[15]

What Paul hopes, he tells the Philippians, is "to send Timothy to you soon" (Τιμόθεον ταχέως[16] πέμψαι ὑμῖν).[17] Of the one hundred or so of Paul's associates and coworkers,[18] he speaks most warmly of this "dear and faithful son in the Lord"[19] (1 Cor 4:17; see also Phil 2:22; 1 Tim 1:18; 2 Tim 1:2). According to Acts, Paul originally met Timothy in Lystra on his second missionary journey (Acts 16:1). Born of a Jewish mother named Eunice, who was a devout believer (2 Tim 1:5), and a gentile father (Acts 16:1), at a young age Timothy was respected as Christ's follower (v. 2). His ministry was endorsed by leaders of the church (1 Tim 1:18; 4:14; 2 Tim 1:6), and he would come to serve as a vital link between Paul and the Philippian church.[20] Paul hopes to send Timothy for the purpose of (ἵνα) receiving encouragement, as he finds out how the church is doing, and to ensure that the needs of the church are being met (Phil 2:19–20). The adjunctive sense of the conjunction ("also") assumes that Timothy himself will find encouragement from the encounter (cf. 2 Cor 7:13) and that Paul anticipates being heartened when Timothy reports back to him.[21] The verb that speaks of encouragement here (εὐψυχῶ) only occurs here in biblical literature and is rare in classical and Hellenistic sources.[22] It could be used of bravery in battle or comfort in trials. But at times it is found in letters or inscriptions, communicating a nuance of joy for having one's spirits lifted by a correspondence or event.[23] It is a good report concerning the Philippians that will boost the apostle's spirits.[24] Here Paul uses the same wording we find at 1:27, where he anticipates

12. E.g., Rom 8:24; 15:12; 1 Cor 15:19; 2 Cor 1:10, 13; 5:11; 1 Tim 5:5.

13. E.g., 1 Cor 16:7; Phil 2:23; 1 Tim 3:14.

14. Harris, *Prepositions*, 130.

15. Campbell, *Paul and Union with Christ*, 171.

16. The adverb ταχέως could communicate speed (i.e., "quickly"), but given the uncertainty of the timing of Paul's release, it probably has the sense of "the brevity of the interval" (i.e., "soon"). See BDAG 992.

17. The aorist infinitive "to send" (πέμψαι) is functioning as complementary to "I hope" (ἐλπίζω) and "Timothy" (Τιμόθεον) as the object of that infinitive.

18. On which, see the In Depth section below.

19. Mixing his family metaphors, Paul also refers to Timothy as "Timothy the brother" (Col 1:1; 1 Thess 3:2; and Phlm 1).

20. On Timothy's role in Paul's mission, and specifically in his ministry to the Corinthians, see Wolf-Henning Ollrog, *Paulus und seine Mitarbeiter: Untersuchungen zu Theorie und Praxis der paulinischen Mission* (Neukirchen-Vluyn: Neukirchener, 1979), 185–87.

21. Contra Hellerman, *Philippians*, 146 (following Fee [*Philippians*, 265] et al.), who assumes the sense that the Philippians will experience joy (2:18) and then Paul "too" will be encouraged upon Timothy's return to him. The problem with this view concerns the delimiting of the verb with the participial phrase, "when I learn what is happening with you" (γνοὺς τὰ περὶ ὑμῶν). Who, in addition to Paul, would be encouraged upon learning how the Philippians were doing? The most straightforward answer would be Timothy himself.

22. It is found in Josephus, *Ant.* 11.241, which speaks of the king encouraging Esther to "be of good cheer."

23. Interestingly, it often occurs in epitaphs, encouraging those who have been left behind at the death of a loved one, but it also is found in letters of condolence. See *TLNT* 2:155.

24. The aorist participle γνούς is temporal ("when I learn" or "once I know"), and τὰ περὶ ὑμῶν ("the things concerning you") is the object of the participle.

hearing about the Philippians standing together for the gospel. He will have his spirits lifted when he hears they are standing in unity for the faith.

**2:20–21 For I have no other kindred spirit available, who will genuinely be concerned about what is happening with you. Indeed, they all look out for their own interests rather than the things that interest Jesus Christ!** (οὐδένα γὰρ ἔχω ἰσόψυχον, ὅστις γνησίως τὰ περὶ ὑμῶν μεριμνήσει· 21 οἱ πάντες γὰρ τὰ ἑαυτῶν ζητοῦσιν, οὐ τὰ Ἰησοῦ Χριστοῦ). Paul explains why Timothy is his envoy of choice. The "for" (γάρ) at the beginning of verse 20 is explanatory, and the clause it introduces makes clear why Paul sent Timothy in particular. He wants to ensure that the spiritual needs of the church will be met by an "others focused" partner in ministry. The apostle confesses, "I have no other kindred spirit available" (οὐδένα . . . ἔχω ἰσόψυχον),[25] alluding to those in his ministry who fit a very particular standard: "who genuinely will be concerned about what is happening with you" (ὅστις γνησίως τὰ περὶ ὑμῶν μεριμνήσε). Here again we find the phrase "what is happening with you" (τὰ περὶ ὑμῶν) functioning grammatically as the object, just as we saw in the previous verse and at 1:27. The repeated use of the phrase reinforces the idea that Paul has in mind significant spiritual matters rather than incidental issues of life in Philippi. In other words, he is not sending Timothy on a multiweek journey simply to ask, "So, how are you?" Rather, Timothy will ascertain the spiritual state of the church vis-à-vis a hostile culture and in terms of their internal unity (1:27–30).

The very rare adjective we have translated as "kindred spirit" (ἰσόψυχος) only occurs here and at Psalm 55:13 [54:14 LXX] in the biblical literature, and seldom elsewhere in the Greek literature of the era. In the context of Psalm 55:13–14 [54:14–15 LXX], the word seems to connote someone who shares aspects of life in common with the writer:[26] "But it is you, my fellow human [ἄνθρωπε ἰσόψυχε],[27] my leader and my familiar friend, who made food sweet together with me; in the house of God we walked in harmony" (NETS).[28] Paul has used several words that are similar in form, including the term translated "I may be encouraged" (εὐψυχῶ) in the previous verse and "having solidarity" (σύμψυχοι) at 2:2.[29]

One thing that Timothy has in common with Paul is a genuine[30] concern about the spiritual welfare of the Philippians. He must have been deeply committed to them to make the journey, for travel was never easy in the ancient world.[31] In this case, the apostle communicates to the Philippians his confidence that Timothy will be concerned[32] about

25. See BDAG 420 on the sense of ἔχω as "to have at one's disposal" (e.g., Matt 14:17; Luke 11:6; 12:17; 1 Cor 11:22).

26. As is the case here. Bruce points out that Erasmus paraphrases this passage with "I will send him as my alter ego" (Bruce, *Philippians*, 94). Paul speaks of Timothy as sharing with him this sense of identity (so, e.g., Reumann, *Philippians*, 420; Silva, *Philippians*, 140), rather than reading the word as speaking of those who share Timothy's perspective (so, e.g., NRSV, ESV, NET, "like him"). See the brief summary in Hellerman, *Philippians*, 147–48.

27. The LXX provides ἰσόψυχε as the translation for the Hebrew עֶרְכִּי, the word in context meaning a man "of my value" or "like me." Of course, this valuation is ironic since the psalmist is being betrayed by his friend.

28. Thus we translate the term as "kindred spirit" here in Phil 2:20, seeking to express not just the idea of sharing a common view but a sense of closeness in life. Similarly, NASB and Bockmuehl, *Philippians*, 165.

29. Fee, *Philippians*, 266; Hansen, *Philippians*, 194; Hellerman, *Philippians*, 147.

30. The adverb rendered "genuinely" (γνησίως) in our translation speaks of sincerity. See BDAG 202.

31. Bruce, *Philippians*, 94.

32. Paul knew that Timothy was "concerned" (μεριμνάω) about the Philippians, a word that could connote anxiety or apprehensiveness (e.g., Matt 6:25–34 [6x]; Luke 10:41), but in our context one that speaks of "attending to" or "caring about" someone or something. So BDAG 632.

"what is happening with you" (τὰ περὶ ὑμῶν). Accordingly, Paul believes that Timothy will tune in to the spiritual dynamics surrounding the situation in Philippi and that he will do so out of a sincere concern for the brothers and sisters in the church there.

The apostle contrasts Timothy's ministerial posture toward the Philippians with that of others. Paul characterizes those ministers (referred to as "all," οἱ πάντες) as seeking "their own interests" (τὰ ἑαυτῶν).[33] He has already characterized a self-centered attitude with the same words at 2:4, encouraging the Philippians that they should not be focused on their "own concerns" (τὰ ἑαυτῶν). Timothy thus serves as a positive role model of an others-focused posture.

Finally, the apostle also sets in contrast the other ministers' "own interests" with "the things that interest Jesus Christ" (τὰ Ἰησοῦ Χριστοῦ).[34] This, of course, is a harsh, unmistakable negation of the ministry of those whom Paul has in mind. So we have an ABA′ pattern:

A "what is happening with you"
τὰ περὶ ὑμῶν (2:19)
B "their own interests"
τὰ ἑαυτῶν (2:21)
A′ "the things that interest Jesus Christ"
τὰ Ἰησοῦ Χριστοῦ (2:21)

One clear implication of these contrasts is that "what is happening with" the Philippians (i.e., their spiritual condition) is of interest to Jesus. The "all," in being focused on their own concerns rather than those of the Philippians, are thus out of line with that which is of interest to Christ himself. Could there be a more condemning assessment of a minister's agenda?! In missing the path of self-sacrificial service, they miss the way of Christ (2:3–8).

Commentators have speculated on the identity of the "all" (οἱ πάντες) to whom Paul alludes. Some suggest that Paul has in mind opponents, preachers with a very different agenda than the apostle (cf. 1:15–17).[35] Others, reading the text straightforwardly, understand "all" to be those who happened to be around Paul at the time of writing, who were available but would not break away from their own work to attend to the need of the Philippians.[36] A third view is that the language is rhetorical, "making Timothy look better in comparison with a sweeping but hypothetical negative example ... hitting whoever is hit."[37] At the end of the day, the key is to focus on Paul's point—the exemplary character of Timothy himself, whom the Philippians should embrace as a stellar example of selfless service to others.

**2:22 You know his proven worth, that, like a son with a father, he has served with me in advancing the gospel work** (τὴν δὲ δοκιμὴν αὐτοῦ γινώσκετε, ὅτι ὡς πατρὶ τέκνον σὺν ἐμοὶ ἐδούλευσεν εἰς τὸ εὐαγγέλιον). The Philippians are aware of Timothy's (αὐτοῦ) character and proven track record in gospel ministry. Accordingly, Paul continues[38]

33. The genitive is read as reflecting "reference" ("things with reference to themselves," i.e., "their own interests").

34. Again, perhaps, a genitive of reference. Many witnesses reverse Ἰησοῦ Χριστοῦ, reading Χριστοῦ Ἰησοῦ (B L 0278. 104. 365. 630. 1175. 1241. 1505 𝔐 vg$^{st}$ sy$^{h}$; Ambst Cass), the more common form for Philippians (Phil 1:1, 6, 8, 26; 2:1; 3:3, 8, 12, 14; 4:7, 19, 21). The order we have here is peppered throughout as well (Phil 1:2, 11, 19; 2:11; 3:20; 4:23), but with four of the six occurrences adding κύριος prior to the formula. The reading as it stands in the text has strong external attestation (𝔓$^{46}$ ℵ A C D F G P Ψ [075]. 33. 81. 326. 1739. 1881. 2464. 2495 it vg$^{cl.ww}$ sy$^{p}$; Cl MVict) and is the more difficult reading in terms of what is most common in the book. Thus, it probably was original.

35. So, e.g., Fee, *Philippians*, 267–68; Bockmuehl, *Philippians*, 166; Witherington, *Philippians*, 173.

36. On which, see Hansen, *Philippians*, 195.

37. So Reumann, *Philippians*, 441.

38. The conjunction δέ, which we have chosen not to translate at this point, marks a continuation rather than a contrast. See Runge, *Discourse Grammar*, 31–32.

by celebrating the young man's "proven worth" (δοκιμή), a term employed seven times total in the New Testament (all in Paul), which could be used to refer to the process of testing (e.g., 2 Cor 8:2). Yet elsewhere the word speaks of either the "proof" of something (2 Cor 9:13; 13:3) or, as here, the closely related idea of character development under duress (Rom 5:4 [2x]; 2 Cor 2:9). Thus the word speaks of the value or worth of one who has proven character. The Philippians "know" (γινώσκετε) this about Timothy from his time among them, beginning with Paul's second missionary journey, during which the church was planted (Acts 16:11–40). Paul refers to Timothy's ministry among the Philippians very personally, writing "that . . . he has served with me in advancing the gospel work" (ὅτι . . . ἐδούλευσεν εἰς τὸ εὐαγγέλιον). That the younger minister "served" (ἐδούλευσεν) the church echoes the description of Paul and Timothy as "slaves" of Messiah Jesus (Phil 1:1) and of the humility of the Lord himself, who took the "outward appearance of a slave" (2:7). Specifically, Timothy served "in advancing the gospel work" (εἰς τὸ εὐαγγέλιον; cf. NET: "in advancing the gospel").[39]

Speaking of how much he values Timothy as a fellow minister, the apostle draws an analogy with the phrase "like a son with a father" (ὡς πατρὶ τέκνον). The apostle employs "family language" a good deal in his letters, using kinship word pictures to describe the relationships he has with churches and individuals. Paul speaks of himself as a spiritual "father" (e.g., 1 Cor 4:15; 1 Thess 2:11) and "mother" (Gal 4:19; 1 Thess 2:7), and to parenthood generally (2 Cor 6:13; 12:14). Yet Timothy seemed to hold a special place in Paul's heart and work (1 Tim 1:18; 2 Tim 2:1).[40] Just like a son, who for years had apprenticed under a loving father in a craft, Timothy had worked faithfully with Paul in his mission for the past decade or so, weathering persecution, carrying out evangelism, and agonizing over the churches' spiritual well-being. Consequently, Paul can hold Timothy before the Philippians as an example, confident that the younger man's character will be obvious to them.

**2:23–24 So this is the person I hope to send as soon as I determine what will happen with me; and I am confident in the Lord that I myself will come soon** (τοῦτον μὲν οὖν ἐλπίζω πέμψαι ὡς ἂν ἀφίδω τὰ περὶ ἐμὲ ἐξαυτῆς· 24 πέποιθα δὲ ἐν κυρίῳ ὅτι καὶ αὐτὸς ταχέως ἐλεύσομαι). Paul wraps up his words about Timothy and expresses confidence of his own release and his return to the Philippians. Structurally the unit is rounded off with the closing of an *inclusio*[41] begun in verse 19, showing it to be a highly crafted, distinct unit. Notice the parallels:

| | |
|---|---|
| 19 | **I hope in the Lord** Jesus **to send** Timothy to you **soon**, in order that I also may be encouraged when I learn **what is happening** with you |
| 23–24 | So this is the person **I hope to send** as soon as I determine **what will happen** with me; and I am confident **in the Lord** that I myself will come **soon**. |

As to timing, Paul writes that he hopes to send Timothy "as soon as I determine what will happen with me" (ὡς ἂν ἀφίδω τὰ περὶ ἐμὲ ἐξαυτῆς). At 1:22–26 the apostle expresses confidence in the outcome of his incarceration, even as he does here in 2:24. Yet the apostle does not know exactly when that will take place. The "as soon as" (ὡς ἂν . . . ἐξαυτῆς) articulates this note of uncertainty.[42] What Paul

39. The preposition εἰς here communicates advantage: "in advancing the gospel work" (BDAG 290–91).

40. Bockmuehl, *Philippians*, 167.

41. An *inclusio* marks the beginning and ending of a unit by using the same or similar language.

42. I agree here with Fee, against Hawthorne and Silva. See his discussion at Fee, *Philippians*, 269.

wants to "determine" (ἀφοράω)[43] before sending Timothy back to Philippi are specifics about his own situation (τὰ περὶ ἐμέ; cf. the similar phrase τὰ κατ᾽ ἐμέ at 1:12).

Verse 24 then concludes Paul's thoughts about Timothy with "and I am confident in the Lord that I myself will come soon" (πέποιθα δὲ ἐν κυρίῳ ὅτι καὶ αὐτὸς ταχέως ἐλεύσομαι). Earlier in the letter at 1:25, the apostle expressed his "confidence" that he would continue his ministry to the Philippians. The verb here, translated as "I am confident" (πείθω), has the sense of being "convinced" of something.[44] The thought in 2:24 is thus very similar to that at 1:25: "Believing this to be the case, I am confident that I will remain and continue with all of you" (τοῦτο πεποιθὼς οἶδα ὅτι μενῶ καὶ παραμενῶ πᾶσιν ὑμῖν). Yet Paul's confidence, rather than resting on his own abilities or the workings of human justice, rests "in the Lord." Consequently, he is confident that he himself (αὐτός) will come quickly, with Timothy's visit in part paving the way for Paul's return to Philippi.[45]

## IN DEPTH: Coworkers in the Pauline Mission

Paul could neither be described as a "loner" nor a "one-man band."[46] Rather, he was constantly surrounded by companions, including some long-term coworkers in his mission. In the New Testament, approximately one hundred people are named as associates with the apostle. If we narrow the list to those who are mentioned in his letters with some form of ministry designation or a particular role, we have a group of about thirty-six, who are referred to with nine different designations.[47] The most commonly used designations include "coworker" (Rom 16:3, 9, 21; 1 Cor 3:9; 2 Cor 1:24; 8:23; Phil 2:25; 4:3; Col 4:11; 1 Thess 3:2; Phlm 1, 24), "servant," which Paul also uses of himself (Rom 16:1; 1 Cor 3:5; 2 Cor 3:6; 6:4; Eph 3:7; 6:21; Phil 1:1; Col 1:7, 23, 25; 4:7; 1 Tim 3:8, 12; 4:6), "brothers," a designation for believers generally but also used of coworkers (1 Cor 16:19–20; Gal 1:2; Eph 6:23–24; Phil 1:14; 4:21–22; Col 1:2; 4:15), and "apostle" (Rom 16:7; 1 Cor 4:6–9; 9:5–6; 15:7; Gal 1:19).[48] Some of Paul's coworkers include Barnabas, Luke, Aquila, Priscilla, Silas, Titus, Tychicus, Achaicus, Andronicus, Apphia, Apollos, Archippus, Aristarchus, Crescens, Demas, Epaphras, Erastus, Fortunatus, Junia, Jesus Justus, John Mark, Mary, Onesimus, Quartus, Persis, Philemon, Phoebe, Sosthenes, Stephanas, Trophimus, Tryphaena, Tryphosa, and Urbanus.[49] Note the number of women in the

43. BDAG 158.
44. BDAG 791.
45. Hansen, *Philippians*, 198.
46. James D. G. Dunn, *Beginning from Jerusalem* (Grand Rapids: Eerdmans, 2008), 571–72.
47. Ellis, *Prophecy and Hermeneutic*, 3–5; for a list of the coworkers, see Eckhard Schnabel (*Early Christian Mission*, 2 vols. [Downers Grove, IL: InterVarsity Press; Leicester: Apollos, 2004], 2:1426–27), who puts their number at thirty-eight.
48. Ellis, *Prophecy and Hermeneutic*, 7–15.
49. Schnabel, *Early Christian Mission*, 2:1426–27.

list, most of whom participated directly in carrying out the apostle's mission by proclamation of the gospel.[50]

In Philippians, Paul mentions Timothy, whom he calls a slave of Christ Jesus (Phil 1:1), celebrating his younger associate as a "son" in ministry (2:22); Epaphroditus, whom he calls "my brother and coworker and fellow soldier, who also is your messenger and minister attending to my need" (2:25; cf. 4:18); Euodia and Syntyche, "women who participated in gospel work at my side" (4:2–3); Clement and the rest of Paul's fellow workers (v. 3); and finally "the brothers and sisters who are with me" (v. 21).

Many of Paul's coworkers served in teaching and preaching, either as local ministers or fellow travelers with Paul on his mission trips. Others played significant roles in the production of his letters, whether as cosenders or secretaries.[51] He also employed coworkers as delegates of newly planted churches (Col 1:7; 4:12–13; Phlm 13) or as those who cared for churches in his forced absence (e.g., Timothy and Titus).[52] Of Paul's ability to lead this vast array of coworkers James Dunn writes, "It follows that he must have been a very accomplished leader of men and women who inspired personal loyalty and commitment to his mission."[53]

**2:25 Now I considered it necessary to send to you Epaphroditus, my brother and coworker and fellow soldier, who also is your messenger and minister attending to my need** (Ἀναγκαῖον δὲ ἡγησάμην Ἐπαφρόδιτον τὸν ἀδελφὸν καὶ συνεργὸν καὶ συστρατιώτην μου, ὑμῶν δὲ ἀπόστολον καὶ λειτουργὸν τῆς χρείας μου, πέμψαι πρὸς ὑμᾶς). Paul now writes of another coworker, Epaphroditus, whom he also celebrates as an exemplary leader. As pointed out above under "Structure," in 2:25–30 Paul accomplishes several things as he writes about Epaphroditus. In 2:26–28 the apostle explains his motivation for sending his coworker back to Philippi. Epaphroditus had been very sick, which evidently caused a great deal of stress for Paul, Epaphroditus himself, and the Philippian church.[54] So Epaphroditus goes in part to relieve that stress. However, 2:25 and 29–30 function to celebrate Epaphroditus before the Philippians, as 2:29–30 lauds his sacrificial service and calls on the church to respect him, while 2:25 reminds the Philippians of the significant role Epaphroditus had played in Paul's ministry and theirs.

In Greek, the whole of verse 25 is sandwiched by its first four and last three words, translated as "now I considered it necessary to send to you Epaphroditus" (Ἀναγκαῖον δὲ ἡγησάμην Ἐπαφρόδιτον . . . πέμψαι πρὸς ὑμᾶς). The conjunction rendered "now" (δέ) signals a new development in the letter,[55] as Paul turns to the topic of sending Epaphroditus.

50. Schnabel, *Early Christian Mission*, 2:1428.
51. E. Earle Ellis, "Paul and His Coworkers," *DPL* 187–88.
52. Schnabel, *Early Christian Mission*, 2:1440–43.
53. Dunn, *Beginning from Jerusalem*, 572.
54. Colin Ogilvie Buchanan, "Epaphroditus' Sickness and the Letter to the Philippians," *EvQ* 36.3 (1964): 157–66.
55. Runge, *Discourse Grammar*, 31.

The main verb (ἡγησάμην) could mean "to lead" but here communicates an "intellectual process"—that is, to "think, consider, regard."[56] In context, the perfective aspect of the verb, often noted as an epistolary aorist, can be rendered as referring to the moment when Paul was writing the words (i.e., "I consider it" or "think it"; e.g., NRSV, NIV). Or, as with our translation, it can be rendered as relative to the timeframe when the Philippians heard it read, Paul's reflections heard as in the past—"I considered it" (as with NASB, CSB, NLT).[57] The apostle reflected on the act of sending Epaphroditus back to the Philippians (Ἐπαφρόδιτον . . . πέμψαι πρὸς ὑμᾶς).[58] Paul deemed this act of sending "necessary" (ἀναγκαῖον),[59] a term that could be used of something "constraining, necessary, indispensable" and that often finds expression in relational contexts involving certain obligations.[60] Paul has already noted that he and Timothy were not going to be able to leave for Philippi yet (2:19, 24), so something compelled the apostle to dispatch Epaphroditus right away. Though commentators offer much speculation as to why Paul sent Epaphroditus when he did, it seems best to focus on the reasons unpacked by the apostle himself in verses 26–28.

We don't know much about Epaphroditus beyond what we have here and at 4:18. His name was common in the first century, and it carried the basic meaning "charming." The name originated from the moniker for Aphrodite, the Greek goddess of beauty, love, and fertility, who was widely worshiped in the Greco-Roman world. It is therefore likely that Paul's coworker had been converted from a pagan background.[61] The remainder of verse 25, however, consists of five ways that Paul describes Epaphroditus, the first three emphasizing the closeness of partnership that Paul enjoys with his fellow worker, and the final two the role that Epaphroditus plays as he ministers to the apostle on behalf of the church at Philippi.[62] Epaphroditus is:

| Paul's | *brother* and |
|---|---|
| | *coworker* and |
| | *fellow soldier,* |
| who also is the Philippians' | |
| | *messenger* and |
| | *minister* attending to Paul's needs. |

The apostle begins by referring to Epaphroditus as "the brother" (τόν ἀδελφόν). Here we have Paul's most basic word for relationships in the body of Christ. Used 133 times in his writings, the word for "brother" occurs thus far in Philippians at 1:12 and 14. He adds the personal pronoun translated "my" (μου), which, as almost all translations suggest, adds a note of intimacy to the triple description, "brother and coworker and fellow soldier."[63] In any case, "brother" anchors Paul's affection and esteem for Epaphroditus in their relationship in Christ. The prefix (συν-) at the beginning of the next two

56. BDAG 434.

57. See Hellerman, *Philippians*, 155; the NET and ESV seem to render the verb as if it is "stative," perhaps combining the past and present ideas: "I have thought" (ESV) or "for now, I have considered" (NET).

58. The substantival infinitive has "Epaphroditus" (Ἐπαφρόδιτον) as its object, and the phrase "to you" (πρὸς ὑμᾶς) as its indirect object.

59. Paul uses this word elsewhere at 1 Cor 12:22; 2 Cor 9:5; Phil 1:24; Titus 3:14.

60. As when at Phil 1:24 the apostle speaks of the necessity of remaining in the flesh in order to continue ministering to the Philippians. So *TLNT* 1:97, which contrasts the term with χρεία, the common necessities of everyday life.

61. Hawthorne and Martin, *Philippians*, 162; Bockmuehl, *Philippians*, 169.

62. Grammatically the five are appositional descriptions of Epaphroditus, and the article τόν relates to all five descriptions, providing an example of Sharp's rule of the article (Wallace, *Greek Grammar*, 271–72).

63. Just as ὑμῶν ("your") encompasses both "messenger" and "minister" later in the verse. The plural form "my brothers" (ἀδελφοί [-ῶν] μου) occurs only nine times in Paul, twice here in Philippians (Phil 3:1; 4:1; see also Rom 7:4; 9:3; 15:14; 1 Cor

Greek terms ("coworker," συνεργόν; "fellow soldier," συστρατιώτην) was a characteristic of "friendship" language.[64] If "brother" (ἀδελφόν) expresses familial affection for a fellow Christian, "coworker" and "fellow soldier" communicate the value that Paul placed on his partnership with Epaphroditus in Christian ministry. The apostle uses the former word variously of those who have joined him in the hard work of building up the church,[65] including Euodia and Syntyche, who, according to Paul, "have participated in gospel work . . . along with Clement and the rest of my fellow workers" (4:3).

The second descriptor, which evokes a military image (συστρατιώτης), Paul uses only here and of Archippus at Philemon 2 (but see 2 Tim 2:3). The word may have been taken up by the apostle as a strong encouragement for Epaphroditus himself and the church, neither of whom should see the Philippians' representative, who now returns to Philippi, as abandoning his post but rather as carrying on the honorable role of someone fully engaged in the "battle" for the cause of Christ.[66] Further, this term and the one rendered "minister" (λειτουργός) were honorary epithets used in the broader culture. Inscriptions throughout Philippi bear witness to the high value that such titles carried as reflecting military or civic achievements.[67] Thus Paul seems to be utilizing common language from the culture to bolster the esteem of one of his key coworkers in Philippi.

For example, this word for "minister" (λειτουργός) was used to refer to a civic administrator in the Roman Empire. Paul uses it elsewhere only at Romans 13:6, speaking of civic authorities, and at Romans 15:16, where he speaks of his ministry to the gentiles. Given the use of "apostle" (ἀπόστολον) here in the present verse in the nontechnical sense of "messenger," and the term translated as "service" and "ministry" (λειτουργία) at 2:17, 30, it may be that "minister" (λειτουργός) not only connotes the nuance of "minister" in a religious sense but also that of "administrator"—one who carried out duties as a respected representative on behalf of the community.[68] Both senses occur in fairly even measure in the LXX,[69] and either sense works with the phrase "attending to my need" (τῆς χρείας μου).[70] The key is that Epaphroditus was caring for Paul's practical needs and to this end had been "sent" by the Philippians, only now to be sent back to Philippi by Paul, for reasons the apostle communicates in the following verses.

**2:26–27 since he was longing for all of you and was very distressed because you heard that he was sick. Indeed, he was sick to the point of death, but God had mercy on him, and not only on him, but also on me, so that I would not have sorrow piled on top of sorrow** (ἐπειδὴ ἐπιποθῶν ἦν πάντας ὑμᾶς καὶ ἀδημονῶν, διότι ἠκούσατε ὅτι ἠσθένησεν. 27 καὶ γὰρ ἠσθένησεν παραπλήσιον θανάτῳ· ἀλλὰ ὁ

1:11; 11:33; 14:39; 15:58). The singular "my brother" is found, e.g., at 1 Cor 8:13 and 2 Cor 2:13. I agree with Fee that with the addition of μου it does seem unlikely that ἀδελφός is used semitechnically as another designator for a coworker, a view suggested by Ellis (*Prophecy and Hermeneutic*, 13–18; see Fee, *Philippians*, 275).

64. Reumann, *Philippians*, 425.

65. Rom 16:3, 9, 21; 1 Cor 3:9; 2 Cor 1:24; 8:23; Phil 2:25; 4:3; Col 4:11; 1 Thess 3:2; Phlm 1, 24; 3 John 8.

66. So Fee, *Philippians*, 275–76.

67. Hellerman, "Brothers and Friends," 20–21.

68. So Hellerman, *Philippians*, 158. Contra Hooker, "Philippians," 520, who reads the word only as reflecting priestly service.

69. For the word as referring to civic administrators or servants, see, e.g., 2 Sam 13:18; 1 Kgs 10:5; 2 Kgs 4:43; 6:15; 2 Chr 9:4; Ps 103:4; cf. Sir 10:2; 3 Macc 5:5. For uses where it is used in more of a religious sense, see, e.g., Ezra 7:24; Neh 10:40; Isa 61:6; cf. Sir 50:14.

70. Perhaps a genitive of reference, "with reference to my need."

θεὸς ἠλέησεν αὐτόν, οὐκ αὐτὸν δὲ μόνον ἀλλὰ καὶ ἐμέ, ἵνα μὴ λύπην ἐπὶ λύπην σχῶ). In verses 26–27 the apostle gives the first of two key reasons[71] for sending Epaphroditus back to Philippi—the man had been longing for them, and this emotion was heightened by the Philippians' distress over his illness. The verb translated as "longing" (ἐπιποθῶν) speaks of a strong desire or yearning, pointing to an intimacy of relationship, such as the longing of an eagle for her chicks (Deut 32:11 LXX), and this seems to be a common use of the word in Paul's writings.[72] Again we have here an inclusive "all of you" (πάντας ὑμᾶς)[73] as the object of Epaphroditus's longing, perhaps underscoring his (and Paul's) commitment to the whole church, not just one group or another. Moreover, Epaphroditus's longing was exacerbated by anxiety; he was distressed or troubled (ἀδημονέω)[74] "because you had heard that he was sick" (διότι ἠκούσατε ὅτι ἠσθένησεν). Unfortunately, we are not given any details about the sickness, other than its seriousness (Phil 2:27). As "part of the fabric of human life," illness weaves its way through the pages of the New Testament, often in contexts focused on a miraculous cure.[75] But the "cure" is not the focus here, although it cannot be ruled out, as Fee notes.[76] Epaphroditus's brush with death reminds us that the early followers of Jesus were susceptible to the devastation of disease and sudden death. Yet in this passage Epaphroditus displays a profoundly "others-focused" mentality, being concerned about the distress his illness caused the church in Philippi.

Paul goes on to explain that the Philippians' anxiety over their representative was not misplaced, writing, "Indeed, he was sick to the point of death" (καὶ γὰρ ἠσθένησεν παραπλήσιον θανάτῳ, v. 27). The conjunction rendered "indeed" (καί) may be read as ascensive, and the conjunction γάρ (untranslated here) as explanatory,[77] as the apostle offers a bit more detail that the illness was "to the point of death" (παραπλήσιον θανάτῳ). Thankfully, what happened could be set in contrast (ἀλλά) to the threat: "God had mercy on him, and not only on him, but also on me" (ὁ θεὸς ἠλέησεν αὐτόν, οὐκ αὐτὸν δὲ μόνον ἀλλὰ καὶ ἐμέ). To show mercy means to be moved with compassion at the suffering of another.[78] That God is merciful to his people is a cornerstone of biblical theology.[79] In the Gospels it is primarily the Lord Jesus who shows mercy,[80] and his followers are called to be merciful as well, making mercy an active virtue (e.g., Matt 5:7; 18:33). In the balance of the New Testament,

71. The subordinating conjunction ἐπειδή ("since," "because") explains *why* sending Epaphroditus was necessary. The construction of the present participle + the imperfect form of εἰμί constitutes a periphrastic imperfect with imperfective aspect, and this carries over to the participle ἀδημονῶν as well.

72. Cf. Rom 1:11; 2 Cor 9:14; 1 Thess 3:6; 2 Tim 1:4; and note Phil 1:8 where Paul expresses his affectionate longing for the Philippians. This is not "homesickness," which would not make sense in most of the apostle's uses; contra Hawthorne and Martin, *Philippians*, 164.

73. Some manuscripts add the complementary infinitive ἰδεῖν ("longing *to see*"; ℵ* A C D I$^{vid}$ 0278. 33. 81. 104. 326. 365. 1175. 1241. 2495 sy bo), but this is probably an accommodation to parallel passages in Paul (Rom 1:11; 1 Thess 3:6; 2 Tim 1:4). The external evidence for the text as it stands carries equal weight (so Metzger, *Textual Commentary*, 546–47).

74. BDAG 19. The verb is used elsewhere in biblical literature only of Jesus's distress in the garden of Gethsemane (Matt 26:37; Mark 14:33).

75. On illness in the biblical world, see Max Sussman, "Sickness and Disease," in *ABD* 6:6–15.

76. Fee, *Philippians*, 279, who suggests gifts of healing may have been involved.

77. The combination of the two conjunctions is a common construction, used for emphasis not only in Paul but also in the NT generally (e.g., Matt 8:9; Mark 10:45; Luke 1:66; 6:32–33; 7:8; John 4:23; Acts 19:40; Rom 11:1; 15:3; 1 Cor 5:7; 2 Cor 2:10; Phil 2:27; 1 Thess 3:4; 2 Thess 3:10; Heb 4:2).

78. *TLNT* 1:472–73.

79. E.g., Gen 33:5, 11; 43:29; Ps 50:3; 56:2; Hos 2:25; Amos 5:15; Isa 30:18; 44:23; 49:13.

80. E.g., Matt 9:27; 15:22; 17:15; 20:30; Mark 5:19; 10:47; Luke 16:24; 17:13; 18:38.

either "the Lord" or "God" displays mercy.[81] In Epaphroditus's case, God's mercy was expressed to him by deliverance from death, and to Paul by God sparing his partner in ministry.[82] The reason (ἵνα)[83] God did this, according to Paul, was so that the apostle might not have "sorrow piled on top of sorrow" (λύπην ἐπὶ λύπην). This word for sorrow (λύπη) can refer to grief, affliction, or sorrow, whether from mental or physical causes.[84] If Epaphroditus had died, Paul would have experienced profound grief, the intensity of which would have overwhelmed the apostle in a compounding effect.

**2:28–30 Therefore, I sent him as soon as possible so that upon seeing him you might be filled with joy again, and I might have less grief. So, welcome him in the Lord with lots of joy, and honor leaders like him since he came very close to death because of the work of Christ, risking his life in order that he might fulfill what was lacking in your ministry to me** (σπουδαιοτέρως οὖν ἔπεμψα αὐτόν, ἵνα ἰδόντες αὐτὸν πάλιν χαρῆτε κἀγὼ ἀλυπότερος ὦ. 29 προσδέχεσθε οὖν αὐτὸν ἐν κυρίῳ μετὰ πάσης χαρᾶς καὶ τοὺς τοιούτους ἐντίμους ἔχετε, 30 ὅτι διὰ τὸ ἔργον Χριστοῦ μέχρι θανάτου ἤγγισεν παραβολευσάμενος τῇ ψυχῇ, ἵνα ἀναπληρώσῃ τὸ ὑμῶν ὑστέρημα τῆς πρός με λειτουργίας). With verse 28 we come around again to the theme of "sending" (ἔπεμψα αὐτόν; cf. 2:25), specifically the manner in which Paul sent Epaphroditus back to Philippi ("as soon as possible"), as well as two reasons given for the dispatch (the joy of the Philippians and the apostle's relief from grief).

The inferential conjunction "therefore" (οὖν) probably points to the result of the information about Epaphroditus given thus far (vv. 25–27) but, given the reasons that follow, perhaps especially relates to the distress that Epaphroditus had experienced (v. 26b–c). That Paul had sent his colleague "as soon as possible" (σπουδαιοτέρως, the comparative form of the adverb σπουδαίως)[85] expresses a sense of urgency, translating a term that variously communicated "haste," the "seriousness" of a situation, or the need for "diligence." Here the word probably carries the sense of heightened urgency, given the context.[86] In dispatching his coworker with a sense of urgency, Paul sought to accomplish two purposes (introduced by ἵνα). First, he sent the man so that "upon seeing him" (ἰδόντες[87] αὐτόν), the Philippians "might be filled with joy" again (χαρῆτε). This verb, of course, reprises the very important "rejoice!" theme in the letter (Phil 1:4, 18, 25; 2:2, 17–18, 28–29; 3:1; 4:1, 4, 10), and as noted in the "Structure" section above, it plays an important structural role in framing 2:18–3:1, both reiterating the exhortations to rejoice in 2:18 and anticipating the exhortation to "rejoice in the Lord" at 3:1. In short, Paul hoped that the Philippians' anxiety about Epaphroditus's illness would be turned to sheer joy when they saw him alive and well.

Second, however, Epaphroditus's return to Philippi was so that Paul himself "might have less grief" (ἀλυπότερος ὦ).[88] The term for "grief free" (ἄλυπος), of which our term is a comparative, has to do with being free from sorrow and in the

81. Rom 9:15, 18; 11:31; 1 Cor 7:25; 2 Cor 4:1; 1 Tim 1:13, 16; 1 Pet 2:10.

82. The οὐκ . . . δὲ μόνον ἀλλὰ καί construction heightens the emphasis on Paul's role as a recipient of mercy.

83. Purpose and reason are often closely related in Philippians. See, e.g., Reed, *Discourse Analysis*, 325.

84. BDAG 605.

85. Also occurring at Luke 7:4; 2 Tim 1:17; Titus 3:13; cf. Wis 2:6.

86. *TLNT* 3:284.

87. The aorist participle is temporal, is derived from ὁράω, and is delimiting the verb χαρῆτε.

88. The word ὦ is a present subjunctive form of the verb εἰμί, the imperfective aspect indicating an open-ended condition.

broader literature is often coupled with being free from fear.[89] It may be that the Philippians' distress over Epaphroditus's illness weighed heavily on Paul, grieving him. Knowing that this fellow minister was back with the church turned this note of grief to joy.

With 2:29, Paul again uses the inferential, this time translated as "so" (οὖν), to lead into an exhortation concerning Epaphroditus: "Welcome him in the Lord with lots of joy" (προσδέχεσθε . . . αὐτὸν ἐν κυρίῳ μετὰ πάσης χαρᾶς). This call for joy, of course, follows directly from the reference to one of Paul's motives for sending Epaphroditus in the previous verse—that they "might be filled with joy." Thus "lots of joy" (μετὰ πάσης χαρᾶς)[90] will be a natural response to Epaphroditus's presence among the Philippians again. Rather than indicating strain in Epaphroditus's relationship with the church, when Paul writes for the Philippians to "welcome" him—that is, to "receive [him] in a friendly manner" (προσδέχεσθε), the apostle uses common cultural language for commendation.[91] The common Pauline phrase "in the Lord" (ἐν κυρίῳ) has the sense of "in view of your common relationship with Christ,"[92] amounting to "as a fellow Christian." Harris, who understands the syntax to reflect "sphere of reference," renders the thought as "give him a joyful Christian welcome."[93]

The Philippians are also to "honor leaders like him" (τοὺς τοιούτους ἐντίμους ἔχετε), valuing Epaphroditus as a type of leader worth following. When applied to people, the term that often had to do with "value" or "worth" (ἐντίμους) could speak of someone who was honored or respected.[94] In the broader Greco-Roman culture, which was based on a system of honor and shame, leaders rose in status by gaining wealth (and showering it on others), by social connections, by great speaking ability, by advanced education, or by making shrewd political moves.[95] Yet in a countercultural expression of values, the Philippians are to honor people like Epaphroditus because he had suffered for the cause of Christ, following the pattern set by the Lord in embodying sacrificial service (Phil 2:6–8). While this may seem a transparent good in a culture profoundly impacted by the Judeo-Christian ethic of sacrificial service, it would have seemed tacitly odd on the streets of Philippi and is an example of countercultural thinking.

Specifically, Paul writes that Epaphroditus should be honored as he "came very close to death because of the work of Christ, risking his life in order that he might fulfill what was lacking in your service to me" (v. 30). Paul here explains why (ὅτι) the Philippians should value Epaphroditus as a leader: Epaphroditus almost died (μέχρι θανάτου ἤγγισεν; lit. "he came near to the point of death") "for the sake of" Christ's work (διὰ τὸ ἔργον Χριστοῦ).[96] This assertion echoes "to the point of death" (μέχρι θανάτου) at 2:8, which beautifully

89. E.g., Epictetus, *Ench.* 12.1; *Diatr.* 3.24.117; Philo, *Cherubim* 86. A number of commentators point out that the idea of "anxiety," the primary gloss in BDAG and a main rendering in English translations (e.g., NASB, ESV, NRSV, CSB, NET, NIV, NLT), has no lexicological basis. For the proper understanding, see, e.g., LSJ 73; Fee, *Philippians*, 281; Hansen, *Philippians*, 207; Hellerman, *Philippians*, 162.

90. The phrase μετὰ πάσης χαρᾶς, "lots of joy," reflects intensity or volume, not variety (i.e., "every kind of joy").

91. Fee, *Philippians*, 281.

92. The preposition perhaps communicates association in this case.

93. Harris, *Prepositions*, 130.

94. BDAG 340.

95. See, e.g., Guthrie, *2 Corinthians*, 16.

96. The external support for this reading is strong ($\mathfrak{P}^{46}$ B F G 88 614 1739), as is the reading κυριου (א A P Ψ 075. 33. 81. 104. 365. 1241. 1505 sy$^{h}$ bo). The addition of the article before Χριστοῦ is the reading in D K L 630 𝔐. Metzger and the committee believe that Χριστοῦ originally was omitted from τὸ ἔργον Χριστοῦ by error. They speculate that κυρίου may have been assimilated to the text by copyists familiar with "the work of the Lord" at 1 Cor 15:58 and 16:10 (Metzger, *Textual Commentary*, 547).

describes the extent to which Christ went to meet the needs of humanity.[97] He went to the point of death and died. That Epaphroditus came to the same point and lived does not lessen the significance of his risk, for the language here expresses exposure to danger or risk.[98] In short, Epaphroditus risked his life (τῇ ψυχῇ).

Though there has been a great deal of speculation concerning how Epaphroditus's life was in danger,[99] the details are lost to us. Nevertheless, the purpose clause (ἵνα) with which verse 30 ends makes it clear that the risk was directly related to Epaphroditus's ministry to Paul on behalf of the Philippian church. He carried out his ministry to the apostle so that "he might fulfill" (ἀναπληρώσῃ) the deficiency (ὑστέρημα)[100] in the Philippians' service to Paul, in effect functioning as a representative on behalf of those who could not attend to the apostle themselves.[101] In other words, it cost Epaphroditus dearly to fill in the gap between the Philippians' commitment to Paul and what had actually been accomplished on behalf of the church. This is why the Philippians should cherish Epaphroditus, honoring and valuing him as a respected example of Christ-like leadership. He and Timothy therefore serve as prime exemplars of self-sacrificial service to others, which the apostle holds up to the Philippians as a key to unity.

## Theology in Application

### *The Need for Living Examples*

At its best, the Western church has emphasized right thinking about the faith. As we have already seen in this letter, "right living" needs the foundation of "right thinking." Exegetical and theological foundation stones offer sure footing for a flourishing church in the ever-shifting sands of the modern world. Yet it cannot be overemphasized how the church's flourishing depends on embodying right teaching in life and especially in the lives of leaders—living exemplars who can be followed down dusty, winding roads through the nitty-gritty realities of the world. As much as good teaching, we need godly leaders who are great examples of how the faith and the advancement of the kingdom are to be lived out.

In Jane Austen's *Sense and Sensibility*, the author depicts two sisters who handle matters of the heart in profoundly different ways. Marianne, the younger sister, is the consummate romantic—all energy and openness, throwing social propriety to

97. So, e.g., Reumann, *Philippians*, 432, 438; Hansen, *Philippians*, 208.

98. BDAG 759.

99. Bockmuehl, *Philippians*, 171; Reumann, *Philippians*, 428; Hawthorne and Martin, *Philippians*, 165. But contra Hawthorne and Martin, the thought that Epaphroditus had somehow brought the illness upon himself and that it thus could have been a source for criticism against him presses beyond anything suggested by the context.

100. For the use of this term communicating a "lack," see Judg 18:10; 19:19; Ps 33:10; Luke 21:4; 2 Cor 8:14; and for the sense of "fulfilling" what was lacking, see 1 Cor 16:17; 2 Cor 11:9; Col 1:24.

101. See Hellerman, *Philippians*, 164, who, following Fee and others, points out that it was not the content of the gift that was lacking but the presence of the Philippians themselves.

the wind. She falls in love with John Willoughby, as flawed in character as he is charming, and he carries her down a road to heartbreak and public humiliation. Elinor, the older sister, is a picture of quiet reserve. She too falls in love, with Edward Ferrars, but must wait for any indication from him that he returns her affections. She also endures long torment at the hands of Lucy Steel, the young woman to whom Edward has been secretly engaged for some years. Yet Elinor does so with poise, supporting Edward in his honorable commitments.

Both sisters come to devastating disappointment (before all comes right in the end). It seems that Edward will marry Lucy. Willoughby jilts Marianne, throwing her off for a rich wife whom he does not love. After Marianne has been distraught and endured a dangerous physical illness, she and Elinor discuss Willoughby's conduct—and her own.

> "I am not wishing him too much good," said Marianne at last with a sigh, "when I wish his secret reflections may be no more unpleasant than my own. He will suffer enough in them."
>
> "Do you compare your conduct with his?"
>
> "No. I compare it with what it should have been; I compare it with yours."[102]

At last Marianne sees herself in a new light, which has been shining from her older sister all along as Elinor lived out a steady, stellar example of how to process love with honor.

Paul's words to the Philippians about Timothy and Epaphroditus raise the question for us: To whom do we look as bright, shining examples of the faith well lived? For whom are we an example? In the Christian church and ministry, we always stand between those who are, and those who are in need of, good examples. How will we live in that place? The Christian faith is an embodied faith, and such embodiment is caught as much as taught, in the context of community, side-by-side with leaders of integrity, and under the transforming power of the Spirit of God.

### *Examples of Self-Sacrifice and Service*

One question that every Christian leader must ask themselves is, "How will I spend my life?" The spending may be in daily tasks, faithfully performed for the good of others, over years. Or the spending may be in a climactic moment of sacrifice on behalf of others that literally means the giving or risking of one's life. Both involve

102. Jane Austen, *Sense and Sensibility*, ed. James Kinsley, Oxford World's Classics (Oxford: Oxford University Press, 2008), 261–62.

a posture of "for the kingdom" and "for others" rather than a self-promoting, self-protecting posture. In the history of the church, we have many wonderful examples of self-giving.

For example, Lilias Trotter was one of the most gifted artists of the nineteenth century and a protégé of art critic John Ruskin. Ruskin had met Trotter while she and her mother were in Venice, and he was impressed with her artistic skill, encouraging her that if she devoted herself to her art "she would be the greatest living painter and do things that would be immortal."[103] Yet Trotter had higher aspirations aimed at other "immortal" concerns. In May of 1879 she decided that she could not give her life to art, since she had already committed her life to "seek first the kingdom of God." Although she and Ruskin continued to interact as friends, she began to devote herself to a Christian organization, teaching during the day and walking the streets at night, ministering to prostitutes.[104] Then in May of 1887 Trotter felt a call to missionary service in North Africa. Although she was denied an official position with the North African Mission due to poor health, they allowed her to be self-supporting and work in conjunction with the mission.[105] So in March 1888 Trotter, along with two other young, financially independent women, arrived in Algiers. She later reflected, "Three of us stood there, looking at our battle-field, none of us fit to pass a doctor for any society, not knowing a soul in the place, or a sentence of Arabic or a clue for beginning work on untouched ground; we only knew we had to come. Truly if God needed weakness, He had it!"[106]

We should celebrate those who have served as great examples for others, even as Paul celebrates Timothy and Epaphroditus. Most of us probably have leaders in our lives who have sacrificed greatly to carry out their ministry. Are we receiving their ministry, warmly embracing their place in our community, with joy and honor? Do we value and affirm those leaders who serve out of interest in the welfare of others rather than self-interest? Or do we take them for granted? Do we consider the impact of such leaders as a unifying, relational force in our communities, celebrating their positive examples? Or do we tend toward celebrating values most spotlighted by the culture around us—winning personalities, great speaking ability, and charismatic leadership? Take a moment today to express to the sacrificial leaders in your life your joy in their service and your celebration of their faithfulness.

103. Miriam Huffman Rockness, *A Passion for the Impossible: The Life of Lilias Trotter* (Grand Rapids: Discovery House, 2003), 83.

104. Rockness, *Passion for the Impossible*, 91.

105. Rockness, *Passion for the Impossible*, 98.

106. Lisa M. Sinclair, "The Legacy of Isabella Lilias Trotter," *International Bulletin of Missionary Research* 26 (Jan 2002): 32.

CHAPTER 9

# Philippians 3:1–14

## Literary Context

The great center section of Philippians addresses the problem of disunity in the church by presenting a series of key exemplars who embody self-sacrificial leadership. Christ himself is Paul's first and preeminent example (2:5–11), which is followed by a block of exhortations (vv. 12–17). Timothy and Epaphroditus, each in their own way, offer stellar examples of sacrificial leadership in the Pauline mission (vv. 18–30), and here, as we move into chapter 3, Paul offers himself as a profoundly Christ-centered example, in contrast to false teachers (3:1–14). The apostle's program of offering exemplars is stated plainly in the exhortation that follows (3:15–4:4a), where he writes, "Be imitators of me, brothers and sisters, and in the same way that you have us as role models, pay careful attention to those who live like we do" (3:17). In this exhortation we see a reprisal of numerous themes that anchor the unit at 1:27–2:4 and close a major *inclusio*, thus bracketing the center section of Philippians.[1] So 3:1–14 offers a climactic moment in the book, as Paul uses himself as a model of Christian commitment. A powerful, exalted reflection on his own Christocentric life and ministry, the apostle in essence says, "If you want to see where your commitments should lie—look to me and those who walk like me." His example then sets up a direct exhortation to those who seem to be disrupting the unity of the Philippian church (4:1–4a), before closing the book with final exhortations and a word of thanks.

1. On which, see above at "Literary Context" of 1:27–2:4.

## Main Idea

In contrast to false teachers, Paul puts his religious credentials in perspective, considering those credentials as loss—on the level of refuse or "crap"—in comparison to knowing or "gaining" Christ and attaining to the resurrection from the dead.

## Translation

### Philippians 3:1–14

| | | | |
|---|---|---|---|
| 1a | Affection. Address | Finally, | my brothers and sisters, |
| b | Exhortation | **rejoice** | |
| c | Relationship | in the Lord. | |
| d | Statement | **I do not hesitate to write** | |
| e | Object | | the same things |
| f | Indirect Object | | to you; |
| g | Expansion/Advantage | **it is stabilizing for you.** | |
| 2a | Exhortation List | **Watch out for dogs;** | |
| b | Exhortation | **watch out for evil workers;** | |
| c | Exhortation | **watch out for those who ritually dismember others.** | |

*Continued on next page.*

| | | |
|---|---|---|
| 3a | Basis/Contrast (of 3:2c) | For **we ourselves are those who have been truly circumcised,** |
| b | Apposit./Action List | people who serve by the Spirit of God, and |
| c | Action | boast in Christ Jesus, and |
| d | Action | do not place confidence |
| e | Standard | in human standards |
| 4a | Concession/Assertion | —although I too have |
| b | | a basis for placing confidence |
| c | Standard | in human standards. |
| d | Condition | If some other person thinks he has the basis to place confidence |
| e | Standard | in human standards, |
| f | Assertation | **I have much more of a basis**: |
| 5a | List (3:5a–6d)/Descr. | circumcised on the eighth day, |
| b | Identification | of the people of Israel, |
| c | Identification | of the tribe of Benjamin, |
| d | Identification | a Hebrew of Hebrews; |
| e | Reference | with respect to the law, |
| f | Association | a Pharisee; |
| 6a | Reference | with respect to zeal, |
| b | Action | a persecutor of the church; |
| c | Reference | with respect to righteousness occurring by means of the law, |
| d | Description | blameless. |
| 7a | Ascensive/ | Yet whatever were gains |
| b | Advantage | for me |
| c | Contra-expectation | **I consider these things as loss** |
| d | Advantage | for the sake of Christ. |
| 8a | Ascensive | Indeed, |
| b | | even more than that, |
| c | Testimony | **I consider all things to be loss** |
| d | Reason | because of the far more valuable knowledge |
| e | Content | of Christ Jesus |
| f | Apposition | my Lord |
| g | Advantage | for whom I have lost all things and |
| h | Perspective | consider them crap |
| i | Purpose 1 | in order that I might gain Christ and |
| 9a | Purpose 2 | be found |
| b | Relationship | in him, |
| c | Circumstan. | not having a righteousness |

| | | |
|---|---|---|
| d | Possession | of my own |
| e | Source | issuing from the law, but rather |
| f | Means | through trust in Christ |
| g | Apposition | a righteousness |
| h | Source | from God |
| i | Basis | on the basis of trust |
| 10a | Expansion (of 3:8c–e)/ Purpose | so that I may know him, and |
| b | List/Object | the power of his resurrection, and |
| c | List/Object | the fellowship of his sufferings, |
| d | Means | as I am being conformed to his death, |
| 11a | Result | in hope that I will reach |
| b | Destination | the goal of the resurrection |
| c | Separation | from among the dead. |
| 12a | Clarification | **Not that I have already taken hold of this or** |
| b | Restatement | **have already reached the goal,** |
| c | Alternative | but |
| d | Testimony | **I am running hard** |
| e | Goal | that I might grab hold of |
| f | Object | that for which I was grabbed by Christ Jesus. |
| 13a | Affection. Address | Brothers and sisters, |
| b | Testimony | **I do not consider myself to have grabbed hold of it yet,** |
| c | Testimony | but **I focus on one thing**: |
| d | Action/Manner | disregarding the things behind me and |
| e | Simultaneous Act. | straining for the things ahead of me, |
| 14a | Testimony | **I am running hard** |
| b | Extension | toward the goal |
| c | Goal | for the prize |
| d | Subject | of the upward call |
| e | Agency | of God |
| f | Relationsh. | in Christ Jesus. |

## Structure

Fee remarks that analysts have struggled to find an internal logic to the organization of all the material in 3:1–4:3, and this includes the unit at 3:1–14. In some ways this subsection of Philippians raises a number of questions structurally—for instance, the reason for the abrupt shift to a focus on false teachers, how Paul's religious credentials in 3:3–6 and his exultation on knowing Christ in 3:7–11 relate to the apostle's status of not having reached the goal of his ministry (3:12–14), and the relationship between the false teachers of 3:2 and the "enemies" he derides in 3:18–19.[2] Yet as Fee points out, the material here clearly reprises themes from earlier in the book. For example, the theme of "gaining" Christ (3:8) echoes 1:21 ("to die is gain"), the theme of participating in the sufferings of Christ (3:10–11) reiterates that theme in 1:29–30 and 2:17, and the eschatological perspective of 3:11–14, 20–21 recalls 1:6.[3] Thus the unit before us should not be considered as a fragment interposed at this point in Philippians.

As for structure, 3:1–14 falls into three general sub-movements. First, Paul begins with a return to his exhortation to rejoice (v. 1), making a smooth transition to the new unit. He then continues with an exhortation to watch out for false ministers, particularly focusing on a contrast of false and true standards for a relationship with God (vv. 2–6), pointing out that according to human standards (that is, the false standards), he himself had led an exemplary life. Third, however, he reflects on loss and gain (vv. 7–11). Here he confesses that those human standards, as lived out by him, he now considers "loss" in view of the surpassing greatness of the great gain of knowing Christ. Paul's thought here is profoundly Christocentric. Fourth, the apostle makes clear that having gained a relationship with Christ does not mean that he has arrived at the ultimate conclusion of the relationship, which would only come at "the upward call of God" at the end of his life. Thus the apostle continues to press on to that goal (vv. 12–14).

2. Fee, *Philippians*, 285.

3. Fee, *Philippians*, 285.

## Exegetical Outline

➦ **5. The Example of Paul's Christocentric Life and Ministry (3:1–14)**
- **a. An Exhortation to Rejoice (v. 1)**
- **b. False and True Standards of Relationship with God (vv. 2–6)**
  - (1) Introduction: An Opening Exhortation concerning False Ministers (v. 2)
  - (2) Basis: Paul's Ministry and True Circumcision (vv. 3–6)
    - a) An Assertion: We Are the Ones Who Have Been Circumcised (v. 3a)
    - b) The Nature of True Circumcision (v. 3b–e)
    - c) Concession: If Anyone Could Boast in Human Standards, It Would Be Paul (vv. 4–6)
- **c. The True Nature of Relationship with God—Knowing Christ (vv. 7–14)**
  - (1) Paul Considers All Things to Be "Loss" Compared to the "Gain" of Knowing Christ (vv. 7–8b)
  - (2) The "Gain" of Knowing Christ (vv. 8c–14)

## Explanation of the Text

**3:1 Finally, my brothers and sisters, rejoice in the Lord. I do not hesitate to write the same things to you; it is stabilizing for you** (Τὸ λοιπόν, ἀδελφοί μου, χαίρετε ἐν κυρίῳ. τὰ αὐτὰ γράφειν ὑμῖν ἐμοὶ μὲν οὐκ ὀκνηρόν, ὑμῖν δὲ ἀσφαλές). Paul once again exhorts the brothers and sisters to rejoice, adding a "hesitation formula." The verse begins with "finally" (τὸ λοιπόν). Generally the term λοιπός refers to what is "remaining" or the "rest" of a group of people, objects, or actions, such as the "rest" of Paul's coworkers, mentioned at Philippians 4:3 (cf. 2 Cor 13:2; Phil 1:13; Rev 8:13; 11:13). Adverbially the word can mean "from now on" or "in the future," or simply "finally" or "in addition." In epistolary contexts the term can be used with the sense of "finally" as an author signals a transition in the letter (e.g., 2 Cor 13:11), or as is the case here, it can be used to introduce a new section (see also, e.g., 1 Thess 4:1).[4] Assuming the integrity of the letter, the use here marks the opening of a new movement in Philippians rather than a letter closing.[5]

Further, here at this key transition, amid his appeal to the Philippians to embrace sound ministers and reject those who are false, Paul once again addresses the Philippians warmly and personally as "my brothers and sisters" (ἀδελφοί μου; cf. Phil 1:12; 3:13, 17; 4:1, 8). His appeals to the church rest in part on their family relationship as children of God. From this "we are family" vantage point, the apostle exhorts them to "rejoice" (χαίρετε; see 2:18)—a heartfelt challenge to which he adds "in the Lord" (ἐν κυρίῳ); he will again repeat this call to "rejoice in the Lord" at 4:4a, marking 3:1–4:4a as a key movement in the letter.[6] The repeated exhortation underpins a key, foundational conviction woven into the fabric of this book: the "choice to

4. BDAG 602–3.

5. As proposed by some who see 3:1 as part of a letter fragment; on which, see the helpful discussion in Reed, *Discourse Analysis*, 239–41.

6. Here again we have a use of *inclusio*, a device by which an author marks the beginning and ending of a unit of discourse.

rejoice" is made possible as the Philippians embrace sound Christian thinking in the context of a unified Christian community.

The term we have translated as having to do with hesitation (ὀκνηρός) is one of several interpretive conundrums in the verse. As Ceslas Spicq points out, in first-century literary Greek as well as the LXX, the verb form related to the word used in our passage normally means "to hesitate."[7] The adjective here, on the other hand, is often used negatively of a lazy or idle person,[8] but it also can convey the sense of "hesitating."[9] Accordingly, in his excellent work on the discourse dynamics in Philippians, Jeffrey Reed unpacks the second half of verse 1 as embodying an epistolary "hesitation formula," which functions to express affection for the Philippians[10] but also to facilitate a transition in the discourse.[11] Such a formula normally consists of the verb (ὀκνέω) or a related term, sometimes combined with a verb of disclosure or writing (e.g., "I write," γράφω).[12] In Philippians 3:1, the formula speaks of open communication: "I do not hesitate to write." But to what does Paul allude when he speaks of "the same things" (τὰ αὐτά) about which he does not hesitate to write? Scholars have suggested, for instance, that he anticipates the warning against false teachers in the next verse,[13] or that he alludes to things he had written or taught them previously. Yet based on the broader context of Philippians, there is another option that seems most likely.

As we have seen, the apostle has already underscored the call for the Philippians to "rejoice" a number of times in the letter (Phil 1:18; 2:17–18, 28). Thus, one way of reading the hesitation formula in 3:1 is as an acknowledgment that this could sound a bit repetitive by this point in the letter. Yet Paul "does not hesitate to write the same" call to rejoice yet again. At a number of places in his letters the apostle reflects on his process of writing, sometimes looking back at what he has already written and its relationship to what he is penning at the moment.[14] The pattern in Philippians 3:1 is similar, for example, to what we find in 2 Corinthians 9:1. There Paul had already been discussing at length the Corinthians' project of collecting funds for the church in Jerusalem. As he continues the theme, he seems to feel the need to acknowledge the redundancy.[15] Something similar is going on here, with the function of marking a shift in the letter's focus—but the shift is not as abrupt as some suggest. Paul has just offered Timothy and Epaphroditus as positive examples of true Christian ministers. As he turns to Philippians 3:2 and following, he mentions false ministers to launch a discussion on the example offered by his own life and ministry. Thus the harshness of tone as we move to 3:2 has more to do with Paul setting up his next movement than it does a radical shift in topic.

Why does the apostle not hesitate to write again, challenging the Philippians to rejoice? Because the act of writing and reminding them to rejoice is "stabilizing" (ἀσφαλές)[16] for them. The adjective has to

7. *TLNT* 2:576. E.g., Num 22:16; Judg 18:9; Tob 12:6, 13; Jdt 12:13; Sir 7:35; 4 Macc 14:4.

8. Prov 6:6, 9; 11:16; 18:8; 20:4; 21:25; 22:13; 26:13–16; 31:27; Sir 22:1–2; 37:11.

9. E.g., Josephus, *Ant.* 2.236; 20.71; *J.W.* 4.584; Philo, *Spec. Laws* 1.99; *Virtues* 83.

10. See esp. Jeffrey T. Reed, "Philippians 3:1 and the Epistolary Hesitation Formulas: The Literary Integrity of Philippians, Again," *JBL* 115.1 (1996): 73–76.

11. Reed, *Discourse Analysis*, 229–39; idem, "Hesitation Formulas."

12. Reed, *Discourse Analysis*, 330.

13. Lightfoot, *Philippians*, 126.

14. E.g., Rom 15:15; 1 Cor 5:9, 11; 14:37; 2 Cor 2:4; 7:12; 9:1; 1 Thess 4:9.

15. Guthrie, *2 Corinthians*, 432.

16. Here we have a neuter singular nominative adjective, which is part of a word-group combining an alpha-privative and the verb σφάλλω, "to slip, fall, or lose out" on something.

do with something that is secure, solid, or safe.[17] Accordingly, most English translations render the adjective with the sense of something that is "safe" or a "safeguard" for the Philippians.[18] At Hebrews 6:19, in the context of an anchor metaphor, this word speaks of something that is "firm" or "secure," and this may be the nuance here also, describing the repeated call to rejoice as a spiritually fortifying dynamic for the Philippians.[19] In other words, the stability of the Philippians depends in part on an ongoing, healthy posture of making the "choice to rejoice" as a pattern of life and community.

**3:2–4c Watch out for dogs; watch out for evil workers; watch out for those who ritually dismember others. For we ourselves are those who have been truly circumcised, people who serve by the Spirit of God, and boast in Christ Jesus, and do not place confidence in human standards—although I too have a basis for placing confidence in human standards. If some other person thinks he has the basis to place confidence in human standards, I have much more of a basis** (Βλέπετε τοὺς κύνας, βλέπετε τοὺς κακοὺς ἐργάτας, βλέπετε τὴν κατατομήν. 3 ἡμεῖς γάρ ἐσμεν ἡ περιτομή, οἱ πνεύματι θεοῦ λατρεύοντες καὶ καυχώμενοι ἐν Χριστῷ Ἰησοῦ καὶ οὐκ ἐν σαρκὶ πεποιθότες, 4 καίπερ ἐγὼ ἔχων πεποίθησιν καὶ ἐν σαρκί. εἴ τις δοκεῖ ἄλλος πεποιθέναι ἐν σαρκί, ἐγὼ μᾶλλον). Paul now offers a triple caution about false teachers, using an exhortation built around the repeated present imperative verb, "Watch out!" (βλέπετε). Notice that the graphically descriptive objects of the verb are alliterated (the *k* sound) in Greek:

| | | |
|---|---|---|
| Watch out for dogs | βλέπετε | τοὺς κύνας |
| Watch out for evil workers | βλέπετε | τοὺς κακοὺς ἐργάτας |
| Watch out for those who ritually dismember others | βλέπετε | τὴν κατατομήν |

This rhetorically powerful triple punch, which spits "invective and sarcasm" against false teachers,[20] should all be read as addressing the same problem group. It should also be read as a strong counterpoint to the positive exhortations in 2:29–3:1 where Paul challenges the Philippians to "welcome" Epaphroditus, to "honor leaders like him," and to "rejoice in the Lord."[21] Although we do not know the exact identity of these opponents,[22] their description as "those who ritually dismember others" (τὴν κατατομήν) seems to point in the direction of Jewish agitators, about which we will say more momentarily. Nevertheless, Paul's concern may not be with an immediate threat to the church in Philippi; he could just as well be giving a strong, general caution based on his ministry in the broader Mediterranean world.[23] While it is true that the word translated here as "watch out"

17. *TLNT* 1:214–15. Elsewhere in Acts, the word connotes the "truth" (i.e., the actual facts or specific information) about a situation, as when the Roman officer was trying to get to the bottom of why Paul was being mobbed in Acts 21:34 (cf. Acts 22:30; 25:26). Victor Furnish has suggested a similar meaning—"specific"—for our passage, but few if any have followed him in the suggestion. See Victor Paul Furnish, "The Place and Purpose of Philippians 3," *NTS* 10 (1963): 87; see also the remark by Fee, *Philippians*, 292.

18. E.g., NASB, NRSV, ESV, CSB, NET, NIV, NLT.

19. BDAG 147.

20. Fee, *Philippians*, 293–94.

21. Reed, *Discourse Analysis*, 260.

22. For the various positions on the opponents' identity, see Hansen, *Philippians*, 217–18 and the In Depth section below.

23. So Bockmuehl, *Philippians*, 183–84. Concerning "an intra-Jewish debate, which involved very real theological commitments," including the reading of Scripture as pointing to the integration of the gentiles into the people of God, see Christopher Zoccali, "Rejoice, O Gentiles, with His People: Paul's Intra-Jewish Rhetoric in Philippians 3:1–9," *CTR* 9.1 (2011): 31. Mikael Tellbe suggests the social context, especially given conflict with the Roman authorities in Philippi, would have made the appeal of Jewish agitators a strong draw for those

(βλέπω) does not necessarily convey a harsh tone of warning, the context—with Paul's edgy descriptors of the false teachers—certainly warrants more than a reading of "pay careful attention to" or "study" these people.[24] The alertness communicated by "watch out for" is probably not far from the apostle's intention.

So the Philippians are to keep on guard against "dogs" (τοὺς κύνας), a common word picture in the biblical literature for "squalor, dismal poverty, and the life of a pariah at the bottom of the social scale."[25] Rather than the clean, domesticated pets of the modern Western world, dogs often were considered disgusting scavengers,[26] consuming and regurgitating that which is vile.[27] The imagery can be applied as a general insult (e.g., 2 Sam 16:9), and it certainly applies to bad leaders (Isa 56:10), as here.[28] Significantly, enemies of God's people were referred to as "dogs" (Ps 22:16, 20; 59:6, 14), and in Revelation the image is associated with "those who practice magic arts, the sexually immoral, the murderers, the idolaters and everyone who loves and practices falsehood" (Rev 22:15). Not a very flattering list!

In the history of interpretation, commentators commonly suggest that Jewish teachers or writers sometimes referred to lapsed Jews or gentiles as "dogs" (Matt 7:6; 15:26–27), the imagery alluding to gentiles' "unclean" eating habits. Yet this idea seems to have little support in ancient Jewish texts.[29] It is clear, nevertheless, that Paul uses "dogs" here as a word picture of contempt for those theological scavengers fixed on advancing aspects of traditional Judaism to the perversion of the gospel.[30]

Second, Paul refers to the false ministers as "evil workers" (τοὺς κακοὺς ἐργάτας). In this letter the apostle consistently celebrates good work (1:6, 22; 2:30) and good coworkers (4:3). But those he has in mind at 3:2 do "evil" (κακός) work—something "morally reprehensible" or even "dangerous."[31] Some read a pun in the passage, associating these false "workers" (ἐργάτας) with "works of the law," thus pointing to their attempt to call gentile converts to law obedience.[32] The problem with this interpretation, however, is that Paul uses "worker(s)" generally as a reference to those "working" in ministry in some way.[33] The negative uses at 2 Corinthians 11:13 ("deceitful workers") and here in Philippians 3:2 may serve simply as caustic, antithetical referents, setting false teachers over against those who do good, honest work as Christian ministers.[34] The bottom line is that these so-called ministers do egregious "work," hurting the church rather than patterning themselves after Paul's mission, which is characterized by "good works."

Third, the apostle employs a harsh play on

longing to be recognized as a legitimate religion in the Roman Empire (*religio licita*). See Tellbe, "Sociological Factors."

24. So Hansen, *Philippians*, 217; Garland, "Composition," 165–66.

25. "Dogs," *DBI* 214.

26. The use of the diminutive at Mark 7:27 may be an exception, where Jesus and the woman seem to have a small house pet in mind. Dogs were also used for hunting, herding, and as watchdogs for herds, so they had a utilitarian purpose. See Reumann, *Philippians*, 460.

27. E.g., Exod 22:31; 1 Kgs 14:11; Prov 26:11; 2 Pet 2:22.

28. *DBI* 214.

29. Mark D. Nanos, "Paul's Reversal of Jews Calling Gentiles 'Dogs' (Philippians 3:2): 1600 Years of an Ideological Tale Wagging an Exegetical Dog?," *BibInt* 17.4 (2009): 448–82. Nanos makes a strong case for caution, and Paul's pejorative use does not depend on a particular cultural phenomenon. However, I believe that Nanos's suggestion that Paul has pagan opponents in mind is mistaken (480).

30. Garland, "Composition," 167–68; Still, *Philippians & Philemon*, 99.

31. BDAG 501.

32. So Bockmuehl, *Philippians*, 188; Fee, *Philippians*, 295–96; Silva, *Philippians*, 147.

33. E.g., 2 Cor 11:13; Phil 3:2; 1 Tim 5:18; 2 Tim 2:15.

34. On the differences between the situation at Corinth and that at Philippi, see Bockmuehl, *Philippians*, 183.

words, calling the false ministers "those who ritually dismember others" (τὴν κατατομήν, lit. "the mutilation"). Playing on the term for "circumcision" (περιτομή) in the next verse, Paul coins this word, used only here in the biblical literature, to make clear his view of their religious ritual. Thus, whoever these opponents were, the commitment to give circumcision a prominent place in their "ministry" was very much in play.[35] Paul coins this term, replacing the περι- in the word for circumcision with the κατα- prefix, shaping a word that speaks of "cutting off" rather than "cutting around." Thus English translations render the word variously as "the false circumcision" (NASB), "those who mutilate the flesh" (NRSV, ESV, CSB, NET), or "mutilators of the flesh" (NIV). The NLT interprets it as "those mutilators who say you must be circumcised to be saved." The apostle seems to echo Jeremiah, who condemned members of God's people who had been circumcised physically but lived like pagans (Jer 4:4; 9:25–26).[36] Paul's term, in fact, may be related to a verb in the LXX, used of pagan self-mutilation.[37] Thus, these false ministers, devoid of the Spirit of God, act more like pagans than God's people.

Furthermore, as with our rendering "dismember," it may also be that Paul has a double entendre in mind, not only cutting off the physical member but also cutting off the recipient from the gospel itself and thus from the true church (cf. Gal 5:2–4). Chrysostom approximates this idea, writing, "For what is he saying? 'That circumcision is mutilation.' For when this happens unlawfully, it is nothing but a curtailment of the flesh, a 'concision.' Either this was the reason or else it was because they were trying to cut up the church in pieces" (*Homily on Philippians* 10).[38] In other words, by the physical cutting of circumcision, the evil workers were cutting people off from the true gospel and the church. Our translation as "dis-member" seeks to get at this double meaning.

With verse 3 comes the explanatory contrast, "for we ourselves are those who have been truly circumcised" (ἡμεῖς γάρ ἐσμεν ἡ περιτομή, lit. ". . . the circumcision"). The apostle's inclusive "we ourselves are" (ἡμεῖς . . . ἐσμεν) is emphatic and includes himself, a circumcised Jew, as well as both Jews and gentiles in the Philippian house churches, some of whom probably had not been circumcised physically.[39] Those who have had their hearts transformed by Jesus in the new-covenant gospel have experienced true circumcision of the heart.

Physical circumcision was originally intended as a sign of membership in the elect people of God (Gen 17:9–14), but the physical mark was never an adequate gauge of the deeper condition of the human heart. Thus, "circumcision of the heart" would be necessary for the true people of God,[40] and this is how Paul uses the imagery here and elsewhere.[41] Further, the apostle's statements here are not a form of "replacement theology," as if Christ-following has replaced the religion of Judaism.

35. Although some, like Hawthorne, read Paul's warning as against Jewish teachers, not Jewish Christians. See Hawthorne, *Philippians*, xliv–xlvi, 125.

36. The Jeremiah text reads in part, "All the nations are uncircumcised in the flesh and all the house of Israel are uncircumcised in their heart" (Jer 9:26 NETS).

37. κατατέμνω; see LXX Lev 21:5; 1 Kgs 18:28; Isa 15:2; Hos 7:14; so *EDNT* 269.

38. Edwards, *Galatians, Ephesians, Philippians*, 254. This passage is mislabeled as homily 11 in the ACCS.

39. In addition to the explanatory use of "for" (γάρ), the construction combines the pronoun as the subject, followed by the verb of being, which is followed by the predicate nominative, "the circumcision" (ἡ περιτομή).

40. E.g., Jer 4:4; Ezek 44:7; cf. 6:10; 9:25; Deut 10:16; 30:6.

41. E.g., Rom 2:25–29; Col 2:11; cf. 1 Cor 7:19; Gal 5:6; 6:15; Eph 2:11; so Frank S. Thielman, *Philippians*, NIVAC (Grand Rapids: Zondervan, 1995), 168.

Rather, Paul's understanding might be termed "fulfillment theology," with the new-covenant realities in Christ fulfilling the deepest intentions of the old-covenant Scriptures. The gospel takes the old covenant's hopes and promises to God's desired end in Christ and his followers, both Jews and gentiles. In the most basic terms, this involves transformation, the "circumcision" of the human heart (Rom 2:28–29; cf. Deut 30:6), making those with faith in Jesus, both Jews and gentiles, the real "seed of Abraham," the "Israel of God" (Gal 3:7, 29; 6:16).[42]

Thus, labeling the true people of God as "the circumcision," Paul expands on this label with three appositional descriptions:

> people who serve by the Spirit of God, and οἱ πνεύματι θεοῦ λατρεύοντες καὶ
> boast in Christ Jesus, and καυχώμενοι ἐν Χριστῷ Ἰησοῦ καὶ
> do not place confidence in human standards οὐκ ἐν σαρκὶ πεποιθότες

The first of these exhibits some textual turbulence in the Greek manuscripts, but the text reflected in the standard editions seems correct.[43] The word rendered as "people who serve" (the substantival participle λατρεύοντες), is sometimes translated as "the ones worshiping" (e.g., ESV, NRSV, NET, NLT), but it should probably be rendered, as with our translation, as referring to service (e.g., NIV), since here Paul contrasts approaches to ministry. This verb has a rich background in religious service to God in the old covenant.[44] Elsewhere, the apostle stresses that true Christian ministry works by the power of the life-giving Spirit (e.g., 2 Cor 3:6, 8).[45]

Second, Christ's true ministers "boast in Christ Jesus" (καυχώμενοι ἐν Χριστῷ Ἰησοῦ). The motif of "boasting" is common for Paul, as noted in the commentary at 1:26 and 2:16, where Paul uses the related noun (καύχημα).[46] The verb used in Philippians 3:3 occurs another thirty-four times in the apostle's writings,[47] and we need to grasp its nuances in Paul and the broader biblical literature, since modern Westerners normally hear the word "boast" as the negative act of a braggart. In fact, in the broader Greco-Roman context and in Judaism, appropriate boasting was viewed positively, as in an important passage for Paul, Jeremiah 9:23–24 (9:22–23 LXX):

> This is what the Lord says: Let not the wise boast in his wisdom, and let not the mighty boast in his might, and let not the wealthy boast in his wealth, but let him who boasts boast in this: that he understands and knows that I am the Lord when I do mercy and justice and righteousness in the earth, because in these things is my will, says the Lord. (NETS)

42. Silva, *Philippians*, 148.

43. The standard Greek texts read οἱ πνεύματι θεοῦ λατρεύοντες, "the ones serving by the Spirit of God" (א*A B C D$^{2}$ G K 33. 81. 614. 1739 it$^{g}$ sy$^{hmg}$ cop$^{sa, bo}$ al). On the other hand, 𝔓$^{46}$ reads πνεύματι, without a reference to God, but this probably should be understood as an accidental scribal omission. And several manuscripts read the dative θεῷ in place of the genitive, "the ones serving God in spirit" (א$^{2}$ D* P Ψ 88 it$^{d, ar}$ vg sy$^{p, h}$ goth eth Speculum), which turns the reference to God into an object. Of these, the first seems the strongest reading, both in terms of external witnesses and the likely scribal activity. So Fee, *Philippians*, 288; Metzger, *Textual Commentary*, 547.

44. So Fee, *Philippians*, 299–300. E.g., part of the contrast in the Pentateuch may be between the Israelites "serving" Pharaoh and them serving God (e.g., Exod 3:12; 4:23; 7:16, 26; 8:16; 9:1, 13; 23:24; Lev 18:21).

45. See Guthrie, *2 Corinthians*, 191–200; the dative of the word for "Spirit" (πνεύματι) may be read as a dative of agency ("through, by"), and the genitive "of God" (θεοῦ) perhaps as a genitive of apposition, "the Spirit who is God." The "Spirit" described as "God" (θεοῦ) also appears at Rom 8:9.

46. The noun is also used at Rom 4:2; 1 Cor 5:6; 9:15–16; 2 Cor 1:14; 5:12; 9:3; Gal 6:4.

47. E.g., Rom 2:17, 23; 5:2–3, 11; 1 Cor 1:29, 31; 2 Cor 5:12; Gal 6:13–14; Eph 2:9.

In this theologically loaded text, there exists a contrast between boasting in inappropriate things and boasting in the Lord himself. The key difference between the two clearly has to do with the *object* of one's boast.[48] The one who boasts must boast in the Lord. Accordingly, in the broader context of our passage, *knowing* the Lord (cf. Phil 3:10)—in light of his glorious mercy, justice, and righteousness—stands as the object of Paul's boast, for he boasts "in Christ Jesus" (ἐν Χριστῷ Ἰησοῦ).[49] Paul's exultation in life focuses preeminently on the grace-work of God in Christ. This stands in profound contrast to those who boast in themselves and their religious works.[50]

Finally, in keeping with those who serve by the Spirit and boast in Christ, Paul describes those associated with his mission as those who do not "place confidence in human standards" (καὶ οὐκ ἐν σαρκὶ πεποιθότες). Clearly, as this chapter unfolds, the apostle reveals that placing confidence in something other than Christ had been his posture prior to meeting Christ. The "human standards" he lists in Philippians 3:5–6 had been his "gain" (κέρδη, v. 7) but now have been reassessed in light of knowing Christ (vv. 8–11). Such had been the object of his confidence, but this is no longer the case.

The verb translated as "place confidence" (πείθω) has to do with "depending on" or "trusting in" someone or something.[51] For the apostle, trusting in something or someone other than Christ constitutes placing confidence "in human standards" (ἐν σαρκί),[52] a phrase often translated as "in the flesh" (ἐν σαρκί). The apostle uses this phrase fifteen times in his writings. It can be employed of the flesh of the human body (e.g., Rom 2:28; Gal 6:12), or of human existence generally (2 Cor 10:3; Gal 2:20; Col 2:1; 1 Tim 3:16; Phlm 16), or as that aspect of human existence in opposition to the ways and workings of God's Spirit (Rom 8:8–9). Here Paul uses this language as shorthand for "human standards," similar to the phrase "according to the flesh" (κατὰ σάρκα) used elsewhere (e.g., Rom 8:12; 1 Cor 1:26; 2 Cor 1:17; 5:16; 10:2; 11:18). Such earth-bound standards are not what true believers place their trust or confidence in; their trust is "in the Lord."

Yet in verse 4 Paul makes a strategic concession: "although I too have a basis for placing confidence in human standards" (καίπερ ἐγὼ ἔχων πεποίθησιν καὶ ἐν σαρκί). The conjunction rendered "although" (καίπερ), only found here in Paul, occurs elsewhere in the New Testament four times, with three occurrences in Hebrews (Heb 5:8; 7:5; 12:17; 2 Pet 1:12). As our translation depicts, the term communicates a note of concession.[53] The apostle's concession, however, does nothing to diminish his conviction concerning "fleshly" standards when it comes to relationship with God. Rather, he uses the concession to spotlight his radical posture concerning such things—his sole object of his confidence in life and death.[54] As noted above, the word for "confidence" connotes a state of reliance, trust, or confidence

48. In the LXX, the preposition "in" (ἐν) plus the dative (ἐν τούτῳ, "in this," LXX Jer 9:22) marks the "referent" of boasting.

49. "In Christ Jesus" (ἐν Χριστῷ Ἰησοῦ) is used with a different nuance from that in 1:26. For a slightly different interpretation, see Campbell, *Paul and Union with Christ*, 99, 101, 104, 111, 370.

50. E.g., see esp. 2 Cor 10:12–18 (see Guthrie, *2 Corinthians*, 486–501).

51. Here a substantival perfect participle used with the dative; BDAG 791–92.

52. For Paul, "flesh" (σάρξ) generally speaks of a human being as a person (e.g., Rom 3:20; Gal 1:16), or of the human body (e.g., 1 Cor 6:16; 2 Cor 7:1; 12:7; Gal 4:13), or simply of human life or human nature (e.g., Rom 4:1; 8:3; 9:8; 1 Cor 1:29). Negatively, the apostle employs "flesh" to connote an independence from or opposition to God (Rom 7:5; 8:8; 13:14; Gal 5:13–19). See Moo, *Epistle to the Romans*, 47.

53. BDF 219.

54. The use of the personal pronoun plus the present participle of the verb rendered "I have" (ἐγὼ ἔχων) is emphatic, as the

in something,[55] and again the basis of Paul's confidence lies elsewhere than "human standards." Nevertheless, although he does not trust in human standards, he too (καί)[56] has the credentials to do so if he wished.

The apostle continues with a "simple condition": "If some other person thinks he has the basis to place confidence in human standards, I have much more of a basis" (εἴ τις δοκεῖ ἄλλος πεποιθέναι ἐν σαρκί, ἐγὼ μᾶλλον).[57] Paul consistently uses the indefinite pronoun ("some other person," τίς) to refer to opponents without naming (and thus dignifying) them. Such references often come couched in a conditional clause, as here.[58] The term translated as "other" (ἄλλος) may serve simply to build up the contrast between Paul and those false teachers who put confidence in the flesh. If they trust in human standards (δοκεῖ . . . πεποιθέναι[59] ἐν σαρκί), Paul has a much stronger basis for doing so, communicated tersely yet intensely[60] with the verbless, punchy little clause, "I [have] much more!" (ἐγὼ μᾶλλον).

## IN DEPTH: The "Opponents" of Paul in Rome and Philippi

One of the most debated issues in Philippians research concerns the identity of the so-called opponents to whom the apostle alludes.[61] His statements are mere allusions, not overt descriptions or identifications, which explains why their identity has been elusive, producing so many interpretations—as many as eighteen, by one count.[62] Some scholars see various groups of opponents in Philippians,[63] while others believe the allusions are to one group.[64] The two passages that generate the most discussion are 1:15–17 and 3:2–3.

For example, concerning the identity of the opponents alluded to at Philippians 1:15–17, scholars have proposed variously that they are:

1. Jewish agitators who have followed (or preceded) Paul to Rome and preach their heresy as they have elsewhere[65]

apostle underscores his credentials. Of course, the object of the participle "placing confidence" (πεποίθησις) is cognate with the participle at the end of v. 3.

55. BDAG 796.

56. The conjunction interpreted adjunctively ("also").

57. It is a first-class conditional clause in the balance of v. 4, with the protasis assumed to be true and the main verb in the indicative.

58. See, e.g., the extensive use in 2 Corinthians at 2:5; 3:1; 10:2, 7, 12; 11:16, 20–21; 12:6, and the comments by Guthrie, *2 Corinthians*, 131, 478.

59. The perfect infinitive is complementary to the main verb δοκεῖ.

60. See 1:15–17, 27–28; 3:2–3, 18–19; Fee, *Philippians*, 306.

61. I do not include 2:21, where Paul primarily celebrates Timothy's integrity over against others in the circle whom he might send rather than addressing the issue of false teachers or opponents.

62. So Fee, *Philippians*, 7.

63. E.g., Robert Jewett, "Conflicting Movements in the Early Church as Reflected in Philippians," *NovT* 12 (1970): 362–90.

64. E.g., Chris Mearns, "The Identity of Paul's Opponents at Philippi," *NTS* 33 (1987): 194–204.

65. So, e.g., Johann Albrecht Bengel, *Gnomon of the New Testament, Tr., with Notes, Revised and Ed. by A. R. Fausset*

2. Christian ministers who were in Rome before Paul, who preach the gospel but, motivated by personal rivalry, also are trying to hurt Paul, treating him as a rival[66]
3. The same troublemakers with whom Paul tangled in the Corinthian correspondence[67]
4. Christian preachers who are speaking against the Roman authorities, proclaiming an anti-imperial message, and thus adding to Paul's troubles[68]
5. Political rivals, whether Jewish antagonists or not, who seek to do Paul harm through public discussions about his person and message[69]

Concerning the identity of the opponents alluded to at Philippians 3:2–3, we find similar suggestions. The most common proposals are that these false teachers are:

1. Gnostic Christian missionaries, who hold a form of perfectionism surrounding the law[70]
2. Gnostic Christian missionaries, who are libertines rather than perfectionists[71]
3. Jewish missionaries, who offer a perfectionism based on law[72]
4. Jewish-Christian missionaries ("Jewish agitators"), who preach circumcision as a means to gain perfection/righteousness[73]

(Edinburgh: T&T Clark, 1857), 4:124; Lightfoot, *Philippians*, 88; Heinrich August Wilhelm Meyer, *The Epistles to the Philippians and Colossians*, trans. John C. Moore and William P. Dicksone (Edinburgh: T&T Clark, 1875), 36; Ellicott, *Commentary*, 17–18.

66. We see this position in Oscar Cullmann's suggestion, based on parallels with 1 Clement, that personal rivalry and animosity toward the apostles in the church at Rome form the backdrop of Paul's situation. See Oscar Cullmann, *Peter, Disciple, Apostle, Martyr: A Historical and Theological Study*, trans. F. Filson (London: SCM, 1953), 104–9; cf. Vincent, *Philippians*, 19; Witherington, *Philippians*, 80.

67. On which, see Guthrie, *2 Corinthians*, 41–46. See also T. W. Manson and Matthew Black, *Studies in the Gospels and Epistles* (Manchester: Manchester University Press, 1962), 161–63, who take Paul as alluding to the factionalism such as that found in Corinth and Galatia. Manson sees the factionalism stemming from Paul's conflict with Jewish-Christian elements in the churches, so there is overlap here with the "Judaizer" position.

68. T. Hawthorn, "Philippians 1:12–19: with Special Reference to vv 15, 16, 17," *ExpTim* 62.10 (1951): 316–17.

69. This is my position, as detailed in the commentary on 1:15–17.

70. E.g., Helmut Koester, "The Purpose of the Polemic of a Pauline Fragment," *NTS* 8 (1961): 317–32.

71. W. Schmittals, "Die Irrlehrer des Philipperbriefes," *ZTK* 54 (1957): 297–341.

72. A. F. J. Klijn, "Paul's Opponents in Philippians iii," *NovT* 7 (1964): 278–84.

73. Jewett, "Conflicting Movements." Jewett sees the situation as hypothetical, these false teachers not having arrived in Philippi as yet; similarly Francis Watson, *Paul, Judaism, and the Gentiles: Beyond the New Perspective* (Grand Rapids: Eerdmans, 2007), 143; Mearns, "Identity." On these and a variety of other positions, see Reumann, *Philippians*, 470.

Obviously, there is overlap between these lists. So what can we say about the myriad of options? Rather than a full-blown treatment, which would have to be book length, I offer a few preliminary points and then make suggestions that attempt to sort through the evidence.

As for preliminary thoughts, consider first that the language of each of these passages is notoriously ambiguous and thwarts any dogmatic certainty. There are tantalizing clues, such as the reference to circumcision at 3:2–3, but specific details on the exact identity of the opponents are few and far between. Therefore, we are constrained by the limits of the text and should be careful about filling out a picture of the opponents that goes beyond the evidence. Second, during his ministry Paul had various types of opponents in the Mediterranean region—some political and others religious—and more than one group could be alluded to in Philippians. While it might be simpler to propose one opponent group behind Paul's comments in the letter—a view that may be accurate—reality is often messier than our theories allow. Finally, in considering Paul's statements at 1:15–17 and those at 3:2–3, we are dealing with at least two primary social contexts—Paul's imprisonment (1:15–17) and the city of Philippi itself (1:27–30; 3:2–3, 18–19). Thus it is possible that we are dealing with two different types of opponents, or at least two groups of opponents, one located in the city of the apostle's confinement and the other in Philippi.

My suggestions concerning the opponents in Philippians are as follows. As detailed in the commentary at 1:15–17, we are unsure of the exact agenda of the opponents whom Paul faces in his imprisonment. Are they Jewish agitators? Political opponents of another orientation? We simply are not sure; but whoever they are, they are embroiled in conflict with Paul in a very public way, in a political context, and in a way that involves discussions and/or proclamations about Christ and the gospel. I do not believe that Paul regards them to be true Christian ministers. They try to hurt the apostle by speaking of Christ and are therefore distinct from those who were encouraged by Paul's imprisonment to preach the gospel (1:14). In 1:18 Paul says that Christ is preached by these opponents, which we understand to mean that the opponents are speaking publicly about Christ. They inadvertently are spreading the message as they speak publicly about Paul and his message.[74]

So we cannot know whether the opponents in Paul's place of incarceration (1:15–17) were Jewish antagonists, Jewish agitators, or political adversaries with other motives. Given Paul's mild response to their message at 1:18,

74. For a defense of this position, see the commentary at 1:15–18.

I doubt they were Jewish agitators or the false teachers of Corinth. Paul did not speak mildly about false teachers, whom he saw as peddling a false gospel to the devastation of the church (e.g., 2 Cor 2:16–17; 11:4; Gal 1:6). In any case, at 1:15–17 there is no evidence of false teaching. It seems clear that the opponents were working against Paul in a public, political context, seeking to do him harm by speaking about Christ publicly, and *this is the key point*. They are not doing Christian evangelism. They speak of Christ *to hurt Paul* (v. 17). It may be that they stir up trouble for Paul by publicly opposing him and his message, even as they inadvertently make that message better known.[75]

In Philippians 1:27–28 we also encounter opponents, but these oppose the church in Philippi. Again, Paul is not explicit as to the nature of the opposition other than it is public, involves intimidation, is causing suffering for the church, and in some way parallels Paul's own situation (vv. 28–30). I take this to mean that this opposition experienced by the Philippians also was in the public square and, at least to some degree, political or civic. Richard Cassidy writes:

> The struggle and suffering that Paul experiences result from measures imposed by the Roman authorities at Rome. Yet at 1:30 Paul's words indicate that the Philippians are engaged in the same struggle and suffering that are Paul's. In what way is it the same? It is the same because these measures are being initiated in both cities by authorities vested with power in the imperial system. The Roman authorities at Philippi are thus the "opponents" of the Philippian Christians that Paul mentions at 1:28. Indeed, only the Roman authorities hold enough power to cause suffering for the Philippian Christian community as a whole.[76]

Thus the Philippians probably were oppressed by the authorities in Philippi, perhaps because they were refusing to celebrate the pagan and imperial cults of the city or were withdrawing from the associations of the city (which often involved pagan worship practices), or a combination of the two. In other words, the followers of Jesus were at odds with the cultural and civic agendas of Philippi and were paying a price for their countercultural lifestyles.

It seems that the opponents to which Paul alludes at 3:2–3, and perhaps at 3:18–19, are more hypothetical. Paul is not dealing with immediate threats but warning the Philippians based on his broader experience of ministry. Unlike Paul's battle with the opponents of 2 Corinthians, for instance, it does not seem that any of the believers in Philippi had been drawn into error. The "watch

75. For a modern example of this dynamic, see the "Theology in Application" section for 1:12–18g.

76. Cassidy, *Paul in Chains*, 169–70.

out for dogs" of 3:2 simply warns against Jewish agitators that the Philippians might encounter at some point, and they serve as a foil for Paul to speak of his own example of committed Christian leadership. The "many" who live as "enemies of the cross of Christ" (3:18–19) are potential opponents who may come to Philippi and set a false example of leadership. Paul speaks of them as a counterpoint to his own example as detailed in 3:2–14.

Thus, I suggest that in Philippians Paul addresses both real and hypothetical opponents. On the one hand, he and the Philippians are publicly opposed, probably in politically charged contexts. Yet, on the other, the apostle warns against future threats, calling for the church to follow his example in life and teaching. This will help them to recognize false teachers when they appear on the streets of Philippi.

**3:5–6 circumcised on the eighth day, of the people of Israel, of the tribe of Benjamin, a Hebrew of Hebrews; with respect to the law, a Pharisee; with respect to zeal, a persecutor of the church; with respect to righteousness occurring by means of the law, blameless** (περιτομῇ ὀκταήμερος, ἐκ γένους Ἰσραήλ, φυλῆς Βενιαμίν, Ἑβραῖος ἐξ Ἑβραίων, κατὰ νόμον Φαρισαῖος, 6 κατὰ ζῆλος διώκων τὴν ἐκκλησίαν, κατὰ δικαιοσύνην τὴν ἐν νόμῳ γενόμενος ἄμεμπτος). Paul now itemizes his credentials from the vantage point of "human standards" (ἐν σαρκί, 3:3–4). Joseph Hellerman has made the case that in this rapid-fire list of status standards, the apostle follows the pattern of a Roman *cursus honorum* (a "course" or "race of honors")—a listing of honors like those found in the inscriptions of Philippi. In Paul's list, the first four honors are associated with his birth, followed by three achieved in adult life, which is the same pattern found in honors lists of the era.[77] Yet rather than playing the "honors game" so valued in the broader culture, Paul offers his credentials to point to their vapidity in comparison to knowing Christ.

First, the apostle notes that he was "circumcised on the eighth day" (περιτομῇ ὀκταήμερος). Given to Abraham as the "sign of the covenant," cutting off the male foreskin served in Judaism as a picture of commitment to God's ways.[78] The word translated as "eighth day" (ὀκταήμερος) is an adjective but functions like a noun, "an eighth-day-person." In the Jewish religion, the eighth day was significant as a day of dedication or "ritual viability,"[79] and Jewish males were circumcised on the eighth day, following the Abrahamic covenant and the law (Gen 17:12; Lev 12:3; cf. Luke 1:59; 2:21).

Underscoring his Jewish pedigree, Paul continues that he was "of the people of Israel" (ἐκ γένους Ἰσραήλ) and "of the tribe of Benjamin" (φυλῆς

77. Hellerman, *Philippians*, 176; idem, *Reconstructing Honor*, 121–27.

78. E.g., one had to be circumcised to participate in the Passover celebration (Exod 12:43–49), and Joshua had all the Israelite males circumcised at Gilgal as Israel entered the land of Canaan (Josh 5:2–9). The practice, rather than a badge of honor, was disparaged in broader Greco-Roman culture, as seen in Tacitus, *Hist.* 5.2; Strabo, *Geography* 16.2.37; Suetonius, *Domitian* 12.2. See David A. Bernat, "Circumcision," in *EDEJ* 471, 474.

79. So Bernat, "Circumcision," 471; e.g., Lev 14:10, 23; 15:14, 29; 22:27; 23:36, 39; Num 6:10; 7:54; 29:35; 2 Chr 7:9; 29:17; Neh 8:18; Ezek 43:27.

Βενιαμίν). The term translated here as "people" (γένος) could be used to refer to a "class" or "kind" of person or thing, or even a smaller group or family with a common ancestry. But here Paul refers to the "nation" or "people" of Israel.[80] The most common self-designation of the Jewish people in the ancient world, it evoked their election as God's chosen race. Paul thus evokes the designation, even though elsewhere he challenges the presupposition that physical descent marks the boundaries of God's people (Rom 9:6; 11:13–24).[81] Nevertheless, it was an important religious designation. So as for race Paul claims to be a religious insider.

The apostle more particularly was of Benjamin's tribe (cf. Rom 11:1), which had nuanced overtones that may have been lost on the Philippians. Nevertheless, even if they knew nothing of Rachel's son, whose tribe was "beloved of the Lord" (Deut 33:12), or of Paul's namesake, King Saul (Acts 7:58), or of the Benjaminite Mordecai (Esth 2:5) celebrated at Purim, they would have placed great value on belonging to an ancient tribe, such as the Voltinia, a group often mentioned in the inscriptions of Philippi.[82]

Further, the apostle writes that he was "a Hebrew of Hebrews" (Ἑβραῖος ἐξ Ἑβραίων), pointing to the purity of his heritage, with both parents hailing from Jewish families. Fee calls this a "swing" term, a hinge "summing up the preceding three" designations "and setting the stage for the final three."[83] Most Jews of the diaspora, and many in Israel, embraced Greek as their spoken language and read the Scriptures in that language. The description "Hebrew" served as technical language for Jews who spoke Hebrew or Aramaic as a primary language and read the Scriptures in that language.[84] A "Hebrew," moreover, was a religious traditionalist who valued the language, the land, and the practices of the Jewish religion.[85] Thus Paul's emphatic label, "a Hebrew of Hebrews," connotes exuberant pride in his heritage.

With the words "with respect to the law, a Pharisee" (κατὰ νόμον Φαρισαῖος), the apostle turns to a particular embodiment of the practice of Judaism that was focused on adherence to the law of God. There were approximately six thousand Pharisees in Israel during Paul's era. The sect of the Pharisees (a term derived from Hebrew, meaning "separatist") taught that an oral Torah had been given alongside the written law at Sinai. Their belief was that the oral law had been handed down through the prophets and teachers of Israel and addressed all aspects of a Jew's daily life, especially issues related to purity.[86] That Paul belonged to the Pharisees (Acts 23:6–9; 26:5; Gal 1:14) means that he took observance of the law with deadly seriousness.[87]

This commitment to the law was manifested in Paul's persecution of the church ("with respect to zeal, a persecutor of the church," κατὰ ζῆλος διώκων τὴν ἐκκλησίαν)—referring to the universal church rather than to a specific local congregation.[88] The term for "zeal" (ζῆλος) could be used to communicate intense, negative feelings such as jealousy (e.g., Rom 13:13; 1 Cor 3:3), but here perhaps refers to "intense positive interest in something . . . marked by a sense of dedication."[89] For instance, elsewhere

80. BDAG 194.

81. Hansen, *Philippians*, 223.

82. Bockmuehl, *Philippians*, 196.

83. Fee, *Philippians*, 307.

84. See Acts 6:1; Philo, *Moses* 2.32; cf. Acts 21:40; 22:22; 2 Cor 11:22.

85. Bockmuehl, *Philippians*, 196, following Martin Hengel and Roland Deines, *The Pre-Christian Paul* (London: SCM; Philadelphia: Trinity Press, 1991), 4–6.

86. Jacob Neusner and William Scott Green, eds., *Dictionary of Judaism in the Biblical Period: 450 B.C.E. to 600 C.E.* (New York: Macmillan Library Reference, 1996), 478–79.

87. Reumann, *Philippians*, 484–85.

88. So Fee, *Philippians*, 308.

89. BDAG 427.

the apostle speaks positively of the Corinthians' interest in him, or of a godly zeal (2 Cor 7:7, 11; 9:2; 11:2). Of course, "positive interest" and "dedication" can be badly skewed or misdirected. Paul had persecuted the church out of such zeal for God, and like some of his Jewish compatriots, he had lacked an appropriate foundation for such zeal (Rom 10:2).

Finally, in this list of credentials the apostle notes that "with respect to righteousness occurring by means of the law" he had been "blameless" (κατὰ δικαιοσύνην τὴν ἐν νόμῳ γενόμενος ἄμεμπτος). The concept of "righteousness" (δικαιοσύνη) in Paul is notoriously complex. At times the apostle points to a righteousness that can only be found in relationship with Christ (e.g., Rom 1:17; 2 Cor 5:21), such as when he speaks of a "righteousness from God" (3:9). More generally, however, Doug Moo points out that the term in the Greek Old Testament functions as "covenant" language, pointing to a pattern of life flowing from the Israelites' covenant commitments,[90] and this understanding fits Paul's use of the term here.

The phrase "by means of the law" (ἐν νόμῳ) functions adjectivally and is instrumental,[91] pointing to a particular form of righteousness. At the end of Philippians 3:5, Paul had already noted that "with respect to the law" (κατὰ νόμον) he had been a Pharisee, focused resolutely on how to live out God's commands. In 3:9 he will speak of his embodiment of this form of righteousness (δικαιοσύνη) as "a righteousness of my own issuing from the law" (3:9). By the standards of Pharisaism, which offered an "in-the-law righteousness," Paul proclaims that he was "blameless" (ἄμεμπτος). As noted in the commentary at 2:15, this word for "blameless" speaks of being "faultless" or "above reproach" and is used to connote righteous living before God and others. Thus this is not a claim of sinlessness—since the law made provisions for repentance and forgiveness—but rather is a claim of scrupulous attention to living according to the written and oral Torah.[92] Thus, Paul caps off this list of honorable qualifications with a claim to have lived out a pattern of conformity to the Mosaic law.

**3:7–8e —whatever were gains for me!—I consider these things as loss for the sake of Christ. Indeed, even more than that, I consider all things to be loss because of the far more valuable knowledge of Christ Jesus my Lord** ([Ἀλλ᾽] ἅτινα ἦν μοι κέρδη, ταῦτα ἥγημαι διὰ τὸν Χριστὸν ζημίαν. 8 ἀλλὰ μενοῦνγε καὶ ἡγοῦμαι πάντα ζημίαν εἶναι διὰ τὸ ὑπερέχον τῆς γνώσεως Χριστοῦ Ἰησοῦ τοῦ κυρίου μου). All things considered an advantage, or markers of worth, Paul considers a "loss" compared to the much greater value attached to knowing Christ.[93] The real culmination of the list may be the summary statement, "whatever were gains for me," followed by the declaration, "I consider these things as loss." The "whatever" (ἅτινα) broadens Paul's list of achievements to anything that might be considered praiseworthy or beneficial from the standpoint of human standards or values.[94]

90. Moo, *Epistle to the Romans*, 80.

91. Wallace, *Greek Grammar*, 357, 372.

92. Hellerman, *Philippians*, 180; see 4QMMT 113, 117 for a "righteousness according to Torah," as noted by Bockmuehl, *Philippians*, 201.

93. As indicated by the brackets in the standard texts, ἀλλ᾽ at the beginning of v. 7 is disputed, with good reason. Michael Holmes's *SBL Edition of the Greek New Testament* includes ἀλλά and, following Westcott and Hort, does so without elision. The word is omitted by 𝔓[46.61vid] א* A G 0282. 33. 81. 1241 b d; Lcf Ambst and included by א[2] B D F K L P Ψ 075. 104. 365. 630. 1175. 1505. 1739. 1881. 2464 𝔐 lat sy co. Certainly, since a strong, contrastive conjunction fits so well in context, the omission is the more difficult reading and the external evidence supports it; thus, Fee suggests the omission is likely the original reading (Fee, *Philippians*, 311). Nevertheless, the contrast is certainly inherent in the context.

94. BDAG 729; Hellerman, *Philippians*, 180. The pronoun,

The content of verses 5 and 6 "was" (ἦν) Paul's "gain" (κέρδη) prior to meeting Christ Jesus. We have already seen this word for "gain" at Philippians 1:21, where Paul notes that "to die is gain" (τὸ ἀποθανεῖν κέρδος)—that is, "gain" in the sense of "to the apostle's advantage." The only other occurrence of the noun in biblical literature is at Titus 1:11, where the apostle speaks of false teachers who minister for dishonest "gain." The term and its cognate verb (κερδαίνω) thus could speak of profit, advantage, or acquisitions of value. In Koine Greek, these words had taken on religious meaning as well. For example, the verb could be used to speak of "gaining" one's brother (Matt 18:15), or Paul himself could write about "gaining" converts (1 Cor 9:20–22).[95] The noun as used here in Philippians 3 tells us something about Paul's past perspective on his human credentials—the list of honors noted in 3:5–6. Personally, he had considered such credentials advantageous (μοι).[96]

Nevertheless, things of worth are a matter of perspective. "These things" (ταῦτα) in his list of credentials (3:5–6)—indeed "whatever" could be seen as advantageous (3:7a)—are assessed differently by Paul after meeting Christ on the Damascus Road. Although the verb translated "consider" (ἡγέομαι) could refer to the practice of leadership, the apostle uses the term here with the sense of "believe, think, consider."[97] "These things" formerly were considered worthy or advantageous but now are regarded from a different perspective—as "loss" (ζημία). Thus Paul's assessment of what matters in life has been radically changed.[98] Whereas "gain" (κέρδος) has to do with gain or advantage,[99] the word rendered "loss" (ζημία) is its opposite, speaking of "disadvantage" or that which one forfeits.[100] We would have to be biblically tone-deaf not to hear the words of Jesus behind Paul's thoughts: "What benefit would it be for someone to gain the whole world, yet lose their soul?" (Mark 8:36//Luke 9:25//Matt 16:26).[101] For Paul, all those things he had considered gain he has now forfeited for the sake of the gospel.[102]

This quote from John Barclay concerns the exchange that takes place when one turns to Christ and correspondingly away from things formerly considered of supreme worth:

> The old taken-for-granted systems of value are here undercut; former taxonomies of worth cease to be significant. This is what makes it possible to create new communities in which "there is neither

moreover, functions as a pendent nominative, with the whole relative clause summed up in the accusative plural ταῦτα ("these things") that follows. See Wallace, *Greek Grammar*, 51–53.

95. *TLNT* 2:157–60.

96. The Gk. pronoun understood as a dative of advantage.

97. *EDNT* 2:113.

98. Contra, e.g., Hansen, *Philippians*, 233; there is no need to overemphasize the intellectual orientation of Paul's new way of looking at the world, although of course he had learned to love the Lord in new ways with his mind. His radical change was more through personal confrontation by Christ on the Damascus Road than the result of "an intellectual process" (Hansen, quoting BDAG).

99. The double accusative construction, ταῦτα . . . ζημίαν, provides the object of the verb and its complement. See Wallace, *Greek Grammar*, 185–86.

100. BDAG 428.

101. In Jesus's words, the verbal cognates κερδαίνω and ζημιόω are used. On the connection with Jesus's teaching here, see Michael B. Thompson, *Clothed with Christ: The Example and Teaching of Jesus in Romans 12.1–15.13*, JSNTSup 59 (Sheffield: JSOT Press, 1991).

102. We also hear considerable echoes of the Christ *hymnos* at 2:6–11. So, e.g., Fee, *Philippians*, 314–15; Silva, *Philippians*, 155. Paul no longer considered or "regarded" the content of his honors list as gain, just as Christ did not "regard [ἡγήσατο] equality with God a status to be used for his own advantage" (2:6; 3:7–8). As Christ "stripped himself of the status" he held, so Paul has turned away from status-building religious markers, considering them "loss" (2:6–7; 3:7–8). Christ was "found" (εὑρεθείς) in appearance to look like a normal person, Paul is now "found" (εὑρεθῶ) to be in Christ (2:7; 3:9). This means "death" for Paul, just as it did for Christ (2:8; 3:10), but also glorious vindication (2:9; 3:11).

Jew nor Gentile, neither slave nor free, no male and female" (Gal 3.28), experimental communities which subvert old hierarchies of value and create new possibilities of mutual enhancement. In these communities, far from the old jostling for position according to criteria of human worth, there is a new anti-competitive spirit, in which each is able to contribute to the other from the security of knowing that their worth is underwritten by the love of God in Christ, a worth that is unaffected by their social status or popularity, by their wealth or success, by their ethnicity or gender. Throughout his letters, Paul is able to undercut the contest culture that ruled his honour-obsessed society, giving value not to being the best, but to humility and service to others, because his communities were not founded on the normal values of competitive worth. Being called in grace, and being found in Christ, was all the worth that counted, and the worth that counted for everything. Part of what Paul means by freedom is this liberation from human criteria of worth.[103]

Accordingly, the key to Paul's thought concerns why he has experienced such a radical reassessment of what he formerly valued. He did so "for the sake of Christ" (διὰ τὸν Χριστόν), which we should hear as having profoundly relational overtones. The phrase is rendered variously as "because of Christ"[104] (e.g., NRSV, CSB, NET) or "for the sake of Christ" (e.g., NASB, ESV, NIV).[105] Deciding between the two options isn't necessary, since both constitute the reason for Paul's radical reevaluation of values. Was it "retrospective," looking back to the impetus for his change—namely, that Christ had met him and changed him?[106] Certainly. Was it prospective, a giving up of all for the goal of gaining Christ? Certainly. Christ was the reason for his radical change in perspective. Initiated on the Damascus Road, this dramatic change continued to shape his life and would culminate with the apostle reaching the "goal" (3:12, 14), as he goes on to elaborate in the following verses.

Verse 8 begins a sentence that runs all the way through verse 11 and sums up the great value that for Paul has replaced all other values—knowing Christ, "the relationship which suffuses, empowers, and motivates all that he is and does."[107] He writes, "Indeed, even more than that, I consider all things to be loss because of the far more valuable knowledge of Christ Jesus my Lord" (ἀλλὰ μενοῦνγε καὶ ἡγοῦμαι πάντα ζημίαν εἶναι διὰ τὸ ὑπερέχον τῆς γνώσεως Χριστοῦ Ἰησοῦ τοῦ κυρίου μου). The sentence begins with a flurry of conjunctions. The first (ἀλλά) can be read as contrastive ("but"), but I prefer to translate it here as ascensive ("indeed"). Carrying a note of correction,[108] Paul puts in place the next conjunction (μενοῦνγε), which communicates the sense of "rather," "on the contrary."[109] Finally Paul adds καί, which here may be adjunctive ("also" or "even").[110] It seems, then, that at the beginning of verse 8 Paul has combined

103. John Barclay, "Paul, Grace, and Liberation from Human Judgments of Worth" (lecture delivered at Concordia Seminary, St. Louis, MO, 2017), 9–10.

104. BDF 119.

105. As noted by Robertson, *Grammar*, 583–84.

106. So, e.g., Fee, *Philippians*, 315; Reumann, *Philippians*, 489.

107. Bockmuehl, *Philippians*, 206.

108. In classical Greek, the construction μεν οὖν or μεν οὖν γε could be used to correct or heighten something just stated; see BDF 234.

109. The constructions ἀλλὰ μεν, ἀλλὰ οὖν γε, and ἀλλὰ καί were common in Greco-Roman literature, as was the construction μεν οὖν. Paul uses μενοῦνγε twice elsewhere (Rom 9:20; 10:18), and there too he sounds a note of emphatic correction. Margaret Thrall understands the complex construction at the beginning of v. 8 as a combination of ἀλλὰ καί and μενοῦνγε, the latter added for emphasis: "not only so but all the more." Yet this is not a normal "not only . . . but" construction. See Silva, *Philippians*, 168; Thrall, *Greek Particles*, 11–16; Fee, *Philippians*, 317.

110. We should note that γε καί in the NT, the LXX, and broader Greco-Roman literature seems to be adjunctive, with

these constructions in a way that is awkward, but they communicate a transition that is ascensive ("indeed"), additive ("even"), contrastive ("on the contrary"), and thus strongly emphatic—"Indeed, even more than that!"[111] In essence, the apostle takes the loss of "these things" mentioned in 3:7 and expands the idea to cover "all things" in verse 8:

I consider **these things** loss
ταῦτα ἥγημαι . . . ζημίαν (v. 7)
Indeed, even more than that!
ἀλλὰ μενοῦνγε καί (v. 8a)
I consider all **things** loss
ἡγοῦμαι πάντα ζημίαν εἶναι (v. 8b)

Thus, Paul's abandonment of the religious worth of his former life is absolute and all-inclusive. He has given up "all things" considered of value by "human standards" (v. 4). They are an absolute or total loss, completely thrown over by the opportunity of gaining Christ: "Because of the far more valuable knowledge of Christ Jesus my Lord" (διὰ τὸ ὑπερέχον τῆς γνώσεως Χριστοῦ Ἰησοῦ τοῦ κυρίου μου). The cause (διά) of Paul's radical commitment? He was confronted with something "far more valuable" (τὸ ὑπερέχον). The word speaks of that which surpasses, excels, or is better than something else.[112]

What, then, was so valuable? First, some form of "knowledge,"[113] particularly knowledge "of Christ Jesus my Lord," which anticipates the expansion of the topic in verses 10–11. Paul first gained the knowledge he has in mind through personal confrontation on the Damascus Road, and he continued to learn of Christ in his life and ministry. Although this is knowledge "about Jesus,"[114] it is no mere gathering of information. Rather, the apostle speaks of a profound relational knowledge. Of course, we must learn about someone in order to know them personally. Accordingly, the apostle sometimes speaks of a basic "understanding" or "knowledge" of Christ or of the Christian faith as essential for discipleship (e.g., Rom 15:14; 1 Cor 1:5; 2 Cor 2:14; 4:6; Col 2:3). Such knowledge is foundational. Yet the knowledge permeating this passage runs deeper than just cognitive assent to a set of ideas.

Paul speaks elsewhere of Judaism having a form of knowledge based on the law (Rom 2:20), but here we have a fundamentally different type of knowledge. Neither is this a type of philosophical knowledge found in the broader Greco-Roman world—an insider's knowledge, both mystical and intellectual. Rather, Paul speaks of an intimate, relational knowledge of another person, as we see further in verse 10. As we have already noted, "knowing the Lord" is a concept with a rich Old Testament background (e.g., Jer 9:23–24). This intimate form of knowledge involves revelation, which leads to personal, intimate relationship with God, about which we will say more momentarily. Thus Christ is not just "Lord"[115] for Paul. He calls him "my Lord" (τοῦ κυρίου μου).[116]

the sense of "even," communicating the idea of something added for consideration.

111. Most of the standard English versions render the combination as "more than that" (NASB, NRSV, CSB, NET; cf. NIV: "what is more") or "indeed" (ESV), but the emphatic nature of the construction demands more.

112. BDAG 1033. Here we have the article plus the present active form of the participle, from ὑπερέχω.

113. Perhaps an attributed genitive—i.e., "the exceedingly great" or "the far more valuable knowledge." On this syntax category, see Wallace, *Greek Grammar*, 90; Hellerman, *Philippians*, 183.

114. BDAG 1033.

115. On Christ as "Lord," see the commentary at 2:11. On "knowing the Lord," see the commentary under 3:9 below.

116. Fee, *Philippians*, 318. The phrase τοῦ κυρίου μου, moreover, is appositional to Χριστοῦ Ἰησοῦ.

**3:8f–9 for whose sake I have lost all things and consider them crap in order that I might gain Christ and be found in him, not having a righteousness of my own issuing from the law, but rather through trust in Christ, a righteousness from God on the basis of trust** (δι᾽ ὃν τὰ πάντα ἐζημιώθην, καὶ ἡγοῦμαι σκύβαλα, ἵνα Χριστὸν κερδήσω 9 καὶ εὑρεθῶ ἐν αὐτῷ, μὴ ἔχων ἐμὴν δικαιοσύνην τὴν ἐκ νόμου ἀλλὰ τὴν διὰ πίστεως Χριστοῦ, τὴν ἐκ θεοῦ δικαιοσύνην ἐπὶ τῇ πίστει). Paul continues an evaluation of the status-marking "honors" of his past life and here writes an especially poignant statement about his motivation. For the sake of Christ, all things have become "loss" and are considered "crap." The apostle has thrown over his past life and accomplishments to "gain" Christ and the righteousness of life that God brings to a person on the basis of trust in Christ. Paul's words hit the reader as profoundly Christocentric, as the apostle drives home this motivation with a repetition of language having to do with Christ:

| | |
|---|---|
| "for the sake of Christ" | διὰ τὸν Χριστὸν (3:7c) |
| "because of the far more valuable knowledge of Christ Jesus my Lord" | διὰ τὸ ὑπερέχον τῆς γνώσεως Χριστοῦ Ἰησοῦ τοῦ κυρίου μου (3:8d–e) |
| "for whose sake" | δι᾽ ὃν (3:8f) |

In each case, Paul's former credentials and assets that afforded a certain status in his world had to be revalued as "loss" for the sake of gaining a relationship with Christ.

| | |
|---|---|
| "I consider these things as loss" | ταῦτα ἥγημαι . . . ζημίαν (3:7b) |
| "I consider all things to be loss" | ἡγοῦμαι πάντα ζημίαν εἶναι (3:8c) |
| "I have lost all things and consider them crap" | τὰ πάντα ἐζημιώθην, καὶ ἡγοῦμαι σκύβαλα (3:8f–g) |

So the repetitions rhetorically drive home the much greater value of knowing Christ and the appropriateness of taking a loss for his sake.[117] In ways that are significant, Paul varies his language in his expressions of loss. When in verse 7 he says that he has "considered" (ἥγημαι) these things as loss, the verb form connotes not only a past decision but one that constitutes an ongoing state. This ongoing commitment is also expressed with present-tense forms of the same verb in verse 8.[118] In other words, when Paul met Christ his value system changed and his new perspective continues to drive his life.

The verb communicating loss (ζημιόω)[119] at times is associated with suffering and hardship, what one has forfeited, or the sustaining of an injury.[120] Paul's meaning is clear. Embracing Christ has cost him everything by which he would have assessed his standing in the world. And yet the apostle does not dwell on the great value of what has been lost—just the opposite. For the sake of knowing Christ, Paul labeled "all things" (τὰ πάντα) as having a value on the level with "crap." We have translated the word (σκύβαλα, a plural form of σκύβαλον)

117. So Hooker, "Philippians," 526–27.

118. In the second set of repetitions, the aspect of the verbs is significant: ἥγημαι in v. 7 is a perfect middle and thus stative, perhaps reaching back to Paul's conversion experience and carried forward to his current posture. In v. 8, however, the apostle switches to a present form of the same verb (ἡγοῦμαι), thus communicating imperfective aspect, an ongoing posture. With the latter part of v. 8, the reevaluation is expressed slightly differently, as the apostle shifts from the noun translated as "loss" (ζημία) to the related verb "I have lost [ζημιόω] all things." Here we have perfective aspect, which offers a summary of his loss. Yet he continues with ἡγοῦμαι again in its present middle toward the end of v. 8, again communicating an ongoing posture toward "all things" that could be set over against Christ.

119. This verb is only found in the passive voice in the NT, and as BDF 87 suggests it may have moved to a middle meaning, to "lose." See, e.g., Matt 16:26; Mark 8:36; Luke 9:25; 1 Cor 3:15; 2 Cor 7:9.

120. BDAG 428.

crudely, for it is crude,[121] intended to jar with its baseness. As some commentators have noted, the English slang "crap"[122] conveys how a person on the street in the ancient world might have heard Paul's language here. The term could refer to table scraps, debris, and refuse and was commonly used of dung or excrement.[123] In other words, Paul refers to stuff fit only for the garbage or to be thrown out as sewage—not only disposable but filthy.

The apostle's point is not to denigrate his Jewish heritage (cf. Rom 3:1–2; 9:1–5) but to explain the abandonment of that heritage as an identity marker of supreme value. Commenting on Galatians 2:15–16, John Barclay notes that for Paul, "Jewish ethnicity is no longer the primary form of self-identification, or the ultimate determinant of norms. Jewishness is not obliterated but relativized in its normative significance by the superior status of belonging to Christ."[124] The same perspective is at work in our passage. All that could be valued above Christ from an earth-bound perspective—including, for Paul, his Jewish heritage with its religious identity and pattern of life—has been thrown over for the vastly greater value of knowing Christ. There is no comparison. Christ is supremely valued, and even things that are "good" or "honorable" in the world's eyes must be put in their proper place. Paul has not replaced his Judaism; he has embraced Christ himself as the true embodiment of and fulfillment of Judaism.

Moreover, Paul has treated *all* things as if they were sewage, "in order that" he "might gain Christ" (ἵνα Χριστὸν κερδήσω).[125] So what does it mean to "gain Christ?" We have already seen in verse 8 that "gaining" in some sense means "knowing the Lord," which will be unpacked further in verse 10. Yet in verse 9 we see another dimension of the apostle's understanding of what it means to have a relationship with Christ—a dimension focused on the concept of "righteousness." Paul expands on "gaining Christ" with the words "and be found in him" (καὶ εὑρεθῶ ἐν αὐτῷ).[126] The verb translated as "found" parallels the word for "gain" (κερδήσω) in the first part of the purpose clause.[127] But the focus is now on God himself (i.e., "be found *by God*"); perhaps Paul has in mind his own coming before God at the last judgment (cf. 2 Cor 5:10).

Thus the language of being found explains, in part, the implications of what it means to gain Christ. Speaking of "being found in Christ" can have spatial connotations; Paul is "in Christ" in the sense of location and identification. Thus Paul lives

121. So Silva, *Philippians*, 157. Silva writes, "There is no need to downplay the meaning of *skybala* with such equivalents as 'rubbish.'"

122. As one who grew up in a home where the term was not allowed, a base crudity not fit for educated people, even writing the word makes me a bit uncomfortable—and that is the point in Paul's use of σκύβαλον. Semantically the English word "crap" works because it has both the meaning of excrement but also could be used of garbage, something disposable, or something of little quality or value. Rhetorically, it is *meant* to cause pause, to demonstrate the radical reassessment demanded for one who would follow Christ.

123. *TLNT* 3:263–65.

124. John M. G. Barclay, *Paul and the Gift* (Grand Rapids: Eerdmans, 2015), 372.

125. The verb κερδήσω is an aorist active subjunctive of κερδαίνω and should be read in its relationship with ἡγοῦμαι, which has imperfective aspect: "He considers . . . in order that he might gain." This means that Paul's words anticipate the consummation of his relationship with Christ at the resurrection, as noted in 3:10–11. Yet Paul's inaugurated eschatology, his "now and not yet" perspective, remains pervasive for his theological framework. In this passage he is neither focused solely on his present relationship with Christ nor solely on the future. Rather, his relationship with Christ was inaugurated at his conversion and continues to shape his life in the present, but always with a view toward its consummation at the end of the age. So, e.g., Fee, *Philippians*, 317–20, 330, 335; Hawthorne, *Philippians*, 139–40.

126. The verb "found" (εὑρίσκω) here echoes the same verb at 2:7, where Christ was "found" to be "like a normal person."

127. I am hesitant about Fee's reading of the two verbs joined by καί as forming a hendiadys, where the second constituent develops the idea of the first: "gain Christ, that is, be found in him." So Fee, *Philippians*, 320.

in a relationship with Christ by which he shares with other believers a corporate union and identity with Christ. By this relationship he is united with Christ in his death and resurrection (e.g., Gal 2:20; Col 2:20; 3:1, 3), and as he goes on to explain, he shares in Christ's righteousness.[128]

Thus the apostle unpacks the circumstances of those who are found "in Christ." Following the analysis of R. B. Matlock in his article on the construction πίστις Χριστοῦ ("faith in/of Christ"), the structure of Paul's thoughts here may be depicted as follows:[129]

| I | μὴ | ἔχων ἐμὴν | δικαιοσύνην | τὴν | ἐκ νόμου ἀλλὰ |
|---|---|---|---|---|---|
| | | | | τὴν | διὰ πίστεως Χριστοῦ |
| | not | having my | righteousness | | issuing from the law but rather |
| | | | | | through trust in Christ |
| II | τὴν | ἐκ θεοῦ | δικαιοσύνην | | ἐπὶ τῇ πίστει |
| | | from God | righteousness | | on the basis of trust |

This is a description of how "righteousness" relates to being found "in Christ." Paul first tells the reader what his righteousness is *not*, followed by an explanation of what the righteousness *is*, presenting faith in Christ as the means of his righteousness and God as its source. According to Matlock's analysis, line "II" parallels line "I," and "righteousness" is the topic in focus. Line I is the more complex and constitutes an antithetical construct, as indicated by a contrastive use of "but rather" (ἀλλά). Here we have a negative statement ("not having a righteousness of my own issuing from the law") contrasted with a positive statement ("but rather through trust in Christ"). The second line (II) amplifies the first as a simpler repetition of line I, focusing only on the positive source and means of the righteousness Paul addresses.

Each of these contrasting forms of righteousness has to do with a "personalized" agent, one human, "having my" (ἔχων ἐμήν)[130] righteousness, and the other divine, a "from God" (ἐκ θεοῦ) righteousness. The righteousness that Paul no longer claims is stated first, as "a righteousness of my own."[131] Earlier he has already said that according to a righteousness evaluated by "human standards" (ἐν σαρκί, v. 4), he had been "blameless" (ἄμεμπτος, v. 6), following the dictates of the Mosaic law to the letter. Accordingly, Paul's own righteousness had been aligned with the law (τὴν ἐν νόμῳ). In verse 5

128. Campbell, *Paul and Union with Christ*, 184–89.

129. With slight variation to bring the similarly sounding μή and τήν, as well as ἔχων and ἐκ in line. See R. Barry Matlock, "The Rhetoric of πίστις in Paul: Galatians 2:16, 3:22, Romans 3:22, and Philippians 3:9," *JSNT* 30.2 (2007): 178–81. Matlock contrasts his approach with both the often-cited quasi-chiastic structure of W. Schenk and the more discursively explained structure of M. Bockmuehl. The chiastic structure is as follows.

μὴ ἔχων ἐμὴν
    δικαιοσύνην
        τὴν ἐκ νόμου
            ἀλλὰ τὴν διὰ πίστεως Χριστοῦ
        τὴν ἐκ θεοῦ
    δικαιοσύνην
ἐπὶ τῇ πίστει

See Schenk, *Die Philipperbriefe des Paulus*, 250–51. The problem here, as Matlock points out, is that while τὴν διὰ πίστεως Χριστοῦ is clearly the focus, its relationship with ἐπὶ τῇ πίστει is skewed. Bockmuehl (*Philippians*, 209), on the other hand, pairs "my own" with "through trust in Christ" and contrasts a righteousness "from the law" with that which is "from God," both of which also seem problematic.

130. We might think of Jesus's words to the Pharisees in Mark 7:1–13, where he describes their traditions as the traditions "of men" (τῶν ἀνθρώπων).

131. The personal possessive pronoun ἐμός, here in a feminine singular form to match δικαιοσύνην, adjectivally delimits the noun.

he described himself as having lived as a Pharisee "with respect to the law" (κατὰ νόμον), which means that he had lived out a strict adherence to the oral and written law. Thus Paul's statements in verses 5 and 6 offer a helpful backdrop to what he means when he speaks of "a righteousness of my own issuing from the law" (ἐμὴν δικαιοσύνην τὴν ἐκ νόμου), which refers to a particular form of law observance that was embodied in Pharisaism. For Paul the ultimate source of that form of righteousness was human and thus inadequate, standing in contrast to "a righteousness from God" (τὴν ἐκ θεοῦ δικαιοσύνην).

Further, the phrase "issuing from the law" (τὴν ἐκ νόμου) contrasts with that which is "through trust in Christ" (τὴν διὰ πίστεως Χριστοῦ),[132] both descriptions speaking of the means by which righteousness is attained.[133] Moreover, the reference to "Christ" (Χριστοῦ) points to the Messiah as the object of Paul's trust.[134] The Greek term translated as "faith" or "trust" (πίστις) at times in Paul speaks of the faithfulness of a Christ-follower or, more often, a stance of trust or confidence in God (e.g., Rom 1:5, 8, 12, 17; 3:27–28; 4:5, 9)—though it can also speak of God's faithfulness (e.g., Rom 3:3). Often Christ is clearly presented as the object of faith (e.g., Rom 3:2), which is the case here in 3:9 as well as at Philippians 1:29: "Because for Christ's sake you have been granted not only *to trust him* [τὸ εἰς αὐτὸν πιστεύειν] but also to suffer on his behalf."

## IN DEPTH: The πίστις Χριστοῦ Debate[135]

Interpretation of the phrase "faith of/in Christ" (πίστις Χριστοῦ) has taken on mammoth proportions as a key topic in Pauline theology. For an overview of the issues, see the excursus in Holloway's commentary,[136] and for an excellent collection of essays on the topic in broader New Testament studies, see *The Faith of Jesus Christ*, edited by Michael Bird and Preston Sprinkle.[137] For obvious

132. The articles at the front of each of these phrases function as relative pronouns. Both nouns are in the genitive case and are fronted by prepositions, with each phrase in the third-attributive position. Matlock, "Rhetoric," 180.

133. The "issuing from" (ἐκ in ἐκ νόμου) communicates either source or means, but Paul's thought seems to prefer the latter. See BDAG 297. Our suggestion that Paul here communicates "means" is based partly on the contrasting structural parallelism found in the passage. The sense is similar to διά + the genitive in διὰ πίστεως, which may also communicate means ("by means of faith"). The variation of prepositions offers stylistic variation and structural balance (cf., e.g., Rom 3:30, where the prepositions function similarly). So Matlock, "Rhetoric," 180–81. He writes:

> In a striking recurrent pattern, Paul sets πίστις and νόμος in antithesis, with instrumental ἐκ or διά (or occasional stylistic variants), where the middle term is δικαιόω or δικαιοσύνη (and variations):
>
> with ἐκ: Gal 2.16; 3.2, 5, 7, 8, 9, 10, 11, 12, 18, 21, 22, 24; 5.5; Rom 3.20, 26, 30; 4.2, 14, 16; 5.1; 9.30, 32; 10.5, 6; Phil 3.9
>
> with διά: Gal 2.16, 19, 21; 3.14, 26; Rom 3.20, 22, 25, 27, 30, 31; 4.13; Phil 3.9
>
> other: Gal 2.20; 3.11; 5.4 (ἐν); Rom 3.28 (simple dative); Rom 3.21, 28; 4.6 (χωρίς); Rom 4.11, 13 (simple genitive); Phil 3.9 (ἐπί).

134. The primary alternative is to read the phrase as a subjective genitive—i.e., "the faith, or faithfulness, of Christ." On the broader debate about this ambiguous construction, see the In Depth section below.

135. Readers not interested in technical grammatical discussions may want to skip this section.

136. Holloway, *Philippians*, 165–68.

137. Michael F. Bird and Preston M. Sprinkle, eds., *The Faith of Jesus Christ: Exegetical, Biblical, and Theological Studies* (Milton Keynes: Paternoster; Peabody, MA: Hendrickson, 2010).

reasons, we can only provide a brief sketch of the issues here. Interested readers should follow up by pursuing more detailed treatments.

Scholars following Richard Hays read the phrase as a subjective genitive, that is, the "faith" or "faithfulness" of Christ.[138] Arguments in favor of this position include (1) that in all other cases where the apostle employs the term πίστις with the genitive (in this case, Χριστοῦ), the genitive is subjective (i.e., functioning as a subject); (2) reading the phrase as an objective genitive is often done to overcome a redundancy, since in the immediate contexts there sometimes exists a statement about the object of faith (e.g., the repetition of "in Christ Jesus" at Gal 2:16); (3) a theology oriented toward the person and work of Christ makes more sense than that oriented to a particular response from those embracing the gospel.[139]

Others, including James Dunn and Barry Matlock, read the phrase as an objective genitive (i.e., Christ as the object of faith), as in my interpretation.[140] Among the strongest arguments for this position are (1) several church fathers (who were Greek speakers), including Origen and Chrysostom, understood the expression as an objective genitive, demonstrating that it is a natural reading of the language; (2) Paul often speaks of Christ as the object of faith rather than one who acts in faith (there are no unambiguous examples in the New Testament of the latter); and (3) the linguistic argument that when πίστις is used "as a head term with a prepositional specifier, without an intervening article and followed by an element in the genitive," the genitive is objective. On this third point see the article by Porter and Pitts,[141] who present a strong grammatical argument to be considered alongside other exegetical and theological evidence. Still others opt for an interpretation that allows for the two positions combined, as seen in the work of Garwood Anderson and in Morna Hooker's updated position.[142]

On balance, the arguments for the objective genitive reading at Philippians 3:9 seem to me to be the strongest, based on a combination of exegetical, grammatical, and contextual factors. Moreover, one misstep in the

138. On which, e.g., see Richard B. Hays, *The Faith of Jesus Christ: An Investigation of the Narrative Substructure of Galatians 3:1–4:11* (Atlanta: Scholars Press, 1983); Morna Hooker, "ΠΙΣΤΙΣ ΧΡΙΣΤΟΥ," *NTS* 35 (1989): 321–42; Ian G. Wallis, *The Faith of Jesus Christ in Early Christian Traditions*, SNTSMS 84 (Cambridge: Cambridge University Press, 2005).

139. Holloway, *Philippians*, 165–66.

140. E.g., James D. G. Dunn, "Once More, Πιστις Χριστου," in *Pauline Theology, Volume IV: Looking Back, Pressing On*, ed. E. Elizabeth Johnson and David M. Hay (Atlanta: Scholars Press, 1997), 61–81; Matlock, "Rhetoric."

141. Stanley E. Porter and Andrew W. Pitts, "Πίστις with a Preposition and Genitive Modifier," in Bird and Sprinkle, *Faith of Jesus Christ*, 33–53.

142. Garwood P. Anderson, *Paul's New Perspective: Charting a Soteriological Journey* (Downers Grove, IL: IVP Academic, 2016), 150–51; Morna D. Hooker, "Another Look at πίστις Χριστοῦ," *SJT* 69 (2016): 46–62.

debate concerns how we understand the nature of "faith," since some who read the construction as a subjective genitive consider a believer's "faith" to be a form of work. Yet if we understand πίστις as having to do with "trust" on the part of the believer, inherent to trust is the *trustworthiness*, or faithfulness, of Christ, which is the emphasis of the subjective-genitive reading. The "trust" involved—rather than a form of work—requires letting go of or relinquishing one's own righteousness. This is what Paul means by "not having a righteousness of my own."

Paul's own righteousness issuing from the law is set in contrast to a righteousness through trust in Christ. Paul now elaborates on this Christ-sourced righteousness, calling it "a righteousness from God on the basis of trust" (τὴν ἐκ θεοῦ δικαιοσύνην ἐπὶ τῇ πίστει). The apostle describes this righteousness in two ways. First, it is a righteousness "from God" (ἐκ θεοῦ), or "brought about by God." That is, it is a righteousness with God as its ultimate agent. Second, it is a righteousness had "on the basis of trust" (ἐπὶ τῇ πίστει). If we read correctly the sense of "through trust" (διὰ πίστεως) in verse 9 as communicating the means by which righteousness might be had, there exists a correspondence between this phrase (διὰ πίστεως) and "on the basis of trust" (ἐπὶ τῇ πίστει) at the end of verse 9. A wonderfully flexible preposition (ἐπί), translated here as "on the basis of," functions as a marker of basis for a state of existence or an action; that is, the righteousness from God is "on the basis of" active trust in God. Thus, the two phrases involving "trust" (πίστις) are roughly equivalent conceptually, both speaking of faith as the means by which one experiences righteousness and is found to be "in Christ."[143] Such are not by means of the law but by trust in Christ. Here lies the basis for a transformed life rooted in relationship with God through Jesus Christ, which constitutes "knowing Christ," as the apostle goes on to explain.

**3:10–11 so that I may know him, and the power of his resurrection, and the fellowship of his sufferings, as I am being conformed to his death, in hope that I will reach the goal of the resurrection from among the dead** (τοῦ γνῶναι αὐτὸν καὶ τὴν δύναμιν τῆς ἀναστάσεως αὐτοῦ καὶ κοινωνίαν παθημάτων αὐτοῦ, συμμορφιζόμενος τῷ θανάτῳ αὐτοῦ, 11 εἴ πως καταντήσω εἰς τὴν ἐξανάστασιν τὴν ἐκ νεκρῶν). As Paul moves toward the end of this long, theologically packed, spiritually rich sentence, his crescendo focuses on that which is both the ultimate purpose and the ultimate gain of his life. Building on the paired ideas of "gaining Christ" (3:8) and being "found in" Christ (3:9), the apostle now culminates his reflections with "knowing" Christ.

As noted above in the commentary, the theological backdrop of "knowing the Lord" has deep Old Testament roots (e.g., 1 Sam 3:7; Jer 31:34; Hos 6:3). Such knowledge would be characteristic of relationship with God under the promised new covenant: "No longer will they teach their neighbor, or say to one another, 'Know the Lord,' because they will all know me, from the least of

143. Matlock, "Rhetoric," 181.

them to the greatest, declares the LORD" (Jer 31:34 NIV). Such "knowledge," therefore, constitutes "a relationship of mutual faithfulness expressed on God's side by grace and election (e.g., Exod 33:12; Isa 45:1) and on the human side by love for God and obedience to his commandments (Hos 4:1–2; 6:6)."[144] For Paul, especially in light of Jeremiah 9:23–24 (9:22–23 LXX), one should reject boasting in anything other than a relationship characterized by knowing the Lord (e.g., 1 Cor 1:29–31; 2 Cor 10:17–18). Thus, the intimate relationship connoted by "knowing" is foundational for Paul's understanding of the gospel. The gospel not only offers knowledge about God; the gospel introduces believers to the person of God himself "in the face of Jesus Christ" (2 Cor 4:6). Paul wants "to know him" (τοῦ γνῶναι αὐτόν).[145]

The apostle then describes dynamics surrounding this relationship with Christ in the language of death and resurrection, the concepts laid out in a chiastic structure. In his desire to know Christ, Paul wants to know:

A the power of his resurrection, and
    B the fellowship of his sufferings,
    B′ as I am being conformed to his death,
A′ in hope that I will experience the resurrection from among the dead.

Some read the conjunction (καί) following "him" (αὐτόν) simply as additive ("and"): "I may know him, *and* the power of his resurrection, and the fellowship of his sufferings" (e.g., NASB, CSB, NRSV, ESV). Others read the language as epexegetical, the experience of resurrection power and the fellowship of suffering constituting the essence of what it means to know Christ: "I may know him—that is, the power of his resurrection and the fellowship of his sufferings."[146] The lack of an article in front of the word for "fellowship" (κοινωνίαν)[147] makes this latter interpretation attractive, since it underscores "the power of his resurrection" and "the fellowship of his sufferings" as structurally parallel concepts. Yet this rendering implies that knowledge of the power of Christ's resurrection and fellowship in his sufferings are *equated* to "knowing him." Are they really the totality of that experience? In light of this hesitation, I prefer the reading of "and" (καί) as additive: "I may know him, and the power of his resurrection, and the fellowship of his sufferings."[148] This interpretation understands the experience of Christ's resurrection power and the fellowship of his sufferings as key aspects of our relationship with Christ, but not as the totality of the relationship.

Thus relational union with Christ has powerful implications. As Paul speaks of "the power of his

144. Bockmuehl, *Philippians*, 205. Bockmuehl points out that this view of "knowledge of God" continued into the post-biblical period of Jewish literature, with works such as Wis 15:3; Bar 2:15, 31; Sib. Or. 3.693; 1QS 1.12; 4.22; 11.16–20.

145. The articular infinitive τοῦ γνῶναι αὐτόν (fronted by the genitive form of the article) reaches back to τῆς γνώσεως Χριστοῦ Ἰησοῦ in 3:8d–e and expands on it. This infinitival construction communicates the "ultimate purpose" in the passage, building on the "penultimate purposes" of gaining Christ and being found in him. The logic looks like this:

| | | | |
|---|---|---|---|
| In order that | I might | gain Christ and | **penultimate purposes** |
| | | be found in him . . . | |
| so that | I may | know him | **ultimate purpose** |

146. So NET, NIV; Fee, *Philippians*, 328; Hansen, *Philippians*, 243; Silva, *Philippians*, 163.

147. If the article is not present (as with $\mathfrak{P}^{46}$ ℵ* A B 1241. 2464)—and on the basis of both external and internal evidence it almost certainly should be omitted—then we should understand the accusative article introducing δύναμιν to carry over to κοινωνίαν as well, highlighting the close relationship between the two (an example of Sharp's rule of the article, which here applies to these nouns as related to Christ); see Wallace, *Greek Grammar*, 270–71.

148. Perhaps as with the NLT: "I want to know Christ *and experience* the mighty power that raised him from the dead. I want to suffer with him, sharing in his death."

resurrection" (τὴν δύναμιν τῆς ἀναστάσεως αὐτοῦ), he certainly has in mind his own experience of that transformation. Christ, as the firstfruits, has paved the way to resurrection for all the sons and daughters of God at the end of the age (Rom 8:11; 1 Cor 15:20, 23); this is the great Christian hope. But the apostle may have more in mind than just resurrection at the consummation of the ages, for in the New Testament broadly and in Paul particularly the power manifested in the resurrection of Jesus (Rom 1:4; Eph 1:20) heralds the power of God at work in his church in the world. Thus, for example, resurrection power enables the believer to live a righteous life (Rom 6:13; 7:4; Col 2:12) and manifests in signs and wonders, bearing witness to the resurrection as the church marches through the world on mission (e.g., Acts 4:30; 5:12; 14:3; 15:12; Rom 15:19; Heb 2:4). Indeed, Paul points to the manifestation of resurrection power as an authenticating sign of his apostleship (2 Cor 12:12; 13:4).

The apostle also embraces "the fellowship of his sufferings" (καὶ κοινωνίαν παθημάτων αὐτοῦ) as a mark of authentic ministry. The term translated as "fellowship" (κοινωνία) speaks of a relationship in which something is shared or of close association or participation. Earlier in Philippians Paul speaks of the church's "participation in the gospel" (τῇ κοινωνίᾳ ὑμῶν εἰς τὸ εὐαγγέλιον, 1:5) and the "participation stemming from the Spirit" (κοινωνία πνεύματος, 2:1). Elsewhere he refers to believers as called into "fellowship with his Son, Jesus Christ our Lord" (1 Cor 1:9 NIV; cf. 1 John 1:3, 6), and in the context of teaching the Corinthians about the Lord's Supper, he refers to "participation" in the blood and body of Christ (1 Cor 10:16).

Paul understands that "being conformed to" Christ's "death" (συμμορφιζόμενος τῷ θανάτῳ αὐτοῦ) through suffering shapes a special form of "fellowship." In his reflections in 2 Corinthians 4:7–15, the apostle celebrates the power of God as manifesting through "cracked pots," the apostles carrying around "the dying of Jesus" bodily, so that the life of Jesus might be made known to people. The apostles are constantly "handed over to death because of Jesus, in order that the life of Jesus might also be made known."[149] Yet death also leads to resurrection, a pattern seen in the life and ministry of Jesus (e.g., Acts 17:3; 26:23), and Paul anticipates his own resurrection even as he shares the sufferings of Christ in his ministry.

The words of verse 11, "in hope that I will reach the goal of the resurrection from among the dead" (εἴ πως καταντήσω εἰς τὴν ἐξανάστασιν τὴν ἐκ νεκρῶν), are not as transparent as they might seem. The construction in Greek rendered in our translation as "in hope" can reflect a "more probable future"[150] and relates grammatically and most directly to "being conformed to his death" in the previous verse. The experience of "death" and the anticipation of resurrection life go together. Further, we have rendered the construction εἴ πως as "in hope," for in the New Testament it often seems to be used in context to convey hope rather than a foreboding sense of uncertainty[151]—a sentiment that could be misread in English if translated "if somehow" (as, e.g., in various forms in the NRSV, NET, NIV). Nevertheless, with its note of

149. On which, see Guthrie, *2 Corinthians*, 252, 258–61.

150. Wallace, *Greek Grammar*, 696. It occurs three other times in the New Testament (Acts 27:12; Rom 1:10; 11:14) and six times in the LXX (2 Sam 14:15; 16:12; 1 Kgs 21:31; 2 Kgs 19:4; Job 20:23; Jer 28:8).

151. Contra Jean-Baptiste Edart, *L'Épître aux Philippiens: Rhétorique et Composition Stylistique* (Paris: Gabalda, 2002), 239–41, 263–64. That doubt is not implied see Judith M. Gundry Volf, *Paul and Perseverance: Staying in and Falling Away*, WUNT 2/37 (Tübingen: Mohr Siebeck, 1990), 257–58.

contingency, the construction also communicates humble reserve even amid rising hope.[152] It is not that Paul doubts his status before God, nor the certainty of his resurrection (e.g., Rom 6:5; 2 Cor 4:14; 2 Tim 1:12), but the apostle crafts his statement with reserve and humility, trumping any appearance of presumption.

Paul anticipates that he "will come to" (καταντάω) the resurrection, the verb carrying the sense of "arriving at" a destination. Accordingly, the word could speak literally of travel, but authors also employ it with the metaphorical sense of reaching a goal or condition.[153] That goal here is "the rising up from among the dead" (τὴν ἐξανάστασιν τὴν ἐκ νεκρῶν).[154] The term implying resurrection (ἐξανάστασις) only occurs here in the New Testament, but in other forms of Greek literature refers to "getting up" or "raising up" or a "rising up" in some sense.[155] Although some regard this an intensification of Paul's more common word for resurrection (ἀνάστασις),[156] it seems, rather, that ἐξανάστασις constitutes a word picture related to the more common ἀνάστασις, resurrection from the dead depicted dramatically as an act of "getting up." The apostle, then, paints this graphic picture of "rising up" as "from among the dead" (τὴν ἐκ νεκρῶν). Because of his identification with the crucified Christ, Paul may be beaten to the ground and even killed, but having been laid out among the dead, he will rise up at the end of the age, participating in that greatest of "uprisings," standing up from among the dead, made alive in resurrection.

**3:12 Not that I have already taken hold of this or have already reached the goal, but I am running hard that I might grab hold of that for which I was grabbed by Christ Jesus** (Οὐχ ὅτι ἤδη ἔλαβον ἢ ἤδη τετελείωμαι, διώκω δὲ εἰ καὶ καταλάβω, ἐφ' ᾧ καὶ κατελήμφθην ὑπὸ Χριστοῦ Ἰησοῦ). Here Paul offers a clarification. He is not suggesting that he has already arrived at the ultimate goal in his relationship to Christ. No, that lies in the future, at God's "upward call" (3:14). The concepts reflected in these verses might be aligned as follows.

| Negative | Act of "Taking Hold" | The Object | Paul's Action |
|---|---|---|---|
| Not that | I have already taken hold of | [this] or | |
| | have already reached | the goal | but I am running hard |
| | that I might grab hold of | that for which | |
| | I was grabbed by Christ Jesus | | |
| I do not | | | consider myself |
| | to have caught up | with it | but I focus on |
| | | one thing: | disregarding what is behind me |

152. Hawthorne, *Philippians*, 148; Silva, *Philippians*, 166.

153. BDAG 523.

154. As noted in BDAG 289, εἰς + the accusative can be used to convey "entry into a state of being with verbs of going, coming, leading."

155. E.g., Gen 7:4 LXX; Josephus, *J.W.* 6.69; Herodotus, *Hist.* 9.106; as does the much more common cognate verb, ἐξανίστημι: e.g., LXX Gen 18:16; 19:1, 32, 34; Exod 10:23; 21:19; Lev 19:32; Num 25:7; Josh 8:7, 18–19; Judg 3:20; 5:7, 12; 1 Kgs 1:49; 2:19; 18:27; Esth 7:7; Job 4:4; 1 Macc 9:40; 11:69; 16:16; 2 Macc 14:45; 4 Macc 6:8; Sir 8:11; Josephus, *Ant.* 17.132; 19.96, 101, 157; 20.256; *J.W.* 2.279; 3.328; 4.174; Mark 12:19; Luke 20:28; Acts 15:5.

156. E.g., Silva, *Philippians*, 169. The word ἀνάστασις is used clearly in this way in the NT: Luke 14:14; 20:27, 33, 35–36; John 5:29; 11:24–25; Acts 1:22; 2:31; 4:2, 33; 17:18, 32; 23:6, 8; 24:15, 21; 26:23; Rom 1:4; 6:5; 1 Cor 15:12–13, 21, 42; Phil 3:10; 2 Tim 2:18; Heb 6:2; 11:35; 1 Pet 1:3; 3:21; Rev 20:5–6.

| Negative | Act of "Taking Hold" | The Object | Paul's Action |
|---|---|---|---|
| | | | straining for |
| | | what is in front of me | I am running hard |
| | | toward the goal | |
| | | for the prize of the upward call of God in Christ Jesus | |

The passage is filled with repetition,[157] and Paul's actions dominate the passage. The apostle presents himself as "running hard," "considering," "disregarding," "straining," as a sprinter running with all his might toward a special goal. The athletic imagery is obvious.[158]

Verse 12 begins with the disclaimer, "Not that I have already taken hold of this" (οὐχ ὅτι ἤδη ἔλαβον). The word translated here as "taken hold" (λαμβάνω) often has to do with "taking" or "receiving" something. But given the word picture painted in the passage, it might be rendered "grasped" or, as with our translation, "taken hold."[159] The thought is clarified with "or have already reached the goal" (ἢ ἤδη τετελείωμαι).[160] The verb (from τελειόω) can mean "to complete" or "finish" something, to "bring to an end," or to "bring to its goal/accomplishment." It thus can express "completion" or "perfection" or reaching "full measure."[161] Paul could be using the word for his own "perfection," but given the athletic imagery, he seems to speak of reaching a goal (cf. Luke 13:32).

Continuing the race imagery, the apostle next writes, "but I am running hard to grab hold of that for which I was grabbed by Christ Jesus" (διώκω δὲ εἰ καὶ καταλάβω, ἐφ' ᾧ καὶ κατελήμφθην ὑπὸ Χριστοῦ Ἰησοῦ). The "and" (δέ) may be continuative, or mildly contrastive,[162] and Paul employs this word for pursuit (διώκω) twenty-one times in his writings, either to speak of pursuing virtues (such as righteousness, hospitality, peace, or love)[163] or to write about persecution, as he does earlier in the chapter at 3:6.[164] Yet here he seems to have the former sense in mind, and with the athletic imagery in view the term conveys a sense of "running hard" after something.[165]

157. Notice the repetition of the negatives, expressed with "not" (οὐχ, οὐ), the verbs for receiving (built on the λαμβ- root; v. 12: ἔλαβον, καταλάβω, κατελήμφθην; v. 13: κατειληφέναι), the repetition of the verb having to do with "pursuing" (διώκω, found in vv. 12, 14), and the repetition of "Christ Jesus" (Χριστοῦ Ἰησοῦ, vv. 12, 14).

158. Cousar, *Philippians and Philemon*, 76.

159. "Obtained" (NASB, NRSV, ESV, NIV) does not work quite as well with the athletic imagery, and "reached the goal" (CSB) is not a normal gloss for the verb; "attained" (NET) or "achieved" (NLT) is a bit better.

160. Paul uses the first-person singular perfect middle indicative form of the verb τελειόω, and the aspect, therefore, is stative. It could be read as passive as well: "have been completed." Some scribes added a theological interpretation by replacing the ἢ ἤδη τετελείωμαι with ἢ ἤδη δεδικαίωμαι, "or have already been justified" or "vindicated" ($\mathfrak{P}^{46}$ D$^{*,c}$ [F G] ar [b; Ir$^{lat}$] Ambst).

161. BDAG 996.The verb also could speak of consecration or initiation of the priests in the Greek OT. See Lev 4:5; 8:33; 16:32; 21:10, and the verb's cognate noun τελείωσις at Lev 7:27; 8:22, 26, 28–29, 31, 33, both of which are used to speak of the validation of a priest in the priestly office.

162. As with Hellerman, *Philippians*, 201, following Hansen, *Philippians*, 251.

163. E.g., Rom 9:30; 12:13; 14:19; 1 Cor 14:1.

164. See also 1 Cor 4:12; 15:9; 2 Cor 4:9; Gal 1:13, 23; 4:29; 5:11; 6:12.

165. E.g., Josephus, *Ant.* 1.178; 2.240, 320, 322, 340; 4.91; Epictetus, *Diatr.* 1.1.124; Philo, *Alleg. Interp.* 3.20; *Cherubim* 74. In the Greco-Roman literature, both the more literal idea of running after someone as well as the figurative use of pursuing virtues are common. The verbs διώκω and καταλαμβάνω are used with similar athletic imagery at Rom 9:30–31. So Bockmuehl, *Philippians*, 221.

Continuing with a wordplay on the verb translated "taken hold" (ἔλαβον) at the beginning of the verse,[166] Paul twice uses a related verb (καταλαμβάνω) that could speak of "winning" or "attaining," "catching up with," or "seizing" something or someone.[167] These various images fit the athletic metaphor well. In short, Paul is running as hard as he can to "grab hold" of that for which Christ had grabbed hold of him.[168] Christ apprehended Paul on the Damascus Road to bring him to the place of knowing his Lord face-to-face at the resurrection of the dead. This is the goal for which Paul strives with all his might. The two "actors" in this scenario, Christ and Paul, reflect "the passive and active aspects of [Paul's] experience of being in Christ,"[169] and the goal of each has to do with the perfect relationship attained at the end of the age. As Fee notes beautifully,

> It is hard to imagine that this could refer to anything other than his final apprehension of Christ. Granted the mention of the resurrection in v. 11; but vv. 20–21 indicate that for Paul it is not resurrection per se that interests him but the final glory. The one whose motto is "to live is Christ, to die is [to] gain [Christ]" is not focusing now on the means to that end, but on the eschatological culmination itself—the ultimate apprehension of Christ.[170]

**3:13–14 Brothers and sisters, I do not consider myself to have grabbed hold of it yet, but I focus on one thing: disregarding the things behind me and straining toward the things ahead of me, I am running hard toward the goal for the prize of the upward call of God in Christ Jesus** (ἀδελφοί, ἐγὼ ἐμαυτὸν οὔπω λογίζομαι κατειληφέναι· ἓν δέ, τὰ μὲν ὀπίσω ἐπιλανθανόμενος τοῖς δὲ ἔμπροσθεν ἐπεκτεινόμενος, 14 κατὰ σκοπὸν διώκω εἰς τὸ βραβεῖον τῆς ἄνω κλήσεως τοῦ θεοῦ ἐν Χριστῷ Ἰησοῦ). Here Paul expands on his disclaimer of verse 12. He does not consider himself to have taken hold of the prize yet, but he runs for that goal with all his might. Throughout most of this chapter, the apostle has been caught up in reflecting on his own relationship with Christ. Yet here the fact that he is addressing the Philippians once again comes to the fore, as Paul writes to them directly for the first time since 3:1. At 1:12 and 3:1 he has already referred to the Philippians with the affectionate familial word translated "brothers and sisters" (ἀδελφοί). The masculine plural form of this word was used in the ancient world of men and women in religious contexts, and the apostle continues to address them in this warm way as the book continues (3:17; 4:1, 8). The verb translated as "consider" (λογίζομαι) is a common one for the apostle,[171] and it can mean "to reckon" or "to think about" something (as at 4:8), but here it speaks of seeing something from a particular vantage point. As such it constitutes overt self-reflection in this very self-reflective passage.

As stressed in verse 12, the apostle does not see himself as having reached the culmination of his relationship with Christ. Here again, for the third

166. The conditional construction εἰ καί + subjunctive communicates expectancy rather than doubt, with the καί used adjunctively and Paul speaking of "laying hold" of the work of Christ. See Fee, *Philippians*, 345.

167. BDAG 519–20.

168. In this sense I am most aligned with those who read the phrase as indicating a consecutive relationship rather than those such as Hansen, Harris, and Silva who read the phrase as reflecting cause (as with the CSB, ESV; Hansen, *Philippians*, 252; Harris, *Prepositions*, 140; Silva, *Philippians*, 176). See, e.g., Bockmuehl, *Philippians*, 221, who follows Joseph A. Fitzmyer, "The Consecutive Meaning of Εφ' Ω in Romans 5.12," *NTS* 39 (1993): 321–39.

169. Osiek, *Philippians, Philemon*, 98.

170. Fee, *Philippians*, 346.

171. Used thirty-four times in his writings (e.g., Rom 2:3, 26; 1 Cor 4:1; 2 Cor 3:5; Gal 3:6).

time since the beginning of verse 12, he uses the verb rendered "grabbed hold" (καταλαμβάνω).[172] The repetition constitutes a rhetorical drumming home of the idea for emphasis. Paul has been apprehended by Christ, but he has not yet reached a state of having "grabbed hold of" the full realization of that relationship—the eschatological culmination, which will only come at the resurrection. His perspective must have been that, should Christ tarry, he would be with Christ upon death (1:23). But he would not fully know him as God intended until the end of the age.

The new clause begins with the Greek word for "one" (ἕν), which is followed by the conjunction, translated in context as "but" (δέ). There is no verb, forming a striking interjection, which we translate periphrastically as "but[173] I focus on one thing." The twin actions that follow speak of Paul's manner or posture as he runs the race. These clauses are knitted together with an "on the one hand . . . on the other hand" construction (μέν . . . δέ):

| | | |
|---|---|---|
| disregarding the things behind me | τὰ μὲν | ὀπίσω ἐπιλανθανόμενος |
| and | | |
| straining for the things ahead of me | τοῖς δὲ | ἔμπροσθεν ἐπεκτεινόμενος[174] |

As used here, the word for "disregarding" (ἐπιλανθάνομαι) communicates a posture for Paul. The term means either to "forget" or "neglect," but the former is in mind. Paul is forgetting, that is, disregarding, "the things behind" (τὰ . . . ὀπίσω)[175]—the events, honors, positions, etc. that lie in his past, some of which he details in 3:5–6. Yet in a continuation of the image of an athletic race, he "is stretching out" or "straining" (ἐπεκτεινόμενος) toward[176] the things ahead of him (τοῖς . . . ἔμπροσθεν). The "things" are not defined, but we can be sure that at their center is "the prize of the upward call of God in Christ Jesus" heralded in the next verse. The verb for "stretching out" or "straining" (ἐπεκτείνομαι), used only here in biblical literature, is an intensification of its more common cousin (ἐκτείνω, "to stretch out")[177] and in this context paints a picture of an athlete straining toward the finish line. The image graphically presents Paul's "now and not yet" moment in life—in between a life of now displaced values and not yet having arrived at the ultimate goal in Christ.

Verse 14 continues with a declaration expressing resolute clarity of purpose: "I am running hard toward the goal for the prize of the upward call of God in Christ Jesus" (κατὰ σκοπὸν διώκω εἰς τὸ βραβεῖον τῆς ἄνω κλήσεως τοῦ θεοῦ ἐν Χριστῷ Ἰησοῦ). The verbal idea at the heart of the verse, "running hard" (διώκω), has already been encountered at 3:6 and 3:12, and this use parallels that in 3:12, as Paul again speaks of running after something with all his might. His metaphorical "running hard" is "toward the goal" (κατὰ σκοπόν).[178]

Only occurring here in the New Testament, the word "goal" (σκοπός) could be used in broader Greek literature to refer to a "watchman," but the apostle's use tracks more with a "mark," or "target,"

172. This time in a perfect active infinitive form, on which see the discussion at v. 12.

173. The contrast is read in the context.

174. Notice the alliteration of the *e* (ε) sound in ἕν, ἐπιλανθανόμενος, ἔμπροσθεν, and ἐπεκτεινόμενος.

175. The article τά is the object of the participle.

176. The article may be read as a dative of destination.

177. It is most often used in NT narratives to refer to someone stretching out a hand (e.g., Matt 8:3; Mark 1:41; Luke 5:13; John 21:18; Acts 4:30).

178. With the preposition κατά + accusative communicating movement "toward" (conceived either in spatial or, more likely here, temporal terms).

or "goal."[179] Thus, one nuance of the noun has to do with what is looked for or focused on. Following Paul's athletic imagery, the term conveys the sense of a "goal" toward which a runner strives as he sees it in the distance.

Of course, having reached such a goal in the "crown games," an athlete was given the "prize" (βραβεῖον)—that is, the "award" of a crown.[180] Similar to our language here at Phil 3:14, the apostle's exhortation in 1 Corinthians 9 reads, "Do you not know that all the runners in a stadium compete, but only one receives the prize [τὸ βραβεῖον]? So run to win [ἵνα καταλάβητε]" (NET). What then is the prize? Even in the crown games, the "crown" itself was not the main point but was a symbol of the great honor given to the victor and the victor's home city. Accordingly, "no mere celery wreath"[181] and no fame or status overflowing with Greco-Roman honor was Paul's goal, for he aims much, much higher. Paul identifies the prize as "the upward call of God in Christ Jesus" (τῆς ἄνω κλήσεως τοῦ θεοῦ ἐν Χριστῷ Ἰησοῦ). That the call is "upward" (ἄνω) puts the focus on the heavenly realm (cf. Col 3:1–2), and later at Philippians 3:20 Paul will evoke the believers' heavenly citizenship. The call "of God" (τοῦ θεοῦ) is almost certainly a subjective genitive; in the biblical literature God is almost always depicted as the initiator of the call.

Yet to what does Paul refer when he speaks of the "upward call of God?"[182] Are the "prize" and "the upward call of God in Christ Jesus" to be understood as the same thing? Do they both simply refer to being with Christ in heaven?[183] Against this common view, it may be pointed out that "calling" for Paul normally comes as God initiates something in the life of the believer rather than the culmination of a process (e.g., 1 Cor 1:26; 7:20; Eph 4:1; 2 Thess 1:11; 2 Tim 1:9), and thus the prize should not be equated with the call of God.[184]

As another possibility, perhaps Paul extends the athletic imagery to include the public presentation of the victor, an "upward call" at which the victor's name, his father's name, and his city or country were recognized; in such a scenario the victor would be given a palm branch by an official of the games.[185] On this reading the prize would be associated with a glorious recognition at the completion of the race but would not be directly identified with it.

A third view understands Paul as called *to* the prize (Gal 4:26; Col 3:1; 1 Thess 2:12).[186] The basic sense here is that God has called Paul to himself in conversion, and he continues to call the apostle in an ongoing way, ultimately calling Paul "upward" (i.e., heavenward) into his presence at the end of his life or at the eschaton (cf. Heb 3:1), at which point he would receive the prize. This view makes

179. For instance, in the LXX the term could be used of an arrow finding its target (e.g., Job 16:12; Lam 3:12; Wis 5:12, 21). The cognate verb σκοπέω means "to look for or notice," as at Phil 2:4, where the apostle exhorts the Philippians to "watch out for" the interests of others.

180. See the crown imagery at 2 Tim 4:7–8. In the Greco-Roman games, the crown was a celery wreath, but after the second century BCE it could have been either pine or dried celery. See O. Broneer, "The Isthmian Victory Crown," *AJA* 66 (1962): 259–63, and Mark Golden, *Sport in the Ancient World from A to Z* (London: Routledge, 2004), 89.

In Phil 3:14, the term is situated in a prepositional phrase, εἰς τὸ βραβεῖον, εἰς + accusative, which is read metaphorically as expressing an "extension involving a goal"—i.e., "to the prize."

181. Fee, *Philippians*, 348–49.

182. The question concerns how the genitive "of the call" (τῆς . . . κλήσεως) functions grammatically in relation to "the prize" (τὸ βραβεῖον).

183. So, e.g., Holloway, *Philippians*, 175.

184. So, e.g., both Fee and Bockmuehl. See Bockmuehl, *Philippians*, 222–23; Fee, *Philippians*, 349. Although cf. Eph 1:18; 4:4.

185. Hawthorne, *Philippians*, 154–55, who sees Christ himself as the prize.

186. E.g., Bockmuehl, *Philippians*, 223; Mark Keown, *Philippians 2:19–4:23*, EEC (Bellingham, WA: Lexham, 2017), 208. This reading interprets the genitive τῆς . . . κλήσεως as subjective.

the best sense of the present context and Paul's theology generally. Paul is always moving toward God, who is the great pursuit of his life. This "calling" cannot be conceived apart from the apostle's being "in Christ Jesus," as the covenant relationship with Christ is the whole ground and essence and goal of Paul's existence,[187] as we have seen throughout this unit. It may be, therefore, that the "prize" is the same as the great "gain" the apostle has already celebrated in this letter—that of knowing Christ, face-to-face, in glory. In short, the prize is the consummative moment of "knowing Christ" fully at the resurrection from the dead, which, for the apostle, is an all-consuming hope.

## Theology in Application

### *Perspective Needed for Joy*

At numerous points throughout the letter, we have heard Paul's joyful reflection or his exhortations to the Philippians to rejoice. At 3:1 Paul reiterates the theme, literarily anticipating further uses at 4:1 and 4:4. Joy is an important motif for the letter both structurally and spiritually. The apostle does not perceive his life "race" (3:7–14) as a grueling, grudging burden; rather, it is shot through with a joy born of a particular perspective—everything assessed in light of *knowing* Christ.

The city of Jos in Nigeria straddles the boundary between the Christian south and the Muslim north. A few years ago, Muslim extremists attacked and burned a Nigerian Baptist church, along with the house of the young pastor, Sunday Gomna. When the members of that church returned for worship on the second Sunday after the attack, they gathered in a little mud-wall community center not far from the ruins of their church building. Professor Danny McCain tells of the pastor's response, which illustrates *perspective*. The pastor said,

> "First, I am grateful that no one in my church killed anyone." Certainly many Christians had blood on their hands. However, Pastor Sunday said that he had gone around through the community, and some of the Muslim people said, "Pastor, thank you for the way you taught your people. Your people helped to protect us." So Pastor Sunday was proud that his people did not kill any Muslims.
>
> "Second, I am grateful that they did not burn my church." We all looked at him a bit incredulously. We were meeting in this little uncomfortable place because the church building had been burned. But Pastor Sunday continued: "Inasmuch as no church member died during this crisis, they did not burn our church. They only

187. Thus the dative here might be read as a "dative of relationship," i.e., in relationship with Christ Jesus. On this very common and potent phrase in Paul, which we have already encountered in this form at Phil 1:1, 26; 2:5; and 3:3, see Campbell, *Paul and Union with Christ*.

> burned the building. We can rebuild the building, but we could not bring back to life any of our members. So I am grateful that they did not burn my church."
>
> He continued, "Third, I am grateful that they burned my house as well." He had been living in the parsonage [which] was burned with everything in it. Pastor Sunday continued, "If they had burned your house and not my house, how would I have known how to serve you as pastor? However, because they burned my house and all my possessions, I know what you are experiencing and I will be able to be a better pastor to you. So I am grateful that they burned my house as well."[188]

These words are born of Christian perspective that sees opposition as an opportunity for rejoicing and for the advance of the gospel message. Tim Keller notes, "All opposition to God will be seen in the end as having done nothing but confirm and further His design."[189] God, rather than being the author of evil, is its redeemer, turning the effects of evil inside out and upside down, making the hurtful useful and the contrary a contributor to God's good and gracious plan. "And we know that in all things God works for the good of those who love him, who have been called according to his purpose" (Rom 8:28). This is why we can rejoice in the face of opposition. God is not only working for our good but for the good of the body of Christ, building it up by his good intentions, even through opposition, as believers are shaped in the image of the Son. Christ is real and on the throne of the universe. This changes everything. We will never understand Paul nor his call from prison to "rejoice" until we grasp the jarring, perspective-shaping Damascus Road reality that Christ is real and can be known and has a goal to which he calls us. Prison becomes a platform because of this life-orienting perspective.

### *The Objective*

My wife and I occasionally watch a program called *Antiques Roadshow* on public television. Traveling from city to city, the producers invite residents to bring artifacts for appraisal on camera. Time and again Grandma's blanket, or Uncle Bill's painting, or the nineteenth-century piece of furniture, the coin, the football card, or the letter from a famous person is shown to be a treasure, appraised at far more than the owner ever imagined. The most valuable items in the show's history have been paintings by Joseph Kleitsch, Robert Henri, Frederic Remington, and Diego Rivera; oriental jade and pottery; nineteenth-century Boston Red Stockings baseball memorabilia; a Navajo blanket; and a 1914 Patek Philippe pocket watch, all ranging in value from a few hundred thousand dollars to $1.5 million. Often handed down by family, sometimes

188. Danny McCain, *To the Ends of the Earth* (Calabar: Flourish Brands, 2010), 164–65.

189. Tim Keller, *Galatians for You* (Epsom, UK: The Good Book Company, 2013), 29.

brought out from an old trunk in a closet or a hook behind a door or a corner of the attic, the owner is shocked that this afterthought has suddenly become a treasure. Posture toward the item changes immediately and dramatically. Insurance against loss is suggested. The possession, hidden in obscurity for decades, is finally seen for what it is—an item of great value.

Paul understood that God calls us to the priceless pearl, the once-in-a-lifetime treasure in a field (Matt 13:44–46), which is sometimes hidden under layers of religious dust or cultural clutter but brought out by the Spirit of God and opened up on a Damascus Road to be appraised. The great prize toward which all of life must lean, for which all else must be abandoned, is offered by a king who brooks no rivals for affection and authority. His pearl of inestimable value will not be counted one bauble among many or one objective among others leading to a perceived "better life." Rather, here is the pursuit that negates all others, the relationship that trumps all others, and the one thing worth counting supreme and all else rubbish. "You cannot serve both God and mammon."

In his collection of Sabbath poems from 1979–1997 titled *A Timbered Choir*, Southern agrarian Wendell Berry laments the modern, relentless drive toward what he calls "the objective," an obsession that obliterates any sense of orientation or meaningful direction or place in life—driven people going nowhere. He describes coming to a city that looks just like every other city, a city filled with people pursuing "the objective," free to be enslaved by their relentless pursuit, to sell themselves to whomever offers the highest bid and opens the doors to "the best-paying prisons," all in the name of promotion, progress, contracts, and completed sales. Such "self-realization" and "self-creation" are deemed by the masses as their "salvation."[190]

In seeking "the objective," to gain "my" life according to what the world assesses as valuable, true life is lost. In seeking "the objective" of the present age to find my ultimate identity in *any* form of religion, enterprise, sense of self, cause, or relationship I eschew the one goal, which is knowing God himself in Christ. By embracing the gods of the age, I relinquish the kingdom come, which permeates and transforms the present. In failing to long for the consummation of my salvation in the face of Jesus Christ but rather longing for salvation in the face of the idols of this age, I debase myself with longings that are beneath me, longings that offer no sustainable foundations. Ironically, it is in losing my life that I find it, with God's whole world (remade) thrown in.

Thus, Paul's whole life—his understanding of his identity and purpose, what he most valued—was grounded, anchored, and oriented by where he had come from and where he was going. His calling and his goal, what he deemed the prize, all flowed

190. Wendell Berry, *A Timbered Choir: The Sabbath Poems, 1979–1997* (Washington, DC: Counterpoint, 1998), 208–9.

from and to Christ. Thus life was evaluated wholly in terms of gaining Christ, participating in Christ's righteousness and sufferings and resurrection. "To live is Christ."

For Paul and for us, Christ is the treasure who has a beginning-less past and an unending future. "All that is not eternal is eternally out of date," as C. S. Lewis famously quipped. "Gaining" him is worth everything we have, and our whole life should be bent in that direction, with our whole effort evaluated in that light, resolutely fixed on that prize.

Dear friend, toward what or whom is your life bent urgently? What is "the objective," large or small, about which you believe in the deepest corner of your heart, "Here is the answer for my life! If only I can have this, all will be well"? Health? Position? Competence? Religion? Wealth? A person? A place? Relief from a stressful situation or an abusive person? Moreover, a "Christian life," active ministry, or right theology is no guarantee that we are focused on the right objective in life either. Paul's key was that he had seen the glory of God in the face of Jesus Christ (2 Cor 4:5–6). Do we have that relationship, and is it *everything* for us?

10 CHAPTER

# Philippians 3:15–4:4a

## Literary Context

We have been walking through the great central corridor of Philippians, in which the apostle Paul proposes an antidote for disunity in the church at Philippi. As we have seen, this great central section of the book presents examples of leaders who embody self-sacrifice. Of course, Christ ranks first as the paradigmatic leader of all leaders in the church; the example of Christ, embodied in the narrative poem of 2:5–11, is then followed by a unit of exhortation (2:12–17). Paul next turns to the example set by his associates, Timothy and Epaphroditus, each of whom in their own way embodies sacrificial leadership (2:18–30). Finally, in 3:1–14, Paul presents himself for imitation and as an appropriate alternative to false teachers. The apostle's "all for Christ" approach to life rings in the readers' ears as the letter now turns again to exhortation (3:15–4:4a).

Here, Paul's call to imitation is overt: "Be imitators of me, brothers and sisters, and in the same way that you have us as role models, pay careful attention to those who live like we do" (3:17). The straightforward encouragement in 3:15–4:4a belies the structural significance of this unit, which echoes extensively both 1:27–2:4, the unit that launched the book's central section, and 2:6–11, the narrative poem focused on Christ. Consequently, 3:15–4:4a brings to a resounding conclusion what Paul has been building throughout the main body of the letter. Following 3:15–4:4a, the apostle closes the letter body in 4:4b–9 with yet another series of exhortations. He then crafts the letter closing, found at 4:10–23. Thus, at 3:15–4:4a we find ourselves at the penultima of the letter body (1:12–4:9), the apostle riveting attention on key concerns of the letter and calling for particular responses from the Philippians.

## Main Idea

Paul calls on the believers in Philippi to embrace his pattern of life, which denies a role for false teachers, relinquishes inappropriate status concerns, and embraces unity in the church for the cause of Christ.

## Translation

### Philippians 3:15–4:4a

| | | |
|---|---|---|
| 15a | Inference | Therefore, |
| b | Extent | as many as are mature, |
| c | Exhortation | **let us embrace this mindset.** |
| d | Condition/ Mitigation | And if any of you think differently, |
| e | Prediction | God will make this clear |
| f | Indirect Obj. | to you. |
| 16a | Contrast/Addition | In any case, |
| b | Exhortation | **let each of us live up** |
| c | Extent | to the level that we have reached. |
| 17a | Exhortation/Affection | **Be imitators of me,** brothers and sisters, |

| | | |
|---|---|---|
| b | Expansion | and, |
| c | Accordance | in the same way that you have us as role models, |
| d | Exhortation | **pay careful attention** |
| e | Object | to those who live like we do. |
| | | |
| 18a | Contr./Reason for 3:17 | For **many live a pattern of life** |
| b | Identification | about whom I have spoken to you many times and |
| c | Manner | mention them now, weeping |
| | | |
| d | Description | —enemies of the cross of Christ!— |
| | | |
| 19a | Description/ | whose end is destruction, |
| b | List (a–d) | whose god is their appetite and |
| c | | glory is in their shame, |
| | | |
| d | | who are intent on earthly things. |
| | | |
| 20a | Explanation | For |
| b | Assertion/Contrast | **our citizenship is in heaven** |
| c | Anticipation | from where we also eagerly await a Savior, |
| d | | the Lord Jesus Christ, |
| | | |
| 21a | Description | who will transform |
| b | Object | our bodies of humiliation |
| c | Objective | to be like his glorious body |
| | | |
| d | Accordance | in accordance with the power |
| e | Means | by which he is also able to subject |
| f | Object | all things |
| g | Ind. Obj. | to himself. |
| | | |
| 4:1a | Inference | For this reason, |
| b | Address/Affection | my brothers and sisters, |
| c | Description/List c–d | loved and longed for, |
| d | | my joy and crown, |
| e | Manner | in this way |
| f | Exhortation | **stand firm** |
| g | Relationship | in the Lord, dear loved ones. |
| | | |
| 2a | Appeal | **I urge Euodia** |
| b | | and |
| c | Appeal | **I urge Syntyche** to see eye to eye |
| d | Relationship | in the Lord. |
| 3a | Affirmation | Indeed, |
| b | Appeal | **I also ask you, true companion, to help these women** |
| c | Description | who have participated |
| d | | in gospel work |

*Continued on next page.*

| | | | |
|---|---|---|---|
| e | Association | | at my side, along |
| f | (List) | | with Clement and |
| g | | | the rest |
| h | | | of my fellow workers |
| i | Description | | whose names are in the book of life. |
| 4a | Exhortation | **Rejoice** | |
| | Relationship | in the Lord | |
| | Constancy | always! | |

## Structure

In 3:15–4:4a a series of exhortations tumbles urgently from the page. The structure of the passage falls into three general movements: 3:15–16; 3:17–21; and 4:1–4a. First, 3:15–16 issues a call to embrace Paul's Christocentric pattern of life. Verse 15 includes an exhortation to "embrace this mindset" (τοῦτο φρονῶμεν), and this "mindset" verb appears again at 4:2, where Euodia and Syntyche are urged "to see eye to eye in the Lord" (τὸ αὐτὸ φρονεῖν ἐν κυρίῳ).[1]

The second movement (3:17–21) focuses on the theme of imitation. In this unit, Paul first exhorts the Philippians to a pattern of life modeled after his life and the lives of those who live as he does (v. 17). He then warns of those who have a very different pattern of life and ministry (vv. 18–19). This second movement concludes with the basis for the Philippians to live this way: their citizenship in heaven and eventual resurrection (3:20–21).

The third and final movement (4:1–4a) makes Paul's main reason for writing Philippians overt. The apostle wants the church to stand firmly in unity, and this includes two female leaders in the church, Euodia and Syntyche, who seem to be at odds. Consequently, this movement ends with a call for these women to "get it together" and an appeal for Paul's coworker, his "true companion," to help them do just that.

1. The use of *inclusio* (the same or similar words at the beginning and toward the end of a passage) plays a significant role in marking 3:15–4:4a as a distinct unit.

## Exegetical Outline

→ **6. Exhortations to Embrace Paul's Christocentric Pattern of Life (3:15–4:4a)**

- **a. A Call to Embrace Paul's Christocentric Pattern of Life (vv. 15–16)**
  - (1) Be Unified around this Mindset (v. 15)
  - (2) Live Up to the Standard of Life You Have Attained (v. 16)
- **b. Imitate the Right Leaders (vv. 17–21)**
  - (1) Imitate Paul and Those Who Follow His Pattern (v. 17)
  - (2) Note Others Who Have a Different Pattern of Life and Ministry (vv. 18–19)
    - a) Identification: Paul Has Mentioned Them Before (v. 18)
    - b) Description (v. 19)
  - (3) The Basis for Imitating Paul's Pattern (vv. 20–21)
    - a) A Different Citizenship (v. 20a)
    - b) A Powerful Savior and Lord (vv. 20b–21)
- **c. Final Exhortations to Stand Firm in Unity (4:1–4a)**
  - (1) For this Reason, Stand Firm in the Lord (v. 1)
  - (2) The Relationship of Euodia and Syntyche (vv. 2–3)
  - (3) Rejoice! (v. 4a)

## Explanation of the Text

**3:15–16 Therefore, as many as are mature, let us embrace this mindset. And if any of you think differently, God will make this clear to you. In any case, let each of us live up to the level that we have reached** (Ὅσοι οὖν τέλειοι, τοῦτο φρονῶμεν· καὶ εἴ τι ἑτέρως φρονεῖτε, καὶ τοῦτο ὁ θεὸς ὑμῖν ἀποκαλύψει· 16 πλὴν εἰς ὃ ἐφθάσαμεν, τῷ αὐτῷ στοιχεῖν). Paul challenges the Philippians to embrace the mindset exemplified in his life and ministry. Following from reflections on his own Christ-centered life in 3:1–14, he now builds on those reflections ("therefore," οὖν) by crafting a series of exhortations. The apostle embodies an all-consuming drive toward life's true goal and ultimate prize and thus serves as a fit model for how the Philippians should think and live. Paul understands, of course, that such a posture will be adopted only to the extent that members of the community are spiritually mature: "as many as are mature."[2] The text seems to reflect a common pastoral situation. Paul knows that the spiritually mature Philippians will "get it," while others will have to grow into a Christocentric posture.[3] Given the apostle's denial that he himself has "reached the

2. The noun for "mature" conveys a more advanced stage of life; so Osiek, *Philippians, Philemon*, 99. The term rendered "as many as" (ὅσος) is a quantitative relative pronoun, often translated in the English versions with the relative "who" (so NRSV, ESV, CSB, NET, NIV, NLT). See Hellerman, *Philippians*, 206.

3. So Reumann, *Philippians*, 559–60; Hellerman, *Philippians*, 206; Cousar, *Philippians and Philemon*, 77.

goal" (τετελείωμαι) in verse 12, his use of a related word, translated as "mature" (τέλειος) in 3:15, is ironic, calling on those who are really "mature" to adopt the perspective that they have not yet "arrived."[4] At the very least he crafts a creative play on words.

Once again Paul calls the Philippians to embrace a particular mindset (φρονῶμεν). This word occurs twice in 3:15 and eight other times in Philippians.[5] As noted elsewhere in the commentary, the term refers to thinking along a certain line, setting one's mind on something, or adopting a perspective.[6] But the apostle often uses the word with the sense of being of one mind with another person or persons[7]—thus our translation "let us embrace this mindset." As is the case earlier in the letter, at 2:2, the exhortation here should be understood as Paul encouraging a unified posture of single-hearted commitment to a common cause—living robustly as a community on mission under the lordship of Christ.

It is a fact of pastoral life that every congregation has a spectrum of maturity among its members. So the apostle qualifies his exhortation:[8] "And if any of you think differently, God will make this clear to you" (καὶ εἴ τι ἑτέρως φρονεῖτε, καὶ τοῦτο ὁ θεὸς ὑμῖν ἀποκαλύψει). Paul mitigates his call to conform to his own life posture[9] with an expression of confidence in the continued growth of those who do not yet share his perspective. This mitigation may anticipate his direct exhortation to Euodia and Syntyche, to which he turns shortly (4:2). Whether or not that is the case, the theologically potent verb, which means "to make fully known," "reveal" (ἀποκαλύπτω), suggests that the apostle's comment here in 3:15 is no mere aside. Revelation from God is a serious matter, and Paul uses the terminology here just as he is about to discuss "enemies of the cross of Christ" (3:18–19).[10] Throughout the main body of Philippians, Paul resolutely calls the Philippians to follow the example of the mature and to adopt a common missional mindset that will unify them. His words in 3:2, 18–19 suggest that one function of unity is to help the Philippians stand against the lure of false teaching. Right theology revealed by God can only thrive in healthy community where the right exemplars are followed (3:17–19). In short, the members of the church need to align their perspectives for the sake of the gospel (4:2–3).

Verse 16 continues with "in any case, let each of us live up to the level that we have reached" (πλὴν εἰς ὃ ἐφθάσαμεν, τῷ αὐτῷ στοιχεῖν). The adverb translated as "in any case" (πλήν) functions as a conjunction, turning attention back to the exhortation "let us embrace this mindset" in 3:15.[11] A rather obscure pair of phrases calling the church back to this focused commitment make up verse 16.[12] The verb in the first phrase (φθάνω, "to arrive, reach") only occurs in the New Testament

4. E.g., Reumann, *Philippians*, 559–60; Silva, *Philippians*, 177.

5. Phil 1:7; 2:2 [2x], 5; 3:19; 4:2, 10 [2x].

6. BDAG 1065.

7. E.g., Rom 12:16; 15:5; 2 Cor 13:11; Phil 2:2, 5; 4:2.

8. Paul shapes the qualification with a first-class conditional sentence.

9. Holloway, *Philippians*, 176.

10. Contra Hansen, *Philippians*, 259.

11. The wording approximates the meaning "our momentary misalignment of perspectives aside." See BDAG 826. In v. 15 Paul switches from a first-person plural hortatory subjunctive (φρονῶμεν) to a second-person plural indicative (φρονεῖτε). He then in v. 16 returns to address the Philippians in first-person plural.

12. The obscurity is in part due to the ambiguity of the second half of the verse, τῷ αὐτῷ στοιχεῖν. This ambiguity gave rise to a variety of scribal additions, evidently seeking to clarify the clause. Yet the form as it stands has strong witnesses ($\mathfrak{P}^{16.46}$ א* A B I$^{vid}$ 6. 33. 1739 b co; Hil Aug). As Fee points out, the ambiguity of the verse has led to much unhelpful speculation on how Paul might be alluding to opponents. See Fee, *Philippians*, 360.

six other times.[13] Here it functions as part of the relative clause:[14] "unto that which we have reached" or, as with our translation, "to the level that we have reached." Paul seems to refer to the degree to which they have been living out the faith, as indicated by the remainder of the verse.

The verb στοιχέω conveys being in line with, agreeing with, or living according to a standard of conduct of some kind.[15] This present infinitive is imperatival in force and, in context, calls the church to a pattern of life.[16] We see the sense of the verb, for instance, at Acts 21:24 where Paul is said to live "in conformity to the law" (στοιχεῖς καὶ αὐτὸς φυλάσσων τὸν νόμον), and from Romans 4:12, which speaks of "those who conform to our father Abraham's footsteps of the faith" (τοῖς στοιχοῦσιν τοῖς ἴχνεσιν τῆς . . . πίστεως τοῦ πατρὸς ἡμῶν Ἀβραάμ). In our current verse, the apostle calls the Philippians "to live in conformity to the same" (τῷ αὐτῷ), almost certainly referring back to the prepositional phrase in the first half of the verse. In other words, the Philippians are called to live according to the pattern of "the level reached" in living out the Christian life.

Anytime there is a breakdown in community relationships, and Christ and the gospel get out of focus, the church runs the risk of spiritual regression.[17] Paul seems concerned that the community friction that has wormed its way into the church at Philippi could pose a real threat to the spiritual lives of its members, so he calls them to focus on a common goal rather than their petty differences.[18] They need to keep in view the real goal of the Christian life—intimacy with Christ himself, which will culminate at the resurrection of the dead. Whether or not everyone in the church has a level of maturity by which they can fully grasp Paul's Christocentric pressing on to the goal, he wants them all to live up to the level of the faith already achieved and not digress spiritually, losing sight of what is important in the heat of interpersonal conflicts. They will do this in part by following good role models, as we see in the next verse.

**3:17–19 Be imitators of me, brothers and sisters, and, in the same way that you have us as role models, pay careful attention to those who live like we do. For many live a pattern of life, about whom I have spoken to you many times and mention them now, weeping—enemies of the cross of Christ!—whose end is destruction, whose god is their appetite and glory is in their shame, who are intent on earthly things** (Συμμιμηταί μου γίνεσθε, ἀδελφοί, καὶ σκοπεῖτε τοὺς οὕτω περιπατοῦντας καθὼς ἔχετε τύπον ἡμᾶς. 18 πολλοὶ γὰρ περιπατοῦσιν οὓς πολλάκις ἔλεγον ὑμῖν, νῦν δὲ καὶ κλαίων λέγω, τοὺς ἐχθροὺς τοῦ σταυροῦ τοῦ Χριστοῦ, 19 ὧν τὸ τέλος ἀπώλεια, ὧν ὁ θεὸς ἡ κοιλία καὶ ἡ δόξα ἐν τῇ αἰσχύνῃ αὐτῶν, οἱ τὰ ἐπίγεια φρονοῦντες). In the main body of Philippians, Paul holds up stellar examples—Christ (2:5–11) and Timothy and Epaphroditus (2:18–30)—for emulation. At 3:2 he gives a counterpoint, warning the Philippians to watch out for false teachers. Then, having written of his own relentless pursuit of Christ in 3:7–14, he now moves toward a culmination in the letter body, offering himself and those who live like him as exemplars who provide a stark contrast to false ministers, "enemies of the cross of Christ."[19]

13. Matt 12:28; Luke 11:20; Rom 9:31; 2 Cor 10:14; 1 Thess 2:16; 4:15.

14. The construction εἰς + accusative pronoun connoting degree, "up to"—i.e., "fully" or "completely" (BDAG 289).

15. BDAG 946.

16. So, e.g., Hellerman, *Philippians*, 209.

17. So Fee, *Philippians*, 361–62.

18. So Reumann, *Philippians*, 561–62.

19. John Chrysostom writes, "Remember above when he said 'beware of dogs' and drew them away from those people? Now he directs them to what they ought to imitate" (Edwards, *Galatians, Ephesians, Philippians*, 262).

Thus Paul's own example to the church is bracketed by his concern about those who, if followed, would prove destructive to the church.

So the apostle offers to his "brothers and sisters" (ἀδελφοί)[20] twin exhortations to imitate worthy models—the first an exhortation to imitate Paul and the second an exhortation to imitate those who follow Paul's pattern of life and ministry. Paul does not speak out of arrogance, seeing himself as having arrived spiritually—a point he categorically denies in 3:12–14. Rather, he knows that he is running the race appropriately—he is on the right track, with the right motives and the right goal in view—and he invites the Philippians to run the race with him, to join him as his partners in life and ministry, in pursuing Christ.[21]

In both the Greek and Jewish contexts of the ancient world, the power of imitation was considered of high pedagogic value. Teachers, for instance, drove home the importance of a child imitating a parent (e.g., Philo, *Sacr.* 68) or a student imitating a teacher.[22] Paul normally uses the noun translated "imitator" (μιμητής; 1 Cor 4:16; 11:1; Eph 5:1; 1 Thess 1:6; 2:14), or the verb rendered "to imitate" (μιμέομαι; 2 Thess 3:7–9), but here he points to imitation as a community dynamic,[23] employing a compound form that means "fellow-imitators" (συμμιμηταί).[24] Imitation in community should also be an ongoing pattern of life.[25]

One of the challenges of Paul's ministry was that it consisted of extended periods of absence from his congregations, just as his current imprisonment had kept him away from Philippi. Thankfully, there were others associated with the apostle's mission who were worthy of imitation, as we have already seen with Timothy and Epaphroditus (Phil 2:18–30). Accordingly, Paul now exhorts the Philippians to "pay careful attention" (σκοπεῖτε) to those who follow his pattern of life. As noted in the commentary on 2:4, this verb[26] calls the reader to take particular notice of something or someone. This could include attending to the activities of false teachers, as at Romans 16:17, where Paul writes, "I urge you . . . to watch out for [σκοπεῖν] those who cause divisions and put obstacles in your way that are contrary to the teaching you have learned. Keep away from them" (NIV). That warning, of course, parallels the triple use of "watch out for" (βλέπετε) at Philippians 3:2: "Watch out for dogs . . . evil workers . . . those who ritually dismember others." In the broader context of Philippians, these false teachers are set over against leaders worthy of emulation who are marked by a noteworthy pattern of life.

The verb for "walk" (περιπατέω) could be used of the literal act of walking (which is the dominant use, for instance, in the Synoptic Gospels),[27] but Paul favors its metaphorical use as connoting a pattern of life or behavior that characterizes a person. Accordingly, here the word serves to call the Philippians to pattern their lives after "those who live like" (τοὺς οὕτω περιπατοῦντας)

20. As noted earlier in the commentary, ἀδελφοί was used to refer to both men and women in ancient religious contexts, and the broader literary context of the book makes clear that the apostle addresses both "brothers" and "sisters" through the letter (e.g., 4:2).

21. So Silva, *Philippians*, 179.

22. Keown, *Philippians 2:19–4:23*, 237; Bockmuehl, *Philippians*, 229.

23. Hansen, *Philippians*, 261; Reumann, *Philippians*, 566; Silva, *Philippians*, 188.

24. Since we do not find the term elsewhere in Greek literature, some think that the apostle may have coined the term (so, e.g., Bockmuehl, *Philippians*, 228).

25. The present imperative translated "be" (γίνεσθε) also could be translated into English with "become," and the verb offers a general instruction calling for an ongoing pattern of life.

26. Cognate of the noun σκοπός, "goal," in 3:14.

27. E.g., Matt 4:18; 9:5; 11:5; 15:31; Mark 2:9; 5:42; 6:48–49, etc.

Paul lives.[28] This notion of a pattern is underscored by a word often translated as "example" or "pattern" (τύπος). In the ancient world, the term could be used of a mark made by a blow or pressure (leaving an imprint that reflects the shape of the object used), or of a physical "copy," "image," or "model." Yet the apostle uses the word here with the figurative sense of an archetype, an example or pattern worth following.[29] The Philippians "have" (ἔχετε) such a pattern with reference to "us" (the accusative pronoun ἡμᾶς), as Paul most likely alludes to himself and those immediately associated with him—that is, "the brothers," with whom he normally travels on mission. But the Philippians also can see the pattern in certain local leaders. Since they have witnessed this type of life in Paul and his mission, they can identify it in sound leaders in the community.[30]

In verse 18 the apostle explains (γάρ) the reason why the Philippians should "pay careful attention" to good examples. There are "many" (πολλοί)[31] influencers who "live a pattern of life" (περιπατοῦσιν) at odds with the model established by Paul and his coworkers. In light of the warnings in 3:2, it may be that Paul has Jewish agitators in mind,[32] but given what Paul says here, other options should be considered. For instance, a lack of virtue seems to be one emphasis of 3:18–19 (i.e., their "walk"), which has suggested to some that Paul is more concerned with this lack of virtue than their aberrant theology.[33]

Also, Paul has mentioned these people on numerous occasions. In fact, he identifies them as those "about whom I have spoken to you many times" (οὓς πολλάκις ἔλεγον ὑμῖν). One can imagine, for instance, that as Paul traveled through Philippi on his so-called third mission trip (Acts 20:1–2, 6), he would have spoken openly about his opponents in Corinth, who engaged in a mix of false teaching and unrighteous living.[34] So as he writes to the Philippians, perhaps he speaks out of past conflicts with the Corinthian interlopers, bad leaders whom he had mentioned before.[35]

The apostle "now" (νῦν) feels the need to mention them again, and he does so "weeping" (κλαίων).[36] The language reflects an intensity of emotion. When Paul weeps in the New Testament, he reflects a deep concern for people, whether the church (Acts 20:31; 2 Cor 2:4) or the people of Israel (Rom 9:1–5; 10:1).[37] As is the case here in 3:18, concern often stems from the threat of the church being led astray via a faulty pattern of life or teaching, drifting from the truth about Jesus and his gospel. These leaders are far more than Paul's intellectual sparring partners. Rather, they are "enemies of the cross of Christ" (τοὺς ἐχθροὺς τοῦ σταυροῦ τοῦ Χριστοῦ).[38]

28. The construction τοὺς ... περιπατοῦντας is functioning as a substantival ("those walking") and is the direct object of σκοπεῖτε.

29. For these various uses, see BDAG 1019–20.

30. The use of οὕτω ... καθώς is correlative (e.g., Luke 24:24; Rom 11:26). The οὕτω (an alternate spelling to οὕτως), meaning "thus" or "so," anticipates καθώς, "just as," referring to the comparison to Paul's mission.

31. The word occurs regularly as a substantive without the article (e.g., Matt 7:22; 12:15; 20:28; Mark 2:2; 3:10).

32. See pp. 230–34 of commentary above.

33. E.g., Hansen, *Philippians*, 264–65.

34. On which see Guthrie, *2 Corinthians*, 41–46. Frank Thielman, who holds to an Ephesian imprisonment, speculates that Paul may have the Corinthian opponents in mind as he writes (Thielman, *Philippians*, 198).

35. Although, as pointed out by Bockmuehl, nowhere does Paul refer to the enemies as "teachers." Their hatred is directed at "the cross of Christ," which could be understood as a theological idea rather than a primarily moral one. Cf. Bockmuehl, *Philippians*, 230–31.

36. An adverbial participle expressing manner. A number of English translations take καί as adjunctive ("even," e.g., NASB, NRSV, ESV, NIV); for an ascensive use of the conjunction, see Wallace, *Greek Grammar*, 670–71.

37. Hellerman, *Philippians*, 216–17.

38. The Greek is truncated, lacking a verb, which is perhaps why 𝔓[46] adds the verb βλέπετε prior to τοὺς ἐχθρούς.

The word for enemy (ἐχθρός) speaks of hostility and hatred, and the enemies' hostility is aimed at "the cross" (τοῦ σταυροῦ),[39] which is associated with Christ himself.[40] The cross stands near the heart of Paul's gospel. It is unclear whether the enemies hate his cruciform message or the cruciform lifestyle to which it calls people. Again, some scholars understand the enemies here to refer to those who have departed from the way of Christ in their lifestyles rather than their teaching, but we suggest that this constitutes a false dichotomy. People live out what they believe. If they are living wrongly, they are thinking wrongly. Given the opportunity, they could draw the Philippians as well into destructive patterns of living.

The shame of the cross was an upside-down enigma in the Greco-Roman world, which valued honor and status. It remains very difficult for modern people to grasp the repulsion that the cross had for both Jews and Greeks in Paul's cultural context. Christ's death by crucifixion constituted a significant stumbling block. Paul preached "Christ crucified: a stumbling block to Jews and foolishness to Gentiles" (1 Cor 1:23 NIV). But to Paul and his brothers and sisters in Christ, both Jews and gentiles, he preached "Christ the power of God and the wisdom of God" (v. 24 NIV). The apostle knew that without the cross there is no true Christ-following. Evidently, the enemies knew this too.

At verse 19 the apostle tags the false leaders with four caustic descriptors:

| | | | |
|---|---|---|---|
| whose | end is destruction | ὧν | τὸ τέλος ἀπώλεια |
| whose | god is their appetite and | ὧν | ὁ θεὸς ἡ κοιλία καὶ |
| | glory is in their shame | | ἡ δόξα ἐν τῇ αἰσχύνῃ αὐτῶν |
| who | are intent on earthly things | οἱ | τὰ ἐπίγεια φρονοῦντες |

There are three main clauses, with the middle one combining two descriptions joined by καί. The first describes the ultimate outcome of their lives and "ministries," the last their life focus. Most damning, the middle two descriptions address the idolatrous condition of their hearts. At the heart of these false leaders' wrongheadedness lies wrong worship and twisted values.

Paul has already spoken in 3:12 of "reaching the goal" (τετελείωμαι); now he uses similar language to describe the false leader's destination: "whose end is destruction" (ὧν τὸ τέλος ἀπώλεια). The apostle uses the word translated "end" (τέλος) fourteen times in his writings, with uses similar to the current context at Romans 6:21 and 2 Corinthians 11:15. In the former, the Romans are said to be ashamed of things that *result* in death. In 2 Corinthians, Paul writes of those "whose outcome will be in line with their works" (my translation; ὧν τὸ τέλος ἔσται κατὰ τὰ ἔργα αὐτῶν). Here in Philippians 3:19 the "outcome" or end will be "destruction" (ἀπώλεια). Although this term could be used of the waste or destruction that a person causes (e.g., Mark 14:4), the word most often speaks of the destruction that a wicked person experiences as a form of judgment (e.g., Matt 7:13; John 17:12; Acts 8:20; Rom 9:22; 2 Thess 2:3; 1 Tim 6:9). At Philippians 1:28, Paul has already mentioned the coming "destruction" of the church's opponents in Philippi. He tags the courage of believers, as they stand together against opposition, as a sure sign of that destruction.

The second clause in 3:19 contains parallel descriptions: "whose god is their appetite and glory is in their shame" (ὧν ὁ θεὸς ἡ κοιλία καὶ ἡ δόξα ἐν τῇ αἰσχύνῃ αὐτῶν). The term translated as "appetite" (κοιλία) referred literally to the stomach but could be used figuratively of the "seat of inward

39. The Greek form functions as an objective genitive.

40. Here τοῦ Χριστοῦ is read as a genitive of association.

life, of feelings, desires" (cf. Rom 16:18).[41] If Paul has the latter in mind, these "desires" certainly could include a literal, physical appetite for food. The false leaders are driven people, yet what drives them is not the mission of God but their own appetites, manifesting a deeper spiritual corruption. In his book *Beyond Words*, Frederick Buechner writes of such a malady when he says, "A glutton is one who raids the icebox for a cure for spiritual malnutrition."[42]

Paul continues: "and glory is in their shame." The language here plays on the "honor-shame" structure of Paul's culture. The opponents treat as glorious what should be treated as shameful.[43] Their values are completely disordered.

Finally, Paul has consistently called the Philippians to adjust their perspective or change their focus, using the language of "thinking" (φρονέω), the verb variously used to speak of "giving careful thought to," "being intent on," or "having an opinion about" something. For example, in the letter he has challenged them to "share a common perspective" (2:2) and to "be intent on" Christ's posture of humility (2:5). At 3:15 he challenged the Philippians to align with his perspective on the "great race." At the beginning of chapter 4 he will exhort Euodia and Syntyche to "see eye to eye in the Lord" (4:2).

In contrast to right patterns of thinking and focus, the opponents mentioned in 3:19 "are intent on earthly things" (οἱ τὰ ἐπίγεια φρονοῦντες).[44] In its normal usage, the word rendered "earthly" (ἐπίγεια) offers a spatial contrast to heavenly things, and this is the case in most New Testament uses.[45] Yet the apostle here associates the "earthly" with that which is "worldly"[46] in the lives of the false teachers, their commitments placed in contrast to a heavenly citizenship mentioned in the next verse.[47] This passage, therefore, tends toward a negative use of the term for "earthly," as at James 3:15, where James speaks of a wisdom that is "earthly, unspiritual, demonic" (NIV). Thus the opponents' earthly focus gives rise to the "heavenly" exultation in the next two verses, even while prompting reflection on how the Christian hope is tied closely to Christ's incarnation, death, resurrection, and exaltation as Lord over the universe.

**3:20–21 For our citizenship is in heaven from where we also eagerly await a Savior, the Lord Jesus Christ, who will transform our bodies of humiliation to be like his glorious body in accordance with the power by which he is also able to subject all things to himself** (ἡμῶν γὰρ τὸ πολίτευμα ἐν οὐρανοῖς ὑπάρχει, ἐξ οὗ καὶ

41. BDAG 550.

42. Frederick Buechner, *Beyond Words: Daily Readings in the ABC's of Faith* (San Francisco: HarperOne, 2004), 130.

43. The only other place where the apostle uses the noun rendered "shame" (αἰσχύνη) is at 2 Cor 4:2, where it is aligned with deception and mishandling the word of God. See his use of the cognate verb αἰσχύνω earlier in Philippians 1:20, where he expresses his desire to not shame himself at his hearing. He also uses the cognate verb ἐπαισχύνομαι at Rom 1:16 and 6:21, along with καταισχύνω, which speaks of "shaming" someone (e.g., Rom 5:5; 9:33; 10:11).

44. Although Paul has switched from the relative pronoun to the article in this third description, the article functions as a relative. He also culminates his descriptions of the false leaders by moving from verbless relative clauses to using a participial phrase.

45. So, for instance, when Jesus speaks to Nicodemus in John 3:12 he notes that he had been speaking of "earthly" things, which Nicodemus should have believed. At 1 Cor 15:40 Paul contrasts "heavenly" bodies with "earthly" bodies. In 2 Cor 5:1 Paul refers to the human body as an "earthly" tent. And, as we have seen at Phil 2:10, the word can be used generally of things associated with earth.

46. One reading of the term ἐπίγεια—rather than referring to common matters of everyday life in the world—speaks of "worldly values" that are set against the will of God. See Thielman, *Philippians*, 198.

47. Structurally, as shown in the "Literary Context" section above, ἐπίγεια and φρονοῦντες echo elements of the Christ hymn in 2:6–11, initiating a series of echoes that continues through 3:21.

σωτῆρα ἀπεκδεχόμεθα κύριον Ἰησοῦν Χριστόν, 21 ὃς μετασχηματίσει τὸ σῶμα τῆς ταπεινώσεως ἡμῶν σύμμορφον τῷ σώματι τῆς δόξης αὐτοῦ κατὰ τὴν ἐνέργειαν τοῦ δύνασθαι αὐτὸν καὶ ὑποτάξαι αὐτῷ τὰ πάντα). Paul now turns to the significance of our heavenly citizenship, focusing attention on Christ as Savior. Thus far in the passage we have seen a short series of exhortations (3:15–17), followed by a contrast between the pattern of Paul's life (along with those who emulate him) and the pattern lived out by the "enemies of the cross of Christ" (vv. 18–19). That contrast, introduced with γάρ at the beginning of 3:18, now leads into another contrast, also introduced by γάρ (v. 20),[48] with the attention now shifting away from the enemies back to the example of those in the Pauline mission. As noted in the introduction to 3:15–4:4a and its "Literary Context" section above, 3:20–21 extensively echoes the narrative poem about Christ in 2:6–11, with the Lord's incarnation and exaltation theologically linked to the believer's transformation through resurrection.

The reference to "earthly things" (τὰ ἐπίγεια) in verse 19 now gives rise to a contrasting spatial reference, "in heaven" (ἐν οὐρανοῖς; the plural; lit. "in the heavens") in verse 20. Rather than pointing to the physical universe, the apostle's referent is to "heaven" as the transcendent dwelling place of God,[49] the place of "our citizenship" (ἡμῶν . . . τὸ πολίτευμα . . . ὑπάρχει[50]). At 1:27 Paul exhorts the Philippians, "Live out your heavenly citizenship" (πολιτεύομαι), and a related noun referring to citizenship (πολίτευμα) occurs here. As noted in our discussion of 1:27, this family of terms could be used to speak of a group or association of citizens, or civil administration. Although the noun form occurs only here in the New Testament, it also appears in such diverse literature as the LXX, Epictetus, Josephus,[51] Philo,[52] and the Pseudepigrapha, each time referring to a group or association of citizens. Notably, it can refer to a group of citizens living abroad.[53]

In our discussion of the verb at 1:27, we note that Paul probably uses citizenship language in light of the high value that the people of Philippi placed on the city's legal status as a Roman colony. As pointed out in that discussion, the "unity" theme, so prominent in the letter, was considered a social value. It appears frequently in inscriptions of the era, celebrating the virtue of unity in the context of a political association.[54] What Paul seems to refer to, however, is heavenly citizenship,[55] not just living out Roman civic values in a "Christian" way. The notion of heavenly citizenship also occurs at Hebrews 11:8–16, where the author celebrates people of faith who trust God in pursuit of "a better place—a heavenly one," a city that God has prepared for them. Only God builds things that are permanent.

So, here in 3:20 Paul's "citizenship" theology is countercultural. Rather than mere citizens of a Roman colony with Caesar as their imperial lord, the Philippians should identify primarily as citizens of Christ's colony, as they live for Jesus, the true

48. In Greek grammar, a series of clauses could be introduced by γάρ, with each supporting a key idea, or in the case of this passage, the twin exhortations of v. 17. The function of γάρ is still explanatory in the general sense of offering bases for the exhortation, even though "contrast" clearly is built into the context as we move from v. 17 to v. 18, and again with the move from v. 19 to v. 20.

49. See, e.g., Matt 5:16; 6:1; 7:11; 10:33; 12:50; 16:17; Mark 11:25; Luke 11:2.

50. Note the echo of the same term at 2:6.

51. It normally refers to a government or commonwealth, e.g., *Ant.* 1.5, 13; 11.157; 12.108; *Ag. Ap.* 2.145, 164–65, 184, 250, 257.

52. *Creation* 143; *Agriculture* 81; *Confusion* 109; *Joseph* 69; *Spec. Laws* 2.45.

53. Bockmuehl, *Philippians*, 233.

54. Winter, *Welfare of the City*, 102–3.

55. So Fee, *Philippians*, 162; Silva, *Philippians*, 80, 88.

lord of all people (cf. Phil 2:10–11).[56] That identity includes the understanding that our Lord, at the culminating moment of human history, will come from "heaven"[57] to put things right in the world and to gather his people to himself.

The second coming of Christ is a consistent theme of the New Testament. During Christ's earthly ministry, the disciples were interested in that event, asking, "When will this happen, and what will be the sign of your coming?" (Matt 24:3 NIV). Jesus noted that the coming would be sudden (vv. 27, 39) and would catch people off guard amid normal, everyday activities (v. 37). By contrast, Christ-followers should live in anticipation of the coming as a time of great joy and community celebration (1 Thess 2:19), preparing themselves for it by living blameless, holy lives (3:13; 5:23; 1 John 2:28). They are to anticipate the coming but are to be patient in doing so (Jas 5:7–8; 2 Pet 3:12).

Paul notes that we "eagerly await" (ἀπεκδεχόμεθα) the second advent of Christ.[58] This verb occurs normally in association with the coming of Christ (so 1 Cor 1:7; Gal 5:5; Heb 9:28); for example, it speaks of the creation's eager expectation of God's children being revealed at the end of the age (Rom 8:19), and of the way that believers long for the resurrection and adoption to sonship (8:23–25). At that coming, not only will Christ be manifested as Lord of the universe (Acts 2:34; 1 Cor 16:22; Phil 2:10–11) and the Messiah (Acts 3:20), but he will act as Savior (σωτήρ) of his people (John 4:42; Acts 5:31; 1 Tim 1:1; 2 Tim 1:10; Heb 9:28).

The noun translated "Savior" (σωτήρ)[59] was used in the Greco-Roman world of deities who delivered, healed, and protected people, and also of generals, kings, and the Caesars, who at times were hailed as "savior of the world."[60] This sense in the broader culture stands in stark contrast to the use of the term in the LXX, where God himself is celebrated as "Savior" (e.g., Ps 24:5; 26:9; Isa 45:15; Mic 7:7). Interestingly, Paul only employs the title here, at Ephesians 5:23, and extensively in the Pastoral Epistles, where it is used interchangeably for "God" and the Lord Jesus.[61] Given the context at the end of Philippians 3, this is almost certainly an instance of anti-imperial rhetoric, drawing on a strand of biblical theology, even as the apostle boldly proclaims Christ as the true "Caesar" of the universe.[62] We long for our Savior, who will consummate our salvation, as he delivers us from the ravages of a dark and fallen world, bringing renewal to all things.

One of the most significant aspects of salvation is celebrated in verse 21, where Jesus is hailed as the one "who will transform our bodies[63] of humiliation to be like his glorious body" (ὃς μετασχηματίσει τὸ σῶμα τῆς ταπεινώσεως ἡμῶν σύμμορφον τῷ σώματι τῆς δόξης αὐτοῦ). Four words in this statement echo the narrative poem in chapter 2, which are translated here as "transform"

56. So Bockmuehl, *Philippians*, 98.

57. The relative construction ἐξ οὗ almost certainly delimits οὐρανοῖς rather than τὸ πολίτευμα. Cf. the parallel thought at 1 Thess 1:10: "And to wait for his Son from heaven, whom he raised from the dead—Jesus, who rescues us from the coming wrath" (NIV).

58. The compound ἀπεκδέχομαι is used eight times in the NT, here and at Rom 8:19, 23, 25; 1 Cor 1:7; Gal 5:5; Heb 9:28; 1 Pet 3:20. With its ἀπ- prefix, the word is an intensification of ἐκδέχομαι, which means to "expect" or "await" the arrival of someone or some event.

59. It is marked as emphatic by its lack of article and its forward position in the clause. So Fee, *Philippians*, 380–81.

60. Reumann, *Philippians*, 577.

61. Eph 5:23; Phil 3:20; 1 Tim 1:1; 2:3; 4:10; 2 Tim 1:10; Titus 1:3–4; 2:10, 13; 3:4, 6.

62. So Hansen, *Philippians*, 270–71; Reumann, *Philippians*, 598; Peter Oakes, *Rome in the Bible and the Early Church* (Carlisle: Paternoster, 2002), 138–39.

63. The use of the singular in Greek is collective, referring to the individual bodies of believers.

(μετασχηματίσει), "humiliation" (ταπεινώσεως), "be like" (σύμμορφον), and "glorious" (δόξης). The verb μετασχηματίσει speaks of "changing the form" of something.[64] At 2 Corinthians 11:13, for instance, Paul uses this term to speak of Satan transforming himself into an angel of light.

Here in verse 21, Paul describes this resurrection transformation in three ways. First, "our bodies of humiliation," our mortal bodies, answers the question, *What will be transformed?* (cf. 1 Cor 15:35–56). The hope of resurrection involves a continuity and discontinuity between the earthly body and the renewed resurrected body. The word rendered "humiliation" (ταπείνωσις) belongs to a family of terms having to do with humility (cf. Luke 1:48; Acts 8:33; Jas 1:10). Our bodies are "humiliated" in the sense of being "corruptible" or "mortal," which we feel increasingly with age or as we experience various kinds of suffering, including persecution. Paul uses the term as a stark contrast to "glorious" (δόξα) later in the verse. Again, we have an echo of the narrative poem in 2:6–11, for Jesus "humiliated (ἐταπείνωσεν) himself by becoming obedient all the way to the point of death," making himself vulnerable in his mortality. His humiliation was directly related to his death on the cross and was a pre-step to his resurrection in a glorious body. So, in the resurrection, the humiliation of our disintegrating, mortal bodies will give way to glory, as did his.

Second, the transformation will involve our bodies being brought to a state of sharing the likeness (σύμμορφος) of Christ's glorious body. This answers the question, *What will our bodies be like?* The term connotes "having a similar form, nature, or style."[65] It only occurs here and at Romans 8:29, which reads "because those whom he foreknew he also predestined to be conformed [συμμόρφους] to the image of his Son, that his Son would be the firstborn among many brothers and sisters" (NET). The use here in Philippians 3:21 echoes the two uses of the related word for "form" (μορφή) at 2:6–7, which refer respectively to the Son "being robed in divine glory" and having "the outward appearance of a slave." It also echoes the conformity to Christ's death (συμμορφιζόμενος) mentioned at 3:10. In contradistinction from both of those other contexts in Philippians, however, the emphasis in 3:21 rests squarely on the nature of the resurrection body.[66] Christ as the "firstfruits" of the resurrection (1 Cor 15:20) precedes that of believers, but believers will receive resurrection bodies like his, which are "of glory," or "glorious" (τῆς δόξης). This could refer to their being fit for the transcendent realm, but given Paul's discussion of the "glory" of various kinds of bodies in 1 Corinthians 15:40–43, he may here refer to their magnificence.[67] Paul's confession is another way of saying that the "mortal will take on immortality" (1 Cor 15:53) or that "when our earthly residence, a tent, is torn down, we have a building from God" (2 Cor 5:1), which is gloriously different from our earthly bodies.

Third, the transformation will be effected by power (ἐνέργεια), the same eschatological power exerted in the rule of Christ over all things: "In

64. The verb is only used elsewhere in the NT at 1 Cor 4:6 and 2 Cor 11:13. In addition to the sense of "transform," the verb could also mean "to show a connection or bearing of one thing on another, apply to" (e.g., 1 Cor 4:6). See BDAG 641.

65. BDAG 958.

66. Contra Fee, who states, "It is especially doubtful whether Paul intended 'glorious body,' as though he were describing the nature of the new body itself," interpreting it rather as a reference to Jesus's glorified state, which "belongs to his glory" (Fee, *Philippians*, 382–83). Yet Paul's parallel discussion in 1 Cor 15:42–44, which describes the natural body over against the spiritual, seems to contradict this assumption. There, "glory" is contrasted with "dishonor," "power" with "weakness," and "perishable" with "imperishable," all of which seem to point to the nature of the body.

67. At 15:43, for instance, Paul contrasts the "glory" of the resurrection body with the "dishonor" (ἀτιμίᾳ) of the earthly body. See BDAG 256–58.

accordance with the power by which he is also able to subject all things to himself" (κατὰ τὴν ἐνέργειαν τοῦ δύνασθαι αὐτὸν καὶ ὑποτάξαι αὐτῷ τὰ πάντα). Here the apostle answers the question, *How are we to be changed?* Elsewhere in the New Testament, this verb for "submit" (ὑποτάσσω) is associated with the exaltation of Christ in reflection on Psalms 8:6 and 110:1 (LXX 8:7 and 109:1). The early church pulled these psalms together via verbal analogy, as both refer to "enemies" or "all things" being submitted under "his feet":

| | | |
|---|---|---|
| Ps 110:1 (109:1 LXX): | ἕως ἂν θῶ τοὺς ἐχθρούς σου ὑποπόδιον | τῶν ποδῶν σου |
| | "until I make your enemies a footstool for your feet" (NETS) | |
| Ps 8:6 (8:7 LXX): | πάντα ὑπέταξας ὑποκάτω | τῶν ποδῶν αὐτοῦ |
| | "you subjected all under his feet" (NETS) | |

At the end of the age, the submission of all things to Christ—already a fact according to Psalm 8 as it is used in Hebrews 2:5–9—will be consummated as all enemies are placed under the feet of Christ (cf. Ps 110:1 in Heb 1:13, etc.). That great end-of-the-age power will have no rival, will leave no enemy unaddressed and no authority still standing, as even death is utterly and finally defeated.[68] That power will also command the death-corrupted atoms of all those dead in Christ to transform into new, immortal bodies, fit for a new heavens and new earth. We have a great deal to which we should look forward.

**4:1 For this reason, my brothers and sisters, loved and longed for, my joy and crown, in this way stand firm in the Lord, dear loved ones** (Ὥστε, ἀδελφοί μου ἀγαπητοὶ καὶ ἐπιπόθητοι, χαρὰ καὶ στέφανός μου, οὕτως στήκετε ἐν κυρίῳ, ἀγαπητοί). The heavenly perspective of 3:20–21 now becomes the basis (ὥστε, "for this reason") of a climactic exhortation, as the apostle turns toward concluding remarks.[69] An effusive string of affectionate terms permeates 4:1, and this seems both sincere and strategic as Paul prepares to confront Euodia and Syntyche in the next verse.

The apostle again draws on "family" language, calling the Philippians "brothers and sisters" (ἀδελφοί), an address he uses six times in the letter (Phil 1:12; 3:1, 13, 17; 4:1, 8).[70] This family term, with the addition of "my" (μου), presents a common and very personal expression in the apostle's writings.[71] Paul continues putting words to his affection for the Philippians, calling them "loved" (ἀγαπητοί).[72] This word is also used vocatively at the end of the verse, addressing the Philippians as "loved," "dear," or "greatly valued" people.[73] They also are "longed for" (ἐπιπόθητοι), and this theme of "longing for" another is a common motif in friendship letters of the ancient world.[74] The adjective speaks of intense desire of some kind.

68. Silva, *Philippians*, 185.

69. Reumann, *Philippians*, 605, although Reumann sees v. 1 as beginning a new unit. Our reason for extending the unit through v. 4a in part concerns the lexical links between 1:27–2:4 and the whole of 3:15–4:4a (see the "Literary Context" discussion above.).

70. Paul also uses the affectionate term of Epaphroditus at 2:25 and "the brothers and sisters" in his mission at 4:21. Some translations render the latter as "brothers," since Paul normally travels with other men (e.g., NASB, ESV, CSB, NET, NLT), but given his current imprisonment in Rome, he may well have members of that Christian community in mind, both men and women.

71. See Rom 7:4; 9:3; 15:14; 1 Cor 1:11; 8:13; 11:33; 14:39; 15:58; 2 Cor 2:13; 8:22–23; Phil 3:1, 13; 1 Thess 3:2; Phlm 20.

72. This heartfelt phrase of address, "my loved brothers and sisters" (ἀδελφοί μου ἀγαπητοί), occurs elsewhere in the Pauline corpus at 1 Cor 15:58, and three times in James (1:16, 19; 2:5).

73. BDAG 7.

74. See Fee, *Philippians*, 387; Stanley K. Stowers, "Friends and Enemies in the Politics of Heaven: Reading Theology in Philippians," in *Pauline Theology*, ed. J. M. Bassler (Minneapolis: Fortress, 1991), 109.

Paul simply means that he "misses" the Philippians terribly, as you and I miss dear friends or family members from whom we are separated for a time.

Further, Paul has already noted that he prays "with joy" on behalf of the Philippians (1:4) and that their unity in the faith gives him joy (2:2).[75] In Paul's letters, joy is most often a relational dynamic, a by-product of interpersonal relationships with God and other believers.[76] Now he calls them "my joy and crown" (χαρὰ καὶ στέφανός μου). Simply put, as his "joy," the apostle delights in his relationship with this church. Yet it is more than this, for both "joy" and "crown" point to eschatological realities (cf. 1 Thess 2:19). Paul will experience joy as the Philippians make it to the ultimate outcome of the faith (cf. Phil 3:14–15). When Paul calls the Philippians "my crown" (στέφανός μου), he draws on imagery from Greco-Roman athletic events, where a weaving of laurel, ivy, oak, or olive branches formed a crown marking a contender's victory. At the eschaton, the Philippians would be representative of Paul's exceptional service, and thus they are his reason for "boasting" in the work of God before the Lord (1 Thess 2:19).[77]

The verse ends with Paul exhorting his "loved ones" (ἀγαπητοί) to "stand firm in the Lord" (στήκετε ἐν κυρίῳ). They are to do so "in this way" (οὕτως), referring back to the string of exhortations at the end of chapter 3.[78] Paul thus caps off the general exhortations that he has just given to the church as a whole. Earlier in the letter, the apostle exhorted the Philippians to "stand firm" (στήκω, 1:27). The term can, of course, be taken literally to describe a standing position, but Paul uses it figuratively in Philippians of being firmly committed, grounded in a particular belief and consequent way of life.[79] In particular, stability in life and the community flow from a common commitment to the gospel and a common relation to the Lord himself, with "in the Lord" (ἐν κυρίῳ) in 4:1 understood as a dative of relationship.[80]

**4:2–4a I urge Euodia and I urge Syntyche to see eye to eye in the Lord. Indeed, I also ask you, true companion, to help these women who have participated in gospel work at my side, along with Clement and the rest of my fellow workers whose names are in the book of life. Rejoice in the Lord always!** (Εὐοδίαν παρακαλῶ καὶ Συντύχην παρακαλῶ τὸ αὐτὸ φρονεῖν ἐν κυρίῳ. 3 ναὶ ἐρωτῶ καὶ σέ, γνήσιε σύζυγε, συλλαμβάνου αὐταῖς, αἵτινες ἐν τῷ εὐαγγελίῳ συνήθλησάν μοι μετὰ καὶ Κλήμεντος καὶ τῶν λοιπῶν συνεργῶν μου, ὧν τὰ ὀνόματα ἐν βίβλῳ ζωῆς. 4 Χαίρετε ἐν κυρίῳ πάντοτε). Paul now offers a very direct, personal exhortation to two leaders in the church. It is unusual and therefore of great significance that Paul *names* these women, exhorting each of them individually (notice the repetition of the verb!). Rather than an act of public shaming, the apostle's exhortation should be read as firm but warmly encouraging, especially in light of the strong commendation in verse 3 of Euodia

75. In addition, his continued presence with them will give them joy (1:25), and they likewise should receive Epaphroditus with joy (2:29).

76. Rom 14:17; 15:13, 32; 2 Cor 1:24; 2:3; 7:4, 13; 8:2; Gal 5:22; Col 1:11; 1 Thess 1:6; 2:19–20; 3:9; 2 Tim 1:4; Phlm 1:7.

77. Hellerman, *Philippians*, 227. In the Gospels the word "crown" (στέφανος) is used of Jesus's crown of thorns (Matt 27:29; Mark 15:17; John 19:2, 5). For the term's various uses in the rest of the NT, see 1 Cor 9:25; 1 Thess 2:19; 2 Tim 4:8; Jas 1:12; 1 Pet 5:4; Rev 2:10; 3:11; 4:4, 10; 6:2; 9:7; 12:1; 14:14.

78. The word could be used to anticipate what comes next (so, Silva, *Philippians*, 186), but it normally is used retrospectively, as suggested by Fee, *Philippians*, 388.

79. See BDAG 944.

80. Another option is to understand the preposition to be reflecting agency, the Philippians enabled to stand "by the Lord" (so Harris, *Prepositions*, 129).

and Syntyche as fellow workers. Paul leaves opponents anonymous; he names friends and associates. Nevertheless, the naming also speaks to the gravity of the strained relationship between these women. The situation must be serious indeed for the letter to come to a point of unmistakable intensity at this juncture.[81]

The name Euodia (Εὐοδία) means "good journey" and was thus associated in Greco-Roman culture with wishes for success.[82] Syntyche (Συντύχη), on the other hand, could mean "chance" or "change of fortune" or "luck."[83] Her name, along with the names of Eutychus (Acts 20:9), Tychicus (Acts 20:4; Col 4:7), and Fortunatus (1 Cor 16:17), were associated with the goddess Fortuna, who was believed to govern human affairs.[84] All that we know of Euodia and Syntyche stems from our current passage, but the context tells us a good bit. Given the strategic placement of this reference to these two women, it seems that their conflict was at the heart of Paul's heartfelt concern about the Philippians' unity. This inference is based on two facts.

First, Euodia and Syntyche are urged by name in strongly worded, twin exhortations "to see eye to eye in the Lord" (τὸ αὐτὸ φρονεῖν ἐν κυρίῳ). The verb translated "urge" (παρακαλῶ) could be used to mean "exhort, appeal to, implore, urge strongly."[85] In urging them to align their perspectives, Paul once again uses a verb that we have seen multiple times in this letter to call the Philippians to think in a certain way (φρονέω; cf. uses and commentary at 1:7; 2:2 [2x], 5; 3:15 [2x], 19; 4:10 [2x]), and here they are encouraged to think "the same . . . in the Lord" (τὸ αὐτό . . . ἐν κυρίῳ). Thus they are to align their perspectives, or "see eye to eye," based on their common relationship with the Lord,[86] which is the most important frame of reference for the exhortation to unity. Their common relationship "in the Lord" provides a powerful incentive and a firm basis for healthy relationship as members of Christ's church. The fact that Paul uses the present active imperative παρακαλῶ ("I strongly urge," "exhort," "implore") twice, addressing each woman individually, suggests an intensity to the exhortation.[87]

Second, as pointed out in the "Literary Context" discussions of 1:27–2:4 and 3:15–4:4a, the exhortation to Euodia and Syntyche plays a critical culminating role in the letter's structure. This exhortation to unity plays an important part in the closing of an *inclusio* around the book's main body. That these two are named and exhorted to unity in this pivotal place in the letter speaks to the relational dynamics about which Paul is concerned. Given the thread of key themes in the letter thus far, the problem between them may stem from "envy, rivalry, self-centeredness, selfish ambition, and pride."[88]

Further evidence of Paul's intense concern for Euodia and Syntyche is found in 4:3, which begins with an appeal: "Indeed, I also ask you, true companion, to help these women" (ναὶ ἐρωτῶ καὶ σέ, γνήσιε σύζυγε, συλλαμβάνου αὐταῖς). As Paul turns from his exhortations to Euodia and Syntyche, he emphatically adds "indeed" (ναί)[89]

81. On this moment in the book's structure, see Garland, "Composition," 173.

82. LSJ 724.

83. LSJ 1729.

84. Hellerman, *Philippians*, 229.

85. BDAG 764–65.

86. See the uses of ἐν Χριστῷ Ἰησοῦ at Phil 1:1, 26; 2:5; 3:3, 14; 4:7, 19, 21; ἐν Χριστῷ at Phil 1:13; 2:1; ἐν κυρίῳ is used elsewhere at Phil 1:14; 2:19, 24, 29; 3:1; 4:1, 4, 10.

87. The verb could be translated "invite" or "speak to in a friendly manner," but the double exhortation in context suggests a bit more urgency than would be communicated by these translations. See BDAG 764–65.

88. Keown, *Philippians 2:19–4:23*, 314.

89. BDAG 665.

to a request (ἐρωτῶ) addressed to an unnamed leader of the church, whom he simply refers to as a "true companion" (γνήσιε σύζυγε). Paul describes this colleague as "true" (γνήσιος), which speaks of something "true" or "legitimate," originally referring to a "legitimate" child, which is the sense of the description at 1 Timothy 1:2 and Titus 1:4. Elsewhere Paul could speak of the genuineness of the Corinthians' love (2 Cor 8:8).[90] Speaking of Euodia and Syntyche, Paul's appeal is that this person "help them" (συλλαμβάνου αὐταῖς). This verb could communicate a variety of meanings, including "to apprehend" or "seize," "to catch," "to become pregnant," any of which would make for an interesting translation here! Yet here Paul uses the term to convey "support, aid, help,"[91] as an appeal for his friend to work with these women toward the restoration of their relationship.[92]

Verse 3 continues with further information about Euodia and Syntyche, as Paul refers to them as members of a broader ministry team. These women "have participated in gospel work" (ἐν τῷ εὐαγγελίῳ συνήθλησάν) alongside their apostle ("at my side," μοι). The verb communicating participation (συναθλέω) speaks of struggle alongside of others in a cause.[93] As with the use of the participial form at 1:27, the struggle probably involved standing resolutely for the gospel in the face of a hostile culture and perhaps engagement in gospel proclamation. In any case, Euodia and Syntyche had labored alongside Paul in advancing the cause of Christ. They had done so "along with Clement and the rest of" his "fellow workers" (μετὰ καὶ Κλήμεντος καὶ τῶν λοιπῶν συνεργῶν μου). Clement's name is from the Latin *Clemens*, but no evidence exists that associates this person with others by that name in the early church.[94] With the word translated as "fellow workers" (συνεργῶν), we have a very common term for partners in Paul's mission (cf. Phil 2:25).[95]

When Paul writes "whose names are in the book of life" (ὧν τὰ ὀνόματα ἐν βίβλῳ ζωῆς), the relative pronoun "whose" (ὧν) probably refers to all those mentioned in the verse, including Euodia and Syntyche. That their "names are in the book of life" alludes to an image used earlier in the Old Testament (Exod 32:32–33; Ps 69:28; Dan 12:1; cf. Rev 3:5; 20:15). Though uncommon for Paul, the language here refers to those whose names had been recorded as recipients of eternal life. Just as there were civic registries of Roman citizens in Philippi, heavenly citizens had their names recorded in God's "book of life."[96]

Paul's exhortations to "rejoice" form a bright thread through this letter (1:18; 2:17–18, 28; 3:1; 4:4, 10), playing important structural and hortatory roles in the discourse. As we have seen throughout the letter, a double exhortation to rejoice occurs at key seams in the discourse, the first in a pair wrapping up one movement and a second introducing the next. Structurally, this encouragement to "rejoice" at 4:4a forms a bracket (*inclusio*) with the same exhortation at 3:1, marking the beginning and ending of this major movement in the letter.

> "Rejoice in the Lord!" (χαίρετε ἐν κυρίῳ) (3:1)
> "Rejoice in the Lord always!" (χαίρετε ἐν κυρίῳ πάντοτε) (4:4a)

90. *EDNT* 255.
91. BDAG 955.
92. The dative plural αὐταῖς may be a dative of association.
93. *EDNT* 296.
94. Hellerman, *Philippians*, 232–33.
95. See also Rom 16:3, 9, 21; 1 Cor 3:9; 2 Cor 1:24; 8:23; Col 4:11; 1 Thess 3:2; Phlm 1, 24. This is the fourth time in this verse that Paul uses a compound word with the συν- ("fellow-"; "with") prefix (σύζυγε, συλλαμβάνου, συνήθλησάν)! The stacking up of such forms creates a not-so-subtle emphasis on the need for unity in the church.
96. Fee, *Philippians*, 396–97.

In this way Paul brings the great center section of Philippians to a close. The rolling, striking examples of sacrificial leadership—the Lord Jesus Christ (2:5–11), Timothy and Epaphroditus (2:18–3:1), and Paul himself (3:2–14)—culminate in a call to the Philippians—particularly specific leaders—to take decisive action to bolster church unity. Such unity will be achieved as the church remembers their common cause in living out the mission for their common Lord as citizens of his heavenly city.

## Theology in Application

### *Community and the Processing of Conflict*

Addressing the conflict between Euodia and Syntyche must not have been easy for Paul, since he went to a great deal of trouble setting up what we know as Philippians 4:2–3. Dealing with conflict in a community is never easy. But we can learn from Paul as he addresses the need for unity between these two women who had stood with him for the gospel. What might we take away that could help us when we are dealing with conflict in the church? First, *Paul has a history with Euodia and Syntyche*. As pointed out in the commentary, that the apostle names them means that he values and trusts them as friends. It is always easier to confront someone if you have a "history" with them. Second, *they have worked together in a common cause*. This becomes a basis for "getting it together" as they move into the future. We need to appeal to people out of a common commitment to the gospel. We need to train them to that commitment and then help them see the supreme value of that commitment in all aspects of life. If that does not exist, it becomes very difficult to find motivation for reconciliation in the church. Third, it is noteworthy that Paul *makes an appeal rather than giving a command*. His public call to these women is not authoritarian. Rather, he urges them—strongly, to be sure—rather than backing them into a corner. As we attempt to lead people to reconciliation with one another, our tone and posture are important. Finally, *Paul's appeal is done in the context of a broader community*. It takes a community to build healthy Christian lives, and it takes healthy Christians to build a community. We always have a greater chance of leading people to reconciliation if they are surrounded by a loving, gospel-focused community.

### *Imitatio Veri (Imitation of Truth)*

As detailed in 3:15–4:4a, the twin themes of "examples to follow" and "imitation" shape the center section of Philippians. At this point in history, at least in North America, it may seem presumptuous for a minister to stand in the pulpit and say, "Imitate me as I follow Christ!" But we should give thought to how we might live out Paul's words on the importance of imitation for healthy patterns of life in the church.

There have been moments during our parenting years that have strained the nerves to a catgut tautness. One such moment involved a family hike years ago atop the white cliffs of Dover in England. Rugged paths wind along what seems to the watching parent to be a death-trap edge, open to sky and sea, with a precipitous drop to the rocks below. All thoughts of, "Well, they have to learn to be careful," and, "Don't be *that* parent," are drowned by a screaming inner protector who knows it only takes one false step. It's a good thing I did not know at the time how many people have fallen from those cliffs to their deaths! There really are moments when it is entirely appropriate to say, "Walk where I walk, take the path I take, do as I do." So much is at stake. We trust God *and* teach. We offer boundless encouragement and opportunities for growth, *and* we set boundaries.

Paul must have felt such tension in his "father" role as apostle to Christ's fledgling churches dotted around the Mediterranean (e.g., 1 Cor 4:15). Given what was at stake, it was therefore entirely appropriate for him to say to these young believers, many of whom had come out of pagan backgrounds, "Walk where I walk, take the path I take, do as I do." Such was not arrogance but appropriate care. In any culture, at any time, there are spiritual lemmings leading unsuspecting believers along the edge of catastrophic, deadly drops. Like the enemies in Philippians 3:18–19, they are headed to destruction and would take others with them if it were not for the counterbalance of sound role models. We need good role models in the church. We need those who embody and integrate sound teaching and sound living. We need those who can say with both confidence and humility, "Walk where I walk, take the path I take, do as I do."

## *Citizens of Heaven*

What does it mean for followers of Christ to live in light of a heavenly citizenship? We might begin by reflecting on the fact that believers, according to Paul, are most fundamentally citizens of heaven (Phil 3:20). Their eager expectation is focused on Christ and his coming rather than the spoils and status of their earthly cultures, and they are committed to Christ's ways rather than the world's ways. By very nature, posture, and commitments, the Christ-follower lives a life oriented to an other-worldly citizenship.

When we speak of "the world," or the cultures of the world, we are not speaking of "culture" in terms of the beautiful manifestations of common grace around the world, distinct in time and place. It is appropriate to value the explosive tastes of Asian food, to enjoy Middle Eastern hospitality, to revel in the beauty of European architecture, to glory in the quiet quaintness of an English village—all of which are expressions of culture. What we live "counter" to, rather, is the co-opting of cultures by the value systems of "the world"—that is, that part of creation that shakes its fist at

God. Evil must also be embodied in places and times, and so it becomes embedded in the cultures of the world, twisting what is good and beautiful. That is what Scripture means when it says "do not love the world or the things in the world" (1 John 2:15 CSB). A higher love calls us to higher ways of living, which press into the cultures around us and speak the gospel into them.

A beautiful expression of heavenly citizenship manifesting in the world occurred in October 2006. One morning a disturbed milkman, Charles Roberts, took hostage a classroom full of girls at West Nickel Mine Amish School. At the end of the standoff, Roberts had killed five of the girls and wounded six others, ending the conflict by killing himself.

Yet into that dark moment shone an exceptionally bright, other-worldly light. The following Saturday, some three dozen members of the Amish community attended Charles Roberts's funeral, experiencing the depth of their own grief and yet offering profound sympathy to the family of a disturbed and violent man. No one would have expected such an expression of grace because it so goes against the grain and against the values of the dominant cultures of the world. Fire department chaplain Bruce Porter reflected, "It's the love, the forgiveness, the heartfelt forgiveness they have toward the family. I broke down and cried seeing it displayed." He noted that Marie Roberts, the wife of the killer, was "absolutely, deeply moved by the love shown."[97] It was heaven touching earth.

97. "Amish Mourn Gunman in School Rampage," *USA Today*, October 7, 2006.

CHAPTER 11

# Philippians 4:4b–9

## Literary Context

The main body of Philippians focuses on the theme of unity, as Paul employs a series of examples and exhortations, urging the church to the imitation of sound patterns of life and ministry (1:27–4:4a). In the body closing (4:4b–9), he presents a series of rapid-fire exhortations that culminate once again in a call to imitation. Having closed out the body with this short unit, the apostle turns to the conclusion of the letter in 4:10–23, in which he addresses the Philippians' partnership in his ministry (vv. 10–20) and offers final greetings. He closes with a blessing (vv. 21–23).

I. The Letter Opening: A Prescript and a Prayer Report (1:1–11)
**II. The Letter Body (1:12–4:9)**
   A. The Body Opening: Paul's Current Situation (1:12–26)
   B. The Main Body of the Letter: A Call for Unity in the Church (1:27–4:4a)
➦ **C. The Body Closing: Exhortations (4:4b–9)**
III. The Letter Closing (4:10–23)

## Main Idea

The Christian life involves godly living, right thinking, and imitation of the right patterns we see in others.

# Translation

## Philippians 4:4b–9

| | | | | |
|---|---|---|---|---|
| 4b | Exclamation | **I will say it again:** | | |
| c | Exhort./Reiteration | **Rejoice!** | | |
| 5a | Exhortation | **Let your reasonableness be common knowledge** | | |
| b | Extent | to all people. | | |
| c | Basis of 4:6 | **The Lord is near.** | | |
| 6a | Exhortation | **Don't be anxious** | | |
| b | Extent | about anything, | | |
| c | Contrast/Extent | but in everything | | |
| d | Means | by prayer and | | |
| e | Means | urgent appeal, | | |
| f | Manner | with thanks, | | |
| g | Exhortation | **make your requests known** | | |
| h | Indirect Obj. | to God. | | |
| 7a | Promise | And **God's peace, . . .** | | |
| b | Description | which surpasses every thought, | | |
| c | Action/Object | **. . . will guard your hearts and** | | |
| d | Object | **your minds** | | |
| e | Relationship | in Christ Jesus. | | |
| 8a | Affection. Address | Finally, brothers and sisters, | | |
| b | List–Attribute–Content (8b–i) | | whatever is | true, |
| c | | | whatever is | worthy of respect, |
| d | | | whatever is | just, |
| e | | | whatever is | pure, |
| f | | | whatever is | lovely, |
| g | | | whatever is | commendable, |
| h | | | if anything is | exceptional in character, and |
| i | | | if anything is | worthy of recognition, |
| j | Exhortation | **think carefully about** | **these things.** | |
| 9a | List - Content/Actions (9a–d) | And | what you have | learned and |
| b | | | | received and |

*Continued on next page.*

| | | | | |
|---|---|---|---|---|
| c | | | | heard and |
| d | | | | seen |
| e | | | | in me, |
| f | Exhortation | **do** | **these things,** | |
| g | | and | | |
| h | Promise | **the God of peace will be with you.** | | |

## Structure

The structure of the unit is rather straightforward. Here we have a series of six exhortations of varied complexity. The first four revolve around prayer (4:4b–7), and the final two—a highly stylized conclusion—focus once again on right thinking and imitation (4:8–9). The six exhortations lay out as follows. The first exhortation is a reiteration of the call to joy (v. 4c; "rejoice!"). In the second, Paul exhorts the church to a public posture of reasonableness (v. 5a). The reflection "the Lord is near" (v. 5c) functions as a rationale ("basis" in the diagram) for the third exhortation—namely, to eschew anxiety (v. 6a–b), which stands in contrast to the fourth exhortation, a call to prayer (v. 6c–h). This call is followed by the promise of peace (v. 7). The final two exhortations are introduced by "finally" (τὸ λοιπόν) and fronted by a flurry of correlative (ὅσα) and conditional (εἴ) clauses. These exhortations sum up two of the main motifs in the letter: to think rightly about "these things" (v. 8) and to "do these things" by imitating Paul (v. 9a–f). If the Philippians think rightly and live rightly, they will know God's peace (v. 9h).

## Exegetical Outline

### ➦ C. The Body Closing: Exhortations (4:4b–9)

1. Rejoice (v. 4b–c)
2. Be Reasonable in Public (v. 5)
3. Don't Be Anxious but Pray (vv. 6–7)
   a. Choose Prayer over Anxiety (v. 6)
   b. A Promise (v. 7)
4. Think about the Right Things (v. 8)
5. A Final Exhortation to Imitation (v. 9)

## Explanation of the Text

**4:4b–7 I will say it again: Rejoice! Let your reasonableness be common knowledge to all people. The Lord is near. Don't be anxious about anything, but in everything by prayer and urgent appeal, with thanks, make your requests known to God. And God's peace, which surpasses every thought, will guard your hearts and your minds in Christ Jesus** (πάλιν ἐρῶ, χαίρετε. 5 τὸ ἐπιεικὲς ὑμῶν γνωσθήτω πᾶσιν ἀνθρώποις. ὁ κύριος ἐγγύς. 6 μηδὲν μεριμνᾶτε, ἀλλ᾽ ἐν παντὶ τῇ προσευχῇ καὶ τῇ δεήσει μετὰ εὐχαριστίας τὰ αἰτήματα ὑμῶν γνωριζέσθω πρὸς τὸν θεόν. 7 καὶ ἡ εἰρήνη τοῦ θεοῦ ἡ ὑπερέχουσα πάντα νοῦν φρουρήσει τὰς καρδίας ὑμῶν καὶ τὰ νοήματα ὑμῶν ἐν Χριστῷ Ἰησοῦ). Paul here moves into a series of exhortations, the first four primarily built around prayer. The first exhortation is a repetition of the call to rejoice: "I will say it again: Rejoice!" (πάλιν ἐρῶ, χαίρετε).[1] As noted throughout the commentary, Paul expresses the call to embrace joy at key seams in the letter (1:18; 2:17–18; 2:28–3:1; 4:4). One way of reading the doubling of the exhortation to rejoice is that the motif is used as a transition device, with the first encouragement concluding one section, and the second initiating the next. In this passage, the double exhortation to rejoice flows naturally from the call to unity in 4:1–3: "For when you are joined in heart you rejoice in the Lord, and when you rejoice in the Lord you are joined in heart and stand together in the Lord."[2]

To "rejoice" in the sense Paul means here[3] has to do with being "deeply glad" or "expressing joy" about something or someone. The "someone" in this case is the Lord himself (ἐν κυρίῳ, see v. 4a)—who he has revealed himself to be and what he has accomplished in the lives of his people. Thus, rather than "glib and cloying advice to 'cheer up' or 'have a nice day,'"[4] this exhortation to joy calls for a depth of spiritual vitality and perspective, which offers the ability to discern God's goodness and work in the varied circumstances of life. Whereas the exhortations to virtues such as forbearance and not being anxious overlap with Greco-Roman values, the call to an "unmitigated, untrammeled joy" is a distinctly Judeo-Christian virtue and the distinctive mark of a genuine follower of Christ.[5] Since Christ is our Lord, we should not be emotionally or volitionally captive to circumstances in this often dark and difficult life. Rather, the exhortation to rejoice "always" (πάντοτε) calls us to be characterized by consistently embracing joy, even in very difficult life situations.[6]

Paul continues in verse 5 with "let your reasonableness be common knowledge to all people"

1. The χαίρετε ἐν κυρίῳ at 3:1 is the opening of the broad section running from 3:1–4:4a.

2. Marius Victorinus as quoted in Edwards, *Galatians, Ephesians, Philippians*, 267.

3. As Bockmuehl points out, the interpretation of the verb to mean "farewell" constitutes an obvious misstep in light of the addition of "always" (πάντοτε). See Bockmuehl, *Philippians*, 244.

4. Bockmuehl, *Philippians*, 244.

5. Fee, *Philippians*, 404.

6. In the LXX there are several approximations to Paul's exhortations to rejoice. Hab 3:18 LXX reads, "Now I will exult in the Lord, I will rejoice because of God my Savior" (ἐγὼ δὲ ἐν τῷ κυρίῳ ἀγαλλιάσομαι χαρήσομαι ἐπὶ τῷ θεῷ τῷ σωτῆρί μου). Similarly Zech 10:7 LXX reads, "And their children shall see it and be glad; their heart shall rejoice because of the Lord" (καὶ τὰ τέκνα αὐτῶν ὄψονται καὶ εὐφρανθήσονται καὶ χαρεῖται ἡ καρδία αὐτῶν ἐπὶ τῷ κυρίῳ). Joel 2:23 puts the thought in an exhortation: "Rejoice and celebrate because of the Lord your God" (χαίρετε καὶ εὐφραίνεσθε ἐπὶ τῷ κυρίῳ θεῷ ὑμῶν). Thus Paul's exhortation to rejoice has a rich OT background.

(τὸ ἐπιεικὲς ὑμῶν γνωσθήτω πᾶσιν ἀνθρώποις). In the New Testament, the word translated as "reasonableness" (ἐπιεικής)[7] stands in contrast to violence (1 Tim 3:3), slander (Titus 3:2), and harshness (1 Pet 2:18). As a virtue, it relates to being peace loving (1 Tim 3:3; Titus 3:2), pure, and full of mercy (Jas 3:17). In its LXX contexts, this term (and the related word ἐπιείκεια) speaks of being just and merciful (e.g., Ps 86:5 [85:5 LXX]; Wis 12:18; Pr Azar 19), demonstrating fairness toward other people. The word, therefore, describes someone who is thoughtful and considerate, one who relates with "good grace" toward others.[8] Such "reasonableness" would be a valued virtue in a conflicted situation like that involving Euodia and Syntyche (4:2–3) or in the face of mounting pressure by opponents in the broader culture (1:27–30). Either of these pressure points—conflict within the church or friction with those outside the church—may be why Paul challenges the Philippians to live so that their amiability stands out as "common knowledge to all people." They are to live in a way that their virtue is obvious to those in the surrounding culture.

"The Lord is near" (ὁ κύριος ἐγγύς) offers a basis for the contrasting exhortations (against anxiety and to prayer) in the next verse. As in the broader context of Philippians, the "Lord" refers to Christ Jesus himself. In the LXX it is the "day of the Lord" that is "near."[9] However, the language of the "Lord" himself being "near" is more in line with a few lines from Psalms. For instance, Psalm 34:18 [33:19 LXX] proclaims, "The Lord is near [ἐγγὺς κύριος] to the brokenhearted, and the humble in spirit he will save" (NETS); and Psalm 145:18 [144:18 LXX] reads, "Near is the Lord [ἐγγὺς κύριος] to all who call on him, to all who call on him in truth" (NETS; see also Ps 119:151 [118:151 LXX]). The wording of our verse matches these psalms closely, which suggests that Paul celebrates the nearness of the Lord to establish the call to prayer and the promise of God's peace in the next verse. The Lord's nearness forms a basis for a life of peace, and the Lord's people need peace in this fractious and fallen world. Certainly, anxiety constitutes one of life's greatest temptations, and the Philippians would have been tempted to it, given the cultural pressures they were facing.[10] Accordingly, in Philippians 4:6–7 the apostle offers complementary exhortations (one negative, "don't be anxious"; the other positive, "make your requests known to God"), followed by a promise ("God's peace . . . will guard your hearts and your minds in Christ Jesus").

In the ancient world, the word used here for being anxious (μεριμνάω) could express appropriate care about someone or something, as we saw at 2:20, where Paul notes Timothy's "concern" for the Philippians' welfare. But here Paul taps that part of the word's semantic range that conveys unnecessary worry or apprehensiveness, the same sense communicated in Jesus's words at Matthew 6:25 where he says, "Therefore I tell you, do not worry [μὴ μεριμνᾶτε] about your life, what you will eat or drink; or about your body, what you will wear" (NIV), or at Luke 10:41 where the Lord gently rebukes his friend: "Martha, Martha . . . you are worried and upset about many things" (NIV). In fact, Paul may be drawing on the gospel tradition as he offers this exhortation not to worry about life's challenges.[11]

7. The adjective ἐπιεικής, used four other times in the NT (1 Tim 3:3; Titus 3:2; Jas 3:17; 1 Pet 2:18), is only found here with the article, grammaticalized as an abstract substantive. See Hellerman, *Philippians*, 236.

8. *TLNT* 2:37–38.

9. Isa 13:6; 57:19; Jer 42:4; Ezek 30:3; Joel 1:15; 2:1; 4:14; Obad 15; Zeph 1:7, 14.

10. Reed, *Discourse Analysis*, 270.

11. Hawthorne and Martin, *Philippians*, 183.

The Philippians are to worry about "nothing" (μηδέν);[12] that is, they are not to be anxious about "anything," making the encouragement comprehensive.[13] This encouragement not to give in to anxiety about anything also stands in sharp contrast (ἀλλ') to "in everything" (ἐν παντί) in the next clause, which probably refers to "every circumstance in life." The idea, of course, is, "Don't worry about anything; instead, pray about everything" (NLT), but the grammar is a bit more involved than that, for as seen in our diagram on the passage, there are five ways that the Philippians are to "make" their requests "known" (τὰ αἰτήματα ὑμῶν γνωριζέσθω), which is the central exhortation of the verse. They are to do so:

- in everything (ἐν παντί)
- by prayer and (τῇ προσευχῇ καί)
- urgent appeal (τῇ δεήσει)
- with thanks (μετὰ εὐχαριστίας)
- to God (πρὸς τὸν θεόν)

First, Paul crafts this call to prayer in the form of two phrases communicating *means*, "by prayer and urgent appeal" (τῇ προσευχῇ and τῇ δεήσει). The first of these terms (προσευχή) is the more common one for prayer, occurring often in the New Testament. As Silva notes, the second term (δέησις) has a great deal of semantic overlap with the first when it is used, as here, as a general reference to prayer. It also can function more narrowly as referring to an urgent request made to God.[14] The use of both words in tandem may simply be for emphasis.

Second, the *manner* or *posture*[15] in which we are to pray is "with thanks" (μετὰ εὐχαριστίας), an expression of gratitude, which serves as an antidote for focusing merely on *our* needs rather than *God's* faithfulness. Thanksgiving pulls us out of a self-centered focus to remember what God has already done, what he is doing presently, and what he can do in the future. Perhaps this is why praying "with thanks" constitutes such a standard aspect of Paul's piety.[16]

Finally, requests are to be made known "to God" (πρὸς τὸν θεόν). Rather than suggesting that God must be informed about our needs, to make requests "known" to God is simply an idiomatic way—and a rather unusual way for Paul[17]—of saying "talk to God about your specific needs." God involves his people in prayer for various reasons, and verse 7 highlights a very important one: for the believers' own peace and emotional stability. Paul writes: "And God's peace, which surpasses every thought, will guard your hearts and your minds in Christ Jesus" (καὶ ἡ εἰρήνη τοῦ θεοῦ ἡ ὑπερέχουσα πάντα νοῦν φρουρήσει τὰς καρδίας ὑμῶν καὶ τὰ νοήματα ὑμῶν ἐν Χριστῷ Ἰησοῦ). The conjunction "and" (καὶ) semantically links this promise concerning the effects of prayer to the twin exhortations of the previous verse.[18]

Writers of the biblical literature, who lived in a violent, tumultuous world, often used the term translated "peace" (εἰρήνη) with reference to an

12. This is perhaps an accusative of reference, "with reference to nothing."

13. BDAG 647.

14. Silva, *Philippians*, 199.

15. So Fee, *Philippians*, 409–10.

16. On which, see Fee, *Philippians*, 409. See the use of this noun elsewhere at 1 Cor 14:16; 2 Cor 4:15; 9:11–12; Eph 5:4; Col 2:7; 4:2; 1 Thess 3:9; 1 Tim 2:1; 4:3–4.

17. The only other place in the NT that this noun is used of prayer is at 1 John 5:15, and Paul normally uses this verb (γνωρίζω) to speak of things "made known" to people (Rom 9:22–23; 16:26; 1 Cor 12:3; 15:1; 2 Cor 8:1; Gal 1:11; Eph 1:9; 3:3, 5, 10; 6:19, 21; Phil 1:22; Col 1:27; 4:7, 9).

18. Runge suggests that καί expresses semantic continuity in such a case. See Runge, *Discourse Grammar*, 23. As Fee points out, beginning a sentence with καί is a rare example of parataxis in Paul's writings (Fee, *Philippians*, 410).

absence of war or acts of violence. They celebrated peace as a blessing from God (e.g., Ps 37:11 [36:11 LXX]; 72:7 [71:7 LXX]; 119:165 [118:165 LXX]) and an expression of God's covenant.[19] For instance, God promises "peace" to the land of Israel, granting his people freedom from assault by wild animals or enemies (Lev 26:6), and the Lord gives peace to those in troubling or frightening situations (Judg 6:23; John 14:27). Thus, peace is something to be sought (Ps 33:15; Luke 1:79), and ultimately "the God of peace" (Phil 4:9) is its source (Luke 2:14). Believers especially know peace in relation to the Lord Christ (Acts 10:36; Rom 14:17; 15:13; 1 Cor 1:3; 2 Cor 1:2).

Paul describes God's peace as that "which surpasses every thought" (ἡ ὑπερέχουσα πάντα νοῦν). The verb translated "surpasses" (ὑπερέχω) could be used by ancient authors with the meaning, "to surpass in quality or value, be better than, surpass, excel."[20] The apostle has already used the word with this sense at 2:3 and 3:8. At 2:3 he speaks of considering others "more significant" than oneself, and at 3:8 he celebrates the privilege of knowing Christ as "far more valuable" than the gains of the world. Now the apostle employs the word again, proclaiming that God's peace "surpasses every thought."

In the ancient world, the term translated as "thought" (νοῦς) could refer to the "mind" or "intellect" as a human faculty—that is, a person's ability to understand or process intellectually. It also could refer to a *way* of thinking, an attitude, or the result of the thinking process—that is, an "opinion" or "thought."[21] Paul almost always uses the word with the sense of a person's "mind" and occasionally with the sense of one's "thoughts."[22] Thus, here in 4:7 the apostle could mean that God's peace is a better source of help in the face of anxiety than a person's "mind" or "thoughts." That is, God's peace transcends circumstances in a way that human intellect or reasoning cannot. It is not that the *peace of God* cannot be understood. Rather, it is that God's peace is a superior means of dealing with anxiety.[23] The term "every" (πάντα), on the other hand, could refer to the intellectual ability of all humans ("all," "every") or to any person's ability ("any," "each").[24]

The interpretation that reads God's peace as superior in terms of ability finds further support in the promise that follows. God's peace will be a powerful sentry, protecting the believer from all assaults on mind and heart. Paul writes that God's peace "will guard your hearts and your minds in Christ Jesus" (φρουρήσει τὰς καρδίας ὑμῶν καὶ τὰ νοήματα ὑμῶν ἐν Χριστῷ Ἰησοῦ). The verb rendered "guard" (φρουρέω), only found here and at three other places in the New Testament (2 Cor 11:32; Gal 3:23; 1 Pet 1:5), could connote guarding, confining, detaining, or protecting. The word was used in military or civil law-enforcement contexts.[25] Since God's peace excels human intellectual ability, it has the strength to guard not only a person's thoughts but the heart as well, protecting two dominant aspects of our inner life as human beings. In broader Judaism, the "heart" (καρδία)

19. Our term is used over 270 times in the LXX. On "peace" as an aspect of God's covenant, see Keown, *Philippians 2:19–4:23*, 348.

20. BDAG 1033.

21. BDAG 679–80.

22. Rom 1:28; 7:23, 25; 11:34; 12:2; 14:5; 1 Cor 1:10; 2:16; 14:14–15, 19; Eph 4:17, 23; Col 2:18; 2 Thess 2:2; 1 Tim 6:5; 2 Tim 3:8; Titus 1:15.

23. Fee and others suggest that Paul speaks of the "merely human, unbelieving mind" (Fee, *Philippians*, 410). But the context rather concerns believers, and the delimiter is "every" (πάντα). It might be suggested that God's peace is available to combat anxiety in a way that our human intellect alone cannot.

24. This is similar to 1 En. 82.2, which speaks of wisdom as surpassing thought (Holloway, *Philippians*, 183).

25. E.g., 2 Cor 11:32; Jdt 3:6; 1 Esd 4:56; Jos., *Ant.* 9.42; 11.345; 13.26, 39.

was considered the center and source of the inner life—a person's thoughts, feelings, and will (Prov 4:23). "Thoughts" (τὰ νοήματα), the product of the mind, what the mind employs in intellectual processes, or the will intends, are closely related to the heart in biblical literature. In the Psalms, for example, the heart is the place where thoughts are processed: "My mouth shall speak wisdom and the meditation of my heart understanding" (Ps 48:4 NETS [49:3 English transl.]). Our hearts and minds, moreover, come under assault by the anxieties of life, as our minds churn through possible solutions to our problems.[26] Yet we have this sure promise that God's peace can guard our inner life from such assault because of our relationship with Christ (ἐν Χριστῷ Ἰησοῦ).[27] As we see in the next two verses, God uses *right thinking* and *right doing*, learned from the example of mentors as agents of God's peace, to buttress believers against life's anxieties.

**4:8 Finally, brothers and sisters, whatever is true, whatever is worthy of respect, whatever is just, whatever is pure, whatever is lovely, whatever is commendable, if anything is exceptional in character, and if anything is worthy of recognition, think carefully about these things** (Τὸ λοιπόν, ἀδελφοί, ὅσα ἐστὶν ἀληθῆ, ὅσα σεμνά, ὅσα δίκαια, ὅσα ἁγνά, ὅσα προσφιλῆ, ὅσα εὔφημα, εἴ τις ἀρετὴ καὶ εἴ τις ἔπαινος, ταῦτα λογίζεσθε). Paul here challenges the Philippians to disciplined thinking, since right thoughts serve as one antidote for anxious thoughts. This will be mirrored by right patterns of "doing" in verse 9. The apostle introduces these twin exhortations and moves to the close of 4:4b–9 with "finally, brothers and sisters" (τὸ λοιπόν, ἀδελφοί),[28] a phrase he also used at 3:1 to earmark a transition in the letter. Verse 8 piles up "whatever" (ὅσος)[29] clauses, which thrum through the verse repetitiously, introducing virtues worthy of thought. The Philippians are to "think carefully about these things" (ταῦτα λογίζεσθε), almost all of which were greatly valued in the broader Greco-Roman culture,[30] but which here the apostle places in the context of Christian discipleship. Paul lists eight kinds of thought that are worthy of deep reflection:

> whatever is true,
> whatever is worthy of respect,
> whatever is just,
> whatever is pure,
> whatever is lovely,
> whatever is commendable,
> if anything is exceptional in character, and
> if anything is worthy of recognition.

Paul begins with "whatever is true" (ὅσα ἐστὶν ἀληθῆ). In the broader Greco-Roman world, moral excellence was seen as a product of a search for truth.[31] Plato, for instance, said the goal was to find truth in order to find perfection in life and death (*Gorg.* 526). In biblical literature, being a person of truth can mean the opposite of being "false" or a person of lies. Thus a focus on truthfulness can occur in relation to oaths or testimony.[32]

26. E.g., Ps 10:11; 13:2; 25:17; 38:10.

27. The phrase again read as connoting relationship.

28. Phil 1:12, 14; 2:25; 3:1, 13, 17; 4:1. On the use of ἀδελφοί as referring to both men and women in the church, see the commentary at 1:12.

29. The term normally functions as a correlative.

30. Plato, Aristotle, the Stoics, Dio Chrysostom, and other writers of the ancient world offered similar lists of virtues. See, e.g., Hansen, *Philippians*, 295–96; Reumann, *Philippians*, 616–17.

31. Epictetus, *Diatr.* 1.4.31; 3.24.40; Thucydides, *History* 1.20.3; Plutarch, *Is. Os.* 2.

32. E.g., John 5:31–32; 8:13, 14, 17; 21:24; Titus 1:13; 3 John 12.

Accordingly, we read of a "truthful" person, or even of God himself as truthful.[33] Thinking on things that are "true," therefore, lies at the very heart of what it means to be God's person, a person of morality and character in the world.[34]

Second, the Philippians are to think carefully about those things that are "worthy of respect" (σεμνός). This term has to do with being "serious," "dignified," "worthy of reverence, respect, or honor." It thus relates to what English speakers mean when they say that a person has *gravitas*, a pattern of life and a personal bearing that demands respectful attention. In the LXX, this word normally communicates a sense of reverence.[35] Elsewhere in the New Testament, it only occurs in the Pastorals, where leaders in the church are to be "worthy of respect" or "dignified" people (1 Tim 3:8, 11; Titus 2:2). So the Philippians are to think about things that are worthy of respect.

Third, believers should think on things that are "just" (δίκαιος). A very common word in the New Testament,[36] this term could be used by ancient authors to describe that which is "right, just, fair," and "equitable."[37] The word was used in broader Greek literature, for instance, of those who conformed to custom or law. The "just" are those who fulfill their obligations to God and human beings.[38] Authors of the Greek Old Testament celebrate God as "just" or "righteous" (Deut 32:4; Ps 11:7 [10:7 LXX]; Jer 12:1; Dan 9:14), in part because he delivers justice (Zeph 3:5).[39] In the New Testament, the word could carry the moral sense of being a fair person who does what is appropriate. We see this nuance, for instance, in a landowner who pays his workers equitably (Matt 20:4). Here in Philippians 4:8 and elsewhere (Eph 6:1; 1 Tim 1:9; Titus 1:8), Paul uses the word to describe a person's character or right action.[40]

The fourth descriptor (ἁγνός) speaks of what is "pure" or "holy," the opposite of that which is corrupt. For instance, at 2 Corinthians 7:11 Paul celebrates the Corinthians' response to his "sorrowful" letter, their repentance demonstrating that they had been "pure" in their handling of the situation addressed in the letter. Also in 2 Corinthians, Paul notes that he wants to present the Corinthians as a "pure" virgin to Christ (11:2), which means that he must guard them against the corrupting influences of false teachers. This sense of being free from corruption can also be seen in the Pastorals, where the apostle instructs Timothy as a public leader (1 Tim 5:22) and young women in terms of holiness of character (Titus 2:5).

Fifth, the word translated as "lovely" (προσφιλής) only occurs here in the New Testament and is absent from Greco-Roman virtue lists. A "delight-full" term expressing pleasure, amiability, or that which is "lovely," this word describes a person who

33. E.g., of a truthful person: Matt 22:16; John 7:18; of God as truthful: Gen 41:32; Dan 2:47; Wis 1:6; John 3:33; 8:26; Rom 3:34.

34. *TLNT* 1:66–83.

35. Prov 6:8; 8:6; 15:26; cf. 2 Macc 6:11, 28; 8:15; 4 Macc 5:36; 7:15; 17:5.

36. E.g., Matt 1:19; 5:45; Luke 5:32; 12:57; John 7:24; 17:25; Acts 3:14; Rom 1:17; Gal 3:11; 1 Pet 4:18; 1 John 2:1; Rev 22:11.

37. BDAG 246–47.

38. *TLNT* 1:320–21.

39. *TLNT* 1:322–23.

40. In Romans the apostle speaks theologically of people being "right" or "just" (δίκαιος) in relation to God. It is the "just" who live by faith (1:17), who are right with God because they do the law (2:13). No one is truly just apart from Christ (3:10), but the just God has demonstrated his righteousness in Christ and the gospel by making people just in his sight (3:26; 5:19). The word can be used of ethical behavior, as in Phil 4:8, of a person as behaving justly; or it can be used forensically, as seen at points in Romans, of God's declaration of a person to be in right standing before him because of the work of Christ. On the relationship between the forensic and ethical, see Richard N. Longenecker, *The Epistle to the Romans: A Commentary on the Greek Text*, NIGTC (Grand Rapids: Eerdmans, 2016), 174–75.

is pleasing in their actions or attitudes.[41] In the LXX the word is used of those who present themselves to others in such a way that they engender a positive response (Esth 15:5; Sir 4:7; 20:13). Josephus uses the word variously to speak of someone being friendly or pleasing to others, and especially of those loved by others.[42] So someone who is "lovely" is a "delightful" person with whom others enjoy associating. As Bockmuehl points out, the term suggests more than mere morality. Rather, the apostle wants these believers to be shaped by *aesthetic truth*—that which is "lovely," extending "to all that is beautiful in creation and in human lives."[43]

Sixth, the Philippians are to think deeply about that which is "commendable" (εὔφημος). Here we have another word only found here in the New Testament, and it occurs but rarely in broader Greco-Roman literature. For instance, in Josephus and Philo the term has to do with speaking well of someone.[44] The emphasis, therefore, is not on a person described as "praiseworthy"[45] but on one who speaks positively about others or about situations they observe. Correspondingly, the cognate noun, which the apostle uses at 2 Corinthians 6:8, refers to "a good report" (εὐφημία) that others give about Paul. This word, of course, forms a very practical exhortation for those in a church tempted to grumble and argue but who are striving for unity.

The seventh and eighth items on which the Philippians should fix their thoughts break the rhythmic "whatever" (ὅσα + adjective) pattern that has characterized verse 8 thus far.[46] The question concerns, however, just how Paul uses these final terms, which we render as "exceptional in character" (ἀρετή) and "worthy of recognition" (ἔπαινος). Might the apostle simply be offering a stylistic variation on the "whatever" pattern used thus far in the verse?[47] Or perhaps he uses these two terms to qualify the previous six descriptions, suggesting that the Philippians must be discerning even as they engage common ideas from their cultural context.[48] Or, as a third option, perhaps Paul summarizes the previous six terms.[49] It might be best, however, to embrace a fourth option, reading these final two words as reinforcing "the all-encompassing character of Paul's exhortation, since no list could be complete," thus evoking any other aspect of upright character not mentioned already.[50]

The word meaning "exceptional in character" (ἀρετή) occurs elsewhere in the New Testament only in the Petrine letters (1 Pet 2:9; 2 Pet 1:3, 5 [2x]), but it occurs thirty-two times in the LXX.[51] In Hellenistic-Jewish literature, it stands as the primary word for "virtue." Interestingly, authors frequently pair the term with the concept of "righteousness" (δικαιοσύνη).[52] Moreover, the word has

41. BDAG 886.

42. *Ant.* 1.258; 2.186; 4.203; 5.189; 17.149; 19.115, 121.

43. Bockmuehl, *Philippians*, 253.

44. Josephus, *Ant.* 15.52; 17.331; *Ag. Ap.* 2.248, 253; Philo, *Confusion* 159; *Flight* 86; *Names* 242; *Dreams* 130; *Joseph* 12; *Virtues* 2; *Rewards* 47.

45. Contra BDAG 414; *EDNT* 86.

46. Even as they mirror the first-class conditional construction (εἰ + indefinite pronoun) seen earlier at Phil 2:1 (see comments there). The two contexts, however, present us with two different situations. The conditional clauses of 2:1 are *presuppositions* affirming core Christian ideas. Here we have *qualifications* of a virtue list primarily taken from the broader Greco-Roman world.

47. Reumann, *Philippians*, 640.

48. Fee, *Philippians*, 416; Hansen, *Philippians*, 299; Hellerman, *Philippians*, 247.

49. A common understanding, as with, for example, Hawthorne, *Philippians*, 186–87.

50. Silva, *Philippians*, 197.

51. See, e.g., Isa 42:8, 12; 43:21; 63:7; Hab 3:3; Zech 6:13; Wis 4:1; 5:13; 8:7; 4 Macc 13:27; 17:12, 23. In 4 Maccabees and Wisdom of Solomon the word normally connotes the idea of "virtue." In the biblical prophets the term seems normally to communicate the idea of "praise."

52. E.g., in Philo the two terms are found together 124 times; See, e.g., *Creation* 73, 81; *Alleg. Interp.* 1.63, 65, 72; 3.150, 247; *Cherubim* 5, 96; *Sacrifices* 27, 37, 57, 84.

ethical connotations.[53] Indeed, it can be used to speak of the goodness and praiseworthy character of God himself (1 Pet 2:9; 2 Pet 1:3). Thus the word connotes the highest standard of character.

The final word in our list (ἔπαινος) describes something as "worthy of recognition" or "praise," but it also could refer to an act of praise, approval, or recognition.[54] Paul commonly uses the term with the latter sense, referring to the praise a person receives from God or people, or that directed to God,[55] the sense seen earlier in Philippians at 1:11. Yet here Paul probably has in mind the former sense—something that is praiseworthy, or worthy of being recognized.

Thus, summing up, the apostle calls on the Philippians to think on anything that is true, worthy of respect, just, pure, lovely, and commendable; indeed, anything exceptional in character or worthy of recognition. These are the things (ταῦτα)[56] on which they are to ponder, to think about carefully (λογίζομαι).[57] Meditation on what is true and good and commendable should constitute an ongoing pattern of life.

**4:9 And what you have learned and received and heard and seen in me, do these things, and the God of peace will be with you** (ἃ καὶ ἐμάθετε καὶ παρελάβετε καὶ ἠκούσατε καὶ εἴδετε ἐν ἐμοί, ταῦτα πράσσετε· καὶ ὁ θεὸς τῆς εἰρήνης ἔσται μεθ' ὑμῶν). Having challenged the Philippians to meditate deeply on a life lived well and beautifully, Paul now returns to the theme of imitation (cf. 3:17–19), calling his brothers and sisters in Philippi to follow his example. Paul mirrors his call to right thinking in verse 8 with an exhortation to right living here in verse 9.[58] Moreover, verse 9 takes the general admonition of verse 8 and refracts it through a very specific lens—the pattern of Christian discipleship and ministry as seen in the apostle's life and teaching. If the Philippians live this pattern of life, embracing it as their own, God's peace will rest on them.

Accordingly, Paul outlines four ways that his work has been embodied in his life and ministry among these believers.[59] Whereas the Philippians are called to "think carefully about" lauded patterns of life in verse 8, in verse 9 they are to "do" (πράσσετε)—that is, "behave according to" the patterns experienced through Paul's life and teaching. The imperfective aspect of the imperative verb, in context, points once again to an ongoing way of living. The apostle offers four "prompts," or dimensions of his life and teaching, that they are to live out:

| | |
|---|---|
| what you have | learned (ἃ καὶ ἐμάθετε) |
| and | received (καὶ παρελάβετε) |
| and | heard (καὶ ἠκούσατε) |
| and | seen (καὶ εἴδετε) |

53. Keown, *Philippians 2:19–4:23*, 364.

54. BDAG 357.

55. E.g., praise received from God: Rom 2:29; 1 Cor 4:5; praise received from people: Rom 13:3; 2 Cor 8:18; or that given to God: Eph 1:6, 12, 14.

56. The word ταῦτα is placed before the verb for emphasis (object-verb pattern) or thematic prominence. See Reed, *Discourse Analysis*, 394.

57. On the use of this verb, see the commentary at 3:13.

58. As seen in our diagram of the passage, in vv. 8–9 Paul culminates each list with an exhortation concerning "these things" (ταῦτα). With reference to the list of v. 8, they are to "think carefully about" these things. In v. 9, they are to "do" these things. In effect, the lists offer the content of the exhortations' immediate objects, "these things" (ταῦτα). Although it is true that a relative clause at the beginning of a sentence generally functions to unpack what has preceded it, here we have a clear pattern in vv. 8 and 9 of relative clauses preceding and summed up by ταῦτα as the object of a hortatory verb. So, e.g., Hansen, *Philippians*, 300; Bockmuehl, *Philippians*, 254.

59. So, e.g., Fee, *Philippians*, 413–14; Hellerman, *Philippians*, 249; Reumann, *Philippians*, 640.

Although these four items fall roughly into two pairs, "learned and received" on the one hand, and "heard and seen" on the other, a strict demarcation of Paul's teaching (the first pair) and his example (the second pair)[60] seems somewhat arbitrary and unnecessary. The apostle's teaching, the Christian traditions he had received and passed on to them, what the Philippians heard from him, and what they had observed of his behavior all would have woven together in a tapestry of pedagogical impact. Paul's whole life was tuned toward proclaiming the crucified and risen Lord. Thus these patterns of instruction and example communicate a multidimensional form of education through which the apostle had mentored the Philippians in the ways of Christ. Each of the four, however, points to nuances of his approach.

From its beginning, the early Christian movement was oriented to learning from the Jewish Scriptures (e.g., Matt 5:19) and the teaching of Jesus himself (Matt 28:19–20). In his ministry, Paul placed emphasis on the importance of learning sound teaching.[61] At times he uses rabbinic language in referring to that which had been "handed down" and thus "received";[62] so his reference here to what the Philippians "received" (παρελάβετε) probably places an emphasis on the right teaching that he had passed on to them.

Of course, what this church had "heard" from Paul certainly included the teaching that they had learned, but they also had "seen" and "heard" of the apostle suffering for the faith (Phil 1:30), and Paul uses that fact to encourage them in their own struggle for endurance. Thus, what they had "heard" and "seen" in Paul (ἐν ἐμοί), "in his example,"[63] includes the pattern of his suffering as he encountered a hostile world for the sake of Christ. This embodiment of the teaching, practices, conversations, and observed patterns they had seen in the life and ministry of Paul makes it possible for the Philippians to imitate that pattern of life. What, then, is the result? Peace. They can know peace, even amid a harsh, hostile world and even amid a sometimes-fractious church.

That peace is known through the presence of God himself: "The God of peace will be with you" (καὶ ὁ θεὸς τῆς εἰρήνης ἔσται μεθ' ὑμῶν). References to "the God of peace" occur four times in the apostle's writings,[64] but he often associates peace with God, especially in letter openings (e.g., Rom 1:7; 1 Cor 1:3; 2 Cor 1:2; Gal 1:3) or in words of blessing (Rom 15:13, 33; Eph 6:23). God is the source of peace and has brought peace through the gospel of Christ (Rom 5:1) and the power of the Holy Spirit (14:17). Living for God brings peace to believers and peace to their relationships with others (1 Cor 7:15; 2 Cor 13:11). When believers think and live in accordance with the thoughts and ways of God, their lives align with the good patterns in which God created human beings to live. Accordingly, peace from being right with God and rightly related to others is the result (cf. Gal 6:16; 1 Thess 5:23).

60. So, e.g., Hansen, *Philippians*, 300; Hellerman, *Philippians*, 249.

61. E.g., Rom 12:7; 15:4; 16:17; 1 Cor 14:31; Eph 4:14; 1 Tim 4:6; 2 Tim 3:14; Titus 1:9.

62. Fee, *Philippians*, 420. See, e.g., 1 Cor 11:23; 15:1–3; 2 Thess 3:6.

63. The preposition ἐν probably conveys the sense "in the case of," i.e., "from my example." See BDF 118; Robertson, *Grammar*, 587.

64. See elsewhere at Rom 15:33; 16:20; 1 Thess 5:23; cf. Heb 13:20.

## Theology in Application

### *Dealing with Anxiety, Living God's Peace*

As I sit writing this afternoon, I find myself in an especially stressful moment of life. In the course of this day I have thought about finishing this manuscript (which is due!), a student facing deep bouts of anxiety and depression, our retirement funds (the market went down yesterday), the classes I am teaching next week, a not-yet-believer friend with whom I have lost consistent contact, a friend who has left the faith, a relative's health, an upcoming lecture that needs to be developed, a sermon I am preaching this Sunday, whether the pandemic will ease so that my children can come to Vancouver this summer, how my current classes are being received, comps and theses that need attention, discussions about important matters in the faculty, whether Pat and I will be able to travel for my upcoming research leave, etc., etc., etc. That is just a partial sampling off the top of my head, and I am confident that you have your own list. For some readers these concerns must seem laughably mild when compared to a devastating, life-threatening illness, financial crisis, or relational breakdown. Anxiety is relative, but for each of us it is real nonetheless. On a beautiful afternoon in British Columbia, with every reason in the world to trust God and to be hopeful about the future, anxieties pound incessantly on the door of my townhouse or circle the building in the middle of the night, niggling, hissing, and scratching against the windows of my mind.

I am tempted to open the door to these pests, and in our often dark and complex world, that temptation seems relentless at times. A plunge in the stock market, a confrontation with a boss, or bad news concerning a child's health can send our hearts racing. Given their constant call for attention, our anxieties must be addressed, for they can distract and disable, and even kill.

Paul Martin in *The Sickening Mind* recounts that during the Gulf War in the early 1990s, the nation of Iraq launched Scud missiles into Israel, killing several citizens. Yet many of the deaths were due to an unexpected cause. Israeli scientists who studied the data after the war found that most died of heart attacks brought on by extreme stress and anxiety rather than the direct physical violence of the missiles themselves. Just prior to the outbreak of war on January 17, 1991 and building to a climax on the first day of the Scud missile attacks, citizens of Israel were terrified that Iraq would use biological and chemical weapons. The Israeli government issued gas masks and atropine syringes to the population and instructed them to prepare sealed rooms in their homes. The initial attacks from Iraq were much less devastating than Israel had feared, and the stress levels among the population dropped almost immediately as people settled into a new normal. With less stress, the death count also went down, remaining at normal mortality levels throughout seventeen missile attacks that followed in the coming weeks. Nevertheless, during the initial phrase of the Iraqi threat, extreme levels of anxiety took their toll.[65]

As followers of Christ, whether we are dealing with the stress of "normal" life, or a major life crisis, or even the threat of war, Philippians 4:4b–9 challenges us to learn to deal with anxieties, primarily by talking to God about them, adjusting our thinking, following the example of other believers who navigate life well, and even by rejoicing. Of course, there is no emotional "off switch" on the back of the soul, but prayer brings us to the feet of the One who has perfect perspective and absolute power, and who offers a secure future. The circumstances of life, whether presenting real threats or imagined, must be confronted by the Greater Reality. Thus Paul calls us to make our "requests known to God" in the face of our anxieties and to do so "with thanks." He exhorts us to think thoughts that are pure and just and beautiful, even in our stress, and to follow the examples of those who have walked the path of anxiety before us. The foundational disciplines of dealing with anxiety, therefore, have to do with space in heart and mind, for time to talk with God on a rhythmic basis, inculcating our requests with heavy doses of thanks; for rhythmic, deep meditation on Scripture, which trains us to think on that which is holy and delightful; to have a coffee and chat with a mentor who can comfort and call us out of ourselves, lifting our hearts above the clouds of doubt and fear.

So, dear reader, if you are struggling with anxiety at present, set aside time today for a walk and talk around the block or a quiet half hour with a coffee or tea in a place of solitude, and lay your concerns and requests before God, making sure to thank him for the small and large ways he has met your needs in the past, is meeting them in the present, and will meet them in the future. Choose to spend time in Scripture—chunks of time—letting it sink deeply into your bruised soul. Reach out to a friend who can help you find perspective and hope.

## *Christianity and the Beautiful Life*

As we have seen in Phil 4:4b–9, and especially verse 8, Paul taps the moral sensibilities of his broader culture, baptizing commonly held virtues into a Christocentric, community-oriented exhortation. This means that Paul weaves aspects of "common grace," in this case the moral conscience that human beings generally share, into his theological framework and anchors that framework in a relationship with God and other believers. In Christian thought, the truth of the gospel has always been embodied—integrated into real life by living out the highest moral standards in

65. Paul R. Martin, *The Sickening Mind: Brain, Behaviour, Immunity and Disease* (New York: HarperCollins, 1997), 3–4.

loving community, living out the holiness that comes from God himself. Truth and morality go together. Irenaeus of Lyons, in his *On the Apostolic Preaching*, writes:

> For what use is it to know the truth in words,
> only to defile the body and perform evil deeds?
> Or what profit indeed can come from holiness of body,
> if truth is not in the soul?[66]

The integration of truth and holiness with the concept of beauty is especially powerful in certain veins of Christian thought and tradition. Notice, for instance, the interplay of truth, moral reflection, beauty, and joy in Augustine's *Confessions*, as he cries out to God concerning his earlier, unregenerate self:

> This was my plight at the age of twenty-six or twenty-seven, when I wrote that book, hugging to me my own conceptions of the physical world, which filled my ears with their outer noise while I was trying to hear your inner music, my sweet truth. By dealing with beauty and decorum, I was trying to lift up and listen to you, gladdened by the call of my spouse, but I could not—the noise of my errors pulled me outside myself, while the weight of my pride sank me below myself, where you could not grant me "news of real happiness and joy," so my bones could not be lifted up because I had not lowered myself.[67]

The rhetor could not hear the "inner music" he sought, even though he was attracted to "beauty and decorum." He sensed the need to be lifted up but was kept down by his errors and pride. Intuitively he knew that beauty had some part in this process of drawing near to God, this endeavor to find "happiness and joy," but immorality was in the mix, spoiling the pot.

The Christian life is meant to be true, and in being true it is meant to be rightly ordered and beautiful. This beauty and order manifest themselves in a variety of ways—in joy, graciousness, peace in the face of anxiety-inducing circumstances, in honor, justice, purity, the lovely, the moral, and the things that cause even the broader world to take notice and sing praises. Accordingly, something we might emphasize more in the twenty-first-century church is living *beautifully* with one another and before the world, for that is a good beginning in approaching the world with the claims of Christ.

66. St. Irenaeus of Lyons, *On the Apostolic Preaching*, translated by John Behr (Crestwood, NY: St. Vladimir's Seminary Press, 1997), 40.

67. Augustine, *Confessions*, translated by Garry Wills, Penguin Classics (New York: Penguin, 2006), 78.

CHAPTER 12

# Philippians 4:10–20

## Literary Context

As noted throughout the commentary, the main body of Philippians focuses especially on the theme of unity, Paul crafting a series of examples interspersed with exhortations (1:27–4:4a). In the body closing (4:4b–9), there are a string of exhortations that revolve around right thinking and right patterns of living, and these come to a head by once again calling the church to imitate the apostle's ministry in pursuit of what is reasonable, honorable, just, pure, and lovely—virtues that can be celebrated. Having closed out the body, Paul now concludes the letter (4:10–23). In 4:10–20, in language echoing that of 1:3–11,[1] the apostle celebrates the Philippians' partnership with him and focuses on their generous gift of resources. But he does so in a way that, once again, subverts cultural assumptions of the day, carefully crafting a nuanced theology of their partnership as oriented to God himself rather than the demands of patron-client reciprocity. Thus, in 4:10–20 the apostle returns to a focus on his relationship with the Philippians, addressing their recent contributions to meeting his needs. Finally, following patterns expected in the letter form of Paul's culture, the postscript at 4:21–23 offers greetings and a concluding blessing.

I. The Letter Opening: A Prescript and a Prayer Report (1:1–11)
II. The Letter Body (1:12–4:9)
**III. The Letter Closing (4:10–23)**
➡ **A. The Philippians' Gift and Partnership in Ministry (4:10–20)**
B. Postscript: Final Greetings and Blessing (4:21–23)

1. As pointed out in the introduction on the unity and structure of Philippians, Gerald Peterman has demonstrated that the unit under consideration boasts extensive verbal and conceptual parallels to 1:3–11, the book thus framed with reflections on particular aspects of the apostle's relationship with the Philippians. For that discussion, please see the introduction to the commentary on pp. 30–32. See Peterman, *Paul's Gift from Philippi*, 91–92.

## Main Idea

Although Paul has learned to be content in a variety of situations, he deeply appreciates the Philippians' financial contributions to his ministry as they partner with him in the work of God.

## Translation

### Philippians 4:10–20

| | | |
|---|---|---|
| 10a | Testimony | **Now I rejoiced** |
| b | Relationship | in the Lord |
| c | Manner | greatly |
| d | Cause | because once again |
| e | Event | you renewed giving careful thought to what might be done |
| f | Advantage | for me |
| g | Clarification | (with regard to which, I might add, you were mindful of my situation but were lacking the opportunity) |
| 11a | Clarification | —not that I am speaking |
| b | Cause | because I am in need! |
| c | Assertion | For **I have learned to be content** |
| d | Circumstance | in my circumstances. |
| 12a | Assertion/Content | **I know** what it is like to be in very humble circumstances and |
| b | Contrast | what it is like to have a wealth of resources. |
| c | Context/Extent | In any and every situation |
| d | Assertion | **I have learned the secret** of how |
| e | Circumstance | to be well fed and how |
| f | Contrast | to go hungry, how |
| g | Circumstance | to have more than enough and how |
| h | Contrast | to do without: |
| 13a | Assertion | **I am able to do all things** |
| b | Agency | with the help of the one enabling me. |
| 14a | | Nevertheless, |
| b | Assertion | **you did well** |
| c | Means | in sharing your resources |
| d | Association | with me |
| e | Situation | in my difficulty! |

| | | |
|---|---|---|
| 15a | Assertion | Now also **you yourselves know**, Philippians, |
| b | Content/Time | that at the beginning of gospel ministry in your area, |
| c | Time | when I left Macedonia, |
| d | Assertion | not a single church shared |
| e | Association | with me |
| f | Reference | in this matter of giving and receiving |
| g | Exception | —except you!— |
| 16a | Expansion/Content | that |
| b | Time | even when I was in Thessalonica, |
| c | Extent | on more than one occasion |
| d | Action | you dispatched someone |
| e | Destination | to me |
| f | Purpose | to address a need. |
| 17a | Caveat | **It is not that I seek the gift**. |
| b | Alternative | Rather, |
| c | | **I am seriously interested in the compounding interest** |
| d | | credited to your account! |
| 18a | Report | **I have the full amount,** |
| b | | indeed, |
| c | Assessment | **I have more than I need.** |
| d | Reiteration | **I have been supplied completely,** |
| e | Cause | since I received from Epaphroditus all that you sent, |
| f | Description | a fragrant aroma, |
| g | Restatement | an acceptable sacrifice, |
| h | Result | pleasing to God. |
| 19a | Expansion | And |
| b | Assurance | **my God will supply your every need** |
| c | Accordance | according to his wealth |
| d | Description | in glory |
| e | Relationship | in Christ Jesus. |
| 20a | | Now |
| b | Recipient | to our God and Father |
| c | Benediction | **be glory** |
| d | Duration | forever and ever. Amen. |

## Structure

The unit presents a string of Paul's personal reflections or assertions, dominated by the first-person singular: "I rejoiced," "I have learned to be content," "I know," etc. (4:10–13, 17–18). These personal reflections are interrupted briefly by the apostle addressing the Philippians: "you did well," "you . . . know," etc. (vv. 14–16). In the final two verses, the unit concludes with a mix of references to Paul, the Philippians, and God: "And *my* God will supply *your* every need," "to *our* God and Father be glory" (vv. 19–20). As to form, these reflections are what we would expect as Paul moves toward the close of his letter, but they especially are grounded in Paul's theological convictions about the three-way relationship between himself as God's apostle, the Philippians as fellow stewards of God's resources, and God, who is the giver of all good gifts and advances his great gospel cause through his people.[2]

## Exegetical Outline

➦ **A. The Philippians' Gift and Partnership in Ministry (4:10–20)**

**1. Paul's Joy in the Philippians' Gift (v. 10)**

**2. Paul's Contentment in His Circumstances (vv. 11–13)**

a. This Is Not about My Need! I am Content! (v. 11)
b. Varied Circumstances (v. 12)
c. A Confession of Contentment (v. 13)

**3. The Philippians' Partnership with Paul (vv. 14–20)**

a. You Did Well! (v. 14)
b. The Philippians' Past Support (vv. 15–16)
c. Paul's Motive: Their Benefit (v. 17)
d. Paul's Celebration of the Gift (v. 18)
e. An Assurance to the Philippians: God Will Meet Your Needs (v. 19)
f. The Goal of Giving: Glory to God the Father (v. 20)

## Explanation of the Text

**4:10–11 Now I rejoiced in the Lord greatly because once again you renewed giving careful thought to what might be done for me (with regard to which, I might add, you were mindful of my situation but were lacking the opportunity)—not that I am speaking because I am in need! For I have learned to be content in my circumstances** (Ἐχάρην δὲ ἐν κυρίῳ μεγάλως ὅτι ἤδη ποτὲ ἀνεθάλετε τὸ ὑπὲρ ἐμοῦ φρονεῖν, ἐφ᾿ ᾧ καὶ ἐφρονεῖτε, ἠκαιρεῖσθε δέ. 11 οὐχ ὅτι καθ᾿ ὑστέρησιν λέγω, ἐγὼ γὰρ ἔμαθον ἐν οἷς εἰμι αὐτάρκης εἶναι). In the first two verses of this unit Paul expresses joy—a consistent theme in the book—with reference to the Philippians' financial support of his ministry. But then the apostle qualifies his celebration by noting that his "need" has not driven him to a desperate place. Rather, he lives in a state of "contentment" in his circumstances—a sense of

2. On which, see especially Briones, "Paul's Intentional 'Thankless Thanks' in Philippians 4.10–20," 62–64.

adequacy grounded in the sufficiency of God. This theme shapes the unit to a great degree.

The passage connects to what has gone before with the conjunction "now" (δέ), which marks a development in the discourse.[3] In this case, Paul shifts from a series of exhortations in 4:4b–9 to directly address the Philippians about their financial support and God's pleasure in their stewardship. The apostle's perspective includes sheer joy ("I rejoiced," ἐχάρην) in the situation, reprising this important theme as he moves into the letter's final phase.[4] The verb "to rejoice" (χαίρω) can express a state of happiness or well-being, as it does here. The gift caused joy—personal pleasure—to bubble up in Paul, and he describes his joy in three ways.

First, his joy was "in the Lord" (ἐν κυρίῳ). Paul has already used this potent phrase eight times in the letter (Phil 1:14; 2:19, 24, 29; 3:1; 4:1–2, 4), and associated phrases expressing the "in Christ" theme occur in the book another dozen times.[5] As Constantine Campbell notes, the motif is complex but generally has powerful relational overtones.[6] Paul uses "in the Lord" (ἐν κυρίῳ) at 4:10, anchoring his comments in a Christ-centered, relational network. Paul is on mission for the Lord; the Philippians have participated in that mission by helping meet their apostle's needs (4:10; see 1:5; cf. 2 Cor 8:1–5), which pleases God; and God will meet the Philippians' needs (Phil 4:19). All this works to God's glory (v. 20) and manifests the "in the Lord" orientation of Paul, his mission, the Philippians, and their participation in that mission.

Second, his experience of joy was exuberant, as indicated by the adverb rendered "very much" or "greatly" (μεγάλως). The term occurs only here in the New Testament, but it is interesting to note that of its twenty occurrences in the LXX, several are also used to emphasize the extent of a person's thanks or rejoicing, as when King David experienced great joy in the contributions that were given for the building of the temple.[7] So Paul's expression of joy has strong biblical precedent.

Third, the Philippians' revived interest in his situation was the *cause* ("because," ὅτι)[8] of Paul's joy: "Because once again you renewed giving careful thought to what might be done for me" (ὅτι ἤδη ποτὲ ἀνεθάλετε τὸ ὑπὲρ ἐμοῦ φρονεῖν). That they were giving "once again" (ἤδη ποτέ) indicates that the Philippians had supported Paul's mission before. As used here, the phrase communicates a reigniting of the Philippians' earlier passion for giving to the mission.[9] They now are "again" (so, e.g., NLT) giving careful thought to the apostle's need. We should not hear Paul speaking in a harsh tone, as if he is chastising the church for not getting with the program sooner.[10] The following words make clear that the apostle genuinely celebrates their involvement and expresses his thanks to God for their help.[11]

Paul celebrates that the Philippians had "renewed" (ἀνεθάλετε) "giving careful thought"

3. Runge, *Discourse Grammar*, 31–36.

4. See Phil 1:18; 1:25; 2:2; 2:17–18, 28–29; 3:1; 4:4. As noted elsewhere in the commentary, the joy motif also plays a structural role in Philippians, marking key seams or transition points in the book. On the theme of joy in biblical literature and in Philippians, see the introduction (pp. 33–35) and the commentary above at 1:4 (p. 67).

5. See Phil 1:1, 13, 26; 2:1, 5; 3:3, 9, 14; 4:7, 19, 21.

6. On a summary of the theme's nuances, see Campbell, *Paul and Union with Christ*, 420.

7. See 1 Chr 29:9; cf. Neh 12:43; 2 Macc 1:11; 15:27; 1 Esd 9:54; 3 Macc 4:16.

8. Although as Fee points out, the use of ὅτι is ambiguous here; this could be a content clause (Fee, *Philippians*, 428–29).

9. So BDAG 434; Hellerman, *Philippians*, 255.

10. In biblical literature the combination ἤδη ποτέ only occurs here and at Rom 1:10, and most translations render it as "now at last." Yet Paul should not be read as being exasperated by the delay. Rather, he celebrates that they are again involved.

11. So Fee, *Philippians*, 429.

to what might be done for him (τὸ ὑπὲρ ἐμοῦ φρονεῖν), given his situation.[12] In ancient literature the word translated as "renewed" (ἀναθάλλω) often conveyed a horticultural word picture of a plant "sprouting" or "blooming" once again.[13] We might think of bulbs that rhythmically appear each spring, forcing their way through the crust of long-barren soil to bless the world with their beauty. The image has to do with the renewal of something that has taken place in the past, in this case the Philippians' careful thought regarding Paul's situation. Thus we render the verb "renewed."

Throughout Philippians, Paul time and again uses the verb φρονέω, employed twice in this passage, translated in the first instance here as "giving careful thought" (Phil 1:7; 2:2, 5; 3:15, 19; 4:2). As noted elsewhere in the commentary, the word has a semantic range that includes "to think" or "hold an opinion," "to be intent on," or "to give careful thought" to something.[14] The sense in verse 10 communicates affection toward a friend in need, as when we say in English, "Let me give some thought to your situation." The church had given careful thought to what needed to be done on Paul's behalf.[15] So we render the first part of verse 10 as "now I rejoiced in the Lord greatly because once again you renewed giving careful thought to what might be done for me."

However, anticipating that some might misunderstand him as being critical of the delay in giving, the apostle qualifies with a parenthetical statement: "with regard to which, I might add, you were mindful of my situation but were lacking the opportunity" (ἐφ' ᾧ καὶ ἐφρονεῖτε, ἠκαιρεῖσθε δέ).[16] In this case the apostle clarifies his comment ("with reference to what I just said . . ."), while acknowledging their previous concern. The conjunction (καί) appears to be adjunctive ("I might add"), functioning to introduce the qualification to the previous statement.

Finally, when Paul notes that they "were mindful" (φρονέω), he acknowledges that the Philippians had been characterized as being concerned about his situation. What then changed that allowed the church to move from a posture of merely being "mindful" to acting thoughtfully? Before, they "were lacking the opportunity" (ἠκαιρεῖσθε). The verb (ἀκαιρέομαι), which only occurs here in the New Testament, speaks of lacking a favorable time or occasion to accomplish something. The term describes the Philippians' situation previously, but evidently circumstances had changed, and the church now experienced an opportunity to address Paul's need.

Verse 11 includes another qualification, "not that I am speaking because I am in need!" (οὐχ ὅτι καθ' ὑστέρησιν λέγω). The term for "need" (ὑστέρησις) communicates the idea of deprivation ("need, lack, poverty") and is only found in the New Testament here and at Mark 12:44, where Jesus speaks of the poor woman who gave to the temple treasury "out of her poverty." Paul makes

12. The neuter singular accusative article marks the infinitival construction as the object of the verb ἀναθάλλω.

13. BDAG 63.

14. BDAG 1065–66. Almost universally, English translations have rendered the verb here as having to do with the Philippians "being concerned" about Paul (so NASB, NRSV, ESV, CSB, NET, NIV, NLT). Yet this sense is unprecedented among the many uses of the verb in Philippians and is not a common gloss elsewhere. Thus, we consider it better to render the verb with its more common sense.

15. The preposition ὑπέρ + genitive almost always is employed in the apostle's writings to speak of something done *for* someone else; see, e.g., Rom 5:8; 8:31–32, 34; 15:30; 2 Cor 1:11; 5:12, 21; 7:7, 12; Gal 2:20; 3:13; Eph 5:2; 6:19; 1 Thess 5:10; Titus 2:14. Yet the use at 1:7 forms a structural parallel with our verse, and the use there seems to be in terms of content of the thought, i.e., "about you."

16. The prepositional phrase ἐφ' ᾧ, a difficult construction in Paul, may be read as flowing from the infinitival clause that precedes it.

clear that he raises the issue of the Philippians' financial support for particular reasons, and his own "need" is *not* one of them. His joy does not stem from a full belly and a roof over his head.

In fact, Paul is content: "For I have learned to be content in my circumstances" (ἐγὼ γὰρ ἔμαθον ἐν οἷς εἰμι αὐτάρκης εἶναι). As the apostle has served Christ through varied ministry circumstances, many of them involving great hardships (cf. 2 Cor 11:24–33), he has learned the secret of contentment. The verb for "learn" (μανθάνω) could connote learning something through instruction or becoming aware of something through experience. Here, the verb probably conveys the latter nuance of learning through one's experience in the normal course of life,[17] Paul referring to the learning process as a whole. In any case, he describes the experiences to which he has been exposed as the context of his contentment: "in my circumstances" (ἐν οἷς εἰμι).[18] In a sense, Paul's circumstances were the "classroom" where he learned contentment but also the context in which he lived it.

The adjective often translated as "contentment" (αὐτάρκης)[19] expresses contentment or self-sufficiency. Although some make much of the background of this word in Cynic and Stoic philosophy, Fee points out that by Paul's day the word had come to be used commonly with the sense of "contentment."[20] For instance, Seneca, a Stoic philosopher who lived in Rome and served as an advisor to Emperor Nero, could write just a few years before Paul wrote Philippians, "The happy man is content with his present lot, no matter what it is, and is reconciled to his circumstances" (*Vit. beat.* 6.2). This is contentment that accepts that one has what is needed for life—one has "enough."[21] In a striking passage from Josephus, who consistently uses the word with the sense of "sufficient" or "self-sufficient,"[22] the historian notes, "The first command is concerning God, and affirms that God contains all things, and is a being every way perfect and happy, self-sufficient [αὐτάρκης], and supplying all other beings; the beginning, the middle, and the end of all things" (*Ag. Ap.* 2.190 [Whiston]). This notion, of God as the one who is truly self-sufficient and the one who provides for all other beings, lies behind Paul's understanding of the concept. It is not that the apostle is self-sufficient. Rather, he is "God-sufficient" and thus able to be content in his circumstances. That is why he can always say, "I have enough."

Significantly for our context, the term for "need" (ὑστέρησις) could be used in patron-client relationships in the Greco-Roman world, in situations involving obligation. In terms of the cultural value system of his day, when Paul notes that the Philippians had met a personal need and thanks them for it, he would be acknowledging his obligation

17. BDAG 615.

18. Lit. "in which I am."

19. This is another *hapax*, only found here in the NT. The cognate noun αὐταρκεία occurs at 2 Cor 9:8 and 1 Tim 6:6, both with the sense of "having what you need."

20. See especially Fee's comments (Fee, *Philippians*, 431–32). The uses in the LXX, e.g., Prov 30:8; Sir 5:1; 11:24; 31:28; 40:18; 4 Macc 9:9, place an emphasis on sufficiency or self-sufficiency. Although Josephus primarily uses the term with this sense of "sufficiency," he also uses it with the sense of a righteous person being "content," as at *Ag. Ap.* 2.291:

> They are enemies to injustice, they take care of righteousness, they banish idleness and expensive living, and instruct men to be content with what they have and to be laborious in their callings.

21. The sense here communicates a very different sentiment from the posture of presumption warned against in Sir 11:24: "Do not say, 'I have enough [αὐτάρκη], and what distress will I suffer from now on?'" (NETS). Paul's use of the term has no presumptuousness that assumes his present supply guarantees a carefree future. Rather, he bears witness to God's provision for the needs of the moment.

22. *Ant.* 2.220, 259; 4.259–60; 12.152; 15.91, 334; 16.117; *J.W.* 1.215; 7.307; *Ag. Ap.* 1.247; 2.190. The same is true of Philo, who uses the term forty-six times, e.g., *Creation* 146; *Alleg. Interp.* 3.163, 165, 198; *Cherubim* 46; *Posterity* 49.

to them as their client—and hinting that he would repay them. Yet Paul understands the relational dynamics differently, in a way that has been shaped by Christ-following and in contradistinction to the culture. He brilliantly shifts attention to God, emphasizing that ultimately God himself is the patron who will supply all the needs of his clients—including both Paul and the Philippians as partners in God's mission (4:13, 18–20).[23] Thus Paul and the Philippians are under obligation to God. From a cultural-backgrounds standpoint, this makes sense of why Paul offers a clarification here and why he does not overtly thank the Philippians for their gift. They were not the ultimate source of the gift.[24]

Greco-Roman conventions of friendship can also help us in our understanding of "need" and "contentment" found in this passage. In that cultural context, a friendship in which one party meets the needs of another was considered inferior to a friendship among equals, who were "self-sufficient" or "content" with their situation (e.g., Cicero, *Amic.* 14.51).[25] In other words, the social pressure of one person's appeal for help from another does not exist between true friends. By claiming "sufficiency" in Philippians 4:10–20, Paul addresses the Philippians as true friends rather than his patrons or his clients, even as he acknowledges them as fellow workers in the cause of Christ. Again, Paul differs from the broader Greco-Roman culture by shifting to a kingdom orientation, in which he and the Philippians share a common patron, God himself. The bond of friendship he and the Philippians enjoy stems in part from their mutual service to God's kingdom work, as noted above. Their relationship *does* involve the flow of resources from the Philippians to Paul's mission. Yet since those resources ultimately are God's, both he and they, as friends, are obligated to God as they live under the lordship of Christ, and God's resources are sufficient to meet the needs of all his people.

**4:12–13 I know what it is like to be in very humble circumstances and what it is like to have a wealth of resources. In any and every situation I have learned the secret of how to be well fed and how to go hungry, how to have more than enough and how to do without: I am able to do all things with the help of the one enabling me** (οἶδα καὶ ταπεινοῦσθαι, οἶδα καὶ περισσεύειν· ἐν παντὶ καὶ ἐν πᾶσιν μεμύημαι, καὶ χορτάζεσθαι καὶ πεινᾶν καὶ περισσεύειν καὶ ὑστερεῖσθαι· 13 πάντα ἰσχύω ἐν τῷ ἐνδυναμοῦντί με). Paul has learned contentment in a wide variety of ministerial circumstances. Now, through a series of contrasts, he adds a bit more specificity to the types of situations he has experienced. These he lays out in three pairs, with the second and third pair filling out and inverting the descriptions of the first pair.[26]

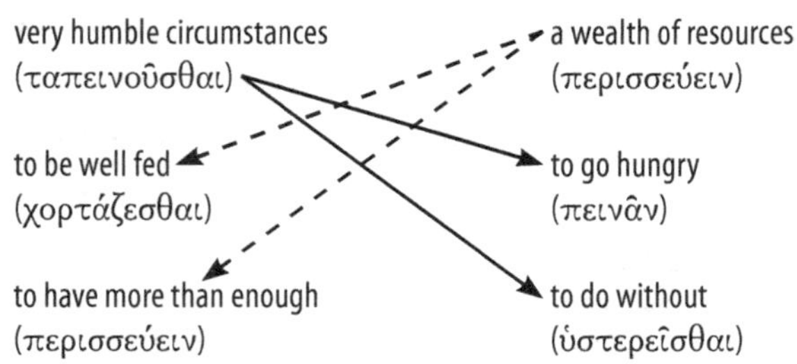


23. So Reed, *Discourse Analysis*, 295; Hellerman, *Philippians*, 257; Fee, *Philippians*, 444; Reumann, *Philippians*, 705.

24. This does not mean that today we need not thank people who have met our needs in some way! Paul is working within the conventions of his own day, and those conventions had strong principles of action between the haves and the have-nots of society.

25. Hellerman, *Philippians*, 256; Hansen, *Philippians*, 311; idem, "Transformation of Relationships: Partnership, Citizenship, and Friendship in Philippi," in *New Testament Greek and Exegesis: Essays in Honor of Gerald F. Hawthorne*, ed. Amy Donaldson and Timothy B. Sailors (Grand Rapids: Eerdmans, 2003), 201.

26. Paul sews each pair together with a series of what

Paul's point is to show that contentment covers a wide spectrum of experiences in his life and ministry, such that seeming opposites are covered by the sufficiency of God. Contentment, rather than being "circumstance dependent," can transcend the varied experiences of life and ministry. Because Paul has "learned" (v. 11) the sufficiency of God's provision, he "knows" (οἶδα) how to live in these widely varying situations.[27] In the present context, the verb has more to do with being enabled to do something rather than possession of information. Of course, experience and knowledge are interrelated.

So, first, the apostle knows how to live in "very humble circumstances" (ταπεινοῦσθαι) as well as with a "wealth of resources" (περισσεύειν). Paul faces these contrasting circumstances from time to time in an ongoing way. The verb communicating the concept of "humble circumstances" (ταπεινόω) has already occurred in Philippians at 2:8, where Paul proclaims that Christ "humiliated himself" by following the path of obedience all the way to the point of death. The verb could connote being at a "lower" place in terms of physical location (e.g., Luke 3:5), but it more often speaks of a humble status (as opposed to moving up in social prestige or glory) or of being humiliated, as seen at Philippians 2:8. The present infinitive may be passive rather than middle in voice, suggesting that Paul's humbling circumstances were forced upon him. Nevertheless, he embraced such circumstances as following in the way of Jesus, who embraced the "shame" of the cross—one of the most shameful forms of death in the ancient world.[28] Thus the path of discipleship could be one of lowly circumstances, and Paul has learned how to live in such situations.

Paul uses this verb (ταπεινόω) elsewhere only at 2 Corinthians 11:7 and 12:21, both of which speak of his Christian ministry.[29] He had "humbled" himself by working with his own hands (2 Cor 11:7) and was concerned that he would be humiliated before God by the behavior of the Corinthians when he returned to the city (12:21). Although the use of the verb here in Philippians 4:12 should not be limited to economic deprivation,[30] the context certainly includes the sense of lacking basic resources for life, as indicated by the descriptive pairs that follow.

Similarly, Paul uses the verb translated "to have a wealth of resources" (περισσεύειν) to speak of abounding or having an abundance of something; the term does not normally speak of economic prosperity.[31] It is only here in 4:12 and 4:18 that the term seems to connote having abundant resources, which in the cultural context would be a marker of "higher status" in contrast to a status of shame. Economic prosperity was often a means of public status and glory. By contrast, "to lack" (ὑστερεῖσθαι) or "to do without" was to be in a position of shame. In the normal course of his ministry, the apostle had experienced both the highs of abundance and the lows of going without. Yet with God as his true patron, Paul was content; he neither gloried in

Denniston calls corresponsive καί ... καί constructions. In such constructions the first καί, often rendered with "both," anticipates a second item added to the thought. The second καί normally is connective ("and"), introducing a second member of the pair. See Denniston and Dover, *Greek Particles*, 323–25.

27. Paul includes "I know" (οἶδα) prior to each of the infinitives in the first contrasting pair to place equal emphasis on each. The verb οἶδα is understood in the second and third pairs of contrasts.

28. As noted in the commentary at 2:8, Isa 53:4, 7–8 probably serves as the backdrop of the *hymnos* in Philippians 2, putting an emphasis on degradation and oppression.

29. But cognates occur eleven more times at Rom 12:16; 2 Cor 7:6; 10:1; Eph 4:2; Phil 2:3, 8; 3:21; 4:12; Col 2:18, 23; 3:12. The family of words is associated with hardship in various ways but also with an appropriate posture in life and ministry.

30. So Fee, *Philippians*, 432–33.

31. Paul uses the verb twenty-six times (e.g., Rom 3:7; 1 Cor 8:8; 2 Cor 1:5; Eph 1:8; Col 2:7; 1 Thess 3:12).

abundance nor felt shame at the lack. Both were part of being God's person on mission.

The apostle's school of contentment had involved "any and every situation" (ἐν παντὶ καὶ ἐν πᾶσιν)—circumstances both varied and comprehensive. In the ancient world, the word translated "I have learned the secret" (μεμύημαι) normally had to do with rites of initiation, as for instance at 3 Maccabees 2:30,[32] where under the rule of Ptolemy Philopator, Jews in Alexandria were given an opportunity to escape persecution by going through initiatory rites in the worship of Dionysus. Here, however, Paul uses the term metaphorically and very much in line with his contemporary Philo, who employs the word to speak of lessons learned in the ways of God.[33] Paul had "learned the secret" of "how to be well fed and how to go hungry, how to have more than enough and how to do without" (καὶ χορτάζεσθαι καὶ πεινᾶν καὶ περισσεύειν καὶ ὑστερεῖσθαι). "To be well fed" (χορτάζω), another word used only here in Paul's letters, speaks of being "full" of food but also carries the connotation of satisfaction.[34] The verb rendered "to go hungry" (πεινάω), on the other hand, can be used metaphorically of the strong desire for something but here speaks of literal hunger.[35] The apostle states that whether he is full or famished, he has learned how to deal with the situation.

As we turn to 4:13, we encounter a much-loved text that, unfortunately, in some cultural contexts has taken on a meaning that veers off the mark: "I am able to do all things with the help of the one enabling me" (πάντα ἰσχύω ἐν τῷ ἐνδυναμοῦντί με). On the surface and taken out of context, the verse *seems* to speak of the Lord granting extraordinary *ability* to a faithful follower who needs enhanced skills. While there are texts that give strong encouragement along such lines, such as Psalm 18:29,[36] this is not one of them. Consider the following.

First, we have already noted that the context of the verse does not deal with ability in terms of skill but with *contentment* in the sufficiency of God. Second, although the verb translated "I am able" (ἰσχύω) can speak of ability,[37] it also can be used of competence, as it is here (see, e.g., Acts 15:10). Paul is saying he has learned *how* to deal with the pendulum swing of ready resources; he has become competent at handling diverse situations. Third, and correspondingly, the participle translated as "the one enabling me" (ἐνδυναμοῦντί) speaks of God as the agent who strengthens Paul at a moment of need.[38] This points not to extraordinary ability in terms of Paul's skills but rather to his possession of God-infused strength to deal with challenging moments of life. The apostle has learned to depend on God—"*with the help* of the one enabling me," with the preposition communicating agency. In other words, Paul has learned to live without dependence on resources supplied by people; his "contentment" rests in his utter dependence on the Lord.[39] This posture undergirds the passage.[40]

**4:14–16 Nevertheless, you did well in sharing your resources with me in my difficulty! Now**

32. The term is only used here in the NT. See also, e.g., Epictetus, *Diatr.* 4.1.106, 140.

33. E.g., *Alleg. Interp.* 3.71, 100; *Cherubim* 49; *Sacrifices* 62; *Giants* 57; *Unchangeable* 61.

34. BDAG 1087. See, e.g., Matt 5:6; 14:20; 15:33, 37; Mark 6:42; 7:27; 8:4, 8; Luke 6:21; 9:17.

35. BDAG 792.

36. "Indeed, with your help I can charge against an army; by my God's power I can jump over a wall" (Ps 18:29 NET).

37. E.g., Matt 26:40; Luke 8:43; Jas 5:16.

38. Cf. Rom 4:20; Eph 6:10; 1 Tim 1:12; 2 Tim 2:1; 4:17.

39. To clarify that the one enabling Paul is Christ himself, several manuscripts add Χριστῷ at the end of the verse ($\aleph^2$ $D^2$ [F G] K L P Ψ 075. 81. 104. 365. 630. 1175. 1241. 1505. 1881. 2464 𝔐 sy; Hier), but the text as it stands has early and varied support ($\aleph^*$ A B $D^*$ I 33. 629. 1739 lat co; Cl).

40. Hellerman, *Philippians*, 261; Hawthorne and Martin, *Philippians*, 266.

**also you yourselves know, Philippians, that at the beginning of gospel ministry in your area, when I left Macedonia, not a single church shared with me in this matter of giving and receiving—except you!—that even when I was in Thessalonica, on more than one occasion you dispatched someone to me to address a need** (πλὴν καλῶς ἐποιήσατε συγκοινωνήσαντές μου τῇ θλίψει. 15 οἴδατε δὲ καὶ ὑμεῖς, Φιλιππήσιοι, ὅτι ἐν ἀρχῇ τοῦ εὐαγγελίου, ὅτε ἐξῆλθον ἀπὸ Μακεδονίας, οὐδεμία μοι ἐκκλησία ἐκοινώνησεν εἰς λόγον δόσεως καὶ λήμψεως εἰ μὴ ὑμεῖς μόνοι, 16 ὅτι καὶ ἐν Θεσσαλονίκῃ καὶ ἅπαξ καὶ δὶς εἰς τὴν χρείαν μοι ἐπέμψατε). Paul here celebrates his partnership with the Philippians in ministry. At the outset of Philippians 4:10–20, the apostle points to how he had celebrated the Philippians' thoughtfulness toward him (v. 10)—only to launch into a multi-verse qualification lest they misread the nature of his relationship with them (vv. 11–13). The celebration did not issue from a perspective of desperate need. Paul did not come to the Philippians "hat in hand" as a client to a patron, nor as a pseudo-friend needing their resources. Rather, his celebration was offered from a posture of theological perspective. He was content and confident in the sufficiency of God, and as he here points out, he primarily celebrates his *shared ministry* with the Philippians.

So with verse 14 the apostle here shifts topic (πλήν, "nevertheless") back to the note of celebration with which he began this passage: "Nevertheless, you did well in sharing your resources with me in my difficulty!" Although Paul has qualified the reason for his celebration of the Philippians' support, this does not mean that he takes their support lightly. In fact, in stating that they "did well" (καλῶς ἐποιήσατε), he underscores the value he places on their contribution.[41] The adverb (καλῶς) has a range of meanings, from the prosaic (e.g., "in the right way," "in a manner free from objection," "acceptably") to the exclamatory (e.g., to act with "excellence," "splendidly"). We should probably hear warmth and enthusiasm in the term's use in this context (which is the reason our translation includes an exclamation point, and which rules out those interpretations that read the section as an apostolic slap on the wrist).[42] By doing something tangible (ἐποιήσατε)[43] in response to Paul's need, the Philippians had expressed continued commitment to their partnership with the apostle in his mission. This is what Paul celebrates. Thus, he weaves into his conclusion of the letter an important acknowledgment with which he began in 1:5—their "participation in the gospel from the first day until now."

Paul next points to an expression of that partnership as "sharing your resources with me" (συγκοινωνήσαντες), which may be read either temporally ("when you shared") or as expressing means ("by sharing" or "in sharing"), as with our translation. In the two other uses of the verb (συγκοινωνέω) in the New Testament, the nuance of "participation" is clear. Ephesians 5:11 speaks of participating in works of darkness, and Revelation 18:4 of participating in the sins of the world. Here the translation "sharing" might be better, since material resources seem to be in view. Yet the note of "participation" is almost certainly present, given that the church's ongoing association with Paul "in"[44] his affliction (μου τῇ θλίψει; cf. 1:17) means

41. The term καλῶς participates in a semantic chain of "value" words in Philippians (δοκιμή, ὑπερέχω, ἀξίως, ἔντιμος, κρείττων). See Reed, *Discourse Analysis*, 315–16.

42. So Fee, *Philippians*, 438.

43. Although ποιέω can connote production (e.g., "produce"), it here speaks of acting to bring something about, "to accomplish" or perhaps "do" something on behalf of someone else. See BDAG 839–42.

44. Note the dative form of the word, which might be read as a dative of association.

that they face social difficulties as well (cf. 1:29–30). Although the word can be used of difficulties in general, Paul often uses the term translated as "difficulty" (θλῖψις) to speak of various challenges surrounding persecution.[45] Although the grammatical construction is a bit odd,[46] the possessive "my [μου] difficulty" points to the apostle's present imprisonment.

One way of celebrating with someone close to us is by *remembering* together, as when a husband and wife or close friends recount significant moments that have marked their relationship. In verses 15 and 16, Paul thus continues to celebrate his friends in Philippi by writing about the history of their partnership with him. He notes, "You yourselves know" (οἴδατε . . . ὑμεῖς), since he is writing a chapter from their own story.[47] Paul continues,[48] by pointing out that this recent round of support was not their first experience of giving to the mission—they *also*[49] had been faithful early on in the apostle's relationship with them. Further, in addressing the church as "Philippians" (Φιλιππήσιοι), Paul transcribes the Latin name for residents of the city into Greek. He has already addressed them as those "in Philippi" (1:1), but the direct address in this verse is both unusual (only occurring elsewhere in 2 Cor 6:11 and Gal 3:1) and expressive of emotional warmth; most interpreters suggest that it communicates affection.

What the Philippians "know" is that 1) only they had supported Paul in his mission as he traveled on from Macedonia (4:15), and 2) (even while he was still in the province) they had supported him when he was carrying out his mission in the much larger city of Thessalonica (v. 16). Thus they had been involved in supporting Paul "at the beginning of gospel ministry" (ἐν ἀρχῇ τοῦ εὐαγγελίου)[50] in their region and beyond (v. 15). As noted in the commentary's introduction, Paul came to Philippi and planted the church there in late 49 or early 50 CE. In that first foray into Europe, Lydia, the Philippian jailer, and their respective households responded to the gospel (Acts 16:6–34). The church started as a relatively small affair. Yet Paul's point in Philippians 4:15 is that the Philippian church was moved to be involved materially in his mission from the very start, and this was vital when he "left Macedonia" (ἐξῆλθον ἀπὸ Μακεδονίας)[51] for his continued mission to the south. The apostle also celebrates the Macedonian generosity elsewhere, in connection with the collection for Jerusalem, at 2 Corinthians 8:1–4:

> Now we want you to be aware, brothers and sisters, of God's grace that has been given in connection with the Macedonian churches, that during a severe test involving affliction their effusive joy and extreme poverty spilled over in extravagant

45. See Rom 5:3; 8:35; 2 Cor 1:4, 8; 4:17; 6:4; 7:4; 8:2; Eph 3:13; Phil 1:17; Col 1:24; 1 Thess 1:6; 3:3, 7; 2 Thess 1:4, 6.

46. A similar construction (the pronoun moved forward in the sentence) is only found at Rom 11:14; 1 Cor 9:27; Phil 2:2; and Phlm 20. So Fee, *Philippians*, 439.

47. Hansen, *Philippians*, 317. In this case the pronoun ὑμεῖς is emphatic. Fee points to passages in Cicero and Seneca on friendship and the exchange of services. The latter notes, "In the case of a benefit . . . the one should straightway forget that it was given, the other should never forget that it was received" (as quoted in Fee, *Philippians*, 439). In accordance with this sentiment, Paul appropriately brings us the Philippians' past service to him.

48. The conjunction (δέ) simply signals here a further development in the discourse; so Runge, *Discourse Grammar*, 31. The construction δὲ καί is common in Paul, occurring thirty-three times and previously in Philippians at 1:15 and 3:18. The δέ is omitted in several witnesses, including 𝔓[46].

49. The addition of καί offers an adjunctive note ("also").

50. Similarly, "in the early days of your acquaintance with the gospel" (NIV), and "when I first brought you the Good News" (NLT).

51. The aorist ἐξῆλθον here should be read as a constative, generally referring to an unspecified period of ministry in Achaia. See Reumann, *Philippians*, 660.

> generosity; I can confirm this—they voluntarily gave according to their resources, even beyond their resources, begging us most emphatically for the privilege of being able to join in this ministry to God's people.[52]

It seems this pattern of enthusiastic giving had marked the Philippians from the very beginning, and when Paul remarks at 2 Corinthians 8:5 that they had first given themselves "to us," he may allude to their deep commitment to his mission, which is a point underscored at 2 Corinthians 11:8–9. In fact, this set the Philippians apart, since at that time "not a single church" (οὐδεμία . . . ἐκκλησία) shared with Paul for the sake of gospel ministry—except the Philippians themselves (μοι[53] . . . ἐκοινώνησεν[54] . . . εἰ μὴ ὑμεῖς μόνοι, Phil 4:15).

There are two points that should be made about the language of "giving and receiving" (εἰς λόγον δόσεως καὶ λήμψεως). First, this turn of phrase stems from the cultural context of financial accounting, the Greek rendering the Latin *ratio dati et accepti*, "an account of giving and receiving."[55] Such language was vernacular of business transactions in Roman colonies and would have been very familiar to street-level merchants in the Philippian church. The term translated "matter" (λόγος) could refer to "computation" or "reckoning," and the phrase "in this matter" (εἰς λόγον) to the settling of a commercial account.[56] Almost certainly Paul does not use the language literally to speak of an account that had been set up, tracking the give and take between the church and Paul's mission.[57] Rather, the apostle uses familiar language and concepts to effect a spiritually rich word picture that would have been meaningful to the Philippians. This is confirmed by verse 17, where he speaks of profit or accrued "interest" (τὸν καρπόν), by which he means not financial but spiritual gain, and by verse 18, where he notes that he has received the full amount. Thus the financial resources they have supplied are literal, but the effects of their exchange are more spiritual than transactional. This fits elsewhere in Paul where material resources and spiritual resources stand side by side in a principle of exchange in the broader work of God; the sowing of spiritual impact should be reciprocated with material support (cf. Rom 15:27; 1 Cor 9:11).

Recent scholarship has clarified that the language also relates to Greco-Roman "friendship" reciprocity,[58] with friends giving and receiving from each other, not as business transactions but in the give and take of healthy, caring relationships.[59] Accordingly, there is a loving mutuality to the friendship between Paul and the Philippians. Shared mission and resources reflect a genuine, warm partnership lived out under God.

Paul also speaks of the help given by the

52. My translation as seen in Guthrie, *2 Corinthians*, 390.

53. The pronoun is probably to be read as a dative of association.

54. We saw at 1:5 the noun related to this verb and there noted that the word group is relationally rich, speaking of sharing in the context of a close relationship. This family of words was used of "sharing" with another or participating with them in a task. Paul uses the verb elsewhere at Rom 12:13, 15:27, and Gal 6:6 to speak of the sharing of resources.

55. The phrase does not have an exact match in ancient Greek literature. See Julien M. Ogereau, *Paul's Koinonia with the Philippians: A Socio-Historical Investigation of a Pauline Economic Partnership*, WUNT 377 (Tübingen: Mohr Siebeck, 2014), 101; Holloway, *Philippians*, 188.

56. So BDAG 601 (see 2.b).

57. For the various interpretations, see Peterman, *Paul's Gift from Philippi*, 11–17; Ogereau, *Paul's Koinonia*, 104.

58. See especially Peterman, *Paul's Gift from Philippi*, 55–89.

59. In a modern Western context, think of friends who go out to lunch from time to time, one saying to the other, "Let me take care of the bill this time." When a friend comes to supper, we never even think of "charging" for the meal. Rather, in such friendships "accounting" gives way to the joy of giving and receiving as a natural part of the relationship.

Philippians when he was in Thessalonica (4:16):[60] "That even when I was in Thessalonica, on more than one occasion you dispatched someone to me to address a need" (ὅτι καὶ ἐν Θεσσαλονίκῃ καὶ ἅπαξ καὶ δὶς εἰς τὴν χρείαν μοι ἐπέμψατε). *Not only*[61] had their support been unique and vital once the apostle left Macedonia, but *even while he was still in the province*, in the city of Thessalonica, they had contributed to his work "on more than one occasion" (καὶ ἅπαξ καὶ δίς; lit. "and once and twice").[62] It is clear from the Thessalonian correspondence that the Philippians did not provide adequate resources for Paul's support while in Thessalonica, for he worked to support himself (1 Thess 2:9; 2 Thess 3:8). But they did supplement his resources. Paul notes, "You dispatched someone to me to address a need" (Phil 4:16). A number of translations render the pronoun as possessive ("my"),[63] but the dative should probably be read to communicate that Paul was the recipient ("to me") of their generosity. The phrase "to address a need" (εἰς τὴν χρείαν), on the other hand, may be read to indicate the purpose of their gift. The point is that the Philippians had shown themselves to be true partners in the mission, giving consistently in support of their apostle when he needed their help.

**4:17–18 It is not that I seek the gift. Rather, I am seriously interested in the compounding interest credited to your account! I have the full amount, indeed, I have more than I need. I have been supplied completely, since I received from Epaphroditus all that you sent, a fragrant aroma, an acceptable sacrifice, pleasing to God** (οὐχ ὅτι ἐπιζητῶ τὸ δόμα, ἀλλὰ ἐπιζητῶ τὸν καρπὸν τὸν πλεονάζοντα εἰς λόγον ὑμῶν. 18 ἀπέχω δὲ πάντα καὶ περισσεύω· πεπλήρωμαι δεξάμενος παρὰ Ἐπαφροδίτου τὰ παρ' ὑμῶν, ὀσμὴν εὐωδίας, θυσίαν δεκτήν, εὐάρεστον τῷ θεῷ). With 4:17 Paul offers a further qualification ("It is not . . .") and a clarification ("Rather, I am seriously interested in . . ."). The qualification concerns the apostle's *motivation* that lies behind his joy in receiving their monetary help.

The verb translated "seek" (ἐπιζητέω) communicates "to be seriously interested in or have a strong desire for"[64] something, and it is fronted with an emphatically placed negative (οὐχ). Here the verb's object refers to the Philippians' financial help, referred to as "the gift" (τὸ δόμα), and Paul makes it clear that this is *not* where his interest lies. He did not ask for their resources and is not discussing these matters as a roundabout way to beg for more.[65] This word for "gift" (δόμα) only finds

60. The ὅτι is read as grammatically parallel to the content clause of 4:15 rather than as a causal clause "justifying what Paul said in v. 15" (so Hellerman, *Philippians*, 265, following Fee, *Philippians*, 445; cf. CSB, NIV, NET, NRSV). The two clauses are temporally distinct, the first indicating a time after Paul left the province and the second a time when he was still in the province. The relationship between the two is ascensive (as Hellerman notes) rather than one of justification. Paul is not underscoring that "even the Thessalonians did not help with the mission once I left Macedonia" but that the Philippians' support had started even while he was still in the province.

61. The first use of the conjunction (καί) functions as ascensive ("even").

62. The statement is idiomatic, and the same phrase is used at 1 Thess 2:18; ἅπαξ καὶ δίς, without the fronting of καί, is seen at LXX Deut 9:13, 1 Sam 17:39; Neh 13:20; 1 Macc 3:30.

63. E.g., ESV, CSB, NASB, NRSV, NET; and the sentiment is reflected as well in the variant μου for μοι (D P 614. 630 et al), clearly a scribal adjustment.

64. BDAG 371. The word is used thirteen times in the NT and often is used in contexts where a note of urgency or intense interest is in play (in addition to the two occurrences in our passage, see Matt 6:32; 12:39; 16:4; Luke 4:42; 12:30; Acts 12:19; 13:7; 19:39; Rom 11:7; Heb 11:14; 13:14).

65. Bockmuehl, *Philippians*, 265; Silva, *Philippians*, 205–6. Silva believes that Paul was insisting that the Philippians not send any more resources at the time.

expression three other times in the New Testament, at Matt 7:11//Luke 11:13 where Jesus speaks of the good "gifts" (δόματα) that fathers give their children, and at Ephesians 4:8 in the quotation of Psalm 68:18: "When he ascended on high, he took the captives captive; he gave gifts [δόματα] to people." As we saw in verses 15–16, the giving and receiving of gifts should be understood to reflect friendship, a "warm and lasting relationship."[66] Yet Paul makes clear that his relationship with the Philippians, their spiritual welfare, and their partnership with him in the gospel are his primary concerns.

The apostle further explains by way of contrast: "Rather, I am seriously interested in the compounding interest credited to your account" (ἀλλὰ ἐπιζητῶ τὸν καρπὸν τὸν πλεονάζοντα εἰς λόγον ὑμῶν). The "rather" (ἀλλά) sets up the contrast, anticipating the appropriate interpretation of his celebration: he has joy in their gift *because of what it is doing for them*. He describes the benefit once again in the language of business, but such vocabulary has been baptized for Christian thought. The word interpreted here as "interest" (καρπός)[67] generally refers to the outcome or product of something, whether literal "fruit," a descendant, or a spiritual by-product, which is always the case in Paul's usage.[68] Already at 1:11 the apostle has prayed that the Philippians would be filled with the "fruit produced by righteousness," and at 1:22 he notes that his continued ministry would result in fruitfulness. At Romans 15:28, 1 Corinthians 9:7, and 2 Timothy 2:6, Paul brings the imagery of "fruit" to bear on financial situations. In fact, the financial framing of Paul's language at Philippians 4:17 leads us to render this word plus the adjectival participle that follows (i.e., τὸν καρπὸν τὸν πλεονάζοντα) as "compounding interest." The participle, translated here as "compounding," has to do with something "increasing" or "becoming more and more." Again, the word translated as "account" (λόγος) is used figuratively of an account or ledger. Paul's point is that as the Philippians invest in his mission financially, the spiritual dividends are piling up, and this constitutes the apostle's real interest—their spiritual welfare.

The first three clauses of verse 18—a mere six words—are terse, strong, and thanks-soaked affirmations of the effect that the Philippians' gift is having on Paul. Notice the alliteration of *p* sounds in this string of Greek words:

| | |
|---|---|
| I have the full amount, indeed, | ἀπέχω δὲ πάντα καί |
| I have more than I need | περισσεύω |
| I have been supplied completely | πεπλήρωμαι |

Continuing with the commercial language that weaves its way through the passage, the first of the verbs means "to have the full amount" or "to be paid in full" (ἀπέχω); in the papyri of the era it conveys the sense of "paid"—that is, "I have received this sum, and here is my receipt."[69] What had been lacking in the Philippians' ministry to Paul (see 2:30) now had been fully discharged, and he had in hand the full amount (lit. "all"; πάντα). Further, the combination of the term meaning "paid" (ἀπέχω) with "the full amount" was used by the Stoic

66. Cousar, *Philippians and Philemon*, 90.

67. Used as the accusative direct object of the second use of the verb ἐπιζητῶ.

68. For fruit, see, e.g., Matt 21:19, 34, 41; a descendant, see Luke 1:42; Acts 2:30; a spiritual by-product, see, e.g., Matt 3:8, 10; 7:16–20; 12:33; Luke 3:8; John 4:36; 12:24; 15:2, 4–5, 8, 16; Acts 2:30; Rom 1:13; 6:21–22; 15:28; 1 Cor 9:7; Gal 5:22; Eph 5:9; Phil 1:11, 22; 2 Tim 2:6.

69. BDAG 102.

writers as synonymous with being "self-sufficient" or "content,"[70] and this takes the readers back to Paul's words in 4:11–13. There he says that he had learned to be "content" (αὐτάρκης) with a wealth of resources (περισσεύειν), and he was talking about his present circumstances, reflected in the verse under consideration. So, he continues, "Indeed, I have more than I need" (καὶ περισσεύω).[71] As noted in the commentary on 4:12, Paul doesn't normally use the term for "abound" (περισσεύω) to speak of financial resources, but he clearly does so here in Philippians 4.

Paul exclaims that he has "been filled" (πεπλήρωμαι)[72]—that is, "supplied completely." Once again this echoes the apostle's prayer of chapter 1, where he asks God that the Philippians might be "filled with the fruit produced by righteousness" (1:11; πεπληρωμένοι καρπὸν δικαιοσύνης). This provision was the result of Epaphroditus having delivered what was sent from the Philippian church: "since I received from Epaphroditus all that you sent."[73]

The apostle next describes the Philippians' gift with sacrificial language taken partially from the Old Testament: "a fragrant aroma, an acceptable sacrifice, pleasing to God" (ὀσμὴν εὐωδίας, θυσίαν δεκτήν, εὐάρεστον τῷ θεῷ). This final movement of verse 18 includes a decisive turn, as the apostle moves beyond the horizontal relationship between him and the Philippians to focus squarely on God. The terms for "fragrance" (ὀσμή) and "aroma" (εὐωδία), used together in a Septuagintal formula, are a *terminus technicus* that speaks of the pleasing smell of sacrifices wafting up to God.[74] The only other time that this technical use occurs in the New Testament is at Ephesians 5:2, where the image is used of Christ's sacrifice for believers.[75] The sacrificial imagery is made explicit with the words "an acceptable sacrifice" (θυσίαν δεκτήν). The verbal adjective translated as "acceptable" (δεκτός, from the verb δέχομαι, "to receive") could speak of something as "acceptable," "welcome," or "approved," and the word could be used in Old Testament contexts to speak of "acceptable" offerings.[76] The adjective is roughly synonymous with what Paul says next—namely, that this sacrificial gift offered by the Philippians is "pleasing to God" (εὐάρεστον τῷ θεῷ), which is common language for Paul[77] but in the New Testament is only found outside the apostle's writings at Hebrews 13:21. In short, God himself

70. Fee, *Philippians*, 450–51; Lightfoot, *Philippians*, 166.

71. The conjunction read as ascensive.

72. This third and final verb is perfect tense, passive in voice, and stative in aspect (a switch from the present tense, active voice, and imperfective aspect of the first two verbs).

73. On Epaphroditus's role, see the commentary at 2:25–30. In both uses of παρά + genitive, the preposition functions as a marker of "one who originates or directs" something, i.e., "from." See BDAG 756.

74. The terms are found together fifty times in the LXX: Gen 8:21; Exod 29:18, 25, 41; Lev 1:9, 13, 17; 2:2, 9, 12; 3:5, 11, 16; 4:31; 6:8, 14; 8:21, 28; 17:4, 6; 23:13, 18; Num 15:3, 5, 7, 10, 13–14, 24; 18:17; 28:2, 6, 8, 13, 24, 27; 29:2, 6, 8, 11, 13, 36; Ezek 6:13; 16:19; 20:28, 41; Dan 4:37; Jdt 16:16; Sir 24:15; 50:15. Only at Sir 24:15 are the two terms found apart from the formulaic, sacrificial use.

75. For the use of the two terms apart from the technical formula (and thus not used of sacrificial language), see 2 Cor 2:14–16a, on which see Guthrie, "Triumphal Procession," and idem, *2 Corinthians*, 152–75. In the Greek literature of the ancient world, when the words are used in the same context but not in this formula, as in 2 Cor 2:14–16, they speak of good or bad smell in the case of ὀσμή, or of a pleasant smell in the case of εὐωδία.

76. See, e.g., Exod 28:34; Lev 1:3–4; 17:4; 19:5; 22:19–21, 29; 23:11. Apart from the current context, the word is used elsewhere in the NT in a quotation of Isa 49:8 at 2 Cor 6:2 (the "acceptable" time designated by the Lord) and in Luke's writings, whether speaking of the "favor" of the Lord (Luke 4:19), a prophet as "accepted" in his home town (4:24), or the person who fears the Lord and does what is right (Acts 10:35).

77. See Rom 12:1–2; 14:18; 2 Cor 5:9; Eph 5:10; Col 3:20; cf. Wis 4:10; 9:10; Philo, *Prelim. Studies* 156–57; *Names* 42, 48; *Joseph* 195, 255; *Spec. Laws* 1.201; *Virtues* 67, 208. The language was picked up by the Apostolic Fathers as well: 1 Clem. 21.1; 35.5; 49.5; 60.2; 61.2; Ign. *Smyrn.* 8.2; Herm. 46.1; 55.2; 56.2.

celebrates the gift given to Paul by the Philippians, receiving it as a sweet smelling, acceptable "sacrifice" offered up to himself.

**4:19–20 And my God will supply your every need according to his wealth in glory in Christ Jesus. Now to our God and Father be glory forever and ever. Amen** (ὁ δὲ θεός μου πληρώσει πᾶσαν χρείαν ὑμῶν κατὰ τὸ πλοῦτος αὐτοῦ ἐν δόξῃ ἐν Χριστῷ Ἰησοῦ. 20 τῷ δὲ θεῷ καὶ πατρὶ ἡμῶν ἡ δόξα εἰς τοὺς αἰῶνας τῶν αἰώνων, ἀμήν). Paul has already called the Philippians to imitate him as he follows Christ (3:17), and verse 19 is a prayerful assurance that calls them to trust that God will provide sufficiently for them, as he has provided for Paul (4:11–13).[78] The very personal reference to God as "my God" (ὁ . . . θεός μου) occurs seventeen times in the New Testament.[79] Three other occurrences with the exact same form as found here are at Mark 15:34, with Jesus's cry from the cross;[80] at John 20:28, where Thomas addresses Jesus as "my Lord and my God"; and at 2 Corinthians 12:21, in Paul's emotional warning of the wayward in Corinth where he writes, "I am also afraid that when I come my God may make me ashamed again in my relationship with you."[81] Yet this personalized reference to God occurs eighty-three times in the LXX and is especially prevalent in the Psalms where it occurs fifty-four times, often as a direct address to the Lord in prayer.[82] Thus Paul draws on the language of the Scriptures as he points his friends to a posture of trust in their profoundly personal God, who is aware of their needs, needs that have been exacerbated by their giving to the mission. From an Old Testament perspective, the sharing of financial resources was an act of virtue rewarded by God. For example, Proverbs 19:17 LXX reads, "He who has compassion on the poor lends to God, and he will repay him according to his gift" (NETS).[83] A similar conviction that God repays the righteous person who shares resources is at the heart of Paul's conviction in Philippians 4:19, as seen in the next part of the verse.

In the broader Greco-Roman world and keeping with the financial language in the broader context, the verb translated as "supply" (πληρόω)[84] could also convey the sense "render" or "pay in full."[85] God will reciprocate to the Philippians by giving to their needs, and he will do so in a comprehensive manner, meeting "every need" (πᾶσαν χρείαν). Paul has already prayed that the Philippians might be filled with the fruit of righteousness (1:11), and elsewhere he writes of God filling people with good things.[86] What God supplies, according to 4:19, is "your every need" (πᾶσαν χρείαν ὑμῶν), which is a unique expression, though the apostle uses the term for "need" (χρεία) elsewhere to speak of the "need" of financial or material resources,[87] including at Philippians 2:25 and 4:16, where he speaks of how the Philippians had met his "need."

So the apostle assures the Philippians that God, in accordance with his vast wealth (κατὰ τὸ

78. Osiek, *Philippians, Philemon*, 123.

79. Matt 27:46; Mark 15:34; John 20:17, 28; Rom 1:8; 1 Cor 1:4; 2 Cor 12:21; Phil 1:3; 4:19; Phlm 4; Rev 3:2, 12.

80. "My God, my God, why have you forsaken me?" (NIV).

81. Translation my own, on which see Guthrie, *2 Corinthians*, 609, 622–23.

82. E.g., Gen 28:3; 30:23; Deut 31:17; Ruth 1:16; 2 Sam 15:31; 1 Kgs 3:7; 1 Chr 28:20; Ps 3:8; 5:3.

83. Peterman, *Paul's Gift from Philippi*, 23–27, 155. Peterman notes the use of the term δόμα in the proverb as at Phil 4:17.

84. The form is a third singular future active indicative; this future form is strongly supported (𝔓[46] ℵ A B D[2] K L P) over against πληρώσαι, in context a third singular aorist active optative (rather than either a second-aorist middle imperative or an aorist active infinitive). Scribes probably thought Paul's assurance needed to be mitigated with a "wish" rather than what sounded like a promise.

85. LSJ 1420 (III.5).

86. E.g., Rom 15:13–14; Eph 1:23; 3:19; 5:18; Col 1:9; 2:10.

87. E.g., Rom 12:13; Eph 4:28; 1 Thess 4:12; Titus 3:14.

πλοῦτος αὐτοῦ), now takes responsibility for reciprocation, just as they have given to Paul in his need. These riches of God are "in glory" (ἐν δόξῃ), but that cannot mean that the answer to this promise lies strictly in the eschaton. Rather, the preposition probably should be read spatially, referring to God's glorious dwelling place. Accordingly, God's provision has its *source* in God's own realm, sent from his presence and by his power.[88] Further, "in Christ Jesus" (ἐν Χριστῷ Ἰησοῦ) has strong relational overtones, pointing to the Philippians' identity as Christ's people. Out of their union with Christ, Paul and his Philippian partners use their resources from God, for God's kingdom, and on mission as God's people. This network of relationships forms the context of giving and receiving.

Paul closes the section at verse 20, breaking out with traditional forms of praise to God,[89] "Now to our God and Father be glory forever and ever. Amen" (τῷ δὲ θεῷ καὶ πατρὶ ἡμῶν ἡ δόξα εἰς τοὺς αἰῶνας τῶν αἰώνων, ἀμήν). The "glory" (δόξα) of this doxology carries over from the "glory" in verse 19 and also echoes the "to the glory and praise of God" (εἰς δόξαν καὶ ἔπαινον θεοῦ) at the end of Paul's prayer in the letter's first chapter (1:11). Whereas the use in 4:19 is spatial, pointing to God's glorious abode, here "glory" refers to the honor due to God, with the dative forms of "God and Father" (τῷ . . . θεῷ καὶ πατρί) marking God as the recipient of this prayerful celebration of his greatness. The apostle speaks of God quite personally, as "*our* God and Father."[90] This brings the letter full circle, for at 1:2 Paul notes that grace and peace come from "God our Father" (θεοῦ πατρὸς ἡμῶν), as well as the Lord Jesus. It is to this glorious, personal God that Paul gives glory, confessing that it will extend "forever and ever" (εἰς τοὺς αἰῶνας τῶν αἰώνων)—a common expression from the LXX.[91] In line with Jewish precedent (e.g., 1 Chr 16:36; Neh 8:6; Ps 41:13), doxologies in the early church were resoundingly answered with a strong affirmation—"Amen!"—adding an exclamation point to the glory ascribed to God.[92] Accordingly, Paul ends with an "amen."

## Theology in Application

The dance between ministers of the gospel on the front lines and those with resources to support them is a very old one, as we see in Paul's correspondence with the Philippians. When we think about strategic kingdom relationships—those providing resources and those putting resources to use in ministry—as people live out a partnership for the gospel under God, perspective is important. The details of such partnerships, in which money flows to areas of need, can be awkward, partners at times unsure of how to respond to requests or gifts. On the other hand, such partnerships can be deeply fulfilling. One of Paul's main points in this passage is

88. Bockmuehl, *Philippians*, 267.

89. I. Howard Marshall, *The Epistle to the Philippians* (London: Epworth, 1992), 122.

90. The affectionate address to God as "our Father" probably stems from the prayer taught by Jesus to his disciples (Matt 6:9–13), and the theme finds wide expression in the literature of the NT (e.g., 1 Cor 8:6; 15:24; Gal 1:4; 4:6; Eph 1:3, 17; 4:6; Col 3:17; Jas 1:27; 1 John 2:14).

91. See, e.g., Ps 9:5 [9:6 LXX]; 45:6 [44:7 LXX]; 84:4 [83:5 LXX]; Dan 12:3.

92. Hansen, *Philippians*, 328; Keown, *Philippians 2:19–4:23*, 459.

that God supplies his people with what they need, whether they are giving or receiving. The key is that we work together, using our resources for work that advances the kingdom.

There is a great deal of money at the disposal of believers around the globe. The 2019 edition of the *International Bulletin of Missions Research* reports that the approximate annual income of Christians around the world is about $60 trillion.[93] As believers we have the responsibility to steward our resources in missional partnerships for the advancement of the gospel at home and abroad. Sometimes we may be on the frontlines of mission work, depending on the resources of partners. At other times, we may be gifted by God to generate resources to support the work. What should not be optional is meaningful involvement in the cause of our missional God.

Through the years, my wife Pat and I have had rich opportunities to give to both short-term and long-term ministry projects in a variety of cultural contexts, and we have had the joy of giving rhythmically through the local church. Having the resources and opportunities to give has been a deeply fulfilling part of our life in the body of Christ. We also have been on the receiving end numerous times in our lives and ministries. For instance, as we moved to Vancouver, BC, in May of 2018, we were blessed by generous people who, believing in our ministry and call to an international context, wanted to help offset some of the exorbitant costs of our move.

In Philippians 4:10–20, Paul provides us with material that is rich in theological insight for our consideration. Many in North America have numerous opportunities each year to give to missions—through major mission agencies and churches, to individuals seeking long-term support, or to those seeking short-term help—and we need to see our involvement in biblical perspective. So let us consider the following theological threads running through this passage and a few questions to consider in light of Paul's words to the Philippians.

First, *our God is missional, enabling the mutual work of partners for gospel ministry.* Ultimately we need to see that valid mission enterprises are driven by the Lord himself, and we need to live out our part faithfully under his direction. This means that we need to *seek God* about where and how we are to be involved, whether going or giving. Do you pray about your involvement in significant work around the world?

Second, it is clear from the passage that *those in a partnership advancing the gospel share resources for the work, whether "at home" or away from home.* We need to evaluate our use of resources for advancing God's kingdom in the world. How are we sharing our resources to support the work of ministry? Have you considered lately the distribution of your resources for kingdom work? How are you using your resources at home to carry out ministry in your context?

93. Gina A. Zurlo, Todd M. Johnson, and Peter F. Crossing, "Christianity 2019: What's Missing? A Call for Further Research," *International Bulletin of Mission Research* 43.1 (2019): 100.

Third, *God richly provides for the needs of the partners in the gospel work, whether those giving or receiving.* God meets the needs of his people for the work he has called them to do. Do you find yourself anxious about your available resources for ministry? Do you find yourself anxious about giving to ministry? How does it affect your attitude toward God himself? Do you trust God to meet your needs as you are faithful to use your resources for kingdom purposes?

Finally, *God enables those engaged in the advancement of the gospel to live contentedly in light of the absolute sufficiency of God to provide what is needed.* Since it takes money to live in this world, it is very easy to become anxious about our resources. If we are engaged in using our resources faithfully for the work of God, we learn that God himself has all that we need—his resources are absolutely sufficient to meet our needs and to give us opportunities to minister to and through others. Are you content? Are you clear about the absolute sufficiency of God to provide for your basic needs?

CHAPTER 13

# Philippians 4:21–23

## Literary Context

We now come to the postscript of Philippians, the final movement in the letter closing, which extends from 4:10 to 4:23. Whereas the book started in 1:2 with a blessing of "grace to you and peace from God our Father and the Lord Jesus Christ" (χάρις ὑμῖν καὶ εἰρήνη ἀπὸ θεοῦ πατρὸς ἡμῶν καὶ κυρίου Ἰησοῦ Χριστοῦ), it now concludes with a blessing of "the grace of our Lord Jesus Christ be with your spirit" (ἡ χάρις τοῦ κυρίου Ἰησοῦ Χριστοῦ μετὰ τοῦ πνεύματος ὑμῶν).

I. The Letter Opening: A Prescript and a Prayer Report (1:1–11)
II. The Letter Body (1:12–4:9)
**III. The Letter Closing (4:10–23)**
A. The Philippians' Gift and Partnership in Ministry (4:10–20)
➦ **B. Postscript: Final Greetings and Blessing (4:21–23)**

## Main Idea

Paul closes the letter with formal greetings and a blessing.

## Translation

### Philippians 4:21–23

| | | |
|---|---|---|
| 21a | Greetings/Exhortation | **Greet every one of God's holy people** |
| b | | in Christ Jesus. |
| c | Greetings | **The brothers and sisters with me greet you.** |
| 22a | Greetings/General | **All God's holy people greet you,** |
| b | Specific | especially those |
| c | Location | from Caesar's house. |
| 23a | Blessing | **The grace of our Lord Jesus Christ be with your spirit.** |

## Structure

The postscript follows a standard form of greeting and blessing at the end of a letter. The triple greetings embody common elements in Pauline letter closings, as does the blessing. The highly crafted parallels may be seen more clearly in the Greek text, as follows.

| | | | |
|---|---|---|---|
| Greet | **every one of God's holy people** | ἀσπάσασθε | **πάντα ἅγιον (object)** |
| | in Christ Jesus. | | ἐν Χριστῷ Ἰησοῦ. |
| greet | you | ἀσπάζονται | ὑμᾶς (object) |
| | The brothers and sisters with me | | οἱ σὺν ἐμοὶ ἀδελφοί. |
| greet | you | ἀσπάζονται | ὑμᾶς (object) |
| | **All God's holy people,** | | **πάντες οἱ ἅγιοι, (subject)** |
| | especially those | | μάλιστα δὲ οἱ |
| | from Caesar's house. | | ἐκ τῆς Καίσαρος οἰκίας. |
| The grace of our Lord Jesus Christ | | ἡ χάρις τοῦ κυρίου Ἰησοῦ Χριστοῦ | |
| be with your spirit. | | μετὰ τοῦ πνεύματος ὑμῶν. | |

Here we have a request to greet others, followed by two expressions of greetings, followed by a blessing. Notice the triple use of the verb meaning "greet" (ἀσπάζομαι), and also the ABBA pattern followed by "all" (πάντα)—"you" (ὑμᾶς)—"you" (ὑμᾶς)—"all" (πάντες), which frames the whole with reference to "Christ Jesus" (Χριστῷ Ἰησοῦ) at the beginning and the inverted "Jesus Christ" (Ἰησοῦ Χριστοῦ) near the end. The "in Christ Jesus" (ἐν Χριστῷ Ἰησοῦ) also balances nicely with the "from

Caesar's house" (ἐκ τῆς Καίσαρος οἰκίας), both offering descriptions of the "saints" or "God's holy people."

## Exegetical Outline

➦ **B. Postscript: Final Greetings and Blessing (4:21–23)**

1. Closing Greetings (vv. 21–22)
2. A Blessing (v. 23)

## Explanation of the Text

**4:21–23 Greet every one of God's holy people in Christ Jesus. The brothers and sisters with me greet you. All God's holy people greet you, especially those from Caesar's house. The grace of our Lord Jesus Christ be with your spirit** (Ἀσπάσασθε πάντα ἅγιον ἐν Χριστῷ Ἰησοῦ. ἀσπάζονται ὑμᾶς οἱ σὺν ἐμοὶ ἀδελφοί. 22 ἀσπάζονται ὑμᾶς πάντες οἱ ἅγιοι, μάλιστα δὲ οἱ ἐκ τῆς Καίσαρος οἰκίας. 23 ἡ χάρις τοῦ κυρίου Ἰησοῦ Χριστοῦ μετὰ τοῦ πνεύματος ὑμῶν). The offering of greetings was a common social convention in the New Testament world,[1] as were words of blessing. In the final three verses of Philippians, Paul offers a triple greeting, followed by a benedictory word of grace. The words, though terse, are common in Paul's letter closings, and the terseness is probably due to the "glorious" praise and "amen" (4:20) that capped off the previous unit.[2] The first clause, a request, reads, "Greet every one of God's holy people[3] in Christ Jesus" (Ἀσπάσασθε πάντα ἅγιον ἐν Χριστῷ Ἰησοῦ). Elsewhere the apostle calls his readers to greet "one another" with a holy kiss (Rom 16:16; 1 Cor 16:20; 2 Cor 13:12; 1 Thess 5:26). Or as here they are to "greet" fellow believers, the "brothers and sisters" (Col 4:15), "those who love us in the faith" (Titus 3:15), or specific believers like Priscilla and Aquila (2 Tim 4:19). In his elaborate greetings at the end of Romans, Paul uses a combination of these forms, sending greetings to a host of specific individuals, collective greetings to members of various households, and a final call for the Romans to "greet one another with a holy kiss" (16:3–16a).

Although a few translations render the two singular adjectives ("every one of God's holy people," πάντα ἅγιον) with "all the saints" or a near equivalent (e.g., NIV, NET), the singular forms are better translated as distributive ("each," or "every," as, e.g., with ESV, CSB, NASB, NLT, NRSV), used perhaps to heighten the focus on each member of the congregation.[4] Further, the very familiar Pauline phrase "in Christ Jesus" (ἐν Χριστῷ Ἰησοῦ),[5]

1. The verb ἀσπάζομαι could be used to mean "to engage in hospitable recognition of another" (BDAG 144). See, e.g., Matt 5:47; 10:12; Luke 1:40; Acts 18:22; Heb 13:24; 1 Pet 5:13; 2 John 13.

2. Among Paul's writings, only Galatians, Ephesians, and 1 Timothy do not offer greetings, and all of his letters close with expressions of grace. See Fee, *Philippians*, 456.

3. On the use of the term ἅγιος, see the commentary on 1:1.

4. Fee, *Philippians*, 457.

5. On which, see the commentary at 1:1. Forms of the phrase occur throughout Philippians at 1:1, 13, 26; 2:1, 5; 3:3, 14; 4:7, 19.

should be read as adverbial,[6] accenting the call to "greet," perhaps stressing the common bond believers have because of their incorporation in Christ, "the source and locus of their common life together."[7]

In verses 21b–22, two groups of people send their greetings to the Philippians via Paul. The first he describes as "the brothers and sisters with me" (οἱ σὺν ἐμοὶ ἀδελφοί). These are gathered around the apostle in his imprisonment, and any guess at the specific identity of these individuals remains speculative.[8] The second group sending greetings constitutes members of the broader church in Rome: "All God's holy people greet you" (ἀσπάζονται ὑμᾶς πάντες οἱ ἅγιοι). What is extraordinary, however, is that he again moves to a specific subgroup by adding, "especially those from Caesar's house" (μάλιστα δὲ οἱ ἐκ τῆς Καίσαρος οἰκίας). Rather than referring to Caesar's family, the reference speaks of the emperor's clients, friends, and servants, some of whom were slaves or freedmen. Such functioned in a variety of capacities in the circle of work and influence surrounding the emperor. Bockmuehl follows Bruce and others in noting the intriguing connections in this regard with the list of names in Romans 16. For instance, "the household of Narcissus" (Rom 16:11) almost certainly refers to those in the house of Tiberius Claudius Narcissus, an influential client of Emperor Claudius (41–54 CE), and "Aristobulus" (v. 10) may be a reference to Herod the Great's grandson, who also had been a member of Claudius's court. Paul's "relative" (συγγενῆς), Herodion, mentioned between these two other prominent households (v. 11), may indicate that the apostle had a family connection within the Roman civil service ranks.[9] These suggestions offer a tantalizing glimpse of those to whom Paul may have referred with his statement at Philippians 4:22. For believers in a Roman colony like Philippi, the penetration of the gospel to the very heart of the empire and to Caesar's own sphere of influence would have been wonderfully encouraging.

The book's final verse reads, "the grace of our Lord Jesus Christ be with your spirit" (ἡ χάρις τοῦ κυρίου Ἰησοῦ Χριστοῦ μετὰ τοῦ πνεύματος ὑμῶν). Whereas standard Greek letters ended with the verb meaning "farewell" (ῥώννυμι; cf. Acts 15:29), Paul almost always ends with a blessing of "grace" as from the Lord Jesus.[10] As at Galatians 6:18 and Philemon 25, Paul here adds "with your spirit" (μετὰ τοῦ πνεύματος ὑμῶν).[11] Thus, as the letter opened in 1:2 with a blessing of "grace to you and peace from God our Father and the Lord Jesus Christ" (χάρις ὑμῖν καὶ εἰρήνη ἀπὸ θεοῦ πατρὸς ἡμῶν καὶ κυρίου Ἰησοῦ Χριστοῦ), it now concludes with a wish-prayer, a form of blessing, "the grace of our Lord Jesus Christ be with your spirit" (ἡ χάρις τοῦ κυρίου Ἰησοῦ Χριστοῦ μετὰ τοῦ πνεύματος ὑμῶν).

6. If read as adjectival, delimiting "God's holy people," the phrase would seem redundant; Paul considers all the people of God as "in Christ."

7. So Fee, *Philippians*, 458.

8. By contrast, in other prison epistles, Paul names individuals. For instance, in Col 4:11–15 he mentions Aristarchus, Mark, Jesus who is called Justus, Epaphras, Luke, and Demas, all of whom send greetings to the Colossians. All of these except Justus are also mentioned as sending greetings in Phlm 23–24.

9. Bockmuehl, *Philippians*, 269–70. Of course, if Paul wrote Philippians after Claudius's rule, these families may well have still been connected to the imperial house.

10. See Rom 16:20; 1 Cor 16:23; 2 Cor 13:13; Gal 6:18; 1 Thess 5:28; 2 Thess 3:18; Phlm 25. Ephesians 6:24 is an exception, where Paul writes, "grace to all who love our Lord Jesus Christ with an undying love" (NIV). Colossians 4:18, 1 Tim 6:21, 2 Tim 4:22, and Titus 3:15 read simply "grace be with you" (cf. Heb 13:25).

11. Although some scholars have thought it was under pressure from the form in Galatians and Philemon that the ending of Philippians was made to conform, the reading as it stands has weighty support ($\mathfrak{P}^{46}$ ℵ* A B D F G P 6. 33. 81. 104. 365. 424. 436. 459. 1175. 1319. 1881. 2127 $it^{d, g, r}$ vg $cop^{sa, bo}$ arm eth). See Metzger, *Textual Commentary*, 550–51.

## Theology in Application

In her wonderful little book, *Caring for Words in a Culture of Lies*, Marilyn McEntyre writes of believers as logocentric people.

> Those of us who preach and teach and minister to each other need to focus on the word—on words—more explicitly, intentionally, and caringly as part of the practice of our trade. This is necessary and urgent activism: to resist "newspeak," to insist on precision and clarity, to love the bald statement, the long sentence, the particular example, the extended definition, the specifics of story, and the legacy of language we carry in our pocket Bibles and on the shelf with Shakespeare. We are stewards of the treasures that have been put into our keeping. We're not doing too well with fossil fuels and wetlands. I commend those causes to you as well. But along with them, conversation itself—the long conversation that is the warp and woof of civil and communal life—is in need of preservation and renovation.[12]

The writing and careful reading of a commentary is a preservation and renovation of a long conversation. We give attention—very focused attention—to the particularity of words, how those words are meaningfully arranged, what makes them sing, and how they might be brought to bear on our lives and the lives of others for good and the glory of God. The conversation surrounding Philippians was initiated by God himself, through Paul, to a relatively small group of Christ-followers in an out-of-the-way agricultural community of the Mediterranean world. The fact that you have this commentary in hand bears witness that the conversation is still going, and I think that matters. How we treat every one of the 1,631 words in the 104 verses of this letter matters.

As I noted in the very first "Theology in Application" section of the commentary, written as a reflection on the book's prescript (1:1–2), when we study a letter like Philippians, we engage a text embodying certain aspects of language and culture in Paul's day, both "secular" and "church." The formality of communication at the beginning and end of Philippians is entirely appropriate for a letter written at that time and place. But the language has been shaped by deeply meaningful relationships—the relationship Paul had with God through Christ as well as the relationship Paul had with the Philippians as part of the broader church.

Consider how the *form* of this postscript communicates particular *living dynamics* with a beautiful economy of language. By its nature the church is translocal

12. Marilyn McEntyre, *Caring for Words in a Culture of Lies* (Grand Rapids: Eerdmans, 2009), 20.

and transcultural. These greetings are sent to fellow believers in another part of the empire—sent collectively from the whole church with Paul, even to those in unexpected places like "Caesar's household." They are sent to those considered brothers and sisters, to be passed on to still others—to do what greetings did: communicate something about a network of relationships. Is that cliché? Are they jotted with no more thought than our "sincerely" posted to a person of marginal acquaintance? I don't think so. The effusive "greetings" here (the verb "to greet" is used three times) flow from dynamics reflected in the broader letter. They speak of relational unity. They reflect a common cause by which the gospel moves outward across the world. They reflect a community of blessing under the lordship of Christ, a community touched by grace, in which the Spirit matters. Even these words communicate a warmth of relationship, if read carefully and contextually. The form has an important function.

And so, dear reader, receive these words as to the extended interpretive community of Christ down through the ages. Let the words of Philippians nourish you, give you encouragement in the face of opposition, give you endurance in the long race, and build unity among your church body. "The grace of the Lord Jesus Christ be with your spirit." We are part of something bigger than ourselves, a group of people that now spans the globe. Greet the brothers and sisters in your place. Tell them those of George's household send their greetings.

CHAPTER 14

# Theology of Philippians

From our walk through Philippians, it is clear that Paul did not write the letter to be a theological treatise but rather to offer various forms of encouragement and exhortation to a church community whom he considered partners in the gospel. Philippians has neither the systematic treatment of theological motifs found, for example, in Romans, nor the rich, protracted theological reflections we find in the first movements of a book like Ephesians. As we have discussed, even Paul's tantalizing allusions to his opponents offer little in the way of specific concerns. Yet Paul's life was so permeated by God that words about him shape, extend, and provide underpinning for every line of this letter. Philippians may be practical in intent (urging the unity of the congregation), rhetorical in approach (using various forms of argument), and profoundly relational in orientation (as a friendship letter), but behind it all stand deeply held theological convictions. So what might we discern about those convictions?[1]

## God the Father

As with his other writings, Paul's letter to the Philippians is God centered, as the apostle uses the term θεός twenty-three times in this brief work (Phil 1:2, 3, 8, 11, 28; 2:6 [2x], 9, 11, 13, 15, 27; 3:3, 9, 14, 15, 19; 4:6, 7, 9, 18–20). God has a "form," which may be understood as his glorious appearance, shared with the preincarnate Christ Jesus (2:6). In sharing his glory and his throne (2:9), God the Father identifies directly with Christ, his Son (1:2). God dwells in heaven, the realm from which he rules the world, from which he sent Christ into the world, and to which he calls his people (3:14). In relation to the rest of creation, God holds supreme authority and power in the universe. He exalted Christ to his heavenly throne and gave him a name above all names. Therefore, all peoples will ultimately bow their knee to Christ and give glory to the all-powerful God, who has the authority and power to enthrone a king to rule over all of reality (2:9–11).

1. Rather than put our reflections on the book's theology into the broader context of Paul's theology, the focus here will be on what might be discerned overtly from the text of Philippians itself.

Rather than being removed from the world, however, God is at work in the world and among his people. Concerning the latter, he works in them to do what pleases him (2:13), and believers may be used by God to have a positive impact on one another (1:3). God, as the ultimate source of the work, is to be thanked. Further, people can have a personal relationship with God, whom Paul refers to personally as "*our* Father" (1:2). Consequently, believers have a family relationship with God through Christ the Son and are considered God's "children" (2:11, 15; 4:20).

One of the primary orientations of Philippians sees God as the supreme source of all that is good and helpful. For his people, God is the source of all grace, peace, and mercy (1:2; 2:27; 4:7, 9, 23). In his mercy, he can deliver a ministry partner from illness (2:27). He provides strength for his people to be content in a variety of circumstances (4:13). And according to his riches he meets the needs of his people (4:19). In terms of ministry, believers serve by the enablement of the Spirit of God rather than putting faith in the flesh (3:3), and the Spirit facilitates dynamic Christian community, building tenderness and compassion in relationships within the church (2:1). Moreover, God is the object of prayer and praise, to whom believers come with their anxiety and needs (4:6), and he is the one who receives glory as believers live well in the world and proclaim his renown (1:11; 4:20).

## Christ Jesus

Paul's world was radically reoriented when he met the Lord Jesus Christ on the road to Damascus (Acts 9:1–22; cf. Phil 3:8). His letters are thus permeated with references to Christ. In Philippians, Paul refers to the Lord as "Christ" (Χριστός) as a stand-alone designation sixteen times (Phil 1:10, 13, 15, 17–18, 20–21, 23, 27, 29; 2:1, 16, 30; 3:7, 9, 18), "Christ Jesus" (Χριστοῦ Ἰησοῦ or related) twelve times (1:1, 6, 8, 26; 2:5; 3:3, 12, 14; 4:7, 19, 21), "Christ Jesus my Lord" (Χριστοῦ Ἰησοῦ τοῦ κυρίου μου) once (3:8), "Jesus Christ" (Ἰησοῦ Χριστοῦ or related) three times (Phil 1:11, 19; 2:21), "Lord Jesus Christ" (κύριος Ἰησοῦς Χριστός or related) four times (1:2; 2:11; 3:20; 4:23), "Lord Jesus" (κυρίῳ Ἰησοῦ) once (2:19), and "Jesus" (Ἰησοῦ) as a stand-alone once (2:10).

In his very nature, Jesus is God, robed with divine glory. Since he refused to consider equality with God something to be used for his own advantage (2:6), he became incarnate to live and die as a human being, taking the role of the Servant (2:7–8; Isa 52:13–53:12). The good news is that Christ made it possible for people to know God (3:8–10) and for God to do a "good work" of salvation in people (1:6). That salvation has a "past," when a person responds to the gospel (1:5), a "present" as God continues to work righteousness in his "holy person" (1:6; 2:12–13; 4:21), and a "future" when the believer comes to the day of Christ and experiences the resurrection (1:10; 2:16;

3:20–21). For believers, righteousness—a right standing before God, which issues in right living for God—comes from God through trust in Christ (3:9).

Because of Christ's obedience even to the point of death on a cross, God the Father exalted him to the place of highest authority in the universe, so that every knee in all the created order will bow and every tongue will confess that Jesus Christ is Lord (2:8–11). Thus, human beings are accountable to God and, through Christ, will submit to God's ultimate authority over the world and humanity. This will bring glory to God.

Currently, in his resurrection body, Jesus is in heaven, and as our Savior he will return from heaven at the end of the age (3:20). That will be "Christ's Day" when he brings believers to the consummation of their spiritual growth (1:6, 10). As the Lord of supreme power, with everything under his control, Christ will transform the bodies of believers to be like his resurrection body (3:21).

By his nature, power, and status Christ Jesus is the source for much that is good for believers. For example, he, along with the Father, is the source of grace and peace (1:2) and is the source of affection that believers have for one another (1:8). He is not only the source of the fruit of righteousness with which believers are to be filled but is also the means by which they give glory and praise to God (1:11; 3:9). Thus Christ is the object of trust or belief, which is given to believers as a gift as Christ takes hold of them (1:29; 3:9, 12), and he is the object of our boasting as we celebrate the work of God (1:26; 3:3, 9). All of life is focused on him as of supreme worth, so that we can say that to live is Christ (1:21; 3:8–9), and all our hope in death is focused on him (1:21; 3:10–11).

## The People of God

Because of the work of Christ, God's people have been incorporated into Christ and have been given the opportunity to share in his sufferings, his righteousness, and his resurrection (2:1; 3:10–11). This is comforting and encouraging for believers (2:1–2). Therefore, it is worth giving up everything for Christ's sake, since Christ can be known—and that is of supreme value (3:7–8). For a believer, to live is Christ and to die is gain, and believers should embrace the goal of Christ magnified in one's body, through life or death (1:20–21). Death can be considered a joy, since to die is to depart and be with Christ. And the hope is to be transformed by the power of Christ and given a resurrection body, in which we will know Christ fully (3:10–11).

At the same time, our spiritual transformation is analogous to a race that requires pressing on to follow Christ (3:12–14). We live in a "now and not yet" reality, in which we have been made the children of God but are still pursuing Christ. The race started with the work of God in us. God has accomplished that work by the Spirit in a way that can be described as "circumcision"—a heart operation of transformation (3:3; cf. Rom 2:29; Col 2:11). God will be working in us until the day of Christ (1:6). We are citizens of heaven (3:20), even as we live out that citizenship in this world (1:27–28). Our orientation in life is godward, thus Christ-ward, thus heavenward (3:14–15), even as God continues to work his will in us so that we might do what pleases him (2:13). We grow in love and knowledge and perception and discernment, so that we can be sincere and blameless, filled with the fruit of righteousness (1:9–11; 3:15). True righteousness comes by trust in Christ alone and has its source in God (3:9).

As his children, God wants us to be blameless and pure as we interact with a corrupt and crooked world (2:15), living in a manner worthy of the gospel (1:27). This is worked out on an interpersonal level as we learn to live well together in the church. We do this in part by maintaining unity, turning away from arguing and grumbling about each other. Maintaining unity comes by serving others humbly, turning from arrogance and selfishness, and thinking of others as more significant than ourselves (2:1–4). As we hold fast to God's good word of life, we live in a way that our lives shine like the stars in the sky. In this way we work out our salvation "with fear and trembling" even as we rest in the fact that God is the one working in us to accomplish what pleases him (2:12–16).

Believers have the privilege of talking to God in prayer—a joyful, relational activity, which involves making requests to God, along with offering praise and thanks (1:9–11; 4:4–6). The foundation of our boldness in prayer is that "the Lord is near" and is concerned about the things that make us anxious (4:5–6). Moreover, prayer is effective, changing things in the world as we pray for fellow believers in need or for the mission of the church (1:7, 19). Prayer is also a means of guarding the heart and mind (4:7). The mind is important for the Christian life, for the way we think is vital for spiritual health (e.g., 2:2, 5; 3:15, 19; 4:2), as is having sound exemplars of the faith to emulate (2:5; 3:17; 4:8–9).

## Mission in the World

As the people of God, we are on mission in the world, participating in the advance of the gospel in a way that is relational and accomplished through living in healthy community with one another as we experience God's grace (1:5, 7). The gospel must be proclaimed fearlessly, defended, and confirmed before the world (1:7, 16), so that it can advance among the people of the world (1:12, 14). This requires the people of God to stand together (1:27–28; 4:3). One expression of mission faithfulness is seen as believers give to support the work. In some sense there is "credit" to the account of believers who give to the work of God, and God reciprocates by supplying the needs of giving believers (4:17–19).

Of course, the mission of the church is opposed by the unrighteous of the world, some of whom do so out of envy, selfishness, and factionalism. Not everyone who speaks about Christ publicly is God's true minister (1:15–17). Some are evildoers, mutilators (3:2), who put confidence in the flesh (3:3) and seek a righteousness based on law. They are enemies of the cross of Christ (3:18–19), and so believers should watch out for them (3:2). The fate of the unrighteous, whether religious or secular, is destruction since they set their minds on earthly things. The things in which they glory are shameful (1:28; 3:18–19).

Opposition to the gospel by the unrighteous means therefore that the advance of the gospel will often involve suffering on behalf of Christ, which actually is considered a gift (1:29–30). False teachers may seek to harm Christ's true ministers (1:17). For believers to "gain" Christ means to experience "loss" in terms of the world (3:7–8). Sometimes ministry involves danger, risk, and sorrow, but God shows mercy amid such things (2:27). Ironically, suffering for the gospel can play a significant role in offering opportunities for gospel proclamation in the world (1:12–14; 18, 20). Since the gospel mission moves forward in the world, and believers know Christ, we live in joy, which can be embraced even amid suffering (1:12–14, 18; 2:17–18, 28; 3:1).

For Paul, sound leadership is key to the mission of the church. There are formal roles within the church, such as overseers and deacons (1:1), but Paul considers those inside the church (1:3–8; 4:1–3, 14), and coworkers external to the local church such as Timothy (2:19–24), to be his partners in the work. Foundational for true Christian leadership is a "servant" posture under Christ's lordship (1:1). Thus leadership is characterized as costly, sacrificial, and service oriented (2:17, 22), putting the needs of others before one's own needs, which really means looking out for Christ's interests, for he is oriented to the needs of his people (2:5–8, 20–21). Good Christian leaders should be celebrated and honored for their sacrificial work (2:29–30), and they should be imitated as offering a pattern of right living for Christ in the world (3:17).

# Scripture Index

## Proverbs



## Ecclesiastes



## Isaiah



## Jeremiah

## Lamentations



## Ezekiel



## Daniel



## Hosea



## Joel



## Amos



## Obadiah



## Jonah



## Micah



## Habakkuk



## Zephaniah



## Zechariah



## Matthew

## Mark



## Luke

## John



## Acts

## Romans

## 1 Corinthians

## 2 Corinthians

## Galatians

## Ephesians



## Philippians

## Colossians



## 1 Thessalonians

## Titus



## Philemon



## Hebrews



## James

# Other Ancient Literature Index

## *Deuterocanonical Works and Septuagint*

## *Old Testament Pseudepigrapha*

### 1 Enoch



### Letter of Aristeas



### 3 Maccabees



### 4 Maccabees



### Psalms of Solomon



### Sibylline Oracles



### Testament of Asher



## *Dead Sea Scrolls*

### 1QS



### 1QSb



### 4QMMT



## *Philo*

### *Agriculture*



### *Alleg. Interp.*



### *Cherubim*



### *Confusion*



### *Creation*



### *Dreams*



### *Drunkenness*



### *Embassy*



### *Flight*



### *Giants*

# Subject Index

# Author Index